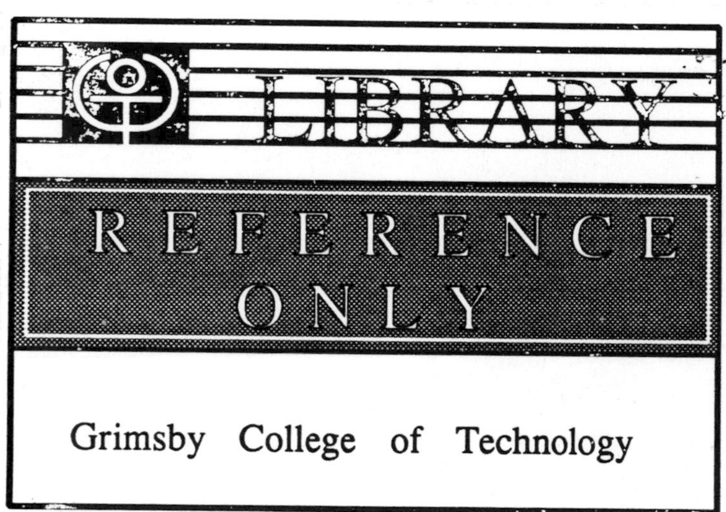
LIBRARY
REFERENCE
ONLY
Grimsby College of Technology

THE ENCYCLOPEDIA OF PHOBIAS, FEARS, AND ANXIETIES

THE ENCYCLOPEDIA OF PHOBIAS, FEARS, AND ANXIETIES

Ronald M. Doctor, Ph.D.,
and
Ada P. Kahn

Facts On File
New York • Oxford

THE ENCYCLOPEDIA OF PHOBIAS, FEARS, AND ANXIETIES

Facts On File, Inc.
460 Park Avenue South
New York NY 10016
USA

or

Facts On File Limited
Collins Street
Oxford OX4 1XJ
United Kingdom

Library of Congress Cataloging-in-Publication Data

Doctor, Ronald M. (Ronald Manual)
The encyclopedia of phobias, fears, and anxieties.

Bibliography: p.
Includes index.
1. Phobias—Dictionaries. 2. Fear—Dictionaries.
3. Anxiety—Dictionaries. I. Kahn, Ada P. II. Title.
RC535.D63 1989 616.85′22′0321 88-31057
ISBN 0-8160-1798-0 (alk. paper)

British CIP data available on request.

Facts On File books are available at special discounts when purchased in bulk quantities for businesses, associations, institutions or sales promotion. Please contact the Special Sales Department of our New York office at 212/683-2244 (dial 800/322-8755 except in NY, AK or HI).

Composition by the Maple-Vail Book Manufacturing Group
Manufactured by R. R. Donnelley
Printed in the United States of America

10 9 8 7 6 5 4 3 2 1

This book is printed on acid-free paper.

CONTENTS

FOREWORD BY ISAAC M. MARKS, M.D. vii
PREFACE ix
ACKNOWLEDGMENTS xi
ENTRIES A–Z 1
BIBLIOGRAPHY 435
INDEX 477

FOREWORD

This is a welcome volume because it brings together many useful and fascinating facts on phobias, fears, and anxieties under one cover. The literature on the topic is vast, so compilation of this encyclopedic reference of relevant terminology provides an important service.

Ronald M. Doctor and Ada P. Kahn have drawn together more than 2,000 entries, including descriptions of things/situations/feelings that some people fear, terms that relate to a diverse range of therapies, and names of some outstanding people in our field. The authors' research has been extensive, and they present their selections of terminology in an easy-to-read style that is interesting as well as informative. I recommend this volume as an adjunct to my own books, including *Fears, Phobias, and Rituals* (New York: Oxford University Press, 1987) and *Living with Fear* (New York: McGraw-Hill, 1978), as well as to those of other researchers and clinicians. Terminology is the key to unlocking many concepts, including the historic and proven as well as the contemporary and experimental.

This is a timely resource as public awareness of phobias, fears, and anxieties has grown sharply recently. It is only in this decade that we have become aware of how surprisingly prevalent these problems are in the general population. Community surveys in the U.S. and Germany have found that up to 10 percent of people suffer from an anxiety disorder at some time in their lives, and that most of these sufferers have had no treatment for the problem. Many are extremely disabled by these so-called "minor" mental disorders. "Minor" is a real misnomer, given that the disability from such problems can be as great as that from "major" mental illnesses. The problems may cause sufferers to become housebound, lose their jobs, and cease carrying out normal family routines so that daily activities have to be shouldered by relatives. Such difficulties can hamper child-rearing badly and create a marked family burden.

We have made great strides in knowledge about phobias and fears in the last few years. Concerning causation, it has become evident that the range of phobias that appears in the population is limited and nonrandom given how frequently we all see a huge variety of different situations in everyday life. Although we all encounter beds, glass, and plants every day, phobias of such objects are very rare. Much more common are phobias of heights, snakes, spiders, strangers, public places, and dirt. Although statistical chances of death from sharks or rabies are minute, those fears are frequent. On the other hand, automobile accidents are the chief cause of death in young people, yet phobias of cars are not very common.

Our range of contemporary fears and the frequent disproportion between the actual danger of a situation and our readiness to fear that situation can be understood from our evolutionary history. Many fears are of evolutionarily dangerous stimuli. Like all species, we humans have been programmed in the course of our evolution to fear certain things more readily than others. New dangers have not been around long enough for natural selection to have modified our neural programs.

However, the fact that behavior is built-in need not mean that it is immutable. Though many of our phobias reflect constraints in our learning capacity that have been shaped by natural selection, we should not despair of overcoming those fears. Research has shown that even obviously programmed fears can be overcome by systematic treatment. Within a few days or weeks of appropriate exposure therapy, "natural" fears of heights, snakes, spiders, and strangers *do* improve, just as much as do fears of more "unnatural" dangers.

What is this treatment that can be so effective? The approach is called exposure. It has been found in many experiments in different countries to help most sufferers from phobias and from phobialike obsessive–compulsive rituals. Moreover, improvement after the completion of explosure treatment has lasted for the four- to eight-year follow-up that has been carried out in many centers in different countries.

The central principle of exposure treatment is persuasion of the sufferer to stop avoiding what he or she fears and instead to start approaching it and staying in its presence until the ensuing panic starts to subside. It can take 20 to 30 minutes of exposure treatment for the panic to come down a bit and an hour or two for it to reduce greatly. This exposure exercise is repeated daily with avoided situations until most of the discomforts and tendencies to avoid them have disappeared, and the phobic individual has obtained freedom from associated work, social, and family disabilities.

Even better news is that recently, phobic sufferers have been found capable of successfully treating themselves without ever needing a clinician to accompany them on their exposure tasks. When phobics applied the self-exposure approach using a self-treatment manual *(Living With Fear),* they improved substantially, as much as when they received such instructions from a psychiatrist. This was true for agoraphobics with panic, for specific (simple) phobics, and for social phobics. Obsessive–compulsive ritualizers, too, treated themselves successfully by self-exposure, improving to the same extent as when clinicians accompanied them into the feared situation. Furthermore, these gains from self-exposure persisted to two-year follow-up.

Medication can help some sufferers when they have depressed mood, which often afflicts phobics and obsessive–compulsives. Antidepressant drugs, given together with exposure instructions, have been useful, but some sufferers have a tendency to relapse when medication is stopped.

Such work illustrates the rapid advances being made in the field of phobias and fears, both in our theoretical understanding and in our ability to help sufferers overcome their problems.

This encyclopedia can assist readers in putting current terminology into appropriate perspective, whether their interest is professional or merely curious. The bibliography included at the back of the book enhances Doctor and Kahn's work with lists of more than 2,500 articles and books of significance to therapists, researchers, and phobic individuals. This book should be considered a standard reference for all who wish to gain more insight into the vast field of phobias, fears, and anxieties.

Isaac M. Marks, M.D., F.R.C. Psych.,
Professor of Experimental Psychopathology,
Institute of Psychiatry,
University of London

PREFACE

This encyclopedia explores in depth diverse aspects of phobias, fears, and anxieties. Information on these subjects has developed along with our knowledge of other areas of mental health. Just as our understanding of the human psyche is far from complete, so too is our understanding of the origins and management of phobias, fears, and anxieties.

This book deals with experiences we all have at times but that for some of us become a persistent and sometimes devastating problem. Although we don't fully understand the causes of the problem, or why some people are more susceptible to it than others, we have been more fortunate in treating phobias, fears, and anxieties. Behavioral therapies have been shown to be particularly effective, and self-help techniques are flourishing. Drugs have also been useful, but the biochemical and physiological mechanisms underlying phobias, fears, and anxieties are still only partially understood. It is clear that anxiety and related disorders are much more than a physical or even behavioral response alone. The complex nature of the problem confronts the clinician and researcher at every turn.

In preparing the contents of *The Encyclopedia of Phobias, Fears, and Anxieites,* we were guided by several purposes. First, we wanted to be inclusive rather than restrictive, and thus we were quite liberal in choosing entries. For example, some entries (such as voodoo, magic, etc.) are sociocultural in emphasis rather than psychological, in order to present a broad perspective. Some entries (such as history of phobias) are historical in nature but again enhance the usefulness of this book. Similarly, some entires concern esoteric manifestations of phobias but are included for purposes of depth. Most of the known technical names of specific phobias are defined and described to the extent that information is available from the literature of psychology and psychiatry. Entries range from descriptions of symptoms, to explanations of treatments for the disorders, to some concepts of historical interest, to some self-help suggestions for phobic individuals.

The Encyclopedia of Phobias, Fears, and Anxieties is intended for both lay readers and health-care professionals. We have tried to use easy-to-understand language without becoming overly simplistic, so that the book can be used by psychologists, social workers, teachers, and family members as well as by individuals who are facing phobias, fears, or anxieties. To give the book an added usefulness for phobic individuals, we have carefully selected some self-tests and self-help suggestions (such as how to relieve fear of flying). Our suggestions are general, but references are included for more complete and specific self-help approaches in each entry. Professionals will find this a convenient reference guide for short descriptions of concepts they want to explain to patients or clients, and for details they may seek in the course of their own writing, teaching, or counseling. For all who seek information to this field, we hope *The Encyclopedia of Phobias, Fears, and Anxieties* will prove a valuable source of information not otherwise available in one place.

Space limitations have dictated conciseness; to assist readers seeking additional information, we have included in many entries references to relevant books and journal articles. We have also included an extensive bibliography at the end of the book.

Preparing this book has given us a deeper appreciation of man's struggle with the elusive force within. We hope that you, too, find it enlightening.

Ronald Manual Doctor, Ph.D.
Northridge, California

Ada P. Kahn, M.P.H.
Chicago, Illinois

ACKNOWLEDGMENTS

We are grateful to Isaac M. Marks, M.D., London, for his encouragement and counsel regarding compilation of this book.

We appreciate the cooperation of the American Psychiatric Association for permitting reproduction of many instructive tables and charts.

We thank many librarians in the reference department of the Skokie Public Library, Skokie, Illinois, for their ongoing assistance in locating research materials and obtaining data sources through the metropolitan Chicago area North Suburban Interlibrary Loan Service, Wheeling, Illinois. Also, we thank librarians in the Division of Library and Information Management, American Medical Association, Chicago, the Northwestern University Medical Library, Chicago, the library of the Institute for Psychoanalysis, Chicago, the Oviatt Library, California State University, Northridge, California, the Wellcome Institute for the Study of the History of Medicine, London, and the library at the Maudsley Hospital, University of London, for their assistance.

We thank Hope C. Apple, Evanston, Illinois and Michael Kite, Waukegan, Illinois, for their research and editorial assistance.

We acknowledge the participation of Heather Yolles and Michelle Williams, Northridge, California, and Marydeanne Wildman, Wilmette, Illinois, in the production of the manuscript.

Finally, we thank Richard Smith, general manager of an electronics firm in Arlington Heights, Illinois, for assistance with computer software utilized in the preparation of this book.

Ronald M. Doctor, Ph.D.
Northridge, California

Ada P. Kahn, M.P.H.
Chicago, Illinois

A

abandonment, fear of Fear of abandonment or loss of love relates to external protection or satisfactions that would overwhelm the child or adult. This is a fear that some children have when they think that one or both parents will neglect or desert them. Some children develop this fear because their parents threaten to send them away as a disciplinary measure. Adults also fear abandonment when they fear losing a loved one on whom they are dependent. Studies of agoraphobics indicate they develop a greater degree of dependency and resentment about it. (See also AGING, FEAR OF; ALONE, FEAR OF BEING; CHILDHOOD FEARS; RETIREMENT, FEAR OF.)

ablutophobia Fear of washing or bathing. The term also relates to incessant preoccupation with washing or bathing. Individuals who have OBSESSIVE–COMPULSIVE DISORDER may be preoccupied with frequent handwashing or an obsession against washing or bathing. Manifestations of this fear would include avoidance (long periods without washing), excessive anxiety when contemplating washing or when actually attempting to wash, and anxiety and dread when seeing others wash. (See also BATHING, FEAR OF.)

Campbell, Robert Jean, M.D., *Psychiatric Dictionary* (New York: Oxford U. Press, 1981).

abreaction Emotional release resulting from remembering a painful experience that has been forgotten or repressed because it was consciously painful. In some cases, the process of abreaction helps an individual gain insight into the roots of a phobia or an anxiety reaction. The therapeutic effect of abreaction is through discharge of the painful emotions, relief from them, and probably some DESENSITIZATION to the emotional expression itself. Freud's colleague BLEULER noted the therapeutic effects of catharsis with his client Anna O. (See also ANNA O.; CATHARSIS; FREUD, SIGMUND.)

abstraction anxiety See MATHEMATICS ANXIETY; NUMBERS, FEAR OF.

Abu Bakr (573–634) An Islamic leader who is said to have died of sorrow after the prophet Mohammed's death. Abu Bakr's death, considered psychosomatic, dramatized an Arabian psychiatric concept that "he who is overcome by worries will have a sick body."

Howells, J.G. and M.L. Osborn, *A Reference Companion to the History of Abnormal Psychology,* (Westport, CT: Greenwood Press, 1984).

acarophobia Fear of small objects, such as INSECTS, worms, mites, and nonliving items such as PINS AND NEEDLES. (See also WORMS, FEAR OF; NEEDLES, FEAR OF; SMALL OBJECTS.)

acceptance A favorable attitude on the part of the therapist toward the phobic or anxious individual under treatment. The therapist conveys an implicit respect and regard for each client as an individual, without necessarily implying either approval of behavior or an emotional attachment toward the client. Acceptance has been defined as "valuing or prizing all aspects of the client including the parts that are hateful to himself or appear wrong in the eyes of society." The term acceptance is used interchangeably with UNCONDITIONAL POSITIVE REGARD by client-centered therapists It is a nonjudgmental condition that is seen as a necessary quality in any therapy. (See also CLIENT-CENTERED PSYCHOTHERAPY.)

accidents, fear of Fear of accidents is known as dystychiphobia. Those who fear having accidents fear behaving in any way that might result in injury to themselves or to other persons, or in damage to property or the environment. Accident phobics associate certain factors with accidents and tend to avoid them. The situations they might avoid include risky jobs, atmospheric conditions, a tiring work schedule, and equipment failure. They also are fearful of personal factors such as inattention, errors of perception, risk-taking, and decision-making. Fear of accidents is related to a fear of decision-making and a fear of errors. Some people who fear accidents also fear injury to themselves. (See also DECISIONS, FEAR OF; ERROR, FEAR OF; INJURY, FEAR OF.)

accommodation A term that describes how a therapist adapts language and specific techniques to the characteristics of the individual patient. Accommodation enhances trust and rapport and therefore helps promote change for the individual or family. (See also FAMILY THERAPY; PSYCHOTHERAPY.)

Minuchin, S., *Families and Family Therapy,* (London: Tavistock, 1974).

acerophobia (acerbophobia) Fear of sourness. The word is derived from the Latin *accer,* meaning "sharp, sour." Such fears would lead to avoidance of acerbic foods or other products. (See also SMELLS, FEAR OF; SOURNESS, FEAR OF; TASTES, FEAR OF.)

acetycholine See LITHIUM.

achluophobia Fear of the dark (also known and NYCTOPHOBIA). Manifestations of this fear include not going out at night, increased anxiety as dusk approaches, not wanting to look out at the darkness (for example, closing shades in order to avoid looking out), avoidance of looking into dark rooms, and having light available constantly. Freud quoted a child who was afraid of the dark as saying, "If someone talks, it gets lighter," implying that darkness is associated with loneliness and separation. (See also DARKNESS, FEAR OF; NIGHT, FEAR OF.)

acid dew, fear of Fear of acid dew is a contemporary fear in technologic societies. Acid dew is a side effect of AIR POLLUTION and is formed when dewdrops absorb chemicals expelled in automobile exhaust or smoke from coal-burning factories. Some people fear the dew because of suspected or unknown health effects and because they feel helpless with regard to avoiding or controlling the presence of the noxious substances in their environment. (See also ACID RAIN, FEAR OF.)

acid rain, fear of Fear of acid rain is a late-twentieth-century fear brought about by high industrialization and AIR POLLUTION in many parts of the world. People fear acid rain because they fear unknown health consequences of breathing the polluted air that results after rain falls. They fear a lack of control over their environment and feel forced to breathe the polluted air. (See also ACID DEW, FEAR OF.)

acousticophobia A morbid fear of noise. Also spelled akousticophobia. This may also be a fear of sounds or particular sounds. (See also PHONOPHOBIA; NOISE, FEAR OF.)

Acquired Immune Deficiency Syndrome (AIDS), fear of According to a 1987 statement issued by the Surgeon General of the United States, "Acquired Immune Deficiency Syndrome is an epidemic that has already killed thousands of people, mostly young, productive Americans. In addition to illness, disability, and death, AIDS has brought fear to the hearts of most Americans—fear of disease and fear of the unknown."

Within just a few years after its discovery, AIDS has all but eclipsed other life-threatening and debilitating diseases in terms of creating fear. Its power to both unify and polarize various groups, to stigmatize, to become an issue of politics and morality, illustrates its pervasiveness. Although some of the anxiety associated with AIDS is reasonable, much has also been irrational, and, as with many fears and anxieties, the best means of controlling the latter lies in education.

Because there is no cure and no vaccine for AIDS, because some people may be infected and never know it, and because symptoms may lie dormant for years, it is especially easy for a person to worry that he or she might have AIDS. Some individuals, especially homosexual men, may experience ANXIETY or PANIC ATTACKS, hypochondriasis, and even some minor, superficial symptoms that mimic AIDS. They may feel certain they are dying and become obsessed with details of the disease or the thought of having to face the stigma it carries. Members of the gay community often experience the anxiety and helplessness of watching friends suffer and die from the disease. Combined with the blame or resentment that a number of uninformed individuals level against them, the resulting anxiety can take on overwhelming proportions.

However, AIDS anxiety is no longer restricted to high-risk groups. A 1987 survey by the American Medical Association (AMA) revealed that almost 50 percent of all Americans believe it is very likely that AIDs will infect and kill a large share of the population. Fifty percent of those questioned said they believed that everything possible needs to be done to prevent the spread of AIDS, even if it means that some people might have their rights violated. Nearly 10 percent believed that AIDS patients should be isolated from the rest of the population.

Heterosexuals may also be overpowered by crippling feelings of fear, shame, and guilt if faced with the possibility of a test for AIDS. Even if there is little chance that they have been exposed to AIDS, such individuals may still be terrified at the thought of AIDS testing. Anxiety about testing may result from three distinct emotions—fear of getting AIDS, shame over past sexual events, and guilt at the thought of harming a loved one. Some people may withdraw emotionally and sexually from their partner.

Because AIDS is transmitted through exchange of bodily fluids, including blood, drug users who share needles, persons receiving or donating blood, and health-care workers have all been subject to anxiety surrounding the disease. With proper precautions, risks to health-care workers, hemophiliacs, and persons receiving blood transfusions are minimal, and risks to blood donors are virtually nonexistent.

As with fear of other diseases, some individuals may attempt to avoid anxiety over AIDS by purposely nurturing their ignorance of the disease. Denial is common. Individuals who believe they might be at risk may go a long way to explain exactly the opposite belief. Some persons may call upon dubious methods of protection, including vitamins, questionable nutritional approaches, or even astrology. Depression and anger are also common reactions. Feelings of hopelessness or helplessness are prevalent, especially in the homosexual community and in other communities where the risk of acquiring AIDS is elevated. Other individuals may resort to "bargaining"—attempting to make deals with health professionals in which they promise to take certain precautions in exchange for a "guarantee" that they will not contract AIDS. Education, in many of these instances, can go a long way in changing such fears or anxieties into informed caution rather than hysteria. (See also DISEASE, FEAR OF; EPIDEMIC ANXIETY; ILLNESS PHOBIA; MASS HYSTERIA; PLAGUE, FEAR OF; PSYCHOSEXUAL ANXIETIES; SEXUALLY TRANSMITTED DISEASES.)

Celovsky, Andree, "AIDS Test May Panic Even Heterosexuals, Suggests Chicago AIDS Psychiatrist" (Chicago: Michael Reese Hospital and Medical Center, November 18, 1987).

Morin, Charles and Malyon, "The Psychological Impact of AIDS on Gay Men," *American*

Psychologist, (November 1984), pp. 1288–1293.
USDHHS, "Surgeon General's Report on Acquired Immune Deficiency Syndrome" (Washington: U.S. Dept. of Health and Human Services, 1987).

acrophobia A fear of heights, also known as hypsosophobia. This is one of the commonest phobias in the general population. According to a study by Agras, about .4 percent of the population has a phobia to heights, and only about 2 percent of those seek treatment. Treatment commonly involves EXPOSURE THERAPY, in which graded exposure to heights is made while in a state of relative relaxation. For example, a person might start exposure with looking out the second-floor window until relaxation or comfort is achieved and then move on to third and subsequent floors in the same manner. In severe cases, a therapist or trained support person may be necessary.

Individuals who have acrophobia fear being on high floors of buildings or on the tops of hills or mountains. They usually feel anxious approaching the edge of precipices such as BRIDGES, rooftops, stairwells, railings, and overlooks. They usually fear FALLING and being injured. Some feel and fear an uncontrollable urge to jump. They may have fantasies and physical sensations of falling even when on firm ground.

Fear of ELEVATORS, ESCALATORS, balconies, and stairways are related to a fear of heights, as is sometimes a fear of FLYING or FALLING. In severe cases, the individual cannot even stand on the lower steps of a ladder without experiencing some anxiety. Often fear of driving on freeways or highways has an acrophobic component in that these roadways are frequently elevated.

In psychoanalysis, fear of falling from high places sometimes represents fear of punishment for forbidden wishes or impulses. (See also HEIGHTS, FEAR OF.)

ACTH (adrenocorticotrophic hormone) A substance secreted by the pituitary gland to control release of steroid hormones from the adrenal cortex. STRESS leads to simultaneous release into the circulation of both ACTH and beta-endorphin, a type of amino acid. ACTH is also known as corticotropin. (See also ENDORPHIN.)

action therapy An approach to psychotherapy that focuses on altering problem or unwanted behaviors by teaching the individual new skills, action therapy is often used in treating phobic conditions. Action therapy is a generic term for exposure treatments, desensitization, and any therapy that actively confronts the feared STIMULUS as opposed to more passive therapies that rely on talk, catharsis, and insight. (See also BEHAVIOR THERAPY; CATHARSIS; DESENSITIZATION; FLOODING; INSIGHT; MODELLING.)

active analytic technique See ACTIVE TECHNIQUE.

active technique A psychotherapeutic approach that differs from the classical or expectant technique of PSYCHOANALYSIS. Active techniques are aimed at modifying the troublesome responses of ANXIETIES, PHOBIAS, and OBSESSIONS in individuals. Active techniques encourage reenactment of events that may have led to development of the habits or phobias that the individual seeks to change. This approach, which stems from psychoanalytic therapies, predates and foreshadowed the behavioral techniques that are more commonly used in treating anxiety today. Names associated with this technique are Sandor Ferenczi, Wilhelm Stekel, Franz Alexander, and Thomas French.

acupressure Acupressure, also known as shiatsu, a cross between acupuncture and massage, is a useful technique for relief of some types of anxieties. The technique was developed in Japan in the latter half of the 20th century. Acupressure emphasizes deeply relaxing tense or exhausted muscles, thus improving blood flow. The technique shares with acupuncture the concept of points on the body that, with stimulation, bring beneficial results. Acupressure has been used successfully to reduce headaches, muscle soreness, and anxieties in many individuals. (See also ACUPUNCTURE.)

acupuncture A technique used to relieve certain disorders or to produce anesthesia in certain areas of the body by piercing the skin with fine needles. The word is derived from the Latin word *acus,* meaning needle. Individuals who have a needle or injection phobia usually fear acupuncture even to the extent of seeing pictures of acupuncture being practiced. Acupuncture has been practiced in China for several thousand years as a form of therapy, to relieve pain, and to induce anesthesia for surgical procedures. It is based on an Oriental concept that certain pathways of energy, known as meridians, flow between places on the skin and possibly nearby nerves and the organ systems in the body. Energy balancing is seen as treatment for anxiety disorders since this system assumes that energy imbalance and blockage are the root of emotional disorders. (See also NEEDLES, FEAR OF.)

Adapin See DOXEPIN.

adaptation Fitting one's needs to the environment. The individual may combine changes in the self with alterations of the external environment. For example, an agoraphobic may find that he is able to do certain things away from home alone, but not others. He or she may restrict going out to only at night, under cover of darkness, so as not to be seen. Or he may be able to go out in the company of a trusted friend or relative. Likewise, each phobic reaction results in adaptation to the fear reaction through avoidant thought or action, use of excuses or crutches such as drugs and alcohol, other people etc. (See also AGORAPHOBIA.)

adaptation mechanisms Adjustment processes one uses to accommodate new information into one's mental framework and self-perception. In psychoanalytic terminology, defense mechanisms protect the psychic system while allowing the individual to adapt to reality. (See also DEFENSE MECHANISMS; EGO DEFENSE MECHANISMS.)

Adaptive Behavior Scale A test developed by the American Association on Mental Deficiency to assess how well developmentally disabled people cope with the demands of the environment. Information on behavior, physical development, language development, independent functioning, socialization, destructive behavior, hyperactivity, and withdrawal is provided by observers. While used primarily for assessing levels of independent functioning, many of these assessment areas can be influenced by anxiety. The role of anxiety in affecting the developmentally disabled is an area that needs considerably more study.

addiction, fear of Fear of dependence on a chemical substance to the extent that one establishes a physiologic need for it. Alcohol, tobacco, caffeine, narcotics, and some sedatives, many of which are prescribed by physicians for the treatment of anxiety, may produce addiction. Some individuals fear addiction and that their bodies will develop a physiological craving for the prescribed substance. Thus, when the substance is removed or withdrawn, he or she develops withdrawal symptoms. Addiction is a physiological condition but has important psychological and social consequences. Some individuals fear that they may become so totally involved in their addiction that they might neglect or harm other people. Others fear the loss of control implied by addiction.

Addiction to antianxiety medications is usually not physiological but psychological. Even after discontinuing a medication, patients may carry the drug with them wherever they go (along with water, gum, and other soteria) because the mere possession of the drug is comforting. (See also ALCO-

HOL, FEAR OF; ANXIETIES; SEDATIVES, FEAR OF.)

Bugelski, B. Richard and Anthony M. Graziano, *Handbook of Practical Psychology,* (Englewood Cliffs, NJ: Prentice-Hall, 1980).

adenosine A naturally occurring chemical in most living cells. Adenosine is a source of energy in metabolic activities at the cellular level, is associated with nerve impulse transmissions, and may be involved in causing some anxiety disorders. (See also BIOLOGICAL BASIS FOR ANXIETY.)

adenylate cyclase An enzyme-linked chemical secreted by the body that affects HORMONE functions.

adjustment Change or accommodation by which the individual can adapt himself to the immediate environment. For example, a phobic individual may make adjustments in his route to work so that he will not encounter a fearful situation along the way, such as a BRIDGE, tunnel, or overpass. An agoraphobic may arrange to have a trusted friend or relative go with him or her to necessary appointments. (See also ADAPTATION.)

Adler, Alfred (1870–1937) A Viennese psychologist and the first disciple of Sigmund Freud. Adler broke away from Freud to form his own school of Individual Psychology. Adler argued that social factors, rather than sexual instincts, were the causes of behavior, including anxiety and phobic reactions. These social factors included concepts such as the striving for superiority, feelings of inferiority, the inferiority complex, compensation and overcompensation, social interests, and creative development at personal and social levels.

Adler occupied the first chair of medical psychology in the U.S., at Long Island University. He called his system Individual Psychology because he intended to treat each patient as an individual worth listening to, rather than as an impersonal problem. He viewed the individual not as a conflict between ego, superego, and id, but as a whole. Of great importance to Adler was the individual client's life-style and his own system of subjective convictions about himself. Adler focused attention on building up the troubled individual's self-esteem through an understanding of his innate potential. Adler called this potential "social interest," another way of stating that individuals are goal-oriented and that working with others produces happiness and success. In the process of striving for their goals, people develop a "sense of life," the courage to judge themselves realistically, and the common sense to confront the social and physical environment constructively. Five critical areas must be mastered: family, work, sexuality, feelings about self, and the spiritual dimension. Adler did not think of a neurosis, such as a phobia, as a disease. An important part of Adlerian therapy is examining the individual's concept of "reality." The prime function of the Adlerian therapist is building up the patient's self-image and optimism, mainly through cognitive aspects of therapy. That is, Adlerian therapy does not focus on anxiety itself but concentrates on identifying thoughts and beliefs, ways of thinking, that produce such emotions. Along with such concepts as sibling rivalry and empathetic understanding, Adler's ideas served as a base for the development of some group-therapy ideals that later became popular.

Adler advocated a multiple-analyst approach to therapy, allowing the individual to interact with two or more therapists, thereby reducing the possibility of psychotherapeutic impasses. There was the added advantage that any patient who was not getting along particularly well with one of his therapists might pursue therapy with one of the other analysts dealing with his case. (See also COMPENSATION; COMPLEX; EGO; EXISTENTIAL THERAPY; FREUD, SIGMUND; ID; INFERIORITY COMPLEX; JUNG, CARL; SUPEREGO.)

Lande, Nathaniel, *Mindstyles/Lifestyles* (Los Angeles: Price/Stern/Sloan, 1976).

adolescent depression See DEPRESSION, ADOLESCENT.

adolescent suicide See SUICIDE, ADOLESCENT.

adrenaline A hormone secreted by the central, or medullary, portion of the adrenal glands that produces an increase in heart rate, a rise in blood pressure, and a contraction of abdominal blood vessels (often leading to "butterflies"). Anxiety and panic are the subjective reactions to these changes. These sympathetic changes can be reversed by activation of the parasympathetic system. (See also EPINEPHRINE; NEUROTRANSMITTERS; NORADRENERGIC SYSTEM.)

adrenergic blocking agents Substances that inhibit certain responses to adrenergic, or adrenalinelike (energizing), nerve activity. The term adrenergic blocking agents (a.b.a.) is also applied to drugs that block the action of the neurotransmitters epinephrine and norepinephrine. Ergot alkaloids were first discovered to alter responses to sympathetic nerve stimulation. A.b.a.s are selective in action and are classed as alpha a.b.a.s (alpha blockers or alpha-receptor blocking agents) and beta a.b.a.s (or beta blockers or beta-receptor blocking agents), depending which types of adrenergic receptors they affect. Medications for anxiety may involve both alpha-receptor blockers and beta blockers, although the beta blockers are used primarily for performance anxiety such as public speaking or test taking. (See also ADRENERGIC DRUGS; ADRENERGIC SYSTEM.)

adrenergic drugs Substances that stimulate activity of adrenaline (epinephrine) or mimic its functions. Adrenergic drugs produce stimulation of the central nervous system, thereby increasing anxiety. A.d.s are part of a group of sympathomimetic amines that includes ephedrine, amphetamines, and isoproterenol. Adrenergic agents are produced naturally in plants and animals but can also be developed synthetically. (See also ADRENERGIC BLOCKING AGENTS; ADRENERGIC SYSTEM; DRUGS.)

adrenergic system The part of the AUTONOMIC NERVOUS SYSTEM that is influenced by adrenergic drugs, which stimulate the activity of epinephrine or mimic the functions of epinephrine. (See also ADRENERGIC BLOCKING AGENTS; ADRENERGIC DRUGS.)

advantage by illness The benefit or relative satisfaction a sick person gains from being ill. Freud differentiated between primary and secondary advantages, or gains, by illness. In primary advantage, the psychic mechanism is preserved because inaction and withdrawal lower ANXIETY and avoid emergence of possibly destructive impulses. In secondary advantage, the individual consciously or unconsciously perceives an environmental gain, such as sympathy and attention from family members, removal of responsibilities or possible failure, and avoidance of frightening situations. Some phobic individuals (especially agoraphobics) experience some advantage to having a phobia, which may cause resistance to therapy. (See also AGORAPHOBIA; PHOBIA; SECONDARY GAIN.)

adverse drug reactions Adverse drug reactions are physical or mental reactions that occur after self-administration of a drug and/or use of a drug for therapeutic purposes. How an individual reacts to drugs depends on many factors, including genetic susceptibility, general health, allergies, attitude in taking the drugs, medical history, tolerance to bodily changes, and other drugs or foods the individual has consumed. An example of an adverse drug reaction is extremely high blood pressure as a result of the combination of a drug in the category known as MONOAMINE OXIDASE (MAO) INHIBITORS with wines, cheeses, or other foods that contain tyramines. Adverse drug reactions may range from mild stomach aches to heart attacks, seizures, hallucinations, and even death. When one receives a prescription for any drug as part of therapy to help deal with a phobia or anxiety, one should ask the physician about any possible adverse reactions. (See also DRUGS; TYRAMINE.)

aelurophobia Fear of cats. Also known as ailurophobia, elurophobia, felinophobia, galeophobia, and gatophobia. (See also CATS.)

aeroacrophobia Fear of open, high spaces. Aeroacrophobia includes fear of being at great heights, such as in an airplane. This should be differentiated from airsickness, which is a vertigo-type disturbance. (See also FLYING, FEAR OF; VERTIGO.)

aeronausiphobia Fear of airplanes; fear of vomiting due to airsickness. (See also FLYING, FEAR OF.)

aerophagia Fear of swallowing air. (See also AIR, FEAR OF.)

aerophobia A fear of air, drafts, gases, or airborne noxious influences. Also known as air phobia. Sometimes this term is used as a label for the fear of flying. (See also AIR, FEAR OF; FLYING, FEAR OF; WIND, FEAR

affective disorders Affective disorders are also known as MOOD DISORDERS and are often associated with anxiety. Affective disorders are so named because they involve changes in affect, a term that is roughly equivalent to emotion, or mood. In this group of disorders, the individual experiences mood disturbances intense enough to warrant professional attention. An individual who has an affective, or mood, disorder may have feelings of extreme sadness or intense, unrealistic elation with the disturbances in mood not due to any other physical or mental disorder. Some affective disorders have been thought to be related to ANXIETY. For example, AGORAPHOBIA is sometimes associated with DEPRESSION. The depression may be a reaction to the demoralization that accompanies the phobic's feelings of incompetence, ineffectualness, and loss of self-respect. Some agoraphobics may feel disappointed and hopeless about themselves and aware of their fearful dependency on their spouses or significant others. However, as phobics gain more mastery over their problems during the course of treatment, the depression that accompanies agoraphobia usually improves.

Mood disorders differ from thought disorders; schizophrenic and paranoid disorders are predominantly disturbances of thought, although individuals who have those disorders may also have some distortion of affect. A disorder of the thought processes is not a common feature in affective disorders; however, if the disorder reaches extreme intensity, there may be a change in thought pattern, but the change in thought will be somewhat appropriate to the extremes of emotion that the person is experiencing.

Affective disorders have been known throughout history. There are descriptions of mood disorders in the early writings of the Egyptians, Greeks, Hebrews, and Chinese. There are descriptions in the works of Shakespeare, Dostoyevski, Poe, and Hemingway. Many historical figures have suffered from recurrent depression, including Moses, Rousseau, Dostoyevski, Queen Victoria, Lincoln, Tchaikovsky, and Freud.

BIPOLAR DISORDERS and depressive disorders sometimes occur according to a seasonal pattern, with a regular cyclic relationship between the onset of the mood episodes and particular 60-day periods of the year.

A mood syndrome (depressive or manic) is a group of associated symptoms that occur together for a short duration. For example, Major Depressive Syndrome is defined as a depressed mood or loss of interest of at least two weeks' duration, accompanied by several associated symptoms, such as weight loss and difficulty concentrating.

A mood episode (major depressive, manic, or hypomanic) is a mood syndrome not due to a known organic factor and not part of a nonmood psychotic disorder such as schizophrenia, schizoaffective disorder, or delusional disorder. A mood disorder is diagnosed by the pattern of mood episodes. For example, the psychiatric diagnosis of Major Depression is made when there have been one or more major depressive episodes without a history of a manic or unequivocal hypomanic episode.

Manic episodes

Individuals who have manic episodes have distinct periods during which the predominant mood is either elevated, expansive, or irritable. They may have inflated self-esteem, decreased need for sleep, accelerated and loud speech, flight of ideas, distractibility, grandiose delusions, or flamboyancy. The disturbance may cause marked impairment in their working or social activities or relationships; an episode may require hospitalization to prevent harm to themselves or others. They may experience rapid shifts of mood, with sudden changes to anger or depression.

The mean age for the onset of manic episodes is in the early twenties, but many new cases appear after age 50.

Hypomanic episodes

These are mood disturbances not severe enough to cause marked impairment in social or work activities or to require hospital care.

Major depressive episodes

Individuals who experience a major depressive episode have either depressed mood (in children or adolescents, irritable mood) or loss of interest or pleasure in all, or almost all, activities for at least two weeks. Their symptoms are persistent in that they occur for most of the day, nearly every day, during at least a two-week period. Associated symptoms may include appetite disturbance, change in weight, sleep disturbance, decreased energy, feelings of worthlessness or excessive or inappropriate guilt, difficulty concentrating, restlessness, such as an inability to sit still, pacing, hand-wringing, pulling or rubbing of hair, and recurrent thoughts of death or of attempting suicide. The average age of onset of depressive episodes is in the late 20s, but a major depressive episode may begin at any age. They are more common among women than among men.

Bipolar disorders

Bipolar disorders (episodes of mania and depression) are equally common in males and females. Bipolar disorder seems to occur at much higher rates in first-degree biologic relatives of people with Bipolar Disorder than in the general population.

Cyclothymia

This is a condition in which there are numerous periods of hypomanic episodes and numerous periods of depressed mood or loss of interest or pleasure that is not severe enough to meet the criteria for a major depressive episode.

Dysthymia

This is a history of a depressed mood for at least two years that is not severe enough to meet the criteria for a major depressive episode.

Causes of affective disorders

Many factors contribute to an individual's affective or mood disorders. The major causative categories are biological, psychosocial, and sociocultural. There seems to be a hereditary predisposition because the incidence of affective disorders is higher among relatives of individuals with clinically diagnosed affective disorders than in the general population. There has been considerable research during the 1970s and 1980s to explore the view that depression and manic episodes both may arise from disruptions in the delicate balance of the levels of the brain chemicals called biogenic amines. Biogenic amines serve as neural transmitters or modulators that regulate the movement of nerve impulses across the synapses from one neuron to the next. Two such amines involved in affective disorders are norepinephrine and 5-hydroxytryptamine (serotonin). Some drugs are known to have antidepressant properties and biochemically increase the concentrations of one or the other (or both) of these transmitters.

Psychosocial and biochemical factors may work together to cause affective disorders. For example, stress has been considered as a possible precipitating factor in many cases. Stress may also affect the biochemical balance in the brain, at least in predisposed persons. Mild depressions frequently follow significant life stresses, such as the death of a family member. Many other life events may precipitate changes in mood, especially those involving lowered self-esteem, thwarted goals, physical disease or abnormality, or ideas of deterioration or death.

Some individuals may have personality characteristics that predispose them to affective disorders, such as negative views of themselves, of the world, and of the future. A stressful life event for these individuals simply activates previously dormant negative thoughts. Generally, individuals who become manic are ambitious, outgoing, energetic, care what others think about them, and are sociable before their episodes and after remission. On the other hand, depressive individuals appear to be more obsessive, anxious, and self-deprecatory. They often have rigid consciences and are prone to feelings of guilt and self-blame.

Depressed individuals tend to interact with others differently from the way manics do. For example, some manic individuals do not want to rely on others and try to establish a social role in which they can dominate others. On the other hand, depressed individuals take on a role of dependency on others and look to others to provide support and care; this is the case with agoraphobics.

According to many researchers, feelings of helplessness and a loss of hope are central to depressive reactions. In severe depression, "learned helplessness" may occur, when the individual sees no way to cope with his or her situation and gives up trying.

Treatment

Affective disorders are treated with behavior therapy as well as drugs. Some behavioral approaches, known as cognitive and cognitive-behavioral therapies, involve efforts to correct the individual's thoughts and beliefs (implicit and explicit) that underlie the depressed state. Therapy includes attention to unusual stressors and unfavorable life situations, and observing recurrences of depression.

Medical intervention includes the use of antidepressant, tranquilizing, and antianxiety drugs. Lithium carbonate, a simple mineral salt, is used to control manic episodes and is also used in some cases of depression where the underlying disorder is basically bipolar. Lithium therapy is often effective in preventing cycling between manic and depressive episodes.

Death rates

The death rate for depressed individuals seems to be about twice as high as that for the general population because of the higher incidence of suicide. Manic individuals also have a high risk of death because of accidents (with or without alcohol as a contributing factor), neglect of proper precautions to safeguard health, or physical exhaustion. (See also ALCOHOLISM; ANTIDEPRESSANTS; ANXIOLYTICS; DEPRESSION, ADOLESCENT; DRUGS; ENDOGENOUS DEPRESSION; EXOGENOUS DEPRESSION; MANIC–DEPRESSIVE DISORDER; SEASONAL AFFECTIVE DISORDER; SUICIDE, FEAR OF; SUICIDE, ADOLESCENT; TRANQUILIZERS.)

American Psychiatric Association, *Diagnostic and Statistical Manual of Mental Disorders* (Washington, D.C.: American Psychiatric Association, 1987).

Coleman, J. et al., *Abnormal Psychology and Modern Life* (Glenview, Il: Scott, Foresman & Co., 1984).

affective neuroses An older term used to describe some of the disorders of MOOD, or affect, now termed mood disorders or AFFECTIVE DISORDERS. The term *neurosis* is no longer used in describing or diagnosing mental and emotional disorders.

age distribution of fears, phobias, and anxiety During their first few weeks of life, infants exhibit fear responses. Sudden, loud noises or loss of support typically result in fearful reactions such as crying and stiffening the body. The number of stimuli to which a child responds with fear increases as the child gets older. During the second half of the first year, and through the second year, fear of strangers is fairly common. After the first two years, fear of animals shows an increasing incidence from around age 3 and by 4 or 5 comprises the largest category of children's fears. After age 4 or 5, animal fears tend to decline. New fears involve more intangible or abstract objects or situations, such as fear of imaginary creatures, monsters, and the dark. Fear of creatures usually declines steadily and becomes negligible after 10 or 11 years for most children. Fears associated with school and social life then become more prominent.

As many as 40 percent of CHILDHOOD FEARS persist into adulthood. In a significant epidemiological study by Stuart Agras et al. in 1969, three different patterns of specific fears occurred over a broad age range. The greatest number of specific fears and phobias was during childhood, usually peaking before age 10. Another cluster of fears, including fears of doctors and medical procedures such as injections, showed a peak occurrence at about age 20. Then there was a rapid decline in prevalence during the adolescent and early adult years. By the sixth decade, the same fears were negligible. Fears of death, injury, illness, separation, and crowds showed a steady increase in prevalence up to age 60, and then also declined. Another pattern, involving fears of ANIMALS, SNAKES, HEIGHTS, STORMS, ENCLOSED SPACES and social situations, showed an increasing prevalence up to age 20 and then declined gradually, suggesting that these fears tend to persist much longer than tne others. Stuart Agras, a Stanford University psychiatrist, suggests that this constellation of fears had survival value to primitive man and therefore are relatively universal reactions.

In 1975, Isaac Marks, a British psychiatrist affiliated with the Maudsley Hospital, London University, and Michael Gelder, a British psychiatrist at the University of Oxford, reported that more severe fears, phobias, and anxiety states also show age-related patterns. For specific phobias involving heights and storms, they reported an average age of onset of about 22.7 years. Social phobias and extreme shyness had a mean onset of 18.9 years, and the average age for the onset of agoraphobia was 23.9 years of age. The latter percentage corresponds closely to age of onset for agoraphobia of 24 years found by Ronald M. Doctor, Ph.D., professor of psychology, California State University, Northridge, California. (See also INCIDENCE OF PHOBIAS; PREVALENCE OF PHOBIAS; SHYNESS; SOCIAL PHOBIA.)

Scarr, S. and P. Salapatek, "Patterns of Fear Development in Infancy," Merrill Palmar Quarterly 16 (1970): pp. 53–90.

Marks, Isaac, *Fears and Phobias* (London: Heinemann Medical, 1969).

Doctor, Ronald M. "Major Results of a Large Scale Survey of Agoraphobics," in R. Du

Pont, *Phobia: Comprehensive Summary of Modern Treatment* (New York: Brunner/Mazel, 1982), pp. 203–214.

aging, fear of Fear of aging is known as gerontophobia. Many people fear aging, which is a normal process throughout life. In older individuals, aging involves some characteristic patterns of late life changes that can be distinguished from diseases and social adversities. Fear of aging is based on fears of being alone, of being without resources, and of being incapable of caring for oneself both intellectually and physically. (See also AGISM.)

agism Stereotyping of old people. In an effort to avoid primitive fears of aging and death, many people discriminate against elderly persons, creating distance between themselves and the social plight of old people. Ageism is distinguished from gerontophobia, a specific fear of old people and aging. (See also AGING, FEAR OF; RETIREMENT, FEAR OF.)

American Psychiatric Association, *Psychiatric Glossary* (Washington, D.C.: American Psychiatric Association, 1988).

agitation Excessive movement, usually nonpurposeful, that is associated with or is symptomatic of tension or anxiety. Examples of agitation are wringing of the hands, pacing, and inability to sit still. (See also ANXIETIES; SYMPTOMS.)

agoraphobia Agoraphobia is the most common phobic disorder for which people seek treatment. It is also the most disabling. According to the National Catchment Interview Study published in 1984 by the National Institutes of Mental Health (NIMH), about one adult in 20 suffers from agoraphobia. More than three quarters of agoraphobics are women. According to the New York State Psychiatric Institute of the Columbia-Presbyterian Medical Center in New York City, 4,000,000 Americans a year seek treatment for this disorder, which may represent only about 20 percent of all agoraphobics. Some therapists say agoraphobia is the most difficult of all phobias to treat. Treatment, however, has been successful for many individuals.

A central component of agoraphobia is fear of fear itself. The agoraphobic syndrome is a complex phobic disorder that usually occurs in adults. The major features are a variable combination of characteristic fears and the avoidance of public places, such as streets, stores, public transportation, crowds, and tunnels.

Agoraphobia is well known in many languages. For example, in German, it is *platzangst;* in French, *peur des espaces* or *horreur du vide.* The English term is derived from the Greek root "agora," meaning the place of assembly, the marketplace. The original definition meant fear of going out into open spaces such as streets or isolated areas. Now the term agoraphobia is applied

The Cycle of Agoraphobia

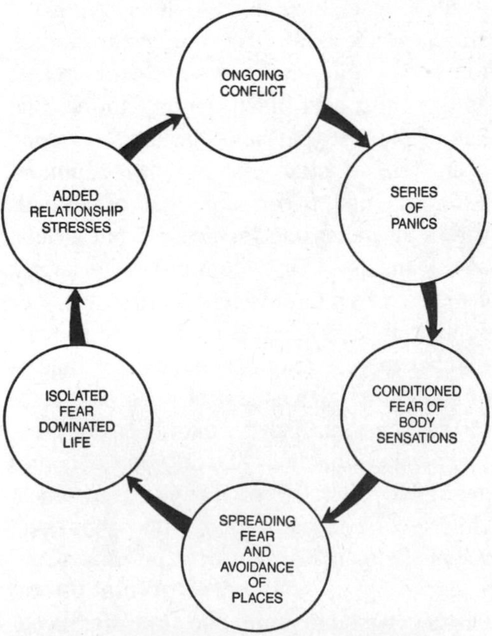

Reprinted by permission, from *Overcoming Agoraphobia,* by Dr. Alan Goldstein and Berry Stainback (New York: Viking Penguin, 1987).

Main Effects of Agoraphobia on Subjects' Lives

112 Men	%	818 Women	%
Unable to work	42	Social restrictions	29
Lack of social contacts	29	Personal psychological effect	23
Personal psychological effect	11	Marital disharmony	14
Marital disharmony	9	Unable to work	14
Travel restrictions	4	Travel restrictions	11
Guilt about children	2	Guilt about children	6

Reproduced from *Fears, Phobias, and Rituals: An Interdisciplinary Perspective,* by I.M. Marks (copyright © 1987 Oxford University Press; reproduced by permission).

Symptoms and Worst Fears During a Panic, as Listed by 100 Patients with Agoraphobia (in England)

Symptoms	%	Worst Fears	Listed as First Fear (%)	Listed as Second Fear (%)
Nervous and tense	93	Death	13	20
Dizzy or faint	83	Fainting/collapsing	38	16
Agitated	80	Heart attack	4	4
Palpitations	74	Becoming mentally ill	6	1
Weak legs	73	Causing a scene	6	7
Trembling/shaking	72	Inability to get home/		
Feeling totally unable to cope	66	to place of safety	6	26
Stomach churning	65	Losing control (e.g.,		
Sweating/perspiring	65	becoming hysterical)	7	9
Shortness of breath	59	Other personal illness	10	7
Confused	58			
Things not quite real	57			
Loss of control	52			
Tightness/pressure in the head	43			
Difficulty with eyes (blurred vision, etc.)	36			
Feeling of becoming paralyzed	19			

Reproduced from *Fears, Phobias, and Rituals: An Interdisciplinary Perspective,* by I.M. Marks (copyright © 1987 Oxford University Press; reproduced by permission).

to many disabling fears, usually involving a group of fears centering around distance from a safe place. Consequently, agoraphobics commonly fear going away from home, going into the street, into stores, occupying center seats in churches, theaters, or public transportation, crowded places, large rooms where many people are gathered, or being far from help.

Although agoraphobia has been recognized as far back as Hippocrates's time, until the latter half of the 20th century, the term agoraphobia and the agoraphobic syndrome were not well defined. Individuals who were afraid to go out were considered unusual or peculiar. Some received sympathy, some received ridicule. Even today, many agoraphobics conceal their disorder for long periods, especially if they work outside the home. Sometimes only family members and close associates are aware of the individual's problem.

Historical background

In 1871, Alexander Karl Otto Westphal (1863–1941), a German neurologist, coined the term agoraphobia, because the most striking symptom of the condition was anxiety that appeared when a phobic individual walked across open spaces or through empty streets. He described this as the "impossibility of walking through certain streets or squares, or possibility of so doing only with resultant dread of anxiety."

The previous year, Moritz Benedikt (1825–1920), an Austrian physician, described the condition but suggested that the central feature was dizziness rather than anxiety. He suggested the name *platzschwindel,* which meant "dizziness in public places." Although the term is no longer used, many individuals still report some of the same symptoms, including palpitations, trembling, sweating, nausea, pressure in the chest, headaches, breathlessness, and blushing. Some individuals have anticipatory anxiety and fear of dying. Some fear that they may attract unwanted attention.

In 1871, Westphal observed that anxiety in agoraphobia is based on ideas (cognitive factors) and not brought about by stimuli in the environment.

In 1885 a clinical description of a female agoraphobic patient appeared in the literature with a comment that the condition was uncommon among women. Interestingly, all five of Westphal's original agoraphobic patients were men! Now, however, the condition is much more common among women than men. Current estimates are that approximately 80 percent to 85 percent of the agoraphobics who seek treatment are women.

In 1912, American psychologist Morton Prince (1854–1929) wrote that such phobias "occur in people of all types and characteristics, amongst the normally self-reliant as well as amongst the timid."

Onset

Agoraphobia usually begins with a panic experience followed by extreme sensitivity to bodily sensations, self-judgment, helplessness, and social anxiety. Social fears, fear of embarrassment, or fear of sensations may lead to avoidance of critical situations and thus the frightening feelings.

Most agoraphobia begins in early adulthood, between the ages of 18 and 35, with 24 years as an average age, but many individuals do not seek treatment until about 10 years after onset. In this regard, agoraphobia differs from most simple phobias, which originate during childhood. Agoraphobia rarely occurs in children. However, it may be that childhood anxieties, such as school phobia, fear of the dark or of leaving parents, or night terrors, might sensitize someone to later agoraphobia; both problems may reflect a generally fearful disposition.

Some people who have agoraphobia can pinpoint the overt onset of their disability to some incident or situation. Typical examples

Locations of First Panic Attacks*

Location	Percentage
Auto	15%
At work	9%
Home	8%
Public places	8%
Restaurant	8%
School	7%
Away from home	7%
Store	6%
Bridge	4%
Public transportation	4%
Street	4%

*Locations in which first panic attack occurred and percent of agoraphobics with first panic in these locations.

Ronald M. Doctor, in R.L. DuPont (ed.), *Phobia: Comprehensive Summary of Modern Treatment* (New York: Brunner-Mazel, 1982).

that have been reported to therapists are a sudden bereavement, losing a baby at birth, the emotional and physical strain of a difficult pregnancy, or a state of acute shock following major surgery and a period of isolation or incapacity.

The death of a parent or spouse is a major crisis for most individuals. For an agoraphobic, however, such an event, or the threat of it, may lead to panic attacks. The same is true when college or a job transfer threatens to separate the agoraphobic from an emotional-support figure.

In many individuals, however, the agoraphobia is not triggered by a major life event. For example, some report relatively insignificant incidents at the onset of their agoraphobia, such as a minor fall on a slippery street, or being startled outdoors in the dark by a lamppost or dog. Many individuals do not recall any single stressful event preceding their first agoraphobic panic attack. However, these attacks usually do occur while the individual is under some nonacute stress, such as marital conflict, the illness of a child, engagement, marriage, pregnancy, bereavement, or physical illness.

Many individuals report that their agoraphobia began suddenly with an unexpected, spontaneous panic attack (usually lasting from two to 10 minutes) during a situation that they later came to fear and avoid. Some say the panic occurred while crossing the street, at a bus stop, or while in a crowded store.

One Australian study reported that more agoraphobia begins in summer weather than in the colder months. It may be that agoraphobic individuals become unusually anxious when they notice physical changes such as sweating and increased heart and breathing rates, which occur in everyone during hot weather.

Agoraphobia may develop within a few hours or over several years after a precursory stage of vague, intermittent anxiety. After the first anxiety attack, some individuals experience anxiety only when they return to the same or similar surroundings. For most, the fear generalizes to other situations that also elicit fear.

Once the phobic reaction happens a few times, a type of learning called *conditioning* occurs, and the reaction tends to happen more frequently in certain places. Conditioning is the process by which the fearful reactions become associated with particular things or places.

The feeling of panic in agoraphobia, like other panics, cannot be controlled easily. Some people who experience panic attacks may be predisposed (due to personality, social learning history, or perhaps genetic factors) to develop agoraphobia while others who have panic attacks do not. Usually agoraphobia becomes chronic, but it may fluctuate, depending on responses to minor occurrences in the environment. An individual may have periods of relative freedom from the disorder, sometimes with complete remissions of the fears. Research shows, however, that over time, without treatment, the agoraphobia will worsen.

Rating of Panic Provocation by Agoraphobics*

Activity	Panic-Provoking	No Problem
Driving freeways	42.6%	29.4%
Airplanes	38.8	17.7
Closed-in places	24.5	17.1
Heights	23.1	17.9
Audiences	22.0	20.2
Department stores	20.4	27.4
Crowds	18.1	15.2
Bridges	14.8	39.3
Supermarket lines	11.2	34.9
Parties	10.8	34.7
Being alone	10.8	50.8
Elevators	10.0	37.2
Restaurants	09.6	36.1
Unfamiliar places	07.9	20.9

*N = 477

Adapted from S.L. Williams, "On the Nature and Measurement of Agoraphobia," in *Progress in Behavior Modification,* 19 (1985), pp. 109–144.

Agoraphobia often develops in anxious, shy people. Some agoraphobics tend to be indecisive, have little initiative, feel guilty, and are self-demeaning, believing they should be able to get out of their situation themselves. They may become increasingly withdrawn into their restricted life. There is some evidence that dependency and perfectionism are associated with a subgroup of people who develop agoraphobia. There is also substantial clinical evidence that emotional suppression is strongly associated with development of agoraphobia.

One theory about the cause of agoraphobia is that experience in certain individuals' learning process conditioned them to regard the world as a dangerous place. Many agoraphobics have had at least one agoraphobic parent, and many have had at least one parent who is somewhat fearful. In some cases, they received mixed messages from their parents; while they were encouraged to achieve, they were not well prepared to deal with the world, either because they were overprotected, taught that home is the only safe place, or underprotected, having to take on too much responsibility at an early age.

When agoraphobics seek treatment, they are often in a constant state of alertness, have a passive and dependent attitude, and show a tendency toward sexual inhibition. Typically, the agoraphobic admits to being generally anxious and often expresses feelings of helplessness and discouragement. However, many agoraphobics were formerly active, sociable, outgoing persons. Some agoraphobics abuse alcohol and drugs, and researchers are beginning to uncover the extent of such abuse. Some current estimates place 30 percent of alcoholics as having a primary anxiety disorder that leads to the chronic use of alcohol.

General symptoms

A common characteristic of agoraphobia is a history of panic attacks in which the individual experiences symptoms of extreme excitement, distortion of perceptions, and an overwhelming sense of imminent catastrophe, loss of control, or fear of public humiliation. A fear of the fear then develops in which the individual begins experiencing anxiety in anticipation of panic reaction. The result is avoidance of the feared situation.

Situations that bring on anxiety in agoraphobia have common themes involving distance from home or other safe places, crowds, and confinement. Crowds and confinement bring on these anxieties because the individual often feels trapped and cannot leave easily, for example, in a waiting line for a bus or train, or in a crowded department store.

Still other agoraphobics are afraid to be home alone or to be outside alone. They require constant companionship. Casual observers sometimes feel the agoraphobic is lazy and shirking routine responsibility, but this is not true. Most individuals who are agoraphobic fear that they will lose control over their own reactions and that their fear may lead to a panic attack. Some are afraid of fainting, having a heart attack, dying among strangers, screaming, attacking someone, or otherwise attracting unwanted attention and causing embarrassment.

Agoraphobic people avoid specific fear-provoking situations in different ways. Most tend to avoid places that might trigger their phobia. Some phobic individuals feel better with someone they trust and may habitually depend on having a companion when they go out because a reassuring person can make a frightening situation seem safer. Some agoraphobics feel better in a public place just knowing there is a policeman or doctor nearby. Generally, stimulation (physical, emotional, perceptual) will trigger anxiety, so agoraphobic individuals generally avoid such situations as crowds, noisy places, traffic, bright lights, and movement.

Symptoms include general anxiety, spontaneous panic attacks, and occasional depersonalization. DEPERSONALIZATION is a change in the perception or experience of the self so that the feeling of one's own reality is temporarily lost. This is manifested in a sense of self-estrangement or unreality, which may include the feeling that one's extremities have changed in size, or a sense of perceiving oneself from a distance (usually from above). Depersonalization occurs in the absence of any mental disorder when an individual is experiencing overwhelming anxiety, stress, or fatigue. Experiences of depersonalization, in and of themselves, are common (nearly 50 percent of adults report having had a depersonalization experience).

For some individuals, anxiety in agoraphobia may be aggravated by certain predictable situations, such as arguments between marital partners and general STRESS. For some, the anxiety is nearly always relieved somewhat in the presence of a trusted companion. Some individuals relieve their anxiety by having with them a dog or an inanimate object such as an umbrella or shopping cart (SOTERIA).

Some agoraphobics develop ways to live more comfortably with their disorder. For example, those who go to movie theaters or churches may be less frightened if they sit in an aisle seat so that they can make a fast exit if they experience a panic attack. Having a telephone nearby is another comfort.

In severe cases, individuals may also have panic attacks, depression, feelings of depersonalization, obsessions, and other symptoms. Historically, other terms that were used to describe agoraphobic symptoms include anxiety hysteria, locomotor anxiety, street fear, phobic-anxiety-depersonalization syndrome, anxiety syndromes, phobic-anxious states, pseudoneurotic schizophrenia, and nonspecific insecurity fears.

Many agoraphobics have episodes of depression. The first episode may occur within weeks or months of the first panic attack. Individuals complain of feeling "blue," having crying spells, feeling hopeless or irritable, with a lack of interest in work and difficulty in sleeping. Agoraphobia is often aggravated during a depressive episode. The increased anxiety may make individuals less motivated to work hard at tasks (such as going out) that they previously did with difficulty.

Some agoraphobics are also claustrophobic. Usually claustrophobia is present before the agoraphobia develops. The common factor between the two phobias is that escape is blocked, at least temporarily. Some people fear confinement in a barber or beautician's chair, or a dentist's chair; some fear taking a bath in the nude. Some individuals who are phobic about bridges fear them because long, narrow bridges with open sides high above a river offer no way out except to

Percentage of Agoraphobic People Reporting Certain Situations That Relieve Anxiety

Situation	%
Being accompanied by spouse	85
Sitting near the door in a hall or restaurant	76
Focusing my mind on something else	63
Taking dog, baby carriage, etc.	62
Being accompanied by a friend	60
Talking problems over with my doctor	62
Talking problems over with a friend	62
"Talking sense to myself"	52

Reprinted with permission from Andrew M. Mathews, Michael G. Gelder and Derek W. Johnston's *Agoraphobia: Nature and Treatment* (New York: Guilford Press, 1981).

Frequency of Symptoms Other Than Phobias in Agoraphobics Compared with Healthy Controls*

	Agoraphobics	Healthy
General anxiety	80%	17%
Depression	30	3
Obsessional symptoms	10	3
Depersonalization	37	13
Loss of libido	53	3

*N = 30 in each group

Modified from Buglass, Clarke, Henderson, Kreitman, and Presley (1977), using their numbers for symptoms "clearly present," in A.M. Mathews, M.G. Gelder, and D.W. Johnston, *Agoraphobia: Nature and Treatment* (New York: The Guilford Press, 1981).

cross. Others fear tunnels and elevators for similar reasons.

Many agoraphobics develop some sexual dysfunctions due to anxiety and depression. Dr. Isaac Marks reported in 1969 that inability to achieve orgasm is not uncommon in agoraphobic women. Some agoraphobic men complain of general impotence or premature ejaculation. Anxiety from any cause reduces capacity for sexual enjoyment, and panic attacks and background tension are features of agoraphobia. Many women report that generalized anxiety and panic in agoraphobia tend to be worse just prior to and during menstruation.

Symptoms of the phobic anxiety in agoraphobia may include the many physical sensations that accompany other anxiety states, such as dry mouth, sweating, rapid heartbeat, hyperventilation, faintness, and dizziness.

The mental sensations an agoraphobic experiences include a fear of losing control and behaving in an disinhibited way, of having a heart attack because of the rapid heart action, of fainting if the anxiety becomes too intense, and of being surrounded by unsympathetic onlookers. Following is a table indicating the thoughts of some agoraphobics.

Cognitions in Agoraphobia

	First Fear	Second Fear
Fainting/collapsing	37.9%	15.8%
Death	13.2%	19.7%
Other personal illness	10.4%	9.7%
Losing control (e.g., becoming hysterical)	7.4%	6.7%
Causing a scene	6.2%	25.8%
Inability to get home to place of safety	5.9%	8.5%
Becoming mentally ill	5.8%	7.0%
Heart attack	4.1%	4.0%
Other	8.9%	3.0%

From Mathews, Gelder and Johnston's *Agoraphobia: Nature and Treatment* (New York: Guilford Press, 1981).

Panic attacks

Panic attacks are specific periods of sudden onset of intense apprehension, fearfulness, or terror, often associated with feelings of impending doom. During panic attacks there are symptoms such as difficulty in breathing (hyperventilation), palpitations, chest pain or discomfort, choking or smothering sensations, and fear of going crazy or losing control. For diagnostic purposes, the panic "syndrome" is characterized by three panic attacks within a two-week span of time. Panic syndrome leads to agoraphobia in many individuals.

Obsessions

Some agoraphobics may develop obsessional thinking about certain situations, objects, or places where the fear reaction might occur. Obsessions are recurrent, persistent ideas, thoughts, images, or impulses that are not experienced as voluntarily produced but rather as ideas that invade consciousness. Obsessional or worry thinking is difficult to control, often gravely distorts or exaggerates reality, and is the source of much anticipatory anxiety. Compulsive (superstitious) behavior may develop in an attempt to reduce obsessional thoughts and the anxiety that results from them. Some agoraphobics often have obsessive symptoms, such as ritual checking or thoughts of harming others by strangling, stabbing, or other means. They may avoid being alone with their own infants because they fear harming them. Some agoraphobics fear that they might jump from heights or in front of an oncoming train. Obsessional behavior is usually present *before* an individual develops agoraphobia.

Effects on social functioning and marriage

When individuals tend to avoid situations that provoke fear, their lives become restricted to varying extents. For example, they give up visiting homes of friends, shopping, and accompanying children to school.

They become fearful even when anticipating these situations. Some individuals report that their anticipatory fear is worse than the fear they actually experience in the situation.

Many agoraphobics become socially disabled because they cannot travel to work, visit friends, or shop. They may refuse invitations and often make excuses for not going out. Various adjustments are necessary to compensate for the phobic's lack of participation in family life and activities outside the home.

At the time they come for treatment, most agoraphobics are married. In most research projects involving agoraphobics, spouses are fairly well adjusted and integrated individuals. In some cases, therapists use the Maudsley Marital Questionnaire to assess the individual's perception of his or her marriage before and after treatment. Questions relate to categories of marital and sexual adjustment, orgasmic frequency, work and social adjustment, and "warmth" items. When agoraphobia improves with treatment, marriages usually remain stable or improve.

Agoraphobia may strain a marriage because the phobic person may ask the spouse to take over any chores that require going out, such as shopping, picking up children, and doing errands, and because spouses often must fulfill social obligations without the companionship of their mates. Spouses are additionally stressed by having to be "on call" in case anxiety attacks occur that require communication or a trip home to soothe the agoraphobic. Thus a couple that may have been happy may be driven apart by the disorder, with each blaming the other for a lack of understanding. The husband may think that the wife is not trying to overcome her phobic feelings, and the agoraphobic wife may think that her husband does not understand her suffering. The wife may become so preoccupied with fighting her daily terrors that she focuses little attention on their marital relationship and her husband's needs. However, in cases where the agoraphobic has an understanding, patient, and loving spouse, this support can be an asset in overcoming the agoraphobic condition. The spouse can attend training sessions with the therapist, attend group therapy sessions, and act as the "understanding companion" when the agoraphobic is ready to venture out.

Agoraphobia and alcoholism

Alcohol plays a significant role in the lives of many agoraphobics. As Hippocrates wrote in his *Aphorisms,* "Wine drunk with an equal quanity of water puts away anxiety and terrors."

In the early 1970s, J.A. Mullaney and C.J. Trippett described "a treatable complication of the phobic-anxiety syndrome: i.e., addiction to various habituating sedatives such as barbiturates, nonbarbiturate sedatives, minor tranquilizers and alcohol." These addictions were viewed as attempts to self-medicate for chronic anticipatory anxiety, believed to develop in response to panic attacks. Alcohol is effective in relieving chronic anticipatory anxiety, and agoraphobics may escalate to alcoholism in a mistaken attempt to prevent panic, for which it is not effective. In fact, alcohol may even exacerbate panic by contributing to a feeling of loss of control and to strange body sensations. Some agoraphobic men say that drinking helps to calm them before they venture out into public and that they avoid social situations where alcohol is not served. Likewise, some agoraphobic men say that drinking helps them to drive, as well as to be able to go to school or hold a job.

Use of alcohol to cope with panic or to overcome withdrawal due to anxiety not only increases the risk of alcoholism but may interfere with effective treatment of the agoraphobia, since central nervous system depressants reduce the efficacy of exposure treatment.

While the hypothesis that alcohol is used as self-medication or a tension reducer is complex and controversial, many researchers agree that alcohol is functionally related to agoraphobia through its capacity to relieve symptoms associated with the phobic syndrome. In one study (Mullaney and Trippet, 1979, noted in Bibb, 1986), the mean age of onset for agoraphobia among inpatient alcoholics preceded that for alcohol abuse. This led to speculation that the alcoholism might result from self-medication for a preexisting phobic disorder. In a later study, however, no consistent order of onsets was found.

In a 1986 study at the American University, Washington, D.C., (Bibb, 1986), findings indicated that outpatient agoraphobics are at clear risk for alcoholism. The research indicated that about 10 percent of agoraphobic patients were alcoholic, with men both somewhat more likely to be alcoholic and more likely to engage in severe pathological drinking. These findings probably underestimate the true extent of alcohol abuse in this population, however, as subjects selected from outpatient treatment settings probably tend to be healthier and more motivated than the wider agoraphobic population. Additionally, self-reports of alcoholism probably provide a conservative estimate due to alcoholic denial, as well as problems identifying alcoholics in remission. Many agoraphobics with a history of alcohol abuse consider themselves recovered, but such individuals may be particularly vulnerable to relapse, since they believe that alcohol helps them cope with anxiety and panic.

In the 1986 study, use of alcohol to self-medicate for phobic discomfort was reported by 91 percent of those with a history of alcoholism and 43 percent of those without such a history, suggesting that it may be a common practice among agoraphobics. Of the individuals who later became alcoholic, 33 percent reported that their earliest use of alcohol was mostly for control of phobic symptoms, indicating that a pattern of alcohol use for phobic control may lead to alcoholism for a substantial minority of individuals. Based on these findings, it appears that self-medication with alcohol for dysphoria associated with the phobic syndrome may represent enduring and intentional patterns.

Alcohol-abusing agoraphobics may differ from their nonalcoholic peers in several ways. Histories of disturbed childhoods are common both for agoraphobics and alcoholics, and such histories are important in determining the causes of combined alcoholism and agoraphobia. Disturbed childhoods of alcoholic agoraphobics frequently include familial alcoholism and depression. Also, children whose early attachments to caretakers are characterized by lack of consistent support as well as by frightening and dangerous interactions may fail to learn a sense of trust and security, and they may be particularly vulnerable to later psychopathology, such as panic attacks and agoraphobia; alcoholism may be one mode of coping for such individuals.

Depression is also frequently evident in the clinical pictures of both agoraphobia and alcoholism, and it appears to be linked to panic attacks.

Agoraphobics who have alcohol-abuse problems may also be more socially anxious than their nonalcoholic peers. High rates of social phobia have been noted among inpatient alcoholics, and major depression has been found to increase both the likelihood and intensity of agoraphobia and social anxieties. According to the American University study, alcoholic agoraphobics are more phobic and anxious on a variety of measures than their nonalcoholic counterparts. More social phobia among outpatient agoraphobics with a history of alcoholism is consistent with previous reports of high rates of social phobia, as well as agoraphobia, among inpatient alcoholics. Also, alcoholic agoraphobics are more avoidant of feared situations when accompanied, not when alone. Their social anxiety and relative failure to benefit from companionship is consistent with their more disordered and abusive childhoods. Children raised in the belief that caretakers are undependable and perhaps frightening may be less likely as adults to believe that companionship in the face of danger is beneficial. They may learn to mistrust or fear social contacts, and perhaps to respond to fearful situations with catastrophic thinking or extreme anticipation of physicial or psychosocial trauma.

The prevalence of alcohol abuse among agoraphobic individuals and its relationship to the development and course of the agoraphobic syndrome are still unclear, but it appears that there may be definite relationships.

Biological basis for agoraphobia

Many autonomic and biochemical changes occur during agoraphobic attacks; these changes may be similar to those experienced during anxiety, depression, and sudden fright. Spontaneous panics are accompanied by physical changes including increased heart rate and elevated blood pressure.

Temporary aggravation of fear may be caused by stimulants such as caffeine and yohimbine, by inhalation of carbon dioxide, infusion of sodium lactate or isoproterenol, or by hyperventilation, heat, and physical or mental effort. This may reflect a general tendency of anxious people to overreact to certain autonomic sensations produced in these various ways. The dexamethasone suppression test (used to diagnose major depression) is generally normal, and mitral valve prolapse (MVP) is not especially frequent among agoraphobics.

Some researchers hold the view that panic attacks associated with agoraphobia may be associated with hypoglycemia or mitral valve prolapse (MVP), a usually benign condition more common in women than in men, in which a defect in the shape of a mitral heart valve may cause a sudden rapid, irregular heartbeat. Some studies have shown a higher incidence of these conditions among agoraphobics, but current evidence indicates that while hypoglycemia (which is clinically quite rare) and mitral valve prolapse can produce body sensations that the individual reacts to with anxiety, they cannot cause agoraphobia, and treatment for these conditions does not cure agoraphobia. Likewise, there is *no* evidence that agoraphobia is caused by or linked to an inner-ear disorder.

In some treatment centers, as part of a diagnostic workup, agoraphobic patients are given a sodium-lactate challenge test. Individuals who have panic disorder have attacks when they are injected with sodium lactate, a substance found in everyone's body that affects the acidity of the blood. Such individuals may have a sensitivity to this or some other substance that triggers neurotransmitters in the brain to set off panic. Sodium lactate is produced by muscles during exercise. Some individuals get panic attacks when they exercise; this condition was once known as "effort syndrome." About eighty percent of those who suffer panic attacks will experience one in reaction to intravenous infusion of sodium lactate; nonpanic sufferers do not feel anything more than tingling or fatigue.

More recent studies have indicated that once a lactate-reactive person completes a behavioral treatment, their reactivity is no longer present. This would suggest that lactate reactivity is a state factor in the individual dependent on the presence of anxiety rather than a causative factor in phobic disorders. (See also LOCUS CERULEUS; NEUROTRANSMITTERS.)

Treatment

Treatment of agoraphobia is more complicated than treatment of simple phobias, because panic attacks themselves are at the root of the disorder (see Table 1).

There are many treatments for agoraphobia. Often several are combined. Most treatments are exposure-based; that is, the major component involves exposing the agoraphobic to situations that are frightening and commonly avoided, in order to demonstrate that there is no actual danger. Treatment may include direct exposure, such as having the individual walk or drive away from a safe place or a safe person, or to enter a crowded shopping center, in a structured way. Indirect exposure is also used; this may involve use of films with fear-arousing cues. Systematic desensitization is included in this category, as this procedure is characterized by exposure (either in imagination or *in vivo*) to the least reactive elements of a situation or object until the anxiety response no longer occurs. Then the next less reactive element or item is presented, and so on until the individual can be exposed to the most critical aspect without a strong anxiety response. Another imaginal procedure for anxiety treatment involves flooding, or continuous presentation of the most reactive elements of a situation until anxiety reduction occurs.

Behavior therapy may involve educating individuals about their reactions to anxiety-producing situations, explaining the physiology and genetics involved (where applicable) and teaching breathing exercises that help correct hyperventilation. Three to six months of behavior therapy is effective in many cases, and supportive and behavioral techniques reduce the anxiety level.

In recent years, exposure behavioral therapy has been used increasingly to treat agoraphobics. This is also known as *in vivo* therapy, meaning that it uses real-life exposure to the threat. It is thought that facing the fearful situation with appropriate reinforcement can help the individual undo the learned fear. Some therapists develop a "contract" with the phobic individual and set up specific goals for each week, such as walking one block from home, then two and three, taking a bus, and progressing after each session. Many therapists accompany the phobic individuals as they venture forth into public places, particularly in the early stages of treatment. In some cases, therapists train spouses or family members to accompany the phobic individual. Structured group therapy with defined goals and social-skill training for agoraphobics and their families is helpful.

Socially anxious agoraphobic individuals may benefit from assertion training while they participate in a therapy program. They may gradually expose themselves to social situations of increasing difficulty after successfully performing social skills during the assertion training sessions.

Psychotherapy can help agoraphobics resolve past conflicts that may have contributed to their condition. Before investigating the causes of the problem, however, the therapist usually tries to relieve symptoms with behavioral therapies. Drug therapy may be used at the same time. By itself, psychotherapy does not seem to be an adequate way to treat agoraphobia.

Drug therapy is sometimes useful for agoraphobics, particularly those who have panic attacks, and it enhances the results of exposure-based treatments for many individuals, at least initially. Ideally, drugs should be used for three to six months and then discontinued once the individual has some control over bodily sensations. In some individuals, attacks never recur, although in others they return months or years later. If they do, a second course of drug treatment is often successful. The treatment of choice today for agoraphobia involves use of behavioral exposure therapy and judicious use of medication, with the latter withdrawn as progress is made in behavioral therapy.

Drugs used in the treatment of panic attacks associated with agoraphobia include the tricyclic antidepressants and the monamine-oxidase inhibitors (MAOIs) (which are also used to treat severe depression), and alprazolam, an antianxiety drug. Research at the National Institutes of Mental Health indicates that drugs such as tricyclic antidepressants are successful in reducing panic attacks. Some anti-anxiety agents, such as Valium, Xanax, and Librium, reduce anticipatory fear but can lead to abuse as individuals take increasing doses to prevent panic attacks.

Self-help is useful for many agoraphobics. Some support groups encourage agoraphobics to go out together and offer one another mutual support. In this way, individuals share common experiences, learn coping tips, and have an additional social outlet. Some agoraphobics get together for outings, help take children to and from school, arrange programs, and retrain themselves out of their phobias. Since recovery from agoraphobia is a long-term process, self-help groups can provide valuable support during this process.

Involvement of spouses and family members in treatment, researchers say, produces more continuing improvement with better results than treatment involving the agoraphobic alone. The reason for greater improvement lies in motivation for continued "practice" in facing feared situations both between sessions and after treatment has ended. Home-based treatment, where patients proceed at their own pace within a structured treatment program, produce fewer dropouts than the more intensive, prolonged exposure or pharmacological treatments, but suffer from lack of necessary support.

Research

Agoraphobia is one of the phobias most actively studied by researchers and clinicians. Researchers believe that developing improved treatments for agoraphobia will be based on better definition of the agoraphobic phenomenon, and on improved measurement of treatment effects.

To assess agoraphobic conditions, researchers have devised many tests, most of which are behavioral in nature. Such tests include STANDARDIZED BEHAVIORAL AVOIDANCE TESTS (SBATs), Individualized Behavioral Tests (IBATs), the Fear Questionnaire,

Kind of Help and Effects

	Psychiatrist	Psychologist	Counselor	Medical Doctor	Other	F	df	P
Whom did you see?	36.6% (149)	22.3% (90)	9% (28)	22% (89)	8.9% (36)	15.42	4/399	.001
How long?								
1 mo. = 1	4.4%	7.3%	25.0%	20.7%	14.3%			
1–3 mo. = 2	7.7%	32.7%	16.7%	10.3%	28.6%			
4–6 mo. = 3	8.8%	12.7%	25.0%	3.4%	7.1%			
7–12 mo. = 4	6.6%	9.1%	8.3%	0	14.3%			
12+ mo. = 5	72.5%	38.2%	25.0%	65.5%	35.7%			
$\bar{x}$ =	4.35	3.38	2.92	3.79	3.29	6.14	4/198	.01
Results on phobias								
much better = 1	6.3%	5.6%	11.5%	2.6%	17.9%			
slightly better = 2	18.7%	19.7%	30.8%	9.1%	21.4%			
none = 3	64.8%	63.4%	53.8%	83.1%	60.7%			
negative = 4	10.2%	9.9%	3.8%	5.2%	0			
$\bar{x}$ =	2.79	2.79	2.50	2.92	2.43	4.22	4/326	.01
Results on non-phobias								
insight = 1	19.4%	16.1%	9.5%	3.3%	19.2%			
awareness = 2	16.3%	21.4%	33.3%	10.0%	15.4%			
skills = 3	2.0%	5.4%	4.8%	0	7.7%			
none = 4	53.1%	42.9%	47.6%	78.3%	53.8%			
negative = 5	9.2%	14.3%	4.8%	8.3%	3.8%			
$\bar{x}$ =	3.16	3.18	3.05	3.78	3.08	3.43	4/257	.01

R.M. Doctor, "Major Results of a Large-scale Survey of Agoraphobics," in DuPont's (ed.) *Phobia: A Comprehensive Survey of Modern Treatments* (New York: Bruner/Mazel, 1982).

the Mobility Inventory for Agoraphobics, Phobic Avoidance Hierarchy Ratings, Agoraphobia Severity Ratings, Agoraphobia Cognitions Questionnaire, Body Sensations Questionnaire, Self-Monitoring Activities Form, Self-Monitoring of Anxiety Form, and the Anxiety Sensitivity Index.

Researchers are also trying to clarify the relationship of agoraphobic behavior to depression, obsessions and compulsions, and depersonalization. One measure to assess these areas is the Beck Depression Inventory, devised in 1961 to assess changes in the level of depression as a function of agoraphobia treatment. The BDI contains 21 groups of statements representing different levels of severity of depression. Another test is the Middlesex Hospital Questionnaire, devised in 1968. This forty-eight-item questionnaire allows assessment of psychopathological features common to many agoraphobics.

Researchers suggest that adequate assessment of agoraphobia should include physiological measures, because agoraphobics often complain about the physiological concomitants of an anxiety reaction: palpitations, sweating, muscular tension, gastrointestinal upset, and labored breathing. Routine physiological recording has become more important since the early 1980s, when panic attacks were recognized as the central feature of the agoraphobic syndrome.

(See also ADDICTION, FEAR OF; ALCOHOLISM; ANTIDEPRESSANTS; ANXIETY; ANXIETY DISORDERS; BARLOW, DAVID H.; BEHAVIOR THERAPY; CLAUSTROPHOBIA; CONDITIONING; CONTEXTUAL THERAPY; DEPRESSION; FLOODING; INDIVIDUALIZED BEHAVIOR AVOIDANCE TESTS [IBATS]; MAUDSLEY MARITAL QUESTIONNAIRE; PANIC; PHOBIA; PHOBIC DISORDERS; PSYCHOTHERAPY.)

Barlow, D.H. and Waddell, Maria T., "Agoraphobia," in Barlow (ed.), *Clinical Handbook of Psychological Disorders* (New York: Guilford Press, 1985).

Bibb, James L. and Chambless, Dianne L., "Alcohol Use and Abuse Among Diagnosed Agoraphobics," *Beh. Res. Ther.*, 24:1 (1986), pp. 49–58.

Doctor, R.M., "Major Results of a Large-scale Survey of Agoraphobics," in Du Pont, *Phobia* (New York: Brunner/Mazel, 1982).

Fishman, Scott M. and Sheehan, David V., "Anxiety and Panic: Their Cause and Treatment," *Psychology Today* (April 1985).

Frampton, Muriel, *Agoraphobia: Coping with the World Outside*, (Wellingstorough, Northamptonshire: Turnstone Press, 1984).

Himadi, William G. et al., "Assessment of Agoraphobic-II, Measurement of Clinical Change," *Beh. Res. Ther.*, 24:2 (1986), pp. 321–332.

Marks, Isaac M., *Fears, Phobias and Rituals* (New York: Oxford U. Press, 1987).

———, "Agoraphobia Syndrome (Phobic State Anxiety)," *Arch. Gen. Psychiat.*, (December 1970).

———, *Fears and Phobias* (New York: Academic Press, 1969).

Mathews, Andrew M. et al., *Agoraphobia: Nature and Treatment* (New York: Guilford Press, 1981).

Mavissakalian, M. and Barlow, D., *Phobia: Psychology and Pharmacologic Treatment* (New York: Guilford Press, 1981).

Mullaney, J.A. and Trippett, C.J., "Alcohol Dependence and Phobias: Clinical Description and Relevance," *Brit. J. Psychiat.*, 135 (1979), pp. 565–573.

Thyer, Bruce A., "Alcohol Abuse among Clinically Anxious Patients," *Behav. Res. Ther.*, 24:3 (1986), pp. 357–359.

agraphobia Fear of sexual abuse. (See also SEXUAL ABUSE; SEXUAL FEARS.)

agrizoophobia Fear of wild animals. (See also ANIMALS, FEAR OF WILD.)

agyiophobia Fear of being in a street. Fear of streets is also known as dromophobia. This fear is related to agoraphobia and topophobia, or fear of specific places. (See also AGORAPHOBIA; LANDSCAPES.)

aha, ah-hah An experience in which an individual realizes sudden insight into a situation or solution to a problem. The aha, ah-hah response occurs during therapy at the particular moment when the features of the problem, such as the original source of ANXIETY or a PHOBIA, suddenly fit together into an understandable pattern. (See also PSYCHOTHERAPY.)

aichmophobia Fear of pointed objects, such as knives, nails, and forks. The word is derived from the Greek term *aichme,* which means "spear, point." Psychoanalytically, an aichmophobic will avoid these objects because they arouse threatening impulses to use them against others. Symptoms of this phobia may lead to unusual eating habits, such as eating alone or without silverware, or to the selection of an occupation in which the phobic individual will not encounter dangerous implements or their symbolic equivalents. (See also BEING TOUCHED, FEAR OF; KNIVES, FEAR OF; POINTS, FEAR OF.)

aichurophobia Fear of points or of pointed objects. (See also POINTS, FEAR OF.)

ailurophobia Fear of cats. The term is derived from the Greek word *ailouros,* meaning cat. Fear of cats is also known as aelurophobia, galeophobia, gatophobia, and cat phobia. In its most intense form, this phobia may cause one to become virtually homebound or confined due to fear of encountering a cat in the street or even seeing one from a vehicle. The term ailurophobia also refers to a dread of being scratched or bitten in the genital area. Shakespeare grasps the cat phobic reaction in *The Merchant of Venice* when he says: "Some men there are love not a gaping pig; some, that are mad if they behold a cat." (See also CATS, FEAR OF.)

air, fear of Air fear, or anemophobia, is the fear of wind or strong drafts. Some individuals have these fears when the weather changes (for example, when dark clouds appear) or at places where they can hear the wind. This fear may be related to a fear of motion, a fear of whirlpools, or a fear of waves. (See also CYCLONES, FEAR OF; WAVES, FEAR OF; WIND, FEAR OF.)

air pollution, fear of Many people fear air pollution because of its negative health effects. Some individuals who have a fear of contamination, or fear of illness, also fear air pollution. This is not an unreasonable fear, however, because prolonged exposure to polluted air has caused headaches, nausea, and possibly cancer, and it aggravates lung conditions. Air pollution causes anxieties because many individuals fear known as well as unsuspected effects of air pollution. (See also ACID DEW, FEAR OF; ACID RAIN, FEAR OF; CONTAMINATION, FEAR OF; POLLUTION, FEAR OF.)

airplane phobia See FLYING, FEAR OF.

airsickness, fear of Fear of airsickness (aeronausiphobia) includes fears of NAUSEA, VOMITING, and DIZZINESS while on an airplane. Individuals who fear vomiting, or seeing others vomit, may also fear being airsick themselves or seeing others afflicted. Some social phobics who fear being seen while vomiting or looking ill also fear becoming airsick. Some who fear FLYING do so out of a fear of becoming airsick. Like seasickness, airsickness is caused by unaccustomed MOTION that overstimulates the semicircular canals, the center for the sense of balance in the inner ear. Airsickness is more likely to happen in turbulent air when the plane rises and drops abruptly. Individuals prone to airsickness can help themselves by choosing a seat between the wings, reclining in the seat with their head still and their eyes either closed or fixed on the ceiling rather than looking out. (See also MOTION, FEAR OF; FLYING, FEAR OF.)

akathisia Restlessness. Akathisia may range from an inability to sit still to a mild feeling of inner unrest. Akathisia is sometimes a side effect from some antipsychotic drugs used to treat anxieties and other psychological disorders. (See also ADVERSE DRUG REACTIONS; AGITATION; ANTIPSYCHOTIC DRUGS.)

Albert B. A well-known case of an eleven-month-old child who was conditioned to fear rats and subsequently all other furry animals by John B. Watson (1878–1958), an American psychologist. Each time the child handled an animal, sudden loud sounds occurred. The phenomenon was referred to as a transfer of conditioned response. Unfortunately, Albert, or Little Albert, moved away before therapeutic deconditioning, thus leaving one of the first conditioned phobic reactions without treatment.

albuminurophobia Fear of kidney disease. (See also DISEASE PHOBIA; KIDNEY DISEASE, FEAR OF.)

alcohol, fear of Fear of alcohol is known as methyphobia. Some people fear alcohol because it is a drug that affects the central nervous system. They also fear becoming addicted to alcohol. Alcohol is a depressant, not a stimulant, as some think. It numbs the brain centers that help control one's behavior. When this occurs, the individual may feel less inhibited, less fearful, and possibly euphoric. Thus, for many, alcohol decreases normal social fears as well as judgment and problem-solving ability. Prolonged abuse of alcohol can result in alcohol addiction and in many serious physical illnesses, such as malnutrition, cirrhosis of the liver, heart failure, high blood pressure, permanent memory loss, and brain damage.

The fear of alcohol addiction is usually a product of a childhood with an alcoholic parent or seeing the destructive personal and familial effects in other loved ones, especially since much of the literature on alcoholism emphasizes the "disease" nature of the disorder and the high incidence rates among family members. Individuals with little personal identity, low self-esteem, or feelings of helplessness and dependence might have exaggerated fears of becoming alcoholic due to their personal qualities. (See also AGORAPHOBIA; ALCOHOLISM; HANGOVER; HEADACHES.)

alcoholism A physiological and psychological dependence on alcohol. Some fearful and anxious people become dependent on alcohol for relief of their symptoms. Because alcohol exerts both mental and physical effects, it becomes a major part of the dependent person's life. Many agoraphobics become alcoholics as a way of coping with their fears. Some agoraphobic individuals do not go out, so it is fairly easy for them to conceal their habit. Likewise, there is evidence emerging that over 30 percent of alcoholics are actually anxiety- or panic-ridden people who use alcohol for its anxiety relief properties. (See also ADDICTION, FEAR OF; AGORAPHOBIA; ALCOHOL, FEAR OF.)

alektorophobia Fear of chickens. This fear may be related to a fear of feathers, of winged creatures, or of flying animals or birds. (See also ANIMALS, FEAR OF; BIRDS, FEAR OF; CHICKENS, FEAR OF; FLYING THINGS, FEAR OF.)

Alexander, Franz (1891–1964) Hungarian-born American psychoanalyst who was a founder of the Chicago Institute of Psychoanalysis during the 1920s. He was a Freudian psychoanalyst and was also known as a contributor to psychosomatic medicine and brief therapy (treatment of a much shorter duration than psychoanalysis). Alexander saw the analyst as taking over the role of the individual's SUPEREGO during the process of therapy. By assuming the role once played by the patient's parents, he enabled the patient to relive past relationships, which gave him an opportunity to teach the patient to be aware of drives and learn to consciously accept or renounce them. The concept of making the individual reexpose, under more favorable circumstances, emotional situations he had been unable to handle in the past—Alexander's main contribution to the therapeutic process—had an effect on later therapies relating to the treatment of anxieties. (See also AUTOGENIC TRAINING; CORRECTIVE EMOTIONAL EXPERIENCE; PERFORMANCE ANXIETY; PSYCHOANALYSIS.)

algophobia Fear of pain. (See also PAIN, FEAR OF.)

alienation The breakdown of an interpersonal or sociological relationship that leads to anxiety and other mental distress. Social psychologists and psychiatrists use the term to denote estrangement from others as well as from one's own feelings. Alienation is a state of conflict within the individual that gives him or her a feeling of loss of identity and of DEPERSONALIZATION. Alienation is a characteristic of OBSESSIVE–COMPULSIVE DISORDER and is also seen in extreme forms of SCHIZOPHRENIA. Phobic and particularly agoraphobic reactions, like many emotional disorders, tend to result in feelings of being different, unacceptable to others, and consequently alienated. (See also AGORAPHOBIA.)

Allegron See NORTRIPTYLINE.

allergic disorders Uncomfortable and sometimes seriously threatening bodily reactions to stimuli, such as airborne substances (pollen or dust), foods (egg yolks or chocolate), or bee stings. Fearful situations can heighten the body's sensitivity and produce allergic reactions that vary greatly between people. Some respond with stomach problems, some with rashes, and others with respiratory disorders such as asthma. Commonly, allergic reactions can trigger anxiety. For example, the asthmatic may become frightened about repeated attacks during which he has trouble breathing. Those who have skin rashes can become so embarrassed, sensitive, and anxious about their appearance that their normal social functioning is impaired during attacks. When allergic disorders are treated medically, some related ANXIETIES usually disappear. Allergic sensitivity heightens the intensity of anxiety. (See also ASTHMA.)

Bugelski, B. Richard and Anthony M. Graziano. *Handbook of Practical Psychology* (Englewood Cliffs, NJ: Prentice-Hall, 1980).

alliumphobia Fear of garlic. (See also GARLIC, FEAR OF.)

allodoxaphobia Fear of opinions. This may relate to hearing or learning opinions of others or fearing one's own opinions. This fear may also be related to a fear of criticism. (See also CRITICISM, FEAR OF; OPINIONS, FEAR OF OTHERS'.)

Allport, Gordon Willard (1897–1967) An American psychologist who specialized in the study of personality. Allport emphasized individual values, uniqueness of personality, and the study of traits (persisting characteristics of personality that can be measured).

In his theory of "functional autonomy," Allport stressed the importance of the present moment and the relative unimportance of genetic explanations of behavior. His definition of an attitude has become famous: "a mental and experiential state of readiness, organized through experience, exerting a directive or dynamic influence upon the individual's response to all objects and situations with which it is related."

Allport identified 20,000 English words (many of which are anxiety traits) that can be used to describe uniquenesses among people. When overlapping meanings were taken into account, this list was reduced to 171 different terms.

Among his works are *Personality: A Psychological Interpretation* (1937) and several books on prejudice. He was coauthor of two personality inventories, the Allport-Vernon-Lindzey Study of Values and the Allport A-S Reaction Study.

Allport, G.S., "Attitudes," in C. Murchison (ed.), *Handbook of Social Psychology* (Worcester, MA: Clark U. Press, 1935).

alone, fear of being Fear of being alone is known as phobophobia and eremophobia. Fear of being alone sometimes relates to AGORAPHOBIA. Another term for the dread of solitude used by American physician and author Benjamin Rush (1745–1813) was "solo phobia." "This distemper is peculiar to persons of vacant minds, and guilty consciences. Such people cannot bear to be alone, especially if the horror of sickness is added to the pain of attempting to think, or to the terror of thinking."* (See also AGING, FEAR OF; SINGLE-ROOM OCCUPANCY AND PHOBIAS.)

*Runes, D.D., *The Selected Writings of Benjamin Rush* (New York: The Philosophical Library, 1947).

alpha adrenergic blockers See ADRENERGIC BLOCKING AGENTS; ADRENERGIC DRUGS.

alpha adrenergic function See ADRENERGIC SYSTEM.

alprazolam An antianxiety drug (also referred to as an ANXIOLYTIC or SEDATIVE). Marketed under the trade name Xanax, alprazolam is a triazolobenzodiazepine belonging to the BENZODIAZEPINE class of drugs. The drug offers effects comparable to tricyclic ANTIDEPRESSANTS and may be better for use as an antidepressant for persons who have a high degree of anxiety and agitation. Because alprazolam seems to have no cardiac side effects, it is of special interest in the treatment of anxious or depressed cardiac patients. A study reported in the *Journal of Clinical Psychopharmacology* (February 1986) showed that alprazolam-treated postcoronary bypass patients experienced rapid beneficial effect from short-term use of the drug. The action of alprazolam and its effects are generally similar to those of the other benzodiazepines. As with other drugs of this class, dependency develops and prominent withdrawal effects can occur.

Freeman, Arthur M., III, et al., "Alprazolam Treatment of Postcoronary Bypass Anxiety," *Journal of Clinical Psychopharmacology* (February 1986).

LaPierre, Y.P., "New Antidepressant Drugs," *Journal of Clinical Psychiatry*, 44 (August 1983), pp. 41–44.

amathophobia Fear of dust. (See also DUST, FEAR OF.)

amaxophobia Fear of being in a vehicle. (See also AUTOMOBILES, FEAR OF; CLAUSTROPHOBIA; TRAINS, FEAR OF; VEHICLES, FEAR OF.)

ambivalence The simultaneous existence of two sometimes contradictory feelings, attitudes, values, goals, or directions. The term was introduced by Eugen BLEULER, a Swiss psychiatrist (1857–1939), to denote the simultaneous occurrence of two antagonistic emotions, such as hatred and love toward the same person, or inclination and disinclination toward the same activity or goal. For example, some individuals have feelings of ambivalence toward parents who dole out love and affection as well as punishment. Some individuals are ambivalent about work, marriage, and other major life issues. Ambivalence is common in PHOBIAS, including AGORAPHOBIA, as there is often a simultaneous approach–avoidance attitude toward potentially fearful situations.

American Board of Medical Psychotherapists An interdisciplinary organization that offers certification and training to a wide range of professionals who practice PSYCHOTHERAPY, many of whom specialize in treatment of fears and phobias. The ABMP was founded in 1982. With the trend toward more generic forms of licensure and certification throughout health-care specialities in the United States, Canada, Western Europe, and Australia, it has become increasingly important for all professionals to identify their most salient areas of expertise in practice. The ABMP, through its credentialing review and continuing-education programs, offers the public; medical, psychiatric and academic institutions; health-care professionals; employers; and insurance carriers a mechanism for identifying well-qualified professionals who are highly trained in the application of medical psychotherapy. The purpose of the ABMP is to apply high standards to the professional credentialing procedure and encourage interdisciplinary excellence in the performance of medical psychotherapy services and related methods of behavioral assessment and change.

For information:
American Board of Medical Psychotherapists
Physicians' Park B, Suite 11
300 Twenty-first Avenue North
Nashville, TN 37203

American Psychiatric Association The largest professional organization of American physicians who specialize in the practice of psychiatry. The organization was founded in 1844 as the Association of Medical Superintendents of American Institutions for the Insane. In 1891 the name was changed to the American Medico-Psychological Association and in 1921 to its present name. Individuals who have phobias, anxieties, and other concerns may contact the association for information.

American Psychiatric Association
1400 K Street, N.W.
Washington, DC, 20005

(See also PSYCHIATRY; PSYCHOTHERAPY.)

amineptine An antidepressant drug. (See also ANTIDEPRESSANTS, NEW.)

Amitid A trade name for the drug amitriptyline. (See also AMITRIPTYLINE.)

amitriptyline An antidepressant drug known as a tricyclic compound (one of two major classes of antidepressant drugs). It is a popular antidepressant that has a moderate to marked SEDATIVE action. Because the sedative effect of amitriptyline interacts additively with the sedative effect of ALCOHOL, alcohol consumption should be avoided by individuals taking amitriptyline, particularly if they drive a car or work in a hazardous occupation. Amitriptyline compounds are also used to treat HEADACHES associated with depression that are the result of nonorganic causes. Amitriptyline also is know by the trade names Endep, Elavil, Amitid, Domical, Lentizol, Triptafen, and Triptizol. (See also ADVERSE DRUG REACTIONS; ANTIDEPRESSANTS; DEPRESSION; DRUGS; TRICYCLIC ANTIDEPRESSANTS.)

American Medical Association, *AMA Drug Evaluations* (Chicago: American Medical Association, 1980).

amnesia, fear of Fear of having amnesia is known as amnesiophobia. Amnesia is an inability to recall past experiences, or loss of memory. There are two basic types of amnesia that people fear. One is anterograde amnesia, or an inability to form new memories, in which the individual either does not consolidate what is perceived into permanent memory storage or cannot retrieve recent memories from storage. The other is retrograde amnesia, which is a loss of memory of events that occurred before the memory disturbance began. Episodic amnesia refers to a particular event or period in one's life that is forgotten. The episode may have been a significant one that may have led to the development of one or more phobias or anxieties. The fear of amnesia is now commonly related to the development of Alzheimer's disease. (See also REPRESSION.)

amnesiophobia Fear of having amnesia. (See also AMNESIA, FEAR OF.)

amoxapine an ANTIDEPRESSANT drug, also used for ANXIETY and to treat HEADACHES due to nonorganic causes. (See also ANTIDEPRESSANTS, NEW.)

amphetamines Amphetamines, popularly referred to as "speed," include dextroamphetamines, methamphetamines, and methylphenidates. Amphetamines are sometimes prescribed for DEPRESSION and to give the user a sense of well-being and increased alertness. In some cases, they may relieve anxiety symptoms. They are sometimes abused by individuals who have depression and anxieties, and they should be prescribed only for a limited time and for a specific purpose. All drugs in this group are associated with dependence, and all can produce one or more organic mental disorders, intoxication, delirium, delusional syndrome, or withdrawal syndrome. These drugs also act as appetite suppressants. Because of the possibility of patients' developing dependency on amphetamines, many physicians have stopped prescribing them. (See also ADVERSE DRUG REACTIONS; APPETITE SUPPRESSANTS; DRUGS.)

amulets Some individuals who fear witchcraft wear amulets, such as stones, bones, nails, rings, or other objects. Wearers believe that the amulets offer them protection and comfort when facing anxiety about feared situations. Some amulets may have special significance, such as objects found at a significant place of burial or under certain astrological configurations. (See also MAGIC, FEAR OF; WITCHES AND WITCHCRAFT, FEAR OF.)

amychophobia Fear of being scratched. Often such fears are associated with avoidance of ANIMALS, particularly cats, dogs, puppies, and kittens. In many cases the fear is irrational and exaggerated; however, for individuals who have severe allergic reactions to animal scratches, animal hair, or fleas, the fear is quite appropriate. (See also ANIMALS, FEAR OF; SCRATCHED, FEAR OF BEING.)

amygdala A tiny, almond-shaped organ deep in the brain that has been implicated in reactions of fear, aggression, defense, attack (fight or flight), and avoidance learning. There is considerable uncertainty about the role of the amygdala in phobias The amygdala is part of the limbic system. (See also LIMBIC SYSTEM.)

anablepophobia See HIGH PLACES, FEAR OF LOOKING UP AT.

anal stage The second stage of psychosexual development during with libidinal energies are derived from anal activity. The child focuses on the pleasurable feelings of retaining and expelling the feces; this usually occurs during the second year of life. Some phobic reactions and phobias (such as contamination and germ fears, fear of lack of resources such as money, and obsessive–compulsive disorder) relate back to this stage in the individual's development, according to psychoanalytic theory. (See also DEVELOPMENTAL STAGES; FREUD, SIGMUND; OBSESSIVE–COMPULSIVE DISORDERS; PSYCHOANALYSIS.)

analgesia Also known as analgia. This is an insensitivity to pain, which may be due to an organic disorder or to psychological factors, while other senses remain intact. Some degree of analgesia can be induced by distraction, such as by light or sound. Analgesia may also occur in hysterical disorders and schizophrenia. Muscle tension associated with ANXIETY can restrict sensitivity to physical sensations.

A second meaning of analgesia is pain relief from medications. Pain-alleviating drugs are referred to as analgesics or analgesic drugs. (See also ANALGESICS; DRUGS; PAIN.)

analgesics Pharmacologic agents used to alleviate pain and treat ANXIETIES without inducing a loss of consciousness. Analgesics were commonly prescribed for anxiety before the advent of modern tranquilizers. Psychic factors are involved in the experience of pain, including expectations, emotions and thoughts. When tranquilizers and neuroleptics are used to alleviate pain, mental elements may be more affected than physical elements Analgesics may induce slight drowsiness. Some analgesics contain narcotics, which may produce drug ADDICTION or dependence. Examples are opium alkaloids, morphine, codeine, and heroin. The morphine antagonists nalorphine and pentazocine are analgesics but are not addictive.

O'Brien, Robert and Sidney Cohen, *The Encyclopedia of Drug Abuse* (New York: Facts On File, 1984).

analysand The individual undergoing psychoanalysis for a phobia or any other reason. (See also PSYCHOANALYSIS.)

analysis See PSYCHOANALYSIS.

analysis, focused A modification of the classical psychoanalytic technique useful for helping individuals with ANXIETIES and PHOBIAS. In focused analysis, also known as selective, directed, or expectant analysis, the analyst waits and follows the spontaneous unfolding of the individual's thoughts with leisurely, unfocused attention. The analyst targets interpretations to a particular aspect of the personality, such as defenses, conflicts that are causing anxieties, or stages of psychosexual development. (See also PSYCHOANALYSIS.)

analysis, fractional A brief therapy method (focused, short-term therapy based on psychoanalytic theory) introduced by Franz Alexander (1891–1964), a Hungarian-American psychoanalyst and pioneer in brief analytic therapy. In fractional analysis, PSYCHOTHERAPY is suspended for prearranged intervals while the individual works through insights already attained, including those related to ANXIETIES and PHOBIAS. (See also ALEXANDER, FRANZ; BRIEF PSYCHOTHERAPY.)

analyst Along with the term psychoanalyst, usually refers to therapists who follow routines of psychoanalysis as outlined by Sigmund FREUD (1856–1939). Analysts who follow concepts of Carl JUNG (1875–1963) are called analytical psychologists. Those who use the concepts of Adolf MEYER (1866–1950) are psychobiologists. Those who follow Alfred ADLER (1870–1937) are individual psychologists. All these types of analysts try to help individuals with anxieties and phobias. (See also PSYCHOLOGY; PSYCHOANALYSIS.)

anamnesis A process by which the individual recalls past events and the feelings associated with them. The word literally means "not forgetting." The term applies to the lengthy process of retrospective investigation into an individual's past prior to diagnosis in long-term treatments for ANXIETY and other disorders. (See also MEDICAL MODEL; MEMORIES.)

anaphylaxis, psychic Reactivation of earlier symptoms by an event similar to the one that initially produced the symptoms, such as anxieties or phobias. The initial event may be the sensitizing agent, and the later event the activating agent. For example, the early event may have been a near-drowning and the later event an incident that happens near water, with the result that the individual fears water.

Anatomy of Melancholy, The An early volume on physical and mental health, compiled by Robert Burton (1577–1640), an English clergyman and writer. The work is of interest to those concerned with the historical background of anxieties and fears. The book contains sections on causes, symptoms, and treatment of melancholy (depression), and melancholy of love and religion. The book indicates early recognized connections between mental disorders and environmental conditions. Burton recommended special hospitals, pensions for the elderly, and free housing for the poor. Burton believed in witches and that witches could cure melancholy. Burton, after suffering from anxieties and depression throughout his life, is said to have hanged himself. (See also DEPRESSION; MELANCHOLY.)

androgens See HORMONES.

androphobia Morbid fear of men. (See also MEN, FEAR OF; SEXUAL FEARS.)

anemophobia See AIR, FEAR OF.

angina pectoris A specific type of discomfort in the chest. Angina pectoris is not a sharp pain, but rather a sensation of pressure, squeezing, or tightness. It usually starts in the center of the chest under the breastbone (sternum) and radiates to the throat area. Angina generally results from the muscle fibers of the heart not getting enough blood through the coronary arteries to nourish them. This condition, known as myocardial ischemia, is associated with coronary heart disease and is usually the result of the narrowing of blood vessels by atherosclerosis, or hardening of the arteries. It may also be related to heart failure, other heart conditions, blood deficiency diseases such as anemia, or low blood pressure.

Angina symptoms appear when an individual exerts himself, and the discomfort disappears when he rests. Attacks usually last for only two or three minutes, but if they are triggered by ANXIETY or other emotional tension and the individual cannot relax, they may last ten minutes or more. The first time an individual has uncomplicated angina pectoris, he may fear that he is having a fatal HEART ATTACK. He may become extremely anxious and even have a PANIC ATTACK, which will aggravate his chest pains. He should be reassured that he has little to fear if he rests both physically and mentally. (See also CHOKING, FEAR OF; HEART ATTACK, FEAR OF; HEART ATTACK, ANXIETY FOLLOWING; NARROWNESS, FEAR OF.)

anginophobia Fear of ANGINA PECTORIS or related heart problems. (See also CHOKING, FEAR OF; HEART ATTACK, FEAR OF; HEART ATTACK, ANXIETY FOLLOWING; NARROWNESS, FEAR OF.)

Anglophobia Fear of England, the English language, and things relating to the English culture.

angst Loosely, anxiety. Angst is a major concept of the existentialist approach to psychology, which tries to understand the essence of human existence by emphasizing basic human values such as love, free will, and self-awareness. The word "angst" is derived from the German term meaning "fear, anxiety, anguish." American psychoanalyst ROLLO MAY (1909–present) described angst as "the inward state of my becoming aware that my existence can become lost, that I can lose myself and my world, that I can become nothing." Anxiety strikes at the center of an individual's existence, whereas FEAR, in contrast, is a threat to the periphery of physical survival. (See also EXISTENTIAL.)

Angyal, Andras (1902–1960) Hungarian-born American psychologist well known as an advocate of HUMANISTIC PSYCHOLOGY, an approach used by some therapists to treat individuals who have phobias and anxieties. Angyal was the author of *Foundations for a Science of Personality* (1941), and *Neurosis and Treatment: A Holistic Theory* (1965).

anhedonia A term that refers to an ongoing lack of emotional responsiveness and pleasure in life events. A quality commonly found in SCHIZOPHRENIA, anhedonia is contrasted with an excitable personality that might become anxious.

animals, fear of Fear of animals is known as zoophobia. Many individuals fear animals in general (zoophobia), wild animals (agrizoophobia), or particular animals such as SNAKES (ophidiophobia), CATS (ailurophobia), DOGS (cynophobia), INSECTS (acarophobia), MICE (musophobia), or SPIDERS (arachneophobia). Animal phobias are often acquired by vicarious modeling—for example, by seeing an animal in a frightening situation, such as a dog attacking a person in a movie or on the street; by having a traumatic experience, such as being bitten, or by generalization (for example, fear of dogs generalized to cats).

The most common animal phobias are of dogs, cats, snakes, worms, spiders, birds, mice, fish, and frogs. While animal fears are prevalent in the general population, fewer people who fear animals seek treatment than do people who have social fears or agoraphobia, because fear of animals, usually considered a specific phobia, does not disrupt one's life to the extent that some other phobias do.

Animal phobias usually develop early in life, around age four, and rarely after age seven or eight. However, if an individual experiences some traumatic event later in life, such as being attacked by a dog, a fear may develop even during adulthood.

Nearly all children show some fear of one animal or another at some time. Many such fears are overlooked because they cause only mild disturbance, and sometimes these fears disappear spontaneously or are outgrown without any disturbing recurrence. It is only when a child's fear of certain animals radically disturbs his or her normal functioning that therapy becomes necessary—for example, when someone is fearful of leaving home because of the possibility of seeing a dog (or other feared animal) on the street.

In *Totem and Taboo,* Sigmund Freud suggested why many children fear animals. The relation of the child to animals, he said, has much in common with that of primitive man. The child does not show any trace of the pride that moves adults to recognize a dividing line between his own nature and that of all other animals. The child unhesitatingly attributes full equality to animals and, in fact, may feel more closely related to animals than to the mysterious adult. However, sometimes there is a curious disturbance in this understanding between child and animal. The child suddenly begins to fear a certain type of animal and to protect himself against seeing or touching any of this species. The result is a clinical picture of an animal phobia. The phobia is usually expressed toward animals in which the child has until then shown the liveliest interest, and it has nothing to do with the animal itself. Sometimes animals known to the child only in picture books and fairy stories become objects of the inordinate anxiety manifested in the phobia.

Psychoanalytically, animals are sometimes considered to represent unconsciously feared parents (for example, a horse might symbolize the father, a bear the mother) or repressed impulses (for example, snakes as phallic symbols).

In his classic analyses of two infantile animal phobias (''Analysis of a Phobia in a Five-Year-Old Boy'' and ''From the History of an Infantile Neurosis,'' *Collected Papers* III), Freud suggested that the essential feature of animal phobia is displacement of the child's fear from a person important in his emotional life onto some animal selected by the child according to individual circumstances. Thus the animal becomes a substitute for the feared person. Moreover, because libidinal striving, as well as feelings of hate toward the feared object, is transferred in this displacement, the relationship to the feared animal is an ambivalent one. To the patient, the animal phobia has a great advantage over the original fear, because with appropriate behavior, the phobia permits avoidance of fear and anxiety. While the child succeeds in staying away from the feared animal, he or she is free from anxiety. The fear reappears only when the child leaves the protected domain and enters the danger zone of the dreaded animal.

Unlike Freudian analysts, behavioral psychologists emphasize the learned nature of animal fears either through direct-traumatic exposure (classical conditioning) or vicariously by observation, via films, television, newspapers, and stories. Traumatic conditioning is relatively less common (e.g., only about 5 percent of snake phobics have had contact with a snake, or even seen one!), but many dog, bird, insect, cat, and common animal phobias begin with a traumatic or frightening experience involving one of these animals. Vicarious conditioning, a far more common means of acquiring a phobia, occurs when the individual observes another person (often a parent) react to a situation, animal, or person with anxiety. One such experience can be enough to instill a permanent fear if identification with the model is strong and the modeling reaction is intense. Viewers of films such as *Jaws* or *Psycho* perhaps understand how such learning can take place.

Prior to adolescence, there are few gender differences relating to animal phobias. However, after adolescence, animal phobias are more prevalent among females. One study (Marks, 1969) reported that upward of 95 percent of animal phobics are female.

There is evidence that some animal phobias (such as fear of snakes) may have an innate component, perhaps a vestige of a survival mechanism that kept small children away from dangerous animals. (See also AMBIVALENCE; CHILDHOOD ANXIETIES, FEARS, and PHOBIAS; LITTLE HANS; SPECIFIC PHOBIAS; SYMBOLISM.)

Freud, Sigmund, *Totem and Taboo* (London: Routledge and Kegan Paul, 1950).

———, "Analysis of a Phobia in a Five-Year-Old Boy," in *Complete Works* (London: Hogarth, N.D.).

Kleinknecht, Ronald A., *The Anxious Self* (New York: Human Sciences Press, 1986).

Marks, Isaac M., *Phobias and Fears* (New York: Academic Press, 1969).

Sterba, Edith, "Excerpt from the Analysis of a Dog Phobia," *The Psychoanalytic Quarterly*, 4(1935), pp. 135–160.

animals, fear of wild Fear of wild animals is known as agrizoophobia. (See also ANIMALS, FEAR OF.)

animism The belief, stemming from primitive times, that inanimate objects possess life, consciousness, and will. Some individuals attribute various life characteristics to things they fear, such as mountains, TREES, RIVERS, stones, etc. Because of this belief, some individuals become fearful of inanimate objects. For example, young children may believe that the SUN is alive because it produces light or that a vacuum cleaner eats because it sucks up items from the floor. Because of such beliefs, children as well as adults may become phobic about certain objects and perpetuate their fears to their own children. (See also CHILDHOOD ANXIETIES, FEARS, AND PHOBIAS; FAIRY TALES.)

ankylophobia See IMMOBILITY OF A JOINT, FEAR OF.

Anna O. (1859–1936) The first case in psychoanalysis. Anna O. was treated by BREUER and written about by Breuer and FREUD in their work, *Studies in Hysteria* (1893–1895). The patient's real name was Bertha Pappenheim. She was a pioneer social worker and feminist who became well known for her work with the sick and poor and later traveled extensively, including to the Henry Street Settlement in New York City. At age twenty-one, after sitting at the bedside of her ailing father for months, Bertha was diagnosed as having a malady then called "hysteria." Her symptoms included inability to eat, hallucinations of snakes and death's heads, limb paralysis, and multiple personalities; she attempted suicide. Breuer used a technique to help her that may have been hypnosis or autohypnosis. Later, as she began to talk about memories from the past, her emotional expression had the effect of CATHARSIS, or of inducing relief from her anxieties. Her squinting eyes relaxed, and she and Breuer surmised that her eyes became frozen in that position because she was crying when she tried to see a clock to tell her ailing father the time. Her inability to drink came from having seen a dog drinking out of a glass, which apparently disgusted her. After she relived a traumatic time during her father's last illness, her paralyzed arm became useful again. She later spent some time in sanatoriums and became addicted to morphine, which had been prescribed for her as a sedative. She never married and dedicated her life to improving conditions for women and children. (See also HYPNOSIS.)

anorexia nervosa A syndrome characterized by a persistent lack of appetite and considerable reduction in food intake. Anorexia nervosa, a way of coping with anxiety about food and body image, occurs mostly among adolescent girls but has been known among all age groups in both sexes. Symptoms include severe weight loss, wasting (cachexia), vomiting, and amenorrhea (cessation of the menstrual period). Girls may "feel fat," deny their illness, and develop an active disgust for food. Anorexia nervosa is a life-threatening condition; there have been many deaths from the syndrome, which requires medical as well as psychological treatment.

The term was proposed by Sir William Gull in 1874 and has been found in medical literature since then. Individuals who have anorexia are known as anorexics. Some psychiatrists believe that girls who refrain from eating wish to remain "thin as a boy" in an effort to escape the burdens of growing up and assuming a female sexual and marital role. Anorexia nervosa also may be related to a fear of SWALLOWING (phagophobia).

Anorexia nervosa and OBSESSIVE–COMPULSIVE DISORDER may be related. Studies have examined the psychiatric symptoms associated with anorexia nervosa, especially DEPRESSION and obsessive–compulsive personality. As many as half of all anorexics may qualify for a diagnosis of obsessive–compulsive disorder based on nonfood or body-related obsessions. (See also EATING DISORDERS; FOOD, FEAR OF.)

Kasvikis, Y.G. et al., "Past History of Anorexia Nervosa in Women with Obsessive-Compulsive Disorder," *Int. J. of Eating Disorders*, 5:6(1985).

Anorgasmia (anorgasmy) Inability to achieve orgasm or the absence of the orgasmic phase in the sexual reaction cycle. Some women fear sexual intercourse because of anorgasmia. Anorgasmia may be caused by fears about sexual intercourse, incompatible sexual attitudes in the partners, anatomical and neurophysiological defects, fear of painful intercourse, and sociocultural conditioning. (See also FRIGIDITY; SEXUAL FEARS; SEX THERAPY.)

anthophobia Fear of flowers. (See also FLOWERS, FEAR OF.)

anthropophobia Fear of people or human society. (See also PEOPLE, FEAR OF.)

antianxiety drugs Drugs used to reduce anxiety and tension; they are known also as minor tranquilizers. Antianxiety drugs are used by individuals during times of stress and in treatment of stress-related physical disorders under the supervision of a physician. (See also ANXIETY; ANXIETY DRUGS.)

antibiotics Drugs used to treat infectious diseases by destroying pathogenic or noxious microorganisms. Antibiotics are generally not effective in treating viral diseases. The best-known antibiotics are penicillin and streptomycin. Antibiotics are produced by or derived from living cells, such as molds, yeasts, or bacteria, or are manufactured as synthetic chemicals with effects similar to natural antibiotics. Some antibiotics act by interfering with the ability of bacteria to reproduce; others disrupt the pathogen's normal life functions.

Since the discovery that ribonucleic acid (RNA) has effects on learning and retention,* antibiotics have been of interest to psychologists. In experiments, some antibiotics seem to block long-term memory with no effect on short-term memory. Some phobias may have origins in long-term memories. Just how antibiotics influence retention is not yet clear. (See also DRUGS.)

anticholinergics Substances that block or interfere with the acetycholine transmission of impulses in the parasympathetic nervous system. The parasympathetic nervous system actively produces relaxation, calmness, digestion, and sleep. The best-known natural substances with anticholinergic effects are atropine (used as a drug to dilate the eyes) and scopolamine (a plant substance used with morphine to induce sleep). Some antidepressants and antipsychotic drugs have anticholinergic properties; anticholinergic effects sometimes include unpleasant side effects, such as extreme dryness of the mouth. Many synthetic anticholinergics are used to treat nervous-system disorders such as Parkinson's disease. (See also AGORAPHOBIA; ANTIDEPRESSANTS; DEPRESSION; DRUGS; DRY MOUTH.)

O'Brien, Robert and Sidney Cohen, *The Encyclopedia of Drug Abuse* (New York: Facts On File, 1984).

anticonvulsives Substances that prevent convulsions or limit their frequency or severity. In high doses, TRANQUILIZERS and hypnotic drugs may act as anticonvulsants. Anticonvulsives are also known as antiepileptics. Many anticonvulsives are central nervous system depressants and also reduce the incidence of anxiety symptoms. (See also DRUGS.)

*As reported by Agranoff, B.S., R.E. Davis, R. Lim and L. Casola, Biological Effects of Antimetabolics Used in Behavioral Studies,'' in *Psychopharmacology, 1957–67* D. Efron, (Washington DC: U.S. Government Printing Office 1968); and J.A. Deutsch, ''The Physiological Basis of Memory,'' *Annual Review of Psychology* 20 (1969), pp. 85–104.

antidepressants There are three major categories of drugs used to treat depression: tricyclic antidepressants (TCAs), monoamine oxidase (MAO) inhibitors, and lithium. Antidepressants are available only by prescription, and because depressive symptoms are merely suppressed, not cured, by these drugs, they are usually prescribed in conjunction with some type of psychotherapy. Commonly, antidepressant medications take up to two to three weeks before having a full effect (although side effects may begin immediately). The time elapsing before the drug becomes therapeutic varies with the drug. Antidepressants may have to be taken regularly for months, even years, if their gains are to persist. Relapse often occurs upon stopping the drug.

Unlike antianxiety drugs, antidepressants generally do not interfere with exposure therapy. Individuals with phobias or rituals are urged to carry out self-exposure treatment in addition to medication. Antidepressants are useful in treatment of panic disorders and seem to have an inhibitory effect on panic. However, antidepressants are generally not used to treat anxiety by itself or agoraphobia.

How antidepressants work

Because most drugs used to treat depression and most psychostimulants either mimic certain neurotransmitters (biochemicals that allow brain cells to communicate with one another) or alter their activity, a general hypothesis is that a decrease in activity or concentration of these neurotransmitters occurs during depression. Two of the major neurotransmitters involved appear to be norepinephrine and serotonin. The precise pharmacologic mechanisms of antidepressant drugs, as well as the balances of neurotransmitters in individuals exhibiting depression, are still open to debate. As newer, more specific antidepressants are developed, our understanding of antidepressants and depression continues to evolve.

Tricyclic antidepressants

Tricyclic antidepressants are generally the preferred drugs for treating depression. They are referred to as "tricyclic" because the chemical diagrams for these drugs resemble three rings connected together. In the late 1940s imipramine (a tricyclic) was first synthesized in the lab. Since then, tricyclics have been heavily tested and used as antidepressants.

Tricyclics elevate mood, increase physical activity and mental alertness, and improve appetite and sleep patterns in depressed individuals. The effect might more accurately be described as a reduction of depression as opposed to euphoric stimulation. When given to a nondepressed person, tricyclics do not elevate mood or stimulate the person; instead, the effects are likely to be feelings of unhappiness and an apparent increase in anxiety.

Tricyclic antidepressants are relatively safe and generally well tolerated. The side effects are minimal. Their antidepressant effects, however, often take several weeks to appear, for reasons not yet well understood. Because of this lag, tricyclics are not prescribed on an "as-needed" basis.

Unfortunately, no clinical signs or aspects of a person's medical history indicate which tricyclic antidepressant is likely to be the best for him or her. Some depressed individuals may respond remarkably well to one tricyclic, but not at all to another. Due to the time lag of several weeks before any beneficial effects show up, the physician must try first one drug for that time, and then, if results are not achieved, prescribe another tricyclic, again for several weeks. Such trials, with their waiting and uncertainty, may lead to some anxiety and frustration for both the individual and his or her doctor.

Use of tricyclics in agoraphobia

When used in the treatment of agoraphobia with panic attacks, tricyclic antidepressants have been shown to cause moderate or marked improvement in reduction of panic attacks in about 25 percent of those who can tolerate the drug.

Use of tricyclics in obsessive–compulsive disorders

In patients who have obsessive–compulsive disorders, including ritualistic or ruminative (persistently pondering problems) behaviors, the tricyclic drug clomipramine has been reported to be effective. Clomipramine effectively reduces most symptoms in at least 20 percent of those who can tolerate the drug, according to a National Institutes of Mental Health report.

Side effects of antidepressants

The chief side effects of tricyclic antidepressants include dry mouth, blurring of vision, headache, urinary hesitation, and constipation. Excessive sweating is also a common side effect. Drowsiness and dizziness, as well as vertigo, weakness, rapid heart rate, and reduced blood pressure upon standing upright, are likely to occur early on but usually disappear within the first several weeks. Tricyclics should be used cautiously in persons with heart problems.

Drug interactions

It is considered good judgment not to combine tricyclic antidepressants with MAO inhibitors. Although very rare, a severe interaction between the two drugs can occur; in extreme cases, convulsions, seizures, and coma can occur. A more common drug interaction involves the combination of tricyclics and alcohol, and possibly other sedatives. Tricyclic antidepressants increase the effects of these substances.

Monoamine Oxidase (MAO) Inhibitors

MAO inhibitors (or MAOIs) are primarily used for persons who do not respond ade-

Common Antidepressant Medicines That Are Used in Treating Anxiety Disorders

Generic Name	United States Brand Name	United Kingdom Brand Name	Relative Sedative Effects	Relative Anticho-linergic Effects	Relative Hypo-tensive Effects
Tricyclic antidepressants					
amitriptyline	Endep Elavil Amitid	Domical Elavil Lentizol Triptafen Tryptizol	High	High	More
amoxapine	Asendin	*Not available in U.K.*	Medium	Low	Less
desipramine	Norpramin Pertofrane	Pertofrane	Low	Low	More
doxepin	Adapin Sinequan	Sinequan	High	Medium	More
imipramine	Janimine SK-Pramine Tofranil	Tofranil	Medium	Medium	More
nortriptyline	Aventyl Pamelor	Allegron Aventyl	Low	Medium	Less
protriptyline	Vivactil	Concordin	Low	High	More
trimipramine	Surmontil	Surmontil	High	Low	More

quately to tricyclic antidepressants. They are generally considered less effective than the tricyclics, and due to a wider range of potential, often unpredictable complications, their use is limited. However, MAO inhibitors may be recommended for certain types of depressions, generalized anxiety, and phobic disorders. They are used to help individuals who have panic attacks.

Due to the potential hazards in combining tricyclics and MAO inhibitors, when a tricyclic antidepressant is tried and discontinued because of its ineffectiveness, a gap of several days is recommended before the monoamine oxidase inhibitor is tried. In the reverse case, where the MAO inhibitor is ineffective and is to be replaced by a tricyclic, a much longer period of two weeks between medications is recommended.

As with many drugs, the discovery of MAO inhibitors' antidepressant effects first occurred by chance. Quite unexpectedly, tuberculosis patients being given the antituberculosis drug iproniazid experienced an elevation of mood. Further testing with related drugs led to the widespread use of MAO inhibitors as antidepressants. Monoamine oxidase is an enzyme that inactivates certain neurotransmitters. The general hypothesis is that MAO inhibitors, by inhibiting the action of monoamine oxidase, may lead to larger quantities of neurotransmitters, which, in turn, may lead to psychostimulation.

Drug interactions and side effects

One of the main drawbacks of the MAO inhibitors, as a group, is that they may lead to unpredictable and occasionally serious interactions with a great variety of foods and drugs (see Chart). Combining MAO inhibitors with a class of drugs called sympathomimetic drugs can lead to serious complications. Common nasal decongestant sprays often include phenylpropanolamine or phen-

Substances That Can Cause a Hypertensive Reaction in Patients Taking an MAOI

Foods

Patients taking MAOIs must avoid these foods:

- Aged cheese in any form. Cottage and cream cheese are permitted.
- Yogurt
- Marmite, Bovril, and similar concentrated yeast or meat extracts (beware of drinks and stews made with these products). Baked products raised with yeast are allowed.
- Pickled herring
- Liver
- Alcohol in more than social (i.e., moderate) amounts. (Limit yourself to one glass of beer, wine, or sherry. Avoid Chianti wines altogether. You might take more if you are drinking only gin or vodka, but remember that one drink of alcohol may have a much greater effect when you are taking an MAOI.)
- Broad bean pods (limas, fava, Chinese, English, etc.) and banana skins
- Canned figs
- Food that is not fresh (or prepared from frozen or newly opened canned food). Take special care to avoid pickled, fermented, smoked, or aged meat, fish, poultry, game, or variety meats (organ meats and offal).
- Caffeine in large amounts (watch out for caffeine in cola drinks)
- Chocolate in large amounts
- Any food that has given unpleasant symptoms previously

Some patients discover that they can consume small quantities of "forbidden" foods without having a hypertensive reaction. Before making any deviations from these dietary restrictions, you should discuss them with your doctor.

yephrine, both sympathomimetics. Other medications to be avoided include cough and cold preparations or any preparation not specifically recommended by your physician.

Dietary restraints, however, tend to be the most bothersome result of taking MAO inhibitors. Individuals must conform to a special diet devoid of the amino acid tryptamine or they may experience a dangerous rise in their blood pressure. Tryptamine turns up in a great variety of foods, including alcoholic beverages, cheese, liver, lima beans, and beverages containing caffeine and chocolate.

An interesting side effect of monoamine oxidase inhibitors is that they lower blood pressure, an effect that is poorly understood. One MAO inhibitor, pargyline, is even used to treat hypertension.

As mentioned in the discussion of tricyclic antidepressants, combining MAO inhibitors and tricyclics is unwise, as there is a remote chance that such a combination might lead to catastrophic results.

Cardiovascular side effects of tricyclic antidepressants and MAO inhibitors (MAOIs)

Due to a number of cardiovascular side effects, including changes in heart rate and rhythm, as well as postural hypotension (a drop in blood pressure upon rising), antidepressants must be prescribed with caution for elderly persons or individuals with heart conditions. Elderly persons generally are more prone to heart disease and often suffer from depression as well. Postural hypotension (reduced blood pressure while standing up-

Monoamine Oxidase Inhibitors That Are Used in Treating Anxiety Disorders

Generic Name	United States Brand Name	United Kingdom Brand Name	Usual Effective Daily Dose (in milligrams)
isocarboxazid	Marplan	Marplan	30–40
phenelzine	Nardil	Nardil	60–90
tranylcypromine	Parnate	Parnate	30–60

right), especially, may be a danger for them, as it can lead to falls, stroke, even heart attack.

Withdrawal of tricyclic antidepressants and MAO inhibitors

Not only do antidepressants require a period of use before they become therapeutic, they also require tapering off to avoid withdrawal reactions. If symptoms of withdrawal should surface, the drug is usually reinstated temporarily and then tapered off even more slowly. A wide range of symptoms may occur during withdrawal reactions, including nausea, headache, insomnia or nightmares, panic, sweating and shaking, diarrhea, and general symptoms of anxiety. More severe, much rarer reactions might include withdrawal mania or psychosis. Generally, longer-term drug use is associated with a greater chance of withdrawal reactions.

Lithium

For reasons not well understood, lithium is effective in countering both depression and mania and preventing future episodes. It acts without causing sedation, but, like the tricyclics and MAO inhibitors, it requires a period of use before its actions take effect. Lithium's side effects may rule it out for use as an antidepressant. Its toxic effects may include nausea and vomiting, muscular weakness, and confusion.

Use of amphetamines and related drugs

Of less importance in treating depression, but worth mentioning, are the amphetamines and related psychostimulant drugs, such as methylphenidate (a mild central nervous system stimulant). While they may bring on temporary mood elevation, their prescription for such purposes is controversial, as they are subject to abuse. Some physicians try amphetamines for short-term use in certain patients They may also employ amphetamines diagnostically to determine more rapidly the worth of moving on to tricyclic antidepressants.

Alprazolam

Although alprazolam is primarily a drug used to treat anxiety, it also may serve to lift depression (with or without anxiety). Alprazolam has been shown to attenuate panic attacks and induce sleep as well. In depressed individuals with a high level of anxiety, alprazolam may be preferred over tricyclic antidepressants. Where alprazolam is effective, results usually appear within seven days. Its side effects are minimal, although the effects of withdrawal may be similar to those of the tricyclics and MAO inhibitors. (See also ANTIDEPRESSANTS, NEW; AGORAPHOBIA; DEPRESSION; DRUGS; MANIC–DEPRESSIVE DISORDERS; BENZODIAZEPINES; ADVERSE DRUG REACTIONS; SEDATIVES; ANXIOLYTICS.)

Ballenger, James C., "Pharmacotherapy of the Panic Disorders," *Journal of Clinical Psychiatry,* 47:6 (June 1986), pp. 27–32.

Hollister, Leo E., M.D., "Pharmacotherapeutic Considerations in Anxiety Disorders," *Journal of Clinical Psychiatry,* 47:6 (June 1986), pp. 33–36.

Mavissaklian, M. and D. Barlow, *Phobia: Psychological and Pharmacological Treatment* (New York: The Guilford Press, 1981).

Mathews, Gelder and Johnston, *Agoraphobia: Nature and Treatment,* (New York: The Guilford Press, 1981).

Cavenar, Jesse O., Jr. and J. Ingram Walker, *Signs and Symptoms in Psychiatry* (Philadelphia: Lippincott, 1983).

Neshkes, Robert E., M.D. and Leo E. Hollister, M.D., "Cardiovascular Side Effects of Antidepressant Agents," excerpted from symposium on "Psychiatric Problems in the Elderly" (New York: Pfizer, 1987).

Marks, Isaac M., *Fears and Phobias* (London: British Medical Association, n.d.).

McMahon, Terry C., "A Clinical Overview of Syndromes Following Withdrawal of Antidepressants, *Hospital and Community Psychiatry* (September 1986), pp. 883–884

Davis, John M. and Garver, David L., *Psychobiology of Affective Disorders* (Chicago: Upjohn, 1978).

antidepressants, new Researchers have been delving into the complex mechanisms of depression and antidepressant drugs since the 1950s, when they first began to use tricyclic antidepressants and MAO inhibitors to combat the condition. Ideally, the new generation of antidepressants should act more quickly and more powerfully, with less frequent and less severe side effects and with a greater ability to ''home in'' on an individual's specific type of depression.

Newer antidepressants do not fall into the tricyclic or the monoamine oxidase inhibitor classes. They are unicyclic, bicyclic, or of other molecular configurations. Where tricyclics and MAO inhibitors are understood to influence chemicals known as neurotransmitters, the newer generation of antidepressants are technically classified by their preferential influence over individual neurotransmitters—norepinephrine, serotonin, and dopamine. Newer drugs indicate a greater sophistication and tailoring to medicine's needs. However, the tricyclics and MAO inhibitors, while lacking some of this fine tailoring, still rank quite high in terms of expectations of outcome and side effects. Traditional antidepressants are also generally less expensive than the newer ones. One must consider also that new drugs may have new and unexpected side effects.

As research into these and newer antidepressants advances it will become more apparent whether the theoretical mechanisms explaining the drugs' effectiveness are truly on target or if, perhaps, research will move off on some alternative tangent.

Below is a chart of new antidepressants.

NEW ANTIDEPRESSANTS
adnazolam
alprazolam
amineptine
amoxapine
bupropion
butriptyline
citalopram
clovaxamine
dibenzepin
dothiepin
fluoxetine
fluvoxamine
iprindole
lofepramine
maprotiline
melatracen
mianserin
nisoxetine
nomifensine
noxiptiline
tandamine
trazodone
viloxazine
zimelidine
zometapine

(See also ANTIDEPRESSANTS; DEPRESSION; ADVERSE DRUG REACTIONS; DRUGS.)

Lapierre, Y.D., M.D., ''New Antidepressant Drugs,'' *Journal of Clinical Psychiatry* (August 1983), pp. 41–43.

Ostraw, David, M.D., Ph.D., ''The New Generation of Antidepressants: Promising Innovations or Disappointments?'' *Journal of Clinical Psychiatry* (October 1985), pp. 25–29.

antihistamines A class of drugs used primarily to counteract the effects of histamine, one of the body chemicals involved in allergic reactions. While they are primarily used for conditions other than ANXIETY, antihistamines also have an antianxiety-sedative effect. The two drugs in this group most likely to be used to treat anxiety are diphenhydramine (brand names: Benadryl, Allerdryl, BayDryl) and hydroxyzine (Atarax, Vistaril, BayRox, Durrax, Neucalm, Orgatrax). Unlike the BENZODIAZEPINES, these drugs do not carry risks of tolerance, habituation, and dependency. This feature may be important for some individuals. However, antihistamines are somewhat less well tolerated than the benzodiazepines and are therefore not as widely used. (See also ALLERGIC DISORDERS.)

Greist, John H. et al., *Anxiety and Its Treatment: Help Is Available* (Washington, DC: American Psychiatric Press, 1986).

antimanic drug A drug, such as LITHIUM, used to alleviate the symptoms of mania. Lithium is particularly effective in preventing relapses in manic–depressive illness. Other drugs with antimanic effects are haloperidol and chlorpromazine. Some phobic individuals suffer from MANIC–DEPRESSIVE ILLNESS and take antimanic drugs. (See also ANTIDEPRESSANTS.)

antipsychotic drugs A group of drugs used to relieve psychotic symptoms such as HALLUCINATIONS and DELUSIONS and to treat individuals who have SCHIZOPHRENIA. Antipsychotic drugs are sometimes prescribed initially in severe acute mania attacks, because while LITHIUM is the drug of choice for treating mania, it has a delayed effect, whereas antipsychotic drugs take effect fairly quickly. Antipsychotic drugs are known as major TRANQUILIZERS; their chief and most noticeable effect is sedation, but there are many variations in individual response.

The classes of drugs that have antipsychotic activity are the phenothiazines, thioxanthenes, butyrophenones, dihydroindolones, dibenzoxazepines, and diphenylbutylpiperidines. Reserpine has some antipsychotic activity but is more likely to produce depression and low blood pressure than the more effective phenothiazines, and therefore it is no longer used as an antipsychotic.

Antipsychotic drugs are believed to work on receptors in the brain to influence emotional behavior. These actions may influence their antipsychotic effects and may account for a number of ADVERSE DRUG REACTIONS. It is generally believed that the antipsychotic drugs are not appropriate for use with anxiety reactions in the absence of severe psychotic symptoms (see chart following). (See also DRUGS.)

American Medical Association, *AMA Drug Evaluations* (Chicago: AMA, 1980).

Antipsychotic Drugs

Nonproprietary Drug Name	Chemical Classification
Fluphenazine Permitil (Schering) Prolixin (Squibb)	Phenothiazine: Piperazine Compound
Haloperidol Haldol (McNeil)	Butyrophenone
Thiothixene Navane (Roerig)	Thioxanthene
Trifluoperazine Stelazine (Smith Kline & French)	Phenothiazine: Piperazine Compound
Perphenazine Trilafon (Schering)	Phenothiazine: Piperazine Compound
Butaperazine Repoise (Robins)	Phenothiazine: Piperazine Compound
Loxapine Daxolin (Dome) Loxitane (Lederle)	Dibenzoxazepine
Molindone Lidone (Abbott) Moban (Endo)	Dihydroindolone
Piperacetazine Quide (Dow)	Phenothiazine: Piperidine Compound
Prochlorperazine Compazine (Smith Kline & French)	Phenothiazine: Piperazine Compound
Acetophenazine Tindal (Schering)	Phenothiazine: Piperazine Compound
Carphenazine Proketazine (Wyeth)	Phenothiazine: Piperazine Compound
Triflupromazine Vesprin (Squibb)	Phenothiazine: Aliphatic Compound
Mesoridazine Serentil (Boehringer Ingelheim)	Phenothiazine: Piperidine Compound

Nonproprietary Drug Name	Chemical Classification
Chlorpromazine Thorazine (Smith Kline & French)	Phenothiazine: Aliphatic Compound
Chlorprothixene Taractan (Roche)	Thioxanthene
Thioridazine Mellaril (Sandoz)	Phenothiazine: Piperidine Compound

antlophobia Fear of floods. (See also FLOODS, FEAR OF.)

ants, fear of Fear of ants is known as myrmecophobia. Individuals who fear ants may also fear other tiny insects. Some individuals who have fears of dirt or contamination may also fear the presence of ants near food or in kitchens. Some who have OBSESSIVE–COMPULSIVE DISORDER may continually wash kitchen counters and the inside of their refrigerators as a RITUAL to assure themselves that no ants or other sources of contamination are present. (See also CONTAMINATION, FEAR OF; DIRT, FEAR OF.)

anuptaphobia Fear of staying single. (See also SINGLE, FEAR OF STAYING.)

anxiety The word anxiety derives from a Greek root meaning "to press tight" or "to strangle." The Latin word *anxius* and its derivatives imply narrowness and constriction, usually with discomfort, particularly in early derivations, in the throat area. Those words denote distress, disquiet, and sadness rather than the uncertainty and fear denoted by the contemporary English word anxious.

Anxiety is an unpleasant feeling of generalized fear and apprehension, often of unknown origin, accompanied by physiological symptoms. This feeling may be triggered by the anticipation of danger, either from thoughts (internal) or from one's environment (external).

Anxiety and fear have similarities and differences. Fear is sometimes defined as a response to a consciously recognized and usually external threat. In a general way, fear is a response to a clear and present danger, whereas anxiety is a response to a situation, object, or person that the individual has come to fear through learning and experience. Anxiety, as noted by the existentialist philosopher Søren Kierkegaard, is the full experience of fear in the absence of a known threat. In both fear and anxiety, however, the body mobilizes itself to meet the threat, and certain physiological phenomena occur. Muscles become tense, breathing is faster, the heart beats more rapidly, and there may be sweating or diarrhea. There may be shakiness, increased breathing and heart rate, and acute sensitivity to environmental stimuli (for example, an intense startle reaction). Some individuals may focus their anxiety on an object, situation, or activity about which they are phobic. For others, general or unknown stimuli may trigger anxiety. This is known as free-floating anxiety. Some individuals may experience a sudden onset of anxiety and notice physical symptoms such as gastrointestinal upset, weakness, or faintness as precursors to a panic attack. Phobic anxiety is the anxiety that occurs only in contact with a particular situation or object.

Anxiety and depression

While anxiety is not among the criteria by which depressive illness is diagnosed and distinguished from other disorders, anxiety is recognized as a major feature in many cases of depressive illness. The diagnosis of anxiety or depression is difficult in some cases, because symptoms of both disorders often coexist. Many individuals who have anxieties also show some of the symptoms of major depression, including:

Sleep disturbance, such as insomnia or hypersomnia

- Eating disturbance—either loss of appetite or increased eating behavior
- Loss of capacity for pleasure in usually pleasurable activities; loss of motivation
- A slowing of thought, speech and movement, or agitation and an increase in movement and speed of speech
- Difficulty in concentration, memory, or decision-making
- Thoughts of self-reproach, guilt, or profound unworthiness
- Profound loss of energy
- Hopelessness, often leading to suicidal thoughts or impulses

Hypochondriasis

When an individual focuses anxiety on physical signs or symptoms and is preoccupied with an unfounded fear or belief that he or she has a disease, that situation is a type of anxiety called hypochondriasis.

Freudian views

Freud made the term anxiety, or angst, popular in the psychiatric literature of his time. In his theory of personality, he viewed anxiety as a danger signal alerting the ego to impending threat. Depending on the source of threat, he proposed three types of anxiety: reality anxiety, neurotic anxiety, and moral anxiety. Freud called anxiety resulting from the perception of threat from the external environment REALITY ANXIETY, OF FEAR, as a response to an actual threat. He called anxiety resulting from a source of threat generated from unconscious id impulses NEUROTIC ANXIETY, which could take on different forms of intensities resulting in phobias or panic reactions. Freud's third type of anxiety was called "moral anxiety," resulting from unconscious conflicts between the id impulses and the superego, or the conscience. He interpreted moral anxiety as shame or guilt, which is also capable of producing panic and intense anxiety responses.

(See also ANXIETY ATTACK; ANXIETY DISORDERS; ANXIETY HIERARCHY; BASIC ANXIETY; CHILDHOOD FEARS; DEPRESSION; AFFECTIVE DISORDERS; PANIC ATTACK; PSYCHOSEXUAL ANXIETY; RESPONSE PROPERTIES; STATE ANXIETY; STIMULUS PROPERTIES; TRAIT ANXIETY.)

Marks, Isaac M., *Fears, Phobias and Rituals* (New York: Oxford University Press, 1987).

Stone, Evelyn M. (ed.), *American Psychiatric Glossary* (Washington, DC: American Psychiatric Press, 1988).

Bromberg, W., *The Mind of Man: A History of Psychotherapy and Psychoanalysis* (New York: Harper and Row, 1959).

Fawcett, Jan and Howard M. Kravitz, "Anxiety Syndromes and Their Relationship to Depressive Illness," *Journal of Clinical Psychiatry,* 44 (August 1983).

Jones, E., *The Life and Works of Sigmund Freud* (Garden City, NY: Doubleday, 1961).

Kleinknecht, Ronald A., *The Anxious Self* (New York: Human Sciences Press, 1986).

Price, R.H., *Abnormal Behavior: Perspective in Conflict* (New York: Holt, Rinehart & Winston, 1978).

anxiety, ancient Symptoms of anxiety have been mentioned in literature since antiquity. Both the Old and New Testaments contain references to fears, as does the Bhagavad-Gita, a sacred Hindu text. Hippocrates mentioned several instances of fears, phobias and anxieties. (See also BIBLE; HIPPOCRATES.)

anxiety, basic A term for a feeling of loneliness and helplessness toward a potentially hostile world. The term was coined by Karen Horney (1885–1952), a German-born American psychiatrist. Basic anxiety originates in disturbed relationships between parents and children and from social and cultural factors. Hence this concept of basic anxiety differs from Sigmund Freud's con cept of anxiety as resulting predominantly

Anxiety: History, Signs, and Features

Disorder	Clinical History	Clinical Examination	Features
Phobia	Specific fear of object	Behavioral observation useful	Can precipitate fear by talking about specific phobia
Hyperventilation Syndrome		Precipitated by hyperventilation and relieved by increase CO_2	May represent secondary complication of anxiety attacks
Posttraumatic Neurosis	Recurrent dreams, nightmares, and day recollections Specific precipitating event More constant and unremitting Secondary alcoholism and drugs	Mixed features of depression Reluctance to discuss traumatic events	Diagnostic interviews with sodium amytal or hypnosis Treatment with antidepressants helpful
Chronic Anxiety State	Chronic, unremitting, and often with no precipitating event Usually no discrete anxiety attacks	Mixed features of depression Obsessive ruminations	Anxiety neurosis may evolve into chronic anxiety state
Early Schizophrenia	Typical age of onset Family history Reports of weird experiences	Thought disorders Delusions, hallucinations	Favorable response to neuroleptic drugs
Mania	Previous episode of affective illness Family history	Euphoria or irritability paramount Flight of ideas Grandiosity	Atypical forms of mania may resemble anxiety attack Favorable response to lithium
Agitated Depression	Depressive symptomatology paramount Biological signs of depression	Poverty of ideas Delusions of sin, poverty, nihilism, and bizarre somatic complaints	Favorable response to antidepressants or ECT
Hyperthyroidism	Intolerance to heat Profound weakness	Palpable thyroid Exopthalmos	May also respond to propranolol
Cardiac arrhythmias	Often precipitated by caffeine or nicotine	Pulse rate reflects arrhythmia or PAT	EKG corroboration
Angina	Characteristic pain distribution and duration		EKG corroboration Relief by nitroglycerine
Mitral valve prolapse syndrome	Symptoms referable to cardiovascular system but also mimics classic anxiety attacks	Extrasystolies, tachycardia Midsystolic click	Prolapse of mitral valve during systole Diagnostic echocardiogram shows abnormal mitral valve movement

Anxiety: History, Signs, and Features (*Continued*)

Disorder	Clinical History	Clinical Examination	Features
Hypoparathyroidism	Often previous thyroid operation	Chvostek and Taussig signs Hyperreflexia	Decrease of serum calcium Poor response to antianxiety agents
Pheochromocytoma	Episodic or sustained	Marked elevations in blood pressure, flushing Severe headaches	Increased urinary catecholamines Induced by phentolamine and relieved by mecholyl
Insulinoma (Hypoglycemia)	Faintness, nausea Seizures		Low blood sugar during attack Abnormal glucose tolerance
Carcinoid Syndrome	Itching Flushing of skin	Skin blotches	Increased 5-HIAA in urine
Acute intermittent porphyria	Acute intermittent attacks of colicky abdominal pain Positive family history Personality change	Transient peripheral neuropathy during attack Sinus tachycardia Decreased deep tendon reflexes Occasional cranial nerve involvement Reddish urine	Increased urinary porphobilinogens
Stimulant Drugs	Drug use	Paranoid ideation or delusions	Drugs in urine
Caffeinism	Ingestion of large amounts of coffee, tea, etc.		Panic Attacks
Hyponotic-Sedative Drug Withdrawal	Ingestion of barbiturates, alcohol, or related agents	Postural hypotension Clouding of consciousness Transient hallucinations	Heightened tolerance to pentobarbital test dose
Presenile Dementia	Older onset with other cognitive and behavioral disturbances	Memory and abstraction deficits Emotional lability Little insight into illness	Other features of dementia
Cerebral Neoplasm	Unremitting headache, vague neurological complaints	Increased intracranial pressure and papilledema Soft or specific neurological signs	
Auras of Migraine, Temporal Lobe Lesions, or Grand Mal Epilepsy	Precede headache, amnesic period, altered mental states or seizures		May be induced by hyperventilation or special provocative procedures

Disorder	Clinical History	Clinical Examination	Features
	No sustained anxiety between attacks Characteristic clinical history for migraine or epilepsy		EEG changes with temporal lobe or grand mal epilepsy

from sexual urges and hostility. (See also ANXIETY; FREUD, SIGMUND; HORNEY, KAREN.)

anxiety, cognitive vs. somatic The symptoms of anxiety fall into two categories: cognitive or somatic. Cognitive symptoms of anxiety display themselves as thoughts in the anxious person's mind. Ideas of impending doom are reported as though a horrible event is at hand but the source cannot be pinpointed. Other examples are racing thoughts, inability to concentrate, and runaway imaginations. The only real measure of cognitive anxiety is through self-report. Somatic anxiety is easily measured by a second party. Common symptoms of somatic anxiety are increased heart rate, respiration, and blood pressure; sweating; and muscle tension particularly in the forehead. Perspiration is measured by the Galvanic Skin Response Test (GSR) which measures electroconductivity of the skin. (See also ANXIETY; GALVANIC SKIN RESPONSE.)

Anxiety, Hamilton (anxiety) scale An interview schedule in which the therapist checks off the presence or absence of self-reported and observed information indicative of an individual's anxieties. Additionally indications of intensity of reactions within broad grouping categories such as mood can be noted. The six broad categories are: anxious mood, tension autonomic symptoms, cardiovascular symptoms, behavior at interview and physiological behaviors.

anxiety, performance See PERFORMANCE ANXIETY

anxiety, postcoronary bypass See POSTCORONARY BYPASS ANXIETY.

anxiety, psychosexual See PSYCHOSEXUAL ANXIETIES.

anxiety, self-reported Therapists use various ways to evaluate an individual's anxiety. Self-report is one technique. This is often done with a questionnaire. The "Self-report of responses to anxiety" table following is a typical example. This scale has no norms. However there is a maximum score of 70 for each column (14 items; 5 is the top score/item). "A" refers to autonomic symptoms, "M" to somatic symptoms, and "C" to central nervous system responses. Generally, total scores above 100 are anxiety reactive. One of the most important factors is the relative values among the three categories which tell the examiner and testee which system responds the most to stimulation and consequently which type of relaxation intervention would be best suited to the individual. "A" responses do best with a breathing technique, "M" responses do best with muscle relaxation, such as progressive relaxation, and "C" responses do best with mental relaxation such as meditation, thought stopping, and other techniques.

Forgione, Albert G. and Frederic M. Bauer *Fearless Flying* (Boston: Houghton Mifflin, 1980).

anxiety, separation See SCHOOL PHOBIA; SEPARATION ANXIETY.

anxiety, signal See SIGNAL ANXIETY.

Self-Report of Responses to Anxiety

This self-test suggests 39 different responses you may have as reactions to anxiety. To determine your individualized and specific pattern, imagine that you are in a situation that causes you anxiety. Write a number from 0 to 5 (depending on how frequently you experience that particular effect) in the spaces after the question. If there are two sets of spaces, write the same number in both spaces. (The "A" column refers to autonomic symptoms, "M" to somatic symptoms, and "C" to central nervous system responses.)

0 = Never have this reaction
1 = Almost never have it
2 = Seldom have it
3 = Occasionally have it
4 = Frequently have it
5 = Almost always have it

	A	*M*	*C*
1. I tap my feet or fingers.		___	
2. My stomach flutters or *feels full.*	___		
3. I stammer or stutter.		___	___
4. I clench my teeth or grind them.		___	
5. I kick my foot or bounce it.		___	
6. I bite my nails.			___
7. I pick at things (lint, hair, etc.).			___
8. I feel nausea.	___	___	
9. I have tightness in my chest or feel like a strap is tight across my chest.		___	
10. My hand or head shakes or trembles.		___	
11. My hands feel cold.	___		
12. My hands sweat.	___		
13. My heart beats fast and noticeably.	___		
14. I feel distant from my surroundings.			___
15. I continually have the same or many thoughts running through my head.			___
16. I move awkwardly, bump into things, or drop things.		___	___
17. It is difficult to concentrate.			___
18. I must be aware of everything around me to keep control.			___
19. My head or jaws ache.		___	
20. My head aches with a pounding either behind my eyes or on one side of my head.	___		
21. My forehead aches or the back of my head aches with a kind of pulling ache.		___	

	A	*M*	*C*
22. The muscles running from my shoulder blades across my shoulders to my neck ache on one side or both sides.		—	
23. My face flushes.	—		
24. I get dizzy.	—	—	
25. I want to be very close to someone.			—
26. I tend to have lapses of awareness.			—
27. I feel like I want to smash something.		—	
28. I have to go to the toilet often.	—		
29. I have difficulty eating or holding down food.	—		
30. My calves, thighs, or feet get tense.		—	
31. I breathe rapidly and shallowly.	—		
32. I have to check things again and again.			—
33. I keep forgetting things.			—
34. I want to retreat and sleep, safe at home.			—
35. I busy myself putting everything in order.			—
36. I have to eat and eat.	—		
37. I produce gas (burp or other).	—		
38. My mouth gets dry.	—		
39. I worry about many things.			—

anxiety attack The sudden onset of acute anxiety, sometimes starting with pounding of the heart, difficulty in breathing, excessive perspiration, and dizziness. Anxiety attacks always begin in response to a stimulus which may be a bodily sensation, something seen or heard, a thought, or imagining any of these stimuli. Anxiety attacks are triggered by different stimuli for each individual, and each individual will show a different response to an anxiety attack. However, in most cases the main response systems at work are the cognitive (thought processes), autonomic, and muscular. In some individuals, an anxiety attack develops into a full-scale panic attack, in which one experiences unbearable tension, fear of suffocation, or a feeling that he or she may die or that some unnameable disaster is going to occur. (See also ANXIETY; ANXIETY DISORDERS; ANXIETY HIERARCHY; PANIC ATTACK.)

anxiety and pain See PAIN AND ANXIETY.

anxiety disorders A group of disorders in which anxiety is either the predominant characteristic or is experienced when the individual confronts a dreaded object or situation or resists obsessions or compulsions. Individuals suffering from anxiety disorders are always apprehensive and worry, ruminate, and expect something bad to hap-

Clinical Signs and Symptoms of Anxiety Attacks

Cognitive	Emotional	Perceptual	Physiological	Behavioral
Decreased concentration	Fear, tension, panic, dread	Blurred vision	Dizziness, sweating, dry mouth	Immobilized, agitated, and frantic
Impaired memory	Imminence of death	Paresthesias	Headache	Decrease in exercise tolerance
Indecisiveness	Feelings of helplessness	Numbness and tingling of lips and fingertips	Difficulty swallowing	Desperate for relief
Thought content fragmented with obsessive ruminations about symptomatology	Depression	Depersonalization, occasionally derealization	Insomnia, nightmares	Avoidance, escape
Dreaded anticipation	Guilt	Perceptual field narrowed	Increased urination, diarrhea	Dependence on others
Catastrophic thinking	Shame	Ringing in ears	Chest discomfort, palpitations	Excessive worry
Thoughts of going crazy	Anger	Tightness in throat	Dilated pupils, increase in blood pressure, pulse, respiratory rate	Superstitious behavior
Thoughts of physical catastrophe	Loss of self-esteem		Weakness	Anticipatory avoidance
Loss of control thoughts	Disengagement		Perspiration	
Impending doom	Embarrassment		Warmth	
			Shakiness, trembling	
			Hyperventilation, shortness of breath	
			Pain, cramps	
			Pallor or flushing	
			Nausea	
			Fatigue	

pen to themselves or loved ones. They feel "on edge," impatient, and irritable and are easily distracted. Some individuals have symptoms so severe that they are almost totally disabled.

Anxiety disorders refers to a group of illnesses: phobias, panic disorders, and obsessive–compulsive disorders.

Phobias

Phobias afflict between 5.1 and 11.5 percent of all Americans, according to the American Psychiatric Association. People who suffer from phobias feel terror, dread, or panic when confronted with the feared object, situation, or activity. Many have such an overwhelming desire to avoid the source of such fear that it interferes with their jobs, family life, and social relationships. For example, they may lose their job because they fear traveling or eating in front of others. Some become fearful of leaving their homes and live hermitlike existences with their window shades pulled down.

Within the category of phobias are simple phobias, social phobias, and other phobias. Simple phobias are fears of specific objects or situations; examples are fear of snakes, fear of flying, or fear of closed spaces. Simple phobias can begin at any age. Social phobias are fears of situations in which the individual can be watched by others, such as public speaking, or in which the individual behavior might prove embarrassing, such as eating in public. Social phobias begin in late childhood or early adolescence. Agoraphobia—the fear of going outside, being in a public place, being in a place with no escape such as a train or plane, or being alone—is the most disabling because sufferers can become housebound. Other phobias might occur to specific stimuli, e.g., belly buttons, or to general stimuli, e.g., textures

Panic disorders

Individuals who have panic disorders have intense, overwhelming terror for no apparent reason. Often people suffering a panic attack for the first time rush to the hospital, convinced they are having a heart attack. Sufferers cannot predict when the attacks will occur, although certain situations such as driving a car can become associated with them because it was in those situations that the first attack occurred. Agoraphobia is now classified as a form of panic disorder resulting from panic experiences. It appears that agoraphobia may relate to premorbid personality characteristics.

Obsessive–compulsive disorders

Some individuals attempt to cope with their anxiety by associating it with obsessions, which are defined as repeated, unwanted thoughts, or compulsive behaviors, which are defined as rituals that themselves get out of control. Individuals who suffer from obsessive disorders do not automatically have compulsive behaviors. However, most people who have compulsive, ritual behaviors also suffer from obsessions.

Individuals who have obsessive–compulsive disorders have involuntary, recurrent, and persistent thoughts or impulses that are distasteful to them. Examples are thoughts of violence or of becoming infected by shaking hands with others. These thoughts can be momentary or they can be long-lasting. The most common obsessions focus on hurting others or violating socially acceptable behavioral standards, such as cursing or making inappropriate sexual advances. They also can focus on religious or philosophical issues that the individual never resolves.

Individuals who have compulsions go through repeated, involuntary ritualistic behaviors that are believed to prevent or produce an unrelated future event. Some people with this disorder also suffer from a complementary obsession, as in the case of worries over infection and compulsive handwashing.

Examples of compulsive rituals include cleaning; if the individual comes in contact with any dirt, he or she may spend hours washing, even to the point that the hands bleed. Hand-washing affects more women than men. Another example is repetitious behavior, such as saying a loved ones' name several times every time that person comes up in conversation. Compulsives also check and recheck that doors are locked or that electric switches, ovens, and water taps are turned off. Others will retrace a route they have driven to check that they did not hit a pedestrian or cause an accident without knowing it. More men than women are affected by the checking compulsion.

Obsessive–compulsive disorders often begin during the teens or early adulthood. Generally they are chronic and cause moderate to severe disability in their victims.

Posttraumatic stress disorder

This can occur in anyone who has survived a severe physical or mental trauma. For example, people who have witnessed a mid-air collision or survived a life-threatening crime may develop this illness. The severity of the disorder increases if the trauma had been unanticipated. For that reason, not all war veterans develop posttraumatic stress disorder, despite prolonged and brutal combat. Soldiers expect a certain amount of violence, whereas rape victims, for instance, may be particularly affected by the unexpectedness of the attack.

Individuals who suffer from POSTTRAUMATIC STRESS DISORDER reexperience the event that traumatized them through nightmares, night terrors, or flashbacks of the event. In rare cases, the person falls into a temporary dislocation from reality, in which he or she relives the trauma for a period of seconds or days. "Psychic numbing," or emotional anesthesia, may occur, in which victims have decreased interest in or involvement with people or activities they once enjoyed. They may have excessive alertness and a highly sharpened startle reaction. They may have general anxiety, depression, panic attacks, inability to sleep, memory loss, difficulty concentrating or completing tasks, and survivors' guilt. There is evidence that neglected and abused children experience PTSD. It is also likely that many anxiety disorders develop as PTSD phenomena.

Generalized anxiety disorder (GAD)

Generalized anxiety disorders consist of excessive, more or less chronic, and relatively nonspecific anxiety and/or worry that occurs over at least a six-month period of time. In adults, GAD includes excessive (unrealistic) worry and anxiety about two or more life circumstances that persist for at least six months. Impairment in social or occupational functioning is usually not greater than mild. The age of onset is commonly between 20 and 40 years of age. Onset sometimes follows a major depressive episode. The GAD is thought to be equally common in males and females. It is important to note that this form of anxiety is not an anxiety or worry about having a panic attack (as found in PANIC DISORDER), being embarassed in public (as might be found in SOCIAL PHOBIA), being contaminated (as in OBSESSIVE–COMPULSIVE DISORDER), or gaining weight (as in ANOREXIA NERVOSA).

Causes of anxiety disorders

Probably no single situation or condition causes anxiety disorders. Instead, a combination of physical and environmental triggers may combine to create a particular anxiety illness.

Psychoanalytic theory suggests that anxiety stems from an unconscious conflict that began in the individual's past. These conflicts arose from discomfort during infancy or childhood. For example, Freud suggests that a person may carry the unconscious childhood conflict concerning sexual desire for the parent of the opposite sex. Or the person may have developed problems as the result of an illness, fright, or other emotionally charged event as a child. By this theory, anxiety can be resolved by identifying and resolving the unconscious conflict; the symptoms that symbolize the conflict then disappear.

Learning theory says that anxiety is a learned behavior that can be unlearned. Individuals who feel uncomfortable in a given situation or near a certain object will begin to avoid it. However, some individuals learn that their anxiety can be reduced by persistently confronting the feared situation or object. This sort of relearning, then, can cure the anxiety.

Recently, research has indicated that biochemical imbalances may be related to some anxiety disorders. According to this theory, medical treatment of biochemical imbalances in the central nervous system should relieve anxiety. Studies have also indicated, conversely, that biochemical changes occur as a result of emotional, psychological, or behavioral changes.

Each of these theories may be true to some extent. A person may develop or inherit a biological susceptibility to anxiety disorders, and events in childhood may teach a person certain fears, which then develop over time into a full-blown anxiety disorder.

Treatments

Anxiety disorders are usually treated with a combination of approaches. Phobias, agoraphobia, and obsessive–compulsive disorders often are treated by behavior therapy. This involves exposing the individual to the feared object or situation under controlled circumstances, until the level of fear is very significantly reduced. Successfully treated with this method, many anxiety disorders have long-term recovery.

Medications can help reduce intense symptoms so that the individual can make better use of behavior therapy or other psychotherapy techniques. In addition to behavioral modification techniques and medication, psychotherapy can be an important component of treatment.

According to the American Psychiatric Association, 90 percent of the phobic and obsessive–compulsive individuals who cooperate with a therapist will recover with behavior therapy. Medications by themselves are not considered adequate treatment for anxiety disorders.

(See also AGORAPHOBIA; DIAGNOSTIC AND STATISTICAL MANUAL OF MENTAL DISORDERS; GENERALIZED-ANXIETY DISORDER; SIMPLE PHOBIA; RESPONSE PROPERTIES; STIMULUS PROPERTIES; STATE ANXIETY; TRAIT ANXIETY.)

anxiety disorders, classification of

The American Psychiatric Association classifies anxiety disorders (or anxiety and phobic neuroses) as follows:

- Panic disorder with agoraphobia
- Panic disorder without agoraphobia
- agoraphobia without history of panic disorder
- Social phobia
- Simple phobia
- Obsessive–compulsive disorder
- Posttraumatic stress disorder
- Generalized anxiety disorder

The characteristic features of this group of disorders are symptoms of anxiety and avoidance behavior.

According to the American Psychiatric Association's *Diagnostic and Statistical Manual of Mental Disorders* (Washington, DC: American Psychiatric Association, 1987), in panic disorder and GENERALIZED ANXIETY DISORDER, anxiety is usually the predominant symptom, and avoidance behavior is almost always present in panic disorder with AGORAPHOBIA. In phobic disorders, the individual experiences anxiety if he or she confronts the dreaded object or situation.

In OBSESSIVE–COMPULSIVE DISORDER, the individual experiences anxiety if he or she attempts to resist the obsessions or compulsions. Avoidance behavior is almost always present in phobic disorders, and frequently present in obsessive–compulsive disorder.

The classification of posttraumatic stress disorder is controversial because the predominant symptom is reexperiencing of a trauma, not anxiety or avoidance behavior. However, anxiety symptoms and avoidance behavior are extremely common, and there are usually symptoms of increased arousal.

Although anxiety related to separation from parental figures is a form of phobic reaction, it is classified as SEPARATION ANXIETY disorder. Similarly, phobic avoidance limited to sexual activities is classified as sexual aversion disorder.

Recent studies indicate that anxiety disorders are those most frequently found in the general population, SIMPLE PHOBIA being the most common anxiety disorder in the general population, but panic disorder the most common among people seeking treatment. Panic disorder, phobic disorders, and obsessive–compulsive disorder are all apparently more common among close biologic relatives of people with each of these disorders than among the general population. (See also PHOBIA; DSM-III-R; POSTTRAUMATIC STRESS DISORDER; SEXUAL FEARS; SOCIAL PHOBIAS.)

anxiety disorders of childhood A group of disorders in which anxiety is the central feature. They include:

Separation anxiety

Separation anxiety is excessive worry about separation from significant others, such as fears that harm will befall parents or the child and nightmares involving separation themes. School phobia is sometimes considered a form of separation anxiety.

Avoidant disorders

Avoidant disorders include extreme shyness that prevents interacting with other children and persistent retreat from contact with strangers

Overanxious disorder

Overanxious disorder is persistant worrying about the future or humiliations that happened in the past, excessive need for reassurance, and many unfounded physical complaints. (See also CHILDHOOD ANXIETIES, FEARS AND PHOBIAS.)

anxiety disorders interview schedule (ADIS) This is a structured interview designed to provide a detailed functional analysis of the anxiety disorder and an accurate diagnosis. The ADIS and the revised version of the ADIS (ADIS-R) were developed from content analysis of clinical interviews with anxiety disorder patients. Questions are branched so that a "yes" or "no" answer will have particular follow-up questions. The interviewer using the ADIS-R (revised) can acquire a reliable set of information on the client for diagnostic purposes, determination of severity, and effective intervention.

The ADIS was developed by Peter DiNardo, David Barlow, Jerome Cerny, Bonnie Vermilyea, James Vermilyea, William Himadi, and Maria Waddell.

anxiety drugs Some individuals who have anxieties, fears, and phobias are advised by their physicians to take medications commonly known as anxiety drugs, antianxiety drugs, or anxiolytic drugs (anxiolytics). Usually these are prescribed in combination with some form of psychotherapy or exposure treatment. Use of the drugs usually makes the individual more receptive to the "talking therapy" used in many forms of psychotherapy, and particularly to exposure therapy, which is effective in counteracting many forms of phobias.

Many drugs fall into the category of "anxiety drugs." One widely used class of drugs is the BENZODIAZEPINES. The generic name of these drugs ends in -pam. Examples are DIAZEPAM (Valium), ALPRAZOLAM, (Xanax), lorazepam, and oxazepam. They usually begin acting within half an hour and may reduce anxieties for a few hours. As the drug gradually passes out of one's body anxiety is likely to return if its cause continues. Benzodiazepines are used to help individuals over a temporary circumstance that brings on anxiety. They are usually less helpful for chronic anxiety, and there is some risk of dependence on them. These drugs do not improve (on a lasting basis) phobias or compulsive rituals (exposure therapy is the recommended treatment). High doses of benzodiazepines may interfere with exposure therapy if the medications are taken up to four hours before or during exposure sessions. The chief side effects of these drugs are drowsiness, possible confusion, and dependence if one takes them regularly for more than a few days. Use of benzodiazepines must be decreased slowly over days, weeks, or months, depending on how long one has been taking them.

Antidepressants are also sometimes referred to as anxiety drugs. Some individuals may not respond to certain antidepressant drugs, and physicians will try one or more before setting up a regular regimen for an individual. Antidepressants fall into two broad classes: (1) Tricyclic antidepressants—examples are imipramine (Tofranil), amitriptyline (Tryptizol), doxepine (Sinequan), and dothiepin (Prothiaden). Chief side effects are drowsiness and dizziness, which improves after a few days, and dry mouth, blurred vision, constipation, and difficulty urinating. (2) Monoamine oxidase inhibitors (MAOIs)—examples of these drugs include phenelzine (Nardil), isocarboxazid (Marplan), and tranlycypromine (Parnate). Individuals who take MAOIs must exclude certain foods from their diet. These foods contain tryptamine, a substance present in most cheeses, yeast extract, and alcohol. Use of these foods along with the drugs may cause a sudden, dangerous rise in blood pressure.

Antidepressants, unlike benzodiazepines, make take up to three weeks before having a full effect. They may have to be taken regularly for many months (or years). When stopping the drugs, relapses are common. Antidepressant drugs are useful for individuals who are anxious as well as depressed. Many phobics and ritualizers also experience moods of depression. Unlike benzodiazepines, high doses of antidepressants do not interfere with exposure therapy.

BETA-BLOCKERS are another group of drugs sometimes used to reduce some of the physical features of anxiety such as rapid heartbeat and palpitations. Commonly used drugs of this type include propranolol (Inderal), atenolol (Tenormin) and oxprenolol (Trasicor). Side effects may include drowiness and dizziness.

(See also ANTIDEPRESSANTS; ANXIETY; DEPRESSION; MONAMINE OXIDASE INHIBITORS; OBSESSIVE–COMPULSIVE DISORDER; PERFORMANCE ANXIETY; PHOBIAS, RITUALS; TRICYCLIC ANTIDEPRESSANTS; VALIUM; WITHDRAWAL EFFECTS OF ADDICTIVE SUBSTANCES; XANAX.)

anxiety hierarchy A list of anxiety-producing stimuli, ranked from least frightening to most, for use in systematic desensitization and exposure therapies. (See also BEHAVIOR THERAPY; EXPOSURE THERAPY; SYSTEMATIC DESENSITIZATION.)

anxiety hysteria An obsolete diagnostic term for what is now generally called phobia, phobic disorders, or somataform disorder. (See also PHOBIA.)

anxiety management training A behavior therapy technique, developed in 1971, to teach control of anxiety responses. The therapy, based on principles of counterconditioning, involves relaxation training followed by modeling of behavior to teach coping responses to many anxiety-producing situations. (See also ANXIETY; ANXIETY DISORDERS; ANXIETY HIERARCHY; BEHAVIOR

THERAPY; COUNTERCONDITIONING; COVERT MODELING; RELAXATION THERAPY; STRESS MANAGEMENT.)

Suinn, Richard M. and Frank Richardson, "Anxiety Management Training: A Non-specific Behavior Therapy Program for Anxiety Control," *Behavior Therapy* (October 1971), pp. 498–510.

anxiety neurosis An obsolete term for ANXIETY DISORDER, no longer used in psychiatric diagnosis or literature.

Anxiety Sensitivity Index (ASI) The Anxiety Sensitivity Index was developed by Steven Reiss, Department of Psychology, University of Illinois at Chicago, during the late 1980s as a self-report measure of fear or sensitivity to anxiety. The authors claim factor and construct validity and behavioral validity. While people who have anxiety disorders score significantly higher on this scale than nonanxiety-prone individuals, those who have AGORAPHOBIA and POSTTRAUMATIC STRESS DISORDERS tend to score even higher (indicating a greater sensitivity to the body sensations of anxiety).

anxiogenic A term denoting drugs, substances, or activities that tend to raise anxiety levels. For example, in studies of panic disorder with or without agoraphobia, anxiety has been raised by CAFFEINE, yohimbine, SODIUM LACTATE or isoproterenol infusion, carbon dioxide inhalation, HYPERVENTILATION, and exercise. Certain stimuli, such as the sight of a dog (if one is dog-phobic) or looking down from the top of a tall building (if one has a phobia of heights) may be anxiogenic. (See also LACTATE-INDUCED ANXIETY.)

anxiolytics Drugs that are used to combat anxiety or as minor tranquilizers. (See also ANTIDEPRESSANTS; ANXIETY DRUGS; BENZODIAZEPINES.)

anything, fear of Fear of anything or everything is known as panphobia, panophobia, pantophobia, and pamphobia. When an individual fears anything or everything, the condition may be an anxiety disorder rather than a true phobia. (See also ANXIETY, BASIC; ANXIETY DISORDERS; ANXIETY HIERARCHY.)

apeirophobia Fear of infinity. (See also INFINITY, FEAR OF.)

aphenphobia Fear of being touched, or of physical contact. (See also BEING TOUCHED, FEAR OF.)

apiphobia See BEES, FEAR OF.

apocalypse, fear of Fear of the apocalypse, or end of the world, has always been a part of mankind's anxieties. Primitive man was frightened by natural disasters such as earthquakes, volcanic eruptions, and hurricanes. This sense of change and danger in the natural order may have given him the fear that all life could come to an end at any time. Many early religious rituals and observances were aimed at the preservation of order in nature, with the implication that the balance could tip in the other direction very easily. Some civilizations, including the Aztecs, Hindus, Buddhists, and Greeks, developed beliefs that divided time into a series of ages, with either possible or certain destruction at the end of these ages. Common to several apocalyptic philosophies is the theme of man's deterioration into immoral, disorganized, destructive behavior at the point just preceding the earth's destruction. Like other religions, the Judeo-Christian tradition contains notions of past destruction. The Old Testament chronicles the rebirth of civilization in the story of Noah and the flood; several books of the New Testament include a prediction of the end of the world and the second coming of Jesus Christ. It was a strong belief in Europe that the world would end in the year 1,000

Contemporary religious groups deemphasize the fear of the end of the world and the anticipation of the rebirth of a new order, but writers and filmmakers during the latter part of the 20th century have picked up on the theme. Novels such as Walter M. Miller, Jr.'s *A Canticle for Leibowitz* and Walker Percy's *Love in the Ruins* and films such as *Dr. Strangelove, Planet of the Apes,* and *Road Warrior* reflect fears about the end of the world, or at least a cataclysmic finish to civilization as we know it. If artistic expression is a genuine reflection of 20th-century fears and anxieties, man is afraid that he is his own worst enemy.

Cavendish, Richard (ed.), "End of the World," in *Man, Myth and Magic* (New York: Marshall Cavendish, 1983).

appetite suppressant Any substance that decreases the urge to eat. Many individuals who are anxious about their weight and who are afraid they will not be able to lose weight with a nutritionally balanced diet seek appetite suppressants as an aid in their efforts. Some appetite suppressants contain a mild anesthetic that dulls the taste buds to reduce the flavor and aroma of normally appealing foods. AMPHETAMINES are common appetite suppressants.

approach–avoidance conflict The conflict that arises when an individual experiences two competing drives simultaneously. Such unresolved conflicts may result in neuroses, such as anxieties and phobias. The term approach–avoidance conflict was developed in the 1950s by Neil Miller, a renowned learning theorist, who together with J. Dollard attempted to translate psychoanalytic theory into learning-theory terms that might be better researchable. The approach–avoidance conflict assumes that each factor has different strengths, or gradients, and that resulting behavior will be decided by the gradient that is stronger at a given time. (See also NEUROSIS.)

approximation conditioning See SHAPING.

aquaphobia See WATER, FEAR OF.

arachibutyrophobia A fear that peanut butter will stick to the roof of one's mouth. (See also PEANUT BUTTER, FEAR OF.)

arachnophobia (arachnephobia) Fear of spiders. The word is derived from the Greek word *arachne,* meaning "spider". Also known as arachneophobia and spider phobia. It appears that spider fears may be a prepared or innate fear. Donald Kleinknecht, for example, found that of 71 spider-phobic people none had had direct fearful exposure, but 61 percent had become afraid through vicarious sources. (See also SPIDERS, FEAR OF.)

arches, fear of Some individuals may be frightened of arches because the structures may appear less stable and more likely to collapse than angular structures. Arches may also be associated with an aversion to other curved or rounded shapes. The fear may relate to a fear of landscapes in which arches appear. (See also LANDSCAPES, FEAR OF.)

arithmophobia See NUMBERS, FEAR OF.

arrhenophobia Fear of men. The fear of women is called gynophobia, while the fear of men is also known as androphobia. (See also MEN, FEAR OF.)

arsonphobia Fear of fire. (See also FIRE, FEAR OF.)

Asendin See AMOXAPINE.

assertiveness training A behavior-therapy technique in which individuals learn how to responsibly express both positive and negative feelings with other people and with a minimum of passivity, aggression, or guilt. Assertiveness training is helpful in treating some agoraphobics, social phobics, speech phobias, and individuals with other phobias, since it focuses on emotional expression that is incompatible with anxiety. (See also AGORAPHOBIA; BEHAVIOR THERAPY.)

asthenic personality A personality disorder characterized by low levels of energy, fatigue, incapacity for enjoyment, lack of enthusiasm, and oversensitivity to physical and emotional stress and anxiety reactivity. (See also PERSONALITY TYPES.)

asthenophobia Fear of fainting, or weakness. (See also FAINTING, FEAR OF; WEAKNESS, FEAR OF.)

asthma A respiratory disorder that is the most prevalent of chronic childhood diseases. While asthma is a medical problem, it causes ANXIETIES in sufferers as well as in their families. Asthma is characterized by pronounced wheezing as the asthmatic tries to pull air through restricted pulmonary passages. Attacks may be frequent or only occasional, lasting for minutes or for hours. Asthma victims may become very anxious and depressed, sometimes fearing they will die during an attack. Extreme anxiety can escalate into panic in both the asthmatic and the family members, thus making the asthma symptoms worse over time. Asthma can be controlled with medication; usually related anxieties subside when the asthmatic symptoms subside. (See also ALLERGIC DISORDERS; CHOKING, FEAR OF.)

Bugelski, B. Richard and Anthony M. Graziano, *The Handbook of Practical Psychology* (Englewood Cliffs, NJ: Prentice-Hall, 1980).

astraphobia (astrapophobia) Fear of lightning; also known as keraunophobia. (See also KERAUNOPHOBIA; LIGHTNING, FEAR OF.)

astrology, fear of Some individuals fear their lives are affected by the positions of various planets, stars, or constellations. They consult astrologers who plot their horoscopes, relating the time of birth to the present positions of specific celestial bodies. Astrologers advise their clients about the advisability of certain actions. While many individuals become fearful and anxious about what they find in their horoscopes, many others follow horoscopes with confidence. The attraction to astrology, as well as the fears aroused by it, probably evolved from ancient fears about the stars and planets and outside or external forces acting on them. (The term ''lunacy'' was coined by Paracelsus to denote astral influence on sanity.) In an attempt to understand these celestial bodies, astronomers gave names of humans or gods to various constellations of stars and added an anthropomorphic feature to the skies. Some discoveries about sun spots, the influence of the moon on the tides, and eclipses, added to the notion that the earth and its inhabitants might be influenced by the stars and planets. Early forms of medicine were heavily influenced by astrology and numerology. Various religious views added more mystification, and early astronomers gained importance because they were the only individuals who could intercede between man and the heavens to predict the future and advise man about how to avoid fearful predictions. (See also MAGIC, FEAR OF.)

Bugelski, B. Richard and Anthony M. Graziano, *The Handbook of Practical Psychology* (Englewood Cliffs, NJ: Prentice-Hall, 1980).

ataraxy Absence of anxiety or confusion; untroubled calmness. Drugs to produce a state of ataraxy are commonly called tranquilizers. (See also ANXIETY; TRANQUILIZERS.)

ataxiophobia Fear of disorder. (See also DISORDER, FEAR OF.)

atelophobia Fear of imperfection. (See also IMPERFECTION, FEAR OF.)

atenolol A beta-blocking drug that has been used in treating some cases of social phobia, social anxieties, and fear of flying. (See also ANTIDEPRESSANTS; BETA-BLOCKERS; CLASSIFICATION OF PHOBIAS; SOCIAL PHOBIAS.)

atephobia Fear of ruins. (See also RUINS, FEAR OF.)

atomic energy, fear of (See WAR, FEAR OF.)

attachment theory A theory that conceptualizes the ability of human beings to develop strong affectional or object bonds to particular individuals. The theory was proposed by British psychiatrist John Bowlby (1907–). Attachment theory or object relations theory also refers to many forms of distress and disturbance that can result from unwilling separation. These include anxieties, anger, and depression. (See also ANXIETY; BIRTH TRAUMA; BOWLBY, JOHN; DEPRESSION; SCHOOL PHOBIA; SEPARATION ANXIETY.)

attention deficit and hyperactivity disorder (ADHD) Attention deficit and hyperactivity disorder (ADHD) is a chronic condition that affects seven percent of the population, more commonly boys. Children who have ADHD are usually overactive, have symptoms of anxiety and impulsiveness, and are easily distracted. The disorder is usually noticed before age five. When ADHD goes untreated in childhood, some children have behavioral and substance-abuse problems later in life. The disorder causes anxieties for parents and teachers because of the child's continuing complicated behavior.

Symptoms of ADHD are often accompanied by other problems, such as learning disabilities (although most of these children have normal intelligence), aggressive behavior, poor sleeping habits, and "difficult" temperaments. Some specialists believe that ADHD may have a genetic base. It was previously thought that the disorder was a result of brain damage.

Treatment includes medication and social skills therapy for the child, training for the parent, and recommendations for the teacher. Medical and psychological treatment can alleviate many of the symptoms. Stimulants, the most common medication for children with ADHD, act on the control mechanisms of the brain to normalize behavior and help the child sustain attention.

attitude, fear See FEAR.

attribution theory A theory regarding the individual's perception of the causes of his or her phobias and anxieties. People assign causes for certain types of behavior and seek information to support their theories. Such attributions have important behavioral consequences, since a significant part of the meaning attached to a situation or behavior is the cause to which it is attributed.

atychiphobia Fear of failure. (See also FAILURE, FEAR OF.)

aulophobia Fear of seeing, handling, or playing a flute or similar wind instrument. To the psychoanalyst, the flute may serve as a phallic symbol and thus may be related to sexual fears. (See also FLUTE; PHALLIC SYMBOL; SEXUAL FEARS; SYMBOLISM.)

aura A signal of an impending migraine headache or epileptic convulsion. The word aura comes from the Greek word for "breeze." An aura may include a feeling of dizziness, nausea, or visions of colored lights. Migraine sufferers' experiences of auras are highly individualized. For example, one may feel numbness or hear strange sounds, while another may be aware of strange tastes or odors. Some individuals become anxious when the aura heralding an attack begins. However, with therapy, an individual can learn to cope with the impending attack and try to abort it with appropriate medication and relaxation. (See also HEADACHES.)

aurophobia Fear of gold. (See also GOLD, FEAR OF,)

auroraphobia Fear of the auoral lights.

authority, fear of Many individuals fear authority. Some fear authority because the individual loses autonomy and feels dominated. Others fear authority when it loses its sense of legitimacy and becomes associated with coercion. Authority figures or groups within the family or government are feared when they are out of touch with the needs of their subordinates. A power structure that is opposed to social needs generally produces fear rather than cooperation and respect. A clash between two authority figures (e.g., two parents) is also disruptive and disturbing. (See also BUREAUCRACY, FEAR OF.)

Sills, D.E. (ed.), *International Encyclopedia of the Social Sciences* (New York: Macmillan, 1968).

autodysomophobia A fear or delusion that the individual himself has a vile or repugnant odor. This phobia, often combined with automysophobia, or a fear of being dirty, is often associated with obsessive–compulsive disorder and may consequently result in excessive washing or in avoidance of social situations. (See also BODY ODOR, FEAR OF; DELUSIONS; DIRTY, FEAR OF BEING; OBSESSIVE–COMPULSIVE DISORDER; ODORS, FEAR OF.)

autogenic training A form of psychotherapy that uses both body and mind to treat anxieties and other mental problems Autogenic training, which originated in Germany in the early 20th century, is a self-help as well as therapeutic technique, involving a variety of breathing and relaxation exercises and exploration of the subconscious, with or without the help of a therapist. The system was developed by Johannes Schultz and was based on earlier work done by German neuropathologist Oskar Vogt. (See also RELAXATION THERAPY.)

Schultz, J. and W. Luthe, *Autogenic Training: A Psychophysiological Approach in Psychotherapy* (New York: Grune & Stratton, 1959).

autohypnosis A form of self-hypnosis sometimes used with anxiety reactions to promote relaxation on cue in fearful situations. In general, autohypnosis by itself will not significantly relieve anxiety responses. It can, however, be used as a supplement to behavioral therapy to make images more vivid and to heighten one's ability to concentrate.

automobiles, fear of Fear of automobiles is known as motorphobia and ochophobia. (See also DRIVING A CAR, FEAR OF.)

automysophobia Fear of being dirty. (See also DIRTY, FEAR OF BEING.)

autonomic nervous system The part of the nervous system that regulates involuntary functions and activates endocrine glands, smooth muscle, breathing, and heart muscle. The autonomic nervous system (ANS) is involved in the physiological changes that are part of expression and emotion; anxiety reactions are primarily those of the ANS. Increases in heart rate, perspiration on the face and palms of the hands, muscle tension, dry mouth, and queasy stomach result from activation of the ANS.

The part of the ANS known as the sympathetic nervous system (SNS) prepares the body for meeting emergencies and to deal with threats to one's well-being. SNS changes include increased respiration, increased heartbeat, perspiration, and muscle tension. When an event is judged as threatening, neural impulses are sent to the adrenal gland (the adrenal medulla), which in turn releases the hormones epinephrine (also known as adrenaline) and norepinephrine (noradrenaline) into the bloodstream, where they are circulated to various organ systems that they stimulate. The physical changes one perceives when anxious or frightened are partly a result of these hormones stimulating organs activated by the SNS.

Another branch of the ANS, called the parasympathetic nervous system (PNS), conserves energy and is most active when the individual is calm, quiet, and relaxed. The PNS helps to slow heart rate, reduce blood pressure, and facilitate digestion. In cases of extreme fright or shock and for some individuals who are fearful of blood or injury, there is a strong PNS response, which results in lowered blood pressure, dizziness, or fainting. (See also BLOOD PRESSURE; DIZZINESS; FAINTING.)

Connolly, J. et al., "Selective Association of Fainting with Blood-injury Fear," *Behavior Therapy*, 7 (1976), pp. 8–13.

Ost, L.-G. et al., "Physiological Responses in Blood Phobics," *Behavior Research and Therapy*, 22 (1984), pp. 109–117.

autonomic side effect Disturbance of the autonomic nervous system. This effect may be a result of the use of antipsychotic and antianxiety drugs. The autonomic side effects include higher or lower blood pressure, blurred vision, nasal congestion, dryness of the mouth, dizziness, seizures, psychotic symptoms, depression, and reduced sexual drive. (See also ADVERSE DRUG REACTION; AUTONOMIC NERVOUS SYSTEM.)

autophobia Fear of being alone, or fear of oneself. (See also BEING ALONE, FEAR OF; SOLITUDE, FEAR OF.)

Aventyl See NORTRIPTYLENE.

aversion therapy A form of BEHAVIOR MODIFICATION to help the individual avoid undesirable behaviors or stimuli by associating them with unpleasant or painful experiences; also known as aversive therapy. This kind of therapy has been used to treat ALCOHOLISM, nail biting, BEDWETTING, smoking, fetishes, and many other "habit" problems as well as obsessive thoughts and compulsive behavior. The primary goal of the therapy is to enable the individual to make a connection between the behavior and the aversive reaction and thereby reduce the frequency of the undesirable behavior. Secondarily, alternative, acceptable behavior must be shaped and reinforced.

Electrical and chemical techniques have been used to create aversions. With electrical

Effects of Autonomic Nervous System on Bodily Systems

Organ System	Sympathetic Branch	Parasympathetic Branch
Eyes/pupils	Dilates	Constricts
Heart rate	Increases	Decreases
Bronchia/Lungs	Dilates	Constricts
Salivary glands	Reduces saliva (thick)	Increases saliva (watery)
Stomach	Inhibits function	Stimulates function
Adrenal Medulla	Secretes epinephrine and norepinephrine	No effect
Sweat glands (hands and feet)	Increases sweating	No effect
Blood flow	Increases to skeletal muscles	No effect

therapy, the therapist administers a mildly painful shock to the patient whenever the undesirable behavior, or its imagined equivalent, is elicited. With chemical therapy, the individual is given a drug to produce nausea and is then exposed to the deviant stimulus or is required to carry out the deviant act at the time the drug produces its maximal effect. Unfortunately, the drug effect cannot be paired with deviant behavior as precisely as electrical stimulation. The chemical method has been used most widely in treatment of alcoholism; the electrical method has been used predominantly in the treatment of sexual disorders.

There are limitations to aversion therapy, which is based on Pavlov's classical conditioning theory, and therapists now place more importance on cognitive factors. A newer form of aversion therapy, based largely on modification of cognitive behavior, is known as covert sensitization. In this form of therapy, the patient is asked to imagine the deviant activity or stimulus and then to imagine some extremely undesirable consequence, such as nausea, shame, or pain. (See also BEHAVIOR THERAPY; CONDITIONED RESPONSE; PAVLOV.)

Blake, B., "The Application of Behavior Therapy to the Treatment of Alcoholism," *Behaviour Research and Therapy,* 5(1967), pp. 78–85.

Cautela, J., "Covert Sensitization," *Psychology Reports,* 20(1967), pp. 459–468.

Feidman, M.P., "Aversion Therapy for Sexual Disorders," *Psychology Bulletin* 65(1966), pp. 65–69.

Lemere, G. and W. Voegtlin, "An Evaluation of the Aversion Treatment of Alcoholism," *Quarterly Journal of Studies of Alcohol,* 11(1950), pp. 199–204.

Rachman, S. and J. Teasdale, *Aversion Therapy and the Behavior Disorders* (Miami: University of Miami Press, 1969).

aversions An aversion is a preparatory response to fear and could lead to anxiety responses. For example, many people have strong dislikes (rather than fears) of touching, hearing, tasting, or smelling certain things that most people are indifferent to or even enjoy. An aversion is not a phobia, because the feelings these people exercise are somewhat different from fear; aversions make one uncomfortable, perhaps feel cold and clammy, short of breath, and nauseated, not fearful. Fairly common aversions are the screechy sound of chalk against a blackboard, the scraping of a knife against a plate, the feel of fuzzy textures, wet wool, or rubber, the feel of raw seafood, or the taste or smell of other foods. Aversions, while not as disabling as fears and phobias, can influence a person's life. For example, a person who has an aversion to the sound of chalk on the blackboard may give up an ambition to be a schoolteacher. One who has an aversion to fuzzy textures may avoid touching the skin of fresh peaches and never eat fruits with fuzzy skins. (See also FUZZ AVERSION; SMELL, FEAR OF; TASTE, FEAR OF.)

Marks, Isaac M., *Fears, Phobias and Rituals* (New York: Oxford University Press, 1987).

Marks, Isaac M. *Living with Fear* (New York: McGraw-Hill Book Co., 1978).

aviatophobia (aviophobia) Fear of flying. (See also FLYING, FEAR OF.)

avoidance learning A procedure used to treat ANXIETIES and PHOBIAS by pairing a warning signal with an aversive event. After repetitions, the individual learns to respond to the signal alone and engages in avoidance behavior whether the aversive event occurs or not. The behavior is then maintained by negative reinforcement (avoidance of aversive stimulation). Fear reduction can result from avoidance responses, and avoidance responses can continue after the feared event no longer occurs. Although avoidance behavior is motivated by fear, it is reinforced by the presence of a new stimulus, indicating that relief has been achieved. (See also AVERSION THERAPY; NEUROTIC PARADOX.)

Bolles, R.C., "The Avoidance Learning Problem," in G.H. Bower (ed.), *The Psychology of Learning and Motivation* (New York: Academic Press, 1972).

Walrond-Skinner, Sue, *A Dictionary of Psychotherapy* (London: Routledge & Kegan Paul, 1986).

avoidance response An observable behavior resulting from an anxiety-provoking situation. For example, a person fearful of elevators might walk up 15 floors rather than enter the elevator. Avoidance occurs in anticipation of aversive stimulation, whereas escape is a response to aversive (anxiety-producing) stimulation. Where avoidance is not possible, a phobic individual might exhibit escape behavior, such as running away from the situation. Both kinds of responses help to reduce the individual's anxiety. (See also BEHAVIOR THERAPY.)

Kleinknecht, Ronald A., *The Anxious Self* (New York: Human Sciences Press, 1986).

avoidant personality disorder As classified by the American Psychiatric Association, the essential feature of this disorder is a pervasive pattern of anxiety, social discomfort, fear of negative evaluation, and timidity, beginning in early adulthood and present in a variety of contexts. Individuals with avoidant personality disorder have anxiety, depression, and anger at themselves for failing to develop social relations. Some individuals have social phobia as a complication, and others who have this personality disorder also have specific phobias. Some individuals who are agoraphobic show relatively pervasive avoidant behavior, but this is usually due to a fear of being in places or situations where help may not be available, rather than to a personality disorder.

Diagnostic criteria for Avoidant Personality Disorder, according to the American Psychiatric Association, are:

- Easily hurt by criticism or disapproval
- No close friends or confidants (or only one) other than first-degree relatives
- Unwilling to become involved with people unless certain of being liked
- Avoids social or occupational activities involving significant interpersonal contact; for example, refuses a promotion that will increase social demands
- Reticence in social situations because of a fear of saying something inappropriate or foolish, or of being unable to answer a question
- Fears being embarrassed by blushing, crying, or showing signs of anxiety in front of other people
- Exaggerates potential difficulties, physical dangers, or risks involved in doing something ordinary but outside his or her usual routine; for example, may cancel social plans because he or she anticipates being exhausted by the effort of getting there. (See also AGORAPHOBIA; ANXIETY; PERSONALITY DISORDERS.)

American Psychiatric Association, *Diagnostic and Statistical Manual of Mental Disorders* (Washington, DC: American Psychiatric Press, 1987).

B

babies, fear of Some people fear babies for many different reasons. For example, some parents fear holding a new baby because of its small size and apparent fragility. Parents have anxieties about first baths and hairwashings because the baby is slippery, squirms, and almost invariably cries. The fact that crying peaks at about the sixth week often causes anxieties for parents. The inability of a baby to communicate his or her feelings except by crying and the possibility of SUDDEN INFANT DEATH (SID) is frightening. A baby's fitful, noisy sleep pattern may make parents suspect that something is wrong or that the infant is not getting enough sleep. The appearance of a newborn baby may cause anxieties for parents who are not prepared for how newborns look. Newborns frequently have an oddly shaped skull, too much or too little hair, and discolored or wrinkled skin.

The psychological impact of a baby's arrival on both parents may cause anxieties. Parents may be frightened by their new responsibilities. New mothers often enter a period of DEPRESSION that is unpleasant for them as well as for the new fathers. A woman may feel that she has been replaced by the baby as the center of attention. A man's feelings of being on the fringe of events, which started with pregnancy, may continue. A couple naturally fears that the baby's birth may come between them and deprive them of the privacy and romance that had been present in their relationship.

The entrance of a new baby into a household also produces anxieties for parents because of the jealousy it produces. Older children and even pets may need special attention to keep them from resenting the presence of a new baby.

These fears usually subside with increased accommodation and experience with the newborn. If they do not, professional intervention may be required.

Christophersen, Edward R., *The Baby Owner's Manual* (Shawnee Mission, KS: Overland Press, 1985).

Eisenberg, Arlene, Heidi Eisenberg Murkoff and Sandy Eisenberg Hathaway, *What to Expect When You're Expecting* (New York: Workman Publishing, 1984).

bacilli, fear of Fear of bacilli or of microorganisms in general is known as bacillophobia. Bacilli are a class of rod-shaped microorganisms, including many species of spore-forming bacteria. (See also CONTAMINATION, FEAR OF; GERMS, FEAR OF; PARASITES, FEAR OF)

bacillophobia Fear of bacilli or of microorganisms in general. (See also BACILLI, FEAR OF; BACTERIA, FEAR OF.)

bacteria, fear of Fear of bacteria is known as bacteriophobia. Many individuals fear bacteria because some bacteria cause infections and can be seen only under a microscope or a magnifying glass. Bacteriophobics often fear many diseases and many have compulsions about hand-washing and cleanliness. Others may be obsessively concerned about coming into contact with germs. Howard Hughes, for example, took elaborate precautions against exposing himself to "germs." Bacteria are tiny, single-celled organisms that reproduce when each cell splits in half to form two completely new organisms. Although bacteriophobics fear many kinds of bacteria, only a few are dangerous to human beings. These, known as pathogens, are responsible for some serious infectious diseases, including tuberculosis, diphtheria, gonorrhea, typhoid fever, pneumonia, and tetanus (lockjaw). Some phobics with illness phobias fear these bacteria specifically. Bacteria also cause many skin infections, leprosy, boils, impetigo, folliculitis, and scarlet-fever blisters. Some who fear skin diseases also are bacteriophobic. (See also GERMS, FEAR OF; DISEASE, FEAR OF; ILLNESS, FEAR OF; OBSESSIVE–COMPULSIVE DISORDER.)

bacteriophobia Fear of bacteria. (See also BACTERIA, FEAR OF.)

badmen, fear of Fear of badmen is known as sclerophobia or pavor sceleris. This term may refer to burglars, robbers, and others who attack or annoy unsuspecting victims. In urban areas where crime is prevalent, such fears are not totally unfounded, and individuals take precautions, such as locking their doors and cars and not walking alone in deserted areas. However, when these fears prevent an individual from going out and participating in normal activities, they can be considered phobias. (See also CRIME, FEAR OF; MUGGERS, FEAR OF; ROBBERS, FEAR OF.)

bald, fear of becoming; baldness, fear of Fear of becoming bald is known as phalacrophobia. This phobia may be related to a fear of loss of strength, fear of aging, fear of loss of attractiveness, or fear triggered by seeing one's own body. Baldness occurs when hair falls out and is not replaced by new hair growth. "Male pattern" baldness is the most common type of baldness and accounts for about 95 percent of all cases of baldness in men. Women also fear hair loss and hair thinning with age, and some seek assistance from beauticians or use artificial hairpieces.

Many people fear other types of temporary hair loss caused by infection, disease, some scalp disorders, and certain drugs (such as those used in chemotherapy). Hair loss may also occur after pregnancy; although this is somewhat frightening, normal regrowth will usually begin again after a few months. An individual who has had a hair loss from a disease will become less anxious about it when he or she realizes that the baldness is temporary.

Parents often become fearful if their babies develop temporary bald spots on the back of their heads caused by the friction of rubbing the head against bedding. Adults also sometimes develop bald spots if their work gear or rough clothing produces friction.

Another type of baldness that causes much anxiety is alopecia areata. In this condition, bald patches suddenly appear on the scalp and occasionally on other hairy areas such as the beard, eyelashes, and eyebrows. The cause of this disorder is unknown, but the hair generally regrows. (See also AGING, FEAR OF; BODY IMAGE; HAIR, FEAR OF.)

bald people, fear of Fear of bald people is known as peladophobia. Those who have this fear may be repelled by the sight of a shiny, bald head. They may also fear going bald themselves. Some who fear bald people may fear contracting the disease that caused the baldness. Other reasons for fearing bald people may be unique to the individual, such as having had a previously frightening experience with a bald person. In psychoanalytic terms, the bald head may be symbolic of eggs, fertility, or lack of fertility. (See also BALD, FEAR OF BECOMING.)

ballistophobia Fear of missiles. (See also MISSILES, FEAR OF.)

Bandura, Albert (1925–) American psychologist who has made contributions to the field in areas of anxiety, social learning theory and its application to personality development, psychopathology, psychotherapy, and social change. Bandura is the author of many journal articles and books, including *Social Learning Theory* (1977), *Psychological Modeling: Conflicting Theories* (1971), and *Principles of Behavior Modification* (1969). (See also SELF-EFFICACY.)

barber's chair syndrome Barber's chair syndrome includes the fear of obtaining a haircut or visiting a barber shop or beauty shop. The fear may be related to a fear of confinement and of restricted musculoskeletal movement (being "trapped") because one must sit still for a period of time. Barber's chair syndrome includes some aspects of agoraphobia, because some individuals who fear going out also fear going to barbershops. The syndrome may be related to social phobia, because social phobics fear being seen in what they consider compromising situations, such as with their hair half cut or covered in the barber's wrap, which also may produce a feeling of confinement. Phobics may also have anxiety about trusting other people (in this case, the barber). Additional fears may relate to being cut with the barber's scissors or razor. Individuals who have barber's chair syndrome sometimes experience sweating, nausea, dizziness, weakness, increased muscle tension, headache, and palpitations. Many individuals have been treated for this syndrome, with varying degrees of success, by relaxation and desensitization therapy, in vivo desensitization, assertiveness training, and drug therapy. (See also AGORAPHOBIA; HAIRCUT, FEAR OF GETTING A; SOCIAL PHOBIA.)

Erwin, William J., "Confinement in the Production of Human Neuroses: The Barber's Chair Syndrome," *Behavior Research Therapy*, 1(1963), pp. 175–183.

barbiturates A group of more than 2,500 psychotropic substances used as antianxiety drugs, sedatives, anticonvulsants, and hypnotics. Derived from barbituric acid, these drugs act by depressing metabolic functions in several body systems, with the most profound effect on the central nervous system.

Shortly after the beginning of the 20th century, use of barbiturates replaced narcotics and other sleep-inducing drugs. Until benzodiazepines were available in the 1950s, barbiturates were the largest and most widely used group of sedatives and hypnotics. They produce increasing sedation with increased dosage, including poorer performance in vigilance tests, increased bodily unsteadiness, decreased intellectual performance, some loss of motor skills, and underestimation of time.

Because barbiturates induce sleep, chronic use may lead to tolerance and psychological and physical dependence. Barbiturates are one of the leading causes of fatal drug poisoning. For this reason, physicians generally prescribe only small quantities of these drugs.

The most commonly prescribed barbiturates for mild anxiety or insomnia are phenobarbital and butabarbital. One barbiturate, pentobarbital sodium, is sometimes used during psychotherapy to help an individual relax and express himself or herself more freely.

Barbiturate addiction is the physical and psychological dependence on barbiturate drugs. Many phobia sufferers were prescribed barbiturates to diminish anxiety symptoms and became addicted and/or experienced extreme withdrawal effects. (See also ANXIETY; BENZODIAZEPINES; DRUGS; SEDATIVES.)

Barlow, David H. (1942–) An American psychologist, Barlow is professor of psychology at the State University of New York at Albany, co-director of the Center for Stress and Anxiety Disorders, and director of the Phobia and Anxiety Disorders Clinic and Sexuality Research Program at SUNY-Albany. He has been a consultant to the National Institute of Mental Health and the National Institute of Health since 1973. He is past president of the Association for Advancement of Behavior Therapy, a member of the Scientific Advisory Board of the Phobia Society of America, and past editor of the *Journal of Applied Behavior Analysis* and *Behavior Therapy*. Barlow is the author of many books on anxieties, phobias, and behavior therapy, including *Clinical Handbook of Psychological Disorders: A Step by Step Treatment Manual* and *Anxiety and Its Disorders*. (See also ANXIETY DISORDERS INTERVIEW SCHEDULE (ADIS); BEHAVIOR THERAPY.)

barophobia Fear of gravity. (See also GRAVITY, FEAR OF.)

barren spaces, fear of Fear of barren spaces is known as cenophobia. Many who have this phobia also have AGORAPHOBIA. Some fear barren spaces while walking or driving a car; others can go through barren spaces in a vehicle but are afraid of walking through such an area. Fear of barren spaces may also be related to a fear of LANDSCAPE or certain types of landscape. (See also LANDSCAPE, FEAR OF.)

basic anxiety An anxiety characterized by vague feelings of loneliness, helplessness, and fear of a potentially hostile world. As conceptualized by German-American psychiatrist Karen Horney (1885–1952), basic anxiety is the source from which neurotic tendencies get their intensity and pervasiveness. (See also ANXIETY; FEAR.)

basiphobia Fear of walking. Also known as basophobia. (See also WALKING; STANDING UPRIGHT, FEAR OF.)

basistasiphobia (or basostasophobia) Fear of walking and standing upright. (See also WALKING, FEAR OF; STANDING UPRIGHT, FEAR OF.)

Bateson, Gregory (1904–1980) British-American anthropologist and philosopher who developed the DOUBLE-BIND THEORY relating to neuroses, such as phobias and fears, but primarily focused on psychoses. The theory sees neuroses as a communication disorder during early years of life. Bateson's therapeutic techniques were directed at bringing submerged patterns of communication to the surface; improvement was based on reorientation into more direct forms of communication that did not contain double messages to which the individual could not successfully respond.

bathing, fear of Fear of bathing is known as ablutophobia. Some who have this fear also fear WATER. Some fear being seen in the nude. Some fear that their bodies will be criticized or compared with those of others. Some fear that harm will come to their skin from the water. Others fear warm water or cold water. This phobia extends to taking baths, taking showers, and swimming. (See also SKIN; WATER, FEAR OF.)

bathophobia Fear of depths. This fear may be noticeable in situations such as looking into a dark room or boating or swimming in deep water. A person who fears depths may be comfortable when he or she can see the bottom of the lake but not in deeper water. Similarly, such an individual may not fear a dark space when he or she is aware of the size of the room. (See also DEPTHS, FEAR OF.)

bathroom phobia Fear of the bathroom or toilet. Some children and some adults who have obsessive–compulsive disorders have this fear. They may be afraid of falling into the toilet, of being attacked by a monster coming from it, or of being infected. Bathroom phobia may also be related to a fear of dirt and germs, of using a toilet other than in one's own home, or of being seen or heard by others while urinating or defecating. Fears of urination or defecation in unfamiliar bathrooms are often not disclosed (or even assessed by surveys) but from clinical reports may be extensive. From the psychoanalytic viewpoint, bathroom phobia may involve ideas of castration. (See also CASTRATION FEAR; DEFECATING, FEAR OF; URINATING, FEAR OF.)

Campbell, Robert J., *Psychiatric Dictionary* (New York: Oxford University Press, 1981).

batophobia Fear of high objects, such as tall buildings. (See also HEIGHTS, FEAR OF; HIGH OBJECTS, FEAR OF.)

battle fatigue Also known as shellshock. A more recent term for this is posttraumatic stress disorder. (See also POSTTRAUMATIC STRESS DISORDER.)

battle fear Also known as posttraumatic stress disorder. (See also POSTTRAUMATIC STRESS DISORDER.)

batrachophobia Fear of frogs. The term also sometimes applies to fear of reptiles. (See also FROGS, FEAR OF.)

bats, fear of Some people fear bats because in folklore, myth, and art bats have become symbolic of black magic, darkness, madness, peril, and torment. The bat has been thought to be a ghost and also a witches' familiar, capable of transporting evil spirits into and out of the human body. Some people believe in a superstition that bats are attracted to women's hair and that once entangled they can be cut out only by a man.

Most bats have gained their malevolent and fear-inducing reputation because of their ghastly appearance, avoidance of light, and ability to hunt in the dark. The vampire bats of Mexico and Central and South America deserve their bad name, as they actually do feed on the blood of humans and animals, sometimes choosing favorite individuals to attack. The bat can draw blood from a sleeping victim because its saliva apparently contains an anesthetic substance that deadens the pain of the bite. (See also FLYING THINGS, FEAR OF.)

Breland, Osmond, *Animal Life and Lore* (New York: Harper & Row, 1972).

Jobes, Gertrude, *Dictionary of Mythology, Folklore and Symbols* (New York: Scarecrow Press, 1961).

Cavendish, Richard, *Man, Myth and Magic* (New York: Marshall Cavendish, 1983).

beards, fear of Fear of beards, or of persons who have beards, is known as pogonophobia. In a classic study during the 1920s, John Watson was able to condition this fear in a young boy by classical conditioning methods. He found that the fear first conditioned to a rabbit generalized to other hairy objects such as beards, animals, and fur coats.

bearing a monster, fear of Fear of bearing a monster is known as teratophobia. The term also relates to fear of giving birth to an infant with a severe birth defect. Some women fear pregnancy and childbirth because they have teratophobia, especially if they have been exposed to rubella or other agents known to cause birth defects. (See also CHILDBIRTH, FEAR OF; MENTAL DISORDER, FEAR OF; PREGNANCY, FEAR OF; RADIATION, FEAR OF; X RAY, FEAR OF.)

beating, fear of Fear of beating or being beaten may have ritualistic or religious significance or, according to psychoanalytic theory, may be related to fantasies of sexual arousal. Freud discussed beating, or flagellation, as a fantasy related to masturbation. According to Freud, girls have three phases of beating fantasies; first the father beats a sibling, next the girl herself, and then boys who are not necessarily siblings. In boys, according to Freud, beating fantasies originate from an incestuous attachment to the father. The boy evades the threat of homosexuality by transforming the beating father into the beating mother, while the girl transforms herself in fantasy into a man and derives masochistic pleasure from what appears on the surface to be a sadistic fantasy. In our culture, fears of beating and personal violence are prevalent among young children and youths. Psychologists point out that we live in a violent society. Surveys of children find that fears of being attacked at home or on the street are very common. (See also FANTASIES; FREUD, SIGMUND; SEXUAL FEARS.)

Deutsch, Albert and H. Fishman, *The Encyclopedia of Mental Health* (New York: Franklin Watts, 1963), p. 75.

beauty shop, fear of Some women fear going to a beauty shop because they fear going out (in the case of agoraphobics), because they fear that they will be judged unattractive by others in the shop (dysmorphophobia), or because they fear being confined in the beautician's chair. Some women fear being helpless during their visit to the beauty shop and fear that they may not be able to make a quick exit if they feel a need to leave the scene. Others fear being at the mercy of another person, in this case the beautician. Some fear that their appearance may be changed drastically by mistake; for example, too much hair cut off, their hair color changed unexpectedly, or the degree of curl not what they expected. Some women fear being seen by others in a vulnerable situation, such as while they are having their hair cut or colored. Fear of going to the beauty shop is related also to social phobia. (See also AGORAPHOBIA; BARBER'S CHAIR SYNDROME; SOCIAL PHOBIA.)

Beck, Aaron T. (1921–) American psychiatrist who has made contributions to the field in areas of anxieties, depression, suicide prevention, cognitive aspects of psychopathology and cognitive change, and behavior therapy. Beck is the author of many books and journal articles on subjects relating to anxieties, including *Cognitive Therapy and the Emotional Disorders* (1976) and *Depression: Causes and Treatment* (1970). (See also BEHAVIOR THERAPY; COGNITIVE THERAPY.)

bed, fear of Fear of beds is known as clinophobia. Fear of beds and of going to bed may be related to sleep phobias or sleep disorders. Persons who fear going to bed may do so because of unpleasant past experiences such as chronic insomnia, night terrors, sleepwalking episodes, or fear of bedwetting. Others may fear beds and going to bed because they are afraid that they will not wake up; for some, fear of going to bed is related to a fear of death. (See also BEDWETTING, FEAR OF; SLEEPTALKING; FEAR OF; SLEEPWALKING, FEAR OF; WAKING UP, FEAR OF NOT.)

bedwetting Bedwetting, medically known as eneuresis, means uninhibited or unconscious urination during sleep by a person over the age of three. The cause of the problem may be either emotional or physical. A child who fears having a urinary accident, who has perhaps been punished for or embarrassed by a past accident, may have nightmares about the accident or about going to the bathroom; during the dream he may urinate into the bed. A child who has had bedwetting accidents at home may be fearful of visiting another child's home, of napping anyplace but at home, or of falling asleep in a car. The best way to relieve a child's fear of bedwetting is through reassurance that if an accident happens, punishment and shaming will not ensue. Physical problems that may cause bedwetting include infections or inflammation of the urinary tract, systemic diseases such as diabetes and hypothyroidism, and exhaustion; these should be treated medically. The child can be given less liquid in the two-hour period before bedtime; if bedwetting occurs about two hours after the child has gone to sleep, he can be awakened a little before that time and accompanied to the bathroom. Gradually, he will develop the habit of waking himself when he feels an urge to urinate. If the cause is emotional (such as parental conflict), contributing factors can be identified and corrected. For example, the child can be retrained in his toilet habits. When an older child or adult urinates involuntarily during waking hours, the problem is known as incontinence. O. Hobart Mowrer developed a "bell and pad" device based on a two-stage classical conditioning model. This device effectively treats bedwetting in almost 90 percent of all situations. The device is commercially available. (See also BED, FEAR OF; SLEEP, FEAR OF.)

bees, fear of Fear of bees is known as apiphobia or melissophobia. Fear of bees, which combines the anxiety of potential injury with a general fear of flying insects, often begins in the preschool or early school years. The fear may result from a child's own experience or from hearing frightening stories or seeing frightening movies. Bee phobics report that flying, stinging insects give the appearance of attacking them. The fact that fear of a tiny insect may seem ridiculous to others is often upsetting to the phobic but may be of assistance in treatment.

The consequences of a fear of bees may mean restricted travel (so as to avoid seeing bees), driving with the windows of the car up at all times, or even staying indoors during daylight hours. (See also FLYING THINGS, FEAR OF; STINGS, FEAR OF.)

Melville, Joy, *Phobias and Obsessions* (New York: Coward, McCann and Geoghegan, 1977).

Sarafino, Edward P., *The Fears of Childhood* (New York: Human Sciences Press, 1986).

behavior analysis A study of the relationship of problem behaviors and their consequences. Behavior analysis is the first step in behavioral therapies, which are based on the principles of operant conditioning. During behavior analysis, the therapist will examine the interaction between stimulus, response, and consequence and plan a program according to the individual's needs. Behavior analysis is an ongoing process that ends only when the treatment goals have been reached. (See also BEHAVIOR MODIFICATION; DIAGNOSIS.)

Mackay, D., *Clinical Psychology: Theory and Therapy* (London: Methuen, 1976).

behavior constraint theory The theory that an individual may develop a helpless attitude or a phobic behavior when he or she cannot gain control over certain events. (See also LEARNED HELPLESSNESS.)

behaviorism School of psychology associated with American psychologist John Broadus Watson (1878–1958), who proposed that observable behavior, not consciousness, is the proper subject of psychology. OPERANT CONDITIONING evolved from this point of view, and the behavioristic approach led to many later techniques of behavior modification and methods for treating phobias. By this time, however, Watson had left psychology to pursue a career in advertising. (See also BEHAVIOR THERAPY; WATSON, JOHN B.)

behavior modification A type of psychotherapy used to treat phobias that stresses the effect of learning on behavior, uses active therapist and client involvement and *in vivo* practices, outlines explicit goals and desired new behaviors, and evaluates progress toward those goals. Behavior modification does not rely on diagnostic labels and deemphasizes the importance of the past in determining current behavior. (See also BEHAVIOR THERAPY.)

behavior psychotherapy See BEHAVIOR THERAPY.

behavior rehearsal A behavior therapy technique in which the patient practices a new behavior in a controlled setting aided by the therapist. The therapist may use techniques of MODELING, coaching, feedback, positive reinforcement, and role playing. Behavior rehearsal is useful in treating SOCIAL PHOBIAS. A widely used form of behavior rehearsal is assertiveness training, in which inhibited, submissive individuals learn to behave more assertively, to express anger, to respond to another's anger, and to not feel guilty or anxious in doing so. (See also ASSERTIVENESS TRAINING; BEHAVIOR THERAPY; PHOBIAS.)

Bootzin, Richard R. and Joan Ross Acocell, *Abnormal Psychology: Current Perspectives* (New York: Random House, 1984).

Martin, Barclay, *Abnormal Psychology* (New York: Holt, Rinehart and Winston, 1981).

behavior shaping See SHAPING

behavior therapy A form of psychological, emotional, and behavioral therapy that stresses learned responses; also known as behavior modification. Unlike a psychoanalyst, a behavior therapist does not regard phobias as symptoms of unconsciously caused, "deeper" problems that require restructuring of the psyche. Behavior therapists regard panic, anxiety, and obsessive–compulsive behavior as something that has a learned component (as well as a biological component) and can be replaced with desirable behaviors. Behaviorists generally do not believe that other drastic symptoms will appear to replace the ones thus eliminated.

Behavior therapy is considered the most effective treatment for AGORAPHOBIA, social phobias, and other specific phobias, as well as for obsessions, compulsions, certain sexual problems, and alcoholism. Many therapists use behavior therapy to treat phobias, sometimes in conjunction with other forms of treatment.

Behavior therapy focuses on measurable aspects of observable behavior, such as frequency or intensity of particular behaviors like compulsive hand-washing, physiological response, and verbal reports. Verbal reports by the patients and self-rating scales are commonly used to describe details of behavior. Specific treatment techniques are tailored by the therapist to the needs of the individual.

Treatment goals are defined by the therapist in conjunction with the patient and the patient's family. In behavior therapy, the therapist is seen as an instructor or coach, and the patient chooses whether to try to learn a new behavior. The goal generally is to develop self-controlled behaviors and an increased repertoire of new, more adaptive behaviors.

Behavior therapy became fairly well established during the latter half of the 20th century. Important individuals in the development of behavioral techniques include Joseph Wolpe, Hans Jurgen Eysenck and Frederick B. Skinner, Ogden Lindsley, and Ted Ayllon, who based much of their work on the earlier works of Ivan Pavlov and John Watson. Lindsley coined the term "behavior therapy" in a research article in the late 1950s. Wolpe, in his book *Psychotherapy by Reciprocal Inhibition,* introduced many of the basic therapies used today, such as systematic desensitization, sexual therapies, and assertiveness training.

Behavior therapy includes many basic learning techniques, such as reduction of anxiety, desensitization, flooding, classical conditioning, modeling, operant conditioning, aversive therapy, and reciprocal inhibition. Therapists often use techniques that gradually expose the phobic individual to the feared objects or situations. Such exposure may take place in real life or in the individual's imagination. The gradualness of the exposure is considered important in making the treatment effective, combined with the simultaneous use of relaxation responses and cognitive changes.

A major development in the treatment of phobias was described in 1958 by American psychiatrist John Wolpe (1914–   ), who had a background in learning theory. Wolpe reported excellent results in treating adults who had a variety of neuroses, including phobic anxiety, hysteria, reactive depression, and obsessive–compulsive disorder, with a procedure called "systematic desensitization," adapted from a technique developed in the 1920s for helping children overcome animal phobias. Based on the principle of "reciprocal inhibition," this technique trains the individual to relax the muscles, imagine increasing degrees of anxiety-producing stimuli, and then face increasing degrees of the fear-producing stimuli in vivo until the maximum stimulus no longer causes great anxiety.

Systematic desensitization requires the individual to learn deep-muscle relaxation and to rank situations that causes anxiety. For example, an individual who fears elevators might place at the top of the list of things that make him or her anxious riding to the top of a high building alone in an elevator; merely looking at the entrance to an elevator from the lobby of a building might rank at the bottom of the list of fear-producing stimuli.

After relaxing, the individual is then asked to imagine, in as much detail as possible, the least fear-producing item from the list. By relaxing while imagining the feared situation, the individual may weaken the association between the phobic situation and anxious feelings. Once he becomes comfortable imagining the least-threatening situation, he gradually moves up the hierarchy.

Some therapists believe that facing a feared situation in the imagination may be just as effective as facing it in reality. However, most therapists have found that there is a gap between imagination and reality. Once the individual has completed densensitization treatment and goes on to face the real fear, he or she is likely to regress slightly back down the list. For example, an individual who has learned to remain calm while riding an imaginary elevator to the top of a building may be able to enter an actual elevator but may not be comfortable riding in it right away. By taking a floor at a time, however, the individual will be able to master the fear and eventually ride to the top of the building alone.

During the late 1960s, another treatment for phobias was developed by Thomas Stampfl, called "implosion" or "implosive therapy." Implosion was a modification of a technique known as "imaginal flooding," or just "flooding."

Flooding

Flooding, like desensitization, involves the individual's experiencing fear-provoking situations in his or her imagination or *in vivo*. In flooding, the individual is exposed directly to a maximum level of the fear-producing stimulus without any graduated approach.

However, in flooding, the therapist, rather than the individual, controls the timing and content of the scenes to be imagined. The therapist describes such scenes with great vividness, in a deliberate effort to make them as disturbing as possible to the phobic person. The individual is not instructed to relax. Rather, the aim is for him to experience his fears and anxieties with maximum intensity, which gradually diminishes. The prolonged experience with these feared objects or situations is designed to help the individual to experience "extinction" of the anxiety response.

Implosive therapy

This is a variation and extension of the flooding technique. The individual is repeatedly encouraged to imagine a fear-producing situation at maximum intensity in order to experience as intense anxiety as possible. Assuming there is no actual danger in the situation, the anxiety response is not reinforced and thus becomes gradually reduced through extinction. However, the therapist also begins to weave into the terrifying images fantasy-based images and thoughts drawn from psychoanalytic theory, presumably to also extinguish these unconscious factors.

Like desensitization, both flooding and implosive techniques reduce phobic anxiety and behavior in persons with simple phobias, but desensitization appears to be more effective and more permanent. There is some evidence that small amounts of flooding are more effective with agoraphobics.

Exposure therapy

This is a term used to describe a variety of behavioral therapies that have in common the use of gradual exposure to a feared situation (such as systematic desensitization), exposure at full intensity (flooding and implosive therapy), and exposure with cognitive modification (contextual therapy). Contextual therapy was developed by American psychiatrist Manual Zane (1913–). The focus of contextual therapy is to keep the person rooted to the present situation and to work with the anxiety-producing internal cues of the person.

Modeling and covert modeling

In this form of therapy, the phobic individual watches another person, often of the same sex and age as the phobic, successfully perform a particular feared action, such as crossing the street or taking an elevator. The phobic presumably experiences vicarious extinction of the feared response. Modeling is also called social learning or observational learning.

In "covert modeling" the phobic individual simply imagines that another individual is facing the same phobic situation and that anxiety reduction is experienced by the model. Such "vicarious" extinction processes have many potential applications in treatment.

Operant conditioning
This technique is based on the principle that individuals will either maintain or decrease the frequency of a particular behavior as a result of responses they receive from their environment. Thus behavior that produces reinforcing consequences is strengthened, while behavior that produces aversive consequences is weakened. Avoidance and approach behavior to feared stimuli are often considered under operant control and thus modifiable through operant shaping.

Hypnosis
Although hypnosis is not based on learning theory, it is classified as a behavioral technique because the role of the therapist is active, rather than passive, as it is in psychoanalysis. Hypnosis can be used to produce a hypnotic trance in which the individual becomes very receptive to suggestion. Through posthypnotic suggestion, an individual may learn to change behavior patterns, such as having phobic reactions to certain stimuli. Hypnosis by itself, however, is not an adequate form of treatment for phobias.

Comparisons of Psychotherapy and Behavior Therapy

Psychotherapy	Behavior Therapy
1. Based on inconsistent theory never properly formulated in postulate form.	Based on consistent, properly formulated theory leading to testable deductions.
2. Derived from clinical observations made without necessary control observations or experiments.	Derived from experimental studies specifically designed to test basic theory and deductions made therefrom.
3. Considers symptoms the visible upshot of unconscious causes ("complexes").	Considers symptoms as unadaptive conditioned responses.
4. Regards symptoms as evidence of *repression.*	Regards symptoms as evidence of faulty learning.
5. Believes that symptomatology is determined by defense mechanisms.	Believes that symptomatology is determined by individual differences in conditionability and autonomic lability, as well as accidental environmental circumstances.
6. All treatment of neurotic disorders must be *historically* based.	All treatment of neurotic disorders is concerned with habits existing at *present;* their historical development is largely irrelevant.
7. Cures are achieved by handling the underlying (unconscious) dynamics, not by treating the symptom itself.	Cures are achieved by treating the symptom itself, i.e. by extinguishing unadaptive C.R.s and establishing desirable C.R.s.
8. Interpretation of symptoms, dreams, acts, etc. is an important element of treatment.	Interpretation, even if not completely subjective and erroneous, is irrelevant.
9. Symptomatic treatment leads to the elaboration of new symptoms.	Symptomatic treatment leads to permanent recovery provided autonomic as well as skeletal surplus C.R.s are extinguished.
10. Transference relations are essential for cures of neurotic disorders.	Personal relations are not essential for cures of neurotic disorder, although they may be useful in certain circumstances.

H. Eysenck, *Behaviour Therapy and the Neuroses* (London: Pergamon Press, 1960).

Biofeedback

Biofeedback, a technique to monitor psychophysiological events by electrical feedback, provides an anxious or phobic individual with a basis for self-regulation of certain processes, such as reaction to fearful situations. The technique is useful in many approaches to therapy for anxieties and phobias. It establishes a diagnostic baseline by noting physiological reactions to stressful events, enables therapists to relate this information to the individual's verbal reports, fills gaps in the individual's history, and encourages relaxation of the body part to which the biofeedback equipment is applied. Relaxation training is often suggested to assist the individual in controlling anxiety reactions. (See also AVERSION THERAPY; DESENSITIZATION; EYSENCK, HANS JURGEN; OPERANT CONDITIONING; PAVLOVIAN CONDITIONING; RECIPROCAL INHIBITION; SKINNER, FREDERICK BURRHUS; WOLPE, JOSEPH.)

Hafner, R. Julian, "Behavior Therapy for Agoraphobic Men," *Behavior Research Therapy*, 21(1983), pp. 51–56.

Ludwig, Arnold M., *Principles of Clinical Psychiatry* (New York: The Free Press, 1980).

World Book, Inc., *The World Book Encyclopedia* (Chicago: World Book, Inc., 1986).

Suinn, Richard M., *Fundamentals of Behavior Pathology* (New York: John Wiley & Sons, 1975).

behavioral family therapy An approach to family therapy using techniques of behavioral therapy. Therapy includes modifying the ways in which the identified patient receives attention from the others in the family. Behavioral family therapy is often used in treating agoraphobia. The therapist helps identify the problem behavior, chooses reasonable goals and alternative adaptive behaviors, and directs and guides the family to change their patterns of reinforcement toward target behaviors. (See also BEHAVIOR THERAPY.)

being alone, fear of Fear of being alone is known as autophobia. The term taphephobia is also used for being alone, but usually refers to fear of being BURIED ALIVE. Some agoraphobic individuals are also afraid of being alone, particularly when they leave the place where they feel secure. Infants and young children fear being alone, generally because they feel helpless and are afraid of being abandoned by their parents or other caretakers. Older people also fear being alone as they see others in their age group retiring and moving away or dying. A fear of being alone and a feeling of being far from anyone who cares about one may sometimes lead to DEPRESSION.

For people of all ages, fears are usually greater when individuals are alone. Even though people who have SOCIAL PHOBIA may avoid particular forms of social contact, they rarely like to be alone most of the time. (See also GROWING OLD, FEAR OF; SEPARATION ANXIETY.)

Marks, Isaac M., *Fears, Phobias and Rituals* (New York: Oxford University Press, 1987), p. 52.

being enclosed, fear of Fear of being enclosed in a very confined space is known as clithrophobia. Somewhat similar to claustrophobia, clithrophobia generally applies to a very small, well-defined space, whereas claustrophobia also can refer to fear of being in a large room without an easy or visible way out. (See also BEING LOCKED IN, FEAR OF; CLAUSTROPHOBIA.)

being locked in, fear of Fear of being locked in is known as claustrophobia. The term clithrophobia might also apply, if the space in which one is locked is very small as well as confining. Some individuals specifically fear being locked in an elevator, a closet, their car, or a room.

being looked at, fear of Fear of being looked at, or stared at, is known as scopophobia. Fear of two staring eyes is common throughout the animal kingdom, including man. Particularly in individuals who have social fears, being looked at means being the object of another's attention and intention; the gaze of others thus may trigger acute discomfort in self-conscious persons. Many social phobics are afraid of being watched by others.

Realizing that eyes are looking at one may be instinctive. The eyes of another are one of the first figural entities perceived by the infant. Of all the features of the face, the eyes possess the greatest combination of those qualities that attract an infant's fixation—figure, color, movement, and light reflection. In human infants, two eyes are the minimal visual stimulus required to elicit the first human social response, the smile. The infant's smile and his fixation on the eyes of the person looking at him may be an instinctual response of the infant that itself elicits further approach and caring behavior by the mother.

The effect of being looked at has been studied in animals. For example, when rhesus monkeys see a human face observing them in the laboratory, they show a change in behavior and in electrical activity in the brain stem. Many species of mammals use their eyes and eye markings to intimidate intruders, and eyes and conspicuous eyelike markings are used by birds and insects as defense against attack. (See also EYES, FEAR OF.)

Marks, Isaac M., *Fears, Phobias and Rituals* (New York: Oxford University Press, 1987).

being oneself, fear of Some individuals live their lives to fulfill expectations of others and fear being themselves. Some individuals tend to mirror the lives of their same-sex parent. Some women are raised to be images of their mothers in terms of appearance, education, interests, and life goals. Such women grow up aspiring to be and have as much as, but no more than, their mothers. They may imitate their mothers even to the extent of having the same number of children. Similarly, some young men grow up following their father's sports, educational, and career examples. Such individuals become accustomed to subordinating their own desires to those of their parent. As adults, they look to their spouse for guidance in everyday decisions and fear following their own desires and making their own choices.

Often people who grew up under domineering parents raise their children to meet their own expectations and perpetuate the fear of being oneself in their children.

The existentialists say that people are afraid that they do not have a true self and live behind a facade. Most therapies, traditional and behavioral, emphasize reduction of the person's facade or conditioned aspects of their behavior.

being poisoned, fear of Fear of being poisoned is known as toxocophobia. This fear may be related to a fear of contamination, dirt, or germs. (See also CONTAMINATION, FEAR OF; DIRT, FEAR OF; GERMS, FEAR OF; OBSESSIVE–COMPULSIVE DISORDER; POISON, FEAR OF.)

being touched, fear of Fear of being touched is known as aphenphobia, haphephobia, and haptephobia. This fear may be a social phobia. In some cases, fear of being touched may relate to sexual fears. Some people fear being touched because they fear contamination. (See also CONTAMINATION, FEAR OF; SEXUAL FEARS.)

belching, fear of Some individuals who have social phobias fear belching in front of others. Belching, or the common burp, occurs when one swallows air or when gas is produced in the stomach by the chemical reactions between food and digestive juices. (See also FLATULENCE, FEAR OF.)

belonophobia Fear of needles and pins is known as belonophobia or belonephobia. (See also ACUPUNCTURE, FEAR OF; NEEDLES AND PINS, FEAR OF.)

bends, fear of Divers and enthusiasts of scuba (self-contained underwater breathing apparatus) diving fear "the bends," which is also known as caisson disease or decompression sickness. Fear of the bends deters many sports enthusiasts from undertaking scuba diving. Fear of developing this condition motivates participants to learn their skills adequately before going underwater and to observe many safety precautions. The bends occur when a person has been under high atmospheric pressure for a prolonged period, usually a matter of hours, and is suddenly exposed to a lower pressure. When a person stays underwater at a considerable depth, body fluids and tissues conform to the pressure, and the individual may have difficulty if he does not decompress himself slowly while rising to the surface. This is a natural fear that is quite logical and adaptive. However, if one begins to excessively avoid scuba diving because of such a fear, then it might be called a phobia. (See also DIVING, FEAR OF; WATER, FEAR OF.)

benzodiazepines A class of drugs used for treating generalized anxiety disorder (GAD). These drugs, known as minor tranquilizers or anxiolytics, have effects that resemble those of classical sedatives, such as barbiturates or meprobamate-like drugs.

The Benzodiazepines (antianxiety agents)

Generic Name	Trade Name
Alprazolam	Xanax
Chlordiazepoxide	Librium
Clorazepate	Tranxene
Diazepam	Valium
Lorazepam	Ativan
Oxazepam	Serax
Triazolam	Halcion

These effects include muscle relaxation, anticonvulsive action, sedation proceeding to hypnosis, development of tolerance, and the potential for psychologic and physical dependence. Benzodiazepines, however, are considered safer substitutes for barbiturates.

There are numerous drugs in this category, including alprazolam, chlordiazepoxide, clorazepate, diazepam, halazepam, larazepam, oxazepam, and prazepam.

Doses of benzodiazepines must be carefully prescribed according to the physical response of the patient. Usually the starting dose is small and is increased as needed. When the dose is appropriately chosen, response is usually noticeable in a week or two.

Most clinicians and investigators working with phobic individuals believe that the benzodiazepines are usually only partially effective. Patients treated with benzodiazepines experience decreased anxiety but not significant resolution of panic attacks or agoraphobic symptoms. (See also ANTIDEPRESSANTS; ANXIETY DRUGS; DRUGS.)

Ballenger, James C., M.D., "Pharmacotherapy of the Panic Disorders," *Journal of Clinical Psychiatry,* 47 (June 1986), pp. 27–32.

Hollister, Leo E., M.D., "Pharmacotherapeutic Considerations in Anxiety Disorders," *Journal of Clinical Psychiatry,* 47 (June 1986), pp. 33–36.

bereavement, phobia following Phobias occurring after the loss of a loved one may be related to separation anxiety. In some individuals, such a loss brings back unresolved feelings from childhood caused by separation from one's parents. (See also DEATH, FEAR OF; GRIEF REACTION; SEPARATION ANXIETY.)

Berne, Eric (1910–1970) A Canadian-American psychiatrist and the founder of Transactional Analysis (TA), which is used in both individual and group therapy. Transactional Analysis is a restatement of psychoanalytic theory in interpersonal rather than intrapsychic terms. Within TA, anxiety results from a conflict between different levels of functioning. (See also TRANSACTIONAL ANALYSIS.)

beta adrenergic blocking agents More commonly referred to simply as "beta-blockers," these drugs have been used to assist in relief of anxiety. Primarily, beta-blockers tend to have a "calming" effect on the heart, reducing heart rate and force of contraction. When used long-term, they usually result in lowered blood pressure. More recently, they are being used to help relieve some symptoms of anxiety, such as shakiness and heart palpitations. Beta-blockers seem to cause an overall reduction in anxiety. The drugs atenolol and propranolol are examples of beta-blockers. (See also BETA BLOCKING AGENTS; PERFORMANCE ANXIETY; PROPRANOLOL.)

beta-blocking agents Drugs used to treat hypertension, cardiac arrythmias, and, in some cases, anxieties. Beta-blockers act on physical symptoms of anxiety by preventing the racing heartbeat and quickened breathing caused by the adrenaline rush that comes with anxiety. Examples of beta-blocking drugs used to treat anxiety are atenolol and propranolol.

The beta-blocking agents, or drugs, are multiple-action drugs that also influence a part of the sympathetic nervous system. They work by blocking the effects of stimulation coming to the heart and blood vessels through a group of sympathetic nerve fibers known as beta adrenergic. These drugs decrease cardiac output by acting on nerve receptor sites in the heart. Once they decrease the amount of sympathetic nervous input into the heart, the heart rate slows, the heart does not work as hard, less blood is pumped, and blood pressure goes down. The beta-blockers also suppress the system of hormones responsible for directly constricting blood vessels and retaining salt and water in the body.

Beta-blockers have been used effectively to prevent anxiety associated with public speaking and test-taking. In these situations, they are used on a situational basis only.

Some beta-blockers may cross into and accumulate in the brain, causing adverse central nervous system effects. Thus some beta-blockers have been shown to cause depression and sleep disturbance. Beta-blockers may have other side effects—for example, aggravating bronchial asthma or causing fatigue, skin rashes, impotence, or low blood pressure. The side effects may in turn cause the individual additional anxieties and social adjustment problems.

Beta-blocking drugs should not be discontinued abruptly if they are to be stopped or replaced by another type of medication; rather, they should be slowly tapered off over a period of one to two weeks or more. (See also PROPRANOLOL.)

Kahn, Ada P., *High Blood Pressure* (Chicago: Contemporary Books, 1983).

Bettelheim, Bruno (1903–) A Viennese psychologist and philosopher best known for his psychoanalytically oriented theories in child psychology. Bettelheim's studies included the function and development of the superego in the young child and its part in the stimulation of fear or anxiety.

Corsini, R.J. (ed.), *Encyclopedia of Psychology* (New York: John Wiley & Sons, 1984).

biased apperception Seeing things as one wants to see them. The term was used by Viennese psychologist Alfred Adler (1870–1937). Adler believed that biased apperception is necessary for participation in society, because without it, individuals are anxious and indecisive. Individuals who fear making a move unless they are certain they are right are usually paralyzed by indecision. Well-adjusted, well-integrated personalities take chances and make choices without undue anxiety according to a subjective evaluation of each situation (See also ADLER ALFRED.)

Bible No conclusions can be drawn as yet regarding the impact of Bible and Biblical teachings on anxiety. Generally, it is believed that the effects of religious works on anxiety depend on the individual. People who are able to cope well with anxiety usually respond more positively to the Bible, while individuals who have poorer coping skills tend to become more anxious in response to the same teachings. Interest in the effects of religion has increased since 1976, when the American Psychological Association officially recognized a group of religiously-oriented therapists.

Both the Old and New Testaments contain references to fear of God and fear of evil spirits, as well as commentary about music therapy, abnormal behavior, and possession by devils. Treatment for possession by devils included exorcism. For example, Jesus is said to have removed the evil spirit from two men and transferred it into pigs who subsequently fell over cliffs into a lake. David's playing the lyre for Saul was an early example of music therapy. Judas Iscariot is the only suicide mentioned in the Bible.

Fears of the Bible may be related to fears of religious ceremonies and holy things. (See also HOLY THINGS, FEAR OF; PHOBIAS, HISTORY OF; RELIGIOUS CEREMONIES, FEAR OF.)

bibliophobia Fear of books. (See also BOOKS, FEAR OF.)

bibliotherapy See BOOKS AS ANXIETY RELIEF.

biodynamic psychology A term that describes an approach to psychotherapy directed toward integrating the individual's physical and social and metapsychological needs. Biodynamic psychology was introduced by American psychoanalyst Jules Homan Masserman (1905). This approach is a holistic one, with a unified approach to the individual's mind, body, and spirit, using psychological, organic, and spiritual methods. A wide range of techniques are used to help an individual with anxieties and phobias. Masserman's "7 Pil-Rs" of therapeutic wisdom are: reputation (of the therapist), rapport, relief, review, re-orientation, rehabilitation, and resocialization.

Masserman, J.H., *Principles and Practice of Biodynamic Psychotherapy: An Integration* (New York: Thieme/Stratton, 1980).

biofeedback A technique to monitor psycho-physiological events by electrical feedback. Biofeedback is useful in many approaches to therapy for anxieties and phobias. It provides an anxious or phobic individual with a basis for self-regulation of certain processes, such as autonomic system reaction to fearful situations. It establishes a diagnostic baseline by noting physiological reactions to stressful events, enables therapists to relate this information to the individual's reports, fills gaps in the individual's history, and encourages relaxation in the part of the individual's body to which the biofeedback equipment is applied. Relaxation training is often suggested to assist the individual in controlling anxiety reactions. (See also BEHAVIOR THERAPY.)

Forgione, A.G. and R. Holmberg, "Biofeedback Therapy," in Corsini, R. (ed.), *Handbook of Innovative Psychotherapies* (New York: Wiley, 1981).

biological basis for anxiety Researchers studying ANXIETY, including FREUD, predicted that the brain and CENTRAL NERVOUS SYSTEM might function abnormally in persons who have serious ANXIETY DISORDERS. Much research focusing on the brain is underway on anxiety and related disorders focusing on the brain.

(See also ADENOSINE; AGORAPHOBIA; ALPRAZOLAM; ANTIDEPRESSANTS; ANTIDEPRESSANTS, NEW; CAFFEINE AS A PANICOGENIC AGENT; CARBON DIOXIDE SENSITIVITY; CHEMOCEPTORS: DIAZEPAM; DRUG EFFECTS; GAMMA AMINO BUTYRIC ACID (GABA); HYPERVENTILATION; LACTATE-INDUCTED ANX-

CIETY; LOCUS CERULEUS; MITRAL VALVE PROLAPSE; MONOAMINE OXIDASE INHIBITORS; NEUROTRANSMITTERS; NOREPINEPHRINE; PANIC ATTACK; PREMENSTRUAL SYNDROME.)

bipolar disorder (bipolar illness) See MANIC–DEPRESSIVE DISORDER.

birds, fear of Fear of birds is known as ornithophobia. Some bird phobics believe that the sudden, unpredictable movements of birds constitute an attack. Phobics commonly fear the swooping motions of birds and the sound and sight of flapping wings in an enclosed space. Other phobics mention the beady eyes and claws of birds as being particularly frightening. Pigeons are the phobic objects for many individuals, as pigeons gravitate toward buildings and people more than other birds do. Some individuals fear only the sight of a dead bird. Some bird phobics are less frightened by the sight of birds in the open and even may be fascinated by them in this situation. Alfred Hitchcock played on the duality of attraction to and revulsion of birds in his film *The Birds*.

This phobia, like many animal and common stimuli phobias, often severely limits the individual's functioning. Fear of birds, for example, in moderate to severe intensities, limits the person's range of movement outside, often restricting him to areas of few birds or to travel at night. Also, travel is accompanied by ANXIETY or dread at the possibility of seeing birds; windows must be tightly closed, and walking in open spaces is impossible. The individual may not even be able to look outside. (See also FLYING THINGS, FEAR OF.)

Kent, Fraser, *Nothing to Fear: Coping with Phobias* (Garden City, NY: Doubleday, 1977).

Melville, Joy, *Phobias and Obsessions* (New York: Coward, McCann and Geoghegan, 1977).

Neumann, Frederic, *Fighting Fear* (New York: Macmillan, 1985).

birthdays, fear of Some individuals fear telling others their birthday and also fear celebrating their birthday in any way. This fear may be related to a fear of aging and fear of getting old. Some individuals fear telling anyone their correct age and consistently say they are younger than they really are. Some even fear celebrating the birthday of another; this may be related to a superstitious fear. (See also AGING, FEAR OF.)

birth trauma A term coined by Otto Rank (1884–1939), an Austrian psychoanalyst, to describe his concept that ANXIETY has roots in the traumatic event of birth. According to Rank, factors in psychoanalysis represent birth SYMBOLS; for example, transference is the reenactment of the oneness with the mother, and the separation from the analyst at the end of the treatment corresponds to the expulsion from the mother's womb. A desire to return to the womb is seen as the universal neurotic wish, and only when this is overcome is the analysis complete. More recently, natural childbirth advocates have expressed interest in the psychological effects of the birth process and have suggested that a calm separation of the baby from the uterus increases the infant's mental health and facilitates the bonding process with the mother. (See also ANXIETIES; ATTACHMENT THEORY; PRIMAL THERAPY; RANK, OTTO.)

black cats, fear of Some individuals fear black cats because they are associated with witchcraft and superstition. Some people avoid letting a black cat cross their path out of superstitious fear of future misfortune. Some fear black cats but not cats of other colors, while other individuals fear only lighter-colored cats. (See also CATS, FEAR OF.)

Bleuler, Eugen (1857–1939) Swiss psychiatrist known for his important studies of SCHIZOPHRENIA, which term he coined (to mean a "splitting" of functions) to replace the previously used term, dementia praecox (a progressive deterioration starting in youth). A colleague of SIGMUND FREUD and CARL JUNG, Bleuler held the first conclave on psychoanalysis in 1908 and was instrumental in organizing the International Psychoanalytic Association two years later. His major contribution was a recognition of the psychological causes of mental illness, as opposed to the prevailing organic theory of EMIL KRAEPELIN.

blennophobia Fear of slime. (See also SLIME, FEAR OF.)

blocking Interruption of a train of speech before a thought or idea has been completed. After a period of silence, which may last from a few seconds to minutes, the individual indicates that he/she cannot recall what he/she has been saying or meant to say. Blocking should be judged as present only if the person spontaneously describes losing his thought or if, upon questioning, he or she gives that as the reason for the pause. Blocking is often due to low levels of ANXIETY that affect concentration.

Blocq's syndrome Fear of standing or walking; also, a hysterical inability to stand or walk. The fear may be motivated by a desire for secondary gains of sympathy and support. Blocq's syndrome is also known as astasia-abasia. The syndrome was named for Paul Oscar Blocq (1860–1896), a French physician. (See also SECONDARY GAIN.)

blood (and blood-injury) phobia Many individuals are afraid of the sight of blood. Fear of blood is known as hematophobia or hemophobia. While susceptible individuals may not say they have a fear of blood, when faced with the sight of their own or another's blood, they may recoil, close their eyes, or even faint. A reaction may occur on hearing a description of blood and gore, such as a war scene, or even imagining seeing someone bleeding. Blood phobia is different from some other phobias in that the individual does not perceive danger of injury or death.

Blood phobics may experience more nausea and faintness than fear or anxiety. They may avoid their phobic stimuli because they fear fainting, and their fear of fainting in turn can cause them anxiety.

With most phobias, the individual's pulse and breathing rate increase in response to the phobic stimulus. However, with blood phobia (and related blood-injury phobias, such as phobia of needles, injection, blood donation, etc.) there is often a sharp drop in heart rate and blood pressure, which is called a diphasic cardiovascular pattern. Why some blood phobics lose consciousness when faced with the stimulus is not clearly understood, but one hypothesis is that it is a "protective" biological mechanism that, in the event of actual injury, prevents the individual from doing anything that might cause further blood loss.

Like phobias of animals, those of blood and injury often begin during childhood. It appears to be relatively common in minor forms, and is excessive in very few instances. Epidemiological studies indicate that approximately 3.1 to 4.5% of the population report blood and blood-injury phobias. In one 1980 study, a high percentage of blood phobics (68%) reported that close relatives had the same fear.

Severe phobia of blood and injury can be seriously handicapping. For example, sufferers may avoid necessary medical procedures or avoid attractive careers as medical professionals. Blood-injury phobic women may even avoid becoming pregnant in order to avoid medical examinations and the sight of blood.

Benjamin Rush (1745–1813), American physican and author, said of blood phobia:

> There is a native dread of the sight of blood in every human creature, implanted probably for the wise purpose of preventing our injuring or destroying ourselves, or others. Chil-

dren cry oftener from seeing their blood, than from the pain occasioned by falls or blows. Valuable medicines are stamped with a disagreeable taste to prevent their becoming ineffectual from habit, by being used as condiments or articles of diet. In like manner, Blood-letting as a remedy, is defenced from being used improperly, by the terror which accompanies its use. This terror rises to such a degree as sometimes to produce paleness and faintness when it is prescribed as a remedy. However unpopular it may be, it is not contrary to nature, for she relieves herself when oppressed, by spontaneous discharges of blood from the nose, and other parts of the body. The objections to it therefore appear to be founded less in the judgments than in the *fears* of sick people.

(See also DEATH, FEAR OF; FAINTING, FEAR OF; FAMILY INFLUENCE; INJURY, FEAR OF.

Beck, Aaron T. and Gary Emery, *Anxiety Disorders and Phobias: A Cognitive Perspective* (New York: Basic Books, 1985).

Ost, Lars-Goran and Kenneth Hugdahl, "Acquisition of Blood and Dental Phobia and Anxiety Response Patterns in Clinical Patients," *Behaviour Research and Therapy,* 23(1985), pp. 27–34.

Runes, D.D. (ed.), *The Selected Writings of Benjamin Rush* (New York: The Philosophical Library, 1947).

blood donating, fear of Fear of donating blood, for many people, is a fear of the sight of their own blood, a fear of needles, or a combination of these fears. Some fear the pain of the needle or fear becoming weak or ill because of the loss of blood. Many blood-donating phobics do not realize that there is very little pain in the actual donation process. Those who have donated blood say that the needle feels something like a pinch on the arm. Some who fear donating blood use the excuse that their blood is not the right type. This usually is a cover-up for their fear, because every type is the right type. Some phobics say that they do not have any blood to spare, although an adult in generally good health has about 10 to 12 pints of blood in his or her body, and one can safely donate one pint of blood every eight weeks. Other phobics say they do not have time to donate blood.

During the 1980s, when the spread of autoimmune deficiency syndrome (AIDS) increased, many individuals became fearful of donating blood because they feared the possibility of acquiring AIDS during the procedure. Authorities have assured donors that it is impossible to get AIDS by donating blood because all materials involved in the donation procedure are used only one time and are completely sterile and disposable. (See also BLOOD PRESSURE PHOBIA.)

blood pressure, fear of high Because high blood pressure (hypertension) is closely linked with heart disease, many people fear having high blood pressure. Many who have illness or disease phobia fear having high blood pressure. The term blood pressure, as used in medicine, refers to the force of the blood against the walls of the arteries, created by the heart as it pumps blood through the body. As the heart beats, the arterial pressure increases. As the heart relaxes between beats, the pressure decreases. High blood pressure is the condition in which blood pressure rises too high and stays there.

Normal blood pressure varies from moment to moment within each individual. Blood pressure may be higher at one time than another. It goes up when one exercises or experiences ANXIETY and goes down when one rests or sleeps. In otherwise healthy adults, however, the generally recognized normal range of systolic (pumping) blood pressure is from 90 to 120 mm HG; the diastolic (resting) blood pressure ranges from 55 to 90 mm HG. In determining whether an individual has high blood pressure, the physician will be concerned with the usual pressure in one's system. The physician may measure an individual's blood pressure more than once during a visit. For example, if one has hurried to the office, one may feel out of breath, which could contribute to a high reading. Later during the visit, as one relaxes, one's blood pressure may go down. Also, a physican may consider the average of several readings taken at different times before making a diagnosis of high blood pressure. If blood pressure is high on only one occasion, the physician will want to measure it again under other circumstances to see if drug treatment is necessary.

Because so many people do not feel any symptoms with high blood pressure, the disease has been called "the silent killer." However, some people with advanced high blood pressure have persistent HEADACHES, DIZZINESS, fatigue, tension and shortness of breath.

Some individuals who have PANIC ATTACKS may have elevated blood pressure at times; they should be checked periodically to be sure that their average blood pressure is within a normal range. (See also HEART ATTACK, FEAR OF; ILLNESS PHOBIA; "WHITECOAT HYPERTENSION.")

Kahn, Ada P., *High Blood Pressure* (Chicago: Contemporary Books, 1983).

blood pressure phobia Fear of blood pressure, usually high blood pressure. (See also "WHITECOAT HYPERTENSION.")

blood transfusions, fear of During the 1980s, fear of blood transfusion became widespread when it was recognized that the human immuno virus (HIV), which is known to carry the dreaded autoimmune deficiency syndrome (AIDS), can be spread through blood transfusions. Others fear blood transfusions because the procedure involves use of needles or tubes placed in the body. Still others who have blood phobia fear seeing blood or blood components being fed into their bodies.

While blood transfusions are feared by many, they are lifesaving for many others. Transfusions are given after great loss of blood in an accident or in a surgical operation, to treat the systemic shock and fluid loss caused by severe burns, in replacing the blood of an Rh-positive newborn infant, and to treat severe anemias.

Since the rapid spread of certain types of hepatitis and AIDS from blood transfusions, blood of donors is tested before it's drawn, and blood is tested again before it is transfused into a recipient. An understanding of how this is done will allay many fears. (See also BLOOD PRESSURE PHOBIA; DISEASE, FEAR OF; ILLNESS, FEAR OF.)

blushing, fear of Fear of blushing, or erythrophobia, can be a painful and difficult symptom for therapists to treat. Fear of blushing is manifest only when other people are present. The phobic individual, most commonly a woman, is terrified that she will blush in the company of others and is convinced that in this state she will be very visible and consequently the center of unwanted, painful attention. If questioned, such an individual cannot say what is so dreadful about blushing, but it is often evident that shame (fear of disapproval of others) is an important component of her anxiety. A change of color may not be at all evident to the observer, despite the fact that the individual insists that she feels bright red; the force of her fear often leads the individual to a severe restriction of her social life.

Edmund Bergler, in 1944, writing in *Psychoanalytic Quarterly,* suggested that blushing in psychiatric literature is usually considered a hysterical conversion symptom within the "embarrassment neurosis" and that blushing is a symptom of unconscious sexual fantasies as well as punishment for those fantasies. Blushing represents an increase in blood volume to the face and head. It is part of the sympathetic nervous system arousal pattern of anxiety/excitement. As with any emotional response, external stimuli, such as the presence of other people, can become conditioned quite easily. (See also NEUROSIS; SOCIAL PHOBIA.)

Bergler, Edmund, "A New Approach to the Therapy of Erythrophobia," *Psychoanalytic Quarterly,* 13(1944), pp. 43–59.

body image, fear of Body image is the mental picture one has of one's body at any moment. Body image is derived from internal sensations, postural changes, emotinal experiences, fantasies, and feedback from others. Fear of deformity of one's own body is known as dysmorphophobia. Some individuals have fears relating to their body image and fear that one or more parts of their body are unattractive and noticeable to others. A misperception of one's body image can lead to eating disorders, such as ANOREXIA NERVOSA OR BULIMIA, in an effort to make oneself thinner. (See also DEFORMITY, FEAR OF; DYSMORPHOPHOBIA; EATING DISORDERS.)

body odor, fear of Fear of body odors is known as osphreisiophobia or bromidrosiphobia. Some individuals fear their own body odor and have an unfounded fear that others wil' notice it. Such individuals may avoid going into crowded places where they must be close to others, may use deodorants and antiperspirants excessively, may bathe, shower, or change clothes excessively, and may seek constant reassurance from family members that they cannot detect any odor. Fear of one's own body odor is considered a SOCIAL PHOBIA and usually responds to appropriate treatment. (See also DYSMORPHOPHOBIA; ODORS, FEAR OF CERTAIN; SOCIAL PHOBIAS.)

body therapies A group of therapies that emphasize the role of physical factors in anxieties and phobias and the resolution of those anxieties and phobias by relaxation, breathing, body manipulation, massage, and changes in posture and position of body parts. Body therapies are used in holistic therapies, which recognize relationships between mind and body in helping individuals overcome anxieties and phobias. (See also AUTOGENIC TRAINING; BIOFEEDBACK; PRIMAL THERAPY; REBIRTHING; REICHIAN THERAPY; RELAXATION THERAPY; ROLFING.)

bogeyman, bogyman, bogey, and bogy An imaginary character possibly possessing supernatural powers. The word has been used to refer to an apparition, hobgoblin, ghost, or the devil. Children fear the bogeyman because they are told that this spirit will punish them for misbehaving. The word *bogy* may have derived from a southern American form of bug, object of terror, or bugbear; it appears often in 19th and 20th-century literature, as early as 1825.

The words *boglie,* meaning haunted, and *boglesome,* meaning shy or skittish, have been developed from the original term.

In psychoanalytic terms, the bogeyman is interpreted as externalized presuperego; that is, a projection onto persons in the external world of the internalized parental prohibitions that are the forerunners of the superego. (See also ANXIETY DISORDERS OF CHILDREN; FREUD; PSYCHOANALYSIS.)

Campbell, Robert, *Psychiatric Dictionary* (New York: Oxford University Press, 1981).

Sarafino, Edward P., *The Fears of Childhood* (New York: Human Sciences Press, 1986).

Oxford English Dictionary, (London: Clarendon Press, 1961).

Wright, John (ed.), *English Dialect Dictionary* (New York: Oxford U. Press, 1970); reprint of 1905 edition.

Random House, Editors of, *Random House Dictionary of the English Language* (New York: Random House, 1987).

Spears, Richard A., *Slang and Euphemism* (Middle Village, NY: David, 1981).

bogyphobia Fear of bogies, or the bogeyman. Bogyphobia can also refer to a generalized fear of demons, goblins, or spirits. It has no relation to boogyphobia, which is a fear of "getting down and rocking." (See also BOGEYMAN; DEMONS; GOBLINS; SPIRITS; WITCHES.)

Bolshephobia Fear of Bolshevism or Bolsheviks. The word was used in popular American slang in the mid-1900s. Bolshevism generally referred to the political philosophy known at that time as communism.

books, fear of Fear of books is known as bibliophobia. Fear of the power of books is often expressed in terms less personal than those used for other fears. For example, government and religious officials rarely feel that reading a book is damaging to them personally but rather believe that society must be shielded from dangerous or obscene material.

Obsessive-compulsives will sometimes fear particular words or numbers or fear reading about particular behavior, thoughts, or emotions.

With the advent of printing and the spread of literacy, books fell into hands other than those of scholars and religious leaders. As a result, both government and church took various measures to control reading of what were considered heretical or treasonous ideas. The 18th century saw a relaxation of control and a gurarantee of freedom of expression in the American Bill of Rights. In the 20th century, however, the burning of "unpatriotic" books was one of the most dramatic indications of the repressive influence of the Nazi regime in Germany. Concentration on obscenity and the efforts of various pressure groups to control publication and distribution of books have characterized recent history in the United States.

Too much or too little association with books also produces a certain type of stigma. Adult illiterates fear situations that will reveal that they cannot hold down a job or perform other daily tasks. On the other hand, to be considered bookish or a bookworm is not particularly complimentary. (See also BOOKS AS ANXIETY RELIEF.)

Haight, Anne Lyon, *Banned Books, 387 B.C to 1978 A.D.* (New York: R.R. Bowker, 1978), pp. i–xxv.

Sills, D.E. (ed.), *International Encyclopedia of the Social Sciences* (New York: Macmillan, 1968), "censorship."

books as anxiety relief Bibliotherapy is an interdisciplinary field that combines the skills of psychotherapists, librarians, and educators. In the course of a bibliotherapy program, books are selected to promote normal development and to change disturbed patterns of behavior. The books may be directly concerned with mental health or may be fiction or nonfiction works relating to and interpreting the readers' problems and concerns. It has been suggested that reading about a disturbing subject such as DEATH, divorce, or AGING gives the reader a sense of control over his problems, a way of working them out in his mind. Use of selected books with children may alleviate fears by clearing up misconceptions and giving information about the UNKNOWN. Reading may also give the child the comforting knowledge that others share his fears and may promote communication with his or her parents.

Rubin, Rhea Joyce, *Bibliotherapy Sourcebook* (Phoenix: Oryx Press, 1978).

Sarafino, Edward P., *The Fears of Childhood* (New York: Human Sciences Press, 1986).

borborygami, fear of Rumbling, gurgling, etc. in the stomach or intestines, produced by gas in the alimentary canal, and audible at a distance. Some individuals so fear that others will hear these sounds that they become social phobics and avoid situations where other people may hear these sounds. (See also PHOBIA; SOCIAL PHOBIA.)

borderline personality disorder A personality disorder characterized by anxiety and unstable moods, behaviors, self-image, and interpersonal relationships. Moods may shift from normal to depressed, and the individual may show inappropriate intense anger or lack of control of anger. There may be impulsive moods, particularly with regard to activities that are potentially self-damaging, such as shopping sprees, psychoactive-substance abuse, reckless driving, casual sex, shoplifting, and binge eating. There may be an identity disturbance noticeable because of uncertainty about self-image, gender identity, or long-term goals or values. The individual may be chronically bored. During periods of extreme stress there may be symptoms of depersonalization. This disorder is more common in females than in males. (See also ANXIETY; DEPERSONALIZATION; PERSONALITY DISORDERS.)

boredom, fear of Boredom is characterized by slow reactions, lack of productivity, wandering attention, and lessened emotional response. In extreme form, boredom may produce depression and hallucination. Boredom is a uniquely individual psychological condition in that what may be fascinating or soothing to one person may be boring or even anxiety-arousing to another. Boredom has been held responsible for ANXIETIES that lead to vandalism, violence, educational and vocational dropping out, marital unhappiness, and even SUICIDE.

Participants in an experiment using an artificial sensory-deprivation environment dropped out in spite of the fact that they were being paid well for doing nothing. Boredom is actually a type of punishment. Solitary confinement for prisoners is a dreaded condition.

Boredom, or lack of stimulation, can be a triggering stimulus for anxiety, particularly with agoraphobics. For example, many agoraphobics fear being alone, which is a state of too little social stimulation. Likewise, quietness, open spaces, and empty rooms are common anxiety triggers characterized by lack of stimulation. (See also TIME, FEAR OF.)

Encyclopedia of Psychology (New York: Herder and Herder, 1972), "boredom."

International Encyclopedia of Psychiatry, Psychology, Psychoanalysis and Neurology (New York: Van Nostrand, 1977), "boredom."

Healy, Sean, *Boredom, Self and Culture* (Rutherford, N.J.: Fairleigh Dickinson University Press, 1984), pp. 9–11.

Boss, Medard (1903–) Swiss psychiatrist and author of *Psychoanalysis and Dasein Analysis.* (See also DASEIN ANALYSIS.)

botonophobia Fear of plants. (See also PLANTS, FEAR OF.)

bound, afraid of being Fear of being bound is known as merinthophobia. This fear is related to a fear of being out of control and a fear of being closed in without escape. (See also ENCLOSED SPACES, FEAR OF; TIED UP, FEAR OF BEING.)

Bowlby, John (1907–) British psychiatrist and author. His work in the area of personality development, object relations, and boundaries has focused on the effects of the experiences of separation and loss on human behavior. His trilogy of works devoted to the subject, *Attachment, Separation,* and *Loss,* was completed in 1980. He has worked primarily at the Tavistock Clinic and Tavistock Institute for Human Relations in London. (See also SEPARATION ANXIETY.)

Bowlby, John, *Loss* (New York: Basic Books, 1980).

May, Hal (ed.), *Contemporary Authors* (Detroit: Gale, 1976).

bradycardia Extremely slow heart rate; the opposite of tachycardia (rapid heart rate). In many blood-injury phobics, bradycardia occurs as a secondary reaction, following an initial phase of rapid heartbeat. Bradycardia can lead to fainting.

brain disease, fear of Fear of brain disease is known as meningitophobia.

brain imaging techniques Brain imaging techniques, like biological imaging techniques in general (such as X rays), allow a physican or researcher to look inside the body without surgically opening it. Techniques include regional cerebral blood flow (RCBF) imaging, nuclear magnetic resonance (NMR) imaging, positron emission tomography (PET), computerized tomography (CT), single photon emission computed tomography (SPECT), and computerized topographic EEG (electroencephalograph) mapping.

Unlike the other imaging techniques, PET can measure body chemistry rather than simply anatomy. Because it measures tracer concentrations up to a million times better than other techniques, it allows the study of microscopic, virtually invisible processes—such as the passage of nutrients through a membrane—as they take place. Thus PET can measure the distribution of psychoactive drugs, such as ANTIDEPRESSANTS, in the brain as well as the sites of trauma from head injuries, brain cancers, strokes, and epileptic seizures. (See also BIOLOGICAL BASIS FOR ANXIETY; DIAGNOSTIC CRITERIA.)

Morihisa, John, M.D. et al., "Atlas of Brain Imaging: Computerized Topographic EEG and Evoked Potential Mapping" (Upjohn Company, 1986).

University of California Clip Sheet, "Tomography Called Twice as Precise," 63:12 (January 5, 1988).

brainwashing The process of inducing an individual to depart radically from his former behavior patterns, standards, and beliefs, and to adopt those imposed on him by others. It is not a technique used to treat phobias, although the intentions of the process are to change the individual's attitude and behaviors. The term has been used since the middle of the 20th century. Brainwashing is a technique feared by servicemen and spies. Although nothing is done directly to the brains of the individuals, much is done to their bodies, including starvation, beating, torture, isolation, prevention of sleep, endless interrogation, and often rewards for acting or speaking along lines indicated by the captors. Brainwashing is not a scientific application of any special psychological techniques and can be successfully done by virtually primitive people who have never heard of psychology. It is basically a physical-abuse technique in which a victim is deprived of health and vigor by the captors The induction of fears and anxieties is a key element in the brainwashing process.

Bugelski, B. Richard and Anthony M. Graziano, *Handbook of Practical Psychology* (Englewood Cliffs, N.J.: Prentice-Hall, 1980).

breakdown, nervous See NERVOUS BREAKDOWN

Breuer, Josef (1841–1925) Viennese physician who had wide scientific and cultural interests. Breuer collaborated with FREUD in studies of cathartic therapy and withdrew as Freud proceeded to introduce PSYCHOANALYSIS. Breuer had a significant effect on psychoanalysis, including the concepts of primary and secondary processes. He introduced FREUD to the case of "Anna O," an hysterical woman whose experience influenced the formulation of Freud's concepts of psychopathology. Although Breuer did not contribute to the area of psychiatry beyond his work with Freud, he stimulated Freud's interest in early events and their relationship to anxieties, fears, and phobias. (See also ANNA O.)

bridges, fear of Fear of bridges is related to fear of being trapped, similar to the fear of being stopped in traffic and unable to turn around. Fear of bridges is also related to fear of heights and narrow spaces. Bridge fear may be considered a fear of childbirth, according to some sources.

"The Angel of the Bridge," a short story by John Cheever, contains an excellent description of panic attack symptoms on a bridge:

"The seizure came with a rush. The strength went out of my legs. I gasped for breath, and felt the terrifying loss of sight. I was, at the same time, determined to conceal these symptoms. . . . I felt the sense of reality ebbing. . . The loneliness of my predicament was harrowing." (See also FALLING, FEAR OF; HEIGHTS, FEAR OF; NARROW PLACES, FEAR OF)

Sills, D.E. (ed.), *International Encyclopedia of the Social Sciences* (New York: Macmillan & Free Press, 1968).

brief focal family therapy An approach to family therapy derived from focal psychotherapy and other brief psychoanalytic approaches to treatment developed at the Tavistock Clinic, London. The therapist develops a focal pattern to serve as a guide in contacts with the family, and the treatment plan is modified as treatment progresses. Treatment for ANXIETY and PHOBIAS would include the family as a unit, with the goal being alleviation of the anxiety by focusing on dynamics within the unit that cause or maintain the anxiety. (See also BRIEF PSYCHOTHERAPY; FAMILY THERAPY.)

brief psychotherapy A form of therapy in which sessions are limited to 10 or 15 in number and during which the therapist uses active and goal-directive techniques and procedures. Brief psychotherapy has been used in individual and group settings to treat phobias and anxieties but is not the treatment of choice for these disorders. Brief psychotherapy has been effective in "crisis management" situations. (See also BEHAVIOR MODIFICATION.)

bromides Bromides are drugs that produce sedation and reduce anxieties. They were first widely used during the mid-1800s. During the second half of the 20th century, however, as many new antianxiety drugs became available bromides have become less popular. Newer drugs avoid a side effect of bromides known as bromism (a subdelirious state). (See also ANTIANXIETY DRUGS; SEDATIVES.)

bromidrophobia (bromidrosiphobia) Fear of offensive odors of the body, either of one's own or of others. (See also PERSONAL ODORS, FEAR OF.)

brontophobia Fear of thunder; also known as astrophobia. Historically, man has dreaded allegedly demonical phenomena in nature, to which he assigned personalities. Fear of thunder, in psychodynamic terms, may be related to fear of real persons in positions of authority, and especially of the father or father figure.

Those who experience fear of thunder (and usually lightning as well) are restricted to interior sections of buildings (away from outside sight or sound) during storms. Sometimes they will retreat to movie theaters or even leave town as a way to avoid exposure to thunder and lightning. (See also STORMS, FEAR OF; THUNDER, FEAR OF.)

bugging, fear of Fear of bugging is a fear that one is being watched, listened to, or otherwise monitored by others. This is a 20th-century fear as highly technologic listening devices, popularly known as "bugs," have been developed and put into use by governments, industry, and others. While the fear is a realistic one in many cases, such as in governmental embassies, where extensive listening devices have been found, some individuals have delusions that they are being listened to by others. Some of these individuals believe that others are pursuing them or are trying to harm them. A fear of "bugging" may be related to OBSESSIVE–COMPULSIVE DISORDER if the individual becomes compulsive about repeatedly checking for listening devices. It could also be an integral part of a delusional system characteristic of paranoid individuals. (See also PARANOID.)

bugs, fear of Fear of insects and spiders is known as bug phobia. From the psychoanalytic point of view, such fears may represent a direct projection of one's own drives, as the tiny creatures may represent genitals, feces, or little children, such as brothers and sisters. More likely, however, fears of insects develop, as do most fears, by traumatic conditioning, repeated aversive exposure, modeling, etc. In its severe form, fear of insects (which is usually quite specific in nature) leads to excessive cleaning of living areas, regular spraying of insecticides (sometimes to an excessive degree), and, if the dreaded insect is seen, complete avoidance of that area, even moving to another living environment.

Many individuals fear bugs because they bite, cause itching, carry disease, and imply less-than-clean conditions. Fear of bugs may be related to a fear of dirt or fear of contamination by germs. Some individuals who have OBSESSIVE–COMPULSIVE DISORDER have obsessions about keeping their environment bug-free. (See also ANIMALS, FEAR OF; INSECTS, FEAR OF; SPIDERS, FEAR OF.)

Campbell, Robert J., *Psychiatric Dictionary* (New York: Oxford University Press, 1981).

building, fear of passing a tall Fear of passing a tall building is known as batophobia. This fear may be related to a fear of HEIGHTS, a fear of looking up at a high place, or a fear of FALLING. Some individuals who have one phobia relating to heights have another of this type.

bulimia An eating disorder characterized by alternate binge eating and purging episodes, either self-induced vomiting, ingestion of laxatives, or fasting. The name "bulimia" is derived from a combination of the Greek words *bous,* meaning "ox," and *limos,* meaning "hunger." Bulimia is more prevalent in women than in men and usually begins during adolescence or young adulthood. Individuals who become bulimic often have anxieties about their body shape, their eating habits, or their lives in general. Low self-esteem, lack of impulse control, emotional instability, and an overall low level of ego strength are characteristics of the bulimic. These factors limit the individual's ability to effectively manage his or her life and environment, causing use of the bingeing-purging behavior as a means of relieving anxiety. The condition itself, however, often creates secondary problems that require immediate treatment, such as esophageal lesions (sores or holes), excessive dental cavities, and intestinal inadequacies. (See also ANOREXIA NERVOSA; EATING DISORDERS.)

bulls, fear of Fear of bulls is known as taurophobia. The bull as a frightening symbol has a long history. The bull's ancestor, the auroch, was a prime source of meat for Paleolithic and Stone Age man. Since hunting the auroch meant first killing the strongest and most powerful bull—the leader of the herd—the image of the bull as the ultimate adversary became prominent in the prehistoric mind. In many ancient cultures, bulls were a symbol of power and authority associated with kings or gods. The strength and temperament of the bull also created symbolic, mythological associations with other fears, such as fear of destruction and fear of natural forces such as THUNDER, LIGHTNING, and EARTHQUAKES. (See also APOCALYPSE, FEAR OF; SYMBOLS.)

Jobes, Gertrude, *Dictionary of Mythology Folklore and Symbols* (New York: Scarecrow, 1961), p. 259.

Cavendish, Richard (ed.), *Man, Myth and Magic* (New York: Marshall Cavendish, 1983), "bulls."

bupropion A newer antidepressant drug with properties similar to those of the tricyclic antidepressants but with more rapid therapeutic effects and apparently no cardiovascular or sedative side effects. (See also ANTIDEPRESSANTS, NEW; DEPRESSION.)

LaPierre, Y.D., "New Antidepressant Drugs," *Journal of Clinical Psychiatry,* 44:8(August 1983), pp. 41–44.

bureaucracy, fear of Many people fear bureaucracy and "red tape," which, to some, mean the same. Bureaucracy is feared because the individual is subordinated to the group or government and loses his own sense of autonomy. He feels a loss of control as he associates bureaucracy with complicated forms, high-handed officials, narrow thinking, failure to assign or accept responsibility, rigidity, lack of attention to the individual, paper shuffling, official blundering, conflicting orders and information, and empire building. Yossarian, the hero of Joseph Heller's antiwar novel, *Catch-22*, was a victim of military bureaucratic thinking. In his efforts to get out of combat duty, he encountered Catch-22, the requirement that a man must ask to be removed from combat duty on the grounds of insanity but that to do so defeated the purpose because a request indicating concern for safety in the face of danger is the product of a rational mind. (See also AUTHORITY, FEAR OF.)

Sills, D.E. (ed.), *International Encyclopedia of the Social Sciences* (New York: Macmillan, 1968).

Heller, Joseph, *Catch-22* (New York: Simon and Schuster, 1961).

burglars, fear of Fear of burglars is known as scelerophobia. In contemporary urban life, many individuals have a fear of burglars and hence take extra precautions to have adequate locks, elaborate burglar alarm systems, and guard dogs. Some obsessive–compulsives who fear burglars may repeatedly check to be sure they have locked their doors and windows. (See also BAD MEN, FEAR OF; OBSESSIVE–COMPULSIVE DISORDER.)

buried alive, fear of being A type of claustrophobia, or fear of being in ENCLOSED PLACES. Individuals fear being buried alive because they fear an inability to escape from such a situation. This fear is also related to a fear of SMOTHERING. (See also CLAUSTROPHOBIA.)

Buspar Trade name for the anxiolythic drug generically known as buspirone. (See also ANTIANXIETY DRUGS; ANXIETY DRUGS.)

buspirone An anxiolythic drug. Its mechanism of action is largely unknown. (See also ANTIANXIETY DRUGS; ANXIETY DRUGS.)

butriptyline An antidepressant drug. (See also ANTIDEPRESSANTS, NEW; DEPRESSION.)

LaPierre, Y.D., "New Antidepressant Drugs." *Journal of Clinical Psychiatry,* 44:8(August 1983), pp. 41–44.

butterflies, fear of Individuals who fear butterflies, moths, and other flying insects fear that the flying insect may attack them. Some phobics avoid enclosed areas out of fear that they may be trapped with the insect. Some phobics actually have accidents while trying to avoid butterflies and moths. (See also BEES, FEAR OF; FLYING THINGS, FEAR OF; INSECTS, FEAR OF.)

Melville, Joy, *Phobias and Obsessions* (New York: Coward, McCann and Geoghegan, 1977).

"butterflies in the stomach" The feeling of uneasiness in the stomach is often referred to as "butterflies." Caused by a contraction of the abdominal blood vessels, this is a common experience among those who must make a speech in public, perform before an audience, appear for a job interview, or participate in any other type of activity that causes feelings of nervousness or apprehension. (See also ADRENALINE; NERVOUS.)

C

caffeine Caffeine is probably the most popular drug in the world. Regular use of over 600 mg a day (approximately eight cups of percolated coffee) may cause chronic IN-

SOMNIA, breathlessness, persistent ANXIETY and DEPRESSION, mild delirium, and stomach upset. Caffeine is a stimulant of the CENTRAL NERVOUS SYSTEM and is primarily consumed in coffee and tea but is also present in cola drinks, cocoa, certain headache pills, diet pills, and patent stimulants such as Vivarin and Nodoz.

Caffeine belongs to the family of methylxanthines (1, 3, 7-trimethylxanthine). A naturally occurring alkaloid found in many plants throughout the world, caffeine was first isolated from coffee in 1820 and from tea leaves in 1827. Both "coffee" and "caffeine" are derived from the Arabic word *gahweh* (pronounced "kehveh" in Turkish).

When taken in beverage form, caffeine begins to reach all the body tissues within five minutes; peak blood levels are reached in about thirty minutes. Normally caffeine is rapidly and completely absorbed from the gastrointestinal tract. Little can be recovered unchanged in urine, and there is no day-to-day accumulation of the drug in the body.

Caffeine increases the heart rate and rhythm, affects the circulatory system, and acts as a diuretic. It also stimulates gastric acid secretion. There may be an elevation in blood pressure, especially during stress. Caffeine inhibits glucose metabolism and may thereby raise blood-sugar levels.

Caffeine is a behavioral stimulant. It may interfere with sleep and may postpone fatigue. It appears to interact with stress, improving intellectual performance in extroverts and impairing it in introverts. When taken before bedtime, caffeine may delay the onset of sleep for some individuals, may shorten sleep time, and may reduce the average "depth of sleep." It also may increase the amount of dream sleep (REM) early in the night while reducing it overall.

While caffeine in moderate doses can increase alertness and talkativeness and decrease fatigue, regular use of 350 mg or more a day may result in a form of physical dependence. (Coffee contains 100 to 150 milligrams of caffeine per cup; tea contains about half, and cola about one third that amount.) Interruption of such use can result in withdrawal symptoms, the most prominent of which may be a severe headache, which can be relieved by taking caffeine. Irritability and fatigue are other symptoms. Regular use of caffeine produces partial tolerance to some or all of its effects.

Research teams at Yale University and the National Institute of Mental Health (NIMH) reported that a dose of caffeine equal to about eight cups of coffee produces far greater increases in anxiety, nervousness, FEAR, NAUSEA, and restlessness among patients diagnosed for AGORAPHOBIA and PANIC DISORDER than among healthy volunteers. Panic attacks are characterized by severe emotional and physical distress that usually lasts for a few minutes; two to five percent of the population have panic disorder—repeated panic attacks with no apparent external cause.

According to researchers at NIMH, among the panic-disorder patients studied, caffeine doses equal to about four cups of coffee brought on panic attacks in 40 percent of the subjects; healthy controls reported no rise in anxiety at the same dose. However, in contrast, a study published in *Psychopathology* (1984) reported no significant difference between the anxiety attacks of the panic patients and healthy controls given a caffeine dose comparable to almost eight cups of coffee. Both groups said that their studies, when combined with related research, suggest that caffeine blocks the action of adenosine, a chemical that reduces the spontaneous firing of neurons in several brain regions. Both caffeine and yohimbine, a drug with similar anxiety-producing effects, may increase the flow of calcium into neurons, a process controlled by adenosine. More calcium may activate more brain cells, leading to greater anxiety.

Researchers at Johns Hopkins University School of Hygiene and Public Health found a modest association between heavy coffee drinking (considered to be five cups or more per day) and myocardial infarction in young women (a condition in the heart muscle resulting from the formation of a blood clot in the coronary arterial system). Excessive use of caffeine has been suspected as a factor in cancer of the bladder and renal pelvis, but the evidence is inconclusive. In addition, caffeine consumption has been linked to fibrocystic breast disease in women, but, again, the evidence so far is inconclusive.

The following chart shows the caffeine content of various commonly consumed products. (See also BIOLOGICAL THEORIES; CAFFEINE INTOXICATION; PANIC ATTACKS; SLEEP.)

Product	Caffeine (mgs)
Coffee (5 oz.)	
Regular Brewed	
percolated	110
dripolator	150
Instant	66
Decaf Brewed	4.5
Instant Decaf	2
Soft Drinks (12 oz.)	
Dr. Pepper	61
Mr. Pibb	57
Mountain Dew	49
Tab	45
Coca–Cola	42
RC Cola	36
Pepsi–Cola	35
Diet Pepsi	34
Pepsi Light	34
Instant/Brewed Tea	
(5 min. brew)	45
Cocoa (5 oz.)	13
Milk Chocolate (1 oz.)	6
Drugs	
Vivarin Tablets	200
Nodoz	100
Excedrin	65
Vanquish	33
Empirin Compound	32
Anacin	32
Dristan	16.2

Source:
Sara J. Carrillo, "Caffeine Versus the Body,' *PharmChem Newsletter* (April 1981); Addiction Research Foundation of Ontario, "Facts About Caffeine" (Toronto, Canada: January 1980); M.B. McGee, "Caffeine Poisoning in a 19-Year-Old Female," *Journal of Forensic Sciences* (January 1980); Mark Wenneker, "Breast Lumps: Is Caffeine the Culprit?" *Nutrition Action* (August 1980), publication of Center for Science in the Public Interest.

O'Brien, Robert and Sidney Cohen, *Encylopedia of Drug Abuse* (New York: Facts On File, 1984).
Science News (March 30, 1985), p. 199.
Archives of General Psychiatry (March 1985).

caffeine as a panicogenic agent Caffeine, a drug common in coffee, tea, cola, and chocolate, as well as other foods, can produce PANIC ATTACKS in susceptible individuals. About half of panic-disorder patients have panic experiences after consuming caffeine equivalent to four or five cups of coffee. Caffeine may produce its effects by blocking the action of a brain chemical known as ADENOSINE, a naturally occurring SEDATIVE. Persons who have panic attacks should avoid caffeine. Future studies may determine whether caffeine has a direct, causative effect on panic or simply alters the body state, which triggers a panic cycle when the individual perceives the change. (See also CAFFEINE.)

caffeine intoxication Also known as caffeinism, caffeine intoxication is an organic disorder due to recent consumption of over 250 milligrams of caffeine and involving at least five of the following symptoms, depending on the individual: restlessness, nervousness, excitement, INSOMNIA, flushed face, frequent and increased urination, gastrointestinal complaints, muscle twitching, rambling thought and speech, cardiac arrythmia, periods of inexhaustibility, and psychomotor agitation. Phobic effects are often heightened when one uses caffeine on a regular basis. (See also CAFFEINE.)

cainophobia: cainotophobia (neophobia) Fear of newness or novelty (See also NEWNESS, FEAR OF; NOVELTY, FEAR OF.)

cancer, fear of Cancer is one of the most feared of human diseases. Many individuals have anxieties regarding their health because they fear cancer. Many do not visit a doctor because they fear the worst, and many others make frequent visits to reassure themselves that they do not have cancer. Many people even fear saying the word. Some people do not want to go near a person known to have cancer; this is an unfounded fear, as cancer is not contagious. However, fear of cancer may motivate more people to obtain check-ups and pay attention to the warning signals of cancer, to stop smoking, avoid excessive exposure to the sun, and avoid other activities known to cause the disease. In Freudian terms, fear of cancer may also represent a fear of castration or a fear of being devoured by an object inside oneself. (See also CASTRATION COMPLEX; DISEASE, FEAR OF.)

carbon dioxide sensitivity When some individuals inhale small amounts of carbon dioxide, they have symptoms of HYPERVENTILATION, trembling, facial flushing, blurring of vision, and dizziness. Carbon dioxide-provoked panic attacks may occur as a result of increased activity in the LOCUS CERULEUS (a small organ of the brain rich in neurotransmitters) in individuals who have an abnormal sensitivity to carbon dioxide. Such panic attacks occur in nearly all predisposed individuals but rarely in normal persons. (Doctors in the armed forces have observed that people who have chronic anxiety cannot tolerate wearing gas masks because the masks make them breathe in some of their own exhaled carbon dioxide.) (See also ANXIETY DISORDERS; CHEMOCEPTORS; LACTATE-INDUCED ANXIETY; NEUROTRANSMITTERS; PANIC ATTACKS.)

cardiophobia See HEART DISEASE, FEAR OF.

cardiovascular symptoms Some of the most frightening and most prominent symptoms of panic disorder are cardiac symptoms. Those who seek consultation with physicians for their cardiovascular symptoms associated with panic disorder may constitute as many as one third of all cardiology patients. (See also MITRAL VALVE PROLAPSE.)

cargo anxiety In New Guinea and Melanesia, "cargo anxiety" occurs out of a belief that ancestral spirits will arrive, bringing valuable cargo. Locals destroy existing food supplies in expectation of better items to come. Insecurity and dissatisfaction with the existing way of life are thought to lead to such delusions.

Howells, J.G. and M.L. Osborn, *A Reference Companion to the History of Abnormal Psychology* (Westport, CT: Greenwood Press, 1984).

carnophobia Fear of meat. (See also MEAT, FEAR OF.)

cars, fear of driving See DRIVING A CAR, FEAR OF.

case control An experimental study design in which groups of phobic individuals are selected in terms of whether they do (cases) or do not (controls) have the particular disorder being studied. (See also COHORT; LONGITUDINAL STUDY.)

castration anxiety Castration is removal of the male testes or female ovaries by surgery, or inactivation of those glands by radiation, infection, PARASITES, or drugs. Castration alters the hormonal function of the individual and generally reduces libido. Castration anxiety involves unconscious feelings and FANTASIES associated with being deprived of the sex organs. Freud believed that boys worry that their penis will be cut off by an angry and jealous father (Oedipal complex) due to sexual interest in the mother. In girls, according to Freud, the castration anxiety is a fantasy that the penis has been removed as a punishment, for which they blame the mother (Electra complex). When castration anxiety persists into adulthood, it may become the cause of a neurotic inability to engage in SEXUAL INTERCOURSE, fear of the opposite sex, impotence in a male and frigidity in a female, or sexual perversions. At the metaphoric level, castration fears relate to loss of contact with the life force and hence life itself.

Castration anxiety was thought by Freud to be a central factor in many phobias. The classic case of LITTLE HANS demonstrated its importance in the etiology of PHOBIAS from the psychoanalytic perspective, although Joseph Wolpe was able to take this case and persuasively show that it actually fit a learning theory analysis. (See also ELECTRA COMPLEX; FRIGIDITY; IMPOTENCE; OEDIPUS COMPLEX; SEXUAL FEARS.)

catagelophobia Fear of ridicule. This is related to a fear of criticism. (See also RIDICULE, FEAR OF.)

catapedaphobia Fear of jumping from both high and low places. (See also HIGH PLACES, FEAR OF; JUMPING, FEAR OF.)

cataract extraction, fear of As cataracts—the cloudiness that forms in the lens of the eye—develop, many individuals experience anxiety, depression, and an acute sense of loneliness. When the condition seriously affects vision, the lens is surgically removed, and vision is restored by an implanted plastic lens, contact lens, or special glasses. About 900,000 people in the United States have this surgery every year. Although 95 percent of them return to routine activity, many fear that the operation will fail and leave them permanently blind. This prospect is particularly frightening to anyone who has already lost the sight of one eye. Some people fear specific aspects of the operation, such as costs, other health problems such as diabetes or heart disease, or anesthesia.

Many fears of cataract extraction are based on misconceptions, such as that age is a hindrance to surgery and that loss of vision may result. In a study of 425 cases of cataract extraction, 92.7 percent were successful.* Increased public information and better understanding of the safety of the operation helps remove many individuals' fears. (See also AGING, FEAR OF.)

catastrophic anxiety Overwhelming anxiety associated with organic brain syndromes when the individual is aware of defects in his or her thinking. (See also ANXIETY; ANXIETY DISORDERS.)

catharsis Release of suppressed or inhibited emotions and tensions that provides temporary relief from ANXIETY. Catharsis is often observed during individual and group therapy; it also occurs outside therapy. The word "catharsis" is derived from the Greek *katharsis,* meaning purification or cleansing. In psychodynamic therapies, catharsis is viewed as an alleviation of fears, problems, and complexes by making them conscious and giving them expression. (See also ABREACTION; CONVERSATIONAL CATHARSIS.)

cathisophobia Fear of sitting. (See also SITTING, FEAR OF.)

cathexis Psychoanalysts use this term to signify an individual's concentration or investment of mental energy in a certain direction—for example, toward some person or object—in an effort to reduce anxieties. (See also FENICHEL, OTTO.)

catoptrophobia Fear of mirrors. (See also MIRRORS, FEAR OF.)

cats, fear of Fear of cats is known as aelurophobia, ailurophobia, elurophobia, felinophobia, galeophobia, or gatophobia. The characteristics of fear of cats are similar

---

*
Clinical Gerontologist (Summer 1984), pp. 68–70.

to those of fears of other animals. Generally, it is a fear of being injured or scratched by them. Some individuals react with shortness of breath, rapid heartbeat, or feelings of panic just at the sight of a cat. For other individuals, the fear is induced only if the cat comes very close or touches them. Some people fear cats' eyes staring at them. One psychiatric interpretation of fear of cats is that it is a repression of dread of injury to a particular part of the body. Henry III of France is said to have feared cats.

With regard to cat phobia, Benjamin Rush (1745–1813), an American physician and author, said: "It will be unncessary to mention instances of the prevalence of this distemper. I know several gentlemen of unquestionable courage, who have retreated a thousand times from the sight of a cat; and who have even discovered signs of fear and terror upon being confined in a room with a cat that was out of sight." (See also ANIMALS, FEAR OF; BEING LOOKED AT, FEAR OF.)

Runes, D.D. (ed.), *The Selected Writings of Benjamin Rush* (New York: The Philosophical Library, 1947).

Marks, Isaac, M., *Living with Fear* (New York: McGraw Hill, 1978).

causality A view that events, such as phobic reactions, are consequences of preceding events. As an explanation of anxieties and phobias, the causality approach suggests that there is always a distinct cause and effect. The causal approach differs from the purely descriptive approach and from the introspective methods. Within the behavioral approach, causality is not a critical issue. The focus is rather on variables that maintain or trigger responses. (See also ANXIETY; PHOBIAS.)

cemeteries, fear of Fear of cemeteries is known as coimetrophobia. Individuals who fear cemeteries usually also fear going to funerals, looking at tombstones, looking at dead bodies, and even hearing about funerals. Some will drive distances out of their way to avoid passing cemeteries. Others will walk on the side of the street away from a cemetery to avoid being near one. (See also DEATH, FEAR OF; TOMBSTONES, FEAR OF.)

cenophobia Fear of empty rooms, open places, and barren spaces. This fear may be related to agoraphobia. (See also AGORAPHOBIA; BARREN SPACES, FEAR OF; EMPTY ROOMS, FEAR OF; OPEN PLACES, FEAR OF.)

center of the row, fear of sitting in the Some individuals fear sitting in the center of the row in theaters, movies, churches, and community meetings. Some who fear being closed in have this fear. Agoraphobics fear being in the center of the row because they fear being trapped and unable to get to a place of safety. Some who fear that they might have to use a toilet in a public place fear being in the center of the row because getting out might be difficult or embarrassing. Some who have social phobias fear being in the center of the row where they must pass many others before getting to their seat. Others fear that they will do something embarrassing, such as cough, sneeze, or vomit, and want to be sure of a safe getaway, which is more difficult from the center of the row. (See also AGORAPHOBIA; CLAUSTROPHOBIA.)

centophobia Fear of newness or novelty. (See also NOVELTY, FEAR OF.)

central nervous system The part of the nervous system that consists of the brain and spinal cord and to which all sensory impulses are transmitted and from which motor impulses originate; the central nervous system also supervises and coordinates the activities of the entire nervous system. Some drugs used to treat phobic reactions and agoraphobia, as well as antidepressants, affect the central nervous system. (See also ANTIDEPRESSANTS; DEPRESSION; DRUGS)

ceraunophobia (keraunophobia) Fear of thunder. (See also THUNDER, FEAR OF; THUNDERSTORMS, FEAR OF.)

CHAANGE CHAANGE is a self-help private organization that disseminates tapes and other materials for treatment of anxiety disorders. CHAANGE distributes educational materials throughout the United States. The program focuses on these four areas of agoraphobia; 1) understanding the condition; 2) learning to relax the body; 3) learning new skills of thought and attitude; and 4) learning to not avoid.

chaetophobia Fear of hair is known as chaeotophobia. This includes fear of hairy objects, animals, or people. (See also HAIR, FEAR OF; HAIR DISEASE, FEAR OF.)

change, fear of Fear of change or of anything new is known as neophobia. Fear of making changes is known as tropophobia. Many individuals feel secure in their daily lives by doing things in a certain routine. They fear introducing new ways of performing daily activities, a new job, new place of residence, or changes in family status. Some individuals who never move may fear moving, or changing residence. Some never travel, because they fear new places, or changing location. Some who remain single throughout life may also fear change. Those who have AGORAPHOBIA may fear change, such as the change in stimulation when going out of their house, where they feel secure. (See also MOVING, FEAR OF; TRAVEL, FEAR OF.)

character analysis Therapy focused on defensive behavior that is an integral part of the personality. Character analysis is a term introduced by Wilhelm Reich (1897–1957), an Austrian-American psychoanalyst, to describe a process the therapist uses in helping an individual to liberate repressed psychic energy. Reich suggested that individuals have a built-in character armor that they use to repress sexual and social freedoms of expression. Some of these repressed freedoms may lead to ANXIETIES and PHOBIAS. Reich identified six character structures that frequently confront the therapist: the phallic-narcissistic male; the passive-feminine male; the masculine-aggressive female; the hysterical female; the compulsive character; and the masochistic character.

Character analysis also refers to psychoanalytic treatment of character disorders and to the study of character traits supposedly revealed by external characteristics, such as the shape of the jaw. (See also CHARACTER ARMOR; CHARACTER TRAINING APPROACHES; REICH, WILHELM.)

character armor Rigid character structures that prevent release of emotions and liberation of an individual's personality. The term was introduced by Wilhelm Reich, who believed that the analyst should identify the individual's character patterns that serve as defense mechanisms against anxiety that block the way to the unconscious levels of the personality. Examples of character armor are cynicism and overaggressiveness. Clues such as facial expressions or posture determine these mechanisms. (See also CHARACTER ANALYSIS; REICH, WILHEIM.)

character training approaches Approaches that share a moral view regarding the origins and treatment of psychological disturbances, including anxieties and phobias. The focus of treatment in such approaches is on changing the individual's attitude and life-style. The therapist helps the individual recognize his own part in forming symptoms and his responsibility for bringing about changes. (See also INTEGRITY GROUPS; MEDITATION; MORITA THERAPY; NAIKAN THERAPY; WILL THERAPY.)

Charcot, Jean M. (1825–1893) French neurologist, noted for treating HYSTERIA by HYPNOSIS. Charcot, who studied the stages of hypnosis and its effect on the nervous system, was the first to induce and remove hysterical symptoms by this means. Freud based much of his early work on Charcot's studies in hysteria. Charcot became head of Salpetiere Hospital in Paris in 1862 and held the world's first Chair of Medical Diseases of the Nervous System. Many phobic and anxious individuals continue to be helped by techniques of hypnosis that have evolved since Charcot's time. (See also FREUD, SIGMUND; JANET, PIERRE.)

checking (as a ritual) Some individuals who have OBSESSIVE–COMPULSIVE DISORDER spend hours checking ordinary situations out of fear of omission of an act—for example, checking that the doors and windows of their houses are locked. They may fear hairs they have dropped and check and recheck for loose hairs on themselves or in their household. Checking (as a ritual) is more common in men than women; overall, a little more than one third of all obsessive–compulsives exhibit excessive checking.

Marks, Isaac, M., *Fears, Phobias and Rituals* (New York: Oxford University Press, 1987)

cheimaphobia (cheimatophobia) Fear of the cold, being cold, cold things, or cold air. (See also COLD, FEAR OF.)

chemoceptors Substances in the brain that monitor acidity in the blood. In normal individuals, these chemoceptors signal serious changes, such as a buildup of carbon dioxide, which may indicate that oxygen is not reaching the organs of the body. The result is likely to be panic, which influences individuals to take action, for example, to avoid suffocation. However, in people with panic disorder, oversensitive chemoceptors create terror without any apparent reason. (See also CARBON DIOXIDE SENSITIVITY; LACTATE-INDUCED ANXIETY; PANIC.)

chemotherapy, fear of Many people fear chemotherapy—the treatment of mental and physical disorders through drugs or other chemicals—because the treatment is associated with CANCER. Cancer patients fear chemotherapy because of unpleasant side effects associated with it. Strong anticancer drugs often cause side effects of repeated episodes of NAUSEA and VOMITING, and this often conditions strong aversion to stimuli associated with chemotherapy, including FOOD eaten before treatments. Some patients begin to vomit even before the drugs are injected and retch as they get a call from the oncology nurse, get dressed, or travel to the hospital.

Although, in the case of mental disorders, chemotherapy addresses only the symptoms of a disorder, it has become a popular way of treating some individuals because it has the effect of at least making the individuals more manageable and amenable to other forms of therapy. The main categories of chemotherapy (drugs) used to treat anxiety disorders, manic–depressive illness, and obsessive–compulsive disorders are ANTIPSYCHOTICS, antianxiolytics, and ANTIDEPRESSANTS. (See also CANCER, FEAR OF; DRUGS, FEAR OF TAKING.)

Marks, Isaac M., *Fears, Phobias and Rituals* (New York: Oxford University Press, 1987).

McConnell, James V., *Understanding Human Behavior* (New York: Holt, Rinehart and Winston, 1986).

Zimbardo, Phillip, *Psychology and Life* (Glenview, IL: Scott, Foresman, 1985).

cherophobia Fear of being happy or of gaiety. Manifestations of this phobia are ANXIETIES that are triggered by experiences of being happy, or by fears that the happiness or gaiety are going to produce disaster or aversive events. (See also GAIETY, FEAR OF; HAPPINESS, FEAR OF.)

chickens, fear of Fear of chickens is known as alektorophobia. These fears can include feathers, eggs, or live or dead chickens. Some people fear chickens because they peck, swoop, and roost above eye level or because they eat their food from the ground, which may contaminate it. Fears of chickens may be related to fears of other birds and feathered animals. It is interesting that such fears usually involve proximity to a live chicken. A cooked chicken or meal would be quite acceptable. Such specificity is common with phobics. (See also CONTAMINATION, FEAR OF; FEATHERS, FEAR OF.)

child abuse Extreme levels of punishment beyond typical spanking that adults inflict on children, either their own or children of others entrusted to their care. Some children develop fears of adults because of punishment they have suffered at the hands of adults. Abused children are highly prone to develop phobias later in life that are related to early childhood experiences. Those who have experienced pain may fear disease, doctors, or surgical operations. Those who have been tied or placed in ENCLOSED PLACES may develop CLAUSTROPHOBIA and fears of DARKNESS. Children can be abused psychologically, too; an example is being told repeatedly that they will be given away. This type of abuse may cause children to grow up with little self-confidence, feelings of worthlessness, and a tendency toward AFFECTIVE DISORDERS, such as DEPRESSION.

childbirth, fear of Many women approach childbirth with fear and apprehension. Horror stories from friends and relatives fuel many such fears. Some first-time mothers, in particular, are disturbed by what seems to be an encounter with the unknown. Women fear the LOSS OF CONTROL inherent in the childbirth experience and are often afraid that they will behave in an embarrassing manner during childbirth. The contemporary expectation that fathers will attend childbirth produces fears and anxieties in some expectant fathers.

Women also fear many of the practical details connected with the experience of childbirth. Some fear that they will not recognize the beginning of labor and that they will not get to the hospital on time. Some fear hospital procedures, such as the use of stirrups, shaving the pubic area, and the episiotomy. Others fear loss of elasticity due to stretching of the vagina, stretch marks on their abdomen, and sagging breasts as a result of pregnancy and childbirth.

The condition of the newborn and the use of a rating scale for infants produces anxiety for some new mothers. Temporary physical conditions of the newborn, such as a misshapen head, skin blemishes, excess hair, or no hair at all, often disturb many new parents.

Women who have cesarean section births have special fears. For example, some fear that the surgery may damage the baby or that a baby born this way will be exceptionally fragile. Some women also fear that the cesarean procedure will damage their body and that it denies them what they believe should be a natural experience for a woman.

Some women anticipate childbirth as a glorious, fulfilling experience and fear disappointment because of their high expectations. Some anticipate a sense of emptiness after a childbirth, a loss of their reason for existence while pregnant. While education for childbirth has generally had a positive influence for most women, in some women, preparation produces the feeling that childbirth is a type of performance with the accompanying implications of success and failure.

Fears of bearing a monster, of bearing a stillborn baby, of dying during childbirth, and of losing a baby to SUDDEN INFANT DEATH SYNDROME also cause anxieties for many women and men. (See also BEARING A MONSTER, FEAR OF; PREGNANCY, FEAR OF.)

de Beauvoir, Simone, *The Second Sex* (New York: Modern Library, 1968).

Eisenberg, Arlene, Heidi Eisenberg Murkoff and Sandee Eisenberg Hathaway, *What to Expect When You're Expecting* (New York: Workman, 1984).

childhood, anxieties, fears, and phobias Childhood fears are related to a child's age. Infants and toddlers have some fears that arise out of inborn fright reaction to PAIN, sudden loud noises, bright LIGHTS, and loss of physical support, as in FALLING. Infants are most likely to fear STRANGERS and will react with a startled response to an unfamiliar face. Infants over six months also develop "separation distress," which makes them fear being left by the persons they love and trust. When left alone they may cry and scream. When the mother or caregiver returns they will show ANXIETY by staying close to her, touching her, and watching her.

Young children have many more fears than adults that start with no apparent cause and subside and change for no clear reason as the child grows older. Childhood fears may be developmental. An example is when a child suddenly fears things it has experienced without fear or trauma, such as small animals or birds. Fear may also come from exposure to a new situation, such as school (viewed as unpredictable, unknown). Illness or stress may cause a child to regress and reexperience earlier, forgotten fears until he or she is well again.

Whereas infants and toddlers often fear tangible and immediate events, fears of preschoolers are more abstract. Preschoolers have an active fantasy life and may have difficulty in distinguishing between real and unreal events and people. Children develop the greatest number of new fears during the preschool and early school years. It is considered normal for children to have specific fears. They are universally sensitive to the familiar in an unfamiliar guise (for example, parents wearing a mask). At these times, they may have actual frightening encounters or learn about frightening experiences of others. Preschool children are warned about possible dangers and learn about monsters from books, movies, and television. Between two and six, many children fear being in the dark or being alone; fear imaginary creatures, such as ghosts and witches; and fear animals. Some of the most common sources of fear are:

animals (dogs are most common) and insects
dark (especially at bedtime)
death (separation, sometimes injury)
doctors and dentists
heights
monsters and imaginary creatures
nightmares
school
storms (and other natural events)
water (deep)

School-age children worry about their schoolwork as well as about acceptance by teachers and schoolmates. There are particular fears during middle childhood and adolescence, such as fears of physical injury, social relationships, individual competence, and nuclear war.

Two adult fears—blood and injury phobias and animal and snake phobias—usually begin in childhood.

School and death fears

Separation anxiety is the basis for two common childhood phobias, SCHOOL and DEATH. School phobia is an intense fear related to attending school. It can begin at any age, even preschool or kindergarten. School-phobic children may describe problems at school, such as being afraid of teachers or classmates. They may claim that special problems await them on the way to school, such as bullies. They may pretend to be ill, and in some cases may have physical symptoms of illness, such as vomiting. When school phobia occurs in older children, it may be related to home life, school performance, or relationships with classmates. In some cases, separation anxiety also may be related to death phobia. Some children fear that one or both parents will die; these children fear being left alone without the care and love of their parents. Children's perceptions of death change between ages three and 10. Young children may consider death to be like living in another place; they anticipate the return of the deceased. At age five to six, some children believe that death is not inevitable, because, for example, they can outwit monsters. Between ages six and ten, children increasingly understand that death is final, and that it can involve pain, injury, and disease. Thus they begin to fear pain or injury from their imaginary "bogeyman." Around age 10, most children fully understand death as inevitable and final. There is a high incidence of school-phobic children who later develop AGORAPHOBIA.

Sex distribution of fears

Girls seem to have more fears than boys, but it is possible that the differences in number are due to our society's acceptance of different behaviors for boys and girls. Girls admit to more fears, are warned about more dangers, and are comforted when they are fearful. Boys tend to hide their anxieties behind a tough facade, but their anxieties often show up later in different ways. For example, boys outnumber girls in some childhood problems, such as stuttering, asthma, and bedwetting. (See also BOGEYMAN, FEAR OF; DEATH, FEAR OF; SCHOOL PHOBIA; SEPARATION ANXIETY.)

Sarafino, Edward P., *The Fears of Childhood* (New York: Human Sciences Press, 1986).

Marks, Isaac M., *Fears, Phobias and Rituals* (New York: Oxford University Press, 1987).

children, anxiety disorders of See CHILDHOOD ANXIETIES, FEARS, AND PHOBIAS.

children, fear of Fear of children is known as pediophobia. Many adults fear that children will be destructive or messy, will leave finger marks, or will be noisy and create a nuisance. Some adults fear children because they do not understand them and their normal development. The fact that some children tend to be noisy, aggressive, emotional, uninhibited, blunt, constantly interrupting, and complaining, makes them unappealing to many landlords and proprietors of some businesses and recreational facilities, as well as to some parents, relatives, and those who come into unwanted contact with children, for example in restaurants or public transportation.

Throughout history, fears of children have taken various forms. Influenced by a strong belief in original sin, the Puritans thought that children were essentially evil and could fall into depravity if not disciplined and put to work. On the other hand, the Victorians saw childhood as an idyllic time. Children were not particularly welcome in adult society but were seen as innocents who could be irreparably damaged by any but the most tactful, gentle references to the body in general and sex in particular. Parents feared bad influences on their children.

A late-19th-century etiquette book laid down rules for privileged families that indicate that children were not thought to be fit company for adults. Children under the age of 13 ate dinner in the nursery with their governess, not with their parents. The only meal eaten with father at all was Sunday lunch. Young children were excluded from the drawing room except on special occasions.

Early-20th-century child development experts promoted the fear that children's behavior and bodily functions would deteriorate if not properly scheduled.

Social and technological changes of the mid-20th century seem to have created a fear that there is no good way to bring up children. The birth rate is falling, and children have become an economic disadvantage to some parents. When most of society was engaged in farming and small-business operation, children served a role as employees. As the possibilities for children to play this role have decreased the cost of raising and educating a child have increased. Because of mixed emotions, possibly including fear, on the part of parents, child abuse and neglect have increased since the 1960s.

The accleration of change has made the younger generation frightening to the older. In 1970, Margaret Mead (1901–1978) reflected the anguish many adults feel when they see a child eagerly and expertly playing with a computer. "Today nowhere in the world are there elders who know what the children know, no matter how remote and simple the societies in which the children live."

Cable, Mary, *The Little Darlings: A History of Child Rearing in America* (New York: Scribner, 1975).

Albert, Linda, *Linda Albert's Advice for Coping with Kids* (New York: Dutton, 1982).

China Fear of China, the Chinese language, and things relating to the Chinese culture is known as Sinophobia.

In ancient China, hypnosis and supernatural practices were included in therapy for mental disorders, such as possession by spirits and demons. Special institutions for the insane existed in Peking (now Beijing) as early as 300 B.C. Western methods of treating anxiety disorders began during the 19th century when medical missionaries arrived.

A 1970 study indicated that Chinese medicine classified mental disorders by cause, including "wind madness," "ghost evil," "possession by devil," "anxiety due to animus," "convulsive madness," "puerperal (postpartum) insanity," and "mental deficiency." (See also SINOPHOBIA.)

Neki, J.S. "Psychiatry in South-East Asia," *British Journal of Psychiatry*, 123(1973), pp. 257–269.

chins, fear of Fear of chins is known as geniophobia. Some individuals characterize personalities by the shape of chins. For example, some individuals believe that in men, a receding chin may be a sign of meekness, while a strong, protruding chin may be a sign of strength and aggressiveness, and perhaps something to be feared. Some people fear others who have double chins. Individuals who have obsessions about their own body and the shape of their body, particularly their face, may believe that changing the shape of their chin will help change their personality or their life. Some individuals seek cosmetic surgery to correct what they perceive as a misshapen chin. (See also BODY IMAGE, FEAR OF.)

chionophobia Fear of snow. (See also SNOW, FEAR OF.)

chlordiazepoxide An antianxiety drug marketed under the trade name Librium. This antianxiety drug (or anxiolytic) falls into a group of drugs known as BENZODIAZEPINES. Chlordiazepoxide is generally one of several drugs of choice for relief of anxiety and tension. Like the other benzodiazepines, it is also useful in alcohol and drug withdrawal syndromes and as a muscle relaxant. (See also ANXIOLYTICS; ANXIETY.)

chlorpromazine Generic term for one of the most widely used MAJOR TRANQUILIZERS, sold under the name Thorazine. It was the first ANTIPSYCHOTIC agent marketed. It is frequently used to treat psychotics and sometimes incorrectly prescribed for ANXIETY, as it is one of the most SEDATIVE antipsychotic drugs. Tolerance to this effect develops rapidly. Individuals under 40 years of age experience the fewest side effects from the drug. In older patients, there is a high incidence of DIZZINESS, low blood pressure, and vision changes. Because of these major side effects individuals who are taking it should be monitored regularly and closely by their physician. (See also ADVERSE DRUG EFFECTS.)

choking, fear of Although both fear of choking and ANOREXIA NERVOSA are eating disorders, they are distinctly different. Individuals who fear choking may have no particular wish to be thin and often remain hungry despite their inability to eat. They gradually lose weight as they limit themselves to what they consider safe foods and safe places to eat. While tightness in the throat is a common symptom of panic disorder and grief, fear of choking may be the only persistent complaint when there are no other symptoms of PANIC DISORDER or DEPRESSION.

The individual may describe one specific time when he or she almost choked; this is probably the episode during which the phobia began because intense fear or panic was elicited. Later on, the individual may describe a history of episodes of rapid pulse, chest pain or tightness, dizziness, tremulousness, tingling and numbness in the arms and legs, and a sense of impending doom or LOSS OF CONTROL. Some have been diagnosed as previously having had HYPERVENTILATION syndrome They may have other phobias such as the fear of CROWDS, CLOSED PLACES, HEIGHTS, or DRIVING A CAR. These fears may have led to other avoidance behaviors.

Most individuals with fear of choking while eating welcome treatment and respond well. Systematic desensitization and a variety of pharmacologic agents have been known to be helpful to individuals who have choking phobia. (See also DESENSITIZATION; DRUGS, FEAR OF TAKING; EATING PHOBIAS.)

Greenberg, Donna B. et al., ''Fear of Choking,'' *The Journal of Family Practice,* 22:6(1986), pp. 547–548.

cholera, fear of Cholera, a disease caused by contaminated water or food supplies that carry the microorganism *ivrio cholerae,* was widely feared during the 19th century. During the European epidemic from 1840 to 1849, cholera victims died in the streets, causing further fears and anxieties among the non-infected population. Cholera is still feared in southcentral and southeast Asia, where it is prevalent because of lack of sanitary conditions. Many individuals who travel to ''third world' countries still fear cholera, and medical authorities often advise inoculations against cholera for some travelers to certain areas. Infection results in such symptoms as diarrhea, muscle cramps, vomiting, dehydration and sometimes shock. The disease may resemble severe cases of food poisoning. (See also DISEASE, FEAR OF; ILLNESS PHOBIA.)

cholesterol, fear of Cholesterol is a fatty substance essential to the cells of the body. Many people fear eating foods high in saturated fats such as meats and egg yolks because a high cholesterol count has been linked with heart disease. Individuals who fear heart disease often fear having a high cholesterol level. High cholesterol levels sometimes lead to deposits of fatty material within the walls of blood vessels and a condition known as atherosclerosis. High blood pressure, heart disease, and other circulatory problems sometimes follow atherosclerosis. An individual who is anxious about cholesterol and the risk of heart disease can reduce his chance of developing heart disease by reducing intake of saturated fats, which are derived largely from meat, egg yolk, butter, high-fat dairy products, and coconut oil. An intake of largely polyunsaturated fats, on the other hand, will lower the cholesterol level. Likewise, high-fiber diets seem to lower cholesterol levels Some cholesterol is essential to health. Drastic low-cholesterol diets should not be tried without reason or without a physician's recommendation. (See also EATING PHOBIAS; FOOD, FEAR OF; HEART DISEASE, FEAR OF.)

chorophobia Fear of dancing. (See also DANCING, FEAR OF.)

chrematophobia Fear of money. Also known as chromophobia, and more commonly as chrematomania. This phobia is often linked to obsessive concerns about cleanliness and avoidance of germs thought to be carried on much-handled money. Sufferers will eventually quit handling money or begin to wear gloves as a safeguard. (See also GERMS, FEAR OF; MONEY, FEAR OF; OBSESSIVE–COMPULSIVE DISORDER.)

chromatophobia Fear of a certain color or colors. (See also COLORS, FEAR OF.)

chronic obstructive lung disease and anxiety Many individuals who have chronic obstructive pulmonary (lung) disease (COPD) such as chronic bronchitis and chronic emphysema frequently fear that they will suffocate, lose control, and die. They also fear having a breathless attack in public and the embarrassment of requiring emergency care. During an attack of obstructed breathing, they may have a panic attack in which they gasp for air, which only worsens their situation and anxiety. Some recall frequent periods of panic and may even have nightmares about being unable to inhale. Some who suffer from COPD have disabling anxiety because of their disease. They may avoid social situations because they fear an obstructed breathing attack and may become depressed and withdrawn.

An understanding of what happens to an individual who has COPD can help others around him or her cope with the anxieties the individual experiences. In many respiratory disorders, there is a narrowing of the bronchial tubes. In chronic bronchitis, the mucous membrane lining the main air passages (bronchi) of the lungs becomes inflamed, leading to breathlessness and heavy coughing. In chronic asthma, the muscles of the bronchial walls contract, leading to partial obstruction of the bronchi and the bronchioles (smaller air passages in the lungs). The individual has attacks of wheezing and difficult breathing. In asthmatics, such attacks may be brought on by stimuli to which they are allergic, or by exercise or stress. With chronic emphysema, the air sacs (alveoli) at the ends of the bronchioles are damaged. Because this is where oxygen and carbon dioxide exchange, the lungs become less and less efficient, and the primary symptom is difficult breathing, which gets worse and becomes more frightening as the individual ages.

R. Reid Wilson includes these self-helps suggestions for COPD anxiety in *Don't Panic: Taking Control of Anxiety Attacks* (New York: Harper & Row, 1986):

1. Find ways to make yourself less fearful of social situations. Be prepared to endure a coughing spell and dispose of sputum while in public, without withdrawing or becoming embarrassed.
2. If you take medications, ask your physician if any of them can lead to increased irritability or nervousness. Some drugs that open up the bronchi activate the sympathetic nervous system and may make one feel a little jumpy. If you understand that this is likely to occur, you will be better prepared to cope with the additional feelings of anxiety.

   Some medications for COPD may cause anxieties as a side effect. For example, the oral medication used for bronchospasm, aminophylline and the beta-Z adrenergic agents, can cause general anxiety and a rapid heart rate. The inhaler form of the beta-Z adrenergic agents can produce general anxiety and shaky hands. Corticosteroids may elevate mood and then cause a shift into depression.
3. Try to face and cope with stressful changes, rather than avoid them. You will feel in better control of your life by coping than avoiding.
4. Try to avoid (without withdrawing from social life) activities that you know may lead to any quick change in your emotional state and bring on anxiety.
5. Use techniques such as relaxation or medication to diminish feelings of nervousness, worry, and depression. If

you are less worried and anxious, you may have fewer severe difficult breathing episodes.

6. Learn the best ways to feel and act during acute episodes. Learn specific techniques to minimize symptoms and help you return to comfortable breathing. Learn a set of response skills and use them.

(See also ALLERGIC REACTIONS; ASTHMA; LUNG DISEASE, FEAR OF; STRESS MANAGEMENT.)

chronic pain, fear of Fear of chronic pain is associated with fear of certain diseases, such as arthritis and cancer, and with aging and growing old. (See also AGING, FEAR OF; CANCER, FEAR OF; PAIN, FEAR OF; PAIN AND ANXIETY.)

chronophobia Fear of time; also known as prison neurosis, because it may be the most common anxiety disorder in prison inmates. Chronophobia is characterized by panic, anxiety, and claustrophobia. Sooner or later, almost all prisoners suffer chronophobia to some degree and become terrified by the duration and immensity of time. This is often called going "stir crazy." Chronophobia appears suddenly, without warning. The introductory phase of imprisonment is ordinarily marked by hopes and plans for a new trial, by uncertainty, and by a studied indifference or carefree attitude. After the novelty of prison wears off, when the prisoner comes to grips with the real length of the sentence, chronophobia sets in. The prisoner goes into a panic, usually while in his cell, and fears his enclosure and restraint; this apparent claustrophobia arises from fear of time, as represented by the prison. After the first attack, the prisoner experiences more or less constant anxiety, restlessness, insomnia, dissatisfaction with life, numerous hypochondriacal complaints, and progressive inability to adjust himself to his surroundings. The intensity of the crisis usually passes within a few weeks or months, though mild relapses may occur. Later the prisoner becomes relatively indifferent to his surroundings and serves the rest of his sentence by the clock and lives wholly in the present, one day at a time. See also ANXIETY; CLAUSTROPHOBIA; PANIC; TIME, FEAR OF.)

Deutsch, A. and H. Fishman, *The Encyclopedia of Mental Health* (New York: Franklin Watts, 1963), pp. 110–111.

churches, fear of Fear of churches is known as ecclesiophobia. The term also refers to fear of clergypersons. (See also HOLY THINGS, FEAR OF.)

cibophobia Fear of food. This is commonly associated with a particular food or class of foods. (See also FOOD, FEAR OF.)

circumspection-preemption-control (CPC) cycle A cyclical process in which an anxious or phobic individual develops a system that enables him or her to interpret the environment and anticipate future events. When faced with a novel situation or new material to learn, the individual may approach it first by loosening his constructs (circumspection), then by tightening them (preemption), and finally, when the situation or material has been integrated, by developing new control. The term was introduced by George A. Kelly (1905–1967), an American psychologist.

Walrond-Skinner, Sue, *A Dictionary of Psychotherapy* (London: Routledge & Kegan Paul, 1986).

Kelly, G.A., *A Psychology of Personal Constructs* (New York: W.W. Norton, 1955).

circumstantiality A term that describes an indirect speech pattern common among individuals who have obsessive–compulsive disorder. The individual delays reaching the point by introducing unnecessary, tedious details and parenthetical remarks. Circumstantial replies or statements may be prolonged for many minutes if the speaker is not interrupted and urged to get to the point. Therapists often respond to circumstantiality by interrupting the speaker in order to complete the process of history-taking. Such interruption may make it difficult to distinguish loosening of associations from circumstantiality. In loosening of associations, there is a lack of connection between clauses, and the original point is lost; but in circumstantiality, the clauses always retain a meaningful connection, and the speaker is always aware of the original point, goal, or topic.

American Psychiatric Association, *DSM-III-R* (1987), p. 393.

classical conditioning A form of learning by which some specific FEARS and PHOBIAS may develop. An understanding of the concept evolved from the work of Ivan P. Pavlov (1849–1936), a Russian physiologist, who conditioned dogs to salivate at a specific STIMULI, such as the sound of a bell. The procedure involves simultaneously exposing the individual to two different stimuli, one of which, known as the unconditioned (or unconditional) stimulus (UCS), automatically or reflexively brings about a specific response, known as the UNCONDITIONED (or unconditional) RESPONSE (UCR). The second stimulus, known as the CONDITIONED STIMULUS (CS), at first has no effect on the response in question. After repeated trials delivering the CS slightly preceding the UCS, the CS alone comes to elicit the response previously brought on by the UCS. If the response is brought about by the CS alone, it is known as a CONDITIONED RESPONSE (CR). This type of learning is by association or stimulus substitution.

John B. Watson (1878–1958), an American psychologist known as the founder of behaviorism, was one of the first and most influential proponents of the theory that classical conditioning could be used to account for acquisition of fears and anxieties.

There has been some controversy about general applicability of the classical conditioning theory to the development of all phobias. Many individuals with specific fears do not recall any conditioning experience associated with the beginning of their fears. Also, many people have phobias out of proportion to the stimulus. For example, fear of snakes is a generally prevalent fear, yet few phobic people have had direct contact with snakes. Fear of dentists is about half as prevalent as that of snakes, and although many people have received unpleasant stimuli on the DENTAL chair, most do not develop conditioned fear reactions. However, classical conditioning is still regarded as a source for some people's phobias and fears.

This particular learning model or method is applicable in situations in which traumatic events have occurred. For instance, people who have severe auto accidents often react to brakes squealing or traffic lights with intense anxiety. In this case, since brake lights or squealing (CSs) have been associated with the accident (and the pain and anxiety elicited by it), they become conditioned stimuli. Likewise, observation of a person in a painful/anxious/frightening situation (such as the shower scene in Alfred Hitchcock's movie, *Psycho*) can classically condition people to fear showers or showering while alone. (See also BEHAVIORISM; CONDITIONING THERAPY; PAVLOV, IVAN P.; WATSON, JOHN B.)

Kleinknecht, Ronald A., *The Anxious Self* (New York: Human Sciences Press, 1986).
Suinn, Richard M., *Fundamentals of Behavior Pathology* (New York: John Wiley, 1975).

classification of anxiety disorders
See ANXIETY DISORDERS, CLASSIFICATION OF.

classification of phobias See PHOBIA.

claustrophobia Claustrophobia is an exaggerated fear of closed places, such as closets, subways, tunnels, telephone booths, elevators, small rooms, crowds, or other enclosed or confined spaces. The word is derived from the Latin word "claustrum," meaning bolt or lock. More people may suffer from claustrophobia than from any other exaggerated fear.

Claustrophobia takes many forms. Some individuals fear being in a car or room in which they cannot open a window or in which the door is closed or the shades drawn. Others fear sitting in the center of a row in a church, theater, or airplane. Some cope with their fears, to some extent, by sitting at the end of the row or at the aisle. Some claustrophobics fear and avoid FLYING because they do not like to be in an enclosed place.

While most people dislike feeling hemmed in or trapped to any extent, claustrophobics react with severe PANIC and physiologic symptoms such as increased pulse when they feel closed in. Persons with this phobia often fear suffocation. There are many reasons why individuals have claustrophobic feelings. Some individuals who have claustrophobia may once have had a frightening experience while enclosed in a small space. While the experience itself is forgotten, the feelings associated with it remain and lead to the phobia. Such individuals tend to avoid, at all costs, being in situations that make them panic. Others may have had a frightening dream of being trapped in a closed place. While the dream is forgotten, the feelings of fear and panic remain.

Some whose phobias include being in tunnels may fear that the tunnel will cave in and they will be buried alive or be killed by the falling structure. While they travel through a tunnel, they imagine what might happen and may actually feel shortness of breath as though something was crushing their chests.

Claustrophobics who are afraid of elevators must make many life choices so that they can avoid taking elevators. This may affect where they work and where they live. Some who fear elevators fear that the elevator will get stuck between floors, that the doors will not open, that they will be trapped, and that they may starve or suffocate to death. Some claustrophobics have similar fears about airplanes.

Another form of claustrophobia is a morbid fear of being below ground level, such as in submarines or underground trains. Some servicemen have been rejected from submarine duty because of their panic at being underwater. Others avoid going in subways or underground trains by taking other means of transportation.

Many individuals who have agoraphobia were first claustrophobic. There is strong evidence that a claustrophobic tendency is an innate human potential that can become activated by (negative) experiences and become a conditioned response. Nevertheless, these reactions are avoidable, and improvement and recovery is possible with a proper treatment approach. (See also AGORAPHOBIA; COUNTERPHOBIA; ELEVATORS, FEAR OF; FLYING FEAR OF.)

Beck, A.T. and G. Emery. *Anxiety Disorders and Phobias: A Cognitive Perspective* (New York: Basic Books, 1985).

Melville, Joy, *Phobias and Obsessions* (New York: Coward, McCann & Geoghegan, 1977).

claustrophoboid A term used to describe one who suffers from claustrophobia, or fear of being in an enclosed place. (See also CLAUSTROPHOBIA; ENCLOSED PLACES, FEAR OF.)

cleaning (as a ritual) Fears of dirt and contamination lead many individuals to excessive cleaning rituals. Some sufferers feel contaminated, for example, each time they urinate, defecate, touch a pet, or pass a hospital. Afterward, they repeatedly wash their hands or disinfect objects they have touched while they feel dirty. Cleaning (as a ritual) appears in about half of all sufferers of OBSESSIVE–COMPULSIVE DISORDER. (See also OBSESSION; RITUAL.)

cleithrophobia (cleisiophobia) Fear of closed spaces or being locked in enclosed places. (See also CLOSED SPACES, FEAR OF.)

cleptophobia A fear of stealing. Also known as kleptophobia. (See also STEALING, FEAR OF.)

client-centered psychotherapy A therapeutic technique that stresses the uniqueness and personal growth of the individual. In this therapy, unconditional regard and communication of emphatic understanding are seen as conditions for self-actualization and greater personal acceptance. This therapy was developed by Carl Rogers. (See also BEHAVIOR THERAPY; ROGERS, CARL.)

cliffs, fear of Fear of cliffs or precipices is known as cremnophobia. It is similar to bathophobia, which is a fear of DEPTH and of looking down from HIGH PLACES. It is also related to batophobia, a fear of being on or passing by HIGH OBJECTS such as skyscrapers. (See also ACROPHOBIA; BATHOPHOBIA; BATOPHOBIA; SIMPLE PHOBIAS.)

climacophobia Fear of stairs or of climbing stairs. (See also STAIRS, FEAR OF.)

climate, fear of Seasonal affective disorder (SAD) is a type of depression that seems to occur more in climates that have long periods of dark, gloomy weather. Individuals who suffer from the anxieties associated with SAD generally feel better during the brighter months of the year. Some people benefit from special treatments with lights used on a regular basis each day. In earlier times, scholars (including Robert Burton, author of *The Anatomy of Melancholy*) believed that cold, damp climates produced more insanity that warmer ones, but statistical studies have not been able to substantiate these concerns. (See also DEPRESSION; SEASONAL AFFECTIVE DISORDER.)

clinical psychology The branch of psychology (study of behavior) that specializes in the study, diagnosis, and treatment of behavior disorders. Many individuals who have anxieties, fears, and phobias receive treatment from clinical psychologists. Clinical psychologists in most states must have a Ph.D. degree and a license in order to offer their services to the public. Graduate training for the Ph.D. emphasizes research knowledge and skills, academic coursework, and clinical practice and internship experiences. Clinical psychology came into prominence after World War II when its emphasis shifted from mental and personality testing to psychotherapy and research. Clinical psychologists are responsible for most of the major research on clinical methods/therapy, psychopathology, and the diagnostic system. (See also BEHAVIOR THERAPY; PSYCHOLOGY.)

clinophobia Fear of beds or of going to bed. (See also BED, FEAR OF.)

clithrophobia Also cleithrophobia. Fear of closed spaces. (See also CLOSED SPACES, FEAR OF.)

clocks, fear of Individuals who fear seeing clocks, hearing clocks, or thinking of clocks may fear the passage of time, or the infinity of time. Some have chronophobia, or fear of a long duration. Some prisoners develop this fear. Looking at clocks may be a COMPULSION for one who has OBSESSIVE–COMPULSIVE DISORDER. The person who watches clocks frequently may have a compulsion to be on time, or a fear of being late. (See also CHECKING; CHRONOPHOBIA; INFINITY, FEAR OF.)

clomipramine A tricyclic ANTIDEPRESSANT that is the drug of choice in treating OBSESSIVE–COMPULSIVE DISORDER. It has been used for many years in Europe and Canada. Clomipramine is reportedly at least twenty percent effective in alleviating symptoms and in significantly helping those who can tolerate the drug. (See also MONOAMINE OXIDASE INHIBITORS (MAOI).)

Greist, J.H. et al., *Anxiety and Its Treatment: Help Is Available* (Washington, DC: American Psychiatric Press, 1986).

clonazepam An anticonvulsant drug of the benzodiazepine group marketed under the trade name Clonapin. It has been tried in the treatment of tardive dyskenesia (a drug-induced neurological disorder). It is also used to treat anxiety disorders in certain individuals. Adverse reactions to the central nervous system occur in many patients. (See also ANTICONVULSIVES; TARDIVE DYSKENESIA.)

clonidine A drug used in the treatment of high blood pressure and relief of anxieties in some individuals. Clonidine (trade name: Catapres) is an adrenergic agonist that acts on the central nervous system and reduces the action of the sympathetic nervous system by altering the chemical balance within the brain. Effects in the brain slow the heart rate and decrease the action in some nerves that control blood vessel constriction. In studies during the early 1980s, clonidine was effective in alleviating anxiety in most patients who had GENERALIZED ANXIETY DISORDER (GAD) and PANIC ATTACKS. Clonidine was more effective in reducing ANXIETY ATTACKS than general physical symptoms. As a side effect, it may cause persistent drowsiness and dryness of the mouth, in which case physicians usually advise cutting down on the medication. Abruptly stopping this medication can trigger a sudden, dangerous rise in blood pressure. Methyldopa is a similar drug. (See also ADVERSE DRUG REACTIONS; HIGH BLOOD PRESSURE, FEAR OF.)

closed spaces Fear of closed spaces, or being locked in an enclosed space, is known as clithrophobia, cleisiophobia, or cleithrophobia. This fear is a form of claustrophobia. (See also CENTER OF THE ROW, FEAR OF SITTING IN; CLAUSTROPHOBIA.)

clothing, fear of Fear of wearing clothing, or the sight of clothing, is known as vestiphobia. This fear is usually associated with particular styles, textures, or colors of clothing. (See also COLORS, FEAR OF.)

clouds, fear of Fear of clouds is known as nephophobia. People who experience this phobia will not look up in the sky at clouds. Occasionally, pilots will feel anxious when flying over clouds or through clouds, whereas they are comfortable in clear skies. This fear may be related to other fears concerning weather, such as impending rain, thunderstorms, or lightning. Some people who feel depressed on gray days also fear clouds, because they anticipate an episode of depression. Some depressions are seasonally related, and for those whose depression occurs during the cloudier months, clouds can be particularly threatening. (See also FLYING, FEAR OF; LIGHTNING, FEAR OF; RAIN, FEAR OF; THUNDERSTORMS, FEAR OF.)

clovaxamine An antidepressant drug. (See also ANTIDEPRESSANTS; ANTIDEPRESSANTS, NEW; DEPRESSION.)

LaPierre, Y.D. "New Antidepressant Drugs," *Journal of Clinical Psychiatry,* 44:8(August 1983), pp. 41–43.

clozapine A medication to treat SCHIZOPHRENIA. After preliminary trials, clozapine appears to be an effective treatment for a substantial number of schizophrenics who do not respond to other drugs. Clozapine rarely causes movement disorders—for example, muscle jerks or cramps, tremors, muscle rigidity, restlessness, or the severe movement disorders known as TARDIVE DYSKENESIA—associated with other ANTIPSYCHOTIC drugs. However, weekly blood tests are necessary to check for a potentially fatal weakening of the immune system in response to the drug. Clozapine does not cure schizophrenia, but it improves symptoms enough so that individuals can function in the community and benefit from rehabilitation services. As of 1987, clozapine is used in research projects but not available for prescription use in the United States. Clozapine has been tried unsuccessfully as a treatment for anxiety. (See also DRUGS.)

Science News (May 23, 1987), p. 131.

cnidophobia Fear of stings. The term applies to stings of bees, wasps, mosquitoes, and other insects. The fear may relate to a fear of flying things and insects that may look threatening to an individual. (See also BEES, FEAR OF; STINGS, FEAR OF.)

coaching The way in which a behavior therapist teaches an anxious or phobic individual or family to develop new behaviors. The procedure helps the individual move toward the defined treatment goal by shaping behavior. While this is a term that comes from family therapy, coaching is also very evident in field work and in *in vivo* desensitization or exposure treatments. (See also BEHAVIOR THERAPY; FAMILY THERAPY.)

Bowen, M., *Family Therapy and Clinical Practice* (New York: Jason Aronson, 1978).

Carter, E and M.M. Orfanidis, ''Family Therapy with One Person,'' in P. Guerin, *Family Therapy: Theory and Practice* (New York: Gardner Press, 1976).

cocaine, fear of Cocaine is a drug that affects the CENTRAL NERVOUS SYSTEM causing a stimulative sensation, inducing feelings of euphoria. In the latter part of the 20th century, abuse of cocaine became a major social problem, feared by parents, employers, and individuals who fear addiction. The effects of cocaine are similar to the effects of the natural substance ADRENALINE as well as to the manufactured stimulants, AMPHETAMINES. The effects, which last a very short time, depend on the size of the dose. Small doses will bring about sensations of extreme euphoria, illusions of increased mental and physical strength and sensory awareness, and a decrease in hunger, pain, and need for sleep. Large doses significantly magnify these effects, sometimes causing irrational behavior. In heavy users, the heightened euphoria is often accompanied by intensified heartbeat, sweating, dilation of the pupils, and a rise in body temperature. Euphoria can be followed by irritability, DEPRESSION, INSOMNIA, and an extreme condition of PARANOIA. Formication, the belief and feeling that ants or other insects are running up and down the skin, is also common. In some cases, a condition similar to amphetamine poisoning may occur, and the user will not only appear extremely restless and nervous but will experience delirium, HALLUCINATIONS, muscle spasms, and chest pain. Male users may become impotent or incapable of ejaculation. If the drug is injected, abscesses may appear on the skin. Many of the symptoms can be reversed simply by stopping the drug.

Fear of use of cocaine involves fear of the economic consequences of the habit. Because of its high cost, cocaine was until recently confined primarily to the upper strata of the economic ladder, particularly to people in the sports and entertainment fields. However, in the latter part of the 20th century, cocaine has been steadily gaining acceptance among the young, among college students, and in many blue- and white-collar circles as well. (See also ADDICTION, FEAR OF; DRUG ABUSE.)

O'Brien, Robert and Sidney Cohen. *Encyclopedia of Drug Abuse* (New York: Facts On File, 1984).

cockroaches, fear of Cockroaches are feared worldwide. They are agents in spreading cholera, dysentery and many species of parasitic worms. Although cockroaches, unlike lice and mites, do not present any physical harm to humans through direct contact, they do feed on food and human feces. Because of this, they often become infected with disease-producing organisms, which they later excrete onto food, thereby spreading disease. Cockroaches are associated with dirt and garbage and are difficult to kill. Cockroaches develop immunities to pesticides easily and can live for days without food and water. They are sensitive to air currents and can run quickly to flatten their bodies and hide in tiny dark cracks, causing frustration and anxiety to the humans trying to rid their living space of the pest. As scavengers, cockroaches can live on such seemingly inedible materials as glue, leather, hair, paper, and starch in bookbindings. (See also DIRT, FEAR OF; CONTAMINATION, FEAR OF.)

Encyclopedia Americana, Editors of, "Cockroaches" entry in *Encyclopedia Americana* (Danbury, CT: Grolier, 1986).

Goldman, Jane, "What's Bugging You?" *New York* (May 27, 1985).

Osmond, Breland, *Animal Life and Lore* (New York: Harper and Row, 1972), p. 313.

cognitive appraisal A process by which the individual attempts to evaluate and consider potential consequences of an upcoming event. The initial components of fear might begin at this point, especially if the individual is unsure of the outcome or expects it to be unpleasant. This appraisal process is also referred to as anticipatory anxiety. An example is starting to feel fearful just after learning that the date for an important examination has been set. (See also ANXIETY; FEAR.)

Lazarus, R.S. *Psychological Stress and the Coping Process* (New York: McGraw-Hill, 1966).

Kleinknecht, Ronald A., *The Anxious Self* (New York: Human Sciences Press, 1986).

cognitive behavior therapy A type of therapy based on stimulus-response-reinforcement. Cognitive behavior therapy is used to help some individuals who have anxieties and phobias. It is considered an OPERANT CONDITIONING approach, with the individual's own statements regarded as stimuli. Cognitive behavior therapy includes self-instructional training, STRESS INOCULATION, and COPING SKILLS INTERVENTIONS. Cognitive behavior therapy recognizes the importance of cognitive processes; it is a form of behavioral therapy. Three prominent innovators in this field are Albert Ellis, Donald Meichenbaum, and Aaron Beck. (See also BECK, AARON T.; BEHAVIOR MODIFICATION; BEHAVIOR THERAPY; COGNITIVE THERAPY; ELLIS, ALBERT; MEICHENBAUM, DONALD.)

cognitive-behavioral approach See COGNITIVE BEHAVIOR THERAPY.

cognitive dissonance A state of conflict and discomfort that occurs when one's existing beliefs or assumptions are challenged or contradicted by new evidence. The individual usually seeks to relieve the discomfort by various means such as denying the existence or importance of the conflict, reconciling the difference, altering one of the dissident elements, or demanding more and more information. An example is smokers, who, when faced with evidence that cigarettes are hazardous to health, say the evidence is not enough. The term was coined by Leon Festinger, an American psychologist (1919–). Cognitive dissonance comes into play as phobic individuals begin to improve substantially. Attitudinally, they often hold to views of self as avoidant and fearful of a situation when in fact the emotional and physiological component may have diminished greatly. (See also BEHAVIOR THERAPY.)

Festinger, L., *A Theory of Cognitive Dissonance* (Stanford, CA: Stanford University Press, 1957).

cognitive restructuring A behavior therapy technique in which one learns to change the way one thinks about life so that one may change one's behavior; often used in treating agoraphobia and many social phobias. Cognitive restructuring is also an important treatment for depression. (See also AGORAPHOBIA; BEHAVIOR THERAPY; PHOBIA; SOCIAL PHOBIA.)

cognitive structure The unified structure of beliefs and attitudes about the world or society an individual holds. Phobias and anxieties may be part of an individual's cognitive structure. The term cognitive structure was introduced during the mid-1970s, and the concept predates cognitive behavior therapy. Cognitive structure is also an individual's mental pattern that maintains and organizes information in a learning situation. (See also BEHAVIOR MODIFICATION; BEHAVIOR THERAPY; COGNITIVE BEHAVIOR THERAPY; COGNITIVE RESTRUCTURING.)

Meichenbaum, D., *Cognitive-Behavior Modification* (New York: Plenum Press, 1977).

cognitive therapy A therapeutic approach based on the concept that anxiety problems result from patterns of thinking and distorted attitudes toward oneself and others and that one can alter one's behavior by changing one's thinking. Cognitive therapy is used to treat depressed individuals and others who have anxieties and phobias. It was introduced during the late 1970s by American psychiatrist Aaron Beck (1921–).

Cognitive therapy, like behavior therapy, has the goal of helping the individual change his unwanted behavior. It differs from radical behavior therapy in that it rejects focus only on overt behavior for therapy. Instead, cognitive therapy emphasizes the importance of the individual's thoughts, feelings, imagery, attitudes, and hopes and their causative relationship to behaviors. (See also BECK, AARON T.; BEHAVIOR THERAPY; COGNITIVE BEHAVIOR THERAPY; DEPRESSION.)

Beck, A.T. et al., *Cognitive Therapy of Depression* (New York: Wiley, 1979).

Beck, A.T., *Cognitive Therapy and the Emotional Disorders* (New York: International Universities Press, 1976).

Wolpe, J., "Cognition and Causation in Human Behavior and Its Therapy," *American Psychologist*, 33(1978), pp. 437–446.

cohort A group of individuals gathered together for an epidemiologic study For example, cohorts (groups) of phobics and individuals who have anxiety disorders are brought together for research purposes to test hypotheses regarding the cause of their disorder. In a cohort, the group or groups of persons to be studied are defined in terms of characteristics evident before the appearance of the disorder being investigated; for example, they may be individuals of the same sex, same age, or identical educational background who became agoraphobic during their mid-twenties. Individuals in a cohort may be observed over a period of time to determine various factors related to their disorder. (See also CASE-CONTROL; CROSS-SECTION; LONGITUDINAL STUDY.)

cohort effect A term used in cross-sectional and longitudinal studies in which group differences may be due to cohort grouping rather than effects of an independent variable. For example, differences in sexual behavior between twenty-year-olds and sixty-year olds would be due to differences in developmental and cultural experiences rather than age per se. (See also COHORT; LONGITUDINAL STUDY.)

coimetrophobia Fear of cemeteries or graveyards. The word is derived from the Greek word "koimeterion," meaning sleeping room or burial place. (See also CEMETERIES, FEAR OF.)

coitophobia Fear of sexual intercourse, or coitus. Coitus means sexual intercourse through the vagina between male and female. In medicine, the words coitus, copulation, cohabitation, and sexual intercourse are used synonymously, although the words have somewhat different meanings in their original context. A wide variety of fears regarding sexual intercourse have been reported, including impotence, inability to achieve and maintain an erection, inability to ejaculate, intercourse without orgasm, coitus interruptus, rectal penetration, vaginal penetration, oral penetration, pain during intercourse, vaginismus or tightening of the vaginal muscles to impair penetration, and intercourse with animals. The best treatment for this is behavioral sex therapy, which involves a gradual desensitization of the fear response to sexual arousal and enhanced stimulation, relaxation, and sexual excitement. (See also COITUS MORE FERARUM; COITUS ORALIS; FEMALE GENITAL FEARS; PAIN; PREGNANCY; PSYCHOSEXUAL ANXIETIES; SEXUAL FEARS, SEXUAL INTERCOURSE.)

coitus more ferarum, fear of A term derived from the Latin words meaning sexual intercourse in the manner of wild beasts. Although the term is obsolete, the fear of the situation, and the anxieties produced by it, are not. The term applies to the act of heterosexual intercourse in the position usual in lower animals, with the male inserting the penis into the vagina from the rear, and usually with the female on hands and knees. When the penis is inserted into the rectum, the act is called anal intercourse. This latter practice is called pederasty when the partner is a boy; sodomy refers either to vaginal or anal copulation with an animal. Although coitus more ferarum is not sodomy, it is often thought of as primitive. The axis of the vagina, in this position, is in direct correspondence with the axis of the penis in erection, which might indicate its primitive biological congruity. (See also SEXUAL FEARS; SEXUAL INTERCOURSE.)

Deutsch, A. and H. Fishman, *Encyclopedia of Mental Health* (New York: Franklin Watts, 1963), p. 116.

coitus oralis, fear of Fear of sexual relations using the mouth. The term is now obsolete, but relates to fellatio, which involves inserting the penis into the partner's mouth. The act of the male using his mouth, lips, and tongue to stimulate the female's vaginal area is known as cunnilingus. Some individuals, whether heterosexual or homosexual, fear sexual relations involving the mouth. (See also SEXUAL FEARS; SEXUAL INTERCOURSE.)

cold, fear of Fear of cold or cold objects is known as cheimaphobia, cheimatophobia, cryophobia, frigophobia, and psychrophobia. Individuals who fear cold may fear being in a cold climate, being outdoors in winter, or not having enough heat indoors, and they may tend to dress too warmly for the circumstances. Such individuals may even avoid cold drinks and particularly ice in their beverages.

collective unconscious Ideas that are common to mankind in general. CARL JUNG (1875–1961), Swiss psychiatrist and philosopher, introduced the term, believing that the collective unconscious is inherited and derived from the collective experience of the species. The collective unconscious transcends cultural differences and explains behavior observed in some individuals who have never been exposed to certain ideas. Certain fears, such as snakes and heights, may be part of the collective unconscious in western civilization.

Kaplan, Harold I. and Benjamin J. Sadock, *Comprehensive Textbook of Psychiatry,* Vol. 2 (Baltimore: Williams & Wilkins, 1975).

colors, fear of Fear of colors is known as chromophobia, chrematophobia, and chromatophobia. Some individuals fear specific colors; others have fears of any items that are not specifically black or white. (See also RED, FEAR OF THE COLOR; WHITE, FEAR OF THE COLOR.)

combat fatigue Anxiety and tension as a result of stresses in battle. (See also POSTTRAUMATIC STRESS DISORDER.)

combined therapy A form of psychotherapy in which the individual is involved in both individual and group therapy with the same or different therapists. Combined therapy is often used to help agoraphobic individuals; the individual, their spouses and families in therapy. (See also FAMILY THERAPY.)

cometophobia Fear of comets. (See also COMETS, FEAR OF.)

comets, fear of Fear of comets is known as cometophobia. A comet is a celestial body, observed only in the part of its orbit that is relatively close to the sun. A comet is thought to consist chiefly of ammonia, methane, carbon dioxide, and water. (See also FLYING THINGS, FEAR OF; METEORS, FEAR OF.)

commitment phobia A term introduced by Steve Carter and Julia Sokol in their book, *Men Who Can't Love: When a Man's Fear Makes Him Run from Commitment and What a Smart Woman Can Do About It* (New York: M. Evans and Company, 1987). The authors see the avoidance of commitment as a true phobia similar to claustrophobia, the fear of being trapped in a small enclosed place. Sustained closeness intensifies this fear since it creates conflict over priorities, work and leisure preferences, and relationships.

compensation A defense mechanism by which the individual, either consciously or unconsciously, tries to make up for an imagined or real deficiency, physical or psychological, or both. For example, a person with social phobias or feeling of incompetence may excel in music, art, or drama.

complex A group of connected conscious and unconscious ideas and feelings that affect an individual's behavior. The most well-known complex may be the Oedipus complex (or Electra complex in girls) as identified in Freudian psychoanalysis, and the superiority and inferiority complexes, as identified by Adler. The oedipus complex begins during the phallic stage of psychosexual development (approximately age three to five), in which the child experiences the conflict of sexual desire for the opposite-sex parent and sees the same-sex parent as a rival. This psychic conflict causes the child anxiety as he or she fears punishment (castration) from the same-sex parent and realizes the inability to fulfill his or her desires. To resolve this conflict, the child represses feelings for the opposite-sex parent and identifies increasingly with the parent of the same sex. This identification with the presumed "aggressor" is an anxiety-reducing mechanism and helps sexual roles and the superego develop.

Resolution of the Oedipus conflict (or the Electra conflict in girls) involves adoption and internalization of social mores and values, and the beginning of the SUPEREGO.

Other well-known complexes are the superiority complex and inferiority complex, which were named by ALFRED ADLER. (See also FREUD, SIGMUND.)

Bootzin, R. et al., *Psychology Today* (New York: Random House, 1983).

Davison, Gerald C. and John M. Neale. *Abnormal Psychology* (New York: John Wiley, 1986).

compulsion Seemingly purposeful, repetitive behavior that an individual performs according to certain internal, idiosyncratic rules or in a stereotyped fashion. The behavior is not an end in itself but is designed to produce or prevent some future state of adversive affairs to which it may not be connected in a realistic way or for which it may be clearly excessive. The person performs the act with a sense of subjective compulsion coupled with a desire to resist it (at least initially). Performing the particular act is not pleasurable, although it may afford some relief of tension. An example is when a person feels compelled to wash his/her hands every time he/she shakes hands because of an excessive fear of contamination. Compulsions are characteristic of OBSESSIVE–COMPULSIVE DISORDER.

compulsive personality A personality type characterized by inability to relax, extreme inhibition, overconscientiousness, and rigidity. Many phobics have compulsive personalities; individuals who have obsessive–compulsive disorder also have compulsive personalities. (See also NEUROSIS; OBSESSIVE–COMPULSIVE DISORDER; PERSONALITY TYPE.)

computer phobia Fear, distrust, or hatred of computers is also known as cyberphobia. Some individuals who are faced with learning to work with computers show symptoms of classic phobia, such as nausea, dizziness, cold sweat, and high blood pressure. Many computer phobics hide their fears because of peer pressure to make efficient use of computers. Results of a 1983 study by the management consulting firm of Booz, Allen & Hamilton showed that a manager who had spent 25 years with a company was more likely to resist the introduction of computers than someone the same age who had just changed jobs. Educational level itself did not seem to be a critical factor in determining anxious reactions. However, as an ability to type is essential for adaptation to computers, secretaries are less likely to suffer from computer phobia. Individuals who fear computers can overcome their phobia by gradually exposing themselves to electronic calculators, games, and eventually simple computer programs. (See also TECHNOLOGY, FEAR OF.)
Psychology Today (August 1983), p. 79.

computer therapy Computer therapy—the treatment of anxieties, phobias, and other mental disorders through special computer programs—is a field wide open to experimentation. Initial studies examining the usefulness of the computer in a therapeutic application are positive, but there have been difficulties in creating a "personable" computer program.

The computer has been very successful, however, as a desensitization tool in treatment of anxiety, particularly test anxiety. In this capacity, the computer is not required to have rapport with "patients." In newer applications currently under development, the computer not only interacts verbally with clients but also makes ongoing physiological assessments of anxiety responses.

Concordin See PROTRIPTYLINE.

condensation A psychological process often present in dreams in which two or more concepts are fused so that a single symbol represents many components. For example, one symbol may represent several phobic objects or situations. Or, a phobia itself may be symbolic of many situations.

conditioned response A learned or acquired response to a stimulus that originally did not elicit the response. A conditioned response, also known as a conditioned reflex, is elicited by a conditioned stimulus. In classical conditioning theory, the conditioned response is brought about as a result of the pairing of a neutral and an unconditioned stimulus. For example, the salivation response that occurred in Pavlov's dogs following the ringing of a bell (conditioned stimulus) is a conditioned response. (See also BEHAVIOR MODIFICATION; CONDITIONED STIMULUS; CONDITIONING; PAVLOV.)

conditioned stimulus A stimulus, or cue, that elicits a response as a result of learning or conditioning. In classical conditioning, the pairing of a neutral stimulus with an unconditioned stimulus produces a conditioned stimulus. The conditioned stimulus is capable of producing approximately the same response as that of the unconditioned stimulus. For example, a child who fears loud noises could be conditioned to transfer that fear to a white rat. The white rat is the conditioned stimulus; after several exposures of the pairing of the noise and the rat, the fear associated with the loud noise is transferred to the rat. (See also BEHAVIOR THERAPY; CONDITIONED RESPONSE; CONDITIONING; PAVLOV; WATSON.)

conditioning Procedures to change behavior patterns. Conditioning techniques are used in therapy for phobias and anxieties. There are three main types of conditioning: classical, operant, and modelling. In classical or Pavlovian conditioning, two stimuli are combined: one adequate, such as offering food to a dog to produce salivation (an unconditioned response), and the other inadequate, such as ringing a bell, which by itself does not have an effect on salivation. After the two stimuli have been paired several times, the inadequate or conditioned stimulus comes to elicit salivation (now a conditioned response) by itself. In operant conditioning, consequences are introduced that strengthen or increase the rate or intensity of the desired activity (reinforcement) or weaken or decrease the rate or intensity of the undesired activity (punishment). Partially reinforcing or punishing the activity will increase its resistance to extinction. Unlike classical and operant conditioning that require repeated trials for new learning or behavior, modelling results in behavior acquisition by observation. Subsequent performance of the new behavior may rely on operant reinforcement and the past history of the observer. (See also BEHAVIOR MODIFICATION; CONDITIONING.)

conditioning therapy A term sometimes used for BEHAVIOR THERAPY. (See also CONDITIONED RESPONSE; CONDITIONED STIMULUS; CONDITIONING.

confinement, fear of Fear of confinement, or of being in a closed space, is known as CLAUSTROPHOBIA. (See also AGORAPHOBIA; BARBER'S CHAIR SYNDROME; ELEVATORS, FEAR OF; FLYING, FEAR OF.)

confrontation A therapeutic technique that requires the individual to face his own attitudes and perceived shortcomings, such as anxieties and phobias. It encourages the individual to face the way he or she is perceived by others and the possible consequences of his or her behavior. The therapist may offer feedback, make interpretations, or attack the individual's defense mechanisms. Confrontation as a technique is used in psychoanalytic therapy, Adlerian therapy, group therapy, existential psychotherapy, encounter groups, and other therapies. (See also ADLER, ALFRED; ENCOUNTER GROUPS; EXISTENTIAL THERAPY.)

conjoint therapy A type of marriage therapy. Also called triadic or triangular, as two individuals and one therapist work together. The therapist sees the partners together in joint sessions; conjoint therapy may be helpful when one spouse has AGORAPHOBIA.

conscience Synonymous with SUPEREGO. The part of the individual that judges one's own values and performance. Conscience plays a role in self-esteem, self-image, and development of some SOCIAL PHOBIAS. Conscience may involve negative evaluations (such as guilt and shame) or positive evaluations (pride, self-pleasure) of behavior. (See also SELF-ESTEEM.)

conscious The part of the mind that is immediately aware of the environment at any time. The conscious is differentiated from the preconscious and the UNCONSCIOUS; Their divisions can best be viewed as degrees of availability of cognitive and emotional material. An individual's functions of reality testing, perception, observation, and evaluation are all conscious activities. Expansion of consciousness is a term and training that is associated with 20th-century psychology and spirituality. (See also EGO.)

consensual validation Ongoing comparison of the thoughts and feelings of members of a group toward one another; the process tends to modify and correct distortions of interpersonal relationships and to allieviate social fears and ANXIETIES. The term was introduced by Harry Stack Sullivan, an American psychiatrist (1892–1949), to refer to the therapeutic process between therapist and patient. Previously, Trigant Burrow, an American psychoanalyst (1875–1951), used the term "consensual observations" to describe this process, which results in effective reality testing.

constipation, fear of Fear of constipation is known as coprastasophobia. Constipation is difficult, incomplete, or infrequent evacuation of the bowels. Some individuals fear constipation if they do not have one or more bowel movement every day. Some who become obsessed with the notion that this is necessary resort to taking laxatives regularly, which leads to a dependence on laxatives for complete evacuation. Fear of constipation may be related to a fear of painful bowel movements (defecalgesiophobia). See GASTROINTESTINAL SYMPTOMS; IRRITABLE BOWEL SYNDROME.

contamination, fear of Fear of contamination is known as misophobia, mysophobia, and molysomophobia. Contamination is a state of being impure or being in contact with unclean or disease-producing substances. Those who fear germs or contracting a disease by touching something also usually fear contamination. Individuals who have OBSESSIVE–COMPULSIVE DISORDER, with frequent hand-washing as a symptom, often fear contamination and thus wash their hands frequently. Contamination obsessions include disease, dirt, germs, mud, excrement, and sputum. It may extend to animals and objects regarded by some as unclean, such as chickens, rats, mice, and insects.

In psychiatry, the term "contamination" also applies to the combining of a part of one word with a part of another, usually resulting in a word that is unintelligible.

content, latent See LATENT CONTENT.

contextual family therapy See TRANSGENERATIONAL FAMILY THERAPY.

contextual therapy A form of BEHAVIOR THERAPY. Contextual therapy is also known as *in vivo* therapy, because it takes place in real life, as opposed to in the imagination. After a phobic individual has been through a series of sessions in the therapist's office during which he vividly imagines himself facing a feared situation, he actually ventures out to face the situation itself. Sometimes the therapist or a trained assistant accompanies the phobic individual. In some cases of AGORAPHOBIA, the agoraphobic's spouse is trained to accompany and assist the individual in facing the feared situation. The individual is trained to focus on his "phenomenology" or direct experience in the moment. The task of the therapist is to help direct attention to the ongoing internal and external context in which anxiety occurs. Contextual therapy was developed by American psychiatrist Manuel Zane (1913–).

Frampton, Muriel. *Agoraphobia: Coping with the World Outside* (Wellingborough, Northamptonshire: Turnstone Press, 1984).

contingency management The therapist's process of changing an individual's possible responses by control (introducing or removing consequences to a behavior) in order to change the rate of intensity of the behavior. For example, by their very nature, anxiety responses are usually aversive to the individual (that is, the individual will work to reduce or eliminate them). Avoidance of anxiety-arousing stimuli becomes a behavior that is reinforced by the ensuing diminishment of anxiety, thus making it very difficult to modify. Behavior therapists using exposure therapies will introduce the phobic individual to anxiety-arousing stimuli in small doses that do not stimulate a lot of anxiety. In this way, approaching (rather than avoiding) the stimulus becomes reinforced. (See also BEHAVIOR THERAPY; OPERANT CONDITIONING; REINFORCEMENT.)

contrectophobia Fear of sexual abuse, or of being touched or fondled by another person, usually involving genital stimulation. The term is derived from the Latin word "contrectare," which means "to handle" or "to take hold of." (See also CHILD ABUSE; SEXUAL ABUSE.)

control group The group in which a condition or factor being tested is deliberately omitted during an experiment. For example, in a study of the effects of a new drug on ANXIETY, the control group may be given a PLACEBO instead of the new drug.

conversational catharsis See CATHARSIS.

conversion The term conversion applies to an unconscious mental conflict that the individual converts into a physical symptom; the physical symptom may represent a disguised drive gratification or wish fullfillment, or both. Freud said that conversion neuroses are "conversion hysteria" and "pregenital conversion neuroses," and that fixations on the later or early anal stages may lie at the root of these illnesses.

A conversion symptom is a loss or alteration of physical functioning that suggests a physical disorder but that is actually a direct expression of an unconscious psychological need or conflict. Such a disturbance is not under voluntary control and, after examination, cannot be explained by any physical disorder. Conversion symptoms, seen in conversion disorder, are relatively rare in their true form. However, as common knowledge about medical conditions improves, conversion symptoms have become more sophisticated. The tendency to develop conversion symptoms is related to stress, past medical history, and observation or personal experience with the particular symptom and a reinforcement in the current environment either through stress reduction, social status, or attention. (See HYSTERIA; NEUROSES; SCHIZOPHRENIA.)

coping behavior Any ADAPTATION that reduces ANXIETY in a stressful situation. Individuals who have anxieties and PHOBIAS can learn new coping behaviors to keep their fears under control. Coping behaviors are also known as COPING MECHANISMS. Coping behaviors include taking a detour to avoid crossing a BRIDGE or ordering groceries by telephone to avoid going out. Some coping behaviors are unproductive, such as REGRESSION, in which the individual resorts to behaviors learned at an earlier developmental stage, or the adoption of the SICK ROLE, which has as its aim the unconscious wish to avoid a situation, or denial, the mental process through which the individual tries to make the anxiety-producing situation disappear. Coping behavior also includes problem solving, choice of alternative methods of coping, selection of one of them, and taking appropriate steps to put it into effect. (See also BEHAVIOR THERAPY; COPING SKILLS INTERVENTION.)

coping mechanism See COPING BEHAVIOR; COPING SKILLS INTERVENTION.

coping skills intervention Techniques that a therapist uses to help an individual develop coping behaviors that can be useful in a variety of anxiety-producing situations. Coping skills intervention focuses on ways to teach the individual to face stress rather than reduce or avoid it. The procedures include covert modeling, a modified form of systematic desensitization in which the individual is taught to cope with, rather than avoid, anxiety-producing imagery, relaxation training, anxiety management training, and stress inoculation. (See also ANXIETY MANAGEMENT TRAINING; BEHAVIOR THERAPY; COPING BEHAVIOR; COPING MECHANISMS; COVERT MODELING; STRESS INOCULATION; SYSTEMATIC DESENSITIZATION.)

coprophobia Fear or revulsion of feces or dirt. Also known as scatophobia and koprophboia. This phobia is interpreted psychoanalytically as a defense against anal erotism, or coprophilia. (See also CONSTIPATION, FEAR OF; DEFECATION, DIRT, FEAR OF; FECES, FEAR OF.)

Coprastasophobia Fear of constipation. (See also CONSTIPATION, FEAR OF.)

corners, fear of Some individuals fear sitting in the corner of a room or fear bumping into corners. Those who fear sitting in corners may be fearful of CONFINEMENT or of being in an enclosed space with no easy exit. Some who have AGORAPHOBIA or CLAUSTROPHOBIA may feel this way. Some who fear injury or ILLNESS may fear bruising themselves with furniture or counters that have corners. Some parents are very fearful when their infants and young children get too close to sharp corners. (See also CLOSED PLACES; ILLNESS/INJURY, FEAR OF.)

coronary bypass anxiety, postoperative Many people are likely to experience anxiety or depression following a coronary bypass operation. This type of anxiety is now fairly common, as nearly 200,000 such operations are performed each year in the United States. An anxiety reaction can bring about serious variations in heartbeat (arrhythmia). Antianxiety drugs that do not adversely affect a postoperative heart patient are often helpful. Alprazolam (Xanax) is one such antianxiety, antidepressant drug. A study reported in the *Journal of Clinical Psychopharmacology* (February 1986) showed that alprazolam-treated postcoronary artery bypass patients experienced rapid therapeutic effects from short-term use of the drug. (See also ALPRAZOLAM; HEART ATTACK, ANXIETY FOLLOWING.)

Freeman, Arthur M., "Alprazolam Treatment of Postcoronary Bypass Anxiety," *Journal of Clinical Psychopharmacology,* 6:1 (February 1986).

Kaufmann, Michael W. et al., "Psychiatric Aspects of Myocardial Infarction: Clinical Implications," *Resident & Staff Physician* (1986).

coronary-prone Type A behavior Coronary-prone type A behavior is characterized by generally aggressive, driven, and competitive behavior. Type A individuals are usually racing against the clock and have little time for relaxation. Type B behavior, on the other hand, is characterized by more easygoing, generally less aggressive behavior. Most individuals are not simply Type A or Type B, but are a combination of both. People exhibiting predominantly Type A behavior are statistically more prone to develop coronary heart disease and suffer heart attacks. Behavior modification can be successful in shifting an individual closer to the Type B end of the continuum. There is some suggestion that there are at least two types of Type A behavior patterns, one with and one without the aggressive component. (See also HEART ATTACK.)

corpses, fear of Fear of corpses, or dead human bodies, or bodies of animals, is known as necrophobia. This fear extends to looking at cadavers and carcasses of animals. Fear of corpses may be related to a fear of death, and many individuals who fear viewing a corpse also fear going into a cemetery, looking at tombstones, or even attending a funeral. (See also CEMETERIES, FEAR OF; DEATH, FEAR OF.)

corrective emotional experience Reexposure to a previously difficult emotional situation under favorable circumstances. Considered a technique of short-term psychotherapy, it may be useful in helping phobic individuals Corrective emotional experience was advocated by Hungarian-American psychoanalyst FRANZ ALEXANDER (1891–1964), who suggested that the therapist temporarily assume a particular role to generate the experience for the individual and facilitate insight and change. (See also BRIEF PSYCHOTHERAPY.)

correlation Correlation is the extent to which two measures vary together, or a measure of the strength of the relationship between two variables, such as treatment of phobias with certain techniques of behavior therapy, and age of the individual. Correlation is expressed by a coefficient that varies between +1.0, indicating perfect agreement, and −1.0, indicating a perfect inverse relationship. A correlation coefficient of 0.0 would mean a perfectly random relationship. The correlation coefficient signifies the degree to which knowledge of one score of variable can predict the score on the other variable. Such results are useful to researchers and therapists in planning treatment for phobic individuals. However, a high correlation between two variables does not necessarily indicate a causal relationship between them; the correlation may occur because each of the variables is highly related to a third unmeasured factor. For example, there is a correlation between sex and age of a person and onset of anxiety. However, is it unknown from a correlation if these are causative factors.

American Psychiatric Association, *Psychiatric Glossary* (Washington, DC: American Psychiatric Press, 1988).

cortisol A hormonelike secretion (a corticoid) from the adrenal cortex, which responds to STRESS. Cortisol is sometimes referred to as a biochemical marker of distress. (See also AUTONOMIC NERVOUS SYSTEM.)

co-therapy A form of PSYCHOTHERAPY in which more than one therapist works with a phobic or anxious individual or a group. Co-therapy is also known as combined therapy, cooperative therapy, dual leadership, multiple therapy, and three-cornered therapy.

counterconditioning Relearning by reacting with a new RESPONSE to a particular STIMULUS. Counterconditioning is achieved by strengthening a response that is antagonistic to or incompatible with an undesirable response, such as a phobic reaction. It is commonly believed that relaxation acts as counterconditioning to ANXIETY, assertiveness to SHYNESS and inhibition, sexual arousal to impotence, etc. The counterconditioning view has been an alternative explanation for Wolpe's "reciprocal inhibition" theory. (See also BEHAVIOR THERAPY; DESENSITIZATION; RECIPROCAL INHIBITION; WOLPE, JOHN.)

counterphobia A preference by the phobic individual for the fearful situation. (See also FEARS; PHOBIAS.)

countertransference An emotional response by the therapist to an individual under treatment. Such a relationship may reinforce the phobic or anxious individual's earlier traumatic history. (See also PSYCHOANALYSIS; TRANSFERENCE.)

covert modeling Mental strategies or internal thought processes a therapist teaches to an anxious or phobic individual who has anxieties and phobias to overcome the anxious feelings and fears. The technique involves a form of mental rehearsal of the fearful real-life situation. Covert modeling may be part of a step-by-step program toward facing and handling successfully the feared situation. Some phobias lend themselves well to covert modeling—for example, ELEVATOR phobia. The individual is asked to imagine standing in front of an elevator, without fear. Next, the individual imagines stepping into it, again without fear. Next, the individual imagines that the elevator goes up one floor, and finally to the top of the building. After successfully imagining the situation, the individual is taken to a real-life situation and may be able to face the elevator with reduced fear. All along the way, positive coping behavior and positive affect are encouraged. (See also BEHAVIOR THERAPY; COVERT SENSITIZATION.)

covert sensitization A form of AVERSION THERAPY in which the individual is asked to imagine a situation or object (to which they are attracted) at the same time as he or she calls up unpleasant feelings by imagination. This fear induction procedure or fear aversive conditioning is used for treatment of addictions. This is an internal mental process, and thus referred to as "covert." (See also BEHAVIOR THERAPY; COVERT MODELING.)

cremnophobia Fear of precipices or cliffs. (See also CLIFFS, FEAR OF; PRECIPICES, FEAR OF.)

crime, fear of Fear of crime has become a fact of life, particularly in urban areas. Crime is feared much more now than it was a generation ago, and fear of crime is one of the most frequent fears of children.

Kadish, Sanford H. et al., *Encyclopedia of Crime and Justice* (New York: The Free Press, 1983).

Guiness Book of World Records (New York: Sterling, 1987).

Pasternak, Stefan, *Violence and Victims* (New York: Spectrum, 1978).

crisis intervention A therapeutic approach that is intended to relieve an urgent psychological problem, such as the onset of panic attacks. As therapy for an emergency, crisis intervention is not intended to be curative in the long run. Treatment may focus on immediate modification of environmental factors as well as interpersonal and intrapsychic factors. Individual, group, family, or drug therapy may be used within a period of time ranging from a few days to a few weeks.

criticism, fear of Many social phobics fear criticism and scrutiny by others. Some fear being criticized for the way they look, talk, act, or eat. They feel that they may be criticized because their hands tremble as they hold their fork or cup. Some may experience this fear most intensely in a crowded restaurant, and some fear even their spouse's criticism of their eating habits and thus cannot eat in front of their spouse. Some fear shaking, BLUSHING, SWEATING, or looking ridiculous on a bus or train. Some fear leaving home during the daylight because they might be seen by others and criticized. Some avoid talking to superiors. Others avoid performing or speaking in public. Some fear criticism of their body shape and avoid swimming so that others will not see their bodies. Those who fear criticism of handwriting may do all their banking by mail. Individuals who fear criticism usually have a low sense of self-esteem. (See also EATING, FEAR OF; PUBLIC SPEAKING, FEAR OF.)

Marks, Isaac M., *Fears, Phobias and Rituals* (New York: Oxford University Press, 1987).

cross sectional A type of experimental study design used in research with phobics and individuals who have ANXIETY DISORDERS. In a cross sectional study, measurements are made in different samples or groups of individuals at the same point in time. A cross-sectional study differs from a cohort study; in a cohort study, all the individuals in the study have something in common before they become part of the study, such as age, sex, or educational background. This is not the case with the cross-sectional study. (See also COHORT; LONGITUDINAL STUDY.)

crossing a bridge See BRIDGES, FEAR OF.

crossing the street, fear of Fear of crossing the street is known as dromophibia. (See also AGORAPHOBIA; STREETS, FEAR OF CROSSING.)

crowds, fear of Fear of crowds, or of a large number of people gathered together, is known as demophobia, enochlophobia, and ochlophobia. Many who have AGORAPHOBIA also fear crowds. Fear of crowds may also be related to a fear of being confined, because in a crowd there may be no quick way for the anxious individual to get to a place he or she regards as safe. (See also CLOSED PLACES, FEAR OF; CONFINEMENT, FEAR OF.)

crucifixes, fear of Fear of crucifixes, or the image of Christ on a cross, or of items in the shape of a cross, is known as staurophobia. This fear may be related to religious fears, superstitious fears, or fear of the supernatural. (See also SUPERNATURAL, FEAR OF.)

crying, fear of Some individuals who are quick to cry in uncomfortable situations may avoid those situations because they fear others will see them cry. They may fear criticism for their tearful reactions. This is a type of social phobia and can be treated with behavior therapy. (See also BEHAVIOR THERAPY; SOCIAL PHOBIA.)

cryophobia Fear of extremely cold temperatures, cold objects, or ice. Also known as psychrophobia and frigophobia. (See also COLD, FEAR OF; ICE, FEAR OF.)

crystallophobia Fear of glass. (See also GLASS, FEAR OF.)

curses, fear of In many cultures, individuals fear that harm will come to them because of verbalizations of such wishes from others. Ancient Greeks and Romans publicly put curses on offenders against the government, traitors, and enemies of the country. William Shakespeare is said to have put a curse on anyone who might disturb his grave. Fears of curses are associated with fears of witchcraft and voodoo. (See also EVIL EYE, FEAR OF; VOODOO, FEAR OF; WITCHES AND WITCHCRAFT, FEAR OF; ZOMBIE, FEAR OF.)

cyberphobia Fear of computers, computerization, or things related to computers. (See also COMPUTER PHOBIA.)

cyclones, fear of Fear of cyclones is known as anemophobia. Individuals who fear cyclones may also fear strong winds or air movements. (See also AIR, FEAR OF; CLIMATE, FEAR OF; WIND, FEAR OF.)

cyclophobia Fear of bicycles.

cyclothymia A chronic mood disturbance in which the individual regularly experiences alternating moods of elation and DEPRESSION, usually unrelated to external circumstances. It is sometimes considered a type of BIPOLAR (MANIC–DEPRESSIVE) DISORDER. A cyclothymic individual has had at least two years of this disorder (one year for children and adolescents) and many periods of depressed mood or loss of interest or pleasure not as severe as the criteria for a major depressive or a manic episode. Cyclothymia differs from DEPRESSION and manic episodes in that the individual is not markedly impaired in social or occupational activities during the hypomanic episodes. However, many cyclothymic individuals experience difficulties in their social relationships, in school, and at work because of recurrent cycles of mood swings and the anxiety that comes about because of the rapid changes in mood. The disorder, which usually begins in adolescence or early adult life and sometimes develops into bipolar disorder, is apparently equally common in males and females. Major depression and bipolar disorder may be more common among first-degree biologic relatives of people who have cyclothymia than among the general population. (See also PERSONALITY TYPES.)

American Psychiatric Association, *Diagnostic and Statistical Manual of Mental Disorder* (Washington, DC: American Psychiatric Press, 1987).

cymophobia Fear of waves or wave-like motions. Derived from the Greek word *kymo,* meaning wave. Also known as kymophobia. (See also MOTION, FEAR OF; WAVES, FEAR OF.)

cynophobia Fear of dogs or fear of rabies; also known as kynophobia. The term is derived from the Greek word *cyno,* meaning dog. (See also DOGS, FEAR OF.)

cyprianophobia Fear of prostitutes; also known as cyprinophobia. (See also PROSTITUTES, FEAR OF; SEXUAL FEARS.)

cypridophobia Fear of venereal disease. The term is derived from the Greek word *kypris,* meaning Venus, the goddess of love. Cypridophobia also means fear of sexual intercourse. (See also SEXUAL INTERCOURSE, FEAR OF; VENEREAL DISEASE, FEAR OF.)

D

daemonophobia See DEMONOPHOBIA.

dampness, fear of Fear of dampness, wetness, moistness, or excessive humidity is known as hygrophobia.

dancing, fear of Fear of dancing is known as chorophobia. Fear of dancing may be a SOCIAL PHOBIA that can be overcome by taking dancing lessons, or it may have more deep-seated causes, such as fear of coming into close contact with another person, being touched, or touching another person, particularly one of the opposite sex. This fear may be related to fears of the opposite sex or sexual fears. (See also SEXUAL FEARS.)

darkness, fear of Fear of darkness is also known as achluophobia, lygophobia, myctophobia, nyctophobia, and scotophobia. Fear of darkness is associated with feelings of uncertainty, helplessness, inability to see what one is doing, and a sense of unfamiliarity because things look different in the dark. Children often develop a fear of darkness at about two years of age. Their first fears of darkness are associated with separation from their parents. Fear of the dark may be partly produced by the sense of being alone. At older ages, children commonly say they hear noises or see images and may imagine ghosts or monsters. As children get older, most lose their fears of the dark, but if they do not outgrow their normal fear, the fear may develop into a phobia in which darkness has unconscious symbolic significance or is associated with danger and threat. Many individuals feel more secure with a night light on during the night; they can assure themselves that they will not bump into anything if they arise in the dark. Some individuals fear darkness when driving; others will only ride in cars and not walk in the dark.

Fear of darkness in children and adults has been successfully treated with behavior modification approaches.

Fear of darkness is the opposite of fear of daylight, which is known as phengophobia. Many agoraphobics feel more comfortable in the dark than in the light.

Individuals who are hearing-impaired have particular fears of darkness, as they depend so much on visual stimuli. They may fear being alone in dark places, fear being robbed, or fear being attacked in dark situations. (See also NIGHT TERRORS.)

dasein A term used in the existential approach to PSYCHOTHERAPY. Dasein is derived from the German word meaning "being there." The term was used originally by Martin Heidegger (1889–1976), a German philosopher, to describe aspects of an individual's experience of awareness of self, others, environment, choices in deciding how to act upon environment, and limitations by history and culture. The individual struggles between freedom and limitation, which may lead to anxieties and fears. Heidegger's approach held that, faced with the inevitability of death, man must find meaning in life, not through outer conformity and adaptation to others, but through self-understanding and self-analysis. By drawing on the uniqueness of experience and the pattern of our potentialities, each individual will develop his or her own kind of life and relief from ANXIETIES. (SEE ALSO DASEIN ANALYSIS.)

Binswanger, L., "The Case of Lola Voss," in *Being in the World* (New York: Harper & Row, 1949).

Boss, M., *Existential Foundations of Medicine and Psychology* (New York: Jason Aronson, 1971).

dasein analysis A form of existential PSYCHOTHERAPY that utilizes classical psychoanalytic technique for relief of ANXIETIES and other psychological concerns. Dasein analysis is particularly associated with the work of Medard Boss (1903–), Swiss psychiatrist and author of *Psychoanalysis and Dasein-analysis.* Boss acknowledged the role of the past and the future in influencing the individual's current behavior. Boss, like HUMANISTIC therapists and other EXISTENTIAL therapists, viewed the therapeutic relationship as requiring full participation of both parties. As in client-centered therapy, Boss stressed the curative power of the enduring, unshakable, benevolent and tactful devotion that an individual receives from the analyst and believed that this relationship, rather than interpretations, leads the individual to relief from anxieties and phobias. (See also DASEIN; EXISTENTIAL THERAPY; PSYCHOANALYSIS.)

Walrond-Skinner, Sue, *A Dictionary of Psychotherapy* (London: Routledge & Kegan Paul, 1986).

Boss, M., *Psychoanalysis and Dasein-Analysis* (New York: Basic Books, 1963).

Boss, M., *Existential Foundations of Medicine and Psychology* (New York: Jason Aronson, 1971).

dawn, fear of Fear of dawn is known as eosophobia. Fear of dawn may be related to fear of daylight or light. Some agoraphobics fear being out during daylight, or after dawn, but are comfortable going out in the dark. Others who fear dawn and daylight may fear being seen by others or fear criticism about their appearance or their actions. (See also DAYLIGHT, FEAR OF; LIGHT, FEAR OF.)

daylight, fear of Fear of daylight is known as phenogophobia or phengophobia. Manifestations of this fear involve secluding oneself in curtained rooms where sunlight cannot enter and permitting only illumination by artificial light. Usually the individual can exit at night and move around at night.

Fear of daylight may be related to a fear of being seen in public, being watched, or of criticism by others for behavior or appearance. Some agoraphobics go out only at night because they are fearful of being seen having a panic attack during the daylight.

Feydeau, the French playwright, is said to have feared daylight; he practically never went out during the day. Fear of darkness is more common than fear of daylight. (See also DAWN, FEAR OF; LIGHT, FEAR OF.)

Marks, Isaac M., *Living with Fear* (New York: McGraw-Hill, 1978).

daymare A term roughly related to ANXIETY ATTACK or PANIC ATTACK.

dead bodies, fear of Fear of dead bodies, corpses and cadavers is known as necrophobia. Individuals who fear looking at dead bodies may indirectly fear that they will also die or that there may be some "contagion." Some necrophobes may also be fearful of disease or injury. (See also CORPSES, FEAR OF; DEATH, FEAR OF.)

death, fear of Fear of death, or thanatophobia, is one of the most universal fears, and may be the basis for many phobias. For example, individuals who fear darkness, choking, suffocation, enclosed places, flying in an airplane, epidemics, having a heart attack, developing cancer or acquired immune deficiency syndrome (AIDS), indirectly fear death under the other feared circumstances. Those who fear having panic attacks also fear death, because at the times when their hearts beat fast and they have difficulty breathing, they are afraid that they will die. Many agoraphobics fear death. The commonly used term "scared to death" probably came about because some individuals are so frightened by circumstances—or their own reactions—that they fear they will die.

Historically, philosophers and psychoanalytic thinkers have considered man's preoccupation with and fear of death, and most religions have incorporated teachings about death into their belief systems. Some people fear death because of its unknown aspects. Some fear their own death and worry that it will be painful and unpleasant. Others fear death because of what might happen to them after the end of life. For those who believe in a hereafter, they worry about where they will go after death. Fear of death and retribution for possible sins during life may influence some individuals toward good behavior.

Others fear the death of a loved one, which would result in the survivor's being left alone. For example, when a spouse does not return when expected, some individuals start fearing an accident or a mugging. Many children fear the death of a parent, because the children fear being left alone. It is not uncommon for a young child to anticipate the return of a dead parent, because young children do not comprehend the finality of death.

Fear of death is common among children, particularly adolescents. Adolescents aged 15 to 18 are more anxious about death than younger children or older adults, while among 12- to 18-year-olds, the most common fear is of nuclear war (a fear of death by nuclear war).

In the United States, many people fear talking about death. As an example, many do not use the words "death" "dying," or "died." Some prefer to refer to another's death as "passing on," or "passing away" or "going to one's reward." People fear death because it is the ultimate unknown. Part of the reason our cultural attitudes about death continue from generation to generation may be that we hide the topic from children. Many adults view death as unspeakable.

In the last decade, however, death has become more commonly talked about out of necessity because of technology that has developed to keep terminally ill patients alive, the development of legal as well as medical definitions of death, questions about euthanasia (mercy killing), organ donation, and the movement toward hospice care for the dying.

The fear of blood and injury is related to a fear of death, as some phobic individuals associate blood, illness and injury with death. Those who fear needles, injections, or having dental work done may also indirectly fear that they will die as a result of the procedure. However, through exposure therapy, by gradually facing the feared circumstance, the individual can learn to reduce these fears. Exposure therapy helps many individuals overcome fear of dentistry and medical examinations to the point where they are able to relax adequately for necessary procedures.

Some of the factors that influence an individual's fear of death are the age of the person, the individual's psychological maturity, and the level of threat of death. Fear of death often becomes more common after age 40. Individuals dread not only the physically destructive aspects of death, but also the expected loss of consciousness, self-control and aloneness that death implies.

Soldiers in combat are afraid of dying but learn to control or repress their fears. Some use defensive coping techniques including the adoption of a fatalistic attitude or the thought that they are invulnerable or immortal. During wartime, fear of death contributes to soldiers' alertness and readiness to use weapons. Because of continually facing this acute fear over a period of time, some servicepeople develop POSTTRAUMATIC STRESS DISORDER, during which they relive their fears of death, even years after active duty. SEE ALSO CHILDHOOD ANXIETIES, FEARS AND PHOBIAS; CLAUSTROPHOBIA; DEATH ANXIETY; DEATH-RELATED FEARS; DENTAL ANXIETY; INJECTION, FEAR OF; PANIC ATTACK.)

Becker, Ernest, *The Denial of Death* (New York: Macmillan, 1975).

Choron, Jacques, Death and Western Thought (New York: Macmillan, 1963).

Henden, David, *Death As a Fact of Life* (New York: Norton, 1973).

death anxiety Fear of death and anxiety over dying; also known as thanatophobia. (See also CEMETERIES, FEAR OF; DEATH, FEAR OF; ILLNESS, FEAR OF.)

death-related fears A fear hierarchy, or arrangement of fears relating to death, from maximum to minimum, is sometimes used during therapy for an individual who has a death phobia. The individual may be asked to name the situation that arouses maximum anxiety; that fear will be given a rating of 100. The situation that causes the least anxiety is given a 5. A fear hierarchy of death-related fears for an individual might be:

Seeing a dead man in a coffin.
Being at a burial.
Seeing a burial assemblage from a distance.
Reading the obituary notice of a young person who died of a heart attack.
Driving past a cemetery (the nearer, the worse).
Reading the obituary notice of an old person.
Being inside a hospital.
Seeing a hospital.
Seeing an ambulance.

(See also CEMETERIES, FEAR OF; DEAD BODIES, FEAR OF; SYSTEMATIC DESENSITIZATION; TOMBSTONES, FEAR OF.)

Wolpe, Joseph, *Our Useless Fears* (Boston: Houghton Mifflin, 1981).

decapitation fear Fear of having one's head cut off. Some psychiatric points of view consider decapitation fear a form of castration anxiety, or fear of having one's genital organs cut off. This bizarre and unlikely concern is usually part of a delusional pattern of obsessive fantasy. (See also CASTRATION ANXIETY; SEXUAL FEARS.)

decaying matter, fear of Fear of decaying matter is known as septophobia. Individuals who have this phobia may be afraid of disease. (See also CONTAMINATION, FEAR OF; DIRT, FEAR OF; FILTH, FEAR OF; GERMS, FEAR OF; INFECTION, FEAR OF.)

decidophobia Fear of making decisions.

See DECISIONS, FEAR OF.

decisions, fear of Fear of making decisions is known as decidophobia Some anxious individuals find it difficult to make choices in life, ranging from simple choices, such as what to wear, to major decisions, such as whether to get married or not, or where to live. Some individuals who fear NEWNESS or NOVELTY have difficulty making decisions regarding changes. ANXIETIES about decision-making are related to FEARS about one's own capabilities and feelings of self-confidence. (See also MOVING, FEAR OF.)

deconditioning A behavior therapy technique in which learned responses such as phobias are "unlearned," or deconditioned. For example, a person who has a phobic reaction to water following a near-drowning experience could be deconditioned by going wading with a trusted friend, taking a small step at a time in very shallow water, and gradually going into deeper water. Desensitization is another term for the deconditioning process. (See also BEHAVIOR THERAPY; DESENSITIZATION.)

deep places, fear of See DEPTH, FEAR OF.

defecalgesiophobia Fear of having painful bowel movements. (See also DEFECATION, FEAR OF; DEFECATION, FEAR OF PAINFUL.)

defecation, fear of Fear of defecation, or of having bowel movements, is known as coprophobia. For some, the fear extends only to the times when the individual perceives that someone is watching or is aware of what is happening, such as in a public bathroom facility. For others, there is a fear of losing part of the body through defecation. Another interpretation is that the individual may have regressed, or perhaps never advanced, from an earlier stage of development in which his or her own feces were considered prized possessions. (See also ANAL STAGE; DEVELOPMENTAL STAGES.)

defecation, fear of painful Fear of having pain during a bowel movement is known as defecalgesiophobia. This fear may be long-standing or may occur at times such as following surgery or during illness, where the pain may be real and not imaginary. (See also DEFECATION, FEAR OF.)

defense mechanisms Patterns of feelings, thoughts, or behaviors that are relatively involuntary and arise in response to perceptions of psychic danger such as ANXIETY, internal conflicts, unacceptable impulses, GUILT, or other threats to the EGO. The term defense mechanisms was first used by SIGMUND FREUD in 1894. Examples of defense mechanisms are AVOIDANCE, COMPENSATION, DENIAL, DISPLACEMENT, RATIONALIZATION, REPRESSION, and substitution. Defense mechanisms may be useful or harmful, depending on their severity, their inflexibility, and the context in which they occur. (See also DISSOCIATION; PROJECTION; SUPPRESSION.)

American Psychiatry Association, *Diagnostic and Statistical Manual* (Washington, DC: American Psychiatric Association, 1987).

deformed people, fear of Fear of deformed people is known as teratophobia. Some individuals have a phobic reaction to deformed people when they see them on the street. Others have anxious reactions just by imagining or thinking of deformed individuals. Some fear giving birth to a deformed child. Fear of becoming deformed oneself is known as DYSMORPHOPHOBIA.

deformity, fear of Fear of a cosmetic defect in one's appearance is known as dysmorphophobia. The individuals who have this condition are in fact well within normal limits in their appearance but complain about some external physical defect they think is noticeable and upsetting to other people. Some individuals are continually concerned with a specific part of the body, e.g., genitals, mouth and smile, breasts, nose, ears, eyes, chin, bald head, buttocks, arms, legs, eyebrows, stomach, etc. Thoughts may be connected with feelings of inferiority. Dysmorphophobia, likeliest to occur in individuals who have sensitive or insecure personalities, may be an early symptom of obsessive–compulsive disorder or schizophrenia.

The term dysmorphophobia was coined in 1886 by Morselli, who described cases of patients concerned over small hands, a dimple on the chin, etc. Pierre Janet in 1908 described patients who had unwarranted feelings of dissatisfaction with their physical appearance. He thought these individuals were neurotic and stressed the obsessional side of their symptoms. (See also NEUROSIS; OBSESSIVE–COMPULSIVE DISORDER; SCHIZOPHRENIA.)

Hay, G.G., "Dysmorphophobia," *British Journal of Psychiatry,* 116(1970), pp. 344–406.

deipnophobia See DINING, FEAR OF.

déjà vu An illusion in which the individual experiences a new event for a moment as something already experienced; such an event may be ANXIETY-producing or cause a PHOBIC REACTION. The word is French and means "already seen." The familiar feeling may be due to resemblance between the present and the past scenes, or to a similar scene pictured in a daydream or night DREAM. Some believe that déjà vu experiences are due to events in a previous lifetime.

delusion An unshakable belief or system of belief based on a faulty premise and maintained in spite of rational evidence to the contrary. The delusion is not a belief ordinarily accepted by other members of the person's culture or subculture; it is not an article of religious faith. Delusions may cause the individual great anxiety and even panic reactions.

Delusions may be transient and fragmentary, as in delirium, or highly systematized and superficially convincing, as in paranoid states, though most of them fall between these two extremes. Though logically absurd, and a symptom of psychosis, delusions sometimes appear to relieve an individual's anxiety, or to counteract feelings of inferiority or insecurity and fill the need some have to blame others for their failures.

Delusions should be distinguished from HALLUCINATIONS, which are false sensory perceptions. Hallucinations may cause the delusion that the perception is true. A delusion should be differentiated from an overvalued idea, an unreasonable belief, or an idea that is not as firmly held as a delusion.

The American Psychiatric Association's *Diagnostic and Statistical Manual of Mental Disorders* lists many common types of delusions. For example, delusions of being controlled involve feelings, impulses, thoughts, or actions that are experienced as originating elsewhere and as being imposed by some external force. A typical case of this type of delusion is the man who claims that his words were those of his father.

Bizarre delusions are false beliefs whose contents are absurd and have no possible basis in fact. An example is a man who believed that when his adenoids were removed in childhood, a box with wires was placed in his head so that the voice he heard was that of the governor.

Grandiose delusions involve an exaggerated sense of one's importance, power, knowledge, or identity. Delusional jealousy may occur, for example, when a person has the delusion that his or her sexual partner is unfaithful. Nihilistic delusion involves the theme of nonexistence of the self or part of the self, others, or the world. An example is the person saying, "There is no need to eat, because I have no insides." The central theme of a persecutory delusion is that a person or group is being attacked, harassed, cheated, persecuted, or conspired against. Usually the subject—or a person or group or institution close to him or her—is singled out as the object of the persecution. A somatic delusion pertains to the function of the body. An example is the belief that one is pregnant despite being postmenopausal.

Delusional thinking is not present in anxiety states; however, people who develop delusions have a severe sense of personal vulnerability and unrecognized fears that they "project" outward. (See also ANXIETIES; PARANOIA; PSYCHOSIS.)

American Psychiatric Association, *Diagnostic and Statistical Manual* (Washington, DC: American Psychiatric Association, 1987).

dementophobia Fear of insanity. (See also INSANITY, FEAR OF.)

demonophobia or daemonophobia Fear of demons, devils, ghosts, and spirits. Also known as phasmophobia. (See also DEMONS, FEAR OF; DEVILS, FEAR OF; GHOSTS, FEAR OF; SUPERNATURAL, FEAR OF; WITCHES AND WITCHCRAFT, FEAR OF.)

demons, fear of Fear of demons is known as demonphobia, demonophobia, daemonophobia, and phasmophobia. Demons, once considered companions or lesser devils of Satan at the time of his fall from heaven, were feared even before the Middle Ages (1220–1400), when church people and later judges and civil authorities sought to detect and rout the devil and other demons that were believed to take over some human bodies and cause diseases and other catastrophes. Those who feared demons feared that powerful forces got inside the human body and that these forces directly caused the possessed person to commit bizarre acts. The victims of demonic possession were not considered responsible for their disturbing mental and physical symptoms, which resemble what are now considered to be attacks of HYSTERIA and SCHIZOPHRENIA. To help the individual, someone or something had to get through to the inner forces, weaken them, and drive them out.

During the Middle Ages, demons were thought to have great knowledge and power. In addition to their potential control over human behavior, they could influence the stars, control weather, and produce earthquakes. Certain areas of learning, such as alchemy, were considered to be the province of demons. Demons were described as being able to assume any form they chose, sometimes having actual physical form, usually that of an animal or a powerful, striking human being.

In some periods, people thought to have made a pact with the devil were considered witches. The procedure for hunting down, detecting, and trying witches included various torturous exorcisms to induce the witches or wizards (male) to recant and break their bonds with the devil. In most cases the presumed witches and wizards possessed by demons were killed. Many individuals were unjustly accused of witchcraft, creating considerable anxiety in the innocent population, many of whom were identified as accomplices or witches themselves, in confessions by torture victims.

In modern therapy, figurative "demons" are driven out when the therapist understands and attempts to change the internal forces that cause observed undesirable behaviors, such as phobic reactions. (See also EXORCISM; WITCHES AND WITCHCRAFT, FEAR OF.)

Bugelski, B. Richard and Anthony Graziano, *The Handbook of Practical Psychology* (Englewood Cliffs, NJ: Prentice-Hall, 1980).

"Demonology," in *Encyclopedia of Occultism and Parapsychology* (Detroit: Gale Research, 1987).

demophobia Fear of crowds. (See also CROWDS, FEAR OF.)

dendrophobia Fear of trees. This fear may be related to fear of forests, or fear of landscape. (See also LANDSCAPE, FEAR OF; TREES, FEAR OF.)

denial A DEFENSE MECHANISM in which the person fails to acknowledge some aspect of external reality that is apparent to others—for example, the existence of a phobia-provoking situation or anxiety-producing event. Denial can be a positive or negative force, depending upon how it is used. For example, in denying that a threat exists, the individual deludes himself or herself into relative calmness and possibly a better ability to cope. Soldiers in battle may use the denial mechanism in this way. An example of a negative adaptation of denial is an agoraphobic who denies that his or her fear of going out of the home may interfere with his or her own economic capacity and may be burdening other family members with chores.

Freud suggested that women's lack of a penis and the anxiety this realization causes in men and women was the basis for the denial mechanism. (see also EGO DEFENSE MECHANISMS.)

Freud, Sigmund, *An Outline of Psychoanalysis,* vol. 23 (London: Hogarth Press, 1940).

dental anxiety Dental anxiety, or fear of dentists and dentistry, is sometimes referred to as dentophobia. A morbid fear of dental treatment is often traceable to at least one traumatic dental experience in childhood but also may be associated in many cases with a lower-than-normal pain threshold, and in some cases with strong personality factors that affect the situation. Dental anxiety ranges from a mild fear of dental treatment to extreme ANXIETY that leads an individual to avoid contact with a dentist entirely. Mild to high dental anxiety may surface as a mild queasy feeling in the stomach, a dryness in the mouth, an increased pulse, sweaty palms, or trembling hands. Persons with extreme dental anxiety may experience difficulty in breathing, dizziness or lightheadedness, choking, chest pain, diarrhea, and PANIC ATTACKS. Some even bolt from the chair during a dental procedure. Most frequently cited fears are the sight of the anesthetic NEEDLE and the sight and sound of the dentist's drill. Dental anxiety often occurs on its own, but it may also be associated with more general fears of BLOOD, INJURY, PAIN, DOCTORS, and HOSPITALS. While many advances in dentistry during the latter part of the 20th century have greatly reduced the anxieties most people have about dentistry, there are still many fearful individuals.

Studies show that persons with high dental anxiety, compared to those with little or no dental anxiety, may have lower pain thresholds or an increased sensitivity to pain.

As with many anxieties, in addition to the stress from the anxiety itself, the potential harm resulting from minor or otherwise preventable problems may become quite serious. Avoiding routine dental care can lead to more severe problems and complications, such as severe tooth decay or periodontal disease. Poor oral health may result in unsightly teeth and thus a reduction in self-esteem. If a dental abscess goes unchecked, the results may even be fatal; as many as 800 people die each year when unchecked bacterial infections travel to and attack other parts of their bodies.

Prevalence of dental anxiety

The American Dental Association (ADA) estimates that 35,000,000 Americans experience moderate to high anxiety about visiting their dentist. An additional 12,000,000 persons experience such intense anxiety that they forgo dental care altogether, sometimes for decades at a time.

Steward Agras, in his large-scale study of anxiety prevalence, found that 19.8 percent of sampled individuals reported moderate anxiety, and an additional 2.4 percent reported intense reaction. Similar results were obtained by Ronald Kleinknecht and associates in a questionnaire survey of 920 persons (see summary table below). Further-

Percentage of Responses to the Question "All Things Considered, How Fearful Are You of Having Dental Work Done?"

Response %	Male %	Female %	Total* %
not at all	29.1	21.8	25.4
a little	40.3	32.7	36.6
somewhat	19.6	21.6	20.5
much	6.1	13.7	10.2
very much	4.0	10.1	7.3

*N=920

more, Kleinknecht found that 44.5 percent of his sample had put off making a dental appointment due to anxiety and that 4.7 percent had done so "nearly every time" an appointment was due or needed.

In this survey, the most feared events were seeing and feeling the needle and hearing, feeling, and seeing the drill. The lack of personal contact, anticipation of pain, feelings of vulnerability and embarrassment, and lack of confidence in the dentist or auxiliary personnel were also contributing factors to the reaction.

Sources of dental anxiety

Some dental anxiety is undoubtedly acquired through direct experience with painful or frightening dental situations. These traumas can produce conditioned emotional reactions so that dental tools or procedures become conditioned stimuli, generalizing further to the dentist, the dental office, and so on. How the patient perceives the dentist's demeanor and reacts personally to him or her also seems to contribute to fear acquisition. For example, if the patient feels embarrassed or belittled, or feels little control of the situation, fear can be heightened. There also seem to be strong cognitive elements of catastrophic or anxiety-engendering thinking that contribute to the reaction.

While various psychoanalytical speculations as to underlying reasons for dental anxiety (some built upon themes of oral fixation or Oedipal authority conflicts) may be valid, the more common line of reasoning is to view dental anxiety as a learned or behavioral response to real, imagined, or anticipated dental stimuli. Firsthand painful or negative experiences during dental treatment are one of the better-documented origins of dental anxiety. Such experiences are certainly subjective and may be perceived as real even if they are not. When origins are not traceable to an unpleasant firsthand experience, they probably lie in vicarious experiences. For many people, dental anxiety is essentially a culturally learned fear. Dental "horror stories" told by friends or relatives or in the media are quite common, as are cartoons or fictional accounts depicting frightening circumstances. Stories told by childhood friends are a significant origin of dental anxiety. Dental "torture" scenes such as those portrayed in *Little Shop of Horrors* or *Marathon Man* are likely to have lasting effects or to reinforce a current dental anxiety. A family member with dental anxiety (most often the mother) might be another cause of an individual's own dental anxiety. In addition, anyone who has had a negative or painful medical experience is likely to generalize that experience to dental treatment. Whether acquired firsthand or vicariously, dental anxiety most often begins in childhood or adolescence.

Components of Anxiety: Dental Fear Surveys

From the dentist's point of view, it may be difficult to tell who suffers from anxiety and who does not. Many people do not outwardly display their fears; they may even go to great lengths to hide them, to avoid the fear of embarrassment. An understanding of the components that make up an individual's dental anxiety can be helpful in deciding which methods might best be employed to break down and treat the anxiety. A number of dental fear surveys have been developed, some for use by dentists or psychologists, others more for use by patients and their dentist together. Such questionnaires, filled out prior to an individual's first appointment, could indicate to the dentist or psychologist how that person would be likely to respond to a dental procedure and what steps might help the person overcome his or her anxiety.

A typical questionnaire assigns point values to specific elements of dental fear. A five- or ten-point scale gauges the range from no reaction or fear to intense reaction or fear. Questions concern the anticipation and avoidance of dentistry, physiological responses to dentistry, fear of individual experiences during specific phases of dental

Sample Anxiety Hierarchy for Typical Dental Phobia

Anxiety-Provoking Situation	SUD (0–100)
1. Being reminded you need a dental appointment	20
2. Calling for an appointment	25
3. Seeing the calendar that shows only 1 day left before appointment	32
4. Driving to the dentist's office	39
5. Entering the waiting room	45
6. Hearing the drill sounds while in the waiting room	54
7. Being taken into the dental chair	60
8. Seeing the dentist walk in	68
9. Dentist uses explorer (probe) to examine your teeth	73
10. Feeling vibrations from the drill on your mouth	80
11. Seeing the local anesthetic syringe	90
12. Dentist begins injection	95

Ronald A. Kleinknecht, *The Anxious Self* (New York: Human Sciences Press, 1986), p. 157.

treatment (such as the sight of the anesthetic needle or sitting in the waiting room), general fear of dentistry, and reactions of family or peers to dentistry.

Using such a scale, Ronald Kleinknecht and D.A. Bernstein found that persons who score high anxiety prior to a dental appointment also report more anxiety when in the office and sweat more during treatment.

Treatment approaches

Management of dental anxiety may include simple communication and explanation of dental treatments, chemical intervention (such as local or general anesthetics, analgesics, or sedatives), behavioral or psychological intervention (ranging from simple relaxation techniques to options such as biofeedback, hypnosis, or psychological consultation), or even acupuncture. Because the mouth is a very sensitive and private part of the body, dental work is likely to be viewed as an aggressive act with the dentist as the aggressor. Dental patients may feel distrust or even hostility toward their dentist. They may hide their anxiety out of embarrassment or fear of criticism. For these reasons, the dentist must be open and communicative; he must encourage patients to view and trust him as a person, not just a clinician. A dentist who is perceived as being critical, judgmental, or insulting will only increase a dental patient's anxiety. People are less likely to anticipate pain from a dentist whom they trust. Because a patient often feels loss of control while undergoing dental treatment, use of hand signals or a pushbutton to get the dentist to stop whatever he is doing can return this element of control and allay that component of anxiety. It is also important for the dentist to appear to be in control. Surprisingly, some people will accept their dentist's authority to the point where their anxiety can actually be reduced simply by the dentist's command. A straightforward explanation of the proposed treatment by the dentist will also lead to a greater feeling of knowledge and control on the part of the dental patient. These basic elements of explanation, understanding, and control are often all that is necessary to relieve dental anxiety for some individuals.

Relaxation and distraction techniques work on opposite principles. Relaxation reduces or inhibits anxiety, while distraction masks anxiety by keeping a person preoccupied. With both techniques, people still report feeling the pain, although not to the same extent. Using relaxation techniques, a person can focus his or her attention on relaxation through a series of muscle-relaxation and deep-breathing exercises. BIOFEEDBACK may also be used. In biofeedback, a machine is used to monitor the individual's state of relaxation or excitation. By a visible or audible signal, the machine relays this information to the person, who in turn concentrates on and responds to the machine's signals and learns to relax. An extension of the

Sample Items from the Dental Fear Survey

Has fear of dentistry ever caused you to cancel or not appear for a dental appointment?

1	2	3	4	5
Never	Once or Twice	A Few Times	Often	Nearly Every Time

When having dental work done:
My muscles become tense:

1	2	3	4	5
Not at all	A little	Somewhat	Much	Very much

My heart beats faster:

1	2	3	4	5
Not at all	A little	Somewhat	Much	Very much

How much fear do you experience when:
Being seated in the dental chair?

1	2	3	4	5
None at all	A little	Somewhat	Much	Very much

When seeing the anesthetic needle:

1	2	3	4	5
None at all	A little	Somewhat	Much	Very much

Ronald A. Kleinknecht, *The Anxious Self* (New York: Human Sciences Press, 1986), p. 101.

relaxation technique is SYSTEMATIC DESENSITIZATION, in which the person first relaxes and then imagines the anxiety-producing situation. The visualized dental treatment thus becomes associated with relaxation.

Distraction techniques focus a person's attention away from the dental work—through, for example, popular music played through headphones; a movie, such as a comedy; or cartoons for children. A video game mounted above the dental chair ensures active participation on the part of the dental patient and thus achieves a greater degree of distraction. In the MODELING technique a person observes someone else receiving dental treatment through a visual presentation, such as a film, slides, pictures, or in person. While the anxiety-producing situation is portrayed, the "model" shows no fear. Modeling leads a person to imitate the same response as the model. This is an excellent preventive technique when it is used with children on their first dental appointments.

HYPNOSIS, or hypnodontics, is capable of providing very deep relaxation in many patients. Despite the popular image created by fiction and magic shows, there is nothing mystical about hypnosis, nor does it cause a person to lose control. There are two major limitations: 1) Only about one-fifth of all dentists have been trained to use hypnosis, and 2) not everyone is equally able to achieve a trance state.

ACUPUNCTURE may be the most controversial technique for relieving dental pain

Only recently has it even been considered seriously to have real analgesic and anesthetic results. If the patient's anxiety is not increased by the use of needles, the apparent pain-relieving effects of acupuncture may help to reduce dental anxiety. Due to the underlying mystery of acupuncture (it is far from clearly understood—the traditional explanation involves yin and yang and energy balance), it is hardly a widespread technique in the U.S. One study suggests that acupuncture's results might be entirely due to a placebo effect.

Not surprisingly, evidence appears to indicate that treating the anxiety and not just the pain is more likely to help an individual free him- or herself from dental anxiety. A study has shown a higher incidence of kept appointments in persons who received behavioral modification than persons who received general anesthesia.

Dentists and fearful patients are not alone when it comes to combating dental anxiety. Recently, many dental fear clinics have opened. These clinics teach behavioral modification techniques to help people get over their dental anxiety. Self-help audiocassette programs and books are also available. In instances of extreme dental anxiety that a dentist is unable to manage or treat, consultation with a behavioral therapist may be helpful. Such persons may refuse sedation, act irrationally or with hostility, or exhibit symptoms of compulsive neurosis.

It is not very surprising that the dental patient's anxiety also affects the dentist. Not only is it likely to make his work more difficult, but it contributes to the dentist's unfortunate high incidence of stress-related diseases and suicide.

Self-help approaches to dental anxiety

Direct experiences that help reduce fear and anticipatory reactions:

1. Expose yourself to a dental office, procedures, instruments, etc., in a nontraumatic way. Visit a dentist to talk, sit in the chair, look at instruments, become acquainted with procedures and personnel; these activities can be helpful in desensitizing yourself to these situations. Begin exposure while relaxed. Several exposure trials may be necessary.
2. Control in the dental situation is advised so that you can learn to stop or delay procedures until you are ready or can cue personnel when you need rest or recovery time.

Indirect experiences:

3. Observe others undergoing cleaning or nontraumatic dental procedures (live or on video) to reduce dental anxiety.
4. Obtain information on modern dental treatment. Develop coping skills to apply in the dental situation.
5. Learn to relax during dental treatment.
6. Learn to pace yourself and breathe to attain relaxation.
7. Develop positive, coping self-statements.
8. Minimize or avoid negative "catastrophizing" self-statements.
9. Learn to distract yourself.
10. Speak up to exercise control if needed.

(See also BEHAVIORAL THERAPY; BLOOD-INJURY FEARS; GAGGING, HYPERSENSITIVE; RELAXATION TRAINING; TOOTHACHE, FEAR OF.)

Seyrek et al., "Comparison of Three Distraction Techniques in Reducing Stress in Dental Patients," *Journal of the American Dental Association* (March 1984), pp. 327–329.

O'Shea et al., "Dental Patients' Advice on How to Reduce Anxiety," *General Dentistry* (Jan.–Feb. 1986), pp. 44–47.

Scott, Donald, and Richard Hirschman. "Psychological Aspects of Dental Anxiety in Adults," JADA (January 1982), pp. 27–31.

American Dental Association, "Ten Steps to More Relaxed Dental Visits," pamphlet (American Dental Association, 1986).

Berggren, U., "Long-term Effects of Two Different Treatments for Dental Fear and Avoidance," *Journal of Dental Research,* 65 (1986):874–876.

Kleinknecht et al., "Origins and Characteristics of Fear of Dentistry." *Journal of the American Dental Association* (April 1973), pp. 842–848.

Stokes, Bill, "Take a Breath, Open Wide: There's Help for Those Who Fear Dentistry," *Chicago Tribune* (August 23, 1987).

Sokol, Sokol and Sokol, "A Review of Nonintrusive Therapies Used to Deal with Anxiety and Pain in the Dental Office," *Journal of the American Dental Association* (February 1985).

Gale, Elliot N. and William A. Ayer, "Treatment of Dental Phobias," *Journal of the American Dental Association* (June 1969), pp. 1304–1307.

Ingersoll et al., "The Use of Contingent Audiotaped Material with Pediatric Dental Patients," *Journal of the American Dental Association* (November 1984), pp. 717–719.

Kroeger, Robert F., "Levels of Fear or Phobia and a Formal Dental Fear Control Program," *General Dentistry* (May–June 1986), pp. 241–242.

Hallstrom, T. and A. Halling, "Prevalence of Dentistry Phobia and Its Relation to Missing Teeth, Alveolar Bone Loss and Dental Care Habits in an Urban Community Sample," *Acta Psychiatrica Scandinavica,* 70 (1984): 438–446.

dentists, fear of See DENTAL ANXIETY.

dentophobia See DENTAL ANXIETY.

dependent personality disorder A personality disorder classified by the American Psychiatric Association. The essential feature of this disorder is a pervasive pattern of dependent and submissive behavior. Anxiety and depression are common. Individuals with this disorder usually lack self-confidence and tend to belittle their abilities and assets. They may at times seek, or stimulate, overprotection and dominance by others. Frequently, individuals with this disorder also have another personality disorder, such as avoidant personality disorder, or histrionic, schizotypal, or narcissistic personality disorders. Dependent personality disorder usually begins in early adulthood and shows up in a variety of contexts, as indicated by *at least five* of the following:

- Unable to make everyday decisions without an excessive amount of advice or reassurance from others
- Allows others to make most of his or her important decisions—for example, where to live, what job to take
- Agrees with people even when he or she believes they are wrong, due to a fear of being rejected
- Has difficulty initating projects or doing things on his or her own
- Volunteers to do things that are unpleasant or demeaning in order to get other people to like him or her
- Feels uncomfortable or helpless when alone, or goes to great lengths to avoid being alone
- Feels devastated or helpless when close relationships end
- Frequently is preoccupied with fears of being abandoned
- Is easily hurt by criticism or disapproval

(See also ANXIETY; AVOIDANT PERSONALITY DISORDER; DEPRESSION; PERSONALITY DISORDERS.)

American Psychiatric Association, *Diagnostic and Statistical Manual* (Washington DC: American Psychiatric Association, 1987).

depersonalization A feeling of unreality or being removed from oneself and the environment. Depersonalization sometimes occurs in agoraphobia. The individual may feel that he or she is someone else or is watching himself, usually from above. Depersonalization may be a "cutoff" mechanism when anxiety, stress, or fatigue reaches an unacceptable level for an individual. It is a temporary condition, lasting a few seconds or minutes or, rarely, several hours.

Depersonalization is also a characteristic of depersonalization disorder, and may also occur in schizotypal personality disorder and schizophrenia. (See also DEPERSONALIZATION DISORDER; SCHIZOPHRENIA.)

depersonalization disorder A disorder characterized by one or more episodes of DEPERSONALIZATION that are severe enough to impair an individual's social and occupational functioning. Onset of depersonalization is rapid and usually shows up in a sensation of self-estrangement, a feeling that one's extremities have changed in size, a sense of being mechanical, perceiving oneself at a distance, and, in some cases, a feeling that the external world is unreal. (See also NEUROSIS.)

depersonalization neurosis See DEPERSONALIZATION DISORDER.

depressants Agents that diminish or slow down any function or activity of a body system or organ. Types of depressants include ALCOHOL, BARBITURATES, and TRANQUILIZERS.

depression An emotional state marked by great sadness and apprehension, feelings of worthlessness and GUILT, withdrawal from others, loss of sleep, appetite, and sexual desire, and either lethargy or agitation. Depression is one of the most common and most treatable of all mental illnesses, according to the American Psychiatric Association. It is estimated that two to three percent of men and four to nine percent of women are suffering a major depression at any given time in the United States. The lifetime risk may be as high as 10 percent for men and 25 percent for women. About 80 percent of those who suffer from depression fail to recognize the illness and get no treatment for it. Many attribute the physical and emotional symptoms of depression to "the flu," or "stress." Many individuals who have AGORAPHOBIA also have some depression

Symptoms

Individuals who are depressed, or who suffer from depression, usually have pervasive feelings of sadness, helplessness, hopelessness, and irritability. Often they do not admit to these symptoms but withdraw from human contact. Other symptoms may include a noticeable change of appetite with either significant weight loss when not dieting or weight gain; noticeable change in sleeping patterns, such as fitful sleep, inability to sleep, or sleeping too much; loss of interest in activities formerly enjoyed; loss of energy; fatigue; feelings of worthlessness; feelings of inappropriate guilt; an inability to concentrate or think; indecisiveness; recurring thoughts of death or suicide, wishing to die, attempting suicide; melancholia (defined as overwhelming feelings of sadness and grief) accompanied by waking at least two hours earlier than normal in the morning, feeling more depressed in the morning, and being significantly slower in motor skills. Some severely depressed persons may develop disturbed thinking.

Many depressed individuals have mental and physical feelings that never go away, appear to have no end in sight, and cannot be alleviated by happy events or good news. Some people are so disabled by depression that they cannot even build up the energy to call a doctor. If someone else calls for them, these people may refuse to go because they are so hopeless that they think there is no point in going. Family, friends, and coworkers of depressed people may become frustrated with victims of depression because their efforts to help and comfort are to no avail. The depressed person will not follow advice, refuses help, and denies comfort. However, persistence is essential, because many doctors believe that depression is the illness that underlies the vast majority of suicides in the U.S. The best prevention for suicide is to recognize and treat the depression.

Depression can appear at any age. Major depressive episodes peak at age 55 to 70 in men and 35 to 45 in women. About 20 percent of major depressions last two years or more, with an average of eight months. About half of those who experience a major depression will have a recurrence within two years.

Some victims have episodes that are separated by several years, and others suffer clusters of the disorder over a short period. Between episodes they can function normally. However, 20 percent to 35 percent of the victims suffer chronic depression that prevents them from functioning totally normally.

Causes

Scientists say that no single cause gives rise to depression. The possibility that depression has a genetic component was explored during 1937, when researchers announced they had located genetic markers for susceptibility to manic–depressive illness. Though they have not found the specific gene or genes for this illness, the existence of genetic markers brought scientists much closer to understanding the biochemical reactions controlled by these genes.

Earlier studies indicated family links in depression. For example, if one identical twin suffers from depression or manic–depression, the other twin has a 70 percent chance of also having the illness. Other studies that looked at the rate of depression among adopted children supported this finding. Depressive illnesses among children's adoptive family had little effect on their risk for the disorder; however, among adopted children whose biological relatives suffered depression, the disorder was three times more common than the norm.

Medications are known to cause some kinds of depression. During the 1950s, doctors realized that some people taking reserpine, a medication for high blood pressure, suffered from depression. Likewise, depression has been noted as a side effect of Valium and Xanax and of many kinds of tranquilizers.

More recent research indicates that people suffering from depression have imbalances of neurotransmitters, natural biochemicals that allow brain cells to communicate with one another. Two of the biochemicals that tend to be out of balance in depressed people are serotonin and norepinephrine. Scientists think that an imbalance of serotonin may cause the sleep problems, irritability, and anxiety many depressed people suffer. Likewise, an improper amount of norepinephrine, which regulates alertness and arousal, may contribute to the fatigue and depressed mood of the illness.

Other body chemicals also may be out of balance in depressed people. Among them is cortisol, a hormone that the body produces in response to extreme cold, anger, or fear. In normal people, the level of cortisol in the bloodstream reaches a peak in the morning, then decreases as the day progresses. In depressed people, however, cortisol peaks earlier in the morning and does not level off or decrease in the afternoon or evening.

Scientists say the environment plays an important role in depression. Historically, depression has been viewed as either internally caused (endogenous) or externally related to environmental events (exogenous). Current thinking, however, views depression from the point of view of the interaction of biological and environmental factors. Some of the environmental correlates to depression are as follows: People most likely to suffer from depression are poor, single, working mothers of young children who live with loneliness, financial stress, and the unrelieved pressures of rearing children and maintaining a household alone. Depression also increases dramatically among older men; one supposition is that men lose their sense of identity and self-worth when they retire. Major changes in the environment, such as a move or job change, or any major loss, such as a divorce or death of a loved one, can bring on depression. Feeling depressed in response to these changes is normal; however, it can become a long-term problem that may require treatment.

Treatments

Between 80 percent and 90 percent of all depressed people can be effectively treated, according to the American Psychiatric Association. There are a variety of therapies and medications that help many depressed people.

Psychotherapies

There are a number of "talk" treatments for depression, including psychoanalysis. In 1986, scientists announced results of research into the effectiveness of short-term psychotherapy in treating depression. Their findings indicated cognitive/behavioral therapy and interpersonal therapy were as effective as medications for depressed patients. Medications relieved patients' symptoms more quickly, but patients who received psychotherapy instead of medicine had as much relief from symptoms after 16 weeks, and their gains were more permanent. The data from this study will help scientists better identify which depressed patients will do best with psychotherapy alone and which may require medications.

Interpersonal psychotherapy is based on the philosophy that disturbed social and personal relationships can cause or contribute to depression. The illness, in turn, may make these relationships more problematic. The therapist helps the individual understand his or her illness and how depression and interpersonal conflicts are related.

Cognitive/behavioral therapy seems to be the most effective psychotherapeutic treatment for depression, based on the understanding that people's emotions are controlled by their views and opinions of the world. Depression results when individuals constantly berate themselves, expect to fail, make inaccurate assessments of what others think of them, overvalue a situation, catastrophize, and have a negative attitude toward the world and the future. The therapist uses various techniques of talk therapy to alleviate negative thought patterns and beliefs.

Psychoanalysis is based on the concept that depression is the result of past conflicts that patients have pushed into their unconscious. Therapists work to identify and resolve the patients' past conflicts that have given rise to depression in later years.

ECT

Some years ago, electroconvulsive therapy (ECT) was used to treat depression. As more effective medications have been developed, use of ECT has declined. However, ECT is still used for some patients who cannot take medications due to heart conditions, old age, severe malnourishment, or inability to respond to antidepressant medication. ECT is considered as a treatment when all other therapies have failed or when a person is suicidal. ECT has been proven effective as a treatment only for psychotic and involutional depression (a major depression that occurs after age 50, usually in a sudden onset), but medications are usually as good or better at alleviating symptoms.

Medications

During the 1950s, several pharmaceutical medications were developed to treat depression. The effectiveness of medication depends on an individual's weight, overall health, metabolism, and other unique characteristics. Several trials of a medication or combination of medications may be needed to learn which work best for each individual. Generally antidepressant medications become fully effective 10 to 20 days after an individual begins taking them.

Usually one of three major types of medication is used to treat depression. They are called tricyclic antidepressants, MAO inhibitors, and lithium.

Tricyclic antidepressants are usually prescribed for individuals whose depressions are characterized by fatique; feelings of hoplessness, helplessness, and excessive guilt; inability to feel pleasure; and loss of appetite with resulting weight loss.

Monoamine oxidase inhibitors inhibitors (MAOIs) are prescribed for individuals whose depressions are characterized by increased appetite, excessive sleepiness, and anxiety, phobic, and obsessive–compulsive symptoms in addition to the depression.

Lithium is used for people who have manic–depressive illness (a severe affective disorder characterized by a predominant mood of elation or depression, and in some cases an alternation between the two states). Occasionally, it is prescribed for people who suffer from depression without mania. Those most likely to respond are depressed individuals whose family members have manic–depression or whose depression is recurrent rather than constant.

Antidepressant medications may have side effects. Common side effects include dry mouth, drowsiness, and constipation; these tend to diminish somewhat or disappear as the body adjusts to the medication.

Self-help

Several techniques have been found effective in prevention of and self-care for depression. These include:

1. A regular program of exercise starting with brief periods and gradually expanding to at least one half hour per day.
2. Interpersonal contact rather than separation and alienation.
3. Coping with exaggerated thoughts, such as self-deprecation, catastrophizing, and overvaluation, by introducing more realistic thoughts and supporting them.
4. Increased activity, gradually adding activities to the day's schedule.

(See also ANTIDEPRESSANTS; DEPRESSION, ADOLESCENT; MANIC–DEPRESSIVE DISORDER; SEASONAL AFFECTIVE DISORDER.)

(Much of the above article reprinted courtesy of the American Psychiatric Association, Washington, D. C.)

Reading List and Other Resources

Greist, John H. and James W. Jefferson, *Depression and Its Treatment: Help for the Nation's #1 Mental Problem* (Washington, DC: American Psychiatric Press, 1984).

Morrison, J.M., *Your Brother's Keeper* (Chicago; Nelson-Hall, 1981).

Winokur, G., *Depression: The Facts* (New York: Oxford University Press, 1981).

Deakin, J.F.W. (ed.), *The Biology of Depression* (Washington, DC: American Psychiatric Press, 1986).

Klerman, Gerald, *Suicide and Depression among Adolescents and Young Adults* (Washington, DC: American Psychiatric Press, 1986).

Sources of information

National Alliance for the Mentally Ill
1901 North Ft. Meyer Drive, Suite 500
Arlington, VA 2209-1604

National Depressive and Manic Depressive Association
P.O. Box 753
Northbrook, IL 60062

National Institute of Mental Health
Public Information Branch
5600 Fishers Lane
Rockville, MD 20857

National Mental Health Association
1020 Prince Street
Alexandria, VA 22314

depression, adolescent For many people, adolescence is a period of complicated and demanding conflicts that lead to ANXIETIES, FEARS about SELF-ESTEEM, and fears regarding the future. Many become overwhelmed by the many changes and pressures and develop depression. Adolescents, neither children nor adults, may experience more loneliness than other age groups; some feel powerless and isolated. Failure in school can lead to a feeling of rejection, a lack of challenge can create BOREDOM, social expectations may be unrealistic, and conflicting messages from family may magnify the struggle for independence.

Depression during adolescence is more than a feeling of being "down in the dumps" or "blue." Depression is an illness and should be treated as such with available help. Recognizing depression in oneself or in one's children or students is important.

Symptoms

Factors relevant to adolescent depression include:

- Feelings of helplessness or hopelessness
- Death wishes, suicidal thoughts, suicide plans or attempts
- Sadness
- Extreme fluctuations between boredom and talkativeness
- Anger, rage, verbal sarcasm, and attack
- Overreaction to criticism
- Guilt; feelings of being unable to satisfy ideals
- Poor self-esteem and loss of confidence
- Intense ambivalence between dependence and independence
- Feelings of emptiness in life
- Restlessness and agitation
- Pessimism about the future
- Rebellious refusal to work in school or cooperate in general
- Sleep disturbances
- Increased or decreased appetite; severe weight gain or loss

Adolescent depression may be difficult to diagnose. Depression in a young person may be somewhat different from that in an adult in several ways. Adolescents do not always understand or express feelings well. Some of their symptoms are often dismissed as "just growing up." The young person, unaware of the concept of depression, may not report anything wrong. Also, there is a strong tie between "getting into trouble" and feeling depressed. It is difficult to sort out if the teenager is depressed because of being in trouble, or in trouble because of being depressed. Depression in the adolescent has been linked to poor academic performance, truancy, delinquency, ALCOHOL and DRUG ABUSE, disobedience, self-destructive behavior, sexual promiscuity, rebelliousness, grief, and running away. The young person may have suffered an increase in the severity of life events, high stress, a number of mental or physical illnesses, a lack of support from family and other significant people, and a decrease in the ability to cope. Adolescents may attempt to escape from depression by denying a need for relationships, or denying that loneliness or depression exist.

Treatment

The most common ways of treating depression in adolescence are medication, psychotherapy, or a combination. For some individuals, the medication (ANTIDEPRESSANTS) is useful in treating symptoms, and a mental-health professional can help them understand why they are depressed and how to handle future stressful situations. PSYCHOTHERAPY is effective in treating stress-related depression. In this treatment, an individual has the opportunity to explore painful events or feelings that might have contributed to the depression. The therapist helps the individual look beyond the problem and explore these feelings. Contemporary therapies also focus on the thought processes that contribute to adolescent depression—for example, exaggerated concerns, misperceptions, and continual self-criticism. Cognitive behavior therapies focus on these processes.

To increase acceptance and a sense of belonging, adolescents who have depression are advised to try to make new and more friends, explore and make better use of existing social connections, and increase their activity in school, community, sports, or job. However, for many young people, these changes are not possible without professional help. Help is available from many community resources, school counselors, and religious advisors. The National Mental Health Association can help interested individuals locate appropriate services locally (in the United States).

Contact:
National Mental Health Association
1021 Prince Street
Alexandria, VA 22314-2971
(703) 684-7722

(See also DEPRESSION; GUILT; SCHOOL PHOBIA; STRESS MANAGEMENT; SUICIDE; SUICIDE, ADOLESCENT; TEST ANXIETY.)

(Adapted with permission from "Adolescent Depression," National Mental Health Association Information Center, Alexandria, Virginia.)

depression and fears across cultures

People of various cultural backgrounds experience symptoms of depression and anxiety. However, depression, fears, anxieties, and phobias are viewed in different ways in different cultures. For example, studies have indicated agitation as a more common symptom among Japanese, South Indian, and North Indian depressives than among Western depressives. Feelings or delusions of guilt are somewhat less common among Indians than Westerners, while fugitive impulse is more common.

Indian studies during the 1970s indicated a fairly high degree of hypochondriasis, which is noticeable as bowel consciousness and concern about sexual potency and the genital organs. Chinese studies during the 1940s described the "Shook Yang," in which an individual fears retraction of the genitals and death because of this process.

In comparison studies of Indian and British depressed persons (1970s), certain differences were noted that may reflect cultural influences. For example, the Indians complained more about physical symptoms than the British. Physical symptoms have also been observed in studies of African depressives.

In determining choice of symptoms, expectancy by the individual concerning what local medical people consider an illness plays a role. Purely psychological symptoms are often dismissed as not of much consequence in less sophisticated groups. Thus rural In-

Patterns of Depression in Three Cultures

	West	Nigeria	India
Incidence	Common	Rare (artifact?)	Common
Sick role	Acknowledged	Not acknowledged (no word for depression)	Acknowledged
Hypochondriasis . .	Less common	Common	Common
Paranoid symptoms . .	Uncommon	Most frequent	Rare
Guilt feelings	Frequent	Almost absent	Rare
Retarded/agitated . .	R > A	A > R	A > R (artifact?)
Fugitive impulse . .	Not described	Common (wander into jungle)	Frequent (renunciation)
Suicide	Common	Rare	Less common

Adapted from J.S. Neki, "Psychiatry in South-East Asia," *British Journal of Psychiatry*, 123 (1973), pp. 257–269.

dians may use the body to express inner tensions and anxieties. Differences in such symptoms were noted among British and Indian soldiers under extreme stress during World War II.

Interpretation of guilt among depressives varies between cultures. For example, some Indians attribute their present suffering to possible bad deeds in a previous life. In the Indian social system, conformity is highly valued and the assumption of self-responsibility for one's acts is less well developed. Thus the individual fears failure because he is concerned what others will say rather than fear of loss of self-esteem.

Contrarily, most Westerners assume a higher degree of individual responsibility, and their guilt may come from a sense of self-failure, causing feelings of shame.

Symptoms of obsession and paranoia appear more frequently in Western studies than among Indian depressives. This may be because rituals are well accepted daily practices in some Indian socioreligious systems, and thus such systems are not considered irregular by the individual or his relatives. Also, Westerners tend to be more competitive than Indians, and this tendency may explain a higher degree of suspicious paranoid attitude.

Following are some specific differences across cultures:

Mourning practices differ between cultures, and the process of grief influences the occurrence of depression. For example, in some societies, religion promises continued interaction with the deceased and the possibility of reparation for whatever wrong may have been done. However, acceptance of loss may be inhibited, if customary rites and beliefs lose significance in rapidly acculturating groups. Whether mourning leads to depression depends on the degree of ambivalence of the individual's relationship to the lost person or object. Such relationships are affected by the interaction between parent and child, and particularly the relationship of father to child in patriarchal, traditional societies, which differs from that in most Western cultures.

Shame and guilt influence depression and anxieties. Depression may be rare among illiterate Africans because of the lack of self-reproach and self-responsibility, fatalistic attitude, and a lack of individual competition. Researchers during the 1950s and 1960s agreed that in Africa, depression is relatively light and short, without feelings of sin and guilt. There is a relative infrequency of manic symptoms and a very low suicide rate.

Early missionary reports indicated that Japanese guilt feelings were not related to sexual and sensual bodily expressions but instead connected with family obligations. The Japanese (according to a 1960 study reported by Yap) have a term that literally means repaying one's parents; infractions of this obligation cause feelings that Westerners call guilt. Different individuals feel guilty about different things, depending on their culture.

In Japanese literature, more first-born than last-born males are among those who become depressed. This may occur because in the Confucian system, the eldest son has a heavy responsibility, especially when the father dies.

Projection (a defense mechanism by which unacceptable impulses are attributed to others or personal failures are blamed on others) is used in many cultures. In some societies in which religion teaches that the individual is evil because of a supernatural cause, there is also a mechanism for absolution, atonement, and relief of guilt in the individual. In the Orient, rites of worship or reverence serve a similiar function. Some individuals will project guilt and depression to some evil "personality" that possesses one. These are alternative reactions to depression and are influenced by differences in education and social class.

Sick role of depressed individuals varies between cultures. For example, the "lost soul" belief in South America may also give cultural support to the depressed person in

Possible Relationships of Sociocultural Variables to Depression

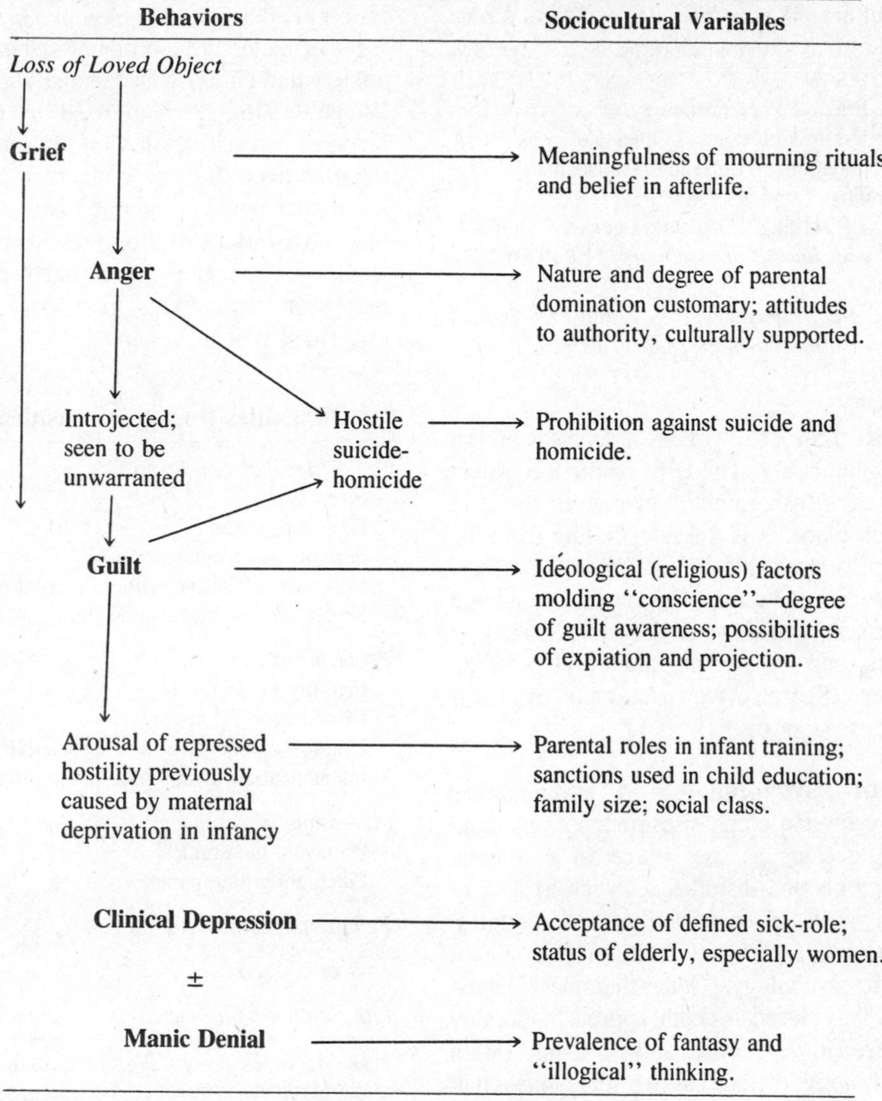

Adapted from P.M. Yap, "Phenomenology of Affective Disorder in Chinese and Other Cultures," CIA Foundation Symposium/Transcultural Psychiatry (London, 1965), p. 98.

the condition called Susto, which does not call for medical attention. Illiterate groups, including the lower classes in advanced cultures, tend to define the sick role in physical terms and visit doctors with physical problems instead of psychological ones.

Child training influences how depression, anxieties, and fears are expressed in later life Guilt feelings may be influenced by parental severity in child training. Withholding of love and affection may increase self-aggression, and aggression seems to turn inward more readily when the mother rather than the father gives punishment. Variables in societies include type of parental dominance, use of verbal, love-oriented techniques or of physical punishment, the size of the family, number of siblings, presence of mother surrogates, and finally, social class or culture pattern. (See also FOLK HEALING; GREECE, ANXIETY DISORDERS IN; INDIA, PHOBIAS IN.)

Yap, P.M., "Phenomenology of Affective Disorders in Chinese and Other Cultures," CIA Foundation Symposium/Transcultural Psychiatry, London, 1965.

Teja, J.S. et al., "Depression across Cultures," *British Journal of Psychiatry,* 119(1970):253–260.

Neki, J.S., "Psychiatry in South-East Asia." *British Journal of Psychiatry,* 123(1973):257–269.

depth, fear of Fear of depths is known as bathophobia. The term commonly refers to fear of losing control of oneself while in a high place. It is a fear of falling from the height and of thus being killed. The fear, common among many people, is considered excessive when the anxiety is intense and lasting and leads to measures to avoid high places. (See also FALLING, FEAR OF; HIGH PLACES, FEAR OF.)

depth psychology A psychological approach that emphasises unconscious mental processes as the source of emotional symptoms and disturbances such as ANXIETIES, PHOBIAS, personality, and attitudes. Freudian psychoanalysis is an example of depth psychology. Other therapies historically have used a depth approach, notably Adler, Horney, Jung, and Sullivan. Depth psychology includes other techniques that explore the unconscious, such as hypnoanalysis, psychodrama, and narcosynthesis. (See also PSYCHODRAMA.)

dermatopathophobia Also known as dermatosiophobia. (See also SKIN DISEASE, FEAR OF.)

dermatophobia See SKIN LESION, FEAR OF.

desensitization (systematic desensitization) Desensitization, or systematic desensitization, is a behavioral therapy procedure that is highly effective in the treatment of excessive emotional states such as anxiety and anger. It originated with Joseph Wolpe (1915–), who used *in vivo* and imaginal desensitization with his patients and reported over 80 percent recovery rates in a variety of anxiety, phobic, and emotional reactions. Desensitization presents particular challenges to patients (see chart). (See also BEHAVIOR THERAPY; SYSTEMATIC DESENSITIZATION; WOLPE, JOSEPH.)

Difficulties During Desensitization

Difficulties during relaxation:
- Sleepiness
- Poor concentration
- Fear of losing control
- Muscular relaxation without mental relaxation
- Severe anxiety and depression

Problems of imagery:
- Inability to obtain images
- Dissociation of anxiety
- Dilution of image to more protective setting
- Intensification of image to panic proportions

Misleading hierarchies:
- Irrelevant hierarchies
- Fluctuating hierarchies

Relapse of desensitized phobias

Lack of cooperation

Life situation influences outside treatment

Isaac Marks, *Fears and Phobias* (London: Heinemann Medical, 1969), p. 187.

desipramine A TRICYCLIC ANTIDEPRESSANT sometimes used to treat HEADACHES due to nonorganic causes. (See also ANTIDEPRESSANTS.)

Desyrel See TRAZODONE.

developmental stages There is some question and debate in scientific circles about whether humans proceed through regular, predictable stages of development. At the physical level, it appears that development occurs in phases or stages, but questions persist about the psychological level.

The two most dominant stage theories are those of Sigmund Freud and Eric Erickson. Freud elaborated stages of "intrapsychic" development to sexual (libidinal) energies and to some extent for aggressive (Thanatos) energies. Freud's psychosexual stages, however, became the best-known developmental phases. Erickson, a student of Freud concentrated on the interpersonal and emotional effects of what he called psychosocial stages of development. neither Freud nor Erickson emphasized anxiety, but they did conclude that it could develop as a result of frustration at any of the stages.

The following chart compares Freud's psychosexual and Erickson's psychosocial stages through the life cycle. (See also FREUD, SIGMUND; PHALLIC STAGE; REGRESSION.)

devil, fear of the Fear of the devil, also known as the supreme evil spirit, has had both a disciplinary and an explanatory role in the Judeo-Christian tradition. In early Judaism, Satan was viewed as God's right-hand man. He was an obstructor, a tempter, and a negative force, but not an antagonist to God's power. Satan began to acquire a more intensely evil character as Judaism came into contact with the Persian belief in Zoroastrianism, a set of religious belief that separated the otherworldly powers into forces of good and evil.

Christian belief made Satan into the angel who led a heavenly revolt and, because of his pride and jealousy, was ejected from heaven and fell into the underworld. The medieval church developed the threatening, grotesque image of the devil with horns and a tail, along with terrifying stories of his ability to tempt the weak and sinful. The

Developmental Stages

Phase	Freud	Erickson
Birth to first year	*Oral stage.* Oral activity is source of psychic energy. Infant needs nurturing physically and psychically or deprivation develops with fixations that affect ability to give and receive love, as well as greediness and dependency.	*Infancy: Trust versus mistrust.* The mode of interaction is incorporative (to get and to take). Insufficiency of meeting physical and emotional needs results in sense of mistrust of others, insecurity, and anxiety.
Age 1–3 years	*Anal stage.* Anal activity is source of psychic energy. Retention and elimination become prototypes for power, independence, and self-control. Fixation can lead to stinginess and obstinacy or disorderliness, impulsivity, and cruelty. Obsessive–compulsive characteristics result from frustration in this stage.	*Early childhood: Autonomy versus shame and doubt.* Child needs to explore, inquire, and test self. Holding on and letting go are modes of activity. Under- or over-gratification results in a sense of self-doubt, inhibition, shame, and feelings of inadequacy to control events. Adequate resolution results in internal locus of control.
Age 3–6 years	*Phallic stage.* Basic conflict develops around incestuous feelings toward opposite-sex parent (Oedipal complex for males and Electra for females). Resolution produces superego and sense of sexuality. Many anxiety reactions stem from inadequate resolution of this stage.	*Preschool age: Initiative versus guilt.* This is an intrusive mode in which self-initiated exploration and discovery are important. Over- and under-gratification stifle initiative and lead to guilt, poor self-concept, and lack of self-worth. Confidence in oneself results from adequate experience.

Developmental Stages (*Continued*)

Phase	Freud	Erickson
Age 6–12 years	*Latency stage.* Sexual energies diminish, resolution of previous stages is possible, efforts are focused outward, and socialization begins.	*School age: Industry versus inferiority.* Understanding of outer world expands, sex role identity develops, achievement and attainment of goals and sense of adequacy develop.
Age 12–18 years	*Genital stage.* Extends from puberty to old age. Ideally, sexual energy should stem from genital sources but may be restricted by previous fixations. Sublimation into socially acceptable activities occurs, as well as sexual role identification.	*Adolescence: Identity versus role confusion.* Self-identity, life goals, and direction develop, as well as breaking of dependency (leaving home) and accepting personal responsibility. Previous frustration or difficulties at this age can lead to an *identity crisis* (an unclear sense of self).
Age 18–35 years	Genital stage continues	*Young adulthood: Intimacy versus isolation.* The task here is to develop intimacy, connection, and commitment to others in the capacity for both love and work. Inadequate resolution results in aloneness, separateness, and denial of need for closeness.
Age 35–60	Genital stage continues	*Middle age: Generativity versus stagnation.* This is a time to focus on the next generation, to adjust to differences between one's dreams and actual achievements, and to achieve a sense of productivity. Inadequate resolution leads to self-indulgence and futurelessness.
Age 60+	Genital stage continues	*Later Life: Integrity versus despair.* Ego integrity is the ability to look back without regret and to feel personally worthwhile and whole. Disappointment and feelings of futility result from inadequate resolution.

Reformation strengthened the image of Satan's evil with its emphasis on the sinfulness of the physical world. Satan's existence became a way of rationalizing the belief in a loving God with the presence of illness, misfortune, and lust in the world. Witches were thought to have gained their power from a pact with the devil. It is believed that many mentally and emotionally disturbed people were identified as witches and burned at the stake. The idea that a man could obtain worldly success by selling his soul to the devil became somewhat widespread. However, at the same time, the devil was thought to be a punisher of evildoers. So great was the fear of the devil that the name Lucifer or ''light bearer'' was applied to him in the belief that using his real name would offend or summon him. (See also DEMONS, FEAR OF; WITCHES AND WITCHCRAFT, FEAR OF.)

Brasch, R. *Strange Customs* (New York; David McKay Co., 1976).

Thomas, Keith, *Religion and the Decline of Magic* (New York: Charles Scribner's Sons, 1971).

dexamethasone suppression test (DST) This test is currently used as a diagnostic tool for identifying depression. The DST measures the degree to which the neurochemicals ACTH and cortisol are suppressed in the brain by the introduction of the synthetic drug dexamethasone. In normal people, dexamethasone suppresses these neurochemicals. Some studies show that depressed people fail to show such suppression. However, the validity of these studies is controversial. Also, dexamethasone suppression in panic-disorder patients has not been shown to be significantly different from than in normal people. (See also ANTIDEPRESSANTS; DEPRESSION; DIAGNOSIS; DRUGS.)

dextrophobia Fear of objects at the right side of the body or fear of the right side.

diabetes, fear of Fear of diabetes is known as diabetophobia. Diabetes is a metabolic disease that develops due to the body's lack of ability to manufacture insulin or to make appropriate use of the foods one eats. Diabetes is not contagious, and there is no need to fear contact with anyone who has diabetes. Normally the food one eats is converted into glucose, which cells use as a source of energy. Glucose causes an increase in blood glucose level, which in turn signals release of the hormone insulin from islet cells of the pancreas, a gland in the abdomen. Insulin regulates the level of glucose in the blood and assists in utilizing and storing glucose in the body. Without enough insulin, glucose is not used by cells and thus builds up in the blood. Diabetes can be controlled but can also be life-threatening. Among the possible consequences of uncontrolled diabetes are poor circulation, high blood pressure, hardening of the arteries, and nerve damage. Having diabetes puts one at greater risk of having heart or kidney disease. Anxiety is also common with diabetics due to bodily reactions and glucose changes.

Kahn, Ada P., *Diabetes* (Chicago: Contemporary Books, 1983).

diabetophobia Fear of DIABETES, either of having the disease oneself or of the disease in someone else.

diagnosis The art of distinguishing one disorder from another, and determining the nature or cause of the disorder. There are many types of diagnoses, such as biological diagnosis, determined by tests performed; clinical diagnosis, based on symptoms shown; and differential diagnosis, determining which one of two or more diseases or conditions an individual suffers from, by systematically comparing and contrasting their symptoms. The word diagnosis come from the Greek words "dia," meaning "through," and "gnosis," meaning knowledge. In cases of anxieties and phobias, diagnosis includes a period of study and evaluation of the individual, including problems, history, and environment, and the individual's own attempts at dealing with problems.

Various professionals have attempted to differentiate FEAR, PHOBIA, and ANXIETY and describe their unique characteristics for diagnostic purposes, although they often differ in their diagnoses because of the intertwining and close appearance of many symptoms. Phobias were first given a separate diagnostic label in the International Classification of Diseases in 1947 and by the American Psychiatric Association in 1952. A standardization of diagnostic criteria is found in the American Psychiatric Association's book, *Diagnostic and Statistical Manual III-R* (Washington, DC: American Psychiatric

Press, 1987). Criteria for diagnosis continue to evolve.

Diagnostic procedures for anxieties and phobias depend largely on the type of therapy that will be used and the style of the therapist. For example, behavior therapists might use one or more of a series of tests to measure level of fear before embarking on a course of treatment. A diagnostic label would not be a part of the behavior therapy. Diagnosis would be a process of discovering the exact eliciting stimuli and response to such stimuli.

In differentiating simple phobias from other disorders, therapists will consider the presence or absence of other symptoms. For example, if the individual has DEPRESSION or OBSESSIVE–COMPULSIVE symptoms, fear may be a symptom of the major disorder. Sometimes fears will precede depressive illness. The diagnosis of SIMPLE PHOBIAS is based on two general findings, PHOBIC ANXIETY and/or AVOIDANCE and exclusion of other definable diagnostic entities. Diagnosing AGORAPHOBIA is more complex. The agoraphobic syndrome is characterized by clinical and psychophysiological similarities to the anxiety neuroses. A clinical difference is that there is a great deal of avoidance behavior in agoraphobia and may be fairly little in anxiety neurosis. There are also personality factors used to diagnose agoraphobia, such as emotional suppression. There is a fine line in diagnosing depression in agoraphobia. This is because agoraphobia restricts an individual's activities, making the person fairly helpless and discouraged. These factors may appear to be depression, but most agoraphobic individuals lack characteristics of an endogenous (self-induced) depression. The individual has not lost his or her interest (which is characteristic of endogenous depression) but is frustrated by not being able to do all the things he or she would like to do. Also, the agoraphobic may be active and productive at home or in his or her restricted environment or when accompanied.

Various researchers during the second half of the 20th century have differed on diagnosing anxieties, fears, phobias, and obsessive–compulsive disorders because of the intertwining and close appearance of many symptoms. A standardization of diagnostic criteria is found in the American Psychiatric Association's book, *Diagnostic and Statistical Manual of Mental Disorders.*

Diagnosis, as we commonly use it for psychiatric purposes, is based on the concept of "topology"—that is, behaviors that are similar in form are categorized together. For example, "depression" is a topological term involving numerous behaviors that are similar in their form (lack of sleep, eating difficulty, etc.) and are symptoms of depression. Likewise, "anxiety" has many topological or symptom categories. The "topological model" or "medical model" is based on the view that these various symptoms derive from a common underlying source (such as childhood trauma, intrapyschic conflict, incongruities, repression, etc.). The underlying cause produces symptoms, which, in turn, can be grouped together or clustered into syndromes, disease entities, or diagnostic categories. Where there is great speculation regarding possible underlying causes, no such causes have been found after almost a century of massive research efforts.

The use of this model has been questioned by many scientists—behavioral therapists as well as psychologists and psychiatrists who have used it for diagnosis. Questions of reliability of diagnosis (which is quite low on some subgroups) and validity have been raised for decades. Others argue that the basic assumptions of this model are flawed, and that a better model—such as the learning-theory approaches of the behavioral scientists—should be developed. Since models are only approximations to reality, they are and should be replaced by more powerful models that afford better prediction and control.

One clear and present danger in the use of these diagnostic categories is that individual differences in etiology and manifestation of psychopathology are ignored or minimized. Yet it is the variations that require a response if treatment is to be effective and the individual is to gain from the experience with the disorder.

These are important issues and should be noted in talking about the diagnostic system. (See also CLASSIFICATION OF ANXIETIES; CLASSIFICATION OF PHOBIAS; DIAGNOSTIC AND STATISTICAL MANUAL.)

Marks, Isaac. *Fears and Phobias* (New York: Academic Press, 1969).

Mavissaklian, M. and D. Barlow, *Phobia: Psychological and Pharmacological Treatment* (New York: Guilford Press, 1981).

Morris, R.J. and T.R. Kratochiwill, *Treating Children's Fears and Phobias* (New York: Pergamon Press, 1983).

Diagnostic and Statistical Manual of Mental Disorders—DSM-III-R—is a handbook for the classification of mental disorders published by the American Psychiatric Association in 1987. The book is useful to physicians, psychiatrists, psychologists, and other individuals who wish to base a diagnosis of mental disorders, including anxieties and phobias, on standardized criteria. It is also helpful for statistical purposes and for insurance reimbursement.

The first edition (DSM-I), published in 1952, was the first official manual of mental disorders to contain a glossary of descriptions of diagnostic categories. Developed by consensus among psychiatrists, this first edition was heavily psychoanalytically based. The use of the term "reaction" throughout the classification reflected the influence of Adolf Meyer's psychobiologic view that mental disorders represented reactions of the personality to psychological, social, and biological factors.

In the second edition (DSM-II), published in 1968, classification of mental disorders was based on the eighth revision of the World Health Organization's International Classification of Diseases, for which representatives of the American Psychiatric Association provided consultation. The DSM-II classification did not use the term "reaction" and, with the exception of the term "neurosis," used diagnostic terms that, by and large, did not imply a particular theoretical framework for understanding the nonorganic mental disorders. The third edition (DSM-III) was issued in 1980. Since then a DSM III-R (revised) was published in 1987 and includes more specific criteria for diagnosing anxiety disorders.

diagnostic criteria Because anxieties, fears, and phobias are highly individual matters, unique to each individual, precise diagnosis of a person's condition is likely to be less than specific. However, the American Psychiatric Association, in its *Diagnostic and Statistical Manual of Mental Disorders* (DSM-III-R) has provided specific diagnostic criteria as guides for making diagnoses, in the belief that such criteria enhance diagnostic reliability. The APA emphasizes, however, that for most of the categories, diagnostic criteria are based on clinical judgment and have not yet been fully validated by data about such important correlates as clinical course, outcome, family history, and treatment response.

Diagnostic criteria (reproduced from the DSM-III-R) follow for the following disorders:

SIMPLE PHOBIA
SOCIAL PHOBIA
GENERALIZED ANXIETY DISORDER
PANIC DISORDER
panic disorder with agoraphobia
panic disorder without agoraphobia
OBSESSIVE–COMPULSIVE DISORDER
POSTTRAUMATIC STRESS DISORDER

Simple Phobia

A. A persistent fear of a circumscribed stimulus (object or situation) other than fear of having a panic attack (as

in panic disorder) or of humiliation or embarrassment in certain social situations (as in social phobia).
Note: Do not include fears that are part of panic disorder with agoraphobia or agoraphobia without history of panic disorder.

B. During some phase of the disturbance, exposure to the specific phobic stimulus (or stimuli) almost invariably provokes an immediate anxiety response.
C. The object or situation is avoided, or endured with intense anxiety.
D. The fear or the avoidant behavior significantly interferes with the person's normal routine or with usual social activities or relationships with others, or there is marked distress about having the fear.
E. The person recognizes that his or her fear is excessive or unreasonable.
F. The phobic stimulus is unrelated to the content of the obsessions of obsessive–compulsive disorder or the trauma of posttraumatic stress disorder.

Social Phobia

A. A persistent fear of one or more situations (the social phobic situations) in which the person is exposed to possible scrutiny by others and fears that he or she may do something or act in a way that will be humiliating or embarrassing. Examples include: being unable to continue talking while speaking in public, choking on food when eating in front of others, being unable to urinate in a public lavatory, hand-trembling when writing in the presence of others, and saying foolish things or not being able to answer questions in social situations.
B. If an Axis III or another Axis I disorder is present, the fear in A is unrelated to it; e.g., the fear is not of having a panic attack (panic disorder), stuttering (stuttering), trembling (Parkinson's disease), or exhibiting abnormal eating behavior (anorexia nervosa or bulimia nervosa).
C. During some phase of the disturbance, exposure to the specific phobic stimulus (or stimuli) almost invariably provokes an immediate anxiety response.
D. The phobic situation(s) is avoided or is endured with intense anxiety.
E. The avoidant behavior interferes with occupational functioning or with usual social activities or relationships with others, or there is marked distress about having the fear.
F. The person recognizes that his or her fear is excessive or unreasonable.
G. If the person is under eighteen, the disturbance does not meet the criteria for avoidant disorder of childhood or adolescence.

Specify generalized type if the phobic situation includes most social situations, and also consider the additional diagnosis of avoidant personality disorder.

Generalized Anxiety Disorder

At least six of the following eighteen symptoms are often present when anxious (do not include symptoms present only during panic attacks):

Motor tension

(1) trembling, twitching, or feeling shaky
(2) muscle tension, aches, or soreness
(3) restlessness
(4) easy fatigability

Autonomic hyperactivity

(5) shortness of breath or smothering sensations

(6) palpitations or accelerated heart rate (tachycardia)
(7) sweating, or cold, clammy hands
(8) dry mouth
(9) dizziness or lightheadedness
(10) nausea, diarrhea, or other abdominal distress
(11) flushes (hot flashes) or chills
(12) frequent urination
(13) trouble swallowing or "lump in throat"

Vigilance and scanning

(14) feeling keyed up or on edge
(15) exaggerated startle response
(16) difficulty concentrating or "mind going blank" because of anxiety
(17) trouble falling or staying asleep
(18) irritability

It cannot be established that an organic factor initiated and maintained the disturbance, e.g., hyperthyroidism, caffeine intoxication.

Panic Disorder

At least four of the following symptoms developed during at least one of the attacks:

(1) shortness of breath (dyspnea) or smothering sensation
(2) dizziness, unsteady feelings, or faintness
(3) palpitations or accelerated heart rate (tachycardia)
(4) trembling or shaking
(5) sweating
(6) choking
(7) nausea or abdominal distress
(8) depersonalization or derealization
(9) numbness or tingling sensations (paresthesias)
(10) flushes (hot flashes) or chills
(11) chest pain or discomfort
(12) fear of dying
(13) fear of going crazy or of doing something uncontrolled

Note: Attacks involving four or more symptoms are panic attacks; attacks involving fewer than four symptoms are limited-symptom attacks.

Panic Disorder with Agoraphobia

A. Meets the criteria for panic disorder.
B. Agoraphobia: Fear of being in places or situations from which escape might be difficult (or embarrassing) or in which help might not be available in the event of a panic attack. (Include cases in which persistent avoidance behavior originated during an active phase of panic disorder, even if the person does not attribute the avoidance behavior to fear of having a panic attack.) As a result of this fear, the person either restricts travel or needs a companion when away from home, or else endures agoraphobic situations despite intense anxiety. Common agoraphobic situations include being outside the home alone, being in a crowd or standing in a line, being on a bridge, and traveling in a bus, train, or car.

Specify current severity of agoraphobic avoidance:

Mild: Some avoidance (or endurance with distress), but relatively normal life-style, e.g., travels unaccompanied when necessary, such as to work or to shop; otherwise avoids traveling alone.

Moderate: Avoidance results in constricted life-style, e.g., the person is able to leave the house alone, but not to go more than a few miles unaccompanied.

Severe: Avoidance results in being nearly or completely housebound or unable to leave the house unaccompanied.

In Partial Remission: No current agoraphobic avoidance, but some agoraphobic avoidance during the past six months.

In Full Remission: No current agoraphobic avoidance and none during the past six months.
Specify current severity of panic attacks:
Mild: During the past month, either all attacks have been limited-symptom attacks (i.e., fewer than four symptoms), or there has been no more than one panic attack.
Moderate: During the past month attacks have been intermediate between "mild" and "severe."
Severe: During the past month, there have been at least eight panic attacks.
In Partial Remission: The condition has been intermediate between "In Full Remission" and "Mild."
In Full Remission: During the past six months, there have been no panic or limited-symptom attacks

Panic Disorder without Agoraphobia

A. Meets the criteria for panic disorder.
B. Absence of agoraphobia, as defined above.
Specify current severity of panic attacks, as defined above

Obsessive-Compulsive Disorder

A. Either obsessions or compulsions.
Obsessions: (1), (2), (3), and (4):

(1) recurrent and persistent ideas, thoughts, impulses, or images that are experienced, at least initially, as intrusive and senseless, e.g., a parent's having repeated impulses to kill a loved child, a religious person's having recurrent blasphemous thoughts
(2) the person attempts to ignore or suppress such thoughts or impulses or to neutralize them with some other thought or action
(3) the person recognizes that the obsessions are the product of his or her own mind, not imposed from without (as in thought insertion)
(4) if another Axis I disorder is present, the content of the obsession is unrelated to it, e.g., the ideas, thoughts, impulses, or images are not about food in the presence of an eating disorder, about drugs in the presence of a psychoactive substance use disorder, or guilty thoughts in the presence of a major depression

Compulsions: (1), (2), and (3):

(1) repetitive, purposeful, and intentional behaviors that are performed in response to an obsession, or according to certain rules or in a stereotyped fashion
(2) the behavior is designed to neutralize or to prevent discomfort or some dreaded event or situation; however, either the activity is not connected in a realistic way with what it is designed to neutralize or prevent, or it is clearly excessive
(3) the person recognizes that his or her behavior is excessive or unreasonable (this may not be true for young children; it may no longer be true for people whose obsessions have evolved into overvalued ideas)

B. The obsessions or compulsions cause marked distress, are time-consuming (take more than an hour a day), or significantly interfere with the person's normal routine, occupational functioning, or usual social activities or relationships with others

Posttraumatic Stress Disorder

A The person has experienced an event that is outside the range of usual human experience and that would be markedly distressing to almost anyone, e.g., serious threat to one's life or physical integrity; serious threat or harm to one's children, spouse, or other close relatives and friends; sudden destruction of one's home or community; or seeing another person who has recently been, or is being, seriously injured or killed as the result of an accident or physical violence.

B. The traumatic event is persistently reexperienced in at least one of the following ways:

(1) recurrent and intrusive distressing recollections of the event (in young children, repetitive play in which themes or aspects of the trauma are expressed)
(2) recurrent distressing dreams of the event
(3) sudden acting or feeling as if the traumatic event were recurring (includes a sense of reliving the experience, illusions, hallucinations, and dissociative [flashback] episodes, even those that occur upon awakening or when intoxicated)
(4) intense psychological distress at exposure to events that symbolize or resemble an aspect of the traumatic event, including anniversaries of the trauma

C. Persistent avoidance of stimuli associated with the trauma or numbing of general responsiveness (not present before the trauma), as indicated by at least three of the following:

(1) efforts to avoid thoughts or feelings associated with the trauma
(2) efforts to avoid activities or situations that arouse recollections of the trauma
(3) inability to recall an important aspect of the trauma (psychogenic amnesia)
(4) markedly diminished interest in significant activities (in young children, loss of recently acquired developmental skills such as toilet training or language skills)
(5) feeling of detachment or estrangement from others
(6) restricted range of affect, e.g., unable to have loving feelings
(7) sense of a foreshortened future, e.g., does not expect to have a career, marriage, or children, or a long life

D. Persistent symptoms of increased arousal (not present before the trauma), as indicated by at least two of the following:

(1) difficulty falling or staying asleep
(2) irritability or outbursts of anger
(3) difficulty concentrating
(4) hypervigilance
(5) exaggerated startle response
(6) physiologic reactivity upon exposure to events that symbolize or resemble an aspect of the traumatic event (e.g., a woman who was raped in an elevator breaks out in a sweat when entering any elevator)

E. Duration of the disturbance (symptoms in B, C, and D) of at least one month.

Specify delayed onset if the onset of symptoms was at least six months after the trauma.

(See also AGORAPHOBIA; GENERALIZED ANXIETY DISORDER; OBSESSIVE–COMPULSIVE DISORDER; PANIC; PHOBIA; POSTTRAUMATIC STRESS DISORDER.)

(The preceding charts were adapted with permission from the American Psychiatric Association, Washington, D.C.)

diarrhea (as a symptom of anxiety) Diarrhea—frequent, loose, watery stools—

is one of many gastrointestinal symptoms anxious individuals experience due to arousal of the AUTONOMIC NERVOUS SYSTEM. When facing or thinking about a feared situation, some may experience stomachaches, diarrhea, weakness, and feeling faint. Those who have test anxiety may experience episodes of diarrhea before taking a test in school or at work. Some who have performance anxiety may experience diarrhea before a performance. Social phobics may have episodes of diarrhea when anticipating a type of social occasion or situation that they fear. Diarrhea induced by anxiety, sometimes referred to as functional diarrhea, can be treated with therapy known as fantasy desensitization, as well as antianxiolytics and medications that act on the gastrointestinal system. (See also ANXIETIES; ANXIOLYTICS; BEHAVIOR THERAPY; DEFECATION, FEAR OF; DESENSITIZATION; GASTROINTESTINAL COMPLAINTS; IRRITABLE BOWEL SYNDROME; NAUSEA; VOMITING.)

diazepam An antianxiety drug. Diazepam, marketed under the trade name Valium, has been used more extensively than other of the benzodiazepines, the class of drugs to which it belongs. Pregnant women should not take diazepam because diazepam crosses the placenta during labor. Use of almost any dose may result in psychological and physical dependence. Withdrawal effects have been pronounced and, at times, dramatic (seizures, hallucinations, etc.), and they can occur over a prolonged period of time (often up to two years). (See also ANTIDEPRESSANTS; BENZODIAZEPINES.)

dibenzepin An antidepressant drug. (See also ANTIDEPRESSANTS; ANTIDEPRESSANTS, NEW; DEPRESSION.)

didaskaleinophobia SCHOOL PHOBIA, or fear of going to school.

dikephobia Fear of JUSTICE is known as dikephobia.

dining (or dinner) conversation, fear of Fear of conversation while dining is known as deipnophobia. Individuals who have this fear usually eat their meal in silence and request silence from their companions at the table. Such individuals may suffer from any of a number of related fears, such as choking, talking with their mouths full, looking ridiculous while they are opening their mouths to talk, saying something ridiculous, or being criticized. (See also CHOKING, FEAR OF; CRITICISM, FEAR OF; LOOKING RIDICULOUS, FEAR OF; SOCIAL PHOBIA.)

dinophobia Fear of DIZZINESS or WHIRLPOOLS.

diplopiaphobia Fear of DOUBLE VISION.

dipsophobia Fear of DRINKING: this usually relates to alcoholic beverages. (See also ALCOHOLISM, FEAR OF.)

directive therapy A term used in psychotherapy to denote activity on the part of the therapist in guiding the phobic or anxious individual. Directive therapy is differentiated from nondirective therapy, such as PSYCHOANALYSIS. (See also BEHAVIOR THERAPY.)

dirt, fear of Fear of dirt is known as mysophobia or rhypophobia. Many individuals who fear dirt fear CONTAMINATION or INFECTION. Some obsessive–compulsives who wash their hands frequently fear dirt. (See also GERMS, FEAR OF; ILLNESS, FEAR OF.)

dirty, fear of being Fear of being dirty is known as automysophobia. Frequent hand-washing is a symptom of this phobia. (See also CONTAMINATION, FEAR OF; DIRT, FEAR OF; GERMS, FEAR OF.)

disease, fear of Fear of disease (or illness) is known as nosemaphobia or nosophobia. (See also CANCER, FEAR OF; HYPOCHONDRIASIS; ILLNESS PHOBIA.)

disease, fear of definite Fear of a definite disease is known as monopathophobia. (See also HYPOCHONDRIASIS; ILLNESS PHOBIA.)

dishabillophobia Fear of undressing in front of someone. (See also UNDRESSING IN FRONT OF SOMEONE, FEAR OF.)

disorientation A state of mental confusion with respect to time, place, objects, or identity of self or other persons. Disorientation sometimes occurs in ANXIETY and AGORAPHOBIA.

disorder, fear of Fear of disorder or disarray is known as ataxiophobia. Some obsessive–compulsives have this phobia. (See also OBSESSIVE–COMPULSIVE DISORDER.)

displacement An unconscious DEFENSE MECHANISM by which one transfers an unacceptable idea or impulse to an acceptable one. For example, a man who fears his own hostile impulses might transfer that fear to knives, guns, or other objects that might be used a weapons. Displacement in psychoanalytic terms is the mechanism by which unconscious fears are transferred to neutral or nonthreatening (but often symbolic) objects, people, or situations.

dissociation A mental process in which thoughts and attitudes unconsciously lose their normal relationships to each other or to the rest of the personality and split off to function somewhat independently. Psychoanalytically, this is a defense mechanism that prevents conflict between logically incompatible thoughts, feelings, and attitudes. It is common for phobic individuals to have the experience of dissociation during periods of intense anxiety and panic. A chronic state of dissociation is usually regarded as pathological. Dissociative disorders are a group of disorders characterized by a sudden, temporary alteration in normal functions of consciousness. These include multiple or "split" personality, depersonalization disorder, certain delusional symptoms, somnambulism (sleepwalking), and hysterical amnesia. (see also DEPERSONALIZATION; NEUROSIS; SCHIZOPHRENIA.)

diving, fear of Fear of diving may be related to a fear of WATER, fear of DEPTHS, fear of swimming, or fear of DROWNING. It may also be related to a fear of the UNKNOWN because often the diver does not know the depth of the water he may enter. Fear of diving for deep-sea divers is related to a fear of getting the "bends," a physical condition that occurs when a diver surfaces too quickly.

The "deep dive" in literature (e.g., the dive taken by the whale in *Moby Dick*) is a universal symbol of moving into the unconscious, dark side, or mysterious aspects of one's life that are frightening because unknown. (See also BENDS, FEAR OF.)

dizziness, fear of Fear of dizziness is known as dinophobia. Many who experience dizziness as a result of phobias fear the dizziness as much as the frightening event that brings it on. Dizziness may also be part of a combination of anxiety-induced gastrointestinal effects, which include nausea and possibly diarrhea and vomiting. It is also a prime symptom of HYPERVENTILATION.

Dizziness as a symptom of anxiety has been treated with behavior therapy and, at times, appropriate medication. Dizziness may be related to a disturbance of the inner ear; therapy may include diagnosis and treatment by an otolaryngologist (eye, ear, nose, and throat specialist). (See also GASTROINTESTINAL COMPLAINTS; MOTION, FEAR OF; NAUSEA.)

doctors, fear of Fear of doctors is known as iatrophobia. Some people who have blood-injury phobias fear doctors because they fear that the doctor may give them a shot or take a sample of their blood. Some who fear undressing in front of others may fear doctors because they are often required to disrobe and cover themselves only with a sheet during a physical examination. Some become so anxious just by being in the doctor's office that their blood pressure increases, a phenomenon known as "white coat" hypertension. Some fear doctors because they associate doctors with illness or injury and with authority figures. Some fear getting germs or a disease from others in the waiting room. Many individuals who fear doctors and doctors' offices also fear hospitals.

Benjamin Rush (1745–1813), American physician and author, commented on doctor phobia: "This distemper is often complicated with other diseases. It arises, in some instances, from the dread of taking physic, or of submitting to the remedies of bleeding and blistering. In some instances I have known it occasioned by a desire of sick people feel of deceiving themselves, by being kept in ignorance of the danger of their disorders. It might be supposed that, 'the dread of a long bill' was one cause of the Doctor Phobia; but this excites terror in the minds of but few people: for who ever thinks of paying a doctor, while he can use his money to advantage in another way! It is remarkable this Doctor Phobia always goes off as soon as a patient is sensible of his danger. The doctor, then, becomes an object of respect and attachment, instead of horror." (See also HOSPITALS, FEAR OF; WHITE COAT HYPERTENSION.)

Runes, D.D. (ed.), *The Selected Writings of Benjamin Rush* (New York: The Philosophical Library, 1947).

dogs, fear of Fear of dogs is known as cynophobia. Many people are afraid of dogs because of the animal's jackal and wolf ancestry, because of its tendencies to be noisy, destructive, and dirty, and because of childhood experiences of being bitten or fearing being bitten that stay with them lifelong. The bark of a dog is frightening to many people, although reassuring to the master who uses the dog, with his protective loyalty, as a burglar alarm. Because of the dog's potential ferocity, combined with the ability to form rapport with humans, dogs are used extensively in police work, instilling fear in all targets of the hunt.

Society has long had a somewhat ambivalent attitude toward dogs, seeing them as both fearsome, unpleasant animals and friends and protectors. Some Biblical references reinforce these ideas. Passages in the Old Testament reflect a feeling that the dog is unclean, sinful, and stupid, and Christian tradition sometimes associates dogs with heresy and paganism. On the other hand, medieval Christian art depicts dogs as symbols of watchfulness and fidelity. Dogs are associated with several of the saints. (See also ANIMALS, FEAR OF.)

Beck, Alan and Aaron Katcher, *Between Pets and People* (New York: G.P. Putnam, 1983).

Jobes, Gertrude, *Dictionary of Mythology, Folklore and Symbols* (New York: Scarecrow Press, 1961).

dogs as anxiety therapy Recent research has reinforced what many people have known for thousands of years: that dogs and other pets can help reduce anxieties in humans and contribute to the human's improvement in physical and mental health. Studies in nursing homes with dogs as pets have indicated reductions in blood pressure and faster recoveries from illnesses when individuals care for or regularly observe the actions of a pet. Dogs provide comfort and stability, and the love they offer is unquestioning and unconditional, unlike close human relationships. Caring for a dog provides the owner with an opportunity for exercise and an object of affection that is totally dependent on and devoted to him. In many cases, the dog gives the owner a sense of self-worth and identity that might otherwise be missing from life. Also, the gluttonous, lustful, comic behavior of dogs is not only entertaining but also allows the inhibited human master to experience release and humor.

dolls, fear of Fear of dolls is known as pediophobia. The fixed, staring eyes of a doll frighten some people. This feeling may be related to a common fear of being stared at or a sense that the lifeless eyes of a doll resemble those of a corpse. Doll phobia frequently extends to fear of other lifeless models of the human figure, such as mannequins, wax figures, statues, and ventriloquists' dummies. Fear of dolls may also stem from certain magical practices and beliefs. A very ancient practice of voodoo and witchcraft involves trying to cause harm to an enemy by piercing or burning a doll made to resemble him or her. (See also VOODOO, FEAR OF.)

domatophobia Fear of being in a house. (See also HOUSE, FEAR OF.)

Domical See AMITRIPTYLINE.

doorknob phobia Fear of touching a doorknob. A doorknob may produce an avoidance reaction because the individual may believe that it is dirty, or that it has germs on it. Doorknob fear may be a fear of contamination. Also, an individual may fear something that may be on the other side of the door, such as a crowd, darkness, a feared object, etc. From the psychoanalytic point of view, the individual who avoids touching doorknobs is protecting himself against an anal-erotic wish to be dirty or to soil. In magic, the characteristics of an object are communicated by touching it. (See also ANAL STAGE; CONTAMINATION, FEAR OF; DEVELOPMENTAL STAGES; DIRT, FEAR OF; FREUD, SIGMUND.)

Campbell, Robert J., *Psychiatric Dictionary* (New York: Oxford University Press, 1981).

dopamine A precursor of the neurotransmitter NOREPINEPHRINE. The role of dopamine in producing anxiety has been studied less than other NEUROTRANSMITTERS. However, some research indicates some role for dopamine in the cause of anxiety.

doraphobia Fear of the SKIN OF ANIMALS.

dothiepin An antidepressant drug. (See also ANTIDEPRESSANTS; ANTIDEPRESSANTS, NEW; DEPRESSION.)

double-bind theory A theory proposed by Gregory Bateson (1904–1980), a British-American anthropologist and philosopher, to explain causes of anxieties, phobias, and schizophrenia. A double bind is a breakdown in communications—for example, a situation in which a child receives contradictory messages from one or both parents and is therefore torn between conflicting feelings and demands. According to Bateson, there are at least two levels of communication present in every message. One of these is the content level, and the other is the intuitive feeling component that is nonverbal. In healthy dialogue, these levels are compatible, whereas in unhealthy dialogue involving a double bind they are inconsistent and contradictory. (See also BATESON, GREGORY; NEUROSIS.)

double-blind A research term used in some studies of ANXIETIES and PHOBIAS. A double-blind study is one in which a number of treatments, usually one or more drugs and/or a placebo, are compared in such a way that neither the individual treated nor the persons directly involved in planning the treatment know which preparation is being administered. An example of a double-blind study is one in which depressed, phobic individuals with many common characteristics are divided into two groups; one group is treated with an antidepressant drug that has known effects and the other group is treated with a newer, experimental drug. Many pharmaceutical products for anxieties and DEPRESSION, as well as many other medical conditions, are evaluated in double-blind studies. While the double-blind is a minimum condition for drug studies, it is often insufficient in that treatment groups may show an obvious drug reaction whereas control (placebo) groups show no behavior.

double vision, fear of Fear of double vision is known as diplopiaphobia. The fear may be founded on a feeling of losing control of one's environment. Double vision may be due to a muscle imbalance or to paralysis of certain eye muscles as a result of inflammation, hemorrhage, or infection. Double vision can be demonstrated by holding two objects straight in front of the eyes, one behind the other. Focusing on the more distant object makes the near object appear double; focusing on the near object makes the more distant object appear double. Double vision can usually be overcome with eye exercises, appropriate eyeglasses, or, in severe cases, muscle surgery.

Unusual fears such as this are sometimes also delusional manifestations of underlying psychosis. (See also EYES, FEAR OF; PSYCHOSIS.)

Andelman, Samuel, *The New Home Medical Encyclopedia* (New York: Quadrangle, 1973).

doxepin A TRICYCLIC ANTIDEPRESSANT that also has a potent antianxiety effect. Safe and well-tolerated, even in elderly patients, doxepin relieves symptoms of anxiety, depression, tension, insomnia, guilt, fear, apprehension, worry, and lack of energy. (See also ANTIANXIETY DRUGS; ANTIDEPRESSANTS.)

drafts or draughts, fear of Fear of drafts is known as aerophobia or anemophobia. Individuals who fear drafts may fear movement, or movement of air, or wind. They may also fear illness, because many people believe that they can get a cold or influenza from sitting in a draft. (See also AIR, FEAR OF; ILLNESS PHOBIA; WIND, FEAR OF.)

dreams, fear of Fear of dreams is known as oneirophobia. Dreaming is a type of thinking that goes on when one is asleep. Dreams are characterized by vivid sensory images, mostly visual, but also involving hearing, motion, touch, and even taste or smell. Since a dreamer accepts a dream as real while he is experiencing it, dreams are a form of hallucination. People are afraid of particular dreams or of nightmares or a sense of losing willful control at night. Fear of dreams can also be connected with nightmare experiences or fright upon awakening.

Psychiatrists believe that dreams serve as a safety valve, permitting partial discharge of repressed, instinctual drive energies, especially the unconscious wishes from the infantile past. Further, Freud believed that dreams preserve sleep through many mechanisms, including displacement and condensation, inhibiting and suppressing disturbing emotions.

Pavor nocturnus are anxiety dreams in the form of nightmares; they are common in young children. For adults and children, phobias may emerge during dreams.

Freud designated a number of dreams that almost everyone has dreamed, and they seem to have the same meaning for everyone. Included in this category are embarrassing dreams of being naked, dreams of the death of loved ones, dreams of flying and falling, examination dreams, dreams of missing a train, tooth extraction, and water and fire dreams.

Dreams are an important part of one's psychic and physical life. Psychically or psychologically, they represent conscious and unconscious preoccupations, conflicts, unresolved fears, and events that either have happened or are to happen. They are symbolic monitors of one's psychological life and therefore can provide important information and direction to those who ponder their symbolic relevance.

Physically, the dream occurs during times of rapid eye movement (REM). Each person goes through three or four periods of REM or dream sleep each night. Depression, stress, drug use, and sleep deprivation or disruption often interfere with REM time or occurrence, and REM time has to be recovered at another sleep period. Important biochemical changes occur at REM and non-REM times that are necessary to normal daytime functioning. (See also CONDENSATION; DISPLACEMENT; DREAM SYMBOLS; FREUD, SIGMUND; INCUBUS; PAVOR NOCTURNUS; POSTTRAUMATIC STRESS DISORDER; SUCCUBUS; WET DREAMS.)

dream symbols In psychoanalytic terms, images in dreams are symbols of unconscious things, objects, or functions. For example, a snake appearing in a dream is conscious, but its meaning is unconscious. Dream symbols may refer to the male and female sexual organs, to birth, death, family members, and primary body functions. Water often symbolizes birth, the mind, and the unconscious. Through interpretations of symbols, a therapist may assist an individual in understanding the causes of his or her phobias and anxieties. Carl Jung pointed out that many dream symbols have universal or archetypal meaning. He pointed out that all the mental energy and interest devoted today by western man to science and technology were, by ancient man, once dedicated to the study of mythology. (See also DREAMS; PSYCHOANALYSIS; SYMBOLISM.)

drink, fear of Fear of taking a drink, or drinking, is known as potophobia. The individual fears swallowing liquid and possibly choking and losing the ability to breathe. (See also CHOKING, FEAR OF; SWALLOWING, FEAR OF.)

drinking alcohol, fear of Fear of drinking alcohol is known as dipsophobia, dipsomanophobia, alcoholophobia, and potophobia. The fear is of ill effects and the body changes that are uncontrollable.

driving a car, fear of Many adults have anxieties while driving. Some individuals actually become phobic about driving and cannot get into the driver's seat without experiencing rapid heart rate, higher blood pressure, faster breathing, and sweating. Some individuals fear driving alone; some fear driving in the dark, on deserted roads, on open highways, or on crowded expressways. Some fear merging into fast-moving freeway or expressway lanes. Fears related to driving a car can be overcome with appropriate behavior therapy. Fears of driving a car may be related to agoraphobia, particularly if they relate to traveling a distance from a safe place such as home. Fears of vehicles are known as amaxophobia or ochophobia.

The fear of driving can occur after an accident or with traumatic conditioning or as part of an agoraphobic syndrome. Fear of driving is prevalent in the United States but less common in countries that rely on other forms of transportation. For example, the fear of trains is more prevalent in England.

Fear of driving may be specific to freeways, busy surface streets, or any street (even quiet residential). In its most severe forms, the individual cannot even sit in an automobile without experiencing anxiety. (See also AUTOMOBILES, FEAR OF DRIVING.)

dromophobia Fear of crossing streets or wandering about is known as dromophobia. (See also STREETS, FEAR OF CROSSING.)

drowning, fear of Fear of drowning is a common fear of individuals who fear WATER. Some fear drowning so much that they will not enter a swimming pool or body of water. Some will not go out in boats. Even if life jackets are available to them, drowning phobics avoid situations in which they might become immersed in water. Some have a PANIC ATTACK when their head goes underwater or even if they get water in their nose or mouth. Fear of drowning is related to a fear of being out of control; most drowning phobics are not good swimmers and fear not being able to save themselves. However, some excellent swimmers have severe fears of drowning and will only swim when others are nearby or will swim only in shallow water. Some swimmers fear DIVING because they fear they will drown. Fear of drowning is a fear of DEATH. (See also LOSS OF CONTROL, FEAR OF.)

drug abuse Some individuals turn to drugs in the belief that they can better cope with their anxieties or depression by using drugs to change their moods and attitudes. Generally, drug abuse occurs when individuals self-prescribe; however, some individuals also misuse substances prescribed by physicians by taking too many doses, or taking them in combination with other medications. Because drugs used to relieve symptoms of anxiety and depression have strong effects on neurotransmitters in the brain, close monitoring by a physician is necessary. (See also DRUG DEPENDENCE.)

drug dependence Individuals who depend on drugs to help them cope with their anxieties, phobias, or depression may develop a dependence on drugs. Dependence refers to a craving or compulsion to continue using a drug because it gives a feeling of well-being and satisfaction. The term habituation is frequently used interchangeably with the term psychological dependence. An individual can be psychologically dependent on a drug and not physically dependent; the reverse is also true. Dependence can occur after a period of prolonged use of a drug, and the characteristics of dependence vary according to the drug involved. (See also ADDICTION, FEAR OF; DRUG ABUSE.)

O'Brien, Robert and S. Cohen, The *Encyclopedia of Drug Abuse* (New York: Facts On File, 1984). Adapted with permission.

drug effects Because we now have a better understanding of how the brain works, drugs have been developed that can alter specific aspects of brain chemistry. Three classes of drugs are known to relieve panic attacks. Two are ANTIDEPRESSANTS—MONOAMINE OXIDASE INHIBITORS (MAOIS) and TRICYCLIC ANTIDEPRESSANTS—and the third is a newer category, BENZODIAZEPINES (for example, alprazolam and diazepam). In research situations, individuals who suffer panic attacks experience less fear if they receive these drugs before they receive lactate infusions because the drugs may change the individual's metabolism, eliminating their abnormal sensitivity to lactate. MAOIs and tricyclics increase levels of the neurotransmitter norepinephrine. Most tricyclic antidepressants decrease activity of the LOCUS CERULEUS (an organ in the brain containing many neurotransmitters), perhaps due to increased availability of noradrenaline at autoreceptor sites. However, because antidepressants affect a wide range of NEUROTRANSMITTERS, many of which have been implicated as causes of anxiety, this mechanism cannot be proved. Antipanic drugs relieve anxiety symptoms, but they may have some undesirable side effects, such as high blood pressure or drowsiness.

The benzodiazepines are used for treating generalized anxiety disorder and have effects resembling those of classical sedatives, such as barbiturates or meprobamatelike drugs. These effects include muscle relaxation, anticonvulsive action, and sedation proceeding to hypnosis. (See also ALPRAZOLAM; ANTIDEPRESSANTS, NEW; CARBON DIOXIDE SENSITIVITY; LACTATE-INFUSED ANXIETY; NORADRENERGIC SYSTEM.)

drugs, fear of taking Fear of taking drugs is known as pharmacophobia. Some individuals have this fear because they are afraid of becoming dependent on drugs, or they fear that the drugs may cause them some harmful side effects, or they fear swallowing pills. A fear of taking drugs may be related to a general fear of doctors, hospitals,

Commonly Abused Drugs

Class	Trade Name* (or Source)	Street Names
Narcotic analgesics		
morphine	morphine sulfate	dope, M, Miss Emma, morpho, white stuff, dollies
heroin	none	girl, H, hard stuff, horse, junk, skag, smack, bags, snow
hydromorphone	Dilaudid	lords, dL's
oxymorphone	Numorphan	blues
meperidine	Demerol	
methadone hydrochloride	Dolophine	dollys, amidone
pentazocine	Talwin	
tincture of opium	paregoric	PG, licorice
cough preparations with codeine	elixir Terpin Hydrate	schoolboy, blue velvet
	Robitussin A-C	Robby
hydrocodone	Hycodan	
oxycodone	Percodan	percs
Nonnarcotic analgesics		
propoxyphene	Darvon	
Barbiturates		barbs, beans, candy, dolls, downers, goofers, peanuts, sleeping pill
amobarbital	Amytal	blue angels, bluebirds, blue devils, blues, lilly
pentobarbital	Nembutal	nebbies, yellow bullets, yellow dolls, yellow jackets
secobarbital	Seconal	pink lady, red devils, reds, seccy, pinks
phenobarbital	Luminal	phennies, purple hearts
amobarbital/secobarbital	Tuinal	Christmas trees, double trouble, rainbows, tooies
Other Sedative Hypnotics		
chloral hydrate	Noctec	
ethchlorvynol	Placidyl	
flurazepam	Dalmane	
glutethimide	Doriden	CIBA's
methaqualone	Quaalude	sopors, ludes, Q
methyprylon	Noludar	
paraldehyde	Paral	
scopolamine	Sominex	truth serum
Muscle relaxants		
meprobamate	Miltown	
Anxiolytics		
chlordiazepoxide	Librium	libbies
diazepam	Valium	Vit V, vals
oxazepam	Serax	
chlorprothixene	Taractan	
alprazolam	Xanax	
lorazepam	Ativan	

Commonly Abused Drugs (*Continued*)

Class	Trade Name* (or Source)	Street Names
Central nervous system stimulants		speed, uppers
d, dl amphetamine	Biphetamine	black beauties, black mollies
amphetamine sulfate	Benzedrine	A's, beans, bennies, cartwheels, crossroads, jelly beans, hearts, peaches, whites
amphetamine sulfate/ amobarbital	Dexamyl	greenies
dextroamphetamine sulfate	Dexedrine	brownies, Christmas trees, dexies, hearts, wakeups
methamphetamine hydrochloride	Methedrine	bombit, crank, crystal, meth, speed, methylphenidate
methylphenidate hydrochloride	Ritalin	
cocaine hydrochloride	cocaine	bernies, big C, coke, flake, happy dust, ice, snow, blow, lady, toot, freebase
cocaine with heroin		speedballs
Drugs with hallucinogenic properties		
d lysergic acid diethylamide	synthetic derivative (ergot fungus)	acid, California sunshine, Micro-dots, pink wedges, purple haze, sandos, sugar cubes
psilocin/psilocybin	mushroom (psilocybe mexicana)	business man's acid, buttons, magic mushroom
dimethyltryptamine (DMT)	synthetic	DMT, DET, DPT
morning glory seeds	bindweed (rivea corymbosa)	flower power, heavenly blue, pearly gates
mescaline	peyote cactus	barf tea, big chief, buttons, cactus, mesc
methyldimethoxy-amphetamine	synthetic derivative	STP, DOM
myristicin	nutmeg	MMDA
muscarine	mushroom (amanita muscaria)	fly
phencyclidine	Sernyl	angel dust, busy bee, DOA (dead on arrival), dust, elephant tranquilizer, embalming fluid, flakes, green, hog, killer weed (K.W.), PCP, peace pills, rocket fuel, super joint (when laced with marijuana), white powder
Tetrahydrocannabinols		
marijuana	cannabis sativa (leaves, flowers)	Acapulco gold, California Sinsemilla, cannabis, Colombian, dope, grass, hay, herb, joint, Mary Jane, Maui Waui, Panama red, pot, reefer, rope, smoke, tea, THC, weed
hashish	cannabis sativa, resin	hash

Class	Trade Name* (or Source)	Street Names
Volatile Solvents and Gases		
benzine	gasoline	
toluol	glue vapor	
carbon tetrachloride	cleaning fluid	
naphtha	cleaning fluid	scrubwoman's kick
amyl nitrite	amyl nitrite	amys, pears, snapper, poppers
nitrous oxide	nitrous oxide	laughing gas, nitrous

*Many of these drugs are sold under a variety of trade names; only a single popular example is used for each.
AMERICAN PSYCHIATRIC GLOSSARY (Washington, DC: American Psychiatric Association, 1988).

and health professionals. (See also DOCTORS, FEAR OF; ILLNESS PHOBIA.)

drugs, fear of new Fear of new drugs is known as neopharmaphobia. Individuals who have this fear do not want to take any medication that is categorized as experimental. They feel safer taking drugs that have been tried and proven effective for their particular disorder. They may fear toxic effects, or adverse interactions with other drugs. Such individuals may question their physicians closely about the track record of drugs being prescribed. Many drugs used for anxiety and depression are relatively new. Fearful people can be assured that such new drugs would not be commercially available if they had not first passed fairly rigorous scrutiny during clinical testing with large numbers of patients.

drugs as treatment See ANTICHOLINERGICS; ANTICONVULSIVES; ANTIDEPRESSANTS; ANTIHISTAMINES; ANXIETY DRUGS; DRUG EFFECTS; LITHIUM; MONOAMINE OXIDASE INHIBITORS (MAOIS); TRICYCLIC ANTIDEPRESSANTS; WITHDRAWAL EFFECTS OF ADDICTIVE SUBSTANCES.

dry mouth Dry mouth is a common symptom of fear, along with a "lump in the throat." In many cultures, there was a test for witchcraft that consisted of asking the suspect to put a pebble in the mouth; if the pebble was dry when it was taken out, it indicated fear and thus the guilt of the suspect.

Dry mouth is a common side effect of some medications, particularly certain ANTIDEPRESSANTS. The sensation may make the patient uncomfortable and lead to NAUSEA or lack of interest in eating. Dry mouth can be helped, to some degree, by sucking on mints or drinking fluids frequently. (See also ADVERSE DRUG EFFECTS.)

Drugs Used in Psychiatry

Generic Names	Trade Names (Examples)
ANTIANXIETY DRUGS	
Antihistamine Derivatives	
hydroxyzine	Atarax, Vistaril
Benzodiazepine Derivatives	
chlordiazepoxide	Librium
clorazepate	Tranxene
diazepam	Valium
lorazepam	Ativan
oxazepam	Serax
halazepam	Praxipam
prazepam	Centrax
alprazolam	Xanax
Sedative Types	
barbiturates (numerous types)	Numerous brands
meprobamate	Equanil, Miltown

Drugs Used in Psychiatry (*Cont.*)

Generic Names	Trade Names (Examples)
ANTIDEPRESSANT DRUGS	
Hydrazine MAO Inhibitors	
isocarboxazid	Marplan
phenelzine	Nardil
Non-hydrazine MAO Inhibitors	
tranylcypromine	Parnate
Tricyclic and Tetracyclic Derivatives	
amitriptyline	Elavil, Endep
desipramine	Norpramin, Pertofrane
doxepin	Adapin, Sinequan
imipramine	Imavate, Janimine, Presamine, SK-Pramine, Tofranil
nortriptyline	Aventyl, Pamelor
protriptyline	Vivactil
trimipramine	Surmontil
amoxapine	Asendin
maprotiline	Ludiomil
Other	
trazodone	Desyrel
STIMULANTS	
Amphetamines	
dextroamphetamine	Dexedrine
Piperidyls	
methylphenidate	Ritalin
COMBINATION ANTIDEPRESSANTS	
Amitriptyline-chlordiazepoxide	Limbitrol
Amitriptyline-perphenazine	Etrafon; Triavil
ANTIMANIC DRUGS	
lithium carbonate	Eskalith, Lithane, Lithonate
ANTIPSYCHOTIC DRUGS	
Butyrophenones	
haloperidol	Haldol
Dibenzoxazepines	
loxapine	Loxitane
Dihydroindolones	
molindone	Moban
Phenothiazine Derivatives	
Aliphatic	
chlorpromazine	Thorazine
triflupromazine	Vesprin
Piperazine	
acetophenazine	Tindal
butaperazine	Repoise
carphenazine	Proketazine
fluphenazine	Prolixin, Permitil
perphenazine	Trilafon
prochlorperazine	Compazine
trifluoperazine	Stelazine
Piperidine	
mesoridazine	Serentil
piperacetazine	Quide
thioridazine	Mellaril
Thioxanthene Derivates	
chlorprothixene	Taractan
thiothixene	Navane

dryness, fear of Fear of dryness and dry places is known as xerophobia. This fear may be related to a fear of lack of water or of landscape. (See also AIR, FEAR OF; LANDSCAPE, FEAR OF.)

DSM-III-R See DIAGNOSTIC AND STATISTICAL MANUAL OF MENTAL DISORDERS.

dual-sex therapy A form of PSYCHOTHERAPY developed by William Masters and Virginia Johnson to treat a particular sexual disorder or fear. In a "round-table session", the male and female therapy team suggest specific exercises for the couple to diminish fears felt by both sexes. Therapy also includes suggestions for improvement in communication in sexual and nonsexual areas. The use of "dual" therapists helps clients feel more at ease since for each partner there is a same-sex therapist. (See also FRIGIDITY; IMPOTENCE; PSYCHOSEXUAL ANXIETIES; SEX THERAPY; SEXUAL FEARS.)

Duncan, Isadora (1878–1927) An American dancer famous for her style of dancing based on classical Greek art. She had a phobia of covered cars. Her first two children drowned in a car that fell into the Seine River. She felt suffocated when she had to ride in a closed car. Ironically, she died by strangulation while riding in an open car when her long scarf became caught in the rear car wheel.

duration, fear of Fear of the duration of an event, or a long block of time, is known as CHRONOPHOBIA. This is a common fear of persons who are imprisoned, or those on long trips. Some have this fear during a school semester or a long academic program. (See also TIME, FEAR OF.)

dust, fear of Fear of dust is known as amathophobia or koniophobia. Some phobics who fear contamination and germs also fear dust. Some who fear dust may keep the windows in their houses closed at all times and install elaborate air-filtering equipment. Some wipe surfaces in their homes frequently and clean their homes thoroughly. Fear of dust may become an obsession with some individuals and may be a symptom of OBSESSIVE–COMPULSIVE DISORDER.

dying, fear of See DEATH, FEAR OF.

dysmorphophobia Fear of a specific bodily defect that is not noticeable to others. Several parts of the body may be involved including faces, breasts, hips, and noses. Dysmorphophobics also complain of body or limbs being too small or too large, misshapen or wrinkled, and of bad odors (imagined) coming from the mouth, underarm sweat, genitals, or the rectum. Sufferers may try to conceal the body part about which they are self-conscious—for example, wearing long hair to hide imagined floppy ears or wearing dark glasses to cover wrinkles around the eyes. Some fear looking in mirrors because they become anxious and upset when they see themselves. Although minor concerns about body shape are common in adolescents as well as adults, dysmorphophobia often occurs in individuals who have always been shy. (See also DEFORMITY, FEAR OF.)

dyspareunia, fear of Fear of painful vaginal SEXUAL INTERCOURSE. This is a common fear of some women. If they have experienced pain in the past, they may fear recurrence of the pain. The pain may be caused by a local irritation, such as from a spermicide or the material of a condom or diaphragm, or by an infection such as moniliasis (yeast) or trichomonas.

A woman who has had little experience with intercourse may feel pain when the penis enters her vagina because of an inadequately stretched hymen. Some women experience pain when the penis contacts their cervix (the neck of the uterus). This pain can be avoided by a change in position or less deep penetration. A pain that is felt deep in the pelvis may come from endometriosis, ovaian tumors or cysts, or some other condition that should be investigated and treated by a physician. Also, ANXIETY, tension, and a lack of stimulation before actual penetration may contribute to a painful experience. With sufficient foreplay (stimulation) before intercourse, the vaginal walls secrete lubricating fluid that will make intercourse more comfortable. After menopause and during breastfeeding secretions may not be sufficient, and a water-soluble jelly may be used as a lubricant. Use of such a lubricant may reduce the woman's fear of discomfort and pain.

Fears of disease and injury are associated with fear of pain during sexual intercourse;

the pain also triggers fears of the UNKNOWN. Some fears can by allayed with a better understanding of human anatomy. A woman's pain during sexual intercourse also arouses fears in the male partner that he may be injuring her. (See also PSYCHOSEXUAL ANXIETIES; SEXUAL FEARS.)

Ammer, Christine, *The A to Z of Women's Health* (New York: Facts On File 1983).

dysthymia Also known as depressive neurosis. Dysthymia is a chronic emotional disturbance involving depressed mood (or irritable mood in children or adolescents) that lasts most of the day and occurs more days than not for at least two years (one year for children and adolescents). During periods of depressed mood, the individual may experience anxiety, poor appetite or overeating, inability to sleep or oversleeping, low energy and fatigue, low self-esteem, poor concentration or difficulty making decisions, and feelings of hopelessness. In making a diagnosis it is difficult to distinguish between dysthymia and major depression, as the two disorders share similar symptoms and differ only in duration and severity. Dysthymia usually begins in childhood, adolescence, or early adult life, with a clear onset. Impairment in social and occupational functioning is usually mild or moderate because the condition is chronic rather than severe, as depression may be. In children and adolescents, social interaction with peers and adults frequently is affected; children with depression may react negatively or shyly to praise and may respond to positive relationships with negative behaviors, such as resentment or anger. Children who have this disorder may not perform and progress well in school. Dysthymia is more common in females than males, although in children it occurs equally frequently in both sexes. It is slightly more common among first-degree biologic relatives of people who have depression than among the general population. (See also AFFECTIVE DISORDERS; DEPRESSED PARENTS, CHILDREN OF; DEPRESSION; DEPRESSION, ADOLESCENT; MOOD.)

American Psychiatric Association, *Diagnostic and Statistical Manual* (Washington, DC: American Psychiatric Press, 1987).

dystychiphobia Fear of accidents (See also ACCIDENTS, FEAR OF.)

E

earthquakes, fear of Individuals who fear earthquakes fear the shaking, rolling, or sudden shock that occurs during an earthquake. They fear losing control of themselves and their environment for the few-second duration of the quake. Some fear motion and hence fear motion of the earth. Some fear the landslides that may bury areas or change mountain shapes or the fires ignited in cities by damage to gas mains, water pipes, and power lines. Some fear falling buildings. Many fear indirect damage from an earthquake, such as falling rubble.

While most earthquakes do not cause damage, fear of earthquakes is a realistic fear in many parts of the world where earthquakes occur with some frequency and have wreaked disaster in past years. Fear of earthquakes is related to fear of the UNKNOWN. Although accurate prediction of earthquakes is almost impossible, scientists do know the regions where earthquakes are most likely to occur. Individuals who have a morbid fear of earthquakes usually avoid such areas or learn to live with their fear. Builders in such areas also fear the damage that might be caused by earthquakes and incorporate certain safety features into new buildings. (See also LOSS OF CONTROL, FEAR OF; MOTION, FEAR OF.)

eaten, fear of being Fear of being eaten originates early in the oral stage of development of the infant's personality. During this stage, when the infant develops the normal aim of satisfaction and pleasure through eating, and, in a more general sense, through the incorporation of objects, frustrations relating to eating or fears of this frustration occur frequently. These anxieties take the form of a fear of being eaten, because in the infant's mind, what he feels and does will also take place in the world around him. In psychoanalytic practice, it has been found that fear of being eaten may also be a disguise for castration anxiety, distorted through regression into the older fear of being eaten. (See also DEVELOPMENTAL STAGES; ORAL STAGE; PSYCHOANALYSIS.)

Campbell, Robert J., *Psychiatric Dictionary* (New York: Oxford University Press, 1981).

eating disorders Eating disorders are maladaptive attitudes and behaviors related to food and eating patterns. The two most common eating disorders are ANOREXIA NERVOSA, characterized by continued abstinence from food and resulting weight loss, and BULIMIA, characterized by alternate binge eating and purging with use of emetics and laxatives.

Eating disorders often are related to body image distortion and/or concern over one's attractiveness and body shape. Other underlying concerns may include low-self-esteem, identity confusion, inability to express anger or aggression, and low ego strength. More women than men are affected by eating disorders. This may be related to the culturally and socially defined "ideal" figure for women, which has grown continually thinner since the 1940s.

Because of the multiple possible causes of eating disorders, successful treatment may vary according to the individual. Behavior modification, individual, group, and family therapy, and occasionally drug therapy have all been used to treat eating disorders. (See also CHOKING, FEAR OF; GAGGING, HYPERSENSITIVE; SWALLOWING, FEAR OF.)

Yudkovitz, E., "Bulimia: Growing Awareness of an Eating Disorder," *Social Work* (Nov.–Dec. 1983).

Bemis, K., "Current Approaches to the Etiology and Treatment of Anorexia Nervosa," *Psychological Bulletin* 85:3 (1978).

Fallon, April, "Standards of Attractiveness: Their Relationship toward Body Image Perceptions and Eating Disorders," *Food and Nutrition News* (Nov.–Dec. 1987), pp. 79–80.

eating phobias Fears of eating are relatively uncommon but troublesome kinds of phobias. They may be limited to a dread of eating in the company of others, or, in more severe cases, the fears may apply to eating food under any circumstances, whether the individual is alone or not. Some who fear eating fear swallowing and choking. Some fear swallowing solid foods but are able to swallow liquids. Phobics have an exaggerated feeling of a lump in their throat and a dry mouth, which are typical phobic responses, making it more difficult to eat.

Another type of eating phobia is food aversion, which involves only certain types of foods. Some food aversions begin in childhood or adolescence.

Some individuals will frequently complain of severe anxiety mounting to panic if they are forced to eat and are able to gain relief only by vomiting or by taking large doses of cathartics in order to get the food out of their bodies. The avoidance of eating to prevent such anxiety is a true phobic mechanism. Cognitive therapists have noted that fear-inducing thoughts accompany eating to produce anxiety and purging (avoidance).

There may be some connection between fears of eating and ANOREXIA NERVOSA. Technically, anorexia nervosa is characterized by a loss of appetite, while an individual with a phobia of eating experiences actual anxiety when eating or even considering eating. Anorexia nervosa is commonly considered either a hysterical phenomenon or a psychophysiological disorder because of the widespread secondary physical changes associated with it, such as slowing of growth and cessation of menstrual periods. However, in many cases the psychological disturbance from which all else follows is a genuine and profound phobia of eating, not a true anorexia. Eating phobias are successfully treated by graded exposure, starting with liquids and moving toward increasingly solid foods. (See also EATING DISORDERS; PHOBIA; SOCIAL PHOBIAS.)

Marks, Isaac, *Fears, Phobias and Rituals* (New York: Oxford University Press, 1987).

eating out, fear of Fear of eating away from home is considered a SOCIAL PHOBIA. This fear takes many forms, including fear of being watched while eating, fear of being seen or heard burping, belching, or vomiting in public after eating, or fear of food contaminated by those who prepare it. Many individuals who have AGORAPHOBIA fear eating out.

Most manifestations of the fear of eating out involve feelings of being trapped in a restaurant by (1) having to wait for one's food, (2) close proximity to others (e.g., one's spouse) about whom one has negative (often unexpressed) feelings, (3) being stared at by others while walking in and out of the restaurant, and (4) physical factors, such as sitting on the inside of a booth or in the rear of the restaurant where exiting is more difficult.

ecclesiaphobia Fear of the church or of organized religion. (See also CHURCHES, FEAR OF.)

echo, fear of Fear of echo is related to a fear of hearing one's own voice, known as phonophobia.

electicism (eclectic therapy) A system of psychotherapy that selects thoughts, suggestions, and procedures of therapy from diverse schools of thought to treat phobic or anxious individuals. Eclecticism is comprehensive psychiatry and draws from the biological, chemical, medical, neural psychological, social, environmental, and cultural points of view

ecophobia, oikophobia Fear of home surroundings. (See also HOME SURROUNDINGS, FEAR OF.)

eczema, behavior therapy for Eczema, a skin disease characterized by an itching rash over a large part of the body, has been relieved in some individuals with BEHAVIOR THERAPY and relaxation techniques. In a research study at the University of California at San Francisco Atopic Dermatitis Outpatient Clinic, patients were asked to record the number of times they scratched each day. The following week they were asked to add a rating of the itching intensity. Next, they were asked to note the time and what they were doing or feeling just before they scratched. Finally, they recorded how good it felt each time they scratched. By examining their records in detail, patients began to see how daily life events that were associated with feelings of ANXIETY, helplessness, anger, or resentment led to increased bouts of scratching that reinforced feelings of hopelessness about their disease and themselves as they looked at their damaged skin after scratching. To lessen the damage to their skin, patients were told to use the relaxation techniques at times of severe itching, such as just before bedtime They were also taught to pat, rub, or slap the skin instead of scratching it. At the end of the study, severity of symptoms was reduced by half. There was a 30 percent average decrease in the use of topical steroids. No patient had to go back to systemic steroids or increase antihistamine dosage, strength of topical steroids, or number of applications. (See also RELAXATION TECHNIQUES; SKIN DISEASE, FEAR OF.)

Cole, W.C., "Group Psychotherapy As An Aid in the Medical Treatment of Eczema," *Journal of the American Academy of Dermatology,* 18:2 (1988), pp. 286–291.

EEG (electroencephalograph) An instrument that receives and records small electrical discharges from the brain through electrodes placed at various points on the skull. Dysfunction within the brain can be identified by examining electrical patterns produced on a graph or a scope. The record of the brain-wave patterns that results, the electroencephalogram, is used in studies of waking activities, the stages of sleep, drowsiness, and DREAMING, and in the detection and diagnosis of brain tumors and EPILEPSY. The EEG is frequently part of the complete physical examination for individuals who have extreme ANXIETIES, repeated INSOMNIA, or severe HEADACHES. (See also DIAGNOSIS.

ego The part of the personality that deals with the external world and practical demands. According to Freud, there are three structural parts to the psychic apparatus: the ego, id, and superego. The ego enables the individual to perceive, reason, solve problems, test reality, delay drive discharge, and adjust instinctual impulses (the id) according to the individual's conscience (the superego). Most of the functions of the ego are automatic. The most important function of the ego is adaptation to reality. This is accomplished by delaying drives until acceptable behaviors are carried out, instituting defense mechanisms as safeguards against release of unacceptable impulses, and conducting executive functions such as memory, planning, thought, etc. Anxiety arises from the ego as a signal that unacceptable unconscious material is building toward conscious discharge. (See also FREUD, SIGMUND; ID; REALITY TESTING; SUPEREGO; SUPEREGO ANXIETY)

ego defense mechanisms A psychoanalytic term referring to the use of unconscious strategies (DEFENSE MECHANISMS) to protect the ego from threatening impulses and conflicts. The most common ego defenses are repression, projection, sublimation, and displacement.

ego integrity The last of Erikson's first eight stages of man. "Ego integrity" seems to mean "the serenity of old age," the looking back on one's life with completeness and satisfaction and the acceptance of one's own death without fear as natural and as part of the life cycle. Without ego integrity, the individual may look back in despair, seeing his life as a series of mistakes and missed opportunities; DEPRESSION may result. (See also DEATH, FEAR OF; DEVELOPMENTAL STAGES; ERIKSON, ERIC.)

ego nuclei The first components of the ego, which begin in infancy during the oral and anal stages of development. The term also refers to integrating new experiences with old ones by relating them to already acquired knowledge. In some individuals, when this mechanism does not function appropriately, fears and phobias result. (See also DEVELOPMENTAL STAGES.)

eidetic psychotherapy A type of therapy that uses eidetic imagery, or mental imagery. Imagery of vivid and detailed memories is usually visual but may also be auditory and closely resembles actual perception. (See also BEHAVIOR THERAPY.)

eisoptrophobia Fear of MIRRORS.

ejaculation, fear of Some men fear the automatic expulsion of semen and seminal fluid through the penis resulting from involuntary and voluntary contractions of various muscle groups during orgasm. Some men have a variety of fears regarding ejaculation, including premature ejaculation, delayed ejaculation, and ejaculatory incompe-

Summary of Some Ego Defense Mechanisms

Compensation	Covering up weakness by emphasizing desirable traits or making up for frustration in one area by gratification in another
Denial of reality	Protecting self from unpleasant reality by refusal to perceive it
Displacement	Discharging pent-up feelings, usually of hostility, on objects less dangerous than those which initially aroused the emotion
Emotional insulation	Withdrawing into passivity to protect self from being emotionally hurt
Fantasy	Gratifying frustrated desires in imaginary achievements (''daydreaming'' is a common form)
Identification	Increasing feelings of worth by identifying self with another person or institution, often of illustrious standing
Introjection	Incorporating external values and standards into ego structure so individual is not at the mercy of them as external threats
Isolation	Cutting off emotional charge from hurtful situations or separating incompatible attitudes into logic-tight compartments (holding conflicting attitudes which are never thought of simultaneously or in relation to each other); also called *compartmentalization*
Projection	Placing blame for one's difficulties upon others, or attributing one's own ''forbidden'' desires to others
Rationalization	Attempting to prove that one's behavior is ''rational'' and justifiable and thus worthy of the approval of self and others
Reaction formation	Preventing dangerous desires from being expressed by endorsing opposing attitudes and types of behavior and using them as ''barriers''
Regression	Retreating to earlier developmental level involving more childish responses and usually a lower level of aspiration
Repression	Pushing painful or dangerous thoughts out of consciousness, keeping them unconscious; this is considered to be the *most basic of the defense mechanisms*
Sublimation	Gratifying or working off frustrated sexual desires in substitutive nonsexual activities socially accepted by one's culture
Undoing	Atoning for, and thus counteracting, unacceptable desires or acts

tence, leading to embarrassment, loss of social status or social value, and perceived male-role inadequacy. (See also PSYCHOSEXUAL ANXIETIES; SEXUAL FEARS.)

Elavil See AMITRIPTYLINE.

Electra complex A term describing a characteristic relationship that presumably occurs between a young daughter and her father during the phallic stage of psychosexual development as described by Freud. According to this Freudian view, female children during the phallic stage develop a strong desire to possess their fathers. This feeling is sexualized and corresponds to the Oedipal feeling young boys presumably develop toward their mothers at this stage. Successful resolution requires identification with the mother and thus allows sexual roles as well as superego structures to develop. (See also DEVELOPMENTAL STAGES; OEDIPAL.)

electricity, fear of Fear of electricity is known as electrophobia. Some who fear electric current, or the passage of electricity along a wire or other electrical conductor, fear the power of electricity. Some fear getting an electrical shock by touching wires or objects that conduct electricity. Some fear fires caused by electricity or faulty wiring or fear being near outdoor electrical wires. Fear of electricity can be a hindrance to enjoyment of modern conveniences, as many labor-saving appliances are electric. Some choose gas appliances as an alternative. Many people with this fear wear insulated shoes and will activate or deactivate wall switches only with wooden sticks or have others do so.

electrocardiogram (EKG) A graph consisting of a wavelike tracing that represents the electrical action of the heart muscle as it goes through a typical cycle of contraction and relaxation. The wave patterns reveal the condition of the various heart chambers and valves. The heart's electrical currents are detected by electrodes placed on the individual's chest and amplified more than 3,000 times in an electrocardiograph, an electronic machine that creates the electrocardiogram. An EKG is usually part of a complete physical examination and may be repeated at intervals for individuals who have ANXIETIES and PANIC DISORDERS. Changes in the EKG may occur as a side effect of taking certain medications and may result from long-term chronic anxiety states. (See also HEART RATE IN EMOTION.)

electrophobia Fear of electricity. (See also ELECTRICITY, FEAR OF.)

electroshock treatment A treatment for mental illness that produces a convulsion by passing an electrical current through the brain; also known an electroconvulsive therapy (ECT). Electroshock treatment has been used to "treat" profound (usually psychotic) and sometimes other symptoms of mental illness. It is typically an unpleasant and occasionally dangerous procedure; today it is not recommended for treatment of phobias, although before clinical and scientific information about agoraphobia was known, agoraphobic patients (usually in a hospital) were sometimes given ECT as an experimental procedure.

electromyographic pattern analysis (EMG) Analysis of the electromyogram (EMG)—a recording of the electrical activity of the muscles through electrodes places in or on different muscle groups when they are relaxed or during various activities—is used in BIOFEEDBACK therapy and in diagnosis and treatment of certain diseases involving the muscles, such as muscular dystrophy and spasmodic torticollis. EMG is used in biofeedback as a measure of muscular tension for people who have anxieties.

elevated places, fear of Fear of elevated places or heights, known as acrophobia, is very common. Some fear standing on elevated places, such as mountains in a distance, while others fear just looking at them. Some fear being at the edge of an elevated place. (See also HEIGHTS, FEAR OF; HIGH OBJECTS, FEAR OF; HIGH PLACES, FEAR OF LOOKING UP AT.)

elevators, fear of Many people fear riding in elevators. Some fear that the elevator cables will break and the elevator will crash. Others fear that the elevator may get stuck between floors, that the doors will not open, or that they will starve or suffocate inside. Some who fear riding in elevators do not fear riding only a few floors and feel safe before the elevator rises above the second or third floors. Some who fear elevators also have fears of closed spaces, such as tunnels, or fears of crowds. Many who have agoraphobia also fear elevators; in both phobias there is a fear of air deprivation. Some elevator phobics fear heights. In most cases, the phobic person feels somewhat trapped in the elevator until it stops and the doors open, which usually brings relief. Crowded elevators produce even greater feelings of being trapped and fears of losing emotional control, resulting in anticipated embarrassment, humiliation, rejection, etc.

There are social as well as physical fears associated with elevators. For example, some fear "going crazy" or fainting and being socially embarrassed if there are other people present in the elevator.

Fear of elevators influences where an individual lives, works, or conducts business. It can be a disabling fear because it limits one's activities. Therapists treat elevator phobia with many techniques, of which the exposure therapies are the most effective. (See also ACROPHOBIA; AGORAPHOBIA; BEHAVIOR MODIFICATION; CLAUSTROPHOBIA.)

Beck, Aaron T. and Gary Emery, *Anxiety Disorders and Phobias* (New York: Basic Books, 1985).

Ellis, Albert (1913–) American psychologist known as the father of rational emotive therapy (RET). Ellis pioneered the rational, or cognitive, movement in psychotherapy, a radical departure from traditional therapy. RET is based on the premise that emotional problems are primarily caused by irrational attitudes and beliefs about oneself, others, and the world at large. This therapy helps the individual focus more clearly on specific irrational patterns of thought that produce unwanted ANXIETIES and PHOBIAS. Ellis's work led the way toward cognitive-behavioral therapy.

In his youth, Ellis had exaggerated fears of public speaking. He applied cognitive-behavioral methods and overcame his fear to the point where he actually enjoyed speaking in public. (See also COGNITIVE THERAPY; RATIONAL EMOTIVE THERAPY (RET).)

elurophobia Fear of cats. (See also CATS, FEAR OF.)

emetophobia Fear of vomiting (See also VOMITING, FEAR OF.)

emotional deprivation Lack of adequate or appropriate interpersonal relationships or exposure to an environment in the early developmental years that may predispose an individual to anxieties and phobias. Emotional deprivation is sometimes caused by separation from the mother or inadequate mothering. (See also SEPARATION ANXIETY.)

emotional flooding approaches Therapies that rely on stimulating intense emotional experiences in the anxious or phobic individual. Emotional flooding approaches include bio-energetics, flooding, implosion, primal therapy, and Reichian therapy. These approaches assume that an individual's emotional and psychological disorders can be helped by encouraging the direct release of blocked emotions. (See also FLOODING; IMPLOSION; PRIMAL THERAPY; REICH, WILHELM.)

"empty chair" A technique used in Gestalt theory to resolve unfinished business or unresolved feelings toward another or to help identify reactions to another (usually someone from the past). The client is asked to talk to an empty chair as though it contained the person he or she reacted to or had unresolved feelings about. The therapist might also ask the client to sit in the empty chair and then to address his or her vacated chair from the point of view of the adversary. Fritz Perls (founder of gestalt therapy) felt that fear was the underlying factor in all unresolved situations and that inhibition was a form of avoidance of the fear. The empty-chair technique is a way of confronting and overcoming fears.

empty rooms and empty spaces, fear of Fear of empty rooms is known as kenophobia or cenophobia. This may be the opposite of CLAUSTROPHOBIA, in which one fears crowded rooms, closed places, or enclosed spaces. (See also AGORAPHOBIA.)

enclosed spaces, fear of Fear of enclosed spaces is known as CLAUSTROPHOBIA. Many people have this fear in elevators, small rooms, or crowded rooms, on airplanes or buses, or in other places where they cannot readily leave if they choose to do so. Some become fearful if there is no window in the room they are in, or if they cannot open a window, as on an airplane.

Some individuals are fearful of going into an enclosed space. Others may easily enter the space and feel comfortable and secure in it and later on become overwhelmed by a feeling of anxiety that something dreadful will happen while in the enclosed space. Sometimes the same individual experiences different feelings at different times. The person might perceive a "closed space" even though he or she is not enclosed. For example, left-turn lanes are often experienced as such.

Some individuals who have fear of enclosed places also have some social phobias or agoraphobia. For example, the individual who is fearful of meeting new people, of being looked at, of being stared at, or of being criticized may anticipate these fears before entering a crowded room from which there is no easy escape and thus become anxious and fearful of entering the room. Some individuals are fearful that they will do something embarrassing or unacceptable, such as faint, lose control, or look stupid, or be unacceptable because they are anxious in public and thus fear being in an enclosed place or an open place without shelter or ease of exit. Fear of enclosed places is a common anxiety symptom, but for some individuals under some circumstances it can produce a panic attack.

Some psychoanalytic points of view relate fears of enclosed places to fantasies of wishing or fearing symbiotic reunion with the mother, or peaceful sleep in the womb. There may be fantasies of being extruded or suffocated by a closing of the birth canal, or being stuck in the birth canal. The basic fear of the claustrophobe is considered by some analysts a castration anxiety. The fear may also be related to a death fear, because the individual, either consciously or unconsciously, fears that there will be no air and he or she will suffocate. Many types of therapies are used to help individuals who fear enclosed places, including behavior therapy, in which the individual learns to face the feared situations and not have a claustrophobic reaction. For some individuals, therapy for generalized anxiety will also help overcome specific fears, such as the fear of enclosed spaces. (See also AGORAPHOBIA; BEHAVIOR THERAPY; CASTRATION ANXIETY.)

Asch, Stuart S., "Claustrophobia and Depression," *Journal of the American Psychoanalytic Association,* 14(1966), pp. 711–729.

Gehl, Raymond H., "Indecision and Claustrophobia," *International Journal of Psychoanalysis,* 54(1973), pp. 4–59.

encounter group therapy A form of training or therapy sometimes used by support groups for individuals who have phobias. Emphasis is on experiences of individuals within the group with minimum input from the therapist-leader. Encounter groups focus on the present, or here-and-now feelings rather than past or outside problems of participants. The term "encounter group" was coined by J.L. Moreno in 1914.

Endep See AMITRIPTYLINE.

endocrine system Many ductless glands that release hormones directly into the blood or lymph. Secretions of some endocrine glands increase during emotional arousal, such as fear and phobic attacks.

end of the world, fear of See APOCALYPSE, FEAR OF.

endogenous depression Profound sadness that may be caused by a biological malfunction, in contrast to a DEPRESSION brought on by an environmental event. Endogenous depression has a more severe set of symptoms than EXOGENOUS DEPRESSION. The term endogenous (quick, "arising from within") is now passing out of use, because

Endocrine System

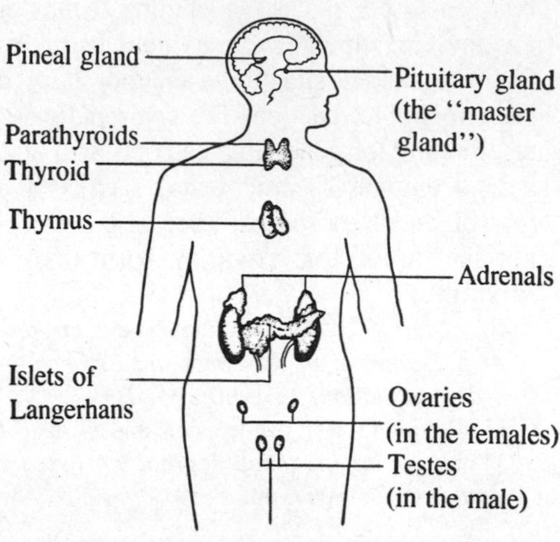

From *Psychology and Life,* by Philip G. Zimbardo. Copyright © 1985, 1979 by Scott, Foresman and Company. Reprinted with permission.

there is no evidence that a major depressive episode has different symptoms just because a precipitating factor was external or internal. (See also ANTIDEPRESSANTS.)

endorphins Naturally occurring morphinelike substances produced in the brain. They play important roles in control of emotional behaviors such as those associated with pain, ANXIETY, tension, and FEAR. Stress, both physical and psychological, seems to stimulate secretion of endorphins.

The binding sites of the endorphins are concentrated in the limbic system. A number of specific endorphins have been identified.

eneuresis See BEDWETTING.

England Fear of England, the English (British) language, and things relating to the English culture is known as Anglophobia.

enissophobia, enosiophobia Fear of sin. (See also SIN, FEAR OF.)

enochlophobia Fear of crowds. (See also CROWDS, FEAR OF.)

entomophobia Fear of insects. (See also INSECTS, FEAR OF.)

eosophobia Fear of dawn. (See also DAWN, FEAR OF; LIGHT, FEAR OF.)

epidemic anxiety Acute anxiety among many members of a given community at the same time. Epidemic anxiety is also known as MASS HYSTERIA. Usually a common factor for the anxiety can be identified, and individuals usually recover without long-lasting effects.

Epidemic anxiety has occurred following chemical explosions and similar crises of public safety. In such cases people commonly report nausea, vomiting, and headaches and attribute all such symptoms (whether correctly or not) to the recent discovery.

Greist, John H., James W. Jefferson and I.M. Marks, *Anxiety and Its Treatment: Help Is Available* (Washington, DC: American Psychiatric Press, 1986).

epidemiology The study of mental and physical disorders and diseases in populations. Epidemiology relates the distribution of disorders (incidence and prevalence), such as anxieties and phobias, to any conceivable factor, such as time, place, or a person existing in or affecting that population. By understanding the magnitude of a disorder and the patterns of risk for the occurrence of a disorder, researchers obtain clues as to what alterations might lead to prevention of the disorder.

The study of population samples includes both treated and untreated persons to obtain a true estimate and better understanding of the disorder. However, for many disorders, only a small fraction of ill persons seek medical treatment, and those who do seek treatment may not be representative of the population with the disorder. This is particularly true of anxiety disorders. (See also INCIDENCE; PREVALENCE OF PHOBIAS AND ANXIETIES.)

Weissman, Myrna M. and Kathleen R. Merikangas, "The Epidemiology of Anxiety and Panic Disorders: An Update," *Journal of Clinical Psychiatry,* 47:6 (June 1986), pp. 11–17.

epilepsy, fear of Fear of epilepsy is known as hylephobia. This is one of many specific disease phobias. Some individuals fear having epilepsy themselves; others fear viewing a person having an epileptic attack.

Fears often accompany epilepsy. For example, after a seizure, an epileptic may become phobic about going to the place where the seizure occurred. Also, the epileptic may fear the social embarrassment of having an attack in the presence of others. (See also ILLNESS PHOBIA.)

epinephrine A hormone secreted by the medulla of the adrenal gland; also called ADRENALINE. The effects of epinephrine are similar, but not identical, to those of stimulating the sympathetic nerves—an increase in blood pressure, an inhibition in peristaltic movements, and a release of glucose from the liver. (See also NEUROTRANSMITTERS.)

epistaxiophobia Fear of nosebleeds. (See also NOSEBLEEDS, FEAR OF.)

equinophobia Fear of horses. (See also HORSES, FEAR OF.)

erectile dysfunction, fear of See SEXUAL FEARS.

erection, failure of See SEXUAL FEARS.

eremophobia (eremiophobia and ermitophobia) Fear of being oneself. This fear is common in a large percentage of agoraphobic individuals. (See also AGORAPHOBIA; ALONE, FEAR OF BEING; SOLITUDE, FEAR OF; STILLNESS, FEAR OF.)

ergasiophobia Fear of work, or of functioning. This is a fear that one's movements will disastrously affect the surrounding world. Sometimes the word ergasiophobia is used to refer to fear of surgical operations. (See also SURGICAL OPERATIONS, FEAR OF; WORK, FEAR OF.)

ergophobia Fear of work. This can be related to social anxieties, perfectionism, and fear of failure as well as anxiety over exertion and effort.

ergot Ergot, a naturally occurring substance derived from a fungus that infests rye plants, is used in medications to treat migraine HEADACHES. It stops the headaches by constricting the blood vessels and reducing the dilation of the arteries. Many individuals find that if they take it early enough in prepain stages of an attack, they can abort their headaches or at least reduce their intensity. Many migraine-headache sufferers become less anxious about having a migraine attack when they begin prophylactic (preventive) treatment.

Erikson, Eric H. (1902–) German-born American psychoanalyst and student of SIGMUND FREUD. Erikson revised the standard psychoanalytic account of ego development to relate stages of life to cultural influences and a search for identity in a changing world. Erikson said that ego identity is gradually achieved by facing positive goals and negative risks during eight stages of life. The psychosocial stages, their goals, and their risks are described more fully under DEVELOPMENTAL STAGES. (See also EGO-INTEGRITY; GUILT.)

Erikson's psychosocial stages See DEVELOPMENTAL STAGES.

erotophobia Fear of sexual love is known as erotophobia. The term also relates to fear of anything that arouses sexual or erotic feelings, such as thoughts, printed matter, or films. (See also DEVELOPMENTAL STAGES; SEXUAL LOVE, FEAR OF.)

error, fear of Fear of errors is known as hamartophobia. Those who have this phobia may fear one of several types of errors, including memory error, which differs from forgetting; false recollection; accidents, such as while driving a car; or minor accidents, such as spilling things or dropping things. From the psychoanalytic point of view, errors stem from repression; the error reveals unconscious feelings and motives (for example, slips of the tongue). Individuals who fear making errors are often perfectionists; some are compulsive about always being right, knowing answers, and always performing correctly. (See also OBSESSIVE–COMPULSIVE DISORDER; PSYCHOANALYSIS; REPRESSION; SLIPS OF THE TONGUE, FEAR OF.)

Campbell, Robert, *Psychiatric Dictionary* (New York: Oxford University Press, 1981).

erythrophobia, erytophobia, ereuthophobia Fear of BLUSHING and fear of the color red. This fear is sometimes associated with a fear of BLOOD. Blushing is often a reaction to social attention, teasing, and emotional expressions that bring on anxiety, self-consciousness, and similar responses that one wishes to hide from others. Blushing is caused by increased blood flow to the facial area and seems to be a physiological response peculiar to some individuals. Relaxation training combined with assertiveness training are usually sufficient to treat this reaction. (See also BLOOD AND BLOOD-INJURY PHOBIA; BLUSHING, FEAR OF.)

Campbell, Robert J., *Psychiatric Dictionary* (New York: Oxford Univ Press, 1981).

escalators, fear of Escalators, moving stairways widely used in stores and train, bus, and airline terminals, are feared by many individuals who fear CONFINEMENT, HEIGHTS, MOTION, STAIRS, or STANDING. The steps on an escalator run up or down on an endless belt, which may cause some who fear INFINITY to fear the endless motion. Some may fear accidents or fear falling on escalators, but most fears are associated with feeling trapped in a social situation in which others might see one's anxiety. This is a common fear in agoraphobics. Fear of escalators is a twentieth-century fear. The first escalator was installed by the Otis Elevator Company at the Paris Exposition in 1900. (See also ACCIDENTS, FEAR OF; FALLING, FEAR OF; MOTION, FEAR OF; STAIRS, FEAR OF; STANDING, FEAR OF.)

escape behavior The actions a phobic person takes to remove him or herself from a phobic object when such an object cannot be avoided. An example is running at the sight of a snake. An alternative to escape behavior would be an AVOIDANCE RESPONSE, which might involve walking around a grassy patch in which snakes may be lurking instead of walking through it. Avoidance and escape behaviors help the individual feel less fearful of a specific situation. Where avoidance or escape behavior is not possible, the phobic individual may show other signs of anxiety or fear, such as trembling hands, shaking, or stammering speech, fidgeting and squirming, or other mannerisms.

Kleinknecht, Ronald A., *The Anxious Self* (New York: Human Sciences Press, 1986).

esodophobia Fear of virginity, either of losing one's own or relating to the loss of virginity in oneself or another. (See also VIRGINITY, FEAR OF.)

ESP See EXTRASENSORY PERCEPTION

eternity, fear of Fear of eternity was described by Otto Fenichel (1899–1946), an Austrian psychoanalyst and disciple of Freud, as part of a group of fears of "surroundings that imply the loss of the usual means of orientation," such as fear of cessation of customary routine, fear of death, fear of uniform noises, etc. The individual who has such fears is particularly afraid of a loss of control over infantile sexual and aggressive impulses and then projects onto the outside world his own fears of losing control. On the other hand, the existential therapists would point out that to experience eternity is to come into contact with our basic sense of alienation and separateness, which engenders great fear.

Campbell, Robert J., *Psychiatric Dictionary,* (New York: Oxford University Press, 1981).

euphobia Fear of hearing good news. This may also be related to the fear of gaiety, fear of laughter, or fear of success. (See also GOOD NEWS, FEAR OF; LAUGHTER, FEAR OF; SUCCESS, FEAR OF.)

eurotophobia Fear of FEMALE GENITALS. (See also PSYCHOSEXUAL ANXIETIES; SEXUAL FEARS.)

everything, fear of Fear of everything is known as panphobia, panophobia, pantophobia, or pamphobia. This may be an anxiety disorder rather than a true phobia. (See also ANXIETY, BASIC; ANXIETY DISORDERS.)

evil eye, fear of Many civilizations have believed in the evil eye, a superstition that certain individuals have the ability to bring on bad luck or injury by looking at another. Belief in the evil eye may stem from the ability of the eye to change color and adapt or from the awareness most people have of being stared at or even stared awake by someone they cannot actually see.

The evil eye is part of witch and voodoo beliefs, which may be an intense occult projection of the feeling of jealousy. Individuals who are prone to disaster and misfortune were thought to have an involuntary evil eye. Both the gods and men were thought be be envious of anyone experiencing good fortune and to wish him ill. The evil eye could cause illness, bad luck, and damage to property and livestock. According to 16th- and 17th-century witch beliefs, the power of the evil eye came directly from a pact with Satan. Babies and children were targets for the evil eye and were sometimes disguised in ragged or inappropriate clothing to protect them. Strings of blue beads and salt carried in a pocket were also thought to protect children. The bridal veil and other marriage customs fended off the power of the evil eye on the happy occasion of a wedding. Sexual functions were thought to be particularly vulnerable to the power of the evil eye. Sexual symbols such as ornaments in the shape of a phallus and a gesture of the hand with thumb between first and second fingers were believed to be powerful protection.

Some people still believe that direct praise, compliments, and discussion of good fortune attracts the attention of the evil eye. A compliment paid in even the most veiled way, according to fearers of the evil eye, should be followed by the act of spitting, which is considered a protective measure against the jealous influence of the evil eye. (See also GREECE, ANXIETY DISORDERS IN; DEPRESSION AND FEARS ACROSS CULTURES; VOODOO, FEAR OF; WITCHES AND WITCHCRAFT, FEAR OF.)

Brasch, R., *Strange Customs* (New York: David McKay, 1976), pp. 127–133.

Hill, Douglas and Pat Williams, *The Supernatural* (New York: Hawthorn, 1965).

Cavendish, Richard (ed.), *Man, Myth and Magic* (New York: Marshall Cavendish, 1983).

evocative therapy A term used in psychotherapy to denote emphasis on evoking responses from the individual rather than guiding the individual toward some therapeutic goal. Therapists often use this approach to treat individuals who have ANXIETIES and PHOBIAS. (See also THERAPIES.)

examination phobia See TEST ANXIETY.

excrement, fear of Fear of excrement (feces) is known as copraphobia or scatophobia. (See also FECES, FEAR OF.)

exercise, compulsion to An irresistible and often abusive impulse to perform physical exercise. This compulsion stems from a national fitness trend in the U.S. during the 1980s coupled with psychological problems and anxieties similar to those found in persons who have eating disorders. The exercise "addict" spends inappropriate amounts of time each day exercising, frequently continuing even when in pain. In contrast to the true athlete in training, the compulsive exerciser has no real athletic goals but instead uses exercise to fill emotional gaps in his or her life, using exercise, for example, to take the place of relationships, to feel in control, or to avoid certain situations. The compulsion pushes one beyond the healthy use of moderate exercise as a means of alleviating tension or anxiety. The compulsive exerciser may also seek the more socially acceptable "high" produced by prolonged exercise rather than turning to drugs or alcohol. The addict who abruptly stops exercising can experience withdrawal symptoms similar to those of a substance abuser—for example, nervousness, depression, and insomnia.

Compulsive exercise can also be a way to distract oneself from the experience of anxiety or a method to reduce anxiety once it occurs. People with anxiety reactions have been known to engage in compulsive strenuous physical exercise to the point of running or working out in the middle of the night. (See also FITNESS ANXIETY.)

Charlier, Marie, "In the Name of Fitness, Many Americans Grow Addicted to Exercise," *The Wall Street Journal* (Midwest edition), Oct. 1, 1987.

exhaustion, fear of Fear of exhaustion is known as kopophobia. Some individuals fear becoming exhausted because they fear being weak, or possibly fainting, and thus being powerless or out of control. (See also LOSS OF CONTROL, FEAR OF.)

existential analysis A phase in existential psychotherapy in which the individual explores his own values, relationships, and commitments. The object of existential analysis is to develop new and more satisfying patterns of life, such as new ways of facing and coping with ANXIETIES and PHOBIAS. Existential anxiety, however, is viewed as a universal experience of humans due to their alienation. (See also EXISTENTIAL THERAPY.)

existential anxiety A term that applies to a normal response to confronting one's life condition. It is differentiated from neurotic anxiety that is out of proportion to the situation, is typically out of awareness, and tends to immobilize the person. Decisions and fundamental changes in one's life produce existential anxiety, which acts as a stimulus for growth and helps to increase awareness and personal freedom. (See also EXISTENTIAL THERAPY.)

existential neurosis A term that applies to a lack of an inner sense of oneself and of meaning in life. The term was popularized by Victor Frankl (1905–), a German-born American psychiatrist, who originated logotherapy, an existential approach that recognizes an inability to see meaning in life as a cause for anxiety, fear, and phobia.

Existential neurosis comes from a failure to experience life on one's own terms. Individuals whose lives are directed solely toward satisfying society's demands or goals without creating their own personally chosen destinies may develop existential neuroses. (See also EXISTENTIAL THERAPY.)

existential therapy A form of therapy for anxieties and phobias in which treatment of the entire person is emphasized. Unlike other therapies that emphasize biology, behavior, or unconscious features, existential therapy focuses on the individual's subjective experiences, free will, and ability to be responsible for his own existence. Existential therapy is also known as humanistic-existential therapy. The therapeutic process encourages the individual to verbalize intimate thoughts, intentions, and convictions in order to reveal the deepest meaning he or she gives to his or her life. The relationship between the therapist and anxious individual becomes a continuous process of sharing, questioning, and probing inner experiences. In the therapeutic situation, there is no transference from individual to analyst, or vice versa, because each relates to the other in a genuine interpersonal expression of feelings. The therapist tries to understand the meaning of a phobic individual's conscious act, for example, as it appears currently in daily life, in the past, and in how the individual perceives that it might happen in the future.

Existential therapists assume that there are four dimensions of mental disturbances: intrapsychic disturbances, disturbed learning processes, systemic disturbances, and existential disturbances. Existentialists believe their aspect of the discipline has been neglected because of the general decline in the use of symbolic language in psychotherapy.

Existential counseling is designed to expand self-awareness and increase the client's concept of the amount of control he or she has making choices in life. Additionally, existential counselors help reduce anxiety in a client's life by helping him or her to transform anxiety from a negative to a positive energy for life.

The founder of existential therapy was Rollo May (1909–), an American psychoanalyst, who was particularly concerned with combating feelings of emptiness, cynicism, and despair by emphasizing basic human values, such as love, free will, and self-awareness. (See also ANGST; ANXIETY; EXISTENTIAL NEUROSIS; FRANKL, VICTOR; GESTALT THERAPY; MAY, ROLLO; PERLS, FRITZ.)

Kleinknecht, Ronald A. *The Anxious Self* (New York: Human Sciences Press, 1986).

Lande, Nathaniel, "On Existential Analysis," in *Mindstyles/Lifestyles* (Los Angeles: Price/Stern/Sloan, 1976), pp. 64–65.

Vontress, C.E., "Existential Anxiety," *American Mental Health Counselors Association Journal*, 8(1986), pp. 100–109.

exogenous depression Profound sadness assumed to be caused by an environmental event. Many agoraphobics have this type of depression, but it recedes as the anxiety diminishes and the person becomes more functional. This term is going out of common use. (See also AGORAPHOBIA; ANTIDEPRESSANTS; DEPRESSION; ENDOGENOUS DEPRESSION.)

exorcism A fear that evil spirits in the form of demons or ghosts can gain control of the human body, places, or animals is the basis for the ritual of exorcism. Exorcism has taken different forms, ranging from a simple prayer to God for deliverance from the power of evil to an elaborate ceremony described in the Roman ritual of the Catholic church. All forms of exorcism attempt to rid the person of evil possession.

Demons, fallen angels who rebelled against God, are believed to have the ability to possess human souls; but demons are supposedly subject to the powers of religious rituals designed to drive them out of their victims. Reports of demonic possession from the past closely resemble modern cases of schizophrenia and hysteria. The dialog between priest and evil spirit, speaking through the victim, also resembles the exchange between psychotherapist and patient and has frequently had similar results. A strong fear associated with exorcism was that the exorcist himself might become possessed by the evil spirit.

In modern times, exorcism is associated with the Catholic church, but it has an ancient history in Greek, Mesopotamian, and Jewish cultures. The New Testament records that Jesus Christ drove demons out of their victims and conferred this power on his Apostles. Early Christians spread the word of the power of Christianity by exorcising evil spirits.

According to some European witch beliefs, witches could inflict demonic possession by contaminating the victims' food with evil spirits. Apples were considered a favorite vehicle for a demon. Simulation of demonic possession was apparently used both by those who feared charges of witchcraft because of their unusual behavior and by those who wished to bring witchcraft charges. Nuns were frequent victims of demonic possession. The condition spread through convents as a type of hysteria. Descriptions of demonic possession included both mental and physical symptoms: sharp pains that made the victim cry out, vomiting, swelling, melancholy, a desire for bad food, wicked, blasphemous language or behavior, and superhuman mental or physical ability.

Interest in exorcism revived in the 1970s partly due to the success of William Blatty's novel *The Exorcist* and the film based on it. Recently, religious leaders and psychotherapists have debated the issue of whether treating devils as entities capable of controlling the human body and soul is helpful or harmful in the treatment of mental cases. The *New Catholic Encyclopedia* makes the following comment: "Exorcisms are rarely performed today, not because the Church has lost its belief in the power and activity of Satan, but because it recognizes that true cases of possession are rare. What often appeared to be possession in earlier ages is now recognized as a pathological state attributable to one or more anxiety disorders and for those the proper remedies are neurology, psychiatry or depth psychology." (See also DEMONS, FEAR OF.)

The New Catholic Encyclopedia, vol. 5 (New York: McGraw Hill, 1976), "Exorcism."

Encyclopedia of Occultism and Parapsychology (Detroit: Gale Research, 1984), "Exorcism."

Hill, Douglas and Pat Williams, *The Supernatural* (New York: Hawthorn, 1965), pp. 94–95, 100–101.

Robbins, Rossel Hope, *The Encyclopedia of Witchcraft and Demonology* (New York: Crown, 1974), "Exorcism" and "Possession."

experiential family therapy An approach to family therapy that focuses on actual experiences between therapist and family and among family members during the therapy session. It is also known as symbolic-experiential family therapy. This therapy may be useful in helping families of agoraphobic individuals or those who have other anxieties or phobias. The therapy is based on existentialism and humanistic approaches and emphasizes the family's "process of becoming," through which the family can learn to use its symptoms and anxieties in constructive ways. (See also FAMILY THERAPY.)

De'Ath, E., "Experiential Family Therapy," in S. Walrond-Skinner ed., *Developments in Family Therapy* (London: Routledge and Kegan Paul, 1981).

exposure therapy A generic term for behavior therapies that focus on altering an individual's reactions and responses to phobic behavior while gradually increasing his or her exposure to the phobic situation. Exposure therapy is effective for many simple phobias, and also for AGORAPHOBIA (sometimes when accompanied by appropriate drug therapy).

Before considering exposure therapy as a

Exposure Therapy Daily Record

This is an example of how one can keep a record of exposure therapy tasks.

Day	Session: Date	Began	Ended	The exposure task I performed was:	(0 = complete calm, 100 = absolute panic) My anxiety during the task was:	Comments, including coping tactics I used:	Name of co-therapist if any: ______ (Co-therapist's signature that task was completed)
Sunday							
Monday							
Tuesday							
				Example from an agoraphobic			
Wednesday		2:30 P.M.	4:30 P.M.	Walked to local supermarket and surrounding stores, bought food and gifts for family, had coffee at a coffee shop	75	Felt worse in crowded stores, practiced deep-breathing exercises	R. Jones (husband)
Thursday		10:00 A.M.	11:30 A.M.	Walked to the park, sat for ½ hour till I felt better, took the bus downtown and back home.	70	Felt faint and giddy. Practiced imagining myself dropping dead.	R. Jones
Friday		2 P.M.	4 P.M.	Rode the bus downtown and back three times till I felt better about it.	60	Worst when bus was crowded. I did deep-breathing exercises.	R. Jones
Plan for next week: Repeat exposure exercises in the bus, park, and stores every day until my anxiety is no higher than 30. After that, start visits to my hairdresser and short car trips.							
Saturday							
Sunday							
Monday							

possible treatment, an individual can test him or herself with the questions that follow to determine if exposure treatment would be appropriate. (See also BEHAVIOR THERAPY; CATASTROPHIC ANXIETY; FLOODING; IMPLOSIVE THERAPY; SELF-HELP; SIMPLE PHOBIA.)

(The charts in this section have been adapted, with permission, from *Living with Fear* by Marks, Isaac M. [New York: McGraw-Hill, 1978].)

*Self-test to determine appropriateness of exposure therapy**

1. Are you very depressed and thinking of suicide?
2. Are you often drinking alcohol to the point of being drunk?
3. Are you having severe heart trouble or severe asthma?
4. Do you find that there aren't any situations or events that you are avoiding?
5. Do you find that you don't have any specific goals for treatment?
6. Do you feel that avoiding less will not really make a difference in your life?
7. Do you find you are unwilling to invest the time and effort necessary to overcome your fears?

* Candidates appropriate for exposure therapy should answer NO to the above questions.

Steps to prepare oneself for exposure treatment

1. Work out exactly what you fear; do not waste time treating the wrong thing.
2. Write down the specific problems and goals you want to work on.
3. Prepare a timetable for exposure to things that frighten you. Record what happens after each exposure session. Revise your goals as you progress.
4. Determine what thoughts or body sensations bother you
5. Plan goals for each particular session.
6. Leave enough time, possibly several hours, to reach a specific goal by the end of a session.
7. Write down the coping strategies (see below) you will use on cards to carry with you.
8. Record your achievements after every session.

Coping tactics during exposure

1. Breathe slowly or steadily. If you find yourself breathing very rapidly, slow your breathing to about 20 breaths a minute.
2. Be aware that even though you may feel tense or even miserable for a while, things will improve. Learn to tense and relax your muscles repeatedly. Eventually you will be able to relax them more easily. Concentrate particularly on muscles you feel are tense.
3. Keep track of your thoughts. During exposure, you may find yourself thinking about your rapid heartbeat and worrying about having a heart attack. Catastrophic thoughts such as these will make you more tense. Tell yourself that this is an unreasonable thought and be assured that your therapist has repeatedly told you that your heart is fine.
4. Watch your anxiety level rise and fall. Construct a scale from one to ten, ten being the worst anxiety feeling, and give yourself ratings while you practice.
5. Here are some sentences to say to yourself:

   I feel terrible now; if I persist, I will get over this.

   I am terrified, as I was told I would be, but the anxiety will subside if I persist.

I am embarrassed by all this, but I will get used to it.

I must remember that dizziness, pounding heart, shaking, sweating, pressure, and pain in my chest is just anxiety. It is the body's natural fear reaction.

I have an impulse to leave the situation. If I do, I will feel worse. If I remain until my anxiety subsides, I will feel better for the effort, and it will probably become easier as I practice.

6. During exposure, monitors give bodily reaction on the ten-point scale. Start response only when your reaction is below a 3 (some mild bodily symptoms and apprehension). Try to keep the reaction down during exposure. If the reaction reaches a 5 or 6, stop the approach and relax. Go on after your reaction is back down below 3. This retreat–approach should be used in any exposure session. If the reaction becomes strong or cannot be brought down by stopping or retreating, then discontinue exposure and return another time.

extrasensory perception (ESP) A feeling of awareness of external events or information by means other than the known sensory channels. This includes mental telepathy, clairvoyance, precognition, and psychokinesis. Although many individuals allege to have ESP, the subject is controversial. The term ESP was introduced by J.B. Rhine during the first half of the 20th century, although the concept has been known for centuries.

eyes, fear of Fear of eyes is known as ommatophobia or ommetaphobia. (See also BEING STARED AT, FEAR OF; DOUBLE VISION, FEAR OF; EVIL EYE, FEAR OF.)

eyes, fear of opening one's Fear of opening one's eyes is known as optophobia. (See also BEING LOOKED AT, FEAR OF; DOUBLE VISION, FEAR OF; EVIL EYE, FEAR OF.)

eyeglasses, fear of Many infants fear people who wear eyeglasses because the glasses distort natural facial features. Most children, however, outgrow this fear as they discover that some people wear glasses and others do not. When children begin to wear glasses, they may fear breaking their glasses or they may fear ridicule and name-calling from other children. Some individuals, particularly those in middle age, fear having to wear glasses, or particularly bifocal eyeglasses, because they associate this type of eyewear with old age. Individuals who must wear glasses for comfortable vision fear losing their glasses because they feel out of control and helpless without them. Goethe (1749–1832), the German poet, novelist, and playwright, is said to have feared bespectacled people. (See also AGING, FEAR OF; CHILDHOOD FEARS; GOETHE, JOHANN WOLFGANG VON; LOSS OF CONTROL.)

Vierordt, Hermann, *Medizinisches aus der geschichte* (Tübingen, Germany: Laupp, 1910).

Eysenck, Hans Jurgen (1916–) German-born British psychologist known for work on personality studies and behavior therapy. He developed the Eysenck Personality Inventory, scales to measure different aspects of personality, and contributed to the analysis of personality and to genetic studies of emotionality, conditioning, and intelligence testing. Eysenck was instrumental in questioning the "base rate" to spontaneous recovery for psychological and emotional disorders (i.e., the proportion of people who recover without therapy). He concluded that only behavior therapy produces recovery rates greater than the base rate for spontaneous recovery, and hence it is the only proven effective form of therapy. Eysenck is the author of *The Scientific Study of Personality* and the founder of the *Journal of Behavior*

Research and Therapy. (See also BEHAVIOR THERAPY; CONDITIONING; EYSENCK PERSONALITY INVENTORY.)

Eysenck Personality Inventory (EPI) Two scales to measure aspects of personality developed by German-born British psychologist Hans Jurgen Eysenck (1916–). One is an extraversion scale; the other is the neuroticism scale known as the N scale, designed to measure the dimension of stability/instability, or trait anxiety. (See also STATE-TRAIT ANXIETY INVENTORY; TAYLOR MANIFEST ANXIETY SCALE.)

Eysenck, H.J. and S.B.G. Eysenck, *Eysenck Personality Inventory* (San Diego: Educational and Industrial Testing Services, 1963).

Kleinknecht, Ronald A., *The Anxious Self* (New York: Human Sciences Press, 1986).

F

fabrics, fear of certain Fear of certain fabrics is known as textophobia. These fears may involve wools, fuzziness, satins, or silks. (See also FUZZ AVERSION.)

failure, fear of Fear of failure is known as kakorraphiophobia, kakorrhaphobia, kakorrhaphiophobia, and atychiphobia. Some individuals fear failure because they lack confidence in themselves; some fear RIDICULE by others for failures. Those who fear RISK TAKING also fear failure. Many who fear failure hold excessive, rigid, or unrealistic expectations or standards for behavior. (See also CRITICISM, FEAR OF.)

fainting, fear of Fear of fainting is known as asthenophobia. Fainting—an abrupt, usually brief loss of consciousness, generally associated with failure of normal blood circulation—is a PHOBIA in its own right and a symptom of other phobias. It is not unusual for otherwise normal people, including medical students and nurses, to faint from slowed heart rate at first sight of BLOOD, surgery, or INJURY. Fainting at the sight of blood may run in families, because some blood-injury phobias are thought to originate in a genetically determined, extreme AUTONOMIC response. Unlike most phobics who experience rapid heartbeat on encountering their phobic stimuli, blood-injury phobics experience a two-phase response to their phobic stimuli, consisting of rapid heartbeat at first and then a period of profound slower heartbeat to the point of fainting. Those who have an extremely slow heartbeat may develop a fear of fainting. The fainting response of blood-injury phobics is similar to that of blood donors, dental patients, and audiences of violent films.

Heart rate also slows in children seeing films of dental procedures for the first time. Children, under such circumstances, have been known to faint and then become fearful that they will faint again, causing embarrassment to themselves. Exposure by video to models of people going through dental experiences while relaxed can help such children. (See also BLOOD AND BLOOD-INJURY PHOBIA; VASOVAGAL RESPONSE.)

fairies, fear of Some children develop a fear of imaginary fairies after reading about curses and wicked spells of bad fairies in stories such as "The Sleeping Beauty." However, even good fairies have habits that may disturb mortals. For example, according to folklore, fairies prize human babies and have been known to steal an unchristened infant and leave a changeling, or substitute, in its place. Some fairies only borrow human possessions, but others steal, especially if they think the victim is bad or underserving. Appropriate treatment would probably include gradual exposure to fairy tales. (See also FAIRY TALES, FEAR OF.)

Briggs, Katharine, *An Encyclopedia of Fairies*, (New York: Pantheon, 1976), "Mortality of Fairies."

fairy tales, fear of Some story books, fairy tales, and even nursery rhymes may lead to some childhood fears and ANXIETIES. Many fairy tales are frightening to children because they contain bad wolves, powerful giants, wicked witches, and abusive adults. For example, some FEARS are created or increased by stories such as the one about the kidnapping WITCH in "Hansel and Gretel," the ferocious wolf in "The Three Pigs," and the SPIDER in "Little Miss Muffet." There is some debate among psychologists about the effects of fairy tales on children. Some point out that children love fairy tales because they enjoy a certain level of fear as stimulation. Bruno Bettelheim (1903–), child psychologist, suggested that encounters with these frightening creatures and circumstances in stories that ultimately reach a happy ending actually help a child's developmental process. By experiencing frightening situations on a fantasy level, the child works out conflicts and accepts adversity in his own life. The happy ending of a fantasy promotes hopeful, positive feelings without the promise and inherent disappointments of the conclusion of a realistic story. While others experts on child development accept the value of folk and fairy tales, they point out that such stories have produced anxiety in some children and should be used with discretion and sensitivity to the individual child's reaction. (See also ANIMISM; CHILD ABUSE, FEAR OF; CHILDHOOD ANXIETIES, FEARS, AND PHOBIAS.)

Bettelheim, Bruno, *The Uses of Enchantment* (New York: Knopf, 1976).

Sarafino, Edward P., *The Fears of Childhood* (New York: Human Sciences Press, 1986).

Zipes, Jack, *Breaking the Magic Spell: Radical Theories of Folk and Fairy Tales* (New York: Methuen, 1984).

falling, fear of Fear of falling is sometimes linked to fear of HEIGHTS. For example, a phobic may be afraid of being drawn over the edge of a height, or over the edge of a platform at a train station. Some people fear falling to the extent that they cannot walk anywhere outdoors without holding on to a wall, furniture, or another person for support. Individuals who fear falling may have a distorted perception of space. Fear of falling may be related to fears of epilepsy; historically, epilepsy has been known as "falling sickness." Fear of falling may also have various psychoanalytic interpretations; for example, it might be related to the figurative sexual "falling." The fear of falling is one of the innate fears of man and usually does not completely vanish with age or therapy. (See also EPILEPSY; SPACE PHOBIA; WALKING, FEAR OF.)

Marks, Isaac, *Living with Fear* (New York: McGraw-Hill, 1978).

false statements, fear of Fear of making false statements is known as mythophobia. This may be related to a social phobia, in that the individual fears criticism or ridicule by others, particularly if he or she unintentionally says something that is incorrect. Fear of lying, or telling something known to be untrue, may be related to a fear of being caught and punished. (See also LYING, FEAR OF; RIDICULE, FEAR OF)

family influence Behaviors or attitudes learned through interaction with other members of the family. For example, parents may influence a child to be fearful of situations or objects that they fear; some fears of ANIMALS, SNAKES, DARKNESS, WATER, etc., may be learned through family influence.

Family influence also relates to how members of a particular family interact with an individual in that family. For example, the family of an agoraphobic may influence the agoraphobic member not to improve because they are providing services that enable the agoraphobic individual to remain housebound. Likewise, improvement may be facilitated by healthy family attitudes and support.

Most research on family data and fears relates to agoraphobia and blood-injury phobias. There is a higher prevalence of anxiety, panic, depressive disorders, and alcoholism among relatives of agoraphobics than those of social and simple phobics. Why agoraphobia runs in families is unclear. However, it is known that more women than men become agoraphobic, and there is an increase in alcoholism among male relatives of agoraphobics.

Blood-injury phobics have the strongest family history of all phobics. A majority of blood-injury phobics report other family members with a similar problem. This strong family history suggests that blood-injury phobia may come from a genetically determined, autonomic response. Unlike the rapid heartbeat that is the common phobic response to phobic stimuli, the heartbeat response of blood-injury phobics to their phobic stimuli is at first fast (tachycardia) and then extremely slow (bradycardia), even to the point of fainting. (See also AGORAPHOBIA; BLOOD-INJURY PHOBIA; LEARNED HELPLESSNESS; SECONDARY GAIN.)

Marks, Isaac M., *Fears, Phobias and Rituals* (New York: Oxford University Press, 1987).

family myth A pattern of mutually agreed-upon, distorted roles adopted by a family. The family myth may be a shared defense against the ANXIETY provoked by some avoided theme, such as denying that one family member is AGORAPHOBIC. The effort to maintain the myth may require continuous collusion of all family members. (See also AGORAPHOBIA; FAMILY NEUROSES; FAMILY PATTERNS; FAMILY THERAPY.)

family neurosis Patterns of emotionally disordered behavior within a family. An example of a family neurosis might be DEPRESSION, fear of closed places, fear of HEIGHTS, AGORAPHOBIA, or a tendency to have generalized ANXIETY DISORDERS or PANIC DISORDERS. Environmental factors are important in developing family neuroses. Some families are more fearful than others and encourage and teach members to be fearful of the same things, on either a conscious or unconscious basis. (See also LEARNED HELPLESSNESS; NEUROSIS; SECONDARY GAIN.)

Torgerson, Svenn, "Childhood and Family Characteristics in Panic and Generalized Anxiety Disorders," American Journal of Psychiatry (May 1986), pp. 630–632.

family patterns Qualities of the relationships between parents and between parents and children in a particular family. For example, some families are affectionate and close, while others keep one another at a distance and exhibit signs of anxiety when they are together or contemplate being together, such as before holidays. Some families are open to friends and relatives, while others remain tightly knit and relatively closed to outsiders or anxious when outsiders are around. Psychotherapists treating individuals who have phobias usually ask about family patterns and try to determine how the family pattern affects the individual's phobia. (See also FAMILY INFLUENCE.)

family therapy Therapy for all members of a family to help one or more phobic individuals in the family. The whole family meets as a group with the therapist and explores its relationships and processes. Psychotherapy is directed to all sources of disturbances that affect the interpersonal relationships and conflicts within the network of the individual family member's most significant and intimate relationships. The emotional relationships of the individual with his family group exert an important influence on the tendency of any one member toward the phobia. The emotional climate of family life may bind a member to a phobia, for example, by rewarding him for maintaining it, or alternately may reinforce his incentive for recovery. In family therapy, the identified patient—i.e., the phobic—is viewed as symptomatic of the family itself so that the family pattern disturbance must be the focus of the treatment and not the patient. (See also ACCEPTANCE; CLIENT-CENTERED THERAPY; SECONDARY GAIN.)

Freedman, Kaplan, Sadock, *Comprehensive Textbook of Psychiatry/II* (Baltimore: Williams and Wilkins, 1975).

fantasy A mental image or figment of the imagination in which individuals fulfill their conscious or unconscious wishes and/or impulses. Fantasies should be differentiated from physical situations that produce PHOBIAS and FEAR reactions, although many fantasies precede anxiety and AVOIDANCE. (See also FAIRY TALES, FEAR OF.)

fat, fear of being Fear of being fat is related to a fear of gaining weight, or obesiophobia. Along with the harmful physical effects associated with obesity, such as HIGH BLOOD PRESSURE and DIABETES, fat individuals fear social discrimination. In an age in which thinness and fitness are considered desirable, fat individuals may be considered lazy and unattractive. Fear of being fat may lead to EATING DISORDERS, such as ANOREXIA NERVOSA and BULIMIA. (See also WEIGHT GAIN, FEAR OF; WEST, ELLEN.)

father-in-law, fear of Fathers-in-law are sometimes feared and disliked by sons-in-law because the young men resent the success of their wives' fathers and feel inadequate. A new husband may also fear a very strong father's retention of control over his daughter. A young bride may also fear her father-in-law if her husband is involved in a family-owned business. A young man entering his father's or his father-in-law's business may be expected to work long hours and meet extremely high standards of achievement to prove that he is worthy of eventually inheriting his father's or his father-in-law's position. (See also RELATIVES, FEAR OF.)

Klamer, Richard H., *Marriage and Family Relationships* (New York: Harper and Row, 1970).

fatigue, fear of Fear of fatigue is known as ponophobia or kopophobia. Some people fear fatigue because they fear that fatigue will interfere with their control of a given situation. For example, an airline pilot will fear fatigue because it will interfere with his judgment and the safety of his passengers. Fatigue, or tiredness, is a normal reaction to physical exertion, BOREDOM, lack of rest, or emotional strain and usually results in a loss of efficiency. Fatigue may be localized and involve only certain muscles, or it may be a general feeling throughout the mind and body. Fatigue is usually a temporary state. (See also FLYING, FEAR OF.)

fear of fear Fear of fear is known as phobophobia. The fear of fear is thought to underlie agoraphobia, since the agoraphobic who fears becoming anxious in a situation and having a panic attack is afraid of fear. Fear of fear was immortalized by Franklin D. Roosevelt in his first inaugural address on March 4, 1933, when he said: "But first of all let me assert my firm belief that the only thing we have to fear is fear itself—nameless, unreasoning, unjustified terror, which paralyzes needed efforts to convert retreat into advance."

fear An emotion of uneasiness that arises as a normal response to perceived threat that may be real or imagined. Fear includes an outer behavioral expression, an inner feeling, and physiological changes. The word "fear" comes from the Old English word "faer," meaning sudden calamity or danger, and refers to justified fright.

Fear may cause any of a variety of unpleasant feelings including terror, a desire to escape, a pounding heart, muscular tenseness, trembling, DRYNESS of the throat and MOUTH, a sinking feeling in the stomach, NAUSEA, perspiration, difficulty in breathing, feelings of unreality, paralyzing WEAKNESS of the limbs, a sensation of FAINTNESS and falling, a sudden urge to URINATE or DEFECATE or a great urge to CRY.

Fear may induce certain types of behavior, such as flight, fighting, or concealment. Chronic fear in healthy people may result in FATIGUE, DEPRESSION, slowing down of mental processes, restlessness, aggression, loss of appetite, INSOMNIA, and NIGHTMARES.

Fear is a normal and useful emotion. When one faces a threat, fear often leads to rapid action, such as fighting back or removing oneself from the scene. Fear also can motivate learning and performance of socially useful responses such as careful driving or completing an examination in school.

Fears, phobias, anxieties, and PANIC, often used inappropriately as interchangeable terms, in fact have distinct meanings. Fear is considered specifically as an appropriate response to a concrete, real, knowable danger. Anxiety usually refers to a fear of uncertain origin; the individual may not know why he is afraid. A phobia is an intense, irrational fear directly associated with specific events or situations that is out of proportion to the potential danger, cannot be explained or reasoned away, is largely beyond voluntary control, and leads to avoidance of the feared situation. Panic refers to a sudden upsurge of acute, intense fear, often associated with frantic attempts to escape. Panic is extreme fear, with all the symptoms of fear intensified. Fear differs from anxiety in intensity but not quality; anxiety is a vague feeling of uneasiness or apprehension, such as anticipation of impending doom that has a relatively uncertain or unspecific source. Sometimes anxieties are related to feelings of low self-worth and anticipation of a loss of either self-esteem or the esteem of others.

There is a difference between "real fear" and "neurotic fear." An individual experiencing neurotic fear feels instinctual urges that are unacceptable to the conscious mind.

Fear can be learned by CLASSICAL, OPERANT, or vicarious conditioning. (See also ANXIETY; PANIC ATTACK; PHOBIA; RESPONSE PROPERTIES; STIMULUS PROPERTIES.)

Marks, Isaac, *Fears and Phobias* (London: Heinemann Medical, 1969).

Marks, Isaac, *Fears, Phobias and Rituals* (New York: Oxford University Press, 1987).

Goodwin, Donald W., *Phobia: The Facts* (Oxford: Oxford University Press, 1983).

Sarafino, Edward P., *The Fears of Childhood* (New York: Human Sciences Press, 1986).

fear, enjoyment of Many people seek out and enjoy the fearful thrill of experiencing and mastering danger. Included in this category are some tightrope walkers, racing car drivers, bullfighters, certain test pilots, and mountaineers who expose themselves to extreme danger. Spectators enjoy watching dangerous sports or frightening films. Others enjoy roller coaster rides and being "scared silly." (See also SCARED STIFF.)

fear, guilty A term for the fear that dire consequences will befall one because of a misdeed or forbidden impulse. The term guilty fear was coined by Sandor Rado, a Hungarian-born American psychoanalyst (1870–1972). Guilty fear is related to a dread of conscience and is a prominent feature of the obsessive syndrome in which the individual represses defiant rage. (See also OBSESSIVE–COMPULSIVE DISORDER.)

fear, impulse A FEAR that comes instinctively from within the individual, as contrasted with real fear, which is associated with some actual object in the environment. For example, the fear of imminent DEATH, while one is in good health, is an impulse fear, while the fear of being in a THUNDERSTORM is a reality fear.

Fear Inventory or Fear Survey Scale The Fear Survey Scale (FSS) was developed by Joseph Wolpe (1915–) and Peter Lang (1936–) as a self-report instrument to assess overall level of anxiety in a person's life, as well as particular areas of anxiety (such as social situations, injury, death, animals, etc.).

The FSS is used by clinicians as an objective measure of overall anxiety and as a measure of change with therapy. The original FSS contained over 100 items. The following is a sample of the types of items used in the scale. As can be seen, it is simple to administer and score. It utilizes a 5 point intensity scale for self-ratings.

1. Noise of vacuum cleaners
2. Open wounds
3. Being alone
4. Being in a strange place
5. Loud voices
6. Dead people
7. Speaking in public
8. Crossing streets
9. People who seem insane
10. Falling
11. Automobiles
12. Dentists
13. Being teased
14. Thunder
15. Sirens
16. Failure
17. Entering a room where other people are already seated
18. High places on land
19. Looking down from high buildings
20. Worms
21. Imaginary creatures
22. Receiving injections
23. Strangers
24. Bats
25. Journeys by train
26. Journeys by bus
27. Journeys by car
28. Feeling angry
29. People in authority
30. Flying insects
31. Seeing other people injected
32. Sudden noises
33. Dull weather
34. Crowds
35. Large open spaces
36. Cats
37. One person bullying another
38. Tough-looking people
39. Birds
40. Sight of deep water
41. Being watched working
42. Dead animals
43. Weapons
44. Crawling insects
45. Dirt
46. Sight of fighting
47. Ugly people
48. Fire
49. Sick people
50. Dogs
51. Being criticized
52. Strange shapes
53. Being in an elevator
54. Witnessing surgical operations
55. Angry people
56. Mice
57. Blood
    a. Human
    b. Animal
58. Parting from friends
59. Enclosed places
60. Prospect of a surgical operation
61. Feeling rejected by others
62. Airplanes
63. Medical odors
64. Feeling disapproved of
65. Harmless snakes
66. Cemeteries
67. Being ignored
68. Darkness
69. Premature heartbeats (missing a beat)
70. a. Nude men
    b. Nude women
71. Lightning
72. Doctors
73. People with deformities
74. Making mistakes
75. Looking foolish
76. Losing control

Fear Survey Schedule II Devel oped by J.M. Geer after extensive factor analytic and statistical studies of the original

Fear Questionnaire

Following is a brief, self-administered fear questionnaire (patterned after Marks's design) identifying common fear areas, particularly for agoraphobics. There are no norms on this scale, but the individual can use it for measuring progress in overcoming phobic problems.

Choose a number from the scale below to show how much you avoid each of the situations listed, because of fear or other unpleasant feelings. Then write the number you chose in the box opposite each situation.

0	1	2	3	4	5	6	7	8
Would not avoid it		*Slightly avoid it*		*Definitely avoid it*		*Markedly avoid it*		*Always avoid it*

1. Traveling alone by bus or train ____
2. Walking alone in busy streets ____
3. Going into crowded stores ____
4. Going alone far from home ____
5. Large open spaces ____
6. Injections or minor surgery ____
7. Hospitals ____
8. Sight of blood ____
9. Thought of injury ____
10. Going to the dentist ____
11. Eating or drinking with other people ____
12. Being watched or stared at ____
13. Talking to people in authority ____
14. Being criticized ____
15. Speaking or acting to an audience ____
16. Other situations (describe, e.g., animals, thunder) ____

GRAND TOTAL ____

Below describe in your own words the *main* phobia you want treated (e.g., "shopping alone in a busy supermarket" or "fluttering birds"):

Isaac M. Marks, *Living with Fear* (New York: McGraw-Hill, 1978).

Fear Survey Schedule. This version has a seven-point intensity scale and covers fifty-one items. Items are nouns relating to animals, social situations, injury and death, objects, noises, and other situations. Mean scores usually center around 100–108 for females and around 75–82 for males.

Geer, J.M., "The Development of a Scale to Measure Fear," *Behavioral Research and Therapy,* 3(1965), pp. 45–53.

The Geer Fear-Survey Schedule II

Item
1. Sharp objects
2. Being a passenger in a car
3. Dead bodies
4. Suffocating
5. Failing a test
6. Looking foolish
7. Being a passenger in an airplane

Item
8. Worms
9. Arguing with parents
10. Rats and mice
11. Life after death
12. Hypodermic needles
13. Being criticized
14. Meeting someone for the first time
15. Roller coasters
16. Being alone
17. Making mistakes
18. Being misunderstood
19. Death
20. Being in a fight
21. Crowded places
22. Blood
23. Heights
24. Being a leader
25. Swimming alone
26. Illness
27. Being with drunks
28. Illness or injury to loved ones
29. Being self-conscious
30. Driving a car
31. Meeting authority
32. Mental illness
33. Closed places
34. Boating
35. Spiders
36. Thunderstorms
37. Not being a success
38. God
39. Snakes
40. Cemeteries
41. Speaking before a group
42. Seeing a fight
43. Death of a loved one
44. Dark places
45. Strange dogs
46. Deep water
47. Being with a member of the opposite sex
48. Stinging insects
49. Untimely or early death
50. Losing a job
51. Auto accidents

fears, childhood See CHILDHOOD ANXIETIES, FEARS, AND PHOBIAS.

fears, minor See MINOR FEARS.

feathers, fear of Feathers in pillows and on clothing arouse fear in certain phobic individuals. Feather phobia, which may be related to BIRD phobia, is frequently embarrassing to the sufferer who is aware of its ridiculous appearance to others. Some feather phobics are afraid to go outdoors for fear of seeing a creature with feathers, such as a bird; and some have disturbing dreams about feathers. Some who fear feathers avoid going to farms and barnyards where they may see chickens, ducks, or other fowl. Fear of feathers is probably a fear of birds or other feathered creatures. (See also BIRDS, FEAR OF; WINGED THINGS, FEAR OF.)

Melville, Joy, *Phobias and Obsessions* (New York: Coward, McCann and Geoghegan, 1977).

febriphobia Fear of fever. (See also FEVER, FEAR OF.)

fecal matter, fear of Fear of fecal matter is known as scatophobia. (See also FECES, FEAR OF.)

feces, fear of Fear of feces is known as coprophobia. Feces—waste matter expelled from the bowels—are also known as excrement and fecal matter. This phobia may include fear of expelling one's own feces, or of coming into contact with or viewing feces. In psychoanalytic terms, witholding the feces is one of the earliest expressions of the drive for aggression and independence. (See also PSYCHOANALYSIS.)

feedback In therapy, information given to the individual about the nature and effects of his or her behavior. Feedback may take many forms, including direct comments, role playing, or videotape replays. Feedback affects correction and self-correction and may change or reinforce behavior. Therapists in some types of therapy offer more feedback than those in others; for example, in behavior therapy there is more feedback than in psychoanalysis. (See also BEHAVIOR THERAPY; PSYCHOANALYSIS; THERAPY)

felinophobia Fear of cats. (See also CATS, FEAR OF.)

female genitalia, fear of Known as eurotrophobia. Female genitalia consist of the vagina, uterus, ovaries, fallopian tubes, and related structures. Those who have this fear may focus their energy on nonsexual objects that resemble or symbolize the female genitalia and may develop FETISHES (neurotic preferences) for them. Fear of female genitalia affects women and men. (See also SEXUAL FEARS.)

feminophobia Fear of women. (See also WOMEN, FEAR OF.)

Fenichel, Otto (1899–1946) An Austrian psychoanalyst and a disciple of SIGMUND FREUD. Fenichel accepted Freud's theory of the LIBIDO and psychosexual development but placed particular emphasis on disturbing emotional experiences in childhood as the primary cause of neuroses. In 1945 he wrote *The Psychoanalytic Theory of Neuroses,* which contained detailed clinical and theoretical material on ANXIETY, PANIC, PHOBIAS, AND AGORAPHOBIA from the psychoanalytic perspective. (See also PHOBIC CHARACTER.)

fetish A nonsexual object or part of the body that arouses sexual interest or excitement by association or symbolization. Common fetishes are feminine undergarments, shoes, or boots. Individuals who have fetishes obtain sexual gratification from fondling, kissing, or licking the object on which they focus. A fetish may develop because of a fear of a part of the body, such as the genitalia. Some individuals fear fetishes or fetishism. Some fetishes are associated with a childhood caretaker, such as a mother's lingerie on the clothesline, etc

The term fetish was derived from the Portuguese word *fetico,* meaning "a charm." Alfred Binet first used the term in the psychoanalytic sense—that is, referring to an object that becomes emotionally charged and, in some cases, is the source of perverted sexual gratification—in 1888. (See also FEMALE GENITALIA, FEAR OF; SEXUAL FEARS.)

fever, fear of Fear of fever is known as febriphobia, fibriophobia, and pyrexiophobia. Individuals who fear ILLNESS may also fear fever. Some who fear fever do so because they fear a LOSS OF CONTROL over their behavior. Some fear the HALLUCINATIONS, DELUSIONS, or CONVULSIONS that may accompany high fever. Such individuals fear doing something to embarrass themselves at those times. (See also HALLUCINATIONS, FEAR OF.)

fibriphobia, fibriophobia Fear of fever. (See also FEVER, FEAR OF.)

fight or flight response The sequence of internal activities triggered when an individual is faced with a threat. The response helps prepare the body for combat and struggle or for running away to safety.

filth, fear of Fear of filth is known as mysophobia, rhypophobia, rypophobia, and rupophobia. This fear may be related to fears of CONTAMINATION and GERMS and to fears of using public toilet facilties. Some obsessive–compulsives fear filth. (See also OBSESSIVE–COMPULSIVE DISORDER.)

fire, fear of Fear of fire is known as arsonophobia or pyrophobia. People who are phobic about fire may avoid striking matches and attending occasions that involve cooking outdoors over a campfire. They may become obsessive about CHECKING the gas supply in their homes and making sure that there is an escape route when they are in an unfamiliar building

Historically, fire has been a fear- and awe-inspiring symbol in the mind of man, with both divine and evil associations. The tradition of a sacred fire tended by virgins was present in early Greek, Irish, and Peruvian cultures. The pantheon of gods in most religions includes a god of fire. Fire was considered to be a test of power or purity, and in many cultures magicians and wizards demonstrated their power by walking over coals or swallowing fire. Christian saints and priests were supposedly immune to injury by fire. Trial by fire was considered a test of virginity, truthfulness, and honesty in general. Fire has also had associations with evil and the powers of darkness. The fires of hell are the fate of sinners. Burning was the method of execution for WITCHES and heretics. Smiths were held in awe and considered possible agents of the DEVIL because of their work with fire. Marsh fires in Britain once were thought to have SUPERNATURAL causes. The strange phenomenon called St. Elmo's fire, a flickering light around ships' masts, was believed to prophesy bad weather.

Psychologically, fire is associated with ANGER and aggression. For example, a "firebrand" is an agitator, a promoter of strife. When someone is angry, he is said to have smoke or steam coming out of his ears. There are many hostile fire-breathing dragons in legends and fairy tales.

Arthur Schopenhauer (1788–1860), a German philosopher, is said to have always lived on a first story because he feared fire.

Modern fears of fire have valid foundations; children playing with matches account for 75,000 fires a year in the United States, which kill about 10,000 people. (See also OBSESSIVE–COMPULSIVE DISORDER; SCHOPENHAUER, ARTHUR.)

Cavendish, Richard (ed.), *Man, Myth and Magic* (New York: Marshall Cavendish, 1983), "Fire."

World Book, Inc., *World Book Encyclopedia* (Chicago: World Book, Inc., 1987), "Fire Prevention."

Melville, Joy, *Phobias and Obsessions* (New York: Coward, McCann, Geoghegan, 1977), p. 146.

fish, fear of Fear of fish is known as ichthyophobia. This fear may include looking at fish, imagining or seeing pictures of fish, or eating fish. Fear of being near lakes or the seashore may be related, if the bodies of water are filled with fish. (See also LAKES, FEAR OF; WATER, FEAR OF.)

fitness anxiety Individuals who have fitness anxiety have a fear of general unfitness or poor health. Fitness anxiety seems to be a result of the 1980s "fitness craze" and the rising popularity of jogging, aerobic exercise, and health clubs, as well as medical evidence that suggests that diet and exercise patterns may be significant in the prevention of heart disease and other major health hazards. Fitness anxiety can lead to obsessive behavior regarding one's own exercise habits or diet. Some individuals—for example, runners—develop compulsions to do their extra mile every day or a given number of miles every week, regardless of weather conditions or how they feel. Some individuals actually overexercise—for example, young women runners who run excessively lose weight, become very thin, and cease to menstruate. (See also EATING DISORDERS; EXERCISE, COMPULSION TO.)

5-Hydroxytroptophan A drug that acts on SEROTONIN receptors and may have a role in the control of anxiety. (See also L-5-HYDROXYTROPTOPHAN; NEUROTRANSMITTERS.)

fixation An obsessional preoccupation with a simple idea, impulse, or aim; sometimes known as an "idée fixe." This may occur in OBSESSIVE–COMPULSIVE DISORDER, AGORAPHOBIA, and other psychological disorders. In PSYCHOANALYSIS, a fixation is the persistence of an early stage of development or an inappropriate attachment to an early psychosexual object or mode of gratification, such as anal or oral activity. Such a fixation persists during adulthood in immature and neurotic form, interfering with other normal attachments. Smoking is sometimes interpreted as an oral fixation, hoarding as an anal-stage fixation, and anxiety as a response to unresolved Oedipal conflicts during the phallic stage. (See also FIXATION PHOBIA.)

fixation phobia Early childhood fears of a specific event or object that a person retains into adulthood without resolving. Although older people tend to fear social harm, the FEARS of children usually involve danger of some kind of physical INJURY or DEATH. Common fears include WATER, THUNDERSTORMS, DOCTORS, and BLOOD. Children usually outgrow fears related to SUPERNATURAL agents such as GHOSTS, WITCHES, CORPSES, or mysterious events, being alone in DARK or strange places, BEING LOST, being attacked by humans or animals, bodily INJURY, ILLNESS, surgical operations, PAIN, FALLING, or traffic accidents. SOCIAL PHOBIAS, such as attending parties, shaking hands, or PUBLIC SPEAKING, may also become fixation phobias.

Fixation phobias may persist into adulthood because phobic children begin to avoid their feared objects or situations at an early age, and their fears may be reinforced by the fears of their parents.

In psychoanalytic theory, a fixation is the arrest of psychosexual development at a particular stage through too much or too little gratification. (See also DEATH, FEAR OF; DEVELOPMENTAL STAGES; ILLNESS, FEAR OF; INJURY, FEAR OF; PHOBIA; PSYCHOANALYSIS; SOCIAL PHOBIA.)

Beck, Aaron T. and Gary Emery, *Anxiety Disorders and Phobias* (New York: Basic Books, 1985).

fixed-interval schedule In OPERANT CONDITIONING (a form of BEHAVIOR THERAPY), a schedule in which the individual receives reinforcement for the first response made after a fixed amount of time has elapsed. Monthly pay would be an example of fixed-interval reinforcement.

fixed-radio schedule In OPERANT CONDITIONING (a form of BEHAVIOR THERAPY), a schedule in which the individual receives reinforcement only after a fixed number of responses. Piecework (that is, work paid for according to the number of items produced rather than by the hour) would be an example of fixed-ratio reinforcement.

flashing lights, fear of Fear of flashing lights is known as selaphobia. This fear may be related in a general way to fear of light, glaring lights, or light and shadows. Some individuals fear driving at night because of flashing lights. (See also LIGHT, FEAR OF; LIGHT AND SHADOWS, FEAR OF.)

flatulence, fear of Flatulence, or the expulsion of air from the digestive tract through the mouth or anus, is a common symptom experienced by individuals who have digestive disorders or IRRITABLE BOWEL SYNDROME. Belching may be caused by unwittingly swallowing large amounts of air during rapid eating, gum chewing, or as a nervous habit. Fear of passing wind (gas), or of BELCHING, are SOCIAL PHOBIAS. The individual fears embarrassing himself or herself, making diagreeable noises, or causing unpleasant odors. Some who have this fear may avoid social situations in which they are near people or in enclosed spaces with other people, such as elevators. (See also BELCHING, FEAR OF.)

flood, fear of Fear of flood is known as antlophobia. This is one of manv fear of natural disasters, which include tornadoes and hurricanes. Some who live in areas that commonly flood after a rainy season have a realistic fear of flood and many take precautions, such as stocking sandbags at the appropriate time. Only when such a FEAR is unreasonable is it considered a PHOBIA.

flooding A technique of BEHAVIOR THERAPY in which the individual experiences the fear-provoking object or situation in his or her imagination without being instructed to relax. The theory behind flooding is that after prolonged exposure the individual will become accustomed to imagined feared objects or situations and thus eventually fear them less. This process is thought to follow the laws of extinction or a gradual diminution with repeated exposure. Exposure to fear-producing stimuli might occur at full intensity for a minimum of two hours and usually three to four hours per session.

In World War II, a group of U.S. soldiers who were severely startled by noise and even music were hospitalized and forced to watch twelve fourteen-minute showings of increasingly loud war films. Reactions to the films gradually changed from terror to boredom, and all but one of the soldiers improved. (See also DESENSITISATION; EXPOSURE THERAPY; IMPLOSION THERAPY.)

flowers, fear of Fear of flowers is known as anthophobia. This fear may be of a particular flower, or of a characteristic of some flowers, such as size or texture.

fluoxetine An antidepressant drug. (See also ANTIDEPRESSANTS; ANTIDEPRESSANTS, NEW; DEPRESSION.)

LaPierre, Y.D., "New Antidepressant Drugs," *Journal of Clinical Psychiatry* (August 1983), pp. 41–44.

flutes, fear of Fear of flutes is known as autophobia and aulophobia. In some societies, flutes are considered to be voices of spirits and therefore represent supernatural beings (who may have been mythological ancestors of the clan). In some cultures, flutes are made of bamboo and cane with a wooden stopper and may be decorated with hair, feathers, and shells. Their motifs may represent clan totems, either human figures or animals, especially birds. Flutes are often played during initiation or cult ceremonies. Because of their shape, for some, flutes may be phallic symbols. Individuals who fear rods or sticks may also fear flutes. (See also RODS, FEAR OF.)

fluvoxamine An antidepressant drug. (See also ANTIDEPRESSANTS; ANTIDEPRESSANTS, NEW; DEPRESSION.)

LaPierre, Y.D., "New Antidepressant Drugs." *Journal of Clinical Psychiatry* (August 1983), pp. 41–44.

flying, fear of Fear of flying, known as aerophobia, represents one of the major fear categories for adults in the United States and probably throughout the world. Estimates of the number of fearful people vary, but the most comprehensive survey concluded that some 25,000,000 Americans—one of every six adults—are afraid to fly.

The fear of flying itself has two points of origin—the anticipatory situation and the flying situation itself. Anticipatory anxiety occurs because a commitment has been made to fly (a reservation has been made, ticket purchased, people informed of trip, etc.). Anticipatory anxiety usually is experienced as feelings of dread, rapid pulse, total body sensations (tension, warmth, etc.), and fear-inducing images and thoughts. Interestingly, the anticipatory fear is usually not of the airplane itself but of uncontrollable outcomes such as fear of losing control of oneself in the airplane and going crazy or embarrassing oneself in public; fear of separation from loved ones, fear of death; fears of relinquishing control to someone else; thoughts of falling from the sky and dying in a crash; and so on. Fear in the plane itself may encompass many of the anticipatory fears just described but also usually involves fears of being enclosed, fears of being alone or away from others one depends on, feeling trapped and unable to leave at will, fears of social rejection due to the reaction, fear of the fear sensations, and sometimes feelings about the place or person the individual is leaving or the place or person the individual may be seeing at the destination.

News reports of air crashes, stories and television and movie depictions can also provide stimuli for fear thoughts and reactions. It has also been pointed out that much of the common language used in the air-travel industry has a fatalistic and fear engendering ring, such as "terminal," "final boarding," "final approach," "departure lounge," and so on; the fears engendered by terminology may be supplemented by insurance desks, oxygen masks, crash procedures, and a number of reminders of possible adverse consequences to flying. Many of these factors are external cues for anxiety while thoughts and sensations represent internal triggers to anxiety.

Treatment for the fear of flying has varied from traditional therapies to hypnosis, flooding, and exposure therapies. The last provide the best long-term success rate at about 75 percent to 80 percent. A "cue-controlled" relaxation procedure in which the phobic learns to produce relaxation on cue seems to offer promise as an effective technique. Success, of course, involves more than just being able to fly. The more rigorous criterion involves flying with progressively increased ease and comfort over a long-term series of trials. Unfortunately, there are very few experimental studies to date that demonstrate comparative therapy effects.

The most commonly used drug for the fear of flying is probably alcohol. Unfortunately, while alcohol reduces autonomic arousal, it tends to produce anxietylike sensations (such as dizziness, loss of balance, mental confusion, lack of control of perceptual-motor functions, and so on), which, in turn, can trigger an anxiety response. PROPRANOLOL and ALPRAZOLAM are two drugs commonly used for fear of flying. They are both fast-acting and produce relatively few side effects. TRIAZOLAM has also been used on a more experimental basis.

Efforts to identify personality qualities associated with the fear of flying have not been fruitful. Interestingly, family trauma associated with flying (such as loss of or injury to a family member—even a distant one—in an aircraft accident) is a significant predictor of phobic reaction. This would support a modeling theory of acquisition. Also, multiphobics or individuals suffering from panic disorders have a higher incidence of aerophobia than uniphobics and seem to be much more difficult to treat than the latter.

Flying fear in aircrew

Flying phobia disables aircrew members as well as some individuals in the public. Fear of flying is a major cause of airline and air force personnel being grounded. Flying phobia may come on gradually along with irritability and insomnia. Some who become fearful of flying report more childhood and other adulthood phobias before the fear of flying began and more flying accidents in their families. Some flying phobics also have more marital or sexual problems than those in the general population and are more neurotic and introverted than aircrew members who do not fear flying.

Experimental comparison studies of phobic and nonphobic aircrews reveals that galvanic skin responsitivity (GSR), history of childhood anxiety and phobias, worries about spouse and children, and family traumas (loss of life) associated with flying were 85 percent predictive of groupings.

Fear of flying has not been noted as a problem in the 8 percent of aircrew who survive ejection from an aircraft despite injuries. Many have had continuing emotional reactions including FEAR, ANXIETY, anger, disgust, or altered motivation. Some aircrew members who become agoraphobic responded well to some form of guided exposure. Behavior therapies are demonstrably effective in aircrews and pilots.

Some members of the military suffer a

FEAR OF FLYING as a symptom of POSTTRAUMATIC STRESS DISORDER. (See also EXPOSURE THERAPY.)

Dean, R.D., and K.M. Whitaker. "Fear of Flying: Impact on the U.S. Air Travel Industry." *Journal of Travel Research* 21 (1982):7–17.

TIPS ON HOW TO FLY MORE COMFORTABLY

1. Make a commitment to fly when you choose to do so. Don't agree to fly with the idea you will back out. See flying as an opportunity for you to become less fearful.
2. Prepare yourself far in advance. Practice relaxation so you build skills in calming yourself. This will not prevent you from becoming anxious, but it will lessen the intensity, allow you to recover faster, and give you some control over the situation. Visualize yourself flying comfortably (as you would like to be able to fly) when you are relaxed.
3. Practice some desensitization. For example, go to the airport to relax yourself in that environment. Watch the planes take off and land and relax yourself. Imagine being comfortable in an airplane that you are watching.
4. Take things with you to occupy yourself when flying. Also, make a tape for relaxation and to remind yourself of thoughts and ideas that will help you cope on the plane.
5. Remember, the fear will not go away without practice, preparation, and continued flying on a regular basis.

flying things, fear of Some people fear flying things, such as birds, flying insects, bats, or butterflies, because such creatures fly at them unpredictably, scare them with sudden motion, and may get in their hair. Those who fear flying things may keep their windows closed tightly and rarely venture outdoors. They also avoid enclosed spaces in which they might become trapped with a flying thing, such as a bat in a barn or belfry. Many people have overcome these fears with exposure therapy. (See also BATS, FEAR OF; BIRDS, FEAR OF; EXPOSURE THERAPY; WINGED THINGS, FEAR OF.)

fog, fear of Fear of fog is known as homichlophobia and nebulaphobia. Fog is frightening because it stimulates near-blindness, distorts shapes, and produces a closed-in, claustrophobic sensation that makes an individual feel a LOSS OF CONTROL over his environment. An object or person can be invisible very close at hand and then appear out of the fog in a startling manner. Fog is associated with confusion and lack of clarity; foggy thinking and language are muddled and imprecise.

Fog is frequently used in suspenseful scenes in horror or mystery films because of its power to inspire fear and apprehension. Fog patches that appear and move suddenly cause particular fear and an impending sense of danger. (See also AIR POLLUTION, FEAR OF.)

Holford, Ingrid, *The Guinness Book of Weather Facts and Feats* (Enfield, Middlesex: Guinness Superlatives, 1982).

folk healers Many individuals around the world consult folk healers for anxiety problems. Before the advent of formalized medical systems, many societies devised ways to cope with fear and phobias. These include use of magic and charms and invocation of divine intervention. Studies during the 1960s indicated that exorcism and antiwitch measures were still prevalent in many Far Eastern cultures. Demonological and astrological remedies were (and still are) prescribed along with recently developed drugs to relieve anxieties. Medicine men are still used extensively by Indians in some societies today.

Additionally, witch doctors, healers, and medicine men are still common in Third World countries. (See also DEPRESSION ACROSS CULTURES; WITCHES AND WITCHCRAFT, FEAR OF.)

Neki, J.S., "Psychiatry in South-East Asia," *British Journal of Psychiatry*, 123(1973), pp. 257–269.

food aversion Many people strongly dislike certain foods, often because they associate them with nausea and vomiting. Most food aversions are taste aversions, but individuals may also dislike a food's appearance, smell, or symbolic aspects. Many people avoid new foods. Individuals decide which foods are acceptable based on cultural and individual rearing patterns. Some who mistakenly eat a taboo food may become terrified of imagined consequences. (See also FOOD, FEAR OF.)

Marks, Isaac M., *Fears, Phobias and Rituals* (New York: Oxford University Press, 1987), pp. 30–31.

food, fear of Fear of food, or certain foods, is known as sitophobia, sitiophobia, and cibophobia. Some individuals fear eating certain foods, such as meat. For some, the fear is related to religious TABOOS. For example, many Hindus are vegetarian, and Muslims and Jews are forbidden to eat pork. If a religious individual eats a forbidden food by mistake or coercion, he or she may vomit or feel nauseous for days. (See also EATING, FEAR OF; NAUSEA; SWALLOWING, FEAR OF.)

foreigners, fear of Fear of foreigners or strangers is known as zenophobia or xenophobia. Many who fear novelty, newness, or anything different may also fear foreigners. (See also NEWNESS, FEAR OF; NOVELTY, FEAR OF; STRANGERS, FEAR OF.)

forests, fear of Fear of forests is known as hylophobia, hylephobia, and xylophobia. Fear of forests may be related to fears of trees or of landscapes. (See also LANDSCAPES, FEAR OF; TREES, FEAR OF.)

Framingham Type A scale See CORONARY-PRONE TYPE A BEHAVIOR.

France and things French, fear of Fear of France and things relating to the French culture is known as Gallophobia. Often such fears relate to hearing the spoken language. (See also FOREIGNERS, FEAR OF; STRANGERS, FEAR OF.)

Frankl, Viktor (1905–) A German-born American psychiatrist, the originator of logotherapy, an EXISTENTIAL approach to life. Frankl's approach stresses the uniqueness and self-determinism of man and the ability of the human being to make decisions, to influence his own life, to be responsible, to achieve personal growth, and to be a significant part of the current world. He suggesested that man can transcend his environment and also distinctly affect it instead of being affected by it. Frankl derived his belief in the importance of meaning in life through his own experiences in a German concentration camp during World War II. He believes that the overly scientific, mechanistic attempt to formulate man's behavior into simple cause-and-effect associations has contributed to a feeling of meaninglessness in life. In Frankl's view, individuals must learn to deal with the here and now, deciding upon the values that are their own and that they will accept. For many therapists, the existential orientation espoused by Frankl is quite compatible with humanism. Frankl is the author of *From Death Camp to Existentialism* (1959) and *Man's Search for Meaning* (1963). (See also EXISTENTIAL THERAPY.)

Suinn, Richard M., *Fundamentals of Behavior Pathology* (New York: John Wiley, 1975).

free association A therapeutic technique in which the individual is encouraged to relax conscious control over his or her thoughts and to say anything and everything that comes to mind. This technique may be useful in associating past events, feelings, and attitudes with phobic behavior. Free association is a key procedure in PSYCHOANALYSIS. The assumption is that over time, hitherto repressed material will come forth for examination by the ANALYSAND and the analyst. (See FREUD, SIGMUND.)

freedom, fear of Fear of freedom is known as eleutherophobia. Such fears were noted after the Civil War in the U.S. when many former slaves returned to work for their masters because they did not want (or were not able) to be free. Similarly, convicts released from prison will sometimes commit another crime in order to return. This phenomenon is also unfortunately associated with "treatment" of the mentally ill in hospitals where they quickly become "institutionalized" by regimes that enforce compliance, passivity, and noninteraction.

free-floating anxiety Continual ANXIETY not easily attributable to any specific STIMULI or reasonable danger. This was a Freudian term used in the first diagnostic system. The current preferred terminology is GENERALIZED ANXIETY, indicating an anxiety state that persists through a person's daily activities (perhaps varying in intensity at different times or locations). (See also FEAR; PHOBIA.)

Freud, Anna (1895–1982) The youngest of SIGMUND FREUD'S six children and the only one to become a psychoanalyst. With her father, she escaped from Vienna to England, where she worked until her death in 1982. She is known for her work on the problems and fears of children separated from their parents by evacuation during World War II. She developed and consolidated her father's theories, despite criticism and opposition from other schools of psychoanalysis. She is the author of many books on diagnostic and analytic work with children, including *The Psychoanalytic Treatment of Children: Lectures and Essays* (London: Imago, 1946). (See also CHILDHOOD FEARS.)

Freud, Sigmund (1856–1939) Austrian neurologist and psychiatrist, creator of PSYCHOANALYSIS, and one of the leading influences on 20th-century thought, attitudes, and behavior. As the creator of psychoanalysis, or the "talking cure," Freud made significant contributions to the study of anxieties and other mental disorders and influenced the development of 20th-century scientific psychology as well as many social science fields, literature, art, business, history, education, and child development.

The term "Freudian approach" has been applied to Freud's emphasis on the view that individuals are driven by UNCONSCIOUS and especially psychosexual impulses. His approach is also known as Freudianism.

Freud's treatment was based on the patient's bringing back to consciousness repressed emotions, and releasing them by reviving and reliving painful experiences that have been buried in the unconscious. As Freud developed his techniques he replaced the use of hypnosis with dream interpretaton, FREE ASSOCIATION, and the analysis of lapses in behavior and speech that came to be known as "Freudian slips."

In Freud's method of free association, unconscious sexual conflicts and their repression are recognized as the major factors in neuroses. These concepts became the essence of the new discipline that he called psychoanalysis, which focused on procedures including the interpretation of DREAMS in terms of hostile or sexual feelings stemming from childhood, analysis of resistances and the transference relationship between the therapist and the patient, and a study of the patient's current symptoms in terms of psychosexual development and early experiences. His theory of personality, known as the Freudian theory of personality, holds that character and personality result from experiences and fixations based on early stages of psychosexual development. The goal of psychoanalysis, which usually takes many years, is to restructure the individual's psychic life.

In his earlier writings in 1895, Freud suggested a differentiation between phobias based on the nature of the object feared and a distinction between common phobias and contingent phobias. Common phobias were those in which there is an exaggerated fear of things "that everyone detects or fears to some extent." Contingent phobias were those "that inspire no fear in the normal man, for example, agoraphobia and other phobias of locomotion."

Freud separated phobic neurosis from obsessive–compulsive neurosis and anxiety neurosis, a separation that still prevails in most psychiatric textbooks.

In Freud's studies, he also applied his psychoanalytic method to historical figures, such as Leonardo da Vinci, and explored primitive cultures; he drew parallels between the childhood of the individual and the childhood of the human race. Freud's views were highly controversial during his lifetime and after. He taught many disciples and helped establish the first psychoanalytical association. His coworkers and pupils included Alfred ADLER, Otto RANK, Carl JUNG, Carl Abraham, and his daughter, ANNA FREUD.

In his writings, Freud frequently mentioned his own agoraphobia. From age thirty-one to forty-three he was anxious about traveling by train but did not avoid it. He is said to have hesitated a long time before crossing a wide street.

Freud published many books, including *The Interpretation of Dreams* (1900), *Three Essays on the Theory of Sexuality* (1905), *Totem and Taboo* (1913), *Beyond the Pleasure Principle* (1920), and *The Ego and the Id* (1923). (See also ABREACTION.)

Goodwin, Donald W., *Phobia: The Facts* (New York: Oxford University Press, 1983).

Schapira, Kurt et al., "Phobias and Affective Illness," *British Journal of Psychiatry*, 117(1970), pp. 25–32.

frigidity A woman's inability to obtain satisfaction (usually orgasm) during SEXUAL INTERCOURSE. This may result from a lack of adequate stimulation or a misunderstanding between the partners concerning sexual behavior and wishes. Cultural rejection of certain practices may also play a part. Freudian psychoanalysts attribute frigidity to many sources, including aggressive inhibition, ill-managed parental love, penis envy, and imperfect transfer of capacity for stimulation from the clitoris to the vagina. Modern sexual therapists reject Freud's theory of two types of orgasms, associated respectively with the vagina and the clitoris, as unproven, and modern sex-therapy treatments for frigidity are behavioral in nature. (See also PSYCHOSEXUAL ANXIETY; SEXUAL FEARS.)

frigophobia Fear of cold and cold things. (See also COLD, FEAR OF.)

frogs, fear of Fear of frogs is known as batrachophobia. This fear may be related to fears of other reptiles, and possibly to slimy things (often snakes). Frogs may be considered any of a number of tailless, chiefly aquatic amphibians. They usually have a smooth, moist skin, webbed feet, and long hind legs adapted for leaping. (See also SLIMY THINGS, FEAR OF; TOADS, FEAR OF.)

Fromm, Erich (1900–1980) German-born American psychologist and sociologist. According to Fromm, one of the ways to deal with fears of loneliness is to seek connection and meaning from external institutions. He defined this process as "authoritarianism," or the development of "symbiotic relationships." However, he believed that the internal resourcefulness of the individual is the true source of fulfillment, and that it requires a breaking away from external authoritarian dependency. In Fromm's system of development, the individual's ability to produce is essential. Those who lack self-fulfillment would be more susceptible to formation of a pseudo-self, somewhat like Karen Horney's "idealized image." Unlike Horney, however, Fromm gave little attention to the concept of the pseudo-self, which he described as "essentially a reflex of other people's expectation" (the "marketing personality"). Fromm said that personal courage allows the individual to face the unknown directly and to go through the "uncertainty" of life. Further, Fromm said that "uncertainty is the very condition to impel man to unfold his powers. If he faces the truth without panic, he will recognize that there is no meaning to life except the meaning man gives his life by the unfolding of his powers." Fromm stressed the eventual despising of the self, the stage when the individual is aware of his insecure existence. The cure for such distortion, or neurotic behavior, was the idea of "relatedness" or the intimacy of love, both of the self and of others in society. His therapy for the neurotic was based upon instilling confidence into the individual who had lost courage. Fromm drew on all techniques of psychoanlaysis in order to uncover the exact reason for the loss. (See also HORNEY, KAREN; PSYCHOANALYSIS.)

frost, fear of Fear of frost is known as pagophobia. Individuals who fear cold things, or fear ice, may also fear frost. (See also COLD, FEAR OF; ICE, FEAR OF.)

functional approach A model of human behavior that achieves prediction and control by analyzing the relationship or function of behavior in the environment.

fur, fear of Fear of touching an animal's fur is known as doraphobia. This fear may be related to a fear of textures or an aversion to fuzz. (See also FABRICS, FEAR OF CERTAIN; FUZZ AVERSION; TEXTURES, FEAR OF.)

fuzz aversion Some individuals do not like to touch certain textures, such as new tennis balls, the skin of a kiwi fruit, or a fuzzy sweater. They tend to avoid fabrics that cause fuzz. (See also FABRICS, FEAR OF CERTAIN; TEXTURES, FEAR OF.)

G

GABA See GAMMA-AMINO BUTYRIC ACID (GABA).

gagging, hypersensitive The feeling that one will gag or choke is often a symptom of anxiety. A fear of gagging is related to the feeling of a lump in the throat that one cannot seem to swallow. Those who are hypersensitive gaggers cannot tolerate foreign objects in their mouths, such as those used during dental treatment. In some cases, individuals may gag, retch, or vomit, if they even hear or think about dentistry or smell an odor associated with dental procedures.

Gagging is a normal protective reflex for the oropharynx; the sensitivity and trigger area is greater in some individuals than in others. In mild cases, gagging can be triggered just by touching near the back of the mouth with the tongue or being touched by a dental instrument. In more severe cases, the trigger can be touching the front of the mouth, the face and the front of the neck, certain smells, or sights associated with unpleasant oral experiences, such as dentistry, or with becoming ill due to certain foods.

Some hypersensitive gaggers swallow with their teeth clenched and thus have difficulty during dental procedures. Such individuals have particular difficulty in swallowing with their teeth apart.

There are several ways that individuals who experience gagging can be helped. General relaxation techniques are beneficial. Communicating one's fears to the dentist before a procedure is important. Use of a rating scale, on which the patient indicates what types of procedures are likeliest to induce the most gagging, will improve communications between patient and dentist. During dental procedures, hypersentitive gaggers can be taught to signal (with a raised hand) whenever gagging is about to occur.

Hypersensitive gaggers can learn to modify their swallowing pattern—for example, swallowing with the teeth slightly apart and the tongue further back in the mouth. When sharp teeth make the tongue hypersentitive, the teeth can be smoothed down somewhat. Some dentists give anxious patients homework assignments, such as learning to hold buttons under the tongue and rolling them around in the mouth, so they become accustomed to having foreign objects in their mouth without gagging. (See also DENTAL FEARS; SWALLOWING, FEAR OF; VOMITING, FEAR OF.)

Wilks, C.G.W. and I.M. Marks, "Reducing Hypersensitive Gagging," *British Dental Journal* (Oct. 22, 1983), pp. 263–265.

gaiety, fear of Fear of gaiety is known as cherophobia.

galeophobia Fear of cats. (See also CATS, FEAR OF.)

Gallophobia Fear of France, the French language, and things relating to the French culture is known as Gallophobia.

galvanic skin response (GSR) Changes in resistance in the skin to psychological stimulation as measured by an electronic device. Emotional arousal (positive and negative) generally leads to increased sweat-gland activity, which, in turn, lowers electrical resistance. Electrodermal responses are taken by pairing a small (imperceptible) electrical current between two electrodes on the skin. Increases in conductance (lowered resistance) are thought to reflect increased autonomic (emotional) activity. The sweat glands are activated by SYMPATHETIC NERVOUS SYSTEM activity, and therefore the GSR measures reflect changes in the sympathetic system.

gambling, fear of; compulsion Individuals who fear gambling usually prefer secure situations to situations involving risks. They may be fearful of losing or making errors, or fearful of what they regard as sin or wrongdoing. They may not feel comfortable when they relinquish a certain amount of control over their circumstances, which is usually involved in gambling. Individuals who feel that they are compulsive gamblers, unable to stop once they get started, may actually fear gambling because of what they perceive as its control over them and the ensuing detrimental effects on their lives. Those who have had bad experiences with gambling may fear it more than those who have never gambled before. (See also RISK TAKING, FEAR OF.)

gamma-amino butyric acid (GABA) A neurotransmitter in the brain that relates to ANXIETY. ALPRAZOLAM, a BENZODIAZEPINE (popularly known as Xanax), binds to the GABA receptors in the brain. (A drug or NEUROTRANSMITTER "binds" to chemical receptors that are shaped to receive and use it rather than other chemicals.) It is known that when taken in therapeutic doses, both Valium (which is not effective in treating panic attacks) and alprazolam change the shape of the receptor molecule (GABA) they share. The chemical interaction between alprazolam and the diazepam receptor changes the metabolism of GABA, which in turn produces a series of changes in the biochemistry of the cell and thus lessens anxiety. Researchers speculate that PANIC DISORDER may be a deficiency disease and may result when a hormone or neurotransmitter that usually regulates anxiety is missing or deficient in some way.

gamophobia Fear of marriage is known as gamophobia or gametophobia. (See also MARRIAGE, FEAR OF.)

garlic, fear of Fear of garlic is known as alliumphobia. This fear may extend to a variety of plants characterized by their pungent odor, including the onion, leek, chive, and shallot. (See also ODORS, FEAR OF.)

gastrointestinal complaints Abdominal discomfort, cramping, DIARRHEA, urgency to defecate, FEAR OF LOSING CONTROL, CONSTIPATION, and NAUSEA are common complaints of many individuals who have ANXIETY DISORDERS, PANIC DISORDERS, and DEPRESSION. Many individuals seek help for gastrointestinal complaints before seeking treatment for their anxieties. In many cases, the gastrointestinal complaints are relieved with antianxiety therapy. (See also IRRITABLE BOWEL SYNDROME.)

Lydiard, R. Bruce et al., "Can Panic Disorder Present as Irritable Bowel Syndrome?" *Journal of Clinical Psychiatry* (September 1986), pp. 470–473.

gatophobia Fear of cats. (See also CATS, FEAR OF.)

geliophobia Fear of laughter. This fear may be related to a fear of gaiety (cherophobia). (See also GAIETY, FEAR OF; LAUGHTER, FEAR OF.)

gender identity An individual's sense of "maleness" or "femaleness," and an acceptance and awareness of one's biological sex. If an individual has internal conflicts regarding his or her gender identity and does not accept his or her biological designation, frustrations and anxieties may develop, leading the individual into practices that may include "cross dressing" and taking on the role of the other sex. (See also GENDER IDENTITY DISORDER; SEXUAL FEARS.)

gender identity disorder A type of psychosexual disorder in which an individual's GENDER IDENTITY is incongruent with his or her anatomical sex. When an individual believes that he or she is a man or woman in the body of the other sex, anxieties often result. Some individuals who have these feelings relieve their anxieties by having a sex-change operation. (See GENDER ROLE; SEXUAL FEARS.)

gender role The set of behaviors and attitudes that are socially associated with being male or female. These attitudes may be expressed to varying degrees by the individual. Historically, in Western cultures, gender role for many women was passive and submissive, which led to many ANXIETIES and frustrations, until the "women's liberation" movement and "sexual revolution" in Westernized countries during the latter half of the 20th century. As a result of many societal changes, gender roles have also changed significantly. For example, child care is no longer exclusively the woman's role, and earning the larger part of the family income is no longer exclusively the man's role. However, changes in gender roles have led to many contemporary anxieties, such as women's feelings of conflict between motherhood and career and men's fears of inferiority when the wife advances rapidly in her career and outearns the husband. (See also "GENERATIONAL" ANXIETIES.)

generalized anxiety disorders (GAD) See ANXIETY DISORDERS.

"generational" anxiety The anxieties faced by millions of middle-aged individuals who care for aging relatives in addition to raising children, holding a job, and trying to live their own lives is sometimes referred to as "generational" anxiety. As the numbers of people above age 65, 75, and even 85 increase dramatically and 95 percent of older people live outside of nursing homes, responsibility for their care falls increasingly to the middle-aged people, and in most cases, women. As these middle-generation individuals see their children entering and finishing college, becoming involved in a career and marriage, they may feel trapped by another long-term burden, which they may view as more demanding that that of raising school-aged children.

Many midlife individuals find that their love of parents turns toward anger as their own lives are pulled in three or four different directions. Many must give up their own time, interests, and relaxation to become caregivers. Thus the "women (or men) in the middle" are three times more likely to suffer DEPRESSION, more likely to become dependent on prescription drugs and alcohol, and more likely to become physically ill. Their spouses and children also suffer restrictions on social and leisure activities, disruption of household routines, and added financial burdens.

To relieve "generational anxieties," individuals in the middle might analyze their situations carefully and consider whether they can fully cope with these demands. A family conference can be called to apprise everyone involved of the burdens and build realistic shared responsibilities, if at all possible. Community support groups for children of aging parents can be helpful. Having a single physician for the entire family may be helpful in tying together all the medical care the aging parent needs and at the same time providing emotional support and encouragement for those in the middle.

Bosey, Linda, *Women in the Middle* (Chicago, IL: American Osteopathic Association, 1987).

geniophobia Fear of chins. (See also CHINS, FEAR OF.)

genital stage The final stage of psychosexual development, also known as genital phase. According to psychoanalytic theory, the genital stage follows the oral and anal phases and is reached during adolescence, when sexual relationships with another becomes the major aim of sexual interest. In some cases, when appropriate transitions from other stages of development do not occur, the individual may develop phobias and anxieties that interfere with later sexual relationships and adjustments to marriage. (See also STAGES OF DEVELOPMENT.)

genitals, female, fear of Fear of the female genital organs is known as kolpophobia or eurotophobia. (See also FEMALE GENITALIA, FEAR OF; SEXUAL FEARS.)

genitals, male, fear of Fear of the male genital organs is known as phallophobia. (See also SEXUAL FEARS.)

genophobia Fear of sexual intercourse. (See also PSYCHOSEXUAL ANXIETIES; SEXUAL FEARS; SEXUAL INTERCOURSE, FEAR OF.)

genuphobia Fear of knees. (See also KNEES, FEAR OF.)

gephyrophobia Fear of bridges. (See also BRIDGES, FEAR OF.)

gerascophobia Fear of growing old. (See also AGING, FEAR OF; OLD, FEAR OF GROWING; RETIREMENT, FEAR OF; WRINKLES, FEAR OF.)

Germanophobia Fear of Germany, German language, and things relating to the German culture. This fear may relate to fear of hearing the German language.

Germany, fear of See GERMANOPHOBIA.

germs, fear of Fear of germs is known as bacillophobia or mikrophobia. The term germs commonly refers to any microorganism that can cause DISEASE. Germs, although a nonspecific term, for the purpose of causing anxieties and phobias, can inlude the many types of bacteria, molds, yeasts, and viruses. Fears of germs can lead to other behaviors, such as OBSESSIVE–COMPULSIVE DISORDER, in which an individual may constantly wash his hands, or specific disease phobias, such as TUBERCULOPHOBIA.

gestalt psychology The study of the formation and function of patterns or configurations in human mental processes. "Gestalt" is the German word for configuration or pattern. In English, the word signifies "a unified whole, picture, or person with specific characteristics that cannot be grasped simply by noting its various parts." Gestalt psychology and therapy was best defined around 1950 by Dr. Frederick Perls (see GESTALT THERAPY). Gestalt psychology emphasizes the whole of experience, which consisted of more than the sum of its parts. For example, in a classic experiment, Edward Kohler describes a monkey given a stick who suddenly ("ah-hah" or insight) realizes that it can be used to pull some desired bananas to him that are out of reach. The whole (use of the stick for this particular purpose) was a configuration that was more than its parts.

gestalt therapy A type of psychotherapy; one of many therapies useful in treating individuals who have phobias and anxieties. Gestalt therapy emphasizes treatment of the person as a whole, including biological aspects and their organic functioning, perceptions, and interrelationships with the outside world. Gestalt therapy focuses on the sensory awareness of the individual's here-and-now experiences, rather than on past recollections or future expectations; it can be used in individual or group therapy settings. Gestalt therapy uses role-playing, acting out anger or fright, reliving traumatic experiences, and other techniques such as the "empty chair" to elicit spontaneous feelings and self-awareness, promote personality growth, and help the individual develop his full potential. Gestalt therapy was developed by Frederic S. PERLS, a German-born American psychotherapist (1893–1970). (See also "EMPTY CHAIR;" GESTALT PSYCHOLOGY; HERE-AND-NOW APPROACH.)

geumaphobia, geumophobia, geumatophobia Fear of taste. (See also TASTE, FEAR OF.)

ghosts, fear of Fear of ghosts is known as phasmophobia or daemonophobia. A ghost may be the spirit of a dead person that haunts living persons or former habitats, or it may be a returning or haunting memory or image.

The fear of ghosts may have been planted in the minds of primitive man because of concern about the afterlife of deceased relatives. Dead ancestors, who were worshipped in many early cultures as gods or near-gods, were thought to be easily angered. Gifts and ceremonies were necessary to sustain their goodwill and decrease hostilities the dead were believed to bear toward the living.

Belief in and fear of ghosts was furthered by desires for a pleasant afterlife, a heaven or Elysian fields, accessible to some but not all spirits. Criminals and witches were condemned to walk the earth rather than enter a restful existence after death. The spirits of murder victims or individuals who had been buried improperly could not rest in peace until the wrong had been righted. Burial customs and rituals indicate a desire to keep the spirits of the dead away from the living. (See also DEMONS, FEAR OF; WITCHES, FEAR OF.)

Runes, D.D. (ed.), *The Selected Writings of Benjamin Rush* (New York: The Philosophical Library, 1947).

Hill, Douglas and Pat Williams, *The Supernatural* (New York: Hawthorn, 1965), pp. 68–100.

Cavendish, Richard (ed.), *Man, Myth and Magic* (New York: Marshall Cavendish, 1983).

girls, fear of Fear of girls (or young girls) is known as parthenophobia. The word is derived from the Greek word *parthenos*, or virgin. Some individuals might have a phobia about young girls because of the survival of a Victorian attitude that children, especially little girls, are pure and vulnerable to corruption by adults. Fear of girls may also be an extension of men's fear of women. (See also CHILDREN, FEAR OF; OPPOSITE SEX, FEAR OF; SEXUAL FEARS; VIRGINS, FEAR OF; WOMEN, FEAR OF.)

Cable, Mary, *The Little Darlings* (New York: Scribner, 1975).

glaring lights, fear of Fear of glaring lights is known as photoaugiophobia. Individuals who have this fear may fear being in the spotlight or fear that others are watching them. They may also fear damage to their eyes. Such individuals usually avoid night driving.

glass, fear of Fear of glass is known as crystallophobia, hyalophobia, hyelophobia, and nelophobia. Some people fear the fragility of glass and fear being injured or cut by broken glass. Others fear their reflections in glass. (See also MIRRORS, FEAR OF.)

Glasser, William (1925–) American psychiatrist and author, Glasser developed REALITY THERAPY in reaction to traditional Freudian treatments. Working with his teacher, G.L. Harrington, Glasser encouraged his patients to accept responsibility for the present and to concentrate on their positive personality traits as a way of overcoming anxieties and behavioral deficiencies. Work with delinquent and inner-city elementary school students led him to apply his ideas to the educational process. *Reality Therapy: A New Approach to Psychiatry* was published in 1965, and *Schools without Failure* in 1969. Glasser is the founder of the Institute for Reality Therapy in Los Angeles.

Contemporary Authors (Detroit: Gale Research, 1978).

The Reality Therapy Reader (New York: Harper and Row, 1976).

globus hystericus The feeling that one has a lump or mass in the throat when nothing is there. The individual usually experiences difficulty in swallowing. This can be a symptom of anxiety arousal. (See also LUMP IN THE THROAT; SWALLOWING, FEAR OF.)

Glover, Edward (1888–1972) A British psychoanalyst, Dr. Glover was a leader in organizing the British Psychoanalytic Society in 1924, and he taught there for 20 years before resigning. He devoted many years to studying and writing about the scientific nature of PSYCHOANALYSIS and the need to exclude unscientific dilutions of psychoanalytic theory and technique introduced in the newer developments. He suggested the concept of EGO-NUCLEI, in which the primitive ego is a compromise formation, consisting of autonomous components that originate in infancy during the oral and anal stages of development. He authored more than 100 scientific works.

goal The object or end toward which therapy for anxieties or phobia is aimed. In different types of therapy there are different types of goals. For example, in BEHAVIOR THERAPY, a goal for an individual who has a specific phobia might be to face the phobic item or situation without fear. In PSYCHOANALYSIS, the treatment goal is to make unconscious material conscious. In FAMILY THERAPY, the goal is to restructure the family system and bring about a better-functioning family group. Goals should be specific, measurable, and attainable. There may be many goals for one individual, and goals may change during the course of therapy. For example, an elevator phobic's first goal might be to face an elevator without fear. A later goal would be to enter the elevator, and then to ride up in it. (See also GOAL ATTAINMENT SCALING [GAS].)

goal attainment scaling (GAS) A research tool to evaluate outcome of treatment for an anxious or phobic individual. It consists of predetermined goals and stages toward those goals. The therapist and individual mutually establish goals before therapy begins. As therapy progresses, attainment of the goals can be assessed, and goals may be revised. Goal attainment scaling is used in family therapy and marital therapy. It is also a valuable research concept that allows researchers to compare various therapies, techniques, modalities, etc. on a common scale. (See also GOAL.)

Kiresuk, T. and R. Sherman, "Goal Attainment Scaling," *Community Mental Health*, 4(1968), pp. 443–453.

goblins, fear of Some people fear the small, grotesque spirits known as goblins, considered by some to be a type of fairy. Goblins are at worst malicious and at best mischievious. They often live in the woods but come into homes to play their tricks. James Whitcomb Riley's poem for children, "Little Orphan Annie," plays on the fears that many children have of goblins and uses these fears to discipline children with the recurring threat, "The gobble-uns'll git you ef you don't watch out!"

> You better mind yer parents, and yer teachers fond an' dear . . .
> Er the Gobble-uns'll get you
> Ef you don't watch out

The poem is frightening to many young children who are not ready to distinguish creatures in their imagination from those in reality. (See also ANXIETY DISORDERS OF CHILDHOOD; CHILDHOOD ANXIETIES, FEARS, AND PHOBIAS.)

Sarafino, Edward P., *The Fears of Childhood* (New York: Human Sciences Press, 1986).

Briggs, Katharine, *An Encyclopedia of Fairies* (New York: Pantheon, 1976).

Maria Leach (ed.), *Standard Dictionary of Folklore, Mythology and Legend* (New York: Funk and Wagnalls, 1972).

Riley, James Whitcomb, *The Gobble-uns . . .* (Philadelphia: Lippincott, 1975).

God, fear of Fear of God is known as theophobia. God as a concept has been both a producer and reducer of fear and anxiety. The mysteriousness and power of God inspires a sense of awe, which is in part fear. Part of many worship rituals are acts of self-abasement; such acts include the lowered eyes, bowed head, and clasped hands, a kneeling or prostrate position, and silence. However, the act of prayer, common to most religions, is, in the end, a reducer of anxiety. In its more primitive form, prayer is a way of asking for help or for some particular desired object or event, rather than facing the reality of luck, chance, and one's own limitations. In a more mystical, meditative form, prayer is a tension-relieving escape, a chance to be in contact with a higher power outside of time and ordinary events.

Acts of propitiation and sacrifice in many religions are indications of the fearful aspect of God. In many religions, dead ancestors were thought to be lower gods who could intercede with higher powers, and in some beliefs they were the sole gods. These spirits, also the enforcers of social taboos, required constant recognition in the form of ceremonies and gifts. Sacrifices and offerings are also common in religions that do not involve ancestor worship. Food, animals, and, in some religions, human lives have all been offered to the higher powers. For example, Aztec Indians believed that the sun would not rise and move across the sky without daily human sacrifice. Sacrifice seems to have performed some psychological functions more positive than alleviation of fear.

The sacrificial victim was considered a messenger to the gods and, at least in some cases, went willingly. The ritual gave the worshiper a satisfying sense of being in touch with God and of vicariously sacrificing himself.

The Western concept of God is far more personal and potentially judgmental than than of Eastern religions, whose moving force is thought of in abstract terms of unity and harmony and, in some Eastern systems of belief, the indescribable. The Judeo-Christian God's role as a loving but judgmental power, a God whose acts are evident in the unfolding of history, who can in fact part the Red Sea for his chosen people, offers tremendous possibilities for emotional response, including fear. In the Christian tradition, juxtaposed to the fearful idea that God can and does punish sins is the belief that God sent His son Jesus to die for man's sins and that through belief in Him everlasting life is attainable. Classical and medieval Christian thinking recognized the power of God, but also that of luck and chance in men's affairs. With the Reformation, a new line of thinking developed: a belief that all actions were a working out of God's will, but admitting that God's ways were nonetheless inscrutable. This would seem to offer a soothing release from anxiety and responsibility, a sense that one's life was in God's hands, but many men and women of that period fell into endless worrisome speculation. When a calamity befell them, they wondered whether God was testing them or punishing them. Some even felt that when life was going well, it was a sign that God had lost interest in their personal situation. Although elements of belief in God's providence continue today, as a rigid set of ideas it became intolerable and dissolved into 18th-century rationalism.

Modern man retains a strong consciousness of the emotion of guilt but has lost the sense of God as a judge or inflictor of punishment. Secular institutions and disciplines now bear a large part of the responsibility for alleviating human suffering and controlling antisocial behavior. Twentieth-century philosophers' speculation that God may be dead has dealt the ultimate blow to God as a source of fear, punishment, or help. On the other hand, there are still those individuals who know that "we are the fulfillment of God; that we are that place in consciousness when God shines through, the realization that every individual is the presence of God."

Goldstein, Joel. *The Infinite Way* (San Gabriel, CA: Willing, 1947).

Hill, Douglas and Pat Williams, *The Supernatural* (New York: Hawthorne, 1965), pp. 28–68.

Sandmel, Samuel, *A Little Book on Religion (For People Who Are Not Religious)* (Chambersburg, PA: Wilson Books, 1975), pp. 46–54.

Spinks, G. Stephens, *Psychology and Religion* (Boston: Beacon Press, 1963), pp. 1–13, 31–46, 117–146.

Thomas, Keith, *Religion and the Decline of Magic* (New York: Scribner, 1971), pp. 51–112.

Goethe, Johann Wolfgang von

(1749–1832) A German poet, novelist and playwright. Goethe hated the "hostile stare" of bespectacled people. Ironically, he was nearsighted after his student years and had to use a lorgnette and later a monocle. Goethe also hated people cleaning candles and lamps in his presence. In an autobiographical note written in 1770, Goethe said the he decided to apply the exposure principle to remedy his phobias of heights, diseased bodies, loud noises, and dark, lonely places. He ascended a cathedral spire and commented: "Such anxiety and pain I repeated so often until the impression became quite different to me."

Marks, Isaac M., "Behavioral Psychotherapy in General Psychiatry," *British Journal of Psychiatry,* 150 (1987), pp. 593–597.

Vierordt, H., Medizinisches aus der Geschichte (Tübingen, Germany: Laupp, 1910), pp. 131 and 180.

going crazy, fear of Many individuals who have ANXIETIES, FEARS, PHOBIAS, and PANIC ATTACKS at times fear that they are going crazy. Their misinterpretation of their situation may be heightened if they do not have any support and understanding from relatives and friends, or particularly if those close to them suggest that the phobic's feelings are "all in the mind." When individuals fear "going crazy," usually they are referring to a severe mental disorder known as SCHIZOPHRENIA. However, most individuals who have phobias, anxieties, panic attacks, depression, and OBSESSIVE–COMPULSIVE DISORDERS are not schizophrenic, and when an individual understands the nature of his or her psychological problem, he or she will have less fear of going crazy. Schizophrenia is a major mental disorder characterized by such severe symptoms as disjointed thoughts and speech, sometimes extending to babbling, delusions, or strange beliefs (for example, that one is receiving messages from outer space), and hallucinations (for example, hearing voices). Schizophrenia usually begins gradually and not suddenly (such as during a panic attack). Schizophrenia is often genetic, and in some people, no amount of anxieties or stress will cause the disorder. People who become schizophrenic usually will show some mild symptoms for most of their lives, such as unusual or bizarre thoughts or speech. Schizophrenia usually first appears in the late teens to early twenties. Individuals who are in therapy for their fears, phobias, and anxieties can be fairly certain that they are not likely to become schizophrenic, for they would have been so diagnosed during examination, interviews, and testing. At a more symbolic level, the fear of going crazy is a fear of becoming disconnected from reality and other people and living in an isolated or alienated state.

Barlow, David, "The Causes of Anxiety and Panic Attacks" (Albany, NY: The Center for Stress and Anxiety Disorders, Phobia and Anxiety Disorders Clinic, 1987).

going to bed, fear of Fear of going to bed, being in bed, or beds in general is known as clinophobia. Such fears may be related to fear of not waking up or fear of dying during sleep. (See also BED, FEAR OF; WAKING UP, NOT, FEAR OF.)

gold, fear of Fear of gold is known as aurophobia. Such fears may relate to fears of success and wealth, fear of shiny things, or fear of textures.

good news, fear of hearing Fear of hearing good news is known as euphobia. Those who have this fear may fear that the good news will not last, that they do not deserve to have good fortune, or that they should have some guilt about the news. Some who fear good news fear that bad news may follow; some fear success. Fear of good news may be related to a fear of gaiety or happiness. (See also SUCCESS, FEAR OF.)

graphophobia Fear of handwriting or writing. (See also WRITING, FEAR OF.)

graves, fear of Fear of graves is known as taphophobia. Those who fear graves also usually fear cemeteries, funerals, and other rituals associated with death, and they may also fear death itself. The source of the fear may be some aspect of "contagion" in the atmosphere around graves. Some individuals who become very anxious avoid going to funerals for this reason, and some will go to the funeral service (if it is held in a place other than the cemetery or burial area), but they will not go near the gravesite. Some individuals avoid walking past cemeteries when funerals are going on, and some avoid cemeteries at all times, even to the extent of driving out of the way to avoid passing one. (See also CEMETERIES, FEAR OF; DEATH, FEAR OF.)

gravity, fear of Fear of gravity is known as barophobia. This fear is related to fear of perceivable changes in air pressure.

Greece, anxiety disorders in As recently as 1966, the idea that a person may become possessed by a demon was still popular in Greece. This was still an accepted church doctrine, and the church offered its services to anyone wishing to help an unfortunate relative with an exorcism. Orthodox dogma taught that one cannot refute the existence of the demon(s) without destroying faith in God, because the two are opposites that cancel each other. If there is a demon, he can take possession of the human soul. The "evil eye" is a related concept that is still blamed in Greece for any personal misfortune, including mental disorders.

The most common cause of suicide, as reported in Greek newspapers (1966), was business worries. The almost-routine explanation for attempted suicide was frustrated love affairs. (See also DEMONS, FEAR OF; EVIL EYE, FEAR OF.)

Hartocollis, P., "Psychiatry in Contemporary Greece," *American Journal of Psychiatry*, 123:4 (October 1966), pp. 457–462.

Greisinger, Wilhelm (1817–1868) A German psychiatrist known for taking the first organic approach to psychiatry. Greisinger believed that mental disorders were due to brain damage and that mental institutions should be centers for medical research. (See also ORGANIC APPROACH.)

grief reaction and grief resolution The feeling of loss and anxiety an individual experiences when a crucial bond is disrupted. Depression often follows. There is a higher death and illness risk for individuals for a year after they lose a spouse. Through the exposure approach of guided mourning the bereaved may be led to reduce avoidance of cues reminiscent of the deceased.

Grief is a type of suffering, a symptom of bereavement and loss, experienced physically, emotionally, and psychologically. Grief may be synonymous with sorrow, or the emotion that accompanies mourning. Individuals who experience grief may have sensations characteristic of emotional disorders such as ANXIETIES, INSOMNIA, DEPRESSION, loss of appetite, and preoccupation with the lost party. As a result of a classic study following the 1942 Cocoanut Grove nighclub fire in Boston, five normal stages of grief reaction were defined as: initial shock, intense sadness, withdrawal from the environment, protest of the loss, and finally, a gradual resolution of the loss. Elisabeth Kübler-Ross identified the stages of emotion experienced after the death of a loved one as: denial, anger, bargaining, depression, and acceptance. Most grieving persons will experience these or similar stages. All stages of mourning are a normal and necessary component to grief resolution. (See also STRESS MANAGEMENT.)

Kübler-Ross, E., *On Death and Dying* (New York: Macmillan, 1971).

Marks, Isaac M., *Fears, Phobias and Rituals* (New York: Oxford University Press, 1987).

Ramsay, R.W. and R. Noorbergen, *Living with Loss* (New York: William Morrow, 1981).

growing old, fear of Fear of growing old is known as gerascophobia. This is a fear shared by many middle-aged people who fear being alone as they get older, deteriorating physically and mentally, and becoming out of control and a burden to their children or others for care and possibly support. Some fear losing their memory, while others fear losing control of bodily functions and being embarrassed by their dependence on others. Many fear the financial costs of care in a nursing home, if that type of care should be needed. More specific fears related to growing old are fear of alzheimer's disease, FEAR OF CATARACT EXTRACTION, fear of HEART ATTACK, and certain disease phobias, such as fear of diabetes, which is more prevalent in older people. (See also AGING, FEAR OF; GENERATIONAL ANXIETY.)

guilt An aversive feeling that an individual experiences as a consequence of an action or in anticipation of performing the behavior. One may feel guilt following commission of an act and omission of an acceptable course of action. Guilt is a form of anxiety. Along with guilt, an individual anticipates punishment; when he or she projects guilt onto others, he or she also anticipates their punishment. Some individuals believe, possibly unconsciously, that they have "sinned," and they fear God will attack and punish them. Guilt keeps individuals trapped because they blame themselves or others. Severe or abnormal guilt feelings may result in DEPRESSION and/or chronic ANXIETIES. Individuals who have obsessive–compulsive neuroses often feel the need to scrutinize their conduct and may have a compulsion to confess to therapists or clergypersons. Some individuals commit suicide out of profound guilt feelings over events for which death seems to be the only appropriate restitution. Guilt is a way to hold onto the past, to produce self-condemnation that keeps the individual under the control of his or her ego and supports a view that he or she is unlovable. (See also NEUROSES; OBSESSIVE–COMPULSIVE DISORDER; SINNING, FEAR OF.)

Jampolsky, Gerald G., *Goodbye to Guilt* (Toronto: Bantam Books, 1985).

gymnophobia Fear of naked bodies. (See also NAKED BODY, FEAR OF; NUDITY, FEAR OF.)

gynephobia Fear of women. (See also WOMEN, FEAR OF.)

H

habit strength The strength of an habitual response (such as fear) that depends on the number and extent of reinforcements and the intervals between stimulus and response and response and reinforcement. The term was coined by Clark Leonard Hull (1884–1952), an American psychologist. Habit strength is the central concept in Hull's theory of learning. He believed that habit strength accumulates as a direct function of the number of reinforced stimulus–response occurrences.

Hadephobia Fear of Hell. (See also HELL, FEAR OF.)

Hagiophobia Fear of holy things. (See also HOLY THINGS, FEAR OF.)

hair, fear of Fear of hair is known as trichophobia or chaetophobia. The most frequently occurring fear regarding hair is BALDNESS, or loss of hair. Also, some individuals fear having the hair on their head touched, pulled, brushed, combed, or washed. Some fear that they will grow bald unless their hair is untouched. Other individuals fear the sight of hair on clothing (their own or the hair of others), on the table, or on a sink. Some fear body hair on themselves or on others. Some fear white or gray hair on themselves or others. As with many fears, hair fear is a conditioned response or a generalized response. (See also BALD, FEAR OF BECOMING; HAIR DISEASE, FEAR OF.)

haircut, fear of having a Fear of having a haircut arises from a number of causes, including a fear of sitting confined in the barber or beautician's chair, a feeling of being out of control while the barber or beautician is working with a scissors or razor, or a fear of injury from these implements. Some who have agoraphobia fear going out to get a haircut. Some fear being seen by others while they are having a haircut or fear being judged and compared unfavorably with others as they sit on the chair. Fear of having a haircut is related to many phobias, including AGORAPHOBIA, SOCIAL

PHOBIA, and fear of blood and injury. ARTHUR SCHOPENHAUER (1788–1860), a German philosopher, is said to have feared his hairdresser. (See also BARBER'S CHAIR SYNDROME; BLOOD PHOBIA; INJURY PHOBIA.)

hair disease, fear of Fear of hair disease is known as chaetophobia. The most common hair disorder is thinning hair or baldness. Hair loss in men is largely due to male-pattern baldness; thinning hair in women is most often due to female-pattern baldness. Most other losses of hair are temporary, such as following illness or as a result of certain drug therapy (e.g., CHEMOTHERAPY). Normal regrowth resumes in most cases.

Some fear unusual hair conditions, one of which is called trichorrhexis, in which the hair shaft may alter, bulge, and narrow; the hair tends to split at regular intervals. The cause of this condition is not known, and there is no cure for it. Some people fear having too oily or too dry hair.

Some hair-related problems involve the scalp. Such conditions include dandruff, psoriasis, seborrheic dermatitis, inflammation of the hair follicles (folliculitis), ringworm, and other infections. Some fear these conditions because, particularly in the case of dandruff, they are socially noticeable. An individual who has any tendency toward social phobia may use dandruff as an excuse to avoid social situations. (See also BALD, FEAR OF BECOMING; HAIR, FEAR OF; SKIN DISEASE, FEAR OF.)

Halloween, fear of The celebration of Halloween has its origins in fear and death. On the night of the end of the summer Druid festival called Samhain, bonfires were kindled on the hills in the British Isles to frighten away witches and the spirits of the dead who were thought to wander free on that night. A Roman holiday that honored the dead, Feralia, was Christianized by Pope Boniface IV to honor saints and martyrs and to serve as a day of prayers of intercession for dead souls who had not been thoroughly purified. In Great Britain, the observations merged into a day called Halligan or All Hallows, and the night before became All Hallows Eve or Halloween.

The American custom of trick-or-treating on Halloween is threatened during the latter part of the 20th century by very real modern fears. Urban crime has made children less likely to be allowed out and adults less willing to open their doors. A rash of incidents of treats adulterated with objects such as pins and razor blades has added still another fear to the celebration of Halloween. (See also CRIME, URBAN, FEAR OF; WITCHES AND WITCHCRAFT, FEAR OF.)

Cohen, Hennig and Tristram Potter Coffin (eds.), *The Folklore of American Holidays* (Detroit: Gale Research, 1987).

McSpadden, J. Walker, *The Book of Holidays* (New York: Thomas Y. Crowell, 1946).

hallucination A perception by any of the senses (visual, auditory, kinesthetic, gustatory, and smell) without relevant and adequate external stimuli. Hallucinations are experiences of an individual and are usually idosyncratic and personal. A group perception is called "illusion." Hallucinations are a central symptom of psychosis and dementias but do not occur with anxiety disorders. (See also SCHIZOPHRENIA.)

hallucinogen A drug or chemical whose effects in the body include HALLUCINATIONS. Hallucinogenic drugs such as LSD (d-lysergic acid diethylamide, lysergide, LSD-25), psilocybin, and mescaline are often called psychedelic drugs. Some individuals try these drugs to relieve anxieties, but in the long run the anxieties remain, and the drug use may result in dependence or unpleasant side effects. (See also DRUGS, FEAR OF.)

hamartophobia A fear of committing an error or sin. The word is derived from the Greek work *hamartia,* meaning "sin." Another word for fear of sin or error is enosiophobia. (See also SIN, FEAR OF.)

Hamilton Anxiety Scale See ANXIETY, HAMILTON SCALE (chart).

handwringing Handwringing is usually a symptom of anxiety and uncertainty. Individuals who constantly wring their hands may have difficulty in making decisions and seem to be expressing physically a worry or concern that they do not express verbally. For many, wringing the hands as though they were constantly washing them or squeezing out a cloth may become an unconscious habit. Some individuals start wringing their hands when faced with a stressful situation, while others may do it at any time. Handwringers tend to be worriers and consider all possibilities of a situation before taking any action. Such individuals are often meticulous about what they do, sometimes to the point of being compulsive. (See also ANXIETY; NERVOUS; OBSESSIVE–COMPULSIVE DISORDER.)

hangover The physical and emotional condition caused by and following excessive intake of alcoholic beverages. Symptoms of hangover include anxiety, uneasiness, HEADACHE, fatigue, NAUSEA, thirst, sweating, and fatigue. These symptoms usually occur several hours after drinking the ALCOHOL. A headache occurs because alcohol causes the arteries in the scalp to stretch. Also, TYRAMINE and HISTAMINE, chemicals in such alcoholic beverages as red wine and brandy, get into the blood, leading to the throbbing pain on one side of the head. Often with the headache comes extreme sensitivity to light and noise (photophobia and phonophobia) and increased vulnerability to anxiety and panic.

The nausea and stomach ache that are part of some hangovers result from irritation of the lining of the stomach by alcohol. (See also ALCOHOLISM; LIGHT, FEAR OF; NOISE, FEAR OF.)

SELF-HELPS FOR TREATING A HANGOVER AND RELATED ANXIETIES

1. Take aspirin or buffered aspirin, or ibuprofen; if the stomach is upset, take acetaminophen.
2. Drink fluids (nonalcoholic). Fruit juices are best because they contain sugar, which may help headaches. Coffee may help at first because of its caffeine content, but after a while the throbbing may get worse as the caffeine leaves the body and a rebound effect takes hold.
3. Wearing a sweatband (not too tight) helps some people because it helps compress some stretched-out scalp arteries. Rubbing one's temples can accomplish the same result. Cold compresses applied to the painful side of the head also may help shrink those arteries.
4. Breathe deeply. Taking in more air, especially fresh air, increases the oxygen level of the blood, which also helps relieve the pain. This may be one reason that a brisk walk often relieves a hangover.
5. Hangovers usually end in 12 to 24 hours without medical help.

(Dr. Daniel B. Hier, chairman, Dept. of Neurology, Michael Reese Hospital and Medical Center, Chicago, Illinois.)

Hans, Little The child patient described in SIGMUND FREUD's "Analysis of a Phobia in a Five-Year-Old Boy" (1909). This was the case that Freud used to formulate his theory of anxiety and phobia. (See also LITTLE HANS.)

haphephobia A fear of being touched. Other words for this phobia are haptephobia and aphephobia. (See also BEING TOUCHED, FEAR OF.)

happiness, fear of Fear of happiness, or fear of gaiety, is known as cherophobia. This fear may be related to a fear of hearing good news, or even a fear of success. (See also GOOD NEWS, FEAR OF; SUCCESS, FEAR OF.)

Hardy, Arthur B. (1910–) An American psychiatrist, best known for his pioneering development of the TERRAP (TERRitorrial APprehensiveness) program for the treatment of agoraphobia and panic-attack syndromes. In the 1960s, when agoraphobia was not well understood as an anxiety condition, Hardy discovered that use of gradual exposure had curative effects. Together with many of his recovered patients, Dr. Hardy developed techniques that became known as the TERRAP self-help treatment program. Dr. Hardy is the founder and past president of the Phobia Society of America, the Mental Research Institute, Palo Alto, CA, and the Mid-Peninsula Psychiatric Society and has served as president of the Counseling and Psychotherapy Center, Palo Alto, CA. He has been in private psychiatric practice in Menlo Park, CA, since 1950. (See also AGORAPHOBIA.)

harpaxophobia A fear of becoming a victim of robbers. (See also ROBBERS, FEAR OF.)

Harrington, G. Leonard (1916–) An American psychiatrist, associate of WILLIAM GLASSER, and a reality therapist. His dissatisfaction with traditional Freudian analysis for the treatment of many anxiety disorders and other conditions led to the development and use of REALITY THERAPY and group therapy. Most of his work has been done at the Los Angeles Veterans Administration Neuropsychiatric Hospital and in private practice.

Harris' syndrome A form of HYPOGLYCEMIA (low blood sugar) or HYPERINSULINISM, due to functional or organic disorders of the pancreas and marked by symptoms of jitteriness, mental confusion, and visual disturbances. The condition may be confused with anxiety and in itself may make the individual feel very anxious.

Hathaway, Starke Rosecrans Hathaway and John Charnley McKinley developed the Minnesota Multiphasic Personality Inventory in the late 1930s, motivated by the lack of a functional, objective, comprehensive, yet simple test of psychopathology. The MMPI uses a true–false self-report format with questions that are empirically keyed against criterion groups. An anxiety scale, called Factor A, was developed later from an amalgamation of several preexisting scales.

Hawthorne effect The effect upon one's behavior when one knows one is in an experiment. The Hawthorne effect is named after a Western Electric manufacturing section in which output increased after experimental changes were made in the working conditions; apparently the increase resulted from the extra attention given to the workers rather than from the specific changes. Changes have been noted in phobics due to contact alone. Any effective therapy must prove it is more effective than contact-only "treatment." (See also BEHAVIOR THERAPY.)

Goldenson, Robert M. (editor-in-chief), *Longman's Dictionary of Psychology and Psychiatry* (White Plains, NY: Longmans, 1984), p. 335.

headaches Headaches, one of the most frequent complaints of individuals who visit physician's offices, are also reported by many who visit therapists for ANXIETY DISORDERS and sleep disorders. An estimated forty-five million Americans suffer from chronic, recurrent headaches. These individuals make more than 50,000,000 visits a year to doctors' offices and spend more than $400 million on over-the-counter-pain relievers. Industry loses at least $55 million a year due to absenteeism and medical expenses caused by headaches. Headaches cause anxieties and stress not only to the sufferer but also to family members who are affected by the sufferer's recurring discomfort. Anxiety, in turn, can cause headaches.

Causes of headaches are not entirely understood. However, heredity is considered important; as many as 75 percent of migraine sufferers come from families in which other members have the same disorder. ANXIETIES, STRESS, diet, and environmental pollutants (including cigarette smoke) are also thought to contribute to headaches.

Anxiety sufferers complain of a variety of headaches, including migraine, cluster, and muscle contraction (tension) headaches.

Migraine headaches

The word *migraine* was derived from the Greek word *hemicrania,* meaning half a head. This kind of headache is called migraine because in many cases, pain is limited to one side of the head. At times it may shift from side to side, and sometimes it may hurt on both sides. Migraine headaches usually recur, causing the sufferer the anxiety of not knowing when an attack will occur, and the fear that an attack will come at a critical time, such as before an important examination, performance, or interview.

Estimates indicate that between 10 and 15 million Americans have migraine headaches. Sometimes the headaches start in childhood, and most begin before the age of 30. Migraine headaches seem to decrease as people age. About six out of every 10 migraine sufferers are women.

Migraine headaches often begin around stressful times, such as during puberty, at the time of a school or job change, around the time of a divorce or death of a mate, or during menopause. In diagnosing a headache, a physician will inquire about stresses in the individual's life, demands on the person's time, and how the individual copes with his or her own anxieties and stresses.

Migraine headaches are vascular; the headache results from distention and dilation of blood vessels of the scalp. Some individuals who have migraines report nausea and vomiting during a migraine attack. Generally, an attack begins with a warning, known as an AURA. This may include some kind of visual disturbance, such as blurring or wavy lines resembling heat waves, or a hearing disturbance. Sometimes this disturbance lasts for 10 to 15 minutes. In some cases, hands, face, arms, or legs feel numb or may twitch. The sufferer may be extremely sensitive to light and sound. When the headache pain begins, it may be aggravated by sudden movement of the head, vomiting, sneezing, or coughing. There may be chills or sweating. Sleep usually provides relief, and many migraine sufferers become sleepy during an attack and go to sleep. The entire attack, including the warning period, pain, and sleep, may last from several hours to several days, leaving the person exhausted afterward.

There are many variations of the headache; only 25 percent of migraine sufferers have classic attacks.

Heredity and personality

Migraine headaches, which often occur in members of the same family, may result from a predisposing genetic biochemical abnormality. Additionally, personality traits may play a role in determining who gets migraine headaches. While there is no typical migraine personality, many migraine sufferers have characteristics of perfectionism and compulsion.

Stress and anxieties as a cause

Emotional tension and stress may lead to migraine attacks, because under extreme stress the arteries of the head and those reaching the brain draw tightly together and restrict the flow of blood. This in turn may result in a shortage of oxygen to the brain. When blood vessels dilate or stretch, a greater amount of blood passes through, putting more pressure on the pain-sensitive nerves in and close to the walls of the arteries. The tension on the wall of a blood vessel depends on the pressure of the blood within it as well as the diameter of the vessel itself. The wider the vessel, the greater the tension produced.

Foods and alcohol

Foods and alcohol can make a difference in the frequency and severity of migraine headaches for certain susceptible individuals. Some foods may provoke a headache because they contain substances that affect the constriction or expansion of blood vessels. One of these substances is tyramine, which is found in aged cheeses, chicken livers, and a variety of other foods. Another is sodium nitrite, a preservative used in ham, hot dogs, and many other sausages. Only about 30 percent of people who have migraine headaches experience this reaction to certain foods. However, some migraine researchers have recommended that all migraine sufferers avoid these foods (see chart at right)

Hormonal effects

Hormones play a role in causing migraine headaches. Many women who have migraine headaches report that attacks come around the time of their menstrual periods, and some have headaches before, during, or at the end of their periods. Some women have migraine headaches during the first months of pregnancy. Some women have them around MENOPAUSE (when menstrual periods cease). Many women who suffer from migraine headaches have found that use of oral contraceptives and hormonal therapies increases the severity and frequency of headaches

Other causes

Some people have headaches as a result of HYPOGLYCEMIA (too little sugar in the blood). Oversleeping and missing a meal can cause hypoglycemia in some individuals. This condition occurs during insulin shock, when the sugar content of the blood is reduced by insulin or by other means, or after fasting. Hypoglycemia causes dilation of the blood vessels of the head and the resulting pain.

Foods To Be Avoided By Migraine Sufferers

- Ripened cheeses: Cheddar, Emmentaler, Gruyère, Stilton, Brie, and Camembert (American, cottage, cream, and Velveeta cheeses are permitted)
- Herring
- Chocolate
- Vinegar (except white vinegar)
- Anything fermented, pickled, or marinated
- Sour cream, yogurt
- Nuts, peanut butter, seeds: sunflower, sesame, pumpkin, etc.
- Hot fresh breads, raised coffee cakes, and raised doughnuts (These are permitted if they are allowed to cool. Toast is permitted.)
- Pods of broad beans: lima, navy, pinto, garbanzo, and pea pods.
- Any foods containing large amounts of monosodium glutamate (Oriental foods)
- Onions
- Canned figs
- Citrus foods (No more than one serving per day: one orange, one grapefruit, one glass of orange juice)
- Bananas (No more than one-half banana per day)
- Raisins
- Papayas
- Excessive tea, coffee, and cola beverages (No more than 2 cups total per day)
- Avocado
- Fermented sausage (Processed meats such as ham, hot dogs, bologna, salami, pepperoni, and summer sausage)
- Chicken livers
- All alcoholic beverages (if possible). If you must drink, limit yourself to two normal-sized drinks selected from among Haute Sauterne, Riesling, Scotch, or Vodka.

Ada P. Kahn, *Headaches* (Chicago: Contemporary Books, 1983), p. 53.

Historical notes

Migraine headaches were known to affect such historical figures as Julius Caesar, Joan of Arc, Thomas Jefferson, Ulysses S. Grant, and Sigmund Freud.

Cluster headaches

Cluster headaches are so called because they occur in repeated groups. The painful episodes may be as short as 30 minutes and usually are not longer than three or four hours. Sometimes attacks occur every day for several weeks or even months. In many cases there is a remission period with no headaches, and then they may start again. There may be several episodes within a 24-hour period, sometimes regularly at the same time each day. The early-morning hours and one or two hours after going to bed are times when these headaches frequently occur.

The cluster headache pain is intense and is more of a steady, boring pain than the pulsating, throbbing migraine headache. The pain is usually on one side and behind the eyes. It usually reaches its peak of intensity soon after the attack begins. Pain in the eye, nasal congestion, and a runny nose may accompany these headaches.

In a general way, people who have cluster headaches are likely to be smokers and to drink more alcohol than the average population, are conscientious, responsible, self-sufficient, tense, anxious, frustrated, and aggressive. Cluster headaches occur eight to 10 times more frequently in men than in women and usually begin in the early twenties.

Cluster headaches differ from migraines in the duration of the attacks, the character of the pain, biochemical changes, and according to the sex of the sufferer, although the pain of both occurs because of changes in the blood vessels. They are similar in that both usually cause pain on one side and may result from use of vasoactive drugs, certain foods or beverages, emotional stress, and possibly hormonal and biochemical changes in the body. Medications that are effective for migraine are usually also effective for cluster headaches.

While the person with a migraine headache will want to lie down in a dark, quiet room and feels overly sensitive to light, noise, or odors, the cluster sufferer may want to become physically active, pace about, or take a walk because the intensity of the pain may prevent him or her from lying down or sitting still.

Muscle-contraction (tension) headaches

Tension or muscle-contractions headaches may be the most frequently occurring type. Most tension headaches are associated with anxiety, depression, or unresolved conflicts, rather than a disease condition. Such headaches may begin during a period of stress, such as a family crisis, or a period of fatigue. They often go away after the stressful stimulus disappears or is resolved. Many people with these headaches have SLEEP DISORDERS in the form of frequent and early awakening, which may also be related to tension and stressful life situations. Some people with muscle-contraction headaches have a depressive illness that contributes to the headaches.

Tension headaches are often associated with contraction of the head and neck muscles. In many cases, such headaches are not severe and do not last long, but in other cases, scalp-muscle-contraction headaches may be incapacitating. Individuals who have these headaches describe them as tight, pressing, squeezing, or aching sensations.

Some individuals have chronic muscle-contraction headaches in which the pain is constant for weeks or longer, and at times there may be feelings of jabbing, stabbing, or piercing. Some sufferers of muscle-contraction headaches also have an associated vascular headache, which is aggravated by jarring of the head due to coughing, sneezing, or bending over.

More women than men have tension headaches, and these headaches often run in families.

Other forms of headache

Traction headaches

The term traction headache applies to many nonspecific headaches that are secondary to a variety of diseases including brain tumors and strokes. An inflammation of the pain-sensitive structures inside and outside the skull may be the cause.

Mixed headaches

Combined or tension-vascular headaches have features of both vascular head pain and muscle-contraction head and neck pain. Some aspects of vascular headaches, such as throbbing pain on one side of the head, nausea, and vomiting, may be present along with the features of tension headache, such as a dull, constant, aching pain or tightness around the head and neck. There may also be tenderness of the scalp or neck.

Caffeine headaches

Individuals who drink too much caffeine in coffee, tea, and soft drinks sometimes have headaches from the caffeine. Excessive coffee drinking can bring on a group of symptoms including headache, sleeping problems, upset stomach, shortness of breath, and shaky hands. Eliminating coffee may eliminate these symptoms for some individuals. However, some people who drink large quantities of coffee and stop abruptly may suffer caffeine withdrawal symptoms, including headache, irritability, depression, and sometimes nausea. Those who want to cut down on the amount of coffee they drink can mix increasing amounts of decaffeinated coffee into their usual brew.

Hangover headaches

A headache is one of the uncomfortable symptoms of an excessive consumption of alcohol. Alcohol causes the headache by making blood vessels swell, brings on nausea by irritating the digestive system, and leads to dehydration by causing excessive urination.

Headaches in depression

Headaches frequently occur during DEPRESSION. Certain ANTIDEPRESSANT medications provide relief from headaches arising from nonorganic causes. Among these are AMITRIPTYLINE HYDROCHLORIDE, IMIPRAMINE HYDROCHLORIDE, DESIPRAMINE HYDROCHLORIDE, NORTRIPTYLINE HYDROCHLORIDE, PROTRIPTYLINE HYDROCHLORIDE, DOXEPIN, MAPROTILINE, TRAZODONE, and AMOXAPINE.

Some headache specialists recommend MONAMINE OXIDASE INHIBITORS (MAOIS) such as PHENELZINE SULFATE as mood elevators for people who have depression. These drugs also help control severe migraine pain in some individuals. However, individuals taking the MAO inhibitors must avoid eating certain foods that contain TYRAMINE (see chart on p. 214). Dangerous side effects of the MAO inhibitors include HIGH BLOOD PRESSURE.

Treatment

Before one takes any medication for headaches, one should be properly diagnosed. Medications that help tension headaches will not help severe migraine headaches, and drugs targeted to relieve migraine headaches may not help any other type. Also, it is important that one does not overmedicate for headaches and bring on other side effects from medications. For many, aspirin or acetaminophen is enough to relieve a headache. Two aspirin tablets every three to four hours may provide some relief for tension headaches. Aspirin relieves pain and reduces inflammation by interfering with substances in the blood that cause them. However, aspirin probably will not have much effect on the persistent pain of migraine or the deep pain of other types of recurring headaches. For many individuals, aspirin can be harmful and cause upset stomach, ulcers, and internal bleeding. Some people are allergic to aspirin and should use an aspirin substitute instead.

Medication for migraine or vascular headaches is directed toward changing the response of the vascular system to stimuli such as stress, hormonal changes, or noise. Such medications interfere with the dilation reaction of the blood vessels. The most popular medication is ergot, a naturally occurring substance that constricts blood vessels and reduces the dilation of arteries, thus stopping the headaches. Ergot is sometimes given by injection, orally, rectally, or by inhalation. Many individuals find that if they take the ergot medication early enough in prepain stages of an attack, they can abort their headaches, or at least reduce their intensity. Persons who are nauseated and vomiting usually take the drug by some means other than orally. In some cases, a SEDATIVE, such as a BARBITURATE, is given along with the ergot to help relax the individual and make him or her more receptive to the action of the ergot.

Vascular headaches are sometimes treated with prophylactic (preventive) measures. Propranolol is the drug of choice for prevention of migraine in carefully selected patients. Propranolol is a vasoconstrictor that can be taken daily for as long as six months. This drug may slow down the vascular changes that occur during the migraine attack. It is frequently prescribed for some individuals who have headaches more than once each week. This drug is helpful for migraine-headache sufferers who have severe high blood pressure, angina pectoris, or conditions for which ergot preparations are contraindicated. In such situations, propranolol relieves the headache as well as the coexisting disorder. Another advantage of propranolol over ergot medications is that discontinuance of propranolol does not cause rebound headaches.

Other drugs commonly prescribed for migraine are cyproheptadine and methysergide.

Medications for tension or muscle-contraction headaches are directed toward relieving muscular activity and spasm. In some cases, injection with anesthetics and corticosteroids is helpful. ANALGESICS (pain relievers) commonly used are aspirin dextropropoxyphene and ethoheptazine. Sometimes a sedative is prescribed along with these medications.

Medications for cluster headaches include methysergide, ergotamine tartrate, and corticosteroids. LITHIUM is also effective for some in controlling chronic cluster headache. However, lithium has multiple possible side effects on the nervous system and kidneys, and its use should be carefully monitored.

Medication for traction or inflammatory headaches usually involves specific treatment for the associated underlying disease and may require consultations with other medical specialists such as neurologists, ophthalmologists (eye specialists), and otolaryngologists (eye, ear, nose, and throat specialists). Treatment may range from surgery to ANTICONVULSANTS, depending on the specific cause.

Nonpharmacological treatments

In addition to medication, there are many other techniques used to treat headaches, particularly those associated with reducing ANXIETIES and STRESS.

Biofeedback

This is a method of treating tension headaches that involves teaching a person to control certain body functions through thought and willpower with the use of machines that indicate how a part of the body is responding to stress. Sensors are attached to the patient's forehead (frontalus muscle) to measure muscle tension, and responses are relayed to an amplifier that produces sounds. While the person is tense, the sounds are loud and harsh. As the person concentrates on relaxing the sounds begin to purr quietly or cease altogether. When the tension disappears, so does the headache.

Meditation

MEDITATION, or TRANSCENDENTAL MEDITATION, is a method for inward contemplation that proponents say helps people relax and relieve their anxieties, and in turn relieve some headaches. As the mind slows down during meditation so do other organs in the body. The heart rate decreases, and breathing becomes quieter. Muscle tensions are relaxed. The goal of meditation is productive rest followed by productive activity. While meditation can relieve headache pain for some people, for many it works as an adjunct to pharmacological therapy, helping the headache sufferer to be more receptive to the effects of medication.

Other therapies

HYPNOSIS is rarely used to treat headaches. However, hypnosis is sometimes used as a beginning for additional psychotherapy on an individual or group basis. ACUPUNCTURE, although controversial, has been successfully used to treat some individuals with headaches. The modern interpretation of why acupuncture works is that the needle insertions somehow stimulate the body to secrete ENDORPHINS, naturally occurring hormone-like substances that kill pain. ACUPRESSURE is a technique that involves pressing acupuncture points with the finger. This can be done oneself or by another lay person.

Self-help organizations:

National Migraine Foundation
5252 North Western Avenue
Chicago, IL 60625

British Migraine Association
178a High Road
London, England

(See also ADVERSE DRUG REACTIONS; ALLERGIES; BIOFEEDBACK; CAFFEINE; ERGOT; FOODS, FEARS OF; HANGOVER; PREMENSTRUAL SYNDROME.)

Adapted with permission from Kahn, Ada P., *Headaches* (Chicago: Contemporary Books, 1983).

headaches in children Headaches in children have been studied separately from adult headaches and often have their own unique set of causes. Children's HEADACHES cause the children themselves and their parents STRESS and ANXIETY. Some children's headaches are in themselves symptomatic of some anxiety conditions, but many headaches have other causes and are just as distressing. By age 15, 5.3 percent of youngsters have migraine headaches, and 5.4 percent have infrequent headaches. U.S. children lost 1.3 million days of school during 1986 because of headaches.

Youngsters have four basic types of headaches: acute, acute recurrent, chronic progressive, and chronic nonprogressive. An acute headache is one single severe headache and may be caused by general infections or infection of the CENTRAL NERVOUS SYSTEM, sinuses, teeth, HIGH BLOOD PRESSURE, or a blow to the head. An acute recurrent headache is a severe headache that returns after pain-free days or months. Migraine headaches fall into this pattern. Some youngsters who have classic migraine headaches report accompanying visual phenomena, such as shimmery lights or halos around objects, and sometimes nausea and vomiting. Chronic progressive headaches are those that increase in severity and frequency over time. These are often caused by a physical problem and should be investigated by a physician.

Chronic nonprogressive headaches are headaches that come and go but do not get worse. These are sometimes referred to as functional headaches because they may have no physical cause. They may be brought on by muscle contractions due to anxieties such as stress at school. A physical cause for this kind of headache may be chronic sinus infection.

Additionally, some children have headaches resulting from dental infections or jaw problems.

Bruckheim, Allan, "Don't Worry Too Much without Good Reason; Children Do Get Headaches," *Chicago Tribune* (Sept. 1, 1987).

headaches, sexually related Some individuals have HEADACHES related to sexual activity, leading to ANXIETIES and discomfort. Such persons do not use the headache to avoid sexual activity but actually do endure discomfort before, during, or after sexual intercourse. Nevertheless, the headaches become involved in a cycle of anxiety and apprehension. Sex-related headaches may include three types: muscle-contraction (tension) headaches, benign orgasmic headaches, and malignant coital headaches. Muscle-contraction headaches cause dull, aching pains on both sides of the head and are relatively brief. More men than women experience these, because many couples use positions during intercourse in which the man is more active, typically above his partner with his head and neck unsupported. In women, muscle contraction headaches can be influenced by premenstrual hormonal changes.

Benign orgasmic headaches are intense, short headaches associated with rises in BLOOD PRESSURE during sexual arousal and ORGASM. These headaches usually occur in individuals who also suffer from migraine headaches. They may be brought on by ALCOHOL and/or certain medications.

Malignant coital headaches are caused by fluid escaping through a defect in a person's spinal-cord sheath that widens during sexual intercourse. Some individuals have these headaches only while participating in sexual activity when standing and/or sitting, but not when reclining.

Sex-related headaches are associated more often with extramarital sexual relations than with intercourse between married partners. The anxiety and guilt caused by having a sexual relationship with someone other than a spouse may be the most significant reason for these headaches.

Bruckheim, Allan, " 'I Have a Headache' Might Be True," *Chicago Tribune,* (Dec. 2, 1987).

heart attack, anxiety following Individuals who have a heart attack (myocardial infarction) are likely to have some anxiety afterward. In the United States alone, over half a million people suffer heart attacks each year, making anxiety following a heart attack a fairly common occurrence. As many as one third of these people may require some psychotherapeutic help to relieve emotional stress.

The anxiety that individuals experience during and after a heart attack often follows a pattern. Upon initial symptoms of a heart attack, a person may, although recognizing the symptoms, deny them. Unfortunately, such denial often delays life-saving medical treatment. Educating individuals known to have coronary-artery disease, as well as educating their friends and family, is an important step toward getting heart-attack victims to seek prompt medical attention.

Once in the emergency ward, a heart-attack victim often experiences much confusion, as well as fear and anxiety. At this point, treatment to minimize these feelings may be limited to a medical explanation of what is happening, plus medications to relieve physical pain. Four emotional responses are fairly common after a person has been admitted to a coronary-care unit: 1) anxiety, 2) denial, 3) depression, and 4) coping. Initially, the person is anxious and fearful of DEATH, the UNKNOWN, and PAIN. As he or she begins to feel better the individual may resort to denial, often even requesting to leave the hospital. Shortly thereafter, the individual realizes the implications of the heart attack and shows signs of depression. Following this, usually by about the fifth day in the hospital, the person is more secure and begins to return to methods of coping typical of persons who have coronary-prone (often referred to as "type A") behavior. Both drugs and nonpharmacologic treatment are often used to relieve anxiety and depression at this point for heart-attack victims. Anxiety, especially if left untreated, can bring about serious arrhythmias (variations in heartbeat). Most commonly, when medication is prescribed for anxiety or depression, it is in the form of a BENZODIAZEPINE, such as ALPRAZOLAM (Xanax). Psychotherapeutic intervention or counseling may be used to help people adapt to new requirements in life-style such as diet, giving up smoking, and management of STRESS resulting from type A behavior. Sexual counseling may also be of help to the heart-attack victim and spouse who have anxieties about resuming sexual activity. (See also CORONARY-BYPASS ANXIETY, POSTOPERATIVE.)

Stern, T.A., "The Management of Depression and Anxiety Following Myocardial Infarction," *The Mount Sinai Journal of Medicine* (October 1985), pp. 623–631.

Kaufmann, M.W. et al, "Psychiatric Aspects of Myocardial Infarction: Clinical Applications," *Resident and Staff Physician* (December 1986).

heart attack, fear of Fear of heart attack is known as anginophobia. Heart attack is the common term for a coronary occlusion. In a heart attack, one of the coronary arteries becomes blocked. The condition may or may not result in a myocardial infarction (heart attack), depending on the extent of the damage to the surrounding muscle. (See also HIGH BLOOD PRESSURE, FEAR OF.)

heart disease, fear of Fear of heart disease is known as cardiophobia. This may be a fear of any disorder or defect that interferes with normal functioning of the heart. Heart disease covers congenital defects, damage caused by diseases such as rheumatic fever or syphilis, or an atherosclerotic condition (hardening of the arteries), angina pectoris, or coronary occlusion. (See also CHOLESTEROL, FEAR OF; HIGH BLOOD PRESSURE, FEAR OF.)

heart rate in emotion Strong emotion, such as fear or anxiety, can increase the rate of the heartbeat through sympathetic impulses (arousal system). Parasympathetic reflexes (calming system) resulting from increased blood pressure during emotion also can alter the heart rate. A strong parasympathetic reflex can slow the heart rate to a point at which it may appear on the verge of stopping. While most phobic individuals experience rapid heartbeat when exposed to their phobic stimulus, those who fear blood often experience a slower heart beat. (See also BLOOD AND BLOOD-INJURY PHOBIA; SYMPATHETIC NERVOUS SYSTEM.)

heat, fear of Fear of heat is known as thermophobia. Some individuals fear hot weather, hot rooms, central heating, hot water, or being hot. They take measures to avoid heat, such as living in a colder climate, staying in air-conditioned places during hot spells, and wearing cool clothing.

heaven, fear of Fear of heaven is known as uranophobia or ouranophobia. Some people fear the idea that they will be judged after life and assigned either the rewards of heaven or the punishment of HELL. Religious skeptics and radical thinkers object on social and ethical grounds to what they consider to be the carrot-in-front-of-the-donkey aspect of a belief in heaven. The prospect of heaven serves as a disciplinary element to promote good behavior and to encourage the feeling that inequities and injustices must be suffered patiently and passively in this life to earn a reward in the next. Some object to the pleasureable, delightful quality of heaven on the grounds that this image of paradise appeals to man's baser, more hedonistic qualities. (See also HELL, FEAR OF.)

Cavendish, Richard (ed.), *Man, Myth and Magic* (New York: Marshall Cavendish, 1983), "Paradise."

Thomas, Keith, *Religion and the Decline of Magic* (New York: Scribner, 1971).

hedonophobia Fear of feeling pleasure. (This term is also used to mean fear of travel.) (See also PLEASURE, FEAR OF.)

heights, fear of Fear of heights is known as acrophobia, altophobia, hypsophobia, and hypsiphobia. It is a very common phobia, especially in its milder forms. Those who have phobias of heights emphasize that their visual space is important. They will not be able to go down a flight of stairs if they can see the open stairwell. They will be frightened looking out of a high window that stretches from floor to ceiling, but not if the window's bottom is at or covered to waist level or higher. They have difficulty crossing bridges on foot because of the proximity of the edge but may be able to cross in a car. Sometimes fear of heights is related to an acute fear of falling (which is innate). Babies usually begin to be wary of heights some time after starting to crawl. Walking, like crawling, also enhances their fear of heights.

Fear of heights, classified as a simple phobia, is not usually associated with other psychiatric symptoms or disorders, such as depression. The heights-phobic person is no more or less anxious than anyone else until exposed to heights, but then he or she becomes overwhelmingly uncomfortable and fearful, sometimes having symptoms associated with a panic attack, such as palpitations, sweating, dizziness, and difficulty breathing. A person who fears heights can also fear just thinking about the possibility that he might be confronted with his phobic stimulus.

Fear of heights is sometimes associated with a fear of airplanes and flying, although the height is only one element in the complex reaction that leads to fear of flying in an airplane. Fear of heights is sometimes involved in many related fears, such as bicycles, skiing, amusement rides, tall building, stairs, bridges, and freeways. (See also FALLING, FEAR OF; FLYING, FEAR OF; HIGH OBJECTS, FEAR OF; HIGH PLACES, FEAR OF LOOKING UP AT; PHOBIA; SIMPLE PHOBIAS.)

Marks, I.M., *Fears, Phobias and Rituals* (New York: Oxford University Press, 1987), p. 130.

Marks, I.M., *Fears and Phobias* (London: Heinemann Medical), 1969.

Goodwin, Donald W., *Phobia* (New York: Oxford University Press, 1983), p. 31.

heliophobia Fear of sunlight. Also known as phengophobia. (See also SUNLIGHT, FEAR OF.)

hell, fear of Fear of is known as hadephobia, stigiophobia, and stygiophobia. Individuals have feared hell for thousands of years before Christianity. Egyptian writings contain some indication of a belief in judgment and punishment after death. The early Greeks believed in an afterlife that was a shadowy realm where almost all of the dead were fated to go, and Plato's writings of the 4th century B.C. indicate a growing fear of punishment after death. The original Jewish concept of the afterlife was Sheol, a dark place removed from God that was everyone's fate after death. Gradually the concept of punishment for a sinful life after death began to enter Judaism, partly to rationlize inequities in this life and partly because Jews wished to think of their oppressors as suffering after death. At this point the image of writhing in flames became part of the fearful description of punishment in the underworld. Gehenna, the term for the place of torment in Judaism, was adapted from the name of the flaming rubbish dump of Jerusalem. Later, Christians produced elaborate descriptions of hell in art and literature as well as religious writings, and these increased fears of hell. The addition of the Devil and his orders of demons as residents of hell provided a rationalization for the theological dilemma of explaining the presence of evil in a world ruled by a loving God.

The fire-and-brimstone image of hell has decreased in the twentieth century. More common fears are either of annihilation after death or that God's mercy will extend to all regardless of their conduct in life on earth. (See also HEAVEN, FEAR OF.)

Cavendish, Richard (ed.) *Man, Myth and Magic* (New York: Marshall Cavendish, 1983), "Hell."

Thouless, Robert H., *An Introduction to the Psychology of Religion* (Cambridge: Cambridge University Press, 1971).

Hellenologophobia Fear of Greek terms or of complex scientific or pseudoscientific terminology.

helminthophobia Fear of worms. (See also WORMS, FEAR OF.)

helplessness Learned helplessness is an experience of fear and indecision and a sense of not being able to personally influence the external world. Freud used the term "psychic helplessness" to describe the experience during the birth process when respiratory and other physiological changes occur; he believed that this psychic helplessness state led to later anxieties. Freud also believed that the baby's helplessness and dependence on the mother created frustration, which in turn led to an inability to cope with later tension. During the 1970s, Martin Seligman developed the concept and coined the term "learned helplessness" to describe an individual's dependence on another. Many phobic individuals have characteristics of learned helplessness, particularly agoraphobics, who cannot go away from home without someone accompanying them. (See also AGORAPHOBIA; LEARNED HELPLESSNESS; SELIGMAN, MARTIN.)

hematophobia Fear of blood or the sight of blood. Also known as hemophobia. (See also BLOOD AND BLOOD-INJURY PHOBIA; ERYTHROPHOBIA.)

hemophobia See HEMATOPHOBIA.

here-and-now approach An emphasis on understanding present feelings and interpersonal reactions as they occur in an ongoing treatment session with little or no attention to past experience or the basic reasons behind the individual's behavior. The approach is often used in treating certain phobic individuals, since it keeps them in the present reality and away from phobic thinking. The behavioral therapies emphasize work in the here and now. (See also BEHAVIOR THERAPY; GESTALT THERAPY.)

heredity, fear of Fear of heredity or of transmitted characteristics is known as patriophobia. Some individuals fear the transmission of genetic characteristics to descendents. Heredity depends upon the character of genes contained in the chromosomes of cells, and upon the particular genetic code contained in the DNA of which the chromosomes are composed. This is a common fear, and many people fear that their children will inherit deformities or mental disorders that have been present in their family.

heresyphobia (heresophobia) A fear of challenges to official doctrine, or a fear of radical deviation.

Spears, Richard, *Slang and Euphemism* (New York: Jonathan David, 1981).

herpetophobia Fear of snakes and reptiles. There is some evidence that humans have an innate aversion to or fear of snakes. Some of this comes from studies of animals (such as chimpanzees, who demonstrate a natural aversion to snakes) and some from epidemiological studies, which show that ninety-five percent of snake phobics have never had direct contact with a snake. This innate tendency, probably coupled with vicarious learning (e.g., stories about the danger or voracity of snakes), can lead to development of an intense anxiety response. Furthermore, since contact with snakes is relatively easy to avoid, new learning and desensitization does not take place, and the fear consequently persists and intensifies. (See also SNAKES, FEAR OF.)

heterophobia Fear of the opposite sex, considered by some psychoanalysists and learning theorists to be a partial explanation of some homosexual behavior.

heterosexuality, fear of Fear of sexual behavior, impulses, and desires in which the object is a person of the opposite sex. (See also SEXUAL FEARS.)

hex, fear of Some individuals fear the hex, a curse or an evil spell meant to kill or harm its victim. Voodoo and witchcraft both contain this frightening idea. Hex comes from the German word for witch, *die hexe*. The Pennsylvania Dutch paint brightly colored hex signs on their barns to keep away evil spirits. (See also VOODOO, FEARS IN.)

Brasch, R., *Strange Customs* (New York: David McKay, 1976), "Hex."

hierarchy A term that describes the organization of a set of behaviors ranked in descending order. In behavior therapy, prior to the start of systematic desensitization or other therapy to reduce phobic behavior, a set of anxieties or behavioral problems is ranked, with the first one the most important. In FAMILY THERAPY, the term describes the relationships of individuals to one another. In biology, the term is used to describe the stratified and organized order of nature. (See also HIERARCHY OF NEEDS.)

hierarchy of needs Some theorists believe that human behavior is motivated by a series of needs that can be arranged in a hierarchical order, beginning with the basic physiological needs, such as food and water; progressing to safety needs, such as protection against danger; social or love needs; esteem or ego needs; and self-actualization. Anxiety and fear can result from incomplete attainment of these levels. The originator of this theory was Abraham Harold Maslow (1908–1970), an American psychologist known as a leader of the human-potential movement because of his emphasis on self-fulfillment.

hierophobia Fear of religious objects. (See also RELIGIOUS OBJECTS, FEAR OF.)

high blood pressure, fear of The fear of having high blood pressure, also known as hypertension, is closely linked with the fear of heart disease. This fear manifests itself with excessive preoccupation with blood pressure. Many fearful individuals are compulsive about having their blood pressure taken frequently and may have equipment for taking their own blood pressure at home in between visits to a physician. The term blood pressure, as used in medicine, refers to the force of one's blood against the walls of the arteries, created by the heart as it pumps blood through the body. As the heart pumps or beats the pressure increases. As the heart relaxes between beats the pressure decreases. High blood pressure is the condition in which blood pressure rises too high and stays there. High blood pressure occurs during anxiety and panic attacks but may become reduced after the panic attack subsides. If it does not, the individual should seek help from a physician. (See also CHOLESTEROL, FEAR OF; HEART ATTACK, FEAR OF; HEART DISEASE, FEAR OF; "WHITE COAT HYPERTENSION.")

high objects, fear of Fear of high objects is known as batophobia. This fear may be related to acrophobia (fear of high places) or to the fear of LOOKING UP AT HIGH PLACES (anablepophobia). Individuals who are fearful of high objects may ask others to reach items from high cabinet shelves, will not climb ladders, and will avoid selecting items from the top shelves in grocery stores. (See also HIGH PLACES, FEAR OF LOOKING UP AT.)

high places, fear of looking up at Fear of looking up at high places is known as anablepophobia. Individuals with this fear avoid looking up at the tops of tall buildings in cities and at the tops of mountains while in the country. This fear may be related to a fear of heights (acrophobia) or a fear of high objects (batophobia). (See also HEIGHTS, FEAR OF.)

Hippocrates (460–377 B.C.) Greek physician and contemporary of Socrates who explored both physical and mental illness. Hippocrates believed that mental disturbances arose from an imbalance of phlegm and bile (the two body "humors") and from the degree of humidity in the brain. Two cases of phobic individuals appear in Hippocrates's writing: a man who was frightened by the sound of flute music only in the evening and a man who was so frightened of looking down from a height that he avoided walking at the edge of a shallow ditch. Rest, exercise, and bloodletting were among Hippocrates's prescribed treatments.

Howells, John G. and Livia M. Osborn, *A Reference Companion to the History of Abnormal Psychology* (Westport, CT: Greenwood Press, 1984).

Kent, Fraser, *Nothing To Fear* (Garden City, NY: Doubleday, 1977).

Hippophobia Fear of horses. (See also HORSES, FEAR OF.)

history of phobias See PHOBIAS, HISTORY OF

hoarding A variant of OBSESSIVE–COMPULSIVE DISORDER. Compulsive hoarding may be a fear of not having enough. Some individuals fear throwing anything away and even store trash and old newspapers. They may store valueless papers from the past or buy vast quantities of food and other supplies when there are no predictable shortages. Such individuals become very anxious if others attempt to remove any of the saved or stored items. (See also RITUALS.)

Marks, Isaac, *Living with Fear* (New York: McGraw-Hill, 1978).

hobgoblin An object that inspires superstitious fear. (See also SUPERNATURAL, FEAR OF.)

hodophobia Fear of travel. (See also TRAVEL, FEAR OF.)

holy things, fear of Fear of holy things or religious objects is known as hagiophobia or hierophobia. (See also RELIGIOUS OBJECTS, FEAR OF.)

home, fear of returning Fear of returning home is known as nostophobia. Some adults fear returning to their childhood home because they are afraid that things will not be as they were, that their parents or other family members may not be there, or that they may not be accepted or welcomed. Some individuals prefer to remember their home as it was in their childhood and have a fear of returning in later years. Sometimes home is associated with conflict with a spouse or other family member, and anxiety occurs in anticipation of returning.

home surroundings, fear of Fear of home surroundings is known as oikophobia or ecophobia and includes fear of household appliances, equipment, electricity, bathtubs, household chemicals, and other common objects in the home.

homichlophobia Fear of fog. (See also FOG, FEAR OF.)

homilophobia Fear of sermons. (See also SERMONS, FEAR OF.)

homophobia Fear of homosexuality or becoming a homosexual. (See also HETEROPHOBIA.)

homosexual panic A panic attack arising out of the fear or the delusional conviction that one is about to be attacked sexually by a person of the same sex. The term also applies to an individual's fear that he or she is thought to be homosexual by fellow workers. Homosexual panic occurs more frequently in males than females. Symptoms may include agitation, conscious guilt over homosexual activity, hallucinations, ideas and threats of suicide, and depression. Such panic attacks may arise out of many different events, including a loss or separation from a member of the same sex to whom the subject is emotionally attached, or from illness, fatigue, fears of impotence, failures in sex performance, or homesickness. This type of panic attack may occur during the first acute episode in schizophrenic disorders. The term was coined by Edward Kempf, an American psychiatrist (1885–1971), in 1920 and has also been known as Kempf's disease. (See also PSYCHOSEXUAL FEARS; SEXUAL FEARS.)

Campbell, Robert J., *Psychiatric Dictionary* (New York: Oxford University Press, 1981).

hormephobia Fear of shock. (See also SHOCK, FEAR OF.)

hormones Hormones are substances produced and secreted by the endocrine glands. Hormones are chemically classified as steroids or proteins (or derivatives of proteins). Hormones are transported in the blood to various sites of action. They influence physiology as well as behavior. To have a sustained effect, hormones must be secreted continuously in precisely controlled quantities. In some glands, secretion is brought about by the nervous system; in others, it is stimulated by other hormones.

The brain has an important influence on hormonal activity. This occurs primarily through the pituitary gland, which is situated at the base of the brain just below the hypothalamus, to which it is neurally connected.

There are two basic kinds of hormones. One may be considered as "local" hormones, which have their effects close to the point of release. The second are "general" hormones, which enter extracellular fluids and may exert effects throughout the body. Hormonal effects can be immediate, occurring within fractions of seconds, or gradual, taking days to get started and continuing for months.

When local hormones—for example, adrenaline—are released and act upon nerve endings, their effect is almost instantaneous. When an individual is frightened, FEAR causes the release of the hormone adrenaline. The heart begins to pound, hands tremble, and the stomach constricts.

General hormones are secreted by a number of endocrine glands and then transmitted throughout the body, causing many physiological effects, often at distant points Some general hormones affect nearly all cells in the body. These include growth hormone from the pituitary gland and thyroid hormone from the thyroid gland.

Other general hormones are more specific, acting at various points. For example, corticotropin is released by the pituitary gland and acts on the adrenal gland. When one secretion acts on a particular site, the site is called the target tissue or target organ.

Hormones are responsible for the development of secondary sex characteristics in males and females, and for the onset of menstruation and menopause in women. Hormones play a role in PREMENSTRUAL SYNDROME and may be responsible for some of the anxieties women experience at this time. Specifically, estrogen and progesterone, secreted by the ovaries, exert control over menstruation, ovulation, conception, and menopause.

Vasopressin, another hormone secreted by the posterior pituitary, affects the kidney and blood pressure. (See also ADRENALINE; BIOLOGICAL BASIS FOR ANXIETY.)

Horney, Karen (1885–1952) A German-born American psychiatrist. Dr. Horney was trained in psychoanalysis by Karl Abraham, a close friend of SIGMUND FREUD. She was the only woman psychoanalyst with enough stature to enter into controversy with Freud and was one of the first psychoanalytical theorists to propose that tensions generated by a culture could be the cause of NEUROSIS. Dr. Horney was influenced by the work of anthropologists Ruth Benedict and Margaret Mead, whose findings she adapted to PSYCHOANALYSIS. She rejected such basic Freudian tenets as penis envy and the libido theory. Her ideas were similar to ALFRED ADLER'S, especially in relation to the drive for superiority. Unlike Adler, however, she believed personality was molded by the mind in its constant sifting through of values that exist in each culture. According to Dr. Horney's view, neurosis, whose core was in human relations, was brought about by conditions of the culture rather than erotic instinctual energy. She believed that certain types of cultural conditions obstructed the child's development, resulting in a "basic anxiety" or a "feeling of being isolated and helpless toward a world potentially hostile." The child, wishing to keep anxiety to a minimum, changes his natural and spontaneous relationships to others, and the movement toward or away from other people becomes artificial, compulsive, and binding. Such compulsive, artificial movements develop into "basic conflicts" or knots of anxiety, which form the neurosis. Horney suggested that in response to the neurosis, the individual sets up a defense mechanism, which she called the "pride system," a facade that gives the appearance of normality. Dr. Horney was the founder of the American Institute for Psychoanalysis. (See also ANXIETY.)

horses, fear of Fear of horses is known as equinophobia or hippophobia. In some individuals, fear of horses may result from incidents such as being kicked or thrown by a horse or simply by the sight of a powerful horse rearing up. Like other animal phobias, fear of horses is most likely to develop in the preschool and early school years. One of Sigmund Freud's most famous cases, LITTLE HANS, involved a five-year-old boy's fear of horses, which Freud interpreted as a fear of his father. Behavioral psychiatrist Joseph Wolpe was able to show, however, that learning theory provided a more powerful explanation of the etiology of this fear and subsequent remission.

An obsessive feeling about horses is the subject of Peter Shaffer's play, *Equus*. Filled with shame because horses (to whom he attributes divine qualities) have watched his first sexual encounter, a young man blinds them with a spike. The drama, based on an actual incident, follows the relationship between the boy and his psychiatrist as they piece together the reasons for the boy's attack on the horses. (See also ANIMALS, FEAR OF; CHILDHOOD ANXIETIES, FEARS, AND PHOBIAS.)

Melville, Joy, *Phobias and Obsessions* (New York: Coward, McCann and Geoghegan, 1977).

hospitals, fear of Fear of hospitals is known as nosocomephobia. Some people fear hospitals because they fear contamination by germs, which they believe are prevalent around hospitals. Some who fear hospitals fear being ill, having pain, and being out of control of their lives. Some who fear hospitals may also fear doctors, nurses, and other health-care providers; they may also fear injury and seeing their own blood or the blood of others. Some people become anxious on seeing individuals who are ill or recovering from surgery.

Many who fear visiting others in hospitals are fearful about their own death. Visiting a hospital, where a certain number of patients die every day, reminds the anxious individual of his or her own mortality. Visiting an ill person makes many individuals anxious because as the visitor, one does not know what to talk about and is afraid to ask about the patient's condition for fear of hearing about pain and suffering.

Another fear of hospitals stems from their impersonal aspects. Many individuals fear being a patient in a hospital for this reason. Patients become known by their injuries or their conditions rather than their names. Strangers must provide very personal care and invade what many individuals view as personal bodily privacy.

Also, some individuals fear hospitals for a practical reason: costs. Hospital costs have escalated astronomically, and a relatively short stay can result in high charges. For those whose costs are not paid for by insurance or a health plan, such as the British National Health insurance, concern about paying hospital costs may also represent a fear of poverty.

Fears of hospitals can be overcome, to some extent, by visiting a local hospital while feeling well, taking a guided tour, and developing a better understanding of what services various hospitals provide for the community. Systematic desensitization also may be helpful. (See also BLOOD AND BLOOD-INJURY PHOBIA; DOCTORS, FEAR OF.)

hot flashes, fear of Many women after age forty begin to fear having hot flashes. Some have anxieties about hot flashes as a symptom of menopause, or the cessation of their menstrual periods. Hot flashes may be one of the first menopausal symptoms a woman notices, even before her periods stop. They may continue after she no longer menstruates. Some women have hot flashes several times a day, once a week, or less frequently. Different women find different things fearful about hot flashes. Some fear the embarrassment of knowing that what they are feeling is visible to others. Some fear being in social gatherings or at work when they break out in a sweat; some fear ruining their clothes because of perspiration. Some fear the sudden onset of perspiration, feeling clammy, or breaking out in a cold sweat at a critical time, such as when they have a business meeting or have to make a public presentation. Some fear wakeful nights due to hot flashes and the tiredness and irritability that occurs the next day. Many women fear that when they visit doctors to seek help for hot flashes, they will be told they are imagining them. For generations, before the function of female hormones was understood, some doctors told women that menopausal symptoms were imagined or strictly psychological. Now, however, hormonal replacement therapies are available to help relieve severe cases of hot flashes.

Understanding what happens in their bodies during and after menopause can reduce the fear of hot flashes for many women.

Women who fear hot flashes can reduce their anxieties by making themselves as comfortable as possible at times when they think hot flashes might occur. For example, they can layer their clothing so that they can remove a jacket or sweater if they become warm. They can learn to use relaxation techniques so that they will feel in control if a hot flash does occur while they are in public. Keeping windows open or a fan on may alleviate some of their feelings of excessive warmth. Above all, having support and understanding from family and friends can be helpful. Many menopausal women seek help from psychotherapists because hot flashes are one of many situations that cause them stress during this period of their lives. When they learn to cope better with other stressors in the lives, they also many become less anxious about hot flashes.

Many women fear menopause, with the accompanying symptoms, such as hot flashes, because they fear growing old and less attractive. While for generations many women based their self-worth on an ability to bear children, this is becoming increasingly less the case as women carry on important jobs in business and industry well past their child-bearing years. (See also AGING, FEAR OF; GROWING OLD, FEAR OF; MENOPAUSE, FEAR OF.)

Kahn, Ada P. and Linda Hughey Holt, *Midlife Health: Every Woman's Guide to Feeling Good* (New York: Facts On File, 1987).

house, fear of being in a Fear of being in a house, or fear of a specific house, is known as domatophobia. This term relates to the fear of the house itself; the term "ECOPHOBIA" pertains to the things inside the house. (See also HOME, FEAR OF RETURNING; HOME SURROUNDINGS, FEAR OF.)

Hughes, Howard (1905–1976) An American film producer, aircraft designer, and businessman publicly known to have OBSESSIVE–COMPULSIVE DISORDER, anxieties, and many phobias. His parents' death before he was 18 years old is said to have led him to fear germs. During his later years, he lived in hermetically sealed rooms. He carried an oxygen supply when he traveled. Because he feared and could not bear even slight pain, he became addicted to codeine. He feared having fingernails and toenails cut and at his death was found with extraordinarily long nails. He died of malnutrition.

Hull, Clark (1884–1952) A famous American psychologist and learning theorist. Hull was one of the first to espouse drive theory, which assumes a biological approach to motivation and learning. Joseph Wolpe's clinical theory of "reciprocal inhibition" is derived from the work of Hull. (See also HABIT STRENGTH; RECIPROCAL INHIBITION, LAW OF.)

human beings and human society, fear of Fear of human beings and human society is known as anthropophobia. (See also PEOPLE, FEAR OF.)

humanistic psychology An approach to psychology that centers on the individual and his personal experience. Humanistic psychology opposes Freudian psychology, which holds that sexual drive is the sole motivating force, and behavioral psychology, which explains human behavior as the product of a multiplicity of organismic and environmental relationships, each of which in turn dominates the others at certain times. In humanistic psychology, emphasis is on human qualities such as choice, creativity, valuation, and self-realization; meaningfulness is the key to selection of problems for study, and therapists oppose primary emphasis on objectivity at the expense of significance. The ultimate concern of humanistic psychology is the development of each person's inherent potential. According to humanistic psychologists, man has a hierarchy of many needs, beginning with physiological needs; safety; love and "belongingness"; esteem needs; esthetic needs; the need to know and understand; and ending in the essential need for self-actualization. The American Association for Humanistic Psychology was founded in 1962 by Abraham Maslow, Kurt Goldstein, Rollo May, Carl Rogers, and others. (See also HIERARCHY OF NEEDS.)

humor, fear of Humor has been studied by psychologists as a form of human behavior and does have some relationship to fears and anxieties. Humor is feared by some individuals who view laughing at rather than with someone as a form of attack. Belittling, sarcastic, or derisive remarks are high on the list of fear producers for individuals who are socially insecure or socially phobic. Laughter can be disturbing if it is an indication that sincere remarks are not being taken sincerely. Laughter and a light joking attitude also may be objectionable and manipulative when used to convince someone that he is not being a good sport about a truly negative, distressing situation. Insincere laughter used to flatter and gain social or professional favor often causes tensions. Laughter may also promote rifts and misunderstandings between social and ethnic groups because what may be funny in one culture and language may not even be amusing in another. (See also HUMOR, USE IN THERAPY.)

Morreall, John, *Taking Laughter Seriously* (Albany: State University of New York, 1983).

Wolpe, Joseph, *Our Useless Fears* (Boston: Houghton Mifflin, 1981).

humor, use in therapy Humor can be a useful way of releasing tension, dispelling anxieties, and momentarily relieving depression during therapy sessions. Humor promotes an individual's hopeful feelings about himself. If an individual can laugh during a therapy session, he will probably more more inclined to open up and reveal more about himself. Humor has known properties of healing. A therapist can employ humor as exaggeration or as a way of adding emphasis. Using a technique called paradoxical therapy, a therapist gives the individual perspective on his or her problems by exaggerating them until they become funny. With a similar exaggeration technique, a therapist assigns the individual a certain time of day to be anxious, depressed, or jealous. Often the silliness of the situation helps to alleviate the individual's distressed feelings. Humor can be used with individuals who are depressed or angry but who will not admit to their true feelings. Thus humor allows the therapist to explore without generating resistance. Since humorous remarks and stories have layers of meaning, such stories can at times be used to reach into the individual's unconscious. (See also HUMOR AS ANXIETY RELIEF.)

Fry, William F. and Waleed A. Salameh (eds.), *Handbook of Humor and Psychotherapy* (Sarasota, FL: Professional Resources Exchange, 1987).

Morreall, John, *Taking Laughter Seriously* (Albany: State University of New York, 1983).

humor as anxiety relief Humor serves to relieve the pressures of anxiety and stress in many ways. Comedians have indicated that they entered the profession because it affords an emotional release and a way of attracting positive attention. The simple absurdity and irrationality of humor is a welcome relief in the usual orderly, serious process of living. If some humor can be found in a negative situation, such as a setback at work or a minor accident, the victim can laugh about it, relax momentarily, and then pick up the pieces instead of uninterruptedly sustaining the stress of the situation. Because of the element of detachment inherent in humor, humor can reduce the stress of an ambitious person trying to reach a goal. Thus having a sense of humor allows the highly motivated person to be objective about the amount of effort and sacrifice necessary to reach the top.

Humor also provides a sense of freedom from political and social constraints. If a powerful figure or government program can be viewed as amusing, the stressful sense of autocratic control is reduced. Studies have shown that BRAINWASHING is impossible as long as the victim retains his ability to laugh. Humor also affords relief from anxieties related to social situations. A witticism can cover complaints and awkward situations that would cause hostility or tension if approached directly.

Shared humor is also a great reliever of anxiety in stressful group situations such as delayed trains. Humor relieves the stress that can result from boredom. When there seems nothing left to talk about, familiar topics can be made new by the use of humor.

Late-twentieth-century studies indicate the actual physical and psychological effects of laughter. The simple act of laughing may actually promote well-being. Norman Cousins's book, *Anatomy of an Illness* (1977), although concerned with physical disease, stimulated interest in the use of humor in recovery from both mental and physical illness. (See also HUMOR, FEAR OF; HUMOR, USE IN THERAPY.)

Morreall, John, *Taking Laughter Seriously* (Albany: State University of New York, 1983).

Ziv, Avner, *Personality and Sense of Humor* (New York: Springer, 1984).

Huntington's chorea A relatively rare, hereditary brain disease. In early stages, symptoms may be similar to those of anxiety and depression. The individual is moody, irritable, and has a poor ability to concentrate or remember. Some individuals who have Huntington's chorea are helped by sedative drugs, but there is no cure, and serious mental illness ensues. (See also DIAGNOSIS.)

hurricanes, fear of Fear of hurricanes is known as lilapsophobia. Those who fear hurricanes will stay indoors with windows, shades, and shutters closed during any period of time in which hurricanes are possible. Some will leave the area and remain in another geographic location for fear of being in the path of a hurricane. Some who fear hurricanes fear not only the destruction of property that occurs, but also a threat to their physical safety. Some fear that they might die as a result of the hurricane. (See also CLIMATE, FEAR OF; LANDSCAPE, FEAR OF.)

hyalophobia or hyelophobia Fear of glass. (See also GLASS, FEAR OF.)

hydrargyophobia Fear of mercurial medicines. (See also MERCURIAL MEDICINES, FEAR OF.)

hydrophobia Fear of water. Hydrophobia is also the technical name for rabies. An individual in the early stages of the disease experiences throat spasms, pain, and fear at the sight of water. (See also RABIES, FEAR OF; WATER, FEAR OF.)

hydrophobophobia Fear of rabies (See also RABIES, FEAR OF.)

hygrophobia Fear of dampness, humidity, or moisture. (See also DAMPNESS, FEAR OF.)

hylephobia Fear of epilepsy. Also, fear of matter (materialism) and wood (forests) (See also EPILEPSY, FEAR OF; FORESTS, FEAR OF.)

hylophobia Fear of a forest, or fear of materialism. Also known as ylophobia. In metaphysical thinking, matter is regarded as the principle of evil. (See also FORESTS, FEAR OF; WOODS, FEAR OF.)

hypengyophobia (hypegiaphobia) Fear of responsibility. (See also RESPONSIBILITY, FEAR OF.)

hyperinsulinism A condition in which too much insulin is produced and secreted by the body. Hyperinsulinism is often due to an overgrowth of the islets of Langerhans, from which insulin is secreted. As insulin promotes the removal and utilization of blood glucose, individuals who have hyperinsulinism become hypoglycemic and must be given massive amounts of glucose. The hypoglycemic condition can produce anxiety symptoms characteristic of anxiety states. Without this therapy individuals will experience "insulin shock," just as a diabetic does if given too much insulin. In such shock, the individual experiences hallucinations, extreme nervousness, trembling and may have convulsions, lose consciousness and pass into a coma. If treatment by injection of glucose is not rapid, there may be permanent damage to nerve cells, which need constant nutrients. Hyperinsulinism can be measured with a glucose tolerance test and a plasma insulin test. (See also DIABETES, FEAR OF.)

Hypersensitivity of gag reflex See GAGGING, HYPERSENSITIVE.

hyperthyroidism Too much thyroid hormone in the body's system. Thyroid overactivity increases the body's ability to convert foods, vitamins, and minerals into secretions, tissues, energy, and heat. Hyperthyroidism is one of the most common problems of the endocrine glands. Some symptoms of hyperthyroidism are similar to some ANXIETY DISORDERS, including an excess of energy, restlessness, nervousness, anxiety, headaches, sweating, and shaky, uncoordinated movements. A hyperthyroid individual may have difficulty sleeping at night and may experience wide changes in mood, varying from very happy to very depressed. An overactive thyroid gland can increase the body's basal metabolic rate (the use of oxygen while resting) 60 percent to 100 percent or more. An individual who has hyperthyroidism burns up food rapidly so that appetite may become ravenous at the same time that weight loss occurs. There may be muscle weakness, loss of calcium, and diarrhea or loose bowels. A hyperthyroid individual has a rapid heartbeat, and in severe cases, congestive heart failure can occur because blood cannot be pumped out of a heart chamber fast enough and collects there. Hyperthyroidism is a condition that requires medical attention and, once diagnosed, close monitoring of treatment.

hyperventilation Very rapid and deep breathing and a feeling of shortness of breath that can bring on high levels of ANXIETY. Hyperventilation causes a reduction in the level of carbon dioxide in the blood, which in turn can lead to feelings of numbness, tingling of the hands, dizziness, muscle spasms, and fainting. Individuals who are anxious or aroused begin to breathe in a rapid, deep manner with shallow exhalations. Gasping may occur. Although they have the sensation of shortness of breath, they are actually overbreathing. Sometimes this experience is accompanied by a feeling of constriction or pain in the chest.

The symptoms of hyperventilation and hyperventilation syndrome are frightening, and sufferers may fear that they are having a heart attack or that they will die. Some agoraphobics experience hyperventilation when they attempt to leave home or even think of going out, particularly unaccompanied by a companion upon whom they depend for security. Hyperventilation, or overbreathing, is also a common symptom among phobics when they face (or even think about) their phobic stimuli. For example, height phobics may hyperventilate when they think about looking out from the top of a tall building.

Hyperventilation is more common in women than in men. Usually, hyperventilation occurs in individuals who are nervous, tense, or having an anxiety or panic attack. Repeated attacks of hyperventilation may occur. Once the individual recognizes that the hyperventilation syndrome is a reaction to anxiety and not a disease itself, the attacks may become fewer or stop because the panic component will be somewhat reduced.

An individual who hyperventilates can help himself by understanding what happens during an attack. By voluntarily hyperventilating (about fifty deep breaths while lying down) and reproducing the symptoms felt during an anxiety attack, the sufferer will see that the symptoms do not indicate a heart attack or a "nervous breakdown." When the fear is reduced, hyperventilation during an anxious time may decrease.

Hyperventilation may also be a response to severe pain, particularly abdominal pain. When there is doubt about the cause of hyperventilation, the sufferer should be examined by a physician.

An Australian investigation of hyperventilation symptoms reported during 1986 compared responses to voluntary hyperventilation by individuals who had panic disorder and generalized anxiety disorder. Those who had panic disorder reported greater distress, a greater number of symptoms, and a lower level of carbon dioxide. Hyperventilation symptoms reported by the panic disorder patients and the generalized anxiety patients are compared in the chart that follows. (See also HEART ATTACK, FEAR OF.)

hypnoanalysis See DEPTH PSYCHOLOGY

Symptoms of Hyperventilation

This table indicates symptoms of hyperventilation and differentiates panic and generalized anxiety disorder.

Following are symptoms listed in the Hyperventilation Questionnaire, showing the percentage of subjects in each group reporting each symptom and the mean distress experienced during the voluntary hyperventilation.

(M = level of distress, a degree of concern or anxiety about the symptom.)

Symptom	Panic Group		Generalized Anxiety Group	
	% Reporting	*M* Distress	% Reporting	*M* Distress
Dizziness	100.0	4.8	69.2	3.2
Breathless	89.5	2.9	53.8	3.3
Tingling hands/feet	73.7	3.6	0.0	—
Dry mouth	100.0	4.3	61.5	3.6
Unsteady on feet	84.2	4.9	23.1	3.3
Nausea	31.6	2.2	7.7	4.0
Little stamina	78.9	3.9	46.2	3.3
Trouble thinking clearly	73.7	3.4	30.8	2.5
Trembling hands/legs	78.9	4.0	7.7	2.0
Tight/pain in chest	31.6	3.3	15.4	2.0
Seeing double	26.3	1.6	15.4	1.5
Fear heart attack	15.8	4.3	0.0	—
Depersonalization/derealization	68.4	2.4	15.4	2.5
Headache	10.5	2.5	7.7	2.0
Tetany (ringing in ear)	26.3	1.8	15.4	1.5
Tingling face	47.4	2.6	7.7	1.0
Breathing too much	68.4	4.2	53.8	3.7
Cold hands	26.3	3.8	7.7	4.0
Difficulty talking	42.1	3.3	15.4	2.0
Feeling far away	57.9	3.0	30.8	2.3
Crying	21.0	3.0	0.0	—
Lump in throat	36.8	3.6	30.8	2.8
Passing out, collapsing	78.9	5.1	38.5	2.8
Blurred vision	42.1	3.0	23.1	1.7
Panic	94.7	3.8	15.4	3.0
Pounding, racing heart	78.9	3.7	38.5	1.8
Nervous stomach	52.6	2.7	23.1	3.3
Burning, tingling, crawling	57.9	2.9	7.7	5.0
Rising agitation	73.7	4.4	30.8	2.5
Feeling want to run	52.6	3.5	0.0	—
Muscular tension	52.6	3.3	38.5	3.4
Feeling of wetting pants	5.3	1.0	0.0	—
Diarrhea	10.5	1.0	0.0	—
Feeling hot or flushed	73.7	2.9	30.8	3.0
Fear may die	21.0	2.8	0.0	—
Feeling trapped/helpless	47.4	3.4	38.5	1.8
Feeling ground moving	21.0	2.5	15.4	2.5

Symptom	Panic Group		Generalized Anxiety Group	
	% Reporting	*M* Distress	% Reporting	*M* Distress
Exhaustion	63.2	3.5	23.1	2.0
Feeling going mad	15.8	2.3	0.0	—
Feeling losing control	31.6	4.2	7.7	2.0
Causing a scene	26.3	4.2	0.0	—

Ron Rapee, "Differential Response to Hyperventilation in Panic Disorder and Generalized Anxiety Disorder," *Journal of Abnormal Psychology*, 95:1(1986), p. 27.

hypnophobia Fear of being hypnotized, or fear of hypnosis in general. The fear may relate to watching another person become hypnotized, or just thinking about HYPNOSIS.

hypnosis Hypnosis is a form of focused attention in which the individual becomes relatively open to receiving new information and exploring the mind–body relationship. It is not a "therapy" but can be a useful supplement to an appropriate anxiety-reduction therapy. Under hypnosis, the individual is in a trancelike state resembling sleep, during which he or she will be more susceptible to suggestion than during the "normal waking" state. While there are theories, no one knows exactly what the trance state represents physiologically or psychologically. Any hypnotizable individual may experience one or more of many hypnotic phenomena. These include sensory, motor, and psychological changes, such as an ability to alter perceptions, capacity to dissociate, amnesia for part or all of the hypnotic experience, a tendency to compulsively comply with suggestions given during the hypnotic state, and a willingness to accept logical incongruities.

There are two types of hypnosis. One is directive or authoritative hypnosis, in which the individual is ordered to give up a symptom, such as a phobic behavior. The second is cathartic hypnosis, in which the individual searches for hidden memories.

Hypnosis is a relatively safe procedure when used by a competent therapist who is specially trained in hypnosis. Practitioners do not have to be medical doctors.

While some people fear that under hypnosis they will do something that they would not do under conscious circumstances, it is generally thought that hypnotized individuals cannot be coerced into actions that go against their values and beliefs.

Most hypnosis is used to help relieve symptoms. Some therapists teach individuals to self-hypnotize themselves, while other therapists prefer to have repeated sessions during which suggestions are given, behavior is supported, and therapeutic gains are rewarded.

Many individuals who have forms of anxiety and phobias are hypnotizable. Individuals can learn to put themselves into the trance state to relax and dissociate psychological and body tension. This can be particularly helpful for those who have specific or simple phobias or performance anxiety. The trance experience can be used to induce physical relaxation in the face of the anxiety-provoking stimulus and to help an individual prepare for an anxiety-producing encounter by focusing on aspects of the experience that are less anxiety-provoking. For example, individuals who fear flying in an airplane can prepare themselves for flight by going into the trance state, thinking about the flight and themselves in the plane, and viewing the plane as an extension of their body, just as a bicycle or car is an extension of their body that enables them to get from one place to another more quickly. Individuals learn to restructure flying from an experience of being trapped in the plane into one of using the plane for their own benefit. Individuals can choose to enter the self-hypnotic trance state repeatedly during the trip, especially at stressful times, such as takeoffs and landings. Hypnosis may also be helpful in conjunction with exposure therapy for simple phobias.

Hypnosis is useful in a variety of pain conditions, such as headache and dentistry. Individuals can be hypnotized to begin their relaxation techniques when they feel a headache coming on. Hypnosis has been used in dentistry with fearful patients. The technique enables such individuals to have necessary care performed without use of drugs and the side effects from them.

It is sometimes helpful to induce hypnosis as an adjunct in psychotherapy to help an individual intensify memories or to relive aspects of the past. However, only individuals who are highly hypnotizable are capable of such regression. Age regression and/or recall can be accomplished with hypnosis when the therapist, usually a psychiatrist, wishes a subject to return to any age in his or her childhood and react as he did then. Regressed to the state of an infant, the individual will go through sucking motions; regressed to age two, he will draw a crude picture as he did at that age and will react to frustrations as he did then. With this method, childhood traumas that might have led to phobic behavior in adulthood but have been consciously forgotten can be uncovered. (See also DENTAL FEARS; HEADACHES.)

Kaplan, Harold I. and Benjamin J. Sadock, *Comprehensive Textbook of Psychiatry* (Baltimore: Williams and Wilkins, 1985).

hypnotics Drugs used to induce sleep by depressing the central nervous system to a greater degree than a sedative. The effect of hypnotic DRUGS is of short duration. They are used for some hospitalized patients and for cardiac patients who cannot sleep through the night because of ANXIETY. An example of a hypnotic drug is sodium secobarbital (Seconal). Because of drug abuse, barbiturates are not prescribed as frequently as in the past. Instead, BENZODIAZEPINES are used more routinely as hypnotics.

hypochondriacal phobia Fear of having a disease when no disease is present. The individual persists in this fear even after a doctor reassures him or her that there are no signs or symptoms of disease (See also DISEASE, FEAR OF; HYPOCHONDRIASIS.)

hypochondriasis Preoccupation with the fear of having, or the belief that one has, a serious disease, based on the individual's interpretation of physical signs or sensations. This is sometimes referred to as hypochondriacal neurosis. A thorough physical examination does not support the diagnosis of any physical disorder that can account for the physical signs or sensations or for the individual's unwarranted interpretation of them, although a coexisting physical disorder may be present. The unwarranted fear or belief of having a disease persists despite medical reassurance but is not of delusional intensity, in that the person can acknowledge the possibility that he or she may be exaggerating the extent of the feared disease or that there may be no disease at all.

The preoccupation may be with bodily functions, such as heartbeat, sweating, or digestion, or with minor physical abnormalities, such as a small sore or an occasional cough. The individual interprets these sensations or signs as evidence of a serious disease. The feared disease or diseases may involve several body systems, at different times or simultaneously. Alternatively, there may be preoccupation with a specific organ or a single disease, as in "cardiac neurosis," in which the individual fears or believes that he or she has heart disease.

Individuals with hypochondriasis frequently show signs of anxiety, depressed mood, and obsessive–compulsive personality traits. The most common age of onset is between 20 and 30 years, and it seems equally common in males and females. (See also DISEASE, FEAR OF.)

American Psychiatric Association, *Diagnostic and Statistical Manual of Mental Disorders* (Washington, DC: American Psychiatric Association, 1987).

hypoglycemia A reduced level of glucose in the blood. Hypoglycemia can produce extreme nervousness, trembling, and hallucinations and many characteristic symptoms of anxiety states. Hypoglycemia was thought to be the medical basis for many anxiety disorders, but research has indicated that true hypoglycemia seldom occurs in anxiety disorders. Some individuals with known blood-sugar-level abnormalities fear reactions to their body's own chemistry. In normal individuals, lowering of blood sugars is performed by the body's insulin, which is produced by the islets of Langerhans in the pancreas. In an individual who has diabetes, the insulin is lacking or is incapable of transporting glucose across cell walls for utilization. In other cases, excessive amounts of insulin may be produced so that blood sugar is almost depleted. If glucose levels fall below certain limits, insufficient amounts are available in the blood for transport to the brain. Unconsciousness can result from too little insulin or too much insulin. It is difficult to tell the difference between the two cases, but the acetone smell on the breath and deep, heavy, rapid breathing are present only in diabetic coma. (See also DIABETES, FEAR OF; HYPERINSULINISM.)

hypothalamus A part of the brain responsible for emotional control, thirst, temperature, and certain endocrine functions. It is the lower part of the thalamus and relays stimuli for most sense organs (except olfactory). The hypothalamus is an endocrine gland.

hypothyroidism A condition in which production of hormones by the thyroid gland is below normal or unable to keep pace with the body's temporary extra needs. In severe hypothyroidism, the individual may become absent-minded, disinterested, and often alternately anxious, nervous, and complacent. Nearly every vital process of the body is affected by the main thyroid hormone, thyroxine. A shortage of this hormone will result in a slowdown of all bodily processes—mental, emotional, and physical—until the hormone is replaced in drug form. Temporary thyroid deficiency can occur during certain periods when the body needs larger amounts of thyroid hormone than usual, such as puberty or menopause. (See also HYPERTHYROIDISM.)

hypsiphobia Fear of heights. (See also HEIGHTS, FEAR OF; HIGH OBJECTS, FEAR OF; HIGH PLACES, FEAR OF LOOKING UP AT.)

hysterectomy, fear of Many women fear hysterectomy, or surgical removal of the uterus. Although it is one of the most common operations in the United States, it is also sometimes a controversial one, because there are often differences of opinion concerning appropriate indications for hysterectomy and the surgical technique used. Some women fear being advised to have a hysterectomy when they do not really need one. Others fear having a premature menopause induced by the removal of the uterus. Actually, if the ovaries are left in place, the hormonal changes women fear with menopause do not occur. Some fear hysterectomy because of lack of information or misinformation. For example, many women fear that they will gain weight after the operation or that their sex lives will change; however, studies have indicated that, in general, hysterectomy has little adverse effect on sexual function and no relation to weight gain. Some women fear pain during sexual intercourse, particularly upon resuming sexual intercourse after surgery. There may be some discomfort at first if there has been some vaginal repair, but this should disappear within a few weeks. Painful intercourse is unusual. Some women may fear depression when they realize that they can no longer bear children. Some fear being less desirable to men when they are no longer able to bear children.

Women who fear hysterectomy can help themselves overcome their fears by getting a second opinion if surgery is recommended and becoming informed about the diagnosis, the reason for the operation, the treatment options, the risks and the benefits of the operation, and the desired improvements in health that will result. (See also MENOPAUSE, FEAR OF; SURGICAL OPERATIONS, FEAR OF.)

Kahn, Ada P. and Linda H. Holt, *Midlife Health: Every Woman's Guide to Feeling Good* (New York: Facts On File, 1987).

Waterfallen, John W., "Hysterectomy: An Overview," *Schumpert Medical Quarterly,* 6(1988), pp. 209–219.

hysteria Hysteria is a medical diagnostic term for illnesses characterized by the presence of physical SYMPTOMS, absence of physical SIGNS or any evidence of physical pathology, and behavior suggesting that the symptoms fulfill some psychological function. Hysteria, considered a neurotic disorder, may be characterized by emotional outbursts, repressed anxiety, and transformation of unconscious conflicts into physical symptoms such as blindness, paralysis, and loss of sensation. These symptoms help the individual blot out primary anxieties and elicit attention and sympathy.

The term hysteria comes from the ancient Greek word *hysteron,* meaning uterus. The Greeks used the term to refer only to diseases of women that they explained as arising from malfunctions of the uterus. Up until the late 1800s, hysteria was thought to be solely a female problem. Sigmund Freud presented a case in the late 1800s of male hysteria that his colleagues did not believe. Now male cases of hysteria often relate to job problems.

From the psychoanalytic point of view, there are two forms of hysteria: conversion hysteria, which corresponds to the traditional medical concept, and anxiety hysteria, the term used at times to denote phobias. Hysteria was first described in medical literature in Freud and Breuer's *Studies on Hysteria* (1895), in which hysterical symptoms were explained as the result of repressed memories and the conversion of ideas into physical symptoms. Freud suggested that symptoms were defenses against guilty sexual impulses, but contemporary therapists recognize many conflicts. (See also CONVERSION; PRIMARY GAIN; REPRESSION; SECONDARY GAIN.)

Rycroft, Charles, *A Critical Dictionary of Psychoanalysis* (Harmondsworth, Middlesex: Penguin, 1986).

hysterical disorder A disorder characterized by involuntary impairment of certain physical functions, such as an inability to speak normally after a highly charged emotional experience. Other hysterical disorders might be a sudden loss of vision, hearing, sense of smell, or sensation in parts of the body. Individuals who have anxiety disorders, phobias, and obsessive–compulsive disorder usually do not have hysterical disorders. (See also HYSTERIA.)

I

---

iatrogenic homosexuality Homosexuality, either in the form of feelings or behavior, which is unconsciously encouraged by the attitude of a doctor or other health professional who is treating or counseling an individual. Some individuals fear having a homosexual relationship with a therapist who is of the same sex. (See also HOMOSEXUAL PANIC.)

iatrogenic illness An illness induced by the examination or comments of a physician, medical practitioner, or therapist. Iatrogenic illness can be real or imagined. Fear of doctors is known as iatrophobia. (See also DOCTORS, FEAR OF; ILLNESS PHOBIA.)

iatrophobia Fear of doctors and places where patients are treated, such as hospitals. (See also DOCTORS, FEAR OF; HOSPITALS, FEAR OF.)

ice, fear of Fear of ice is known as cryophobia or papophobia. (See also COLD, FEAR OF; FROST, FEAR OF.)

icthyophobia See FISH, FEAR OF.

id The psychoanalytic term for the instinctual, biological drives that give the individual his basic psychic energy. FREUD suggested that the id is the most primitive component of PERSONALITY and operates in the deepest level of the UNCONSCIOUS. Freud believed that the id's psychic energy (a hypothetical energy that runs psychic processes) was derived from biological processes, but he did not understand or speculate on how they worked. According to Freud, the id operates irrationally in accordance with the pleasure principle—i.e., immediate discharge. Thus the infant's life centers around the desire for immediate gratification of instincts, such as hunger, thirst, elimination, rage, and sex, until the conscious ego develops and operates in accordance with reality and the SUPEREGO.

Goldensen, Robert M. (ed.), *Longman Dictionary of Psychology and Psychiatry* (New York: Longman, 1984).

id anxiety Sigmund FREUD's concept of ANXIETY resulting from instinctual drives and a primary cause of anxieties.

ideas, fear of Fear of ideas is known as ideaphobia.

ideas of influence A type of DELUSION. Ideas of influence involve ideas that something—usually television messages, voices from audio speakers, animals, or other potential sources—is telling the individual what to do or is having an influence over his or her behavior. The New York murderer known as "Son of Sam" said he heard a machine that told him to kill people. (See also IDEAS OF REFERENCE; PARANOID.)

ideas of reference Ideas of reference, also referred to as DELUSIONS of reference or delusions of observation, are misinterpretations in which one believes that others are smiling, talking, or whispering about one, or that one is being referred to in the newspaper, on television or radio news, or in movies. Ideas of reference are projections of feared situations onto the outside world; phobic individuals thus attribute their fears to an outside source rather than to their own experience. Ideas (or delusions) of reference commonly occur in paranoid SCHIZOPHRENIA.

idée fixe A rigidly held idea, such as an irrational fear. An idée fixe may become an OBSESSION and dominate the individual's mental life. For example, COMPULSIVE handwashing may stem from an idée fixe that the water is CONTAMINATED. The term was used by Pierre Janet in 1882. (See also CONTAMINATION, FEAR OF; OBSESSION; OBSESSIVE–COMPULSIVE DISORDER.)

ideaphobia, fear of Fear of ideas.

illness phobia Fear of illness is known as nosemaphobia and nosophobia. Individuals who have illness phobia are frequently anxious and worry about having a disease. They fear dying and illnesses such as cancer, heart disease, and venereal disease. They may avoid anything that reminds them of diseases, such as programs on television or articles in newspapers. These individuals may frequently search their bodies for outward signs and misinterpret unusual sensations. They may seek frequent medical examinations because of their fears. Some illness phobics fear a disease that is most popular at a given time. For example, in earlier generations, many people feared tuberculosis or poliomyelitis. During the latter half of the 20th century, the most frequently feared diseases seem to be cancer and AIDS (acquired immunodeficiency syndrome).

Fear of illness is most prevalent among middle-aged and older persons. Women seem to fear illness more than men. Illness phobia may be considered as intermediate between simple phobia and obsessive–compulsive disorder, and it may also be regarded as a form of focused hypochondriasis. (See also CANCER, FEAR OF; HYPOCHONDRIASIS; INJECTIONS, FEAR OF.)

Kleinknecht, Ronald A., *The Anxious Self* (New York: Human Sciences Press, 1986).

Marks, Isaac M., *Fears, Phobias and Rituals* (New York: Oxford University Press, 1987).

illyngophobia Fear of vertigo, or fear of feeling dizzy when looking down from a high place. (See also ACROPHOBIA; VERTIGO.)

imipramine Imipramine, or imipramine hydrochloride, is the prototype tricyclic ANTIDEPRESSANT drug. Imipramine has been found to be effective in treating endogenous DEPRESSION. Many phobics notice that their phobias and anxieties get worse during periods of depression, and treatment of depression produces good results in the anxiety as well, as the anxiety subsides along with the depression. Like other drugs in this class, imipramine may take up to three to four weeks to become effective. Side effects of imipramine may include dryness of the mouth, slight blurring of vision, and tiredness. No special diet is required while taking imipramine or other TRICYCLIC ANTIDEPRESSANTS. Imipramine, like other drugs in its class, is identified by the molecular structure consisting of three conjoined benzene rings with varied radicals attached to the middle ring.

Marks, I.M., *Living with Fear* (New York: McGraw-Hill, 1978).

immobility of a joint, fear of Fear of immobility of a joint is known as ankylophobia.

imperfection, fear of Fear of imperfection is known as atelophobia. Some individuals who have OBSESSIVE–COMPULSIVE DISORDER fear that they are not doing everything "right," or that they will make some ERROR in their daily routines unless they check and recheck. Many phobias stem from a fear of being imperfect. Many individuals are unduly concerned with what others think of them and hence develop a phobia of imperfection. Examples of fears of imperfection are talking on the telephone, going for a job interview, writing in front of others, eating in front of others, or speaking in public. (See also SOCIAL PHOBIAS.)

implosion/implosive therapy A behavior-therapy technique in which the individual is explosed to anxiety-producing stimuli by thoughts and imagery rather than the real situation. Implosion is also called FLOODING. The technique is based on CLASSICAL CONDITIONING principles, with ANXIETY as the CONDITIONED RESPONSE to images and thoughts about fearful situations or objects as the CONDITIONED STIMULI. The real situation is the unconditioned stimulus. The purpose of implosion is to prevent the individual from avoiding the conditioned stimuli Implosion is based on principles of learning theory and psychoanalytic theory. The latter is used as a theoretical guide to develop fantasies or fantasy images about the phobic event that relate to conscious fears (such as castration, separation, etc.). This method was developed by Thomas Stampfl, an

American psychologist. (See also ABREACTION; BEHAVIOR THERAPY; CATHARSIS; SYSTEMATIC DESENSITIZATION.)

impotence, fear of Fear of impotence is a relatively common SEXUAL FEAR. Primary impotence is the physical or psychological condition of a man who has never had an erection sufficient for penetration or sexual intercourse. Secondary impotence is an inability of the male to have an erection sufficient for intercourse, although he has a history of at least one successful intromission.

imprinting Experiences during infancy that influence fear responses (separation, incomplete bonding, or traumatic events, for example). Imprinting can occur very early in life, raising the question of whether genetic or environmental factors are greater influences upon later PHOBIAS. In 1873, an English naturalist, D.A. Spalding, observed that newly hatched chicks tended to follow the first moving object, human or animal, that caught their attention—behavior that was later described as imprinting. The term imprinting was coined by Konrad Lorenz, an ethologist, in 1937. The theories regarding human bonding are, at a psychological level, similar to the theory of imprinting. (See also ATTACHMENT THEORY.)

incest, fear of Some individuals fear incest, or sexual relations between blood relatives. Each society determines the prohibited degree of relationship. Many victims of child abuse realistically fear sexual assault by a blood relative. In many cases, fear of incest and retribution keeps children from reporting attempted molestation by relatives. (See also CHILD ABUSE, FEAR OF; RELATIVES, FEAR OF.)

incidence An epidemiologic term meaning the rate of occurrence of new cases of a given condition, such as agoraphobia, in a particular population in a given period of time. Incidence rates are usually expressed per 100,000 population per year. Incidence differs from PREVALENCE, which is the total number of cases of a disorder existing in a given population at a given point in time or during a specified time. (See PHOBIA; also SOCIAL PHOBIA.)

incontinence, fear of Incontinence is an inability to control the evacuation of liquids or solids from the body. Incontinence may occur for many reasons, such as problems related to muscles, the nervous system, or infection, as well as an injury or complications of surgery. Many individuals at an advanced age fear incontinence and may become fearful of going out socially because they will be embarrassed if they wet themselves in public. Incontinence is one of many fears associated with aging. Women around the menopause also fear incontinence; many notice loss of slight amounts of urine during physical stress, such as running, laughing, or coughing. Incontinence in men and women, in many cases, can be improved by surgical means. (See also AGING, FEARS OF.)

incubation of fears The period between the time an individual experiences events that cause ANXIETY or GUILT and the subsequent PHOBIAS or RITUALS that arise from the experience. In many cases, the problem begins even years after the first event. Some individuals relive the event in their mind and begin avoiding the painful situation. They go through an addictive cycle of avoidance to lessen tension and thus strengthen the tendency to further avoidance. An example is a fearful woman who, when given improper change in a store, was too uneasy to complain. After a few weeks she felt uncomfortable when returning to the store and later avoided going into the store or even passing the store for fear that she might see the man who had shortchanged her.

Marks, Isaac, *Fears, Phobias and Rituals* (New York: Oxford University Press, 1987).

incubus Historically, a male demon feared because he seduces sleeping women. In reality, incubus is a sleep disorder recognized since the time of Aristotle in which the victim has feelings of suffocation and impending death, exhaustion and fear upon awakening.

The term "incubus syndrome" has been used to describe patients suffering from the DELUSION that they have been sexually approached at night by an unseen lover. (See also SUCCUBUS; WITCHES AND WITCHCRAFT, FEAR OF.)

Raschka, L.B., "The Incubus Syndrome," *Canadian Journal of Psychiatry* (October 1979), pp. 549–553.

India, phobias in One recent study comparing phobic individuals in India and those in the United Kingdom indicated several differences. The British sample contained more individuals with agoraphobia and social phobias. The Indian sample contained more individuals who had phobias of illness and sudden death. The lower incidence of agoraphobia among the Indians may be explained by the fact that while agoraphobia generally occurs more among females than males, Indian women are traditionally housebound, and an inability to venture out by themselves may not be considered unusual behavior.

More important, this difference may be explained by the differences in social structure between India and the United Kingdom. In India, for example, social life is defined by one's roles, such as son, husband, father grandson, or neighbor, whereas in Western cultures the focus is on individuality and independence. Thus the Indian may feel less social pressure than Westerners, and this lack of social pressure may play a role in the incidence of agoraphobia and social phobias. It may also be that fear of social situations is not recognized as a condition requiring medical help. Also, poor health education and less-than-adequate health services in general may heighten anxieties about illness and death. (See also DEPRESSION AND FEARS ACROSS CULTURES.)

Chambers, J. et al., "Phobias in India and the United Kingdom," *Acta Psychiatrica Scandinavica,* 74(1986), pp. 388–391.

Individualized Behavior Avoidance Tests (IBATs) Tests used by researchers in AGORAPHOBIA. Some researchers prefer IBATs over STANDARDIZED BEHAVIORAL AVOIDANCE TESTS (SBATs) because agoraphobics have so many different phobic difficulties that may be measured. Another advantage of the IBAT is that it assesses personally relevant behaviors in naturalistic situations in phobic individuals' homes and clinics. An example of an individualized test is one that is initially developed from a 10-item hierarchy of phobic situations. Five items representing a range of severity are selected from this hierarchy, and assessment is conducted from the phobic individual's home. The individual is instructed to attempt all five items in the order of increasing difficulty. Each item is scored on a three-point scale, with the interpretation of each score as follows: (0) individual avoided the item; (1) partial completion of the item (escape); (2) successful completion of the item. The total score, therefore, has a range from one to 10. Additionally, Subjective Units of Disturbance (SUDS) ratings on a scale of zero to eight points may be obtained for each item. The IBAT allows assessment in many personally relevant situations and should, if the phobia hierarchy is properly constructed, possess a high enough ceiling to deal with distraction levels, sensitivity to treatment changes, and generalizability to other situations. (See also BARLOW, DAVID.)

Himadi, William G. et al., "Assessment of Agoraphobia—II, Measurement of Clinical Change," *Behavior Research and Therapy,* 24:3(1986), pp. 321–332.

individual psychology An approach to PSYCHOTHERAPY and PERSONALITY. Individual psychology is based on the theory that each individual is governed by a conscious drive to develop goals and create his or her own style of life, as opposed to the view that individuals are dominated by UNCONSCIOUS instincts. The term was introduced by ALFRED ADLER. The goal of individual psychology is to help the individual adopt a more socially useful life-style and thus improve interpersonal relationships. ANXIETIES and PHOBIAS can be overcome with changes in life-style brought about by therapy. (See also COMPENSATION.)

infants, fear of Fear of infants is known as pedophobia. (See also CHILDREN, FEAR OF.)

infection, fear of Fear of infection is known as molysmophobia or mysophobia. Some individuals who fear CONTAMINATION or GERMS or have ILLNESS PHOBIA fear infection. Also, those who fear BACTERIA or BACILLI usually fear infection. Those who have a phobia about contracting autoimmune deficiency syndrome (AIDS) fear infection, as do some individuals who have OBSESSIVE–COMPULSIVE DISORDER.

infecting a sexual partner, fear of See PSYCHOSEXUAL FEARS; SEXUAL FEARS; SEXUALLY TRANSMITTED DISEASES.

inferiority complex Originally this was a term used by ALFRED ADLER to describe the cluster of ideas and feelings that arise in reaction to the sense of "organ" inferiority. Now it is a popular term for a general sense of inadequacy. A sense of inadequacy accompanies DEPRESSION or a mood disorder in which the individual feels a low sense of self-esteem and low self-worth. The opposite of the inferiority complex is a superiority complex; individuals who have BIPOLAR DISORDER or MANIC–DEPRESSIVE DISORDER often exhibit a superiority complex while they are in the manic phase of their illness. (See also COMPLEX.)

infinity, fear of Fear of infinity is known as apeirophobia. Individuals who fear infinity like to have terms defined and distances measured, and appreciate predictability in their lives. They may fear looking far into the distance where they cannot anticipate what lies ahead or looking ahead into time with UNKNOWN, unpredictable circumstances. This fear may relate to a fear of change or newness. Some agoraphobics may have fears related to infinity. (See also AGORAPHOBIA; CHANGE, FEAR OF; UNKNOWN, FEAR OF.)

informed consent Voluntary agreement to a therapy plan. Individuals who seek therapy for ANXIETIES or PHOBIAS should be informed about the types of therapy or treatment to be used, possible side effects, and desired outcome before going ahead with the therapy plan. Also, informed consent refers to the right of the therapist to give out information learned in therapy sessions only with the consent of the individual patient.

inhibition Inhibition is an inner restraint that keeps an individual from following through on feelings or thoughts, such as anger or lust. Inhibition may be caused by real or imagined fear of the consequences of expression. Individuals who have inhibitions in specific areas may experience increased ANXIETY when confronted with the feared object or situation. Inhibitions often lead to SHYNESS; some social phobics have many inhibitions and consequently avoid many situations in which they feel uncomfortable. (See also SOCIAL PHOBIA.)

injection phobias Fear of injections is known as trypanophobia. A fear of injection may be one reason many individuals fear doctors and dentists. Many individuals say their fear of dentists arises from fear of injection of local anesthetic. Usually fear of injections begins before age ten or eleven and diminishes with age. Some who fear acupuncture do so because they fear needles. Some who fear donating blood or having blood transfusions also fear injection. Injection phobias include fear of vaccination and fear of inoculation and immunizations. (See also ACUPUNCTURE, FEAR OF; DENTAL ANXIETY; NEEDLES, FEAR OF.)

Kleinknecht, Ronald A., *The Anxious Self* (New York: Human Sciences Press, 1986).

Kleinknecht, R.A. and D.A. Bernstein, "Assessment of Dental Fear," *Behavior Therapy*, 9(1978), pp. 626–634.

injury, fear of Fear of injury is known as traumatophobia. (See also BLOOD AND BLOOD-INJURY, FEAR OF.)

inkblot test See RORSCHACH TEST.

innate behavior Behavior resulting from genetic causes.

innovation, fear of Fear of innovation, or of something new, is known as neophobia. Many anxious individuals like to keep to the same routine and avoid doing, seeing, or using anything new. (See also NEWNESS, FEAR OF.)

inoculation, fear of Fear of inoculation is known as trypanophobia. Those who fear inoculations fear needles. They fear being vaccinated or having any kind of immunization via a needle. (See also INJECTION, FEAR OF.)

insanity, fear of Fear of insanity is known as dementophobia, lyssophobia, and maniaphobia. (See also GOING CRAZY, FEAR OF; SCHIZOPHRENIA.)

insects, fear of Fear of insects is known as acarophobia and entomophobia. Some individuals are so afraid of insects that they seal off their windows, vacuum and sweep twice a day, and feel uncomfortable outside their "cleansed" environment. There is no instinctual basis or symbolism for fear of insects. (See also BEES, FEAR OF; STINGS, FEAR OF.)

insight A special kind of understanding of a situation. In therapy, the term implies depth and suddenness of understanding of, for example, the origins of one's PHOBIA or ANXIETY. Insight means seeing beneath the surface of one's behavior or ideas. In cognitive insight, an individual understands a relationship between cause and effect and achieves new ways to solve behavioral problems. In emotional insight, one gains new awareness about feelings, motives, and relationships. In PSYCHOANALYSIS, insight is an awareness of the relationship between past experience and current behavior, particularly with regard to UNCONSCIOUS conflicts brought into the CONSCIOUS. In all therapies, insight involves accepting the conceptual system of the therapist to a large extent. Insight therapies are not effective for anxiety disorders and are not the treatment of choice. (See also ATTRIBUTION THEORY; BANDURA, ALBERT; BEHAVIOR MODIFICATION; BEHAVIOR THERAPY.)

insomnia, fear of Insomnia is an inability to sleep or stay asleep. Some individuals fear insomnia, and for others insomnia is a symptom of other disorders. Insomnia is a frequent symptom of individuals who have ANXIETIES. Many moderately or severely depressed individuals complain of fitful sleep with early-morning wakening. However, some depressed individuals sleep more than normal. Many people suffer from temporary insomnia when faced with a particular situation that causes them anxiety or great excitement, but there are also chronic insomniacs.

There are four main categories of insomnia: (1) light-sleep insomnia, characterized by an overabundance of light sleep and less or an inadequate amount of deep sleep; (2) sleep-awakening insomnia, in which the individual wakes up repeatedly during the night and spends at least thirty minutes trying to go back to sleep; (3) sleep-onset insomnia, in which the individual has trouble initially falling asleep; and (4) early-termination insomnia, in which the individual awakens after less than six hours and cannot go back to sleep at all.

Treatment

Treatment of insomnia is usually focused on the main condition causing the sleeplessness, whether a physical condition such as pain or itching, or a psychological concern. Some depressed individuals react well to a sedative ANTIDEPRESSANT such as AMITRIPTYLENE, DOXEPIN, or MIANSERIN taken at night. Similarly, some BENZODIAZEPINES have prolonged effects; one dose at night acts both as an immediate HYPNOTIC and as an ANXIOLYTIC the next day. For occasional use—for example, with travel and time-zone changes—a short-acting benzodiazepine is often recommended. However, use and misuse of sleeping pills is one of the greatest dangers facing chronic insomniacs. Since the pills are addictive and the body builds up a tolerance to them, the insomniac must take more and more of them to put him- or herself to sleep. Another danger of constant use of sleeping pills is that these drugs disturb the normal pattern of dreaming, which is essential to good mental health. Disturbing the dream pattern for several nights may result in neurotic daytime behavior.

Routine administration of drugs known as hypnotics is also a common cause of insomnia. If a drug is taken intermittently or the dose is not kept constant, mild withdrawal symptoms, including insomnia or nightmares, may follow. Drugs known as anxiolytics may make some children's sleep worse and may increase their anxieties. In children who have situational anxiety such as school phobia, anxiolytics may impair their intellectual function, outweighing any emotional benefits they might derive from the drugs.

In elderly individuals who have insomnia, barbiturates and benzodiazepines are sometimes prescribed for sleep problems, but their use should be limited to short courses related to definite periods of stress. To avoid toxicity, short-acting benzodiazepines or a chloral derivative are preferred.

Behavior treatment for insomnia has been effective in eliminating sleep disturbance within a relatively brief therapy duration. Behavioral therapists try to build an association between bed and sleep, and the individual who cannot sleep is asked to get out of bed until sleep is possible. Modification of cognitions (e.g., excessive worries) is often necessary, as well as training in relaxation (which is used preceding attempts to sleep). (See also BARBITURATES; DEPRESSION; DREAMS; SEDATIVES; SLEEP; SLEEPWALKING; SYMPTOMS.)

Andelman, Samuel L., *New Home Medical Encyclopedia* (New York: Quadrangle Books, 1973).

Lader, Malcolm, *Introduction to Psychopharmacology* (Kalamazoo, MI: Upjohn, 1980).

insomnia in cancer patients Insomnia is a frequent complaint of cancer patients. It may be a side effect of treatment, fear of the disease, fear of the unknown, uncertainty about the future, or pain, which interferes with comfortable rest. Vomiting, nausea, fever, and positional discomfort also may interfere with a cancer patient's sleep. Medications that may help a person overcome cancer are themselves frequent causes of sleep disturbances, while anxieties that come with this dreaded diagnosis also may produce insomnia. While cancer patients may be able to stay occupied all day long, at night they focus on concerns over cancer. Often an individual thinks of other family members or friends who have died of cancer. They feel restless, trapped, and not in control of their lives. Therapy to overcome this anxiety may include a short course of antianxiety medication. Some cancer patients stay awake at night because they fear dying in their sleep. They may find nighttime activities, household chores, and other things to do to avoid sleep. This creates an abnormal sleep cycle in which a patient falls asleep during daytime but stays awake all night. Nightmares also may be frequent in a cancer victim. Fears about the future are uncovered and addressed. (See also UNKNOWN FEAR OF THE.)

Bruckheim, Allan, "Insomnia May Accompany Cancer," *Chicago Tribune* (December 11, 1987).

integrity groups SELF-HELP mental health groups developed by O. Hobart Mowrer during the 1960s. Integrity groups were one of the early forms of self-helps for individuals who have anxieties. Mowrer believed that relationships with significant people in an individual's life can be affected by social ANXIETIES and FEARS, particularly the operation of guilt. He believed that the inability to keep commitments to other people was at the root of many psychosocial disorders. His idea in developing integrity groups was to provide a support group in which individuals could deal with these problems. In integrity groups, approximately eight persons met weekly for three-hour sessions during which they participated in open transactions with one another. Mowrer believed that shared honesty and involvement in the group encouraged a sense of community and raised self-esteem; group members thus developed a secure base on which they could then make changes in thoughts, feelings, and behavior toward others. The integrity group motto was: "You alone can do it, but you can't do it alone," which emphasizes the values of self-responsibility along with mutual support.

Corsini, Raymond J. (ed.), *Encyclopedia of Psychology,* (New York: John Wiley, 1984).

interpersonal anxiety An old term used to describe SOCIAL ANXIETY. (See also PHOBIA; SOCIAL PHOBIA.)

intoxication See ALCOHOLISM, FEAR OF.

in vivo desensitization A technique for treating phobias in real-life situations, as opposed to work in a laboratory or in imagination. Phobic individuals are led through the actual situations that arouse their ANXIETIES. The goal is for the phobic individuals to learn to relax in the presence of anxiety-causing stimuli. Whenever it is possible to use it, this is the more effective form of DESENSITIZATION therapy. Also known as *in vivo* therapy. (See also BEHAVIOR THERAPY; SYSTEMATIC DESENSITIZATION.)

in vivo therapy *In vivo* literally means "in life." This is the preferred form of desensitization, as contrasted with imaginal psychotherapies using images. *In vivo* desensitization was used by Wolpe, who then developed imaginal sensations as a more convenient tool in some situations. (See also EXPOSURE THERAPY; *IN VIVO* DESENSITIZATION; WOLPE, JOSEPH.)

iophobia Fear of poisons, or of rust. (See also POISON, FEAR OF; RUST, FEAR OF.)

iprindole An antidepressant drug. (See also ANTIDEPRESSANTS; ANTIDEPRESSANTS, NEW; DEPRESSION.)

iproniazid An antidepressant drug in the monoamine oxidase (MAO) inhibitor class. Iproniazid is also known by the trade name Marsilid. This drug, like others in its class, may take weeks to help depression and is less effective than tricyclic antidepressants, although it sometimes helps individuals in whom tricyclics have been unsuccessful. One disadvantage of this drug (and other MAO inhibitors) is that individuals taking the drug must avoid foods containing quantities of tyramine, such as hard cheese, red wine, and red meat, because tyramine sometimes reacts with MAO inhibitors to cause high blood pressure. (See also

ANTIDEPRESSANTS; DEPRESSION; MONOAMINE OXIDASE INHIBITORS [MAOIS].)

Greist, J.H. and J.W. Jefferson, *Depression and Its Treatment: Help for the Nation's #1 Mental Problem* (Washington, DC: American Psychiatric Association, 1984).

Marks, I.M., *Living with Fear* (New York: McGraw-Hill, 1978).

irrational beliefs, fear of Some individuals who have anxiety disorders harbor more irrational beliefs than those who do not have such disorders. Such irrational beliefs include thinking that it is important to be loved or approved by virtually everyone in one's community; that one must be perfectly competent, adequate, and achieving to consider oneself worthwhile; that past influences cannot be eradicated; and that some people are bad or villainous and therefore should be blamed or punished. (See also SUPERNATURAL, FEARS OF.)

Encyclopedia of Unbelief (Buffalo, NY: Prometheus, 1985).

Davison, G.C. and J.M. Neale, *Abnormal Psychology* (New York: John Wiley, 1986), p. 123.

irritable bowel syndrome A chronic gastrointestinal condition in which the individual experiences abdominal discomfort or pain and a change in bowel habits, such as cramping, DIARRHEA, or CONSTIPATION, without weight loss or gastrointestinal disease. The syndrome may affect eight to seventeen percent of the American population. Some physicians say that the condition is of "nervous" origin and have described irritable bowel syndrome patients as "neurasthenics." Among individuals who have irritable bowel syndrome, many have ANXIETY and DEPRESSION. Conversely, functional gastrointestinal complaints are so common in individuals who have anxiety disorders that gastrointestinal distress has been included as a symptom of panic disorder in the American Psychiatric Association's *Diagnostic and Statistical Manual of Mental Disorders*. In both conditions, onset most often occurs in young and middle-aged adults. Both affect predominantly women, are associated with a variety of complaints, appear to be familial, and are often chronic conditions. In research studies, many individuals found relief from both irritable bowel syndrome and panic symptoms with antipanic therapy. Panic disorder and irritable bowel syndrome both improved with BENZODIAZEPINES and tricyclic ANTIDEPRESSANTS. Researchers hypothesize that gastrointestinal symptoms experienced by some individuals may be symptoms of panic disorder or may be irritable bowel syndrome worsened by a coexisting anxiety disorder. PANIC DISORDER patients often report one particular symptom, such as diarrhea or DIZZINESS, as particularly troublesome and seek a specialist to treat that particular symptom.

Lydiard, R. Bruce et al., "Can Panic Disorder Present as Irritable Bowel Syndrome?" *Journal of Clinical Psychiatry* (September 1986), pp. 470–473.

isocarboxazid A potent ANTIDEPRESSANT in the MONOAMINE OXIDASE (MAO) INHIBITOR class of antidepressants. Isocarboxazid, also known by the trade name Marplan, is used for relief of moderate and severe DEPRESSION in adults. It is not used for mild depression or depression that is an appropriate response to temporary stress. Individuals taking MAO inhibitors must watch their diets to avoid foods containing TYRAMINE, which is found in many foods, including hard cheeses and red wines.

isolation A defense mechanism by which an individual separates feelings from the events to which they are attached. The feelings are repressed, and the events are viewed without emotion. This term is used in Freudian PSYCHOANALYSIS. Isolation mechanisms would enhance anxieties. (See also FREUD.)

isolophobia Fear of solitude or of being alone. (See also SOLITUDE, FEAR OF.)

isopterophobia Fear of termites or of other insects that eat wood and are destructive. (See also TERMITES, FEAR OF.)

itch, fear of Fear of itching, having itchy skin, or having the "seven-year itch" is known as scabiophobia or acarophobia. (See also SCABIES.)

ithyphallophobia Fear of seeing, thinking about, or having an erect penis. (See also PENIS, ERECT; SEXUAL FEARS.)

J

Janet, Pierre (1859–1947) A French psychologist known as a pioneer of psychodynamic psychiatry. He was appointed director of the psychological clinic at Salpetriere Hospital by JEAN-MARTIN CHARCOT. He attributed some psychiatric disorders, such as hysteria and multiple personality, to physical disability and stress, rather than unconscious factors. He is well known for his description of the clinical features of hysteria and use of cathartic treatment. Believing that treatment should provide stimulation, he investigated many methods of treatment, including hypnosis, suggestion, and discussion and guidance aimed at "reeducation." Modern therapies to treat anxieties and phobias include further developments of Janet's work (See also IDÉE FIXE.)

Harre, R. and R. Lamb, *Encyclopedic Dictionary of Psychology* (Cambridge, MA: The MIT Press, 1983).

Janet, P., *The Major Symptoms of Hysteria* (New York: Hafner, 1965)

Janimine See IMIPRAMINE.

Janov, Arthur (1924–) An American psychologist and author who developed the controversial technique known as PRIMAL THERAPY, which is based on the concept that the frustration of basic human needs brings about pain from which the individual can be released by reliving the experience through therapy. Primal therapy is an intense, emotional therapy used in treatment of anxiety disorders to get at early psychological roots of problems. Janov practiced traditional psychotherapy until an encounter with a patient led to the development of his theory and the publication of *The Primal Scream* in 1970. He is the founder and director of the Primal Institute in Los Angeles.

Contemporary Authors (Detroit: Gale Research, 1986).

jealousy, fear of Fear of jealousy is known as zelophobia. Jealousy is an emotion that includes feelings of loss of self-esteem, envy, hostility, and self-blame. Jealousy frequently first appears at the age of two or three when a new child arrives in the family. There may be hostile feelings toward the newborn because he or she is getting more attention. In adulthood, many types of jealousy persist. In the more extreme types it may take the form of a paranoid DELUSION. Many people have observed jealousy in others and may develop a fear of becoming jealous.

Jones, Ernest A. (1879–1958) A British psychoanalyst, a disciple of Sigmund FREUD, the founder of the British Psychoanalytic Society, and its president between 1920 and 1924. Jones is the founder of the *International Journal of Psychoanalysis*. He is the author of the definitive three-volume biography of Freud as well as many other books concerning interpretation of folklore, literature, and art in psychoanalytic concepts. Therapists who treat individuals who have anxieties and phobias study Jones's works.

Jones, Mary Cover (1896–1987) One of the early contributors to behavioral psychology who demonstrated, in two research reports in 1924, behavioral techniques for elimination of fears in young children. The first paper described a direct conditioning treatment for three-year-old Peter, who showed fear of white rats and other furry objects. Using food as a counterconditioning method, Mary Cover Jones was able to produce fear reduction with Peter. This work was a forerunner of the BEHAVIOR THERAPY movement. JOSEPH WOLPE described her as the "mother" of behavior modification.

jumping (from both high and low places), fear of Fear of jumping from both high and low places is known as catapedaphobia. This fear may be related to a fear of heights, a fear of falling, or a fear of being injured. (See also CLIFFS, FEAR OF; HEIGHTS, FEAR OF.)

Jung, Carl Gustav (1875–1961) A Swiss psychiatrist and philosopher known as the originator of analytical psychology. Jung was associated with Sigmund FREUD and the psychoanalytic school of psychotherapy, but he differed with Freud over theories of infantile sexuality. Jung believed that individuals are molded by "racial" as well as personal history and motivated by moral and spiritual values more than by psychosexual drives. Jung did not utilize free association, as Freud did. Jung's theory of "analytic psychology" included concepts of the ego, in which conscious and unconscious forces are integrated and individualized. Jung believed that the unconscious consisted of half-forgotten memories and experiences that in some cases become fragmented into complexes because of traumatic experiences or internal conflicts. He used the term "collective unconscious" to refer to the store of inherited foundations of our intellectual life and personality. He viewed personality as a collection of opposing forces, such as conscious–unconscious, introversive–extroversive, and rational–irrational processes. He called our basic psychic energy the libido, which he believed is responsible for resolving personality conflicts. When conflicts are not resolved, Jung advocated therapy to face and overcome difficulties, such as anxieties and phobias, by studying dreams and drawings and exploring new activities to express the individual's personality. Jung, whose collected works are published in English in twenty volumes, was the first president of the International Psychoanalytic Society. (See also LIBIDO; PERSONALITY TYPES; TELEOLOGY.)

justice, fear of Fear of justice or fear of seeing justice applied is known as dikephobia. Justice involves concepts of moral rightness, honor, and fairness. (See also AUTHORITY, FEAR OF.)

K

kainophobia (kainotophobia) Fear of novelty, change, or newness. (See also CHANGE, FEAR OF; NEWNESS, FEAR OF; NOVELTY, FEAR OF.)

kakorrhaphiophobia (kakorraphiophobia) Fear of failure. (See also FAILURE, FEAR OF.)

katagelophobia Fear of ridicule. This fear is related to a fear of criticism; both may be social phobias. (See also RIDICULE, FEAR OF.)

kathisophobia Fear of sitting down. (See also SITTING DOWN, FEAR OF.)

Kempf's disease See HOMOSEXUAL PANIC.)

kenophobia Fear of empty spaces. (See also EMPTY SPACES, FEAR OF.)

keraunophobia Fear of lightning and thunder. (See also LIGHTNING, FEAR OF; STORMS, FEAR OF; THUNDER, FEAR OF.)

kidney disease, fear of Fear of kidney disease is known as albuminurophobia. The major functions of the kidneys are cleaning the blood of metabolic waste products and controlling the amount of water in the body. Both functions are done by formation and excretion of urine. Some individuals fear that they have kidney disease when their urinary habits change or if they have vague pains in their abdomen or back. Some individuals worry that they are urinating too much, and others worry that they are not urinating enough. Urinalysis usually is part of routine physical examinations, and many phobic individuals are reassured when they learn test results. (See also DISEASE, FEAR OF; HIGH BLOOD PRESSURE, FEAR OF.)

kinesophobia (or kinetophobia) Fear of motion. (See also MOTION, FEAR OF.)

kissing, fear of Fear and anxieties about kissing range from feelings of social awkwardness, to rejection, to concern about disease. The AIDS (Autoimmune Deficiency Syndrome) epidemic during the 1980s has made actresses and actors fearful of engaging in the intimate kissing required in many films. Kissing is endowed with an element of performance anxiety for young people who may be more strongly motivated by a desire to appear adept and sophisticated than by genuine romance or passion. Kissing in social rather than romantic situations also creates a certain type of anxiety and confusion, since there is such a variation in method and expectations in different ethnic and social groups. Kissing is also an unpleasant prospect for some people because of a strong, but seldom freely expressed, social fear: bad breath.

The term "kiss of death," meaning a betrayal or generally damaging action, has its origin in the kiss given by Judas Iscariot to identify Jesus as the man to be arrested and ultimately crucified. (See also SOCIAL PHOBIA.)

Encyclopedia Americana (Danbury, CT: Grolier, 1983).

McCoy, Kath, "How Do I Know If I'm Doing This Right?" *Seventeen* (Jan. 1987), p. 12.

Morrow, Lance, "Changing the Signals of Passion," *Time* (Jan. 13, 1987), p. 74.

Powell, Joanna, "Smack Attack," *Harper's Bazaar* (Feb. 1985), p. 11.

Klein, Melanie (1882–1962) An Austrian child psychologist. Klein worked in England to develop a school of psychoanalysis whose goal was the resolution of children's anxieties, particularly their feelings of ambivalence toward their parents. Her theories were based on a belief that feelings of hostility toward parents start in early infancy. Klein's work included the study of schizoid (split personality) and depressed children.

Howells, John G. and M. Livia Osborn, *A Reference Companion to the History of Abnormal Psychology* (Westport, CT: Greenwood Press, 1984).

kleptophobia, cleptophobia Fear of stealing. (See also STEALING, FEAR OF.)

knees, fear of Fear of knees is known as genuphobia. While this fear seems quite unnatural to most people, sufferers feel equally perturbed. However, fears related to parts of the body do develop, just as fear of other objects develops. These fears, while rare,

are treated with a behavioral, desensitization approach, with a high degree of success.

knives, fear of Fear of knives is known as aichmophobia. Individuals who are phobic about knives usually are also phobic about various objects with points, such as letter openers, spears, and daggers. This fear may interfere with eating, since sufferers will avoid using knives or placing knives on a table.

koinoniphobia See ROOM, FEAR OF.

kolpophobia Fear of genitals, particularly female genitals. (See also GENITALS, FEMALE, FEAR OF.)

koniophobia Fear of dust. (See also CONTAMINATION, FEAR OF; DUST, FEAR OF.)

Kraepelin, Emil (1856–1926) A German psychiatrist best known for his classification of mental illnesses based upon thousands of case studies. He accepted the somatic viewpoint and attributed his first major category, dementia praecox (later known as schizophrenia), to organic brain changes arising within the organism, and resulting in irreversible deterioration. Kraepelin's second major category, manic–depressive psychosis, was differentiated from schizophrenia. He regarded personality factors as by-products of a diseased brain or faulty metabolism. These organic interpretations were later challenged by the adherents of a psychodynamic approach. (See also BLEULER, EUGEN; MANIC–DEPRESSIVE DISORDER; ORGANIC APPROACH.)

kymophobia Fear of waves. (See also WAVES, FEAR OF.)

kynophobia Fear of rabies. (See also RABIES, FEAR OF.)

kyphophobia Fear of stooping. (See also STOOPING, FEAR OF.)

L

L-5-Hydroxytryptophan A drug used to treat individuals who have phobic disorders, with and without panic attacks and generalized anxiety disorders. It is abbreviated as 5-HTP. Research has indicated that some individuals experience a significant reduction in anxiety on this therapy in conjunction with carbidopa (a brain chemical). Clinical trials with other drugs used in controlled populations have not been conducted, so general utility of this drug has not been determined. (See also ANTIDEPRESSANTS; BIOLOGICAL BASIS FOR ANXIETY.)

Kahn, Rene S. and Herman G.M. Westenberg, "L-5-Hydroxytryptophan in the Treatment of Anxiety Disorders," *Journal of Affective Disorders,* 8(1985), pp. 197–200.

lachanophobia Fear of vegetables. (See also VEGETABLES, FEAR OF.)

lactate-induced anxiety Sodium lactate is one of the substances researchers have identified that can produce PANIC ATTACKS in people who have already experienced them. Chemical induction of panic provides a means of evaluating new treatments as well as the opportunity to closely monitor patients, both by psychophysiological and biochemical techniques, during the panic attack itself. Individuals who are subject to panic attacks may be biologically somewhat different than other people. For example, they may differ in sensitivity to sodium lactate or CARBON DIOXIDE and have differences in CHEMOCEPTOR activity.

Sodium lactate is one of the most studied of the known anxiety-producing chemicals. During the 1940s, researchers observed that individuals with chronic anxiety produced excessive amounts of lactate with standard exercise. For such individuals, exercise can actually set off a panic attack.

The anxiety level of anxiety-prone individuals increases as the level of lactic acid rises in their blood, while people in the nonanxious group experience no such anxiety. Researchers have injected chronically anxious patients with sodium lactate, which produces panic similar to their usual attacks, while normal individuals do not respond to the lactate. When lactate is given to anxiety sufferers in the form of an infusion (a constant flow of sodium lactate), their panic can be stopped by turning off the flow.

Researchers at Washington University School of Medicine (St. Louis, Missouri) observed a difference in blood flow in the brains of people who suffer panic attacks and of those who do not. Using positive-emission tomography (PET scans), they measured blood flow in seven areas of the brain that are thought to control panic and anxiety reactions. In one of these areas, the parahippocampal gyrus, researchers observed that in very lactate-sensitive people, blood flow on the right side of the gyrus was much higher than on the left side. Changes in blood flow appeared to reflect differences in the activity of nerve cells on the two sides. These differences were not seen in nonlactate-sensitive individuals.

Other researchers have suggested that sodium lactate triggers panic attacks in 80 percent of patients with panic disorder but in less than 20 percent of normal people. Lactate infusions were thought to provide a means of identifying people biologically prone to panic attacks and thus likely to respond to drug treatments. However, recent evidence casts doubt on the causative role of lactate, since susceptibility varies less after a person has completed behavior exposure treatments for anxiety. This suggests that lactate susceptibility is a variable factor and that psychophysiology can be altered by behavioral treatment and anxiety-coping skills. In light of this research, the most fruitful approach seems to be to study the relationship between physiology and emotion rather than each separately. (See also CARBON DIOXIDE SENSITIVITY; PANIC.)

Fishman, Scott M. and David V. Sheehan, "Anxiety and Panic: Their Cause and Treatment," *Psychology Today* (April 1985), pp. 26–32.

Mazza, Dominic L. et al., "Prevalence of Anxiety Disorders in Patients with Mitral Valve Prolapse," *American Journal of Psychiatry* (March 1986), pp. 349–352.

Marks, Isaac M., *Fears, Phobias and Rituals* (New York: Oxford University Press, 1987).

lakes, fear of Fear of lakes is known as limnophobia. This fear may extend to being on a lake, looking at a lake, either in actuality or in a film or picture, or imagining a lake. Fear of lakes may relate to fear of water or fear of landscape. (See also LANDSCAPE, FEAR OF; WATER, FEAR OF.)

laliophobia, lalophobia Fear of talking, of speaking, or of stuttering. (See also TALKING, FEAR OF; SPEAKING, FEAR OF; STUTTERING, FEAR OF.)

landscapes, fear of Some individuals fear a particular kind of land arrangement or a specific locale—for example, mountains, the seaside, an open prairie, or a desert. Such individuals avoid a particular type of landscape that they may associate (consciously or unconsciously) with something extremely unpleasant or unfortunate in their past. Agoraphobics tend to experience more intense fear in landscape that is high and wide, but their fear tends to diminish when the view is interrupted by trees, irregularities in land, or rain. (See also LAKES, FEAR OF; RIVERS, FEAR OF; TREES, FEAR OF.)

Campbell, Robert J., *Psychiatric Dictionary* (New York: Oxford University Press, 1981).

languages, fear of Fears of foreign places are often manifested in the form of fears of foreign languages. Following are some commonly used terms relating to fears of specific languages (as well as those specific cultures):

China	Sinophobia
England	Anglophobia
France	Gallophobia
Germany	Germanophobia
Russia	Russophobia

(See also STRANGERS, FEAR OF.)

large objects, fear of Fear of large objects is known as megalophobia.

latent content A term used in psychoanalytic theory for the unconscious material of a dream that the individual expresses in a disguised way through the symbols noticed in the dream. In some cases, an understanding of the latent content of a dream helps an individual understand the causes of phobias and anxieties. Latent content is contrasted with manifest content, which relates to the meaning of contemporary events in DREAM content. (See also DREAM SYMBOLS; DREAMS, FEAR OF.)

laughter, fear of Fear of laughter is known as gelophobia. This fear may be related to other fears, such as fear of gaiety, or cheerfulness, or good news. (See also GAIETY, FEAR OF; GOOD NEWS, FEAR OF.)

lavatories, public, fear of Fear of public lavatories is common. Many individuals fear urinating or moving their bowels in a place where another person might be aware of what they are doing. Some fear contracting a disease from a toilet seat or from a towel or sink in a public lavatory. Some fear producing odors themselves, and others fear encountering odors in public lavatories. Some individuals have an inability to pass urine or move their bowels in a place other than their bathroom at home. With the advent of AIDS (Autoimmune Deficiency Syndrome), fear of public lavatories has increased in incidence. (See also CONTAMINATION, FEAR OF; DEFECATION, FEAR OF; URINATION, FEAR OF.)

lead poisoning, fear of Fear of lead poisoning is a 20th-century fear that is prevalent in many older neighborhoods in the United States. Lead poisoning, as well as all heavy metal poisoning, such as that by mercury and arsenic, is a significant problem, especially for children, who tend to put things in their mouths or chew on many things, such as toys, furniture and chips of paint that fall from ceilings or walls, especially in old buildings. Some newsprint such as colored comic pages, is made from leadbased paint. In some areas, there is a heavy concentration of lead in the air. Children are at greater risk than adults of permanent brain damage from lead and other heavy metal poisoning because their brains and nervous systems are still developing. They may become permanently mentally retarded. When an individual ingests too much lead, he may hallucinate and become delirious; he may have convulsions and uncontrollable tremors. To alleviate parents' fears regarding lead poisoning, children who live in high-lead areas can be tested. If high levels are found, children can be detoxified; the procedure may help to slow down and prevent continued brain deterioration. (See also AIR POLLUTION, FEAR OF.)

Bugelski, B. Richard and Anthony Graziano, *Handbook of Practical Psychology* (Englewood Cliffs, NJ: Prentice Hall, 1980).

learned helplessness Feeling of fear and indecision and a sense of not being able to influence the external world. An individual may find that his helpless responses elicit sympathy and assistance from others. Martin Seligman (1942–), who developed the concept of learned helplessness during the 1970s, noted that self-initiated behavior is learned If initiation is thwarted, the individual begins to feel helpless (that is, that he or she has no influence over his or her environment), and anxiety becomes intensified. (See also HELPLESSNESS.)

learning, fear of Fear of learning is known as sophophobia.

learning theory Learning theory is the study of the circumstances under which habits are formed or eliminated; it is the framework of behavior therapy and behavior modification. Learning theory is a set of principles that seeks to explain how behavior is modified in response to changes in the individual's environment. BEHAVIOR THERAPIES used to treat individuals who have anxieties and phobias are derived from the learning principles developed by PAVLOV, Thorndike, Watson, Tolman, Hull, SKINNER, WOLPE, and others whose work contributed to the theory of conditioning, motivation, and habit formation. (See also BEHAVIOR MODIFICATION; CLASSICAL CONDITIONING; CONDITIONING; HULL, CLARK; MODELING; MOTIVATION; OPERANT CONDITIONING.)

left, things to the, fear of Fear of things to the left is known as sinistrophobia or levophobia. Rituals related to the rising sun may have contributed to the feeling that the left is the inferior side because the sun rises in the east, or on the right as one faces north. Many religious ceremonies contain a movement to the right, or toward the sun. By contrast, evil spells of witchcraft and black magic frequently involve a left or counterclockwise motion.

Lentizol See AMITRIPTYLINE.

leprophobia, lepraphobia See LEPROSY, FEAR OF.

leprosy, fear of Fear of leprosy is known as leprophobia or lepraphobia. Leprosy is a communicable bacterial disease that primarily affects the skin and nerves, often producing severe disfigurement. This type of physical deformity is the main reason why the disease has been so feared in the past. In ancient times leprosy was well known and feared through Asia, Africa, and Europe. Today a few cases are still found in Europe and a few in the United States, particularly around the Gulf of Mexico and in Hawaii. The bacterium that causes leprosy was discovered in 1873 by G. Armauer Hansen, a Norwegian. The disease is also known as Hansen's disease. The factors influencing contraction of leprosy are unknown. There is some speculation that genetic factors determine a person's susceptibility to leprosy. Several drugs are used to treat leprosy. (See also DEFORMITY, FEAR OF.)

leukophobia Fear of the color white. (See also WHITE, FEAR OF THE COLOR.)

leukotomy, leucotomy A surgical operation on the brain in which the nerve pathways in the prefrontal lobes of the brain—the areas associated with emotion—are severed from the rest of the brain in an effort to reduce ANXIETY or violent behavior. Leukotomy is also known as prefrontal lobotomy. In recent years, this treatment has been replaced with tranquilizing medications and psychotherapy. In any case, it is not recommended as a treatment for phobias. (See also TRANQUILIZERS.)

levophobia Fear of things at the left side of the body. (See also LEFT, THINGS TO THE, FEAR OF.)

Lewin, Kurt (1890–1947) A German-born American psychologist whose work on the field theory has been a major contribution to the study of human behavior. Lewin influenced the development of social psychology. T-group training and encounter groups were used to treat anxieties. He emigrated to the United States in the early 1930s and was affiliated with Cornell University and then became director of the Research Center for Group Dynamics, Massachusetts Institute of Technology. Lewin's major publications are *A Dynamic Theory of Personality* (1935), *Principles of Topological Psychology* (1936), and *Contributions to Psychological Theory* (1938). (See also ENCOUNTER-GROUP THERAPY.)

libido Sigmund FREUD's term for the drives of the sexual instinct, love-object seeking, and pleasure. In many phobic and anxiety disorders, as well as affective disorders, particularly depression, there is a reduction of libido. The word is derived from the Latin words for "desire, lust." Freud believed that the libido was one of two vital human instincts, the drive toward self-preservation and the drive toward sexual gratification. Freud suggested that when an individual represses libido because of social pressures, continued repression leads to changes in personality and to neuroses such as ANXIETIES and PHOBIAS. Later, Freud gradually broadened the concept to include all expressions of love and pleasure. Jung expanded Freud's original concept to apply the term to the general life force that provides energy for all types of activities, including sexual, social, cultural, and creative. (See also JUNG, CARL; SEXUAL ANXIETY.)

Andelman, Samuel L., *The New Home Medical Encyclopedia* (New York: Quadrangle Books, 1973).

Goldenson, Robert M. (ed.), *Longman Dictionary of Psychology and Psychiatry* (New York: Longman, 1984).

Librium A tradename for CHLORDIAZEPOXIDE hydrochloride, an ANTIANXIETY DRUG.

lice, fear of Fear of lice is known as phthirophobia or pediculophobia. Lice include a number of tiny insects that live on warm-blooded creatures, among them man. Though lice are more common in people among crowded conditions without good facilities for bathing, they are also found in all walks of life, particularly where many children congregate, such as schools and movie theaters. Head lice are particularly feared because anyone can pick up the pests from the clothing of another or from the headrest of a public vehicle. One of the first signs of lice is itching. There may be some skin eruptions containing pus. Bacteria may invade these lesions, leading to other skin diseases. Pesticides in shampoo, powder, or ointment form are available for eliminating lice.

The pubic louse (also known as crab) is found in the hairy region around the sex organs and the anus; this is transmitted by bodily contact with a person who is infested, or from toilet seats.

Individuals who fear contamination, dirt, filth, or public toilets may also fear contracting lice. (See also CONTAMINATION, FEAR OF.)

light, fear of Fear of light is known as photophobia or phengophobia. This fear may be related to fear of light and shadows, fear of dawn, or fear of landscape. (See also DAWN, FEAR OF; LANDSCAPE, FEAR OF; LIGHT AND SHADOWS, FEAR OF.)

light and shadows, fear of Just as some individuals fear certain landscapes, some fear light-and-shadow effects. This may relate to a fear of twilight and the onset of darkness. From a psychoanalytic point of view, there may be deeper meaning to such fears. FENICHEL, an Austrian psychoanalyst (1899–1946), said, "Probably many phobias of darkness or twilight contain memories of PRIMAL SCENES."

lightning, fear of Fear of lightning is known as astraphobia, astropophobia, and keraunophobia. Many people fear lightning so much that they will not go outdoors on days when lightning is predicted. When rain is forecast, many even call the weather bureau to check for the possibility of lightning. During a storm that includes lightning, many take refuge in a closet or in bed, feeling safer in an enclosed place. Fear of lightning is related to fear of storms in general, and many who fear lightning also fear thunder and noise.

Some individuals acquire the fear of lightning from observing their parents or grandparents. Others have experienced traumatic incidents in connection with lightning or thunderstorms.

Fears of specific natural phenomena, such as lightning, have been treated successfully in many cases with exposure therapy. (See also CLIMATE, FEAR OF; STORMS, FEAR OF; THUNDER, FEAR OF.)

Ost, Lars-Goran, "Behavioral Treatment of Thunder and Lightning Phobias," *Behavior Research and Therapy,* 16(1978), pp. 197–207.

ligyrophobia Fear of noise. See NOISE, FEAR OF.

lilapsophobia Fear of hurricanes or tornadoes. (See also HURRICANES, FEAR OF.)

limbic system Part of the midbrain that controls expression of emotional behavior and basic motivational urges. The limbic system, part of the parasympathetic nervous system, also controls speed of heartbeat and breathing, trembling, sweating, and alterations in facial expression, as well as drives including defense, attack (fight or flight), hunger, thirst, and sex.

limnophobia Fear of lakes. (See also LAKES, FEAR OF.)

linonophobia Fear of string. (See also STRING, FEAR OF.)

lithium carbonate A drug used in treating MANIC–DEPRESSIVE DISORDER. Lithium acts by altering the metabolism of NOREPINEPHRINE in the brain. Lithium preparations are used routinely to treat manic and hypomanic individuals and to prevent attacks in individuals who have recurrent affective disorders. These attacks include both manic and depressive episodes in bipolar individuals, episodes of mania in recurrently manic patients, and depressive attacks in unipolar (only depressed) patients. Other conditions in which lithium treatment has been claimed effective include aggressive behavior, schizophrenia, epilepsy, alcoholism, Huntington's chorea, and premenstrual tension. However, as these claims are based mainly on clinical impressions and uncontrolled trials, they remain controversial.

Historical background

During the nineteenth century, lithium salts were known as important constituents of some spa waters to which many medicinal properties were ascribed. In the 1940s, lithium salts were used as a taste substitute for sodium chloride for cardiac patients on salt-free diets. When severe side effects and some deaths were reported, its use was stopped. Then, in the late 1940s, researchers in Australia discovered that lithium had certain tranquilizing properties. In later experiments, lithium safely quieted manic patients to whom it was administered. However, because of the known toxicity of lithium, there was little interest in it for almost a decade. In the 1950s and 1960s, several studies in Europe led to the acceptance of lithium in European and English psychiatric practices as a highly effective and safe treatment for manic–depressive illness. Lithium was accepted into American practice during the 1970s after the need for careful monitoring of blood levels to overcome side effects was understood.

Lithium also has been used in the U.S. since the 1970s because of its prophylactic qualities, preventing not only manic attacks and depressive episodes, but perhaps schizoaffective attacks as well. There is ongoing evaluation of the effectiveness of lithium in treating episodes of depression. Some uncontrolled studies suggested that perhaps 50 percent of depressed individuals might respond. Individuals who have endogenous depression—mainly those who have bipolar illnesses—respond best, but still at a lesser rate than with standard tricyclic antidepressant therapy. The improvement with lithium is often only partial, suggesting the value of combining lithium and tricyclic therapy; however, this is still controversial and under research.

How lithium works
The major ways in which lithium works are uncertain. However, it is known that lithium alters many electrolyte and neurotransmitter functions. For example, synthesis and release of acetycholine are depressed. Also, because lithium interferes with calcium, release of many neurotransmitters, including monoamines, is diminished. In normal individuals, lithium produces mild subjective feelings of lethargy and inability to concentrate. Sometimes it causes a decrease in memory function. Slow waves in the electrocardiogram increase.

Lithium as a prophylactic
On current evidence, lithium therapy is most suitable for individuals who have a long history of many typical affective episodes. Any individual who has had two or more distinct manic–depressive episodes during one year or one or more separate attacks each year during the preceding two years should be evaluated and considered a candidate for lithium treatment. Individuals who have bipolar illnesses are more likely to respond than are patients who have unipolar depression, and the more closely the individual fits the bipolar stereotype, the better the chance of a good response. Some psychiatrists try maintenance therapy with tricyclic antidepressant, especially in unipolar individuals, before initiating lithium therapy. If an individual does not show an adequate response to lithium within the first year of treatment, the drug should be discontinued because it may be unwise to expose the individual to the risks of lithium treatment without benefit. While there is complete prevention for some individuals, lithium provides maintenance therapy for others, in whom the attacks are only reduced to the point at which the individual can be managed as an outpatient instead of being admitted to a hospital.

Treatment
Dosage depends on both the severity of the illness and the particular preparation; dosage should be governed by serum concentrations. Before initiating lithium therapy, the individual should have a complete physical examination. Suggested contraindications include chronic kidney failure, high blood pressure, and a history of heart problems, although in some cases individuals who have these symptoms can take lithium successfully if carefully monitored by their physicians. Lithium is not appropriate therapy for children.

Side effects
Mild neurological side effects, especially during initial treatment, include general and muscular fatigue, lethargy, and mild shaking. The shaking, or tremor, usually begins early in treatment and may or may not resolve or lessen. Lowering the dose or adding a small dose of a beta-adrenoceptor antagonist such as propranolol usually minimizes the tremor. Early signs of toxicity include incoordination, difficulty in concentration, mild disorientation, muscle twitching, dizziness, and visual disturbances. Lithium affects thyroid function at several sites. The main effect is inhibition of release of thyroid hormones; hypothyroidism follows in some cases. Also, lithium use may be associated with alterations in bone-mineral metabolism, leading to osteopororsis in women. (See also AFFECTIVE DISORDERS; ANTIDEPRESSANTS;

BIPOLAR DISORDER; DRUGS; ELECTROCARDIOGRAM; ENDOGENOUS DEPRESSION; HUNTINGTON'S CHOREA; HYPOTHYROIDISM; PREMENSTRUAL SYNDROME (PMS); PROPHYLACTIC; TRICYCLIC ANTIDEPRESSANTS.)
Lader, Malcolm, *Introduction to Psychopharmacology* (Kalamazoo, MI: Upjohn Company, 1980).

litigaphobia Excessive fear of litigation or lawsuits. Twentieth-century American society has shown a rise in litigation as a means of solving interpersonal and societal difficulties. Many professionals now extensively document all procedures because of this fear.

Breslin, Frances A. et al., "Development of a Litigaphobia Scale: Measurement of Excessive Fear of Litigation," *Psychological Reports,* 58(1986), pp. 547–550.

Little Albert See ALBERT B.

Little Hans In the case of Little Hans, titled "Analysis of a Phobia in a Five-Year-Old Boy," Sigmund FREUD interpreted a young boy's horse phobias as a repressed fear of his father. In his conversation with Freud, Hans revealed that "what horses wear around their eyes" and "the black around their mouths" were disturbing to him. Freud related these remarks to the appearance of Hans's father, who had a mustache and wore glasses. Since Hans had a clinging relationship with his mother, Freud believed that Hans resented his father and also feared punishment in the form of castration because of his love for his mother. This case is significant because of the psychiatric implication that the phobic is not really disturbed by the thing ostensibly feared but has displaced his actual feelings onto something that can be avoided. Freud, who never saw Little Hans and really did not conduct therapy with him, obtained information through correspondence (and an occasional meeting) with Hans's father. JOSEPH WOLPE, who has reinterpreted this case from a classical-conditioning theory standpoint, convincingly demonstrates why this approach has a more powerful explanation.

Kaplan, Harold I., *Comprehensive Textbook of Psychiatry* (Baltimore: Williams and Wilkins, 1985).
Stoodley, Bartlett, *The Concepts of Sigmund Freud* (Glencoe, IL: The Free Press, 1959).

lizards, fear of Fear of lizards is known as herpetophobia. This fear is related to fear of snakes. (See also SNAKES, FEAR OF.)

lobotomy A surgical operation on the brain in which the nerve pathways from the frontal lobes of the brain and the thalamus (part of the forebrain that serves as a relay point for nerve impulses between the spinal cord, the brainstem, and the cerebral cortex) are cut in the hope of bringing about beneficial behavior changes. This operation is not recommended as a treatment for phobias; the operation was rarely performed toward the end of the 20th century. Instead, psychotherapy and tranquilizing drugs are used to control unwanted behaviors. In the absence of any treatments, lobotomies were occasionally used on patients with chronic anxiety problems. (See also LEUKOTOMY.)

lockjaw, fear of Fear of lockjaw, or tetanus, is known as tetanophobia. The condition is particularly feared because one of the first signs of the disease is a spasm or cramping of the muscles that close the jaw, making it difficult for the individual to open his or her mouth. The condition can be prevented by immunization.

locus ceruleus (coeruleus) The locus ceruleus (also known as the pons) is a tiny organ in the brain that is thought to play a role in the development of fearful behavior. The locus ceruleus, rich in norepinephrine, contains nearly half the noradrenergic neurons and produces over 70 percent of the total adrenaline in the brain. Overactivity of the locus ceruleus and the noradrenergic system may be linked to the cause of anxiety attacks in some individuals.

Eugene Redmone's research on the relationship between brain activity and anxiety attacks at Yale University in the 1980s, using monkeys, indicated that when the locus ceruleus was electrically stimulated, the monkeys showed anxious and fearful behavior. However, when the same area was surgically stimulated, the monkeys were unresponsive to threats and did not show normal fear when approached by humans or dominant monkeys. In other studies, destruction of the locus ceruleus also reduced naturally occurring fear reactions. Findings from this research were significant because they indicated that the locus ceruleus is vulnerable to the influence of substances in the blood, indicating a possible physiological basis for panic attacks. Researchers speculate that panic, anxiety, and fear may be controlled by changes in norepinephrine metabolism in the brain.

Fishman, Scott M. and David V. Sheehan, "Anxiety and Panic: Their Cause and Treatment," *Psychology Today* (April 1985), pp. 26–32.

Marks, Isaac M., *Fears, Phobias and Rituals* (New York: Oxford University Press, 1987).

locus of control A concept that attempts to explain why some people behave the way they do and why some have more anxieties than others. An individual with an "internal" locus of control believes that whatever happens in his life is the direct result of his own actions, and that he has some control over these events and his behavior. A person who believes that God, destiny, or outside forces determine his fate is said to have an "external" locus of control. People who have an external locus of control are more likely to develop anxieties. Most people are not entirely internalists or externalists but feel more or less in control of their lives. An individual's belief about his locus of control affects his behavior, emotional condition, and manner of dealing with anxieties. The concept was developed in the late 1960s by Julian Rotter (1916–).

McConnell, James V., *Understanding Human Behavior* (New York: Holt, Rinehart and Winston, 1986).

Bootzin, Richard R. et al., *Psychology Today* (New York: Random House, 1983).

lofepramine An antidepressant drug. (See also ANTIDEPRESSANTS; ANTIDEPRESSANTS, NEW; DEPRESSION.)

logophobia Fear of words. (See also WORDS, FEAR OF.)

logotherapy A technique for dealing with the spiritual and existential aspect of psychopathology. The therapist confronts individuals with their own responsibility for their existence and their obligation to pursue the values inherent in life. The technique, useful in treating some phobics, was developed by VICTOR FRANKL, a German-born American psychiatrist (1905–). See also EXISTENTIAL THERAPY; PARADOXICAL INTENTION.)

lonely, being, fear of Fear of being lonely is known as monophobia. This fear seems to increase with age as an individual sees friends and loved ones dying and anticipates having few contemporaries around. Fear of loneliness is compounded by the fear of illness. (See also GROWING OLD, FEAR OF).

long waits, fear of Some agoraphobics fear long waits, such as for buses and trains. This fear may prevent them from going out. In some cases, agoraphobics develop such a feeling of panic while waiting for a bus or train that when it finally arrives, they cannot board. However, if there is no wait, they can get on without anxiety. (See also AGORAPHOBIA.)

longitudinal study A study in which observations of the same group of individuals are made at two or more different points in time. An example of a longitudinal study is one in which observations are made about a group of agoraphobics and then the same variable is observed after a particular pharmacological therapy has been initiated. (See also CASE CONTROL; COHORT.)

looking-glass self The concept of the self as a reflection of how other people react to and what other people think of the individual. The looking-glass-self concept is significant in many phobias, including agoraphobia and social phobias.

looking ridiculous, fear of Fear of looking ridiculous is a social phobia that includes many specific fears, such as fear of shaking, blushing, sweating, fainting, vomiting, performing in front of an audience, entering a room, and looking inappropriate or unattractive. Some may not swim because they think they look ridiculous in a swimsuit. Some fear that their hands will tremble while writing a check or handling money in front of someone else. Fear of shaking may prevent a secretary from typing, or a teacher from writing on the blackboard. In such cases, the phobics fear that their hands or heads might shake; in reality, these fears rarely materialize. However, individuals who have tremors such as that of Parkinson's disease, who shake vigorously and unconsciously, usually do not fear doing anything in public despite their regular shaking. Generally, individuals who fear looking ridiculous have fewer positive and more negative thoughts and consider themselves awkward and less skillful. This fear is treated in the same ways social phobias and shyness are treated, specifically with behavior modification, cognitive modification, and other therapies aimed at improving the individual's self-esteem. (See also BEHAVIOR MODIFICATION; SELF-ESTEEM; SHYNESS; SOCIAL PHOBIA.)

Marks, Isaac M., *Fears, Phobias and Rituals* (New York: Oxford University Press, 1987).

losing control, fear of Many phobic individuals avoid their feared situations because they fear "losing control." For example, during a panic attack, some people fear that they might become totally paralyzed and not be able to move, or that they will not know what they are doing and will embarrass themselves or others in some way. Some agoraphobics who experience panic attacks have this fear. This feeling occurs because during intense anxiety the entire body becomes prepared for action and escape. This "fight or flight" response often makes people feel confused and distracted; however, individuals in such situations are still able to think and function normally. In fact, others rarely notice another individual experiencing a panic attack. (See also AGORAPHOBIA; PANIC.)

lost, fear of being Fear of being lost is common among children as well as adults. In childhood, the fear of being lost is reinforced by such fairy tales as "Hansel and Gretel," in which the children lose their way in the forest. Fear of being lost is a fear of being out of control of one's destiny and may be related to fears of the dark, of animals, of injury, and of being far from safety. Fear of being lost may prevent individuals from visiting certain areas in major cities or from visiting the cities themselves. Fear of being lost also prevents many people from driving their cars in certain areas or on unfamiliar roads. Those who do not speak the language of the country in which they consider traveling may fear being lost and not being able to communicate well enough to ask for directions.

love, fear of Fear of love is known as philophobia. Love is a complex emotion comprising trust, respect, acceptance, strong affection, feelings of tenderness, pleasurable sensations in the presence of the love object, and devotion to his or her well-being. Love as an emotion takes many forms, such as concern for one's fellow humans, responsibility for the welfare of a child, sexual attraction and excitement, and self-esteem and self-acceptance. (See also COMMITMENT PHOBIA; FROMM, ERICH.)

love play, fear of Fear of love play, or foreplay before sexual intercourse, is known as sarmassophobia or malaxophobia. (See also SEXUAL FEARS.)

Ludiomil See MAPROTILINE.

luiphobia A fear of lues, a synonymn for SYPHILIS. Lues is derived from the Latin word for "infection" or "plague." (See also SEXUALLY TRANSMITTED DISEASES.)

lump in the throat A feeling of a "lump in the throat" (medically known as globus hystericus) is one of the most common symptoms of ANXIETY. Most people, whether phobic or not, have experienced this sensation at one time or another. Some people experience it before a job interview or a public speech and fear that they will not have their usual strong voice. The "lump" may actually cause some difficulty in swallowing, although the sufferer usually can make enough effort to eat. However, when one concentrates on swallowing, the problem may worsen. Lump in the throat is more often noticed in young adults, particularly women. The symptom, while unpleasant and uncomfortable, can usually be relieved with relaxation techniques and completion of the stressful event.

Lump in the throat should not be confused with symptoms of several serious diseases that can cause difficulty in swallowing first solid foods and then liquids, resulting in weight loss. In these cases, a physician should be consulted. X rays of the esophagus may be recommended. (See also GAGGING, HYPERSENSITIVE; SWALLOWING, FEAR OF.)

lung disease, fear of Fear of lung disease is related to health anxieties in general and fear of illness. Some people fear lung diseases because the lungs are particularly vulnerable to particles floating in the air. Those who fear contamination by bacteria or other germs may fear lung diseases for this reason. Those who fear AIR POLLUTION, ACID RAIN, and ACID DEW may also fear lung disease. Fear of tuberculosis is included in many people's fears of lung diseases, but because of improved public health measures, pasteurization of milk, and routine examination of cattle, tuberculosis is becoming rare in developed countries. However, some individuals, particularly older people, still fear tuberculosis because they remember when the disease was widespread and less curable than it is today. At its height tuberculosis affected one half of the world population. (See also ASTHMA; TUBERCULOSIS, FEAR OF.)

Kunz, Jeffrey R.M. and Asher J. Finkel (eds.), *The American Medical Association Family Medical Guide* (New York: Random House 1987).

lygophobia Fear of being in dark or gloomy places. Derived from the Greek word *lyge,* meaning twilight. (See also DARKNESS, FEAR OF.)

lying, fear of Fear of lying is known as mythophobia. Lying—making false statements with conscious intent to deceive—may be considered nonpathological or pathological. An example of nonpathological lying is when adults or children seek to avoid punishment or to save others from distress; these are sometimes referred to as "white lies." Pathological lying is a major characteristic of an antisocial personality and may be a symptom of many psychophysiological disorders due to guilt and fear reactions. The lie detector (polygraph) is based on physiological reactions. Many individuals fear lying because they fear being caught in a lie and being punished.

lyssophobia Fear of becoming insane or of dealing with insanity. This fear is also known as maniaphobia and lissophobia. (See also GOING CRAZY, FEAR OF; SCHIZOPHRENIA.)

M

machinery, fear of Fear of machinery is known as mechanophobia. This fear is somewhat related to fears of technical things, such as computers. (See also COMPUTER PHOBIA.)

macrophobia Fear of long waits. (See also LONG WAITS, FEAR OF.)

magic, fear of Fear of magic is primarily concerned with the fear of and desire for supraconscious power and striving for connection with a greater power. Magicians consider themselves capable not of working miracles, but of using the powers of their minds and their knowledge of the laws and secrets of nature as a way of exerting control over nature and human events. Some magicians believe that man is a miniature replica of God and capable of expanding his powers accordingly, not in the rational path of progress provided by science, but by ascending a hierarchy of mysterious secrets; this process is an individual matter and cannot be taught.

Prehistoric cave paintings indicate that early man believed in and feared magic. The Egyptians, Greeks, and Romans combined magical beliefs and practices with their religious observances. Early Christians successfully claimed the superior power of their magic to gain pagan converts. For a time Christianity rejected magic, but the medieval church revived it, claiming the power to exert a certain degree of control over God's will and the course of events. During the Reformation Protestants branded as superstitions the use of holy water and belief in the intercession of the saints.

The power of black magic, to a certain extent, may be a self-fulfilling prophecy. An individual cursed by a person he believes to be a witch or magician may become mentally or physically ill from sheer anxiety. See also WITCHES AND WITCHCRAFT, FEAR OF.)

Arieti, Silvano et al., *American Handbook of Psychiatry,* Vol. 3 (New York: Basic Books, 1974), pp. 195–222.

Shepard, Leslie (ed.), *Encyclopedia of Occultism and Parapsychology* (Detroit: Gale Research, 1984); see "Magic."

Hill, Douglas and Pat Williams, *The Supernatural* (New York: Hawthorn Books, 1965), pp. 39–63.

Deutch, Yvonne E., "Magic" and "White Magic," in Richard Cavendish (ed.), *Man, Myth and Magic* (New York: Marshall Cavendish, 1983).

magical thinking A primitive thought process based on the illusion that thinking can influence events, fulfill wishes, or ward off evil or feared objects or situations. There is a lack of realistic relationship between cause and effect in magical thinking. Magical thinking begins in childhood and shows up later as obsessive thoughts, ritual acts, dreams, fantasies, and superstitions. (See also CHILDHOOD FEARS, PHOBIAS, AND ANXIETIES.)

maieusiophobia Fear of childbirth. (See also CHILDBIRTH, FEAR OF.)

MAOIs See MONOAMINE OXIDASE INHIBITORS

major affective disorders Disorders in which there is a noticeable and persistent disturbance of MOOD, such as DEPRESSION, MANIA, BIPOLAR DISORDERS, and many other symptoms. Major affective disorders may be episodic or chronic. Affective disorders are also known as mood disorders. (See also AFFECTIVE DISORDERS; MANIC–DEPRESSIVE ILLNESS.)

major tranquilizer A drug that strongly suppresses arousal and is used primarily to calm psychotic individuals. Also known as antipsychotic drug. See also ANTIPSYCHOTICS.)

malaxophobia Fear of love play. (See also LOVE PLAY, FEAR OF; SEXUAL FEARS; SEXUAL INTERCOURSE, FEAR OF.)

man, fear of See MEN, FEAR OF.

mania An affective or mood disorder in which the individual is excessively elated, agitated, and hyperactive and has accelerated thinking and speaking. The more up-to-date term is manic episode or manic syndrome. (See also AFFECTIVE DISORDERS; BIPOLAR DISORDER; MANIC–DEPRESSIVE DISORDER.)

maniaphobia Fear of INSANITY. Also known as lyssophobia.

manic–depressive disorder Manic depression, or manic–depressive disorder, also known as BIPOLAR ILLNESS, is the most distinct and dramatic of the depressive or affective disorders (mood disorders). Unlike major DEPRESSION, which can occur at any age, manic–depressive disorder generally strikes before the age of 35. Nearly one in 100 persons will suffer from the disorder at some time. Many people who have manic depression also have phobias.

What distinguishes bipolar illness from other depressive disorders is that the individual swings from depression to mania, generally with periods of normal moods in between the two extremes. Some patients, however, cycle from mania to depression and back within a few days and without a period of normal mood. People with this condition are called rapid cyclers. Phobias may come and go during the cycles.

When an individual experiences a manic phase, he or she will feel a sudden onset of elation or euphoria that increases in a matter of days to a serious impairment. Symptoms of the manic phase include a mood that is excessively good, euphoric, or expansive. The individual feels "on top of the world," and not even bad news will change his or her happiness. The mood is way out of bounds, given the individual's personality.

A manic lacks judgment and will express unwarranted optimism. Self-confidence reaches the point of grandiose delusions in which the person thinks he or she has a special connection with God, celebrities, or political leaders. He or she may think that nothing, not even the laws of gravity, can stop him or her from accomplishing any task. As a result, he or she may feel capable of stepping off a building or out of a moving car without being hurt.

Other symptoms are hyperactivity and excessive plans or participation in numerous activities that have good chances for painful results. The manic becomes so enthusiastic about activities or involvements that he or she fails to recognize there isn't enough time in the day for all of them. For example, he or she may book several meetings, parties, deadlines, and other activities in a single day, feeling able to make all of them on time. Added to the expansive mood, mania also can result in reckless driving, spending sprees, foolish business investments, or sexual behavior unusual for the person.

The manic person's thoughts race uncontrollably. When the person talks, his or her words come out in a nonstop rush of ideas that abruptly change from topic to topic. In its severe form, the loud, rapid speech is hard to interpret because the individual's thought processes have become so totally disorganized and incoherent.

The manic will experience a decreased need for sleep, allowing him or her to go with little or no sleep for days without feeling tired. The manic will also experience distractibility in which his or her attention is easily diverted to inconsequential or unimportant details. At times, the manic will become suddenly irritable, enraged, or PARANOID when his or her grandiose plans are thwarted or excessive social overtures are rebuffed.

Untreated, the manic phase can last as long as three months. As it abates, the individual may have a period of normal mood and behavior. But eventually the depressive phase of the illness will set in. This phase has the same symptoms as major or unipolar depression, namely feelings of worthlessness, hopelessness, helplessness, total indifference, and/or inappropriate guilt, prolonged sadness or unexplained crying spells, jumpiness or irritability, and withdrawal from formerly enjoyable activities, social contacts, work, or sex. Further, in the depressive phase, the individual may be unable to concentrate or remember details and may experience thoughts of death or suicide attempts, loss of appetite or noticeable increase in appetite, persistent fatigue and lethargy, insomnia or noticeable increase in the amount of sleep needed, and aches and pains, constipation, or other physical ailments that cannot be otherwise explained.

Causes

Depressive illnesses often run in families. In early 1987, researchers discovered a genetic marker among members of the Old Order of Amish that made them susceptible to manic–depressive illness. In a second study that year, scientists found an aberrant gene on another chromosome (the material that contains genes). The researchers emphasized that their findings do not account for every case of manic–depressive illness because their results have not been repeated for other populations. However, these studies provide important clues for identifying the precise genes linked to these genetic markers. Now scientists can work toward identifying the genetic defects in other forms of manic–depressive illness among other populations. They also can work toward understanding the biochemical reactions that are controlled by these genes and that contribute to the disorder.

Although the genetic picture of the disease is still far from complete, we do know that close relatives of people who have biopolar illness are 10 to 20 times more likely to develop either depression or manic–depressive illness than the general population. Between 80 and 90 percent of individuals who have manic–depressive disorder have relatives who also have some form of depression. If one parent has manic–depressive illness, a child has a thirty percent risk for suffering from a depressive disorder; if both parents have a manic–depressive illness, the children have a 75 percent chance of developing a depressive disorder.

Other studies have suggested that environmental factors can trigger the illness. Comprehensive psychoanalytic studies indicate manic–depressive individuals were reared to become achievers in order to bring honor to their families; however, at the same time, they were never allowed to become fully autonomous. Research suggests these people grow up with a need to achieve and a contradictory need to depend on others. Failure to reach a goal or to maintain a needed relationship triggers the manic–depressive illness.

Some studies suggest that imbalances in the biochemistry that controls a person's mood could contribute to manic–depressive illness. For example, people suffering from either manic–depressive or major depressive disorders often respond to certain hormones or steroids in a way that indicates they have irregularities in their hormone production and release. Other research suggests that bipolar patients' neurotransmitters—chemicals by which brain cells communicate—become imbalanced during various phases of the disease. Finally, some people who have depressive illnesses have sleep patterns in which the dream phase begins earlier in the night than normal. Such research helps scientists develop scientific theories about how medications work.

Treatment

Some other physical and mental disorders mimic manic–depressive illnesses. For example, an individual with symptoms of manic–depression might be reacting to substances such as amphetamines or steroids or could suffer from an illness such as multiple sclerosis. An individual who has symptoms of bipolar disorder should have a thorough medical evaluation to rule out any other mental or physical disorders and to ensure accurate diagnosis and appropriate treatment.

While manic–depressive disorder can become disabling, it is also among the most treatable of the mental illnesses. The combination of psychotherapy and medications returns the vast majority of manic–depressive individuals to happy, functioning lives. The most common medication, LITHIUM carbonate, successfully reduces the number and intensity of manic episodes for 70 percent of those who take the medication. Twenty percent become completely free of symptoms. Those who respond to lithium best are individuals who have a family history of depressive illness and who have periods of relatively normal mood between their manic and depressive phases. Lithium is effective in treating the manic phase, and it also appears to prevent repeated episodes of depression. One theory for this is that in controlling the mania, lithium helps prevent the swing into depression. Lithium works by bringing various neurotransmitters in the brain into balance. Scientists believe the medication may affect the way or the speed at which brain cells break down the neurotransmitters that are thought to control moods. However, like all medications, lithium can have side effects, including weight gain, excessive thirst and urination, stomach and intestinal irritation, hand tremors, and muscular weakness. More serious side effects are hypothyroidism, kidney damage, confusion, delirium, seizures, coma and, in patients who are not closely monitored by a physician, even death. Such monitoring is essential for anyone taking this medication.

Medications can control the symptoms, but individuals often need psychotherapy to work out the side effects of the illness and to live with their new range of emotions, including changes in phobic patterns. The patient and therapist work out the problems created by the disorder and reestablish the relationships and healthy self-image that are shaken by the illness. (See also ANTIDEPRESSANTS; BIOLOGICAL BASIS FOR ANXIETY; DEPRESSED PARENTS, CHILDREN OF; DRUGS; LITHIUM.)

(Adapted with permission from "Facts about: Manic Depression," published by the American Psychiatric Association.)

manic episode A reaction characterized by a recurring period of extreme elation, extreme euphoria without reason, and grandiose thoughts or feelings about personal abilities. The manic episode may be a phase of manic–depressive disorder.

many things, fear of Fear of many things is known as polyphobia. Individuals who are very anxious often have many phobias. Such individuals may have related phobias, such as fear of precipices, fear of heights, and fear of looking up at tall buildings. Others have unrelated fears, such as fear of water and fear of dogs. (See also EVERYTHING, FEAR OF.)

maprotiline An antidepressant drug. Also known by the tradename Ludiomil, maprotiline is similar in action to the TRI-

CYCLIC ANTIDEPRESSANTS but generally has fewer side effects. (See also ANTIDEPRESSANTS, NEW; DEPRESSION.)

LaPierre, Y.D., "New Antidepressant Drugs," *Journal of Clinical Psychiatry* (August 1983), pp. 41–44.

marijuana Marijuana is a common drug that many individuals use and abuse with the assumption that it will help relieve their anxieties and stresses. One source of panic is the loss of control resulting from euphoric feelings associated with marijuana use; marijuana use has been implicated in the onset of PANIC ATTACKS. Marijuana is smoked in cigarettes and pipes, chewed, and can be made into baked products, such as cookies. Marijuana *(Cannabis sativa)* is a hemp plant that was used as a medication for a variety of disorders during the 1800s. The green leaves are dried and ground up to make the drug commonly known as "grass." Extraction and further drying of the plant's resin is used to make hashish, an even more powerful drug. Marijuana has an intoxicating effect, depending on the amount used. Some individuals say they achieve a feeling of relaxation, a feeling of mild euphoria, and a sharpness in perception. Physiologically, there is a slight increase in heart rate and an increased appetite. Some users believe that marijuana and other drugs make them more creative and allow them to think more clearly. Such claims are probably unfounded.

Smoking marijuana may have the same harmful health effects as smoking tobacco, which is now recognized to cause cancer and other severe illnesses. Another danger of marijuana use as a way to control ANXIETIES is that users may become so dependent on its use for feeling good that they lose interest in all other aspects of life. (See also DRUG ABUSE.)

Marks, Isaac M. (1935–) British psychiatrist who qualified in medicine in 1956 at the University of Cape Town and settled in London in 1960, where he qualified as a psychiatrist at London University in 1963. He joined the Maudsley Hospital in 1960 and the Institute of Psychiatry (University of London) in 1963 and has been affiliated with both institutions since. He became Professor of Experimental Psychopathology in 1978. For more than 25 years he has researched extensively in the field of anxiety disorders and has published 11 books and 220 scientific papers. Many of them concern the causes, classifications, phenomenology, and drug and psychological treatments of phobic, panic, and obsessive–compulsive disorders. He has also researched into the treatment and origin of sexual disorders, and into the delivery of mental-health-care services. He helped to develop exposure treatments for anxiety into their current enduringly effective forms and promoted them in a manner that helps sufferers to help themselves lastingly.

Marplan See ISOCARBOXAZID.

marriage, fear of Fear of marriage is known as gamophobia or gametophobia.

Marsilid See IPRONIAZID.

Maslow, Abraham Harold (1908–1970) An American psychologist, originator of the concept of a HIERARCHY OF NEEDS that motivate all individuals. He suggested that once a person's physiological needs are met, he or she may devote his or her efforts toward other needs, such as safety, belonging, love, esteem, understanding, and self-actualization. By placing a greater emphasis on the positive features of man, such as joy, creativity, success, and love, Maslow offered to correct what he felt was the undue focus of the Freudians and others on the pessimistic features of conflicts, deprivation, emotionality, and aggression. Maslow preferred to understand pathology through the study of normalcy and viewed the healthy person as one who has been able to reach his fullest potential. He believed that psychological disorder results from the inability of a person to successfully satisfy needs within each level. Pressure from the environment, threats to needs, or frustrations can all prevent the person from reaching an integration within himself.

Maslow's emphasis on self-fulfillment made him a leader in the human-potential movement.

Suinn, Richard *Fundamentals of Behavior Pathology* (New York: John Wiley, 1975).

mass hysteria Mass hysteria is also known as EPIDEMIC ANXIETY, a condition in which many people are simultaneously affected by extreme, often unfounded ANXIETY. Mass hysteria was recognized during the latter part of the Middle Ages, when whole groups of people were affected by similar anxieties—for example, dance manias involving raving, jumping, and convulsions. Some thought they had been bitten by a tarantula (spider) and would jump up and run out to dance in the street. This activity became known as *tarantism* in Italy and St. Vitus's Dance in the rest of Europe.

Another example of mass hysteria occurred during the 16th century when individuals imagined themselves being a wolf and then acted like a wolf. In the 1950s, there was also a mass hysteria incident in the state of Washington involving pitting of auto windshields. Groups of people feared that pitting (a normal phenomenon) developed from radioactive material in the air.

masturbation Sexual self-gratification without a partner. Until recently, many people considered masturbation harmful. Many young people were told that masturbation would lead to bad consequences, ranging from acne to impotence. Because of the taboo against masturbation, many people became fearful and anxious about the practice. The more morally restrictive the culture or the environment in which people live, the more likely they are to develop fear and guilt about masturbation. Now it is recognized that masturbation is an almost universal practice before sexual maturity is reached, and a frequent practice in older age when a sexual partner is not available. In Kinsey's research in the 1960s, more than 90 percent of men reported masturbatory experiences in their adolescence. In the early 1980s, results of a research project by Shere Hite on female sexuality indicated that about 82 percent of American women masturbate. In most cases, men masturbate their penis and women the clitoris by hand. (See also SEXUAL FEARS.)

Redlich, Fredrick C. and Daniel X. Freedman, *The Theory and Practice of Psychiatry* (New York: Basic Books, 1966).

material things Fear of materialism is known as hylophobia.

mathematics anxiety An individual's anxiety about mathematics can be broken down into three main components: numerical anxiety, mathematical test anxiety, and abstraction anxiety. Numerical anxiety involves the practical application of mathematics and numbers to one's everyday concerns (real-life "story problems")—items such as personal budgeting, timetables, counting change, and even odds for betting at a horse race.

Nearly everyone in an academic setting has experienced some degree of anxiety about mathematical tests—from multiplication flash cards to a pop quiz in a calculus class.

The third component, abstraction anxiety, is concerned with an individual's anxiety when confronted with methods of abstract mathematical reasoning involving mathematical schemas, theorems and proofs, or symbols and letters in place of numbers.

Questionaires and anxiety scales can help to refine an approach to diminish or eradicate an individual's mathematics fears. (See also NUMBERS, FEAR OF.)

Ferguson, Ronald D., "Abstraction Anxiety: A Factor of Mathematics Anxiety," *Journal for Research in Mathematics* (March 1986), pp. 145–150.

Maudsley Marital Questionnaire (MMQ) A questionnaire used in assessment of agoraphobic individuals. The MMQ is a series of questions grouped into five sections, including marital adjustment, sexual adjustment, orgasmic frequency, work and social adjustment, and warmth. The questionnaire is often given to the agoraphobic individual and his/her spouse before therapy and after therapy to measure changes and improvements. It was developed at Maudsley Hospital, London. (See also AGORAPHOBIA.)

Monteiro, W. et al., "Marital Adjustment and Treatment Outcome in Agoraphobia," *British Journal of Psychiatry,* 146(1985), pp. 383–390.

Maudsley Personality Inventory (MPI) One of the most frequently used and widely standardized research instruments for personality assessment in Britain. The MPI is a forty-eight-item self-rating questionaire designed to measure two personality factors of neuroticism–normality and extraversion–introversion. The MPI is one of many tests therapists use in assessing an anxious or phobic individual's personality. The MPI was developed by HANS JURGEN EYSENCK (1916–). (See also PERSONALITY TYPES.)

May, Rollo (1909–) American psychologist and author known as the father of EXISTENTIAL PSYCHOTHERAPY in the United States because of his views about the breakdown of myths and symbols in modern life and the role of psychology. May turned from a religious vocation to clinical psychology because he believed that religious training had not adequately prepared him to offer sound counsel. A bout with tuberculosis deepened his philosophical and psychological questioning and led to his concentration on the subjects of ANXIETY and the human will. May's theory about therapy places emphasis on the individual exploring his or her current values and developing a more meaningful and fulfilling life by confronting his or her own being, becoming more aware of feelings and relationships, and redefining his or her own identity. Some of May's best-known and most influential books are *The Meaning of Anxiety* (1950), *Man's Search for Himself* (1953), *Love and Will* (1969), *The Courage to Create* (1971), and *Freedom and Destiny* (1981).

Contemporary Authors (Detroit: Gale Research, 1984).

McKinley, John Charnley See HATHAWAY, STARKE ROSECRANS; MINNESOTA MULTIPHASIC PERSONALITY INVENTORY.

meat, fear of Fear of meat is known as carnophobia. Some individuals fear the sight of raw meat or cooked meat; others fear eating meat in any form. (See also EATING, FEAR OF.)

mechanophobia See MACHINERY, FEAR OF.

medical model Also known as "disease model." As applied in the treatment of ANXIETIES and PHOBIAS, the medical model is a set of assumptions in which abnormal behavior is viewed as similar to physical diseases. According to the medical model, symptoms of phobias (e.g., phobic object, anxiety, etc.) represent internally caused manifestations. The internal causes might be early childhood experience, psychodynamic interplay, and even biological predisposition. These internal (and usually unconscious) factors, given the right conditions, produce symptoms. In psychodynamic therapies, the symptoms symbolize something about the internal causes. In its simplest form, it presumes a single or limited number of causes (internal psychological or biological) for each "disease." In this sense it is a reductionist position that minimizes individual differences and multidetermined causation.

Psychodynamically, phobias are seen as displaced stimuli arising from unresolved Oedipal conflict. The classic case described by Freud was of Little Hans, a boy who developed a phobia about horses that Freud analyzed as a displaced fear of castration from his father.

The medical model, the dominant view of psychopathology, has influenced views of etiology, diagnosis, treatment, and research.

Contemporary psychology questions the medical model. Part of the dissatisfaction is that the diagnostic system and therapies based on this model have not proven reliable or effective in leading to behavior change methods.

Instead of the medical model, psychologists prefer a functional approach that relates behavior to environmental events including the internal cognitive environment of the individual either as trigger or consequence. The focus is individualized rather than categorized; treatment is based on principles of learning and behavior change developed through empirical study; the goals of therapy are defined and objectively evaluated. In the functional approach, diagnosis is an integral part of treatment (rather than a procedure in and of itself with little treatment relevance). The functional model is exemplified by the various behavior therapies that have revolutionized treatment and provided highly effective methods for treatment of all forms of anxiety. (See also FUNCTIONAL APPROACH.)

medicine, fear of taking (See also DRUGS, FEAR OF NEW; DRUGS, FEAR OF TAKING.)

meditation therapy Therapists have attempted to use meditation therapy in the treatment of numerous disorders, but anxiety is the only disorder that has been successfully treated in this way. The therapist encourages the client to breathe deeply and concentrate on the repetition of a single syllable, which helps the client to focus and clear extraneous thoughts from his or her mind and to lessen anxiety. As as result, the client sleeps better, feels more relaxed, has better self-esteem, and is less inclined to use drugs. Meditation therapy is most helpful when used by people with mild anxiety disorders. (See also TRANSCENDENTAL MEDITATION.)

Delmonte, M.S. and V. Kenny, "An Overview of the Therapeutic Effects of Meditation," *Psychologia*, 28(1985), pp. 189–202.

medomalacophobia Fear of losing an erection. (See also ERECTION, FEAR OF LOSING; SEXUAL FEARS.)

medorthophobia Fear of an erect penis. (See also PENIS, ERECT, FEAR OF; SEXUAL FEARS.)

megalophobia Fear of large objects. (See also LARGE OBJECTS, FEAR OF.)

Meichenbaum, Donald (1940–) American psychologist and author who developed the concept of STRESS INOCULATION as a preventive method for anxiety situations. With the method, individuals are given practice with mild stress to modify beliefs and self-statements in order to be more successful and less resistive; stress situations are gradually increased in difficulty. Ultimately, the individuals develop better coping skills and strategies. In the late 1980s, Meichenbaum was affiliated with the University of Waterloo, Ontario, Canada, working and writing in areas of stress prevention and reduction, cognitive development, and cognitive factors in BEHAVIOR MODIFICATION.

American Men and Women of Science: Social and Behavioral Sciences (New York: Bowker, 1978).

melancholia A term used throughout history to denote a severe form of DEPRESSION. The word derives from the Greek prefix *melas*, meaning black. In a state of melancholia, the individual feels loss of interest or pleasure in all, or almost all, activities, has low self-esteem, and is preoccupied with self-reproaches and regrets. *Diagnostic and Statistical Manual of Mental Disorders* differentiates between the major melancholic type of major depressive episode and seasonal-pattern major depressive episodes. The long-standing lay definition of melancholia is close to the diagnostic criteria for the melancholic type of major depressive episode. (See also AFFECTIVE DISORDERS.)

Diagnostic and Statistical Manual of Mental Disorders (Washington, DC: American Psychiatric Association, 1987).

melissophobia Fear of bees or insects (See also BEES; INSECTS.)

melitracen An antidepressant drug. (See also ANTIDEPRESSANTS, NEW; DEPRESSION.)

LaPierre, Y.D., "New Antidepressant Drugs," *Journal of Clinical Psychiatry* (August 1983), pp. 41–44.

memories, fear of Fear of memories is known as mnemophobia.

memory loss, fear of Older adults often fear memory loss as something that is inevitable. Health-care professionals use the term "age-associated memory impairment" to describe those minor glitches in memory that affect older adults' experience. Rather than remaining anxious and dwelling on this, many individuals find that written reminders, such as lists, and repeating names or other information aloud helps relieve these fears. Studies of older people actually find little memory loss but some decreases in psychomotor speed. (See also AGING, FEAR OF.)

men, fear of Fear of men is known as androphobia or arrhenophobia. This fear may stem from a variety of factors, including unpleasant experiences with men or particular characteristics of men.

meningitophobia Fear of brain disease. (See also BRAIN DISEASE.)

menopause, fear of Some women fear menopause, or the cessation of the menses. Some women fear that they will become unattractive to men at the time when they are no longer able to bear children. They fear having hot flashes and other symptoms of menopause, such as vaginal dryness, depression, and dry skin. Treatments involving estrogen replacement can alleviate many of the uncomfortable symptoms of menopause. Advances in estrogen products have made them safer to use with fewer side effects. Fewer women fear menopause than in earlier generations, because women now have longer life expectancies and anticipate satisfying lives after menopause. The average age for menopause in the United States is fifty to fifty-one; in the United Kingdom it is forty-nine years and nine months. (See also AGEISM; AGING, FEAR OF; WRINKLES, FEAR OF.)

Kahn, Ada P. and Linda Hughey Holt, *Midlife Health: Every Woman's Guide to Feeling Good* (New York: Facts On File, 1987).

Kahn, Ada P. and Linda Hughey Holt, *Menopause: The Best Years of Your Life* (London: Bloomsbury, 1987).

menophobia Fear of menstruation. (See also MENSTRUATION, FEAR OF.)

menstruation, fear of Fear of menstruation is known as menophobia. Some uninformed young women may fear menstruation because they have not learned about their bodies and sexuality. Since blood flow is usually a signal of physical injury, and a common fear of young children, adolescent girls may become alarmed at the first sight of monthly bleeding with the onset of menstruation at puberty. Some women who fear menstruation reflect anxiety felt by their mothers and generations of women before them: They feel shame if men around them know they are menstruating, they resent men for not having to endure menstruation, and they dread the repetition of what they regard as unpleasantness.

Historically, some men have had fears of menstruating women. Some men fear castration by having intercourse with a menstruating woman. They fear that menstrual blood should have formed the body of a child, and therefore it is charged with potent and dangerous energy. Some fear that menstruation is a punishment for sexual activity. Men who have blood phobia fear menstruating women. Others who fear menstruation are jealous of women's reproductive process. Some fear that women have cosmic power because of the connection of menstruation with the powerful rhythms of nature, such as the moon, sun, and tides.

In some cultures, largely as a result of men's fears of menstruating women, menstruating women were excluded from society during their periods and excluded from contact with religious people or ceremonies. Over centuries, women's fears regarding menstruation have included the notion that sexual intercourse during menstruation is harmful to both men and women's health, that deformed children result from intercourse at this time, that intercourse during menstruation is a sin against God; there has also been an assumption that women are not sexually aroused during menstruation.

Fears of menstruation can be overcome with appropriate information and reassurance that monthly periods are normal and part of female development. Notions that many people have that women are "unclean" during menstruation should be described and dismissed.

de Beauvoir, Simone, *The Second Sex* (New York: Modern Library, 1968).

Delaney, Janice et al., *The Curse, a Cultural History of Menstruation* (New York: E.P. Dutton, 1976). p. 15–19.

Deutch, Yvonne C., "Menstruation," in R. Cavendish (ed.), *Man, Myth and Magic* (New York: Marshall Cavendish, 1983).

Sarafino, Edward P., *The Fears of Childhood* (New York: Human Sciences Press, 1986).

Weideger, Paula (ed.), *Menstruation and Menopause: The Physiology and Psychology, the Myth and the Reality*. (New York: Knopf, 1976). p. 100.

mental disorder, fear of Some individuals fear mental disorder or that they may be becoming mentally ill. This is a common—and commonly unfounded—reaction to PANIC ATTACKS. The American Psychiatric Association, in its *Diagnostic and Statisical Manual of Mental Disorders,* conceptualizes each of the mental disorders as a clinically significant behavioral or psychological pattern that occurs in an individual and that is associated with present distress (a painful symptom) or disability (impairment in one or more important areas of functioning), or a significantly increased risk of suffering death, pain, disability, or an important loss of freedom. Additionally, to qualify as a mental disorder, this syndrome or pattern must not be merely the expected response to a particular event—for example, the death of a loved one. Whatever its original cause, it must currently be considered a manifestation of a behavioral, psychological, or biological dysfunction in the individual. Neither deviant behavior—political, religious, or sexual, for example—nor conflicts that are primarily between the individual and society are mental disorders unless the deviance or conflict is a symptom of a dysfunction in the individual.

Such fears often arise from lack of information regarding types of mental illness, the state of the mentally ill during episodes, forms of treatment, and rights of patients. (See also BEHAVIOR; DIAGNOSIS.)

mercurial medicines, fear of Fear of mercurial medicines is known as hydrargyrophobia. This fear may be related to the fear of taking medicines. For example, mercury cyanide is a crystalline mercuric compound that is used as a medicine in small dosages but is quite poisonous in larger doses, hence inducing fear. (See also LEAD POISONING, FEAR OF.)

merinthophobia Fear of being bound or tied up.

merital See NOMINFENSINE.

Mesmer, Franz (1734–1815) A German physician known for techniques that led to a later understanding of hypnosis. Mesmer, who was educated for the priesthood but changed to law and subsequently to medicine, developed a theory of animal magnetism and believed that magnetic pull could control fluids in the human body. Mesmer treated patients who had anxieties and mental and physical illnesses with magnets. His treatments were a grand show in which he would dress in velvet robes, walk around a tub containing magnet rods, and apply them to afflicted areas of people's bodies while stringed instruments played in the background in his salon. His work was disapproved by the French academic medical community after an investigative committee (which included Benjamin Franklin) examined his salon and methods. However, his work led to an understanding of the power of suggestion and hypnotic techniques. The English verb "mesmerize"—to hypnotize or spellbind—derives from his name. (See also MESMERISM.)

Dictionary of Scientific Biography (New York: Scribner, 1974).

mesmerism An archaic name for HYPNOSIS. The term mesmerism was applied to work done by Franz Anton MESMER (1734–1815), a German physician who used the power of suggestion, as well as magnetic rods, to treat anxious and mentally disordered individuals. Mesmer's work later led to the development of hypnotic techniques.

metallophobia Fear of metals (See also METALS, FEAR OF.)

metals, fear of This fear usually involves a reaction to particular metals or characteristics of some metals—for example, smooth or shiny surfaces, or such characteristics as color or the tendency to conduct cold. (See also LEAD POISONING, FEAR OF.)

meteors, fear of Superstitions and traditional beliefs associate meteors, also known as falling stars, with death and bad luck. Meteors are chunks of matter from outer space, probably pieces of disintegrated comets that burn when they enter the earth's atmosphere. Meteorites are the remainders of meteors that are not completely destroyed by their blazing fall to earth. Asian tribes thought meteors were disembodied souls, some believing optimistically that they carried treasure, others that their purpose in coming to earth was to feed on the blood of the living. An American Indian belief links meteors with the moon; seeing a meteor was thought to cause one's face to become pockmarked like the surface of the moon.

Meteors are also feared because they can cause injury. A meteor may weigh over 2,000 pounds, and a shower may consist of 100,000 stones. There are unsubstantiated reports of human deaths caused by meteors from periods before the early 20th century. Meteorites have fallen through the roofs of houses, and animals have been killed by them.

Heide, Fritz, *Meteorites* (Chicago: University of Chicago Press, 1964), pp. 60–61.

Cavendish, Richard (ed.), *Man, Myth, and Magic* (New York: Marshall Cavendish, 1983).

meteorphobia Fear of meteors. (See also METEORS, FEAR OF.)

methyphobia Fear of alcohol. (See also ALCOHOL, FEAR OF.)

metrophobia Fear of poetry. (See also POETRY, FEAR OF.)

Meyer, Adolf A pathologist who founded the field of psychobiology for the study of mental illness.

MHPG 3-methoxy 4-hydroxy phenylethylene glycol, a noradrenergic metabolite. It is increased during fear and panic attacks. After imipramine or clonidine is given,

MHPG diminishes if phobic anxiety falls but not if it continues.

mianserin An antidepressant drug. Mianserin also has sedative properties. Although it has relatively few side effects and is safe for persons who have heart conditions, the drug has fairly weak effects. (See also ANTIDEPRESSANTS, NEW; DEPRESSION; SEDATIVES.)

Lapierre, Y.D., "New Antidepressant Drugs," *Journal of Clinical Psychiatry* (August 1983), pp. 41–44.

mice, fear of Fear of mice is known as suriphobia or musiphobia. Some people fear mice because they are considered to carry dirt and filth, because they can hide in small places, and because they destroy stored food and leave droppings around homes and stores. Some people who fear mice have fainted or run at the sight of one, or at least jumped away to avoid contact with them.

microbes, fear of Fear of microbes is known as bacillophobia. Those who fear microbes probably have a fear of contamination and a fear of germs. (See also MICROBIOPHOBIA.)

microbiophobia, microphobia, mikrophobia Fear of GERMS or SMALL OBJECTS. The word is derived from the Greek word *micros,* or small, and *bios,* meaning life.

migraine headaches See HEADACHES.

milieu therapy Behavior change procedures that attempt to make the total environment conducive to psychological improvement. Milieu therapy is useful in treating some agoraphobics and their families. While this form of therapy began as an approach to a large number of patients in a hospital ward, the term is now used in many different settings to describe generically environmental intervention. (See also BEHAVIOR THERAPY.)

mind, fear of Fear of the mind is known as psychophobia. This fear may be related to fear of thinking, fear of memory, or fear of memory loss.

Minnesota Multiphasic Personality Inventory (MMPI) A self-rating questionnaire to determine personality types. The MMPI may be of some use to therapists in helping anxious or phobic individuals. The MMPI was developed by Starke Rosecrans Hathaway (1903–1984), an American pychologist, and John Charnley McKinley (1891–1950), an American psychiatrist, in 1942. Results of the questionnaire point toward nine personality scales: hypochondria, depression, hysteria, psychopathic deviate, masculine–feminine interest, paranoia, psychasthenia, schizophrenia, and hypomania. The subject of the test indicates agreement or disagreement with 550 statements; results are scored by an examiner or by computer to determine the individual's personality profile as well as any tendency to fake responses. The MMPI is widely used in clinical research. (See also HATHAWAY, STARKE; PERSONALITY TYPES.)

minor fears Most people have minor fears that are not considered phobias; for example, they are nervous in a job interview or in some new social situations. They may be a little apprehensive as they drive along a road at the edge of a cliff. Such fears are common and even protective. Most people are clean and organized because they feel better, look better, and work better that way. Only when a habit becomes overwhelming—for example, avoiding going outdoors because one might see a bird, or endlessly washing hands—does the fear become abnormal and handicapping, and hence a phobia. Although it hasn't been studied extensively, clinically it is thought that minor fears can escalate.

minor tranquilizer Drugs (e.g., the BENZODIAZEPINES) that reduce moderate to low levels of anxiety; sometimes used to treat individuals who have various phobias. Some tranquilizers are prescribed for phobic individuals so that they can deal more calmly with their fears during behavior-therapy sessions. Treatment with minor tranquilizers is often combined with programs of graduated exposure. Some therapists prefer to use deep relaxation techniques rather than tranquilizers.

One drawback to using minor tranquilizers in the treatment of phobias is that some individuals become fearful of discontinuing their tranquilizers. Abuse of drugs is not uncommon in phobic people. (See also ADDICTION; ALPRAZOLAM; ANXIOLYTICS; LIBRIUM; VALIUM.)

mirroring A BEHAVIOR MODIFICATION technique in which an individual sees himself portrayed by another person, usually the therapist, thereby acquiring a better idea of how he is viewed by others. Mirroring is used in helping some people overcome SOCIAL PHOBIAS. It is especially helpful in desensitizing a person to speech phobias. (See also BEHAVIOR THERAPY.)

Some Examples of Minor Tranquilizers (also known as anxiolytics)

Generic Name	U.S. Brand Name
alprazolam	Xanax
chlordiazepoxide	Librium
	SK-Lygen
chlorazepate	Tranxene
diazepam	Valium
halazepam	Paxipam
hydroxyline	Atarax
	Vistaril
lorazepam	Ativan
meprobamate	Equanil
	Miltown
oxazepam	Serax
prazepam	Centrax
tybamate	Tybatran

mirrors, fear of Fear of mirrors is known as catoptrophobia, eisotrophobia, and spectrophobia. Many modern fears of mirrors are based on ancient fears and superstitions about reflections. The earliest known looking-glasses, or mirrors, were the still waters of lakes and pools. Primitive people believed that when a man saw his own image in a pool, or any other reflective surface, he saw not a mere reflection, but his soul looking back at him. The notion that the soul could be separated from the body without causing death, and that it was sometimes visible as a reflection or a shadow, was widespread in early times and appears in many well-known folktales. As long as the separated spirit was unharmed, the man whose body normally contained it was safe; but if it was injured in any way, misfortune, evil, and very often death would follow. The broken reflection of the human image has long been interpreted as a symbol of disaster. Many people fear seeing a broken or distorted image of themselves because they view distortion as a sign of disintegration, or of impending trouble and even death. Ancient Greeks considered it an omen of death to dream of seeing one's reflection in the water, because the water spirits might drag the soul into the dark depths below, leaving its owner to perish.

Basutos of southern Africa believe that crocodiles can kill a man by snapping at his reflection in water. Zulus of the Bantu nation of southeastern Africa consider it dangerous for anyone to look in a dark pool, because the spirit that dwells within it might seize the reflection and beat away the soul.

Some people fear breaking mirrors because they believe it brings seven years of bad luck, or a misfortune of a particular kind, such as the loss of a close friend, or a death in the house. Another superstition prohibits a child of less than a year from seeing its likeness in a mirror because to do so would cause it to languish, stunt its growth, or bring about an early death. The custom of veiling mirrors after a death is partly due to the fear that whoever sees his reflection then will die soon after, or if not he, then someone else in the house. Brides have been warned not to look at themselves in their wedding clothes, lest something happen to prevent the marriage. However, after the ceremony, it is considered lucky for the married couple to look at themselves together in the mirror. Actors fear looking into a mirror over another's shoulder. They fear seeing two reflections together, because doing so will bring bad luck to the one overlooked. Some individuals who have dysmorphophobia (a fear that part of their body is misshapen) fear looking in mirrors because seeing their reflection provokes anxiety.

Mythology and literature abound with references about fears of mirrors. For example, in a Greek myth, Narcissus's image reflected in a mirror was his own consciousness projected onto the world. In Lewis Carroll's *Alice in Wonderland—Through the Looking Glass,* a mirror symbolized the doorway through which the soul could pass to the other side. Merlin's mirror warned of treason, the mirror of Cambuscan in Chaucer's *Canterbury Tales* told of misfortunes to come, and the all-seeing mirror of Al-Asnam in the *Arabian Nights* indicated by the lightening or darkening of the mirror's surface whether or not the girl reflected was chaste.

In the 1600s and 1700s, catoptromancy, or mirror divination, was practiced, encouraging fears of mirrors and images. The seers dipped a metal mirror into water; depending upon whether the reflection of the sick person who looked into it was disfigured or clearly defined, the seer would decide if the person would live or die. During the Elizabethan era, mirror divination was used to detect witches.

The use of the mirror to deflect the rays of the Evil Eye was once a very common European practice. Among the Chinese, small mirrors were hung up in the house to scare away evil spirits because presumably the spirits would be shocked at the sight of their own reflections.

In dreams the mirror may be a symbol of sight, of the imagination, or of thought, as thought is a reflection of the universe. Also, mirrors may symbolize self-examination, truth, or vanity.

Mirrors have been thought of as doors through which the souls may find freedom. However, the Greek legend of Narc... does not follow this pattern. Narcissus became enamoured of his reflection in a fountain, leaned down to embrace it, and then was embraced by death. Narcissism remains the symbol of self-love. The fear of mirrors is often a symptomatic complaint of schizophrenics. (See also EVIL EYE, FEAR OF; SYMBOLS.)

Holes, Christina, *Encyclopedia of Superstitions* (London: Hutchinson, 1981).

Jobes, Gertrude, *Dictionary of Mythology, Folklore and Symbols* (Metuchen, NJ: Scarecrow Press, 1961).

Cirlot, J.E., *A Dictionary of Symbols* (New York: Philosophical Library, 1962).

Deutch, Yvonne D., ''Mirror,'' in R. Cavendish (ed.), *Man, Myth and Magic* (New York: Marshall Cavendish, 1983).

misophobia Fear of contamination with dirt or germs is known as misophobia. (See also CONTAMINATION, FEAR OF.)

missiles, fear of Fear of missiles is known as ballistophobia. Those who fear missiles may fear nuclear war, or war in general. Many who have lived through wars fear missiles. Ballistophobia also refers to a fear of being shot. (See also POSTTRAUMATIC STRESS DISORDER; SHOT, FEAR OF BEING.)

mist, fear of The fear of moisture is known as hygrophobia, and this fear may extend to mist and fog, forms of moisture. Both obscure one's view, which can create feelings of uncertainty, powerlessness, and loss of control, thus serving as sources of isolation, loneliness, and disorientation. (See also, FOG, FEAR OF; WATER, FEAR OF.)

mites, fear of Fear of mites is known as acarophobia.

mitral valve prolapse (MVP) A heart defect that has sometimes been linked with anxiety. In this condition, the mitral valve does not close sufficiently, and blood is forced back into the atrium as well as through the aortic valve. About 40 percent of normal adults have MVP. The condition can lead to a feeling of palpitations, anxiety, and difficult breathing. Research to study the relationship between anxiety disorders and mitral valve prolapse has unequivocally demonstrated that MVP is not a precursor, cause, or even related to panic and agoraphobia. While there is some symptom overlap, the overwhelming majority of MVP reactors do not develop panic or anxiety. However, individuals who have an anatomic vulnerability of their mitral valves may develop prolapse as a result of increased demands placed on their cardiovascular systems by anxiety. (See also LACTATE-INDUCED ANXIETY; PANIC ATTACK.)

Mazza, Dominic et al., "Prevalence of Anxiety Disorders in Patients with Mitral Valve Prolapse," *American Journal of Psychiatry* (March 1986), pp. 349–352.

Marks, Isaac M., *Fears, Phobias and Rituals* (New York: Oxford University Press, 1987).

mnemophobia Fear of memories. (See also MEMORIES, FEAR OF.)

modeling The acquisition of behavior by observation of a real or symbolic model. Acquisition can occur in one observation if the individual identifies with or is attracted to the model. Modeling or observational learning may be produced by stories, television, or movies, or by direct observation (e.g., of a parent or friend). It is also possible to acquire emotional responses through observation. In this case, the model would be displaying emotional reactions in a particular stimulus situation, such as the ocean or showers. Many people, for example, developed fears of swimming in the ocean after seeing the movie *Jaws*. Likewise, people developed fears of taking showers alone after seeing the Hitchcock thriller *Psycho*. Behavior theorists make a distinction between acquisition (which occurs through observation) and performance (which requires repeated trials, reinforcement, etc., and is affected by the individual's learning history). In other words, a person might acquire a fear through observation, but whether they avoid the situation and consequently become phobic might depend on other factors, such as reinforcement. (See also BEHAVIOR THERAPY.)

molysmophobia, molysomophobia Fear of contamination or infection. (See also CONTAMINATION, FEAR OF; INFECTION, FEAR OF.)

money, fear of Fear of money is known as chrematophobia. Money can help an individual maintain esteem. Fear of loss of money represents a fear of losing the external validation of one's worth provided by money. After the Great Depression, many people committed suicide because they viewed lack of money as a loss of self-worth.

monoamine oxidase inhibitors (MAOIs) A class of ANTIDEPRESSANT drugs (used to treat depression). MAOIs reduce excessive emotional fluctuations and may stabilize brain chemistry by inhibiting the action of the enzyme monoamine oxidase, which in turn inactivates NOREPINEPHRINE. When more norepinephrine becomes available in the SYMPATHETIC NERVOUS SYSTEM, mood is elevated. Individuals taking MAOIs should avoid the foods listed in the chart of foods to be avoided by migraine sufferers. (See also HEADACHES.)

monopathophobia Fear of definite disease. (See also DISEASE, FEAR OF DEFINITE.)

monophobia Fear of being lonely; also fear of desolate places; fear of one thing. (See also BEING ALONE, FEAR OF; ONE THING, FEAR OF.)

monotony, fear of Fear of monotony is a fear of sameness or unchanging situations and consequently has been called homophobia. (This term has also been applied to fear of homosexuality.) This may be related to a fear of boredom and a fear of time, known as chronophobia. Interestingly, monotony—or lack of stimulation—can trigger anxiety in agoraphobic individuals susceptible to react to lack of stimulation.

monstrosities, fear of Fear of monstrosities is known as teratophobia. Teratophobia also refers to fear of giving birth to a monster. (See also CHILDBIRTH, FEAR OF.)

mood A sustained or pervasive emotion that markedly colors the individual's perception of the world. Examples of moods include depression, anxiety, anger, or elation. Moods may be significance in diagnosing anxieties and phobias, and therapists discuss moods with individuals who seek help for such problems. The American Psychiatric Association (in *Diagnostic and Statistical Manual of Mental Disorders*) describes moods as:

Dysphoric: An unpleasant mood, such as depression, anxiety, or irritability.

Elevated: A mood that is more cheerful than normal. It does not imply pathology (as in manic–depressive illness).

Euphoric: An exaggerated feeling of wellbeing. Euphoria occurs in manic–depressive disorder. As a technical term, euphoria implies a pathological, or diseased, mood. Whereas an individual with a normally elevated mood may describe himself or herself as being in "good spirits," "very happy," or "cheerful," the euphoric person is likely to exclaim that he or she is "on top of the world," "up in the clouds," or "high."

Euthymic: A mood in the "normal" range, which implies the absence of depressed or elated mood.

Irritable: Internalized feeling of tension associated with being easily annoyed and provoked to anger. (See also AFFECTIVE DISORDERS; MANIC–DEPRESSIVE DISORDER; MOOD DISORDERS.)

American Psychiatric Association, *Diagnostic and Statistical Manual of Mental Disorders* (Washington, D.C.: American Psychiatric Association 1987).

mood disorders In *Diagnostic and Statistical Manual of Mental Disorders* (American Psychiatric Association), AFFECTIOVE DISORDERS are classified as mood disorders. Mood disorders include depression, manic–depressive disorder, bipolar illness, hypomanic episodes, cyclothymia, and others. (See also MANIC–DEPRESSIVE DISORDER; MANIC EPISODE.)

moon, fear of Fear of the moon is known as selenophobia. The effects of the moon on human behavior, especially as causing insanity, have been noted for centuries. The word "lunatic," coined by the physician Paracelsus in the Middle Ages, derives from the Latin word for moon. In some countries there is a fear that the man in the moon is the biblical Cain, accounting for the observation that as the moon becomes fuller and stronger, human behavior becomes more violent and erratic. People who are mentally unstable are thought to be particularly affected by the moon. Although scientific proof is lacking, professionals such as nurses, police, and firemen who deal with large numbers of people in emergency situations report an upsurge in activity and more extreme behavior at the time of the full moon.

Ancient Greeks and other cultures believed that the rays of the moon contained damaging power that could be collected by witches and magicians and used for their own evil purposes.

The observation that the moon's cycles parallel those of a woman's body led to the belief in some cultures that the moon was a lecherous man who ravished women and caused abortive or abnormal pregnancies each month. Other cultures identified the moon with a feminine emotional influence. In medieval Europe, the Roman moon goddess Diana became the patroness of witches.

Many fear-inducing superstitions are connected with the moon. For example, a full moon on Christmas prophesies a poor harvest; on Sunday, bad luck. A red moon foretells murder or war. Sleeping in the moonlight is thought to produce a twisted face.

Fear of the moon is often related to fear of the night or situations that might occur at a full moon. In any case, critical anxiety stimuli can be seeing darkness or emptiness, being out at night, looking at pictures of the moon, and sometimes, even seeing circles or circular objects that resemble the shape of the moon.

Daniels, Cora Linn and C.M. Stevans, *Encyclopedia of Superstitions, Folklore, and the Occult Sciences of the World* (Detroit: Gale Research, 1971).

Deutch, Yvonne D., "Moon," in R. Cavendish (ed.), *Man, Myth and Magic* (New York: Marshall Cavendish, 1983).

Moreno, Jacob Levi (1889–1974) A Hungarian-American philosopher and major contributor to the field of group psychotherapy, which term he coined in 1932. Moreno went on to develop "psychodrama." In 1936 Moreno founded the Moreno Sanitorium, at which psychodrama was practiced and taught, and in 1942 he established institutes in New York City and Beacon, New York, for training group therapists and psychodrama practitioners. He founded the journal *Sociometry,* later titled *Group Psychotherapy, Psychodrama and Sociometry.* Moreno wrote a three-volume treatise on psychodrama that is used by therapists who treat individuals who have anxieties and phobias. (See also PSYCHODRAMA.)

Morita therapy A form of behavior therapy originated by Shoma Morita (1874–1938), a Japanese psychiatrist and contemporary of Freud. Morita therapy was developed as a treatment for many anxiety-related problems, which Morita referred to as "nervosity problems," characterized by hypochondriacal sensitivity and reactions to threats to health, introversion, self-preoccupation, perfectionistic self-expectations, intellectualized and dogmatic world views and expectations, and egocentric perceptions and reasoning. Morita therapy is centered on positive reinterpretation of anxiety in order to stimulate attentional, attitudinal, and behavioral change in self-preoccupied anxious individuals. This therapy promotes individuals' behavioral commitment to constructive and productive activities. It is currently practiced in Japan in various settings, such as supportive group guidance, directive outpatient therapy, correspondence guidance, guidance through diary commentaries, and also in structured residential treatment. Morita therapy is not widely integrated into Western therapy, largely because of the scarcity of literature on the outpatient application of the therapy.

Morita therapists have observed that Morita therapy often changes individuals' lifestyles. Instead of being mood-governed and feeling-oriented in thinking and action, such individuals become more purpose-oriented. They accept their emotional experiences as facts without suppressing or disputing them and start recognizing an abundance of tasks to be done in daily life that they have been neglecting because of their own self-preoccupation. Instead of allowing temporary moods and feelings to decide or interfere with action, individuals in Morita therapy learn to make pragmatic purposes their priorities They learn to modify, by actual experiences outside therapy sessions, their acceptance of anxiety at cognitive, behavioral, and emotional levels. (See also BEHAVIOR MODIFICATION; BEHAVIOR THERAPY; COGNITIVE THERAPY.)

Morita, S., *Nature and Treatment of Nervosity* (Tokyo: Hakuyosha, 1960). In Japanese.

Ishiyama, F. Ishu, "Morita Therapy: Its Basic Features and Cognitive Interventions for Anxiety Treatment," *Psychotherapy* (Fall 1986), p. 375.

mother-in-law, fear of Fear of a mother-in-law is known as pentheraphobia. Fears of mothers-in-law frequently are expressed in jokes, which may perpetuate the mother-in-law mystique and fear. The most common themes are mothers-in-law as meddlesome troublemakers, ego deflators, unwanted guests, and often mean, unattractive women. Such jokes may have some historical basis, because some primitive societies actually prohibited contact between a man and his mother-in-law.

Hostile feelings toward the mother-in-law may arise from one spouse complaining to the other about mistreatment by his or her mother or a feeling that the irritating or unattractive qualities of the spouse are a direct result of his or her upbringing.

Though mothers-in-law are the butt of jokes, there seems to be some basis in fact for the belief that they present the most frequent in-law problems, with conflict most frequently arising between daughter-in-law and husband's mother. In some young couples, however, the conflict is between husband and the wife's mother because of the young bride's continuing dependence on her mother. In some cases, sources of these conflicts may be children's repressed resentments of their own parents being projected toward in-laws; ethnic, social and religious differences; and the mother-in-law's own difficulty in adjusting to the departure of her children and to the aging process. (See also FATHER-IN-LAW, FEAR OF; RELATIVES, FEAR OF.)

Arnstein, Helene, *Getting Along with Your Grown-up Children* (Philadelphia: M. Evans, 1970).

Klemer, Richard H., *Marriage and Family Relationships* (New York: Harper & Row, 1970).

motion, fear of Fear of motion is known as kinesophobia. Persons may fear motion for many reasons. They may fear the motion of race cars and roller coaster rides because of the danger involved. They may fear plane, train, car, or other vehicular motion because they fear motion sickness, and they may fear the physical discomfort they have previously experienced. Some fear having a lack of control over what may happen during the movement experience. Some individuals fear looking at or being in a whirlpool. Individuals who have balance problems or inner-ear disorders may have a greater fear of motion because of their reduced ability to accommodate to it physically. Some individuals who fear movement are startled by sudden changes, such as a loss of support, changes in altitude in an airplane, or being plunged into darkness. Infants and young children may react with fear when they see a live or toy animal rushing toward them. Movement also means increases in stimulation, and for anxiety-prone individuals, stimulation can be a trigger for anxiety. (See also AUTOMOBILES, FEAR OF; FLYING, FEAR OF; TRAINS, FEAR OF; WHIRLPOOL, FEAR OF.)

Marks, I.M., *Fears, Phobias, and Rituals* (New York: Oxford University Press, 1987).

motivation Motivation is the force or energy that causes individuals to behave in a particular manner. Motivation may include satisfaction of basic drives, such as hunger, thirst, or sex, or desire for praise, power, money, or success. Anxiety or fear may act as motivation for FIGHT OR FLIGHT, causing the anxious individual either to stand up to the feared stimulus or to flee from it. Anxiety may motivate very different behaviors in different individuals depending on their underlying personality structure

Also, reduction of anxiety can serve as a powerful reinforcer or motivator for the behavior of avoidance. This built-in reinforcement for avoidance is what makes treatment of anxiety reactions difficult. Furthermore, only a small group of sufferers (less than twenty percent) ever seeks treatment. (See also STIMULUS.)

motorphobia Fear of automobiles. The fear may also extend to a fear of other vehicles, such as buses. (See also AUTOMOBILES, FEAR OF.)

movement, fear of See MOTION, FEAR OF.

moving, fear of Fear of moving is known as tropophobia. This fear may be related to a fear of newness or of new things. A move from one home to another brings with it the anxiety of facing the unknown. People anticipating a move fear the possibilities of hidden defects in a house or apartment and noisy or disagreeable neighbors. The sheer number of details and responsibilities in moving and the necessity of focusing energy on one project may be physically as well as mentally exhausting. Seeing their parents faced with unaccustomed anxieties and fears, children may sense the uneasiness and become anxious themselves.

A move that involves a complete change of location can cause many anxieties as the sense of the familiar vanishes. Differing customs, a change from rural to urban living or vice versa, or change of climate may create difficulties, including unexpected expenses. Activities that formerly were almost automatic, such as going to the grocery store, visiting the library, or getting a haircut, take more time and investigation in a new place. Children feel lonely and depressed after leaving friends and abandoning group activities such as sports and clubs in which they had created a place for themselves. Anxiety can arise from newness and from the emergence of these aversive feelings.

The reasons for moving may create anxieties. Some moves are made for negative reasons, such as death in the family, divorce, or a reduced economic situation. Even though the move may be an advantage to one member of the family, others may feel dragged along and become resentful and anxious. (See also LANDSCAPE, FEAR OF; NEWNESS, FEAR OF.)

Nida, Patricia Cooney and Wendy M. Heller, *The Teenager's Survival Guide to Moving* (New York: Atheneum, 1985).

mugging, fear of Mugging is a realistic contemporary fear. Many people fear mugging because victims are confronted unexpectedly and suffer physical harm as well as loss of possessions. Fear of being mugged leads many people to avoid wearing expensive, attention-getting clothing or jewelry on the street. In major cities, some individuals have been known to change their clothes before riding the subway, putting on clothes that "disguise" their mission as a business person or partygoer. They carry their "good clothes" in a plain paper bag so that they will not be the victim of a thief. Some individuals may carry this "avoidance" response to an extreme. (See also BAD MEN, FEAR OF; BURGLARS, FEAR OF.)

Pasternack, Stefan A., *Violence and Victims* (New York: Spectrum, 1978).

multimodal behavior therapy A form of behavioral therapy developed by Arnold Lazarus (1932–) that views psychological disorders from seven modalities: behavior, affect, sensation, imagery, cognition, interpersonal relationships, and drug/biological aspects. The acronym BASIC ID was coined for these modalities. A comprehensive, individualized program is developed for each client to assess each of these modalities and to provide consecutive therapies in an eclectic array.

multiple personality disorder A type of dissociative disorder in which the individual adopts two or more personalities. Some writers have noted that multiple personalities develop as a defense mechanism against extreme fears or anxieties. According to *Diagnostic and Statistical Manual of Mental Disorders*, diagnostic criteria for this disorder include the existence within the individual of two or more distinct personalities or personality states, each with its own relatively enduring pattern of perceiving, relating to, and thinking about the environment and the self. Further, at least two of these personalities or personality states recurrently take full control of the individual's behavior. Frequently, one or more of the personalities shows some symptoms of a coexisting disorder, such as a mood disorder, complaints of anxiety suggesting an anxiety disorder, or marked disturbance in personality functioning suggesting BORDERLINE PERSONALITY DISORDER. It is often unclear whether these in fact represent coexisting disorders or are associated features of multiple personality disorder. Multiple personality disorder occurs three to nine times more frequently in females than in males. Several studies have shown that the disorder is more common in first-degree biologic relatives of people with the disorder than in the general population. (See also DISSOCIATION.)

Diagnostic and Statistical Manual of Mental Disorders (Washington, DC: American Psychiatric Press, 1987).

Munch, Edvard (1863–1944) A Norwegian artist who painted *The Shriek*, depicting a nameless, unidentifiable fear or panic reaction. This was one of a series of paintings called the *Frieze of Life*, which Munch, who suffered from mental illness, called "a poem of life, love and death." In *The Shriek*, an abstract, almost featureless woman, standing by a railing, covering her ears, screams because of some unknown, unseen fear as blood-red clouds hover over her head. Commenting on the inspiration for this unique work, Munch wrote, "I hear the scream of nature."

Howells, John G. and M. Livia Osborn, *A Reference Companion to the History of Abnormal Psychology* (Westport, CT: Greenwood Press, 1984).

Messer, Thomas M., *Edvard Munch* (New York: Abrams, 1970).

Oxford Companion to 20th Century Art (Oxford: Oxford University Press, 1981).

Arnson, H. Harvard, *History of Modern Art* (New York: Abrams, 1986).

murophobia, musophobia Fear of mice. (See also MICE, FEAR OF.)

music, fear of Fear of music is known as musicophobia and melophobia. Music phobics usually fear only one type of music, such as organ music, which may have unpleasant associations for the individual. Historically, music has created a number of social fears and has been subjected to cen sorship. For example, operas hinting at revolution were censored in nineteenth-century Europe, as was music of Jewish composers in Nazi Germany and music expressing subjectivity or individuality in Soviet Russia. Social and religious leaders have objected to jazz because of its association with sensuous dancing and because of its development in lower-class dance halls that served as contact points for prostitutes. Jazz was particularly looked down upon by white southerners because of its origin in black culture, and some blacks attempting to rise in a white world have rejected it. Similarly, many have objected to and feared rock music for its associations with commercialization, violence, sex, unbridled primitive energies, and drugs. Folk music became associated with radical, left-wing political movements, frequently labeled subversive, in the United States in the 1930s and 1940s and again in the 1960s and 1970s.

In Hippocrates's (460–377 B.C.) writings, there is mention of a man frightened by the sound of a flute. Mozart is said to have feared the sounds of trumpets.

Denisoff, R. Serge, *Great Day Coming* (Urbana: University of Illinois, 1971).

Kent, Fraser, *Nothing to Fear* (Garden City, New York: Doubleday, 1977).

Nanry, Charles (ed.), *American Music from Storyville to Woodstock* (New Brunswick, NJ: Transaction Books, 1972).

Raynor, Henry, *Music and Society since 1815* (New York: Schocken Books, 1976).

music as anxiety therapy Since antiquity, benefits of music as a soother of anxieties have been known. Music probably has powers to relieve anxieties because it involves nonverbal communication and fills physiological and psychological needs for pattern, form, and sensory stimulation. Music is a way to make the external environment more appealing and acceptable to the individual. Music can provide a focus for therapeutic activity and motivate and reinforce participation in therapy.

In Greek mythology, Apollo was god of both medicine and music. Apollo's son, Aesculapius, god of medicine, was said to cure diseases of the mind by using music and song. The Greek philosopher Plato believed that music affected the emotions and could influence the individual's character. In the Bible, David played his harp to relieve King Saul's melancholy (depression). Music was used during the Middle Ages to exhaust crowds of people suffering from MASS HYSTERIA (probably because the music encouraged them to keep on dancing until exhaustion). Shakespeare made reference to the healing powers of music in his plays.

The first book in English on the subject was *Medicina Musica,* written by Richard Browne, an apothecary, in the early 1700s. In the book, music was said to "soothe the turbulent affections" and calm "maniacal patients who did not respond to other remedies."

During the 19th century, music therapy in the form of brass bands and concerts was used for patients with all the then-identified mental disorders, including anxiety. In the 20th century, particularly during World War II, many American psychiatric hospitals used active music therapy programs. The National Association for Music Therapy (NAMT) was organized in 1950, and in 1954 the NAMT recommended a curriculum for preparation of music therapists. Subsequently, organizations of music therapists were formed in England, Europe, South America, and Australia.

Contemporary music therapists use music and musical activities to bring about desirable changes in an individual's behavior and help the individual adjust to his environment. (See also POETRY AS THERAPY.)

musophobia Fear of mice. (See also MICE, FEAR OF.)

myctophobia Fear of darkness. (See also DARKNESS, FEAR OF.)

myrmecophobia Fear of ants. (See also ANTS, FEAR OF.)

mysophobia Fear of dirt, germs, contamination, or filth. (See also CONTAMINATION, FEAR OF; DIRT, FEAR OF.)

mythophobia Fear of FALSE STATEMENTS, lying, or myths. (See also LYING, FEAR OF.)

myxophobia Fear of slime. (See also SLIME, FEAR OF.)

N

Naikan therapy An approach to therapy developed by Isshin Yoshimoto, a Japanese priest and businessman, during the 1950s. The goal of Naikan therapy is to help individuals gain a new outlook on their current behavior and a new awareness of positive influences in their lives and to face responsibilities. The therapy may be of interest to phobic or anxious individuals, because it encourages them to gain control of responses to their environment. Naikan therapy involves reflection on themes of what has been received from others, what has been returned to them, and the troubles that the individual has caused them. Usually the first topics for reflection include mothers and significant others. The individual is encouraged to confess deficiencies and misdeeds, first to the therapist, then to a peer group, then to the significant others; to make reparation to those he has wronged; and to show his gratitude to those from whom he has received help and nurturance. Naikan therapy does not treat symptoms but expects them to disappear as a result of the character-building process of the therapy. (See also MORITA THERAPY.)

Reynolds, D.K., *Naikan Therapy: Meditation for Self-Development* (Chicago: University of Chicago Press, 1983).

naked body, fear of Fear of the naked body is known as gymnophobia. (See also NUDITY, FEAR OF.)

names, fear of Fear of specific names is known as nomatophobia or onomatophobia. The fear may have developed from a primitive time when men guarded their first name as a precious secret and assumed another name to mislead those who might be able to gain power over them by knowing one's first name. Among gypsies, it is said, individuals were never told their first names, except at birth, when their mothers whispered it to them. Among ancient Hebrews, the name of God was never written down and never spoken.

In certain obsessive–compulsive individuals, hearing a name might stir up anxieties. Historically, names have been tied to numerology and astrology and the belief that names can determine the destiny of the individual. Fears develop about the effect of a name on a child and the outcome of the child's life, as well as the effect of the name on others. (See also WORDS, FEAR OF.)

Brasch, R., *Strange Customs* (New York: David McKay, 1976).

narcolepsy, fear of Some individuals fear sleep attacks, known as narcolepsy. An individual who has narcolepsy may fall asleep suddenly and involuntarily without warning. Sleep attacks appear to be triggered by strong emotions and may be accompanied by visual or auditory hallucinations at the onset. The attacks may occur up to several times per day and often include the type of muscle paralysis common in REM sleep. Individuals who have narcolepsy may experience increased anxiety throughout the day due to their inability to control their actions. (See also HALLUCINATIONS; SLEEP, FEAR OF; SLEEP, FUNCTION OF.)

narcosynthesis See DEPTH PSYCHOLOGY.)

Nardil See PHENELZINE.

narrowness, fear of Fear of narrowness is known as anginaphobia. This may relate to a fear of being in narrow places, of viewing scenery from a narrow vantage point, or of having any narrowing of the body, such as a narrowing of the arteries. The fear may also relate to fear of being in a tunnel and fear of crossing a bridge.

Fear of narrow places is known as stenophobia. This fear is related to the fear of narrowness and may be related to a fear of enclosed places, such as occurs in CLAUSTROPHOBIA. Some who fear narrow places also fear being in tunnels, riding on escalators, using moving walks at airports, and crossing bridges. (See also ANGINA PECTORIS, FEAR OF; BRIDGES, FEAR OF.)

narrow places, fear of See NARROWNESS, FEAR OF

National Institutes of Mental Health (NIMH) A component of the Alcohol, Drug Abuse, and Mental Health Administration, Public Health Service, Department of Health and Human Services, NIMH conducts and supports research into the causes, treatment, and prevention of mental and emotional disorders, including anxieties and phobias, and research on many public-health problems related to mental health. Research is carried out through the Mental Health Intramural Research Program. Additionally, the broad spectrum of biological, genetic, psychological, social, and environmental factors that affect and shape mental health and mental disorders are studied through NIMH-supported research in hospitals, universities, mental-health centers, and community settings.

The Institute's Division of Scientific and Public Information plans and directs the acquisition and dissemination of scientific and technical information related to mental health. This division also maintains the National Clearinghouse for Mental Health Information, which collects, stores, and retrieves information on mental health for dissemination to the lay public, clinicians, and the scientific community.

For information, contact:
National Institutes of Mental Health
5600 Fishers Lane
Rockville, MD 20857

National Mental Health Association The National Mental Health Association, founded in 1909, is the only private volunteer advocacy organization in the U.S. concerned with all aspects of mental health, including research and information on anxiety disorders. Goals of the organization include protecting rights of individuals who have mental disorders, educating the public about mental health, and promoting research into the causes, prevention, treatment, and cure of mental disorders. With over 600 affiliates, NMHA has a network of volunteers who work to maintain and increase federal, state, and local funding for mental-health programs. The NMHA Information Center provides referral and educational information in response to more than 20,000 inquiries each year.

For information contact:
National Mental Health Association
1021 Prince Street
Alexandria, VA 22314–2971
Phone: (703) 684–7722

(See also DEPRESSION; MANIC-DEPRESSIVE DISORDER.)

nature vs. nurture controversy An ongoing debate in psychology involving the relative importance of heredity, or nature, and learning, experience, or nurture, in determining human development and behavior. Currently, this is seen in the controversies between strictly biological and behavioral points of view in causes of agoraphobia, obsessive–compulsive disorder, other phobias, and many anxieties. No conclusions have been reached, but there seems to be mutual influence between biological and psychological factors.

nausea Nausea is a common symptom of ANXIETY and anxiety disorders. Nausea is experienced as a feeling of sickness in the stomach and a feeling that one wants to vomit. Nausea may be accompanied by DIZZINESS or lightheadedness, SWEATING, and muscular weakness. Nausea may accompany anxiety attacks and can appear either as a precursor to or at the onset of an actual bout with anxiety. Nausea may occur on contact with a food that is associated with an anxiety-producing experience from childhood, or in response to certain odors. Nausea may be involved with many specific phobias, such as SOCIAL PHOBIAS, PERFORMANCE ANXIETY, SPORTS ANXIETY, and EXAMINATION ANXIETY. Many individuals experience nausea before an important appointment, before job interviews, before speaking in public, before playing an important game, and before taking tests, whether academic or a type of physical examination. Various forms of BEHAVIOR THERAPY are used to help individuals overcome nausea that does not have physical causes.

Some individuals whose religions proscribe meat (for Hindus) and pork (for Muslims and Jews) fear having reactions of nausea or actually do have nausea when they eat their forbidden food by mistake or coercion. Mahatma Gandhi, a vegetarian, described this reaction after eating meat. (See also FOOD AVERSION; ODORS, FEAR OF; SMELLS, FEAR OF.)

Marks, Isaac M., *Fears, Phobias, and Rituals* (New York: Oxford University Press, 1987).

nebulaphobia Fear of fog. (See also FOG, FEAR OF.)

necrophobia Fear of corpses or dead bodies. (See also CORPSES, FEAR OF; DEAD BODIES, FEAR OF.)

needles, fear of Fear of needles is known as belonephobia. Some fear being pricked by a sewing needle, while others fear injections by hypodermic needles. Some fear dentists because they fear an injection of an analgesic substance with a needle. Some fear needles because needles have been strongly implicated in the transmission of autoimmune deficiency syndrome (AIDS).

Because of fear of needles, some individuals are reluctant to donate blood. Some fear having or seeing a blood transfusion because of their needle fear.

Individuals who have a phobia of needles should, if possible, advise any health-care professionals who treat them. For example, if a dentist knows that a patient has a phobia of needles, he or she will ask the patient to relax first, or to look away, and will keep the needle out of the patient's view rather than provoke a panic attack or make the patient scream or faint. EXPOSURE THERAPY has been effective in successfully treating many individuals who fear needles. (See also ACUPUNCTURE; BLOOD AND BLOOD-INJURY PHOBIA; BLOOD DONATION, FEAR OF; BLOOD TRANSFUSION, FEAR OF; DENTAL ANXIETY; DOCTORS, FEAR OF; INJURY, FEAR OF; TOOTHACHE, FEAR OF.)

negative ambition A type of behavior in which the individual avoids competition, misses opportunities for success, and follows a line of maximum resistance. The term was coined by THEODOR REIK (1888–1970), an Austrian-American psychoanalyst. This behavior leads to anxieties in some individuals.

negative practice A therapy procedure in which the individual is encouraged to intentionally repeat an error for the purpose of overcoming it. The technique was originally used to help individuals overcome stuttering. Deliberate repetition of a habit enables the individual to control it willingly at a later time. Researchers who have compared this practice to FLOODING suggest that negative practice is less effective. (See also BEHAVIOR THERAPY.)

Boudewyns, P.A. and R.H. Shipley, "Confusing Negative Practice with Flooding: A Cautionary Note," *Behavior Therapist*, 5(1982).

neglect of duty, fear of Fear of neglect of duty is known as paraliphobia. Those who have this fear may feel guilty if they do not do what is expected of them and what they expect of themselves. Such individuals may even be compulsive about fulfilling obligations.

nelophobia Fear of glass. (See also GLASS, FEAR OF.)

neopharmaphobia Fear of new drugs. (See also DRUGS, FEAR OF NEW.)

neophobia Fear of newness, novelty, innovation, or change. (See also CHANGE, FEAR OF; INNOVATION, FEAR OF; NEWNESS, FEAR OF; NOVELTY, FEAR OF.)

nephophobia Fear of clouds. (See also CLOUDS, FEAR OF.)

nervous An informal term indicating a state of tension, apprehension, and restlessness. Nervousness is a form of anxiety. The term comes from Freud's theory that neurological weaknesses (neurasthenias) developed as a result of unconscious conflicts.

nervous breakdown A popular term referring to any one or more of a variety of mental-health disorders in an acute phase. It is a type of collapse during which the individual has lost ability to function at his or her previous level of adjustment. Some phobic individuals fear a nervous breakdown when their fears increase or when they have a panic attack.

nervous stomach A common term for feelings of NAUSEA, diarrhea, and abdominal discomfort that an individual experiences when feeling anxious. Nervous stomach is also a common symptom of a panic attack. (See also IRRITABLE BOWEL SYNDROME.)

nervous system An informal term for the AUTONOMIC NERVOUS SYSTEM. Neuropharmacology is the study of the effects of drugs on the nervous system. Neuropathology is the study of diseases of the nervous system. Neuropathology may include examination of the brain, microscopic studies of tissue cells (Chart follows.) and laboratory analysis of the neurochemistry of tissues.

neurosis A now-obsolete term used interchangeably with neurotic disorder (also considered obsolete). A neurosis is a mental condition characterized by anxiety, fears, obsessive thoughts, compulsive acts, dissociation, and depression. Neuroses are considered exaggerated, unconscious ways of coping with internal conflicts. The symptoms are distressing and unacceptable to the individual. The more current term for neurosis in anxiety disorder. (See also ANXIETY DISORDERS.)

neurotic disorders An obsolete diagnostic term now replaced by several terms,

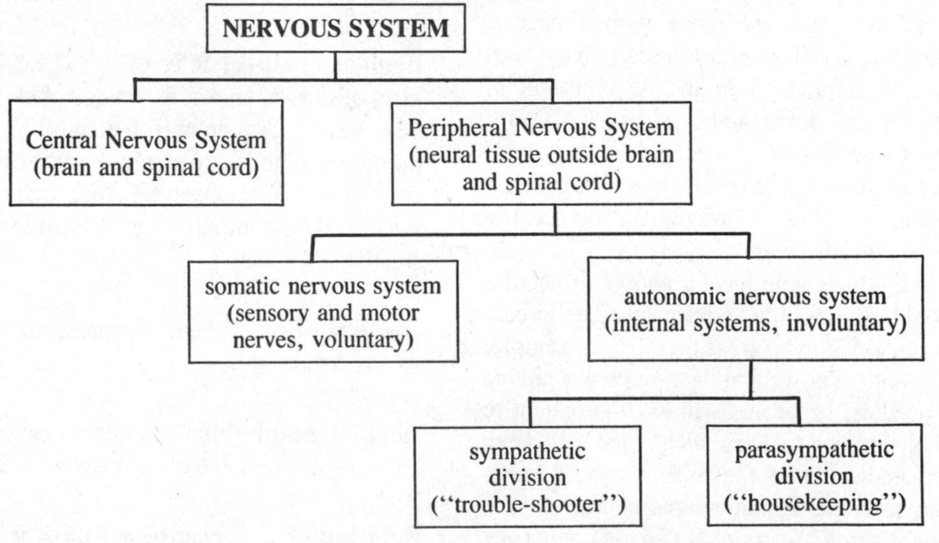

including ANXIETY DISORDERS. The term "neurotic disorders" comes from psychoanalytic theory and was used in the first diagnostic systems. (See also FUNCTIONAL APPROACH; MEDICAL MODEL; NEUROSIS.)

neurotic paradox A term developed by O. Hobart Mowrer (1902–1982) to account for the apparent paradox of why an individual would maintain a "self-defeating," limiting symptom. Mowrer suggested that the punishment or self-defeating nature of the behavior is less aversive than facing the anxiety situation. Facing the feared situation is more aversive than the avoidance, thus the paradox. The tendency is a paradox because in the long run, defenses prevent overall optimal function and development. An example is avoiding areas of life (such as shopping, driving, being alone, etc.) that are self-defeating. However, avoidance, although self-defeating, is more reinforcing than facing the fear situation and getting better.

neurotransmitters Chemical substances that are important in transferring nerve impulses from one cell to another. Neurotransmitters are released at nerve-fiber endings to help nerve impulses across the gap between neurons. At least 30 different substances are known, produced in systems that link various parts of the brain. Several neurotransmitters are involved with fear and anxiety, particularly SEROTONIN, acetylcholine, and dopamine. (Chart on p. 286.) (See also, LOCUS CERULEUS; NOREPINEPHRINE.)

newness, fear of Fear of newness or of anything new is known as neophobia. Individuals who have this fear tend to have fairly routine lives and avoid doing new things, going to new places, or perhaps even wearing new clothes. This fear is related to fear of change, fear of traveling, and fear of moving. (See also INNOVATION, FEAR OF; NOVELTY, FEAR OF.)

Neurotic Disorders*

Type	Major Symptom Patterns
Phobic neurosis	Extreme fear and avoidance of an object or situation which the person himself is able to recognize as harmless
Anxiety neurosis	Anxiety felt in so many situations that it appears to be "free-floating," without specific cause
Hysterical neurosis, conversion type	Paralysis, lack of sensation, or sensory disturbances without organic pathology
Hysterical neurosis, dissociative type	Alterations in consciousness, manifested as amnesia, fugue, somnambulism, and multiple personality
Obsessive–compulsive neurosis	Flooding of the mind with persistent and uncontrollable thoughts, or the compulsion to repeat a certain act again and again
Existential neurosis	Alienation; the feeling that life is meaningless
Neurasthenic neurosis	Chronic fatigue and weakness
Depersonalization neurosis	Feelings of unreality and estrangement from the self and the environment
Depressive neurosis	Extreme sadness in reaction to a specific event
Hypochondriacal neurosis	Preoccupation with bodily functions and with imagined illnesses

From Gerald C. Davison and John M. Neale's *Abnormal Psychology: An Experimental Clinical Approach* (New York: John Wiley, 1974), p. 122.
*These terms are largely obsolete.

Chemicals Thought to Be Neurotransmitters

For a chemical to be designated a neurotransmitter, several criteria must be met. It must be manufactured in the presynaptic terminal of a neuron and be released when a nerve impulse reaches the terminal. Its presence in the synaptic gap must generate a biological response in the next neuron, and if its release is blocked, there must be no subsequent response. Among the chemicals so far identified as neurotransmitters are the following:

Acetylcholine (''asséetil-cóleen'')—found in many synapses of the central and peripheral nervous systems and the parasympathetic division. Excitatory at most central synapses and neuromuscular synapses; inhibitory at heart and some other autonomic nervous system synapses.

Serotonin—produced in the central nervous system, involved in circuits that influence sleep and emotional arousal. Can be either excitatory or inhibitory.

Catecholamines—three chemicals found in synapses in the central nervous system and sympathetic division.

- Dopamine—found in circuits involving voluntary movement, learning, memory, and emotional arousal. Inhibitory.
- Norepinephrine or chemically similar noradrenaline—both a hormone and a transmitter. Found in circuits controlling arousal, wakefulness, eating, learning, and memory. Can be either excitatory or inhibitory.
- Epinephrine or chemically similar adrenaline—both a hormone and a transmitter. Either excitatory or inhibitory; actions include increased pulse and blood pressure.

Amino acids—widely found in brain.

- GABA—the main inhibitory transmitter in the brain.
- Glutamic acid—possibly the chief excitatory transmitter in the brain.

Neuropeptides—chains of amino acids found in the brain.

- Enkephalins—mostly inhibitory, as in pain relief, but excitatory in some locations.
- Beta-endorphin—the most powerful pain reliever produced in the brain. Mostly inhibitory but excitatory in some locations; contained in the stress hormone, ACTH.

night, fear of Fear of night is known as noctiphobia or nyctophobia. Fear of night is related to fear of the unknown, or fear of the dark. Night fear is common in young children. While children may fear the night because they fear separation from their parents, being alone, or imaginary monsters and DEMONS, adults may fear the night for more realistic reasons, such as BURGLARS, who operate under cover of darkness, fear of becoming lost in the dark, or fear of driving a car during the dark hours. Some who fear night fear SLEEPING and DREAMING or fear having NIGHT TERRORS. Some fear SLEEPWALKING or SLEEPTALKING. Some fear going to bed at night for fear that they will not wake up in the morning. People who fear the night usually begin to avoid their fear by going home as dark nears. Night to many primitive people symbolized death, the color black, and unknown forces. (See also DREAMS, FEAR OF; NIGHTMARES; WAKING UP, FEAR OF NOT.)

night terror A nightmare, sometimes containing a phobic object or situation, from which the dreamer, usually a child, awakens screaming with fright. The terror may continue for up to 15 minutes while the child is in a state of semiconsciousness. He or she may scream or talk loudly and show intense fear. The child may appear to be asleep or in a trance, be difficult to awaken, be sitting up, walking around, or lying in bed thrashing about. If the child is wakened, he or she cannot recall what was frightening him or her. Night terrors can make parents anxious. Most children outgrow these episodes without treatment. The Latin name for night terrors is pavor nocturnus. (See also DREAM SYMBOLS; DREAMS, FEAR OF; NIGHT, FEAR OF; NIGHTMARE.)

nightmare A frightening dream during the night. Nightmares resemble phobias in that they are unpleasant stimuli that individuals avoid thinking or talking about in detail. Those who have had a nightmare awaken with a vivid memory of the DREAM and a deep sense of ANXIETY. Nightmares affect about 6 percent of the population. A controlled study of students (as reported by Isaac Marks) found that desensitization decreased nightmare frequency and intensity more than did discussion of the nightmares or mere recording of their frequency. Those who suffer from nightmares often tend to have other forms of sleep disorders and high scores on the TAYLOR MANIFEST ANXIETY SCALE. Children as well as adults fear nightmares that leave them with acute feelings of extreme anxiety, terror, or helplessness. Normal children may have an occasional nightmare after an alarming experience, but constant nightmares may reflect more deep-rooted anxieties or emotional conflicts.

In some cases, nightmares may be the expressions of waking fears, such as BRIDGES or HEIGHTS, and can be reduced by gradual exposure to the frightening stimuli. EXPOSURE THERAPY, which helps phobias, also eases nightmares when applied as rehearsal relief.

Recurrent nightmares are a pronounced feature of acute and chronic POSTTRAUMATIC STRESS DISORDER, which often follows massive trauma and can persist for many years. Fantasy FLOODING, a form of behavioral therapy, has helped Vietnam veterans and victims of physical and sexual assault. Other sufferers of PTSD have improved with fantasy desensitization, and battle dreams have been reported to fade after the individual talks about them. (See also BEHAVIOR THERAPY; FEARS; NIGHT, FEAR OF; NIGHT TERRORS.)

Marks, Isaac, "Nightmares," *Integrative Psychiatry*, 5(1987), pp. 71–81.

———, *Fears, Phobias and Rituals* (New York: Oxford University Press, 1987), p. 393.

nisoxetine An antidepressant drug. (See also ANTIDEPRESSANTS, NEW; DEPRESSION.)

noctiphobia Fear of night. (See also, NIGHT, FEAR OF.)

noise, fear of Fear of noise is known as acousticophobia or ligyrophobia. Noise PHOBIA goes beyond just being startled by loud noises. The individual reacts with FEAR because he feels that the environment is in control of him and he is powerless to stop it. Some individuals fear specific noises, such as sonic booms, whistling, or balloons popping. Some individuals with the last fear avoid going to birthday parties.

Some fears of noises may be related to POSTTRAUMATIC STRESS DISORDER. For example, soldiers who have been in battle may fear loud noises later on. Individuals who have been involved in serious automobile accidents may recall only the noise of the impact and fear loud noises later on. Behavior therapy can be helpful to such individuals. (See also CHILDHOOD ANXIETIES, FEARS, AND PHOBIAS; NIGHTMARES.)

nomatophobia Fear of names is known as nomatophobia. (See also NAMES, FEAR OF.)

nominfensine An antidepressant drug. Common side effects may include mild insomnia or restlessness and nausea, and few cardiac side effects. Nominfensine is also known by the tradename Merital. (See also ANTIDEPRESSANTS, NEW; DEPRESSION.)

LaPierre, Y.D., "New Antidepressant Drugs," *Journal of Clinical Psychiatry* (August 1983), pp. 41–45.

noradrenergic system See LOCUS CERULEUS.

norepinephrine A hormone and NEUROTRANSMITTER to the nervous system. It is also known as noradrenaline. It is found in circuits that control arousal, wakefulness, eating, learning, and memory. Norepinephrine can be either excitatory or inhibitory. Its actions include increased pulse and blood pressure. Disturbances in the level of norepinephrine in the brain may be associated with DEPRESSION and MANIC states. One viewpoint suggests that depression is the result of too little norepinephrine (and too much leads to mania), while another viewpoint suggests that depression results from too little SEROTONIN, another neurotransmitter. There are receptors in the central and sympathetic nervous systems that are sensitive to norepinephrine or substances that mimic its actions. Some receptors accept agents that mimic or inhibit norepinephrine-like qualities. Norepinephrine is a strong vasoconstrictor.

norpramin See DESIPRAMINE.

nortriptylene A TRICYCLIC ANTIDEPRESSANT drug, also known by the tradenames Aventyl, Allegron, and Pamelor. Nortriptylene is also used to relieve symptoms of HEADACHES not due to organic causes. (See also ANTIDEPRESSANTS.)

Griest, J.H. and J.W. Jefferson, *Depression and Its Treatment: Help for the Nation's #1 Mental Problem* (Washington, DC: American Psychiatric Association, 1984).

nosebleeds, fear of Fear of nosebleeds is known as epistaxiophobia. Some blood phobics become fearful when they see anyone else having a nosebleed. For some of these individuals, the sight of blood lowers blood pressure, reduces breathing rate, and induces a feeling of weakness or even a fainting spell. Others fear having nosebleeds themselves, which may be related to a fear of more serious disease, or even fear of bleeding to death. Nosebleeds may have many causes. Among the most common causes of nosebleed are physical injuries to the nose, dryness of the nasal lining, picking at the nasal passage with the fingernails, or too-forceful blowing of the nose. However, persistent or recurring bleeding from the nose may be a symptom of a systemic disease, such as high blood pressure, or of an infection in the nasal passages. (See also BLOOD AND BLOOD-INJURY PHOBIA; INJURY, FEAR OF.)

nosemaphobia Fear of illness is known as nosemaphobia. (See also ILLNESS, FEAR OF.)

nosocomephobia Fear of hospitals is known as nosocomephobia. Some fear that they will go in healthy for an examination and later need treatment for an infection they contracted while in the hospital. This fear is related to a fear of ILLNESS, a fear of CONTAMINATION, and a fear of GERMS. (See also CONTAMINATION, FEAR OF; HOSPITALS, FEAR OF; ILLNESS, FEAR OF.)

nosophobia Fear of disease is known as nosophobia. (See also DISEASE, FEAR OF; ILLNESS, FEAR OF.)

nostophobia Fear of returning home is known as nostophobia. (See also HOME, FEAR OF RETURNING.)

novelty, fear of Fear of novelty is known as cainophobia, cainotophobia, kainophobia, and kainotophobia; also as neophobia and centophobia. For some, novelty implies greater danger, and the strange and unfamiliar provoke fear in many individuals. Individuals who fear novelty tend to have repetitive patterns in their lives. They do not move often, usually live in the same place for a long time, keep the same job, and wear the same clothes. They tend to take vacations in the same places each year to avoid the novelty of something different. They tend to resist change of any sort. (See also CHANGE, FEAR OF; NEWNESS, FEAR OF.)

Marks, Isaac M., *Fears, Phobias and Rituals* (New York: Oxford University Press, 1987).

novercaphobia Fear of a stepmother. (See also RELATIVES, FEAR OF; STEPMOTHER, FEAR OF.)

noxiptiline An antidepressant drug. (See also ANTIDEPRESSANTS, NEW; DEPRESSION.)

nuclear war, fear of See NUCLEAR WEAPONS, FEAR OF; WAR, FEAR OF.)

nuclear weapons, fear of Fear of nuclear weapons is known as nucleomitophobia. The same term applies to fear of atomic energy. This is a 20th-century fear related to the development of atomic and nuclear power. The fear is based on a feeling by individuals that they have no control over the fate of the world and that nuclear weapons can kill off all of human life and civilization. This fear is also related to a fear of DEATH and a fear of APOCALYPSE, or the end of the world. (See also APOCALYPSE, FEAR OF; DEATH, FEAR OF.)

nucleomitophobia Fear of nuclear weapons. (See also NUCLEAR WEAPONS, FEAR OF.)

nudity, fear of Fear of nudity is known as gymnophobia and nudophobia. Some individuals fear being nude themselves, fear seeing others nude, or fear having their bodies looked at by others. This fear may be related to a SEXUAL FEAR or may be a social fear of being without the superficial "cover-up" through which one obtains identity.

nudophobia See NUDITY, FEAR OF.

numbers, fear of Fear of numbers is known as numerophobia. Some individuals have fears of particular numbers, such as thirteen. Some individuals fear working with numbers, as in doing mathematics. Many people fear the modern tendency to give everything a number instead of a name. They fear namelessness and anonymity. (See also MATHEMATICS ANXIETY; THIRTEEN, FEAR OF THE NUMBER.)

numerophobia Fear of numbers is known as numerophobia. (See also MATH PHOBIA; NUMBERS, FEAR OF; THIRTEEN.)

nyctophobia Fear of night or darkness. (See also DARKNESS, FEAR OF; NIGHT, FEAR OF.)

O

obesophobia Fear of gaining weight is known as obesophobia. (See also BODY IMAGE, FEAR OF; WEIGHT GAIN, FEAR OF.)

objective anxiety One form of ANXIETY, postulated by Sigmund FREUD, that is due to a natural fear of a certain object or event. This is contrasted with neurotic anxiety (a signal that unconscious material is being stimulated toward consciousness) and moral anxiety (which is a feeling of deviating from superego standards).

obsessions The insistent, unwanted thoughts that recur despite active resistance against their intrusion. For example, a mother may be plagued by urges to strangle her baby while it sleeps. The word obsession is derived from the Latin word *obsidere*, meaning "to besiege." Individuals who have obsessions usually also have compulsive rituals that they feel compelled to repeat against their will—for example, checking and rechecking that the lights are turned off before leaving home. (See also OBSESSIVE–COMPULSIVE DISORDER; RUMINATIONS; SENSITIVE IDEAS OF REFERENCE.)

Marks, Isaac M., *Living with Fear* (New York: McGraw-Hill, 1978).

obsessive–compulsive disorder OBSESSIONS are persistent, intense, senseless, worrisome, and often repugnant ideas, thoughts, images, or impulses that involuntarily invade consciousness. The automatic nature of these recurrent thoughts makes them difficult for the individual to ignore or restrain successfully. Furthermore, there is a strong emotional component that affects frequency and intensity.

COMPULSIONS are repetitive and seemingly purposeful acts that result from the obsessions. The individual performs certain acts according to certain rules or in a stereotyped way in order to prevent or avoid aversive consequences. However, the compulsive act is not connected in a realistic way with what it is designed to produce or prevent and is usually clearly excessive. While the individual may recognize the senselessness of the behavior and does not derive pleasure from carrying out the activity, doing so may provide a release of tension.

Obsessive PHOBIAS tend to have distinctive features. According to Isaac Marks, "They are usually part of a wide variety of fears of potential situations rather than objects or situations themselves. Because of the vagueness of these possibilities, ripples of avoidance and protective RITUALS spread far and wide to involve the patient's lifestyle and people around him. Clinical examination usually discloses obsessive rituals not directly connected with the professed fear; instead, the obsessive fear is part of a wider obsessive–compulsive disorder."

Common obsessions are repetitive thoughts of violence, contamination, and doubt. The most common compulsions involve handwashing, cleaning, counting, checking, touching, repeating, avoiding, slowing, striving for completeness, and being meticulous. CHECKING and CLEANING are the two major forms of compulsive behaviors.

This disorder was described in a classic publication in 1903 by Pierre Janet, a French physician and psychologist. He used the term "psychasthenia." Later Sigmund Freud described obsessions and compulsions in his patients as complex psychological defenses used to deal with unconscious sexual and aggressive conflicts.

DEPRESSION and ANXIETY are often associated with obsessive–compulsive disorder (and vice versa). There may be a phobic avoidance of situations that involve the content of the obsessions, such as CONTAMINATION or DIRT.

Obsessive–compulsives fear LOSS OF CONTROL. The obsessive–compulsive seems to need structures and ridigity more than others. He or she usually checks, filters, and censors all ingoing and outgoing stimuli. Obsessive–compulsives rarely drink ALCOHOL excessively because they fear becoming out of control while under the influence. Further, they endeavor to extend their sense of control to their immediate environment, and some try to force family and close friends into ritualistic patterns.

In addition to fearing loss of control, obsessive–compulsives fear uncertainty. They are constantly in doubt about how their behaviors will influence their environment and activities and they constantly ask for reassurance from others. Because of the fear of uncertainty and the need for reassurance, they are somewhat resistant to any form of medication. When medicated, they resist the effects of a drug, which takes more effort in control, with the net result that they become more, not less, anxious.

Causes

A 1984 National Institutes of Mental Health epidemiological survey found that some 2.5 percent of the population, or 5,000,000

Americans, have this disorder. In 1987, *Science News* reported that an estimated 2 percent of the adult population in the United States suffers from obsessive–compulsive disorder at some time in their lives, with one third of them developing the disorder during childhood. The disorder, which occurs equally in males and females, is less common than panic disorder.

The disorder usually begins in adolescence or early adulthood. The syndrome may begin suddenly but usually has a slow intensification over time. It usually follows a fairly chronic course, with some waxing and waning of symptoms. Impairment may be moderate to severe, and in some cases, compulsions may become the individual's major life activity. Obsessive individuals may be secretive about their symptoms.

There may be a genetically determined personality factor that influences obsessive–compulsive behavior. Generally, obsessive–compulsives indicate by scores on questionnaires that they have high degrees of emotional liability and tendencies toward long periods of high arousal. With high arousal there is a tendency toward narrowing of the span of attention, which may partially explain the obsessive–compulsive's focus on one aspect of the environment. An ability to distinguish between what is safe and what is unsafe breaks down under high levels of arousal, and the individual views all situations as potentially unsafe.

Scientists have suggested that there may be a biological explanation for some obsessive–compulsive disorders. There may be an imbalance in the frontal lobes of the brains of obsessive–compulsives that prevents the two brain regions from working together to channel and control incoming sensations and perceptions. This speculation occurred after positive emission tomography (PET) scans were used on groups of obsessive–compulsives, depressives, and those with no diagnoses. PET scanning devices transform quantitative measures of metabolic activity through the brain into color-coded pictures Metabolic rates in the forward portion of the frontal cortex were different in obsessive–compulsive individuals and individuals with serious forms of depression. However, since symptoms of severe depression, as well as anxiety, often occur among obsessive–compulsives, diagnosing the disorder with certainty can be difficult. Further studies on the range of environmental and physiological origins of obsessive–compulsive disorder are underway.

Obsessive–compulsive disorder also occurs at a high rate among victims of the brain disorder known as TOURETTE'S SYNDROME, which results in TICS and the involuntary shouting of obscenities.

Treatment

Obsessive–compulsive disorder is treated in many ways. BEHAVIOR THERAPY gained favor as a treatment during the early 1960s, and many studies of advances in treatment modalities were carried out during the 1970s and 1980s. In the course of research with obsessive–compulsives, scientists have found many differences between subgroups of obsessional–compulsive individuals. For example, researchers noted that those who have checking rituals differ from those with washing rituals, and that they respond differently to treatment. Also, differences were found between those who display overt compulsive behaviors and those who do not show such ritualistic behavior. One subgroup was found to have slowness (slow, methodical approach to activities of daily living) as a primary characteristic, and they differ significantly from the checkers, washers, and ruminators. Several major studies have investigated these subgroups of obsessive–compulsives.

Imagery is an important part of obsessive–compulsive disorder and its treatment. Commonly, there are obsessional images, compulsive images, disaster images, and disruptive images. The disaster image has been well-suited for a habituation-training approach. The disaster image is a secondary event arising from an obsession or a compulsive urge and serves to increase the anxiety and distress of the individual. In many cases, content of disaster images is of future disasters and catastrophes. Habituation training to these images may prove to be helpful in treating individuals whose symptoms include this particular type of image. Researchers have found that with checkers, imaginal exposure to feared disasters, when used in combination with response prevention procedures, leads to better long-term outcomes. Perhaps the fears of these individuals are the same as, or closely associated with, the disaster images others have.

The anxiety caused by an obsession is partially the result of its unwantedness and intrusiveness. When the individual can gain mastery or control over it, such anxiety can be alleviated.

When the class of drugs known as MAO INHIBITORS were developed during the sixties, treatment for obsessive–compulsive disorder began to include them. One such drug, CLOMIPRAMINE, is at least 20 percent effective in curing all cases and a significant help in most others.

Studies have also been underway to determine the possible use of tricyclic drugs in curing obsessional disorders. It may be that individuals who are treated and cured of a clinical or subclinical depressive illness will be able to reduce their ritualistic behavior.

Pharmaceutical therapy must be administered cautiously to obsessive–compulsives. Researchers have found that some obsessive thoughts may rapidly worsen after the individual takes a drug that stimulates a specific class of brain receptors. (See table following this entry.) (See also ANTIDEPRESSANTS; ANXIETY DISORDERS; DRUGS; FLOODING; IMAGERY; JANET, PIERRE; MODELING.)

American Psychiatric Association, *Diagnostic and Statistical Manual of Mental Disorders,* 3rd ed. (Washington, DC: American Psychiatric Association, 1986).

Goodwin, Donald W., *Phobia, the Facts* (Oxford: Oxford U. Press, 1983).

Boulougouris, J.C. and A.D. Rabavilas, *The Treatment of Phobic and Obsessive Compulsive Disorders* (Oxford: Pergamon Press, 1971).

Marks, Isaac, *Fears and Phobias* (New York: Academic Press, 1969).

Bower, Bruce, "Images of Obsession," *Science News* (April 11, 1987), pp. 236–237.

deSilva, Padmal, "Obsessional–Compulsive Imagery." *Behavior Research and Therapy* 24(1986): 333–350.

ochlophobia Fear of crowds or being in crowded places is known as ochlophobia. (See also AGORAPHOBIA; CROWDS, FEAR OF.)

ochophobia Fear of being in an automobile or other moving vehicle is known as ochophobia. (See also AUTOMOBILES, FEAR OF; MOTION; FEAR OF.)

odonophobia Fear of teeth is known as odonophobia. (See also DENTAL ANXIETY; TEETH, FEAR OF.)

odors, certain, fear of Fear of particular odors is known as chromophobia, chromatophobia, olfactophobia, and osmophobia. Individuals may develop fears of certain odors because of traumatic experiences, associations with fearful situations or objects, or for many other reasons. Some fear odors of foods in general or those of particular foods. Usually the phobic individual reacts to particular smells, such as types of foods, perfumes, stale odors, etc., and becomes anxious in the presence of these odors. Some fear body odors from themselves or others. Some fear odors in nature, such as flowers, trees, grasses, or molds. Most develop this type of phobia through CLASSICAL CONDITIONING.

Benjamin Rush (1745–1813), American physician and author, commented on "the odor phobia": "The Odor phobia is a very frequent disease with all classes of people.

Obsessive–Compulsive Self-Test

Many individuals who have obsessive–compulsive symptoms have difficulty with some of the following activities. Answer each question by writing the appropriate number next to it.

0 No problem with activity—takes me same time as average person, I do not need to repeat or avoid it.

1 Activity takes me twice *as long as most people, or I have to repeat it* twice, *or I* tend *to avoid it.*

2 Activity takes me three *times as long as most people, or I have to repeat it* three *or more times, or I* usually *avoid it.*

A high total score indicates the severity of the disorder.

Score	Activity	Score	Activity
____	Having a bath or shower	____	Visiting a hospital
____	Washing hands and face	____	Turning lights and tapes on or off
____	Care of hair (e.g., washing, combing, brushing)	____	Locking or closing doors or windows
____	Brushing teeth	____	Using electrical apparatus (e.g., heaters)
____	Dressing and undressing	____	Doing arithmetic or accounts
____	Using toilet to urinate	____	Getting to work
____	Using toilet to defecate	____	Doing own work
____	Touching people or being touched	____	Writing
____	Handling waste or waste bins	____	Form filling
____	Washing clothing	____	Posting letters
____	Washing dishes	____	Reading
____	Handling or cooking food	____	Walking down the street
____	Cleaning the house	____	Traveling by bus, train or car
____	Keeping things tidy	____	Looking after children
____	Bed making	____	Eating in restaurants
____	Cleaning shoes	____	Going to cinemas or theaters
____	Touching door handles	____	Going to public places
____	Touching own genitals, petting or sexual intercourse	____	Keeping appointments
____	Throwing things away	____	Looking at and talking to people
		____	Buying things in shops
____	= ____ Total	____	= ____ Total

There are few men or women to whom smells of some kind are not disagreeable. Old cheese has often produced paleness and tremor in a full-fed guest. There are odors from certain flowers that produce the same effects: hence it is not altogether a figure to say, that there are persons who 'die of a rose in aromatic pain.' " (See also SMELL, FEAR OF; TASTE, FEAR OF.)

Runes, D.D. (ed.), *The Selected Writings of Benjamin Rush* (New York: The Philosophical Library, 1947).

odors, fear of body Fear of body odors is known as osphreisiophobia or bromidrosiphobia. (See also BODY ODOR, FEAR OF.)

odynesphobia Fear of pain is known as odynesphobia, odynephobia, and odynophobia. (See also PAIN, FEAR OF.)

Oedipus complex Attachment of the child to the parent of the opposite sex, accompanied by envious and aggressive feelings toward the parent of the same sex. These feelings are largely repressed, or made UNCONSCIOUS because of the fear of displeasure or punishment by the parent of the same sex. Many individuals have PHOBIAS and ANXIETIES resulting from an unresolved Oedipus complex. The Oedipus complex, originally described by Sigmund FREUD, is a crucial component of Freudian psychology. It derives from the Greek myth of Oedipus, who unwittingly killed his father and married his mother. In its original use, the term applied only to the boy or man in his relationship with his mother. The term Electra complex applied to girls and women and their relationships with their fathers.

American Psychiatric Association, *Psychiatric Glossary* (Washington, DC: American Psychiatric Association, 1988).

oenophobia Fear of wine is known as oenophobia or oinophobia. (See also ALCOHOL, FEAR OF; WINE, FEAR OF.)

oikophobia Fear of home surroundings is known as oikophobia. (See also HOME SURROUNDINGS, FEAR OF.)

old, growing, fear of Fear of growing old is known as gerascophobia. (See also AGING, FEAR OF; RETIREMENT, FEAR OF; WRINKLES, FEAR OF.)

olfactophobia Fear of odors is known as olfactophobia. (See also ODORS, FEAR OF; SMELL, FEAR OF.)

ombrophobia Fear of rain is known as ombrophobia. (See also RAIN, FEAR OF; STORMS, FEAR OF.)

ommatophobia Fear of eyes is known as ommatophobia and ommetaphobia. (See also BEING LOOKED AT, FEAR OF; EYES, FEAR OF.)

oneirophobia Fear of dreams is known as oneirophobia. (See also DREAMS, FEAR OF; NIGHT TERRORS; NIGHTMARES.)

oneirogmophobia Fear of wet dreams is known as oneirogmophobia. (See also DREAMS, FEAR OF; SEXUAL FEARS; WET DREAMS, FEAR OF.)

one's own voice Fear of one's own voice is known as phonophobia. Some individuals fear hearing their own voice on a recording or in an ECHO. Some fear that their voice does not project a powerful image, and thus fear of one's own voice may be related to a fear of PUBLIC SPEAKING, speaking over the TELEPHONE, and in speaking out loud in social situations. (See also SOCIAL PHOBIA.)

one thing, fear of Fear of one thing is known as monophobia. Many individuals who have SIMPLE PHOBIAS, such as fear of DOGS, fear of THUNDERSTORMS, etc., have fear of only one thing. Some individuals who have SOCIAL PHOBIAS also fear only one thing, such as PUBLIC SPEAKING or entering a crowded room. (See also PHOBIA.)

oneself, fear of being See BEING ONESELF, FEAR OF.

onomatophobia Fear of names, or of hearing certain names. (See also NAMES, FEAR OF.)

Open Door Association, The One of the largest societies for agoraphobic individuals in the world, The Open Door has helped thousands of individuals recover from their fears. Membership details and lists of area secretaries throughout Britain are available from:

Mrs. Mona Woodford
The Open Door Association
447 Pensby Road
Haswall, Merseyside
England

(See also PHOBIA SOCIETY OF AMERICA.)

open places and open spaces See EMPTY ROOMS, FEAR OF.)

open spaces See AGORAPHOBIA.

opening one's eyes, fear of See EYES, FEAR OF.

operant conditioning A method of learning. Operant conditioning involves the strengthening or weakening of some aspect of a response (for example, its form, frequency, intensity, etc.) based on the presentation of consequences. The two basic forms of operant learning are CONTINGENCY MANAGEMENT and operant shaping. Contingency management involves the manipulation of existing stimuli that precede or signal the behavior (such as taking cookies out of the cupboard to stop a child from climbing and opening the cupboard), or manipulation of stimuli that follow it as consequences (reinforcement or punishment). Shaping involves selective reinforcement for approximation to a particular behavior until the final behavior is emitted.

The term was coined by Burrhus Frederic SKINNER, an American psychologist (1904–), who applied understanding of operant conditioning to psychotherapy, language, learning, educational methods, and cultural analysis. In 1950, Ogden Lindsley, a student of Skinner's, made the first systematic attempts to apply the techniques of operant conditioning in a psychiatric ward to develop speech and cooperation. Teodoro Ayllon (1929–), a researcher at Anna State Hospital, Anna, Illinois, later developed a TOKEN ECONOMY that could be applied in a controlled setting such as a mental-hospital ward or a classroom setting. The principles of operant conditioning have been the basis for programs that successfully treat a wide range of human behavior problems, habit problems, and behavioral deficiencies, and that elicit and maintain new behavior development. Operant conditioning researchers have applied this methodology to study in the development and treatment of behavioral and cognitive manifestations of anxiety. (See also BEHAVIOR MODIFICATION; CONDITIONING.)

ophidiophobia Fear of snakes and/or reptiles. Fear of snakes is also known as ophiophobia, ophiciophobia, herpetophobia, and snake phobia. (See also SNAKE QUESTIONNAIRE; SNAKES, FEAR OF.)

ophthalmophobia Fear of being stared at. (See also STARED AT, FEAR OF BEING.)

opinions, fear of others' Fear of others' opinions is known as allodoxaphobia. Individuals who fear CRITICISM OR RIDICULE fear opinions of others. Some social phobics have this fear. (See also CLASSIFICATION OF PHOBIAS; SOCIAL PHOBIA.)

opposite sex, fear of Fear of the opposite sex is known as sexophobia. Some individuals fear those of the opposite sex in business and/or social situations. For some this fear may be a fear of sexual activity, a fear of a mother, a fear of a father, or a repressed feeling of sexual desire toward the parent of the opposite sex. The fear seems unrelated to the development of homosexuality. (See also SEXUAL FEARS.)

optophobia Fear of opening one's eyes. (See also EYES, FEAR OF OPENING.)

oral stage In psychoanalytic theory, the first psychosexual stage of human development. The oral stage, as first described by SIGMUND FREUD in 1905, occurs during the first one to two years of life. During this period, the infant maintains a relationship with the outside world through its mouth. Also, the mouth acts as an erogenous zone from which the infant derives sexual pleasure from eating, sucking, and kissing. Successful transition through the oral stage is necessary for development into later stages. Without successful transition, later ANXIETIES, FEARS, and PHOBIAS may develop, according to psychoanalytic thinking. (See also ANAL STAGE; GENITAL STAGE; PHALLIC STAGE.)

orderliness (as a ritual) Some individuals, out of fear, feel compelled to organize and arrange objects in a particular way, such as items on a desk or on a kitchen counter. They become fearful and upset if anyone moves an item or attempts to interfere with their compulsion. The fear of disorder and disarray is known as ataxiophobia. (See also DISORDER, FEAR OF; OBSESSIVE–COMPULSIVE DISORDER; RITUAL.)

organic approach The theory that all disorders, mental and physical, have a physiological, biological, or biochemical basis. The organic approach is also known as organic viewpoint and organicism. In psychiatry, those who hold this view say that all psychotic disorders, including MANIC–DEPRESSIVE DISORDER and SCHIZOPHRENIA, as well as all anxiety disorders, result from structural brain changes or biochemical disturbances of the nervous or glandular system. The organic approach was suggested by Hippocrates (460 B.C.?) and Galen (Greek physician, A.D. 130?) and was systematically developed by Wilhelm Griesinger and Emil KRAEPELIN during the latter half of the 19th century. It has been the dominant but less obvious viewpoint in psychiatry within the last century. (See also BIOLOGICAL BASIS FOR ANXIETY.)

ornithophobia Fear of birds is known as ornithophobia. (See also BIRDS, FEAR OF; FEATHERS, FEAR OF.)

Orr, Leonard Founder of Theta, a San Francisco group that grew out of the EST (Erhard Seminars Training) therapy movement. In 1968 Orr went from sales work to reading and experimenting with self-improvement ideas. He worked as an EST counselor and eventually developed his own concept of "rebirthing," which proposes that the only way to get rid of the anxieties or negative feelings resulting from the birth trauma is to experience simulated birth as an adult. In 1977, with coauthor Sondra Ray, Orr published *Rebirthing in the New Age*.

Corsini, Raymond, *Handbook of Innovative Psychotherapies* (New York: Wiley, 1981).

"Leonard Orr," *New York Times* (Nov. 19, 1976), p. 36.

orthophobia Fear of propriety is known as orthophobia. (See also PROPRIETY, FEAR OF.)

osmophobia Fear of odors is known as osmophobia. (See also ODORS, FEAR OF; SMELL, FEAR OF.)

osphreisiophobia Fear of body odor, either one's own or that of someone else, is known as osphreisiophobia. (See also BODY ODOR, FEAR OF; ODORS, FEAR OF.)

ostraconophobia Fear of shellfish is known as ostraconophobia. (See also FISH, FEAR OF; SHELLFISH, FEAR OF.)

ouranophobia Fear of heaven or thoughts related to heaven is known as ouranophobia. (See also GOD, FEAR OF; HEAVEN, FEAR OF; THEOLOGY, FEAR OF.)

outer space, fear of Fear of outer space is known as spacephobia. This fear is based on a fear of the UNKNOWN. Man has fearfully wondered for years if there is life in the alien, totally dark, soundless, and airless environment known as outer space. Discovery of the immensity and shape of the universe, the possibilities of other universes, theories about black holes, white holes, and "worm holes" that might connect one universe to another are disturbing because they are difficult concepts to comprehend. Scholarly theologians have interpreted these findings in light of their beliefs, but many people find these matters not only incomprehensible but somewhat frightening.

While some books and films portray extraterrestrials as highly advanced, nonthreatening beings, others have portrayed beings from outer space as violent invaders or exploiters of the earth. An example is Orson Welles's radio play of H. G. Wells's *War of the Worlds,* which caused a national panic in 1938 when listeners thought Martians had invaded earth in spite of announcements preceding and during the program indicating that the broadcast was fictional. Unidentified flying object sightings started during World War II; these produced many theories of alien observation of earth, including interest in the atomic bomb and in colonizing earth. Kidnappings by extraterrestrials were reported. Fears were expressed that the United States government was covering up evidence regarding UFOs and even hiding the side of a crashed alien space ship. (See SPACE TRAVEL, FEAR OF; UNKNOWN, FEAR OF.)

Newlon, Clarke, *1001 Questions Answered about Space* (New York: Dodd, Mead, 1962).

Oberg, James E., *UFOs & Outer Space Mysteries* (Norfolk, VA: Donning, 1982).

Steiger, Brad and John White (eds.), *Other Worlds, Other Universes* (Garden City, NY: Doubleday, 1975).

Story, Ronald, *The Space Gods Revealed* (New York: Harper and Row, 1976).

P

pagophobia Fear of ice or frost. (See also FROST, FEAR OF; ICE, FEAR OF.

pain, fear of Fear of pain is known as algophobia, odynesphobia, and odynophobia. Pain is a sensation that hurts enough to make one uncomfortable; it may be mild distress or severe discomfort, acute or chronic. Acute pain is usually severe and lasts a relatively short time. Chronic pain may be mild or severe and is present to some degree for long periods of time. Pain is often a signal that body tissue is being damaged in some way. Pain can only be defined by the person who is feeling it. It cannot be verified by someone else.

Mankind has suffered and feared pain since the beginning of time. Although a wide variety of drugs are now available to ease pain, pain is still a fearful subject, and the prospect of having pain makes people anxious. Fear of pain is evidenced by avoidance of potentially painful situations such as visits to doctors or dentists and dislike or avoidance of hospitals, rehabilitation centers, etc. The phobic individual's reaction is usually anticipatory and often not the result of any traumatic event in his or her life. This phobia is a good example of how reactions become sensitized and expanded by cognitive processes that operate during avoidance.

Some people find pain very difficult to explain. The fact that they cannot explain it to their doctor or others around them contributes to their anxiety and feelings of tension.

pain, anxiety and depression in

ANXIETY or DEPRESSION are rarely the only causes of pain. Both can make pain seem worse. Most people with pain have some emotional reaction to it. Some feel depressed, worried, or easily discouraged when they have pain. Some feel out of control, hopeless, or helpless. Others feel alone or embarrassed, inadequate, angry, or frightened.

Anxiety or depression that accompany the pain of illness or injury may be caused by problems other than pain. For example, one may have concerns over family or friends, spiritual problems, or difficulties with insurance or money because of illness.

Fatigue can intensify pain. If one is tired, one may not be able to cope with pain as well as when one is rested. Some individuals who have chronic pain fear fatigue or fear getting too tired to cope with their painful condition.

Relief of pain and accompanying anxiety

Drugs

In addition to prescription pain relievers and over-the-counter medications for pain, tricyclic ANTIDEPRESSANTS such as Sinequan, Elavil, and Tofranil, taken daily, can help relieve depression associated with pain for some individuals. This antidepressant action is usually noticeable in about fourteen to twenty-one days. Antidepressants may also help stimulate appetite in a person whose pain or condition makes him or her uninterested in eating. Individuals with pain and depression who take antidepressant medications should be aware that the side effects of tricyclic antidepressants include dry mouth, bad dreams, dizziness, and nausea. The dizziness and nausea usually end within two weeks, but dry mouth may continue.

Some individuals who have pain that makes them feel anxious and irritable take tranquilizers to calm them and make it easier for them to cope with pain. Tranquilizers can make nonmedical methods of pain relief more effective and might enable one to take lower doses of analgesics (pain relievers).

Marijuana has been reported to reduce anxiety and control nausea so that a person in pain feels better. However, some individuals with cancer have reported that smoking marijuana actually increased their pain. In experimental studies, tetrahydrocannabinol (THC), the active substance in marijuana, has been found to have mild analgesic effects, but it cannot be recommended for pain relief because it causes HALLUCINATIONS and extreme drowsiness. THC is now available to physicians on an investigational basis for the treatment of nausea and vomiting in cancer patients who are receiving CHEMOTHERAPY.

Non-medication techniques to relieve pain include relaxation, imagery, transcutaneous electric nerve stimulation (TENS), biofeedback, and acupuncture.

Relaxation

Relaxation relieves pain or keeps it from getting worse by reducing tension in the muscles. Relaxation can reduce ANXIETY and help one fall asleep, become more energetic or less tired, and make other pain-relief methods work better. For example, some people find that a pain medicine or a cold or hot pack works faster and better if they are able to relax at the same time.

Imagery
Imagery is a mental picture or situation an individual creates by using his or her imagination. How imagery relieves pain is not completely understood. Imagery can be thought of as a deliberate daydream that uses all of one's senses: sight, touch, hearing, smell, and taste. Some believe that imagery is a form of self-hypnosis. Certain images may reduce one's pain both during the time one imagines them and for hours afterwards. When using imagery, one can decrease anxiety, relax, relieve boredom, and fall asleep more easily.

Transcutaneous electric nerve stimulation (TENS).
TENS is a technique in which mild electric currents are applied to selected areas of the skin by a small power pack connected to two electrodes. The sensation is described as a pleasant buzzing, tingling, or tapping feeling; it does not feel like a shock. The small electric impulses seem to interfere with pain sensations. Pain relief usually lasts beyond the time that the current is applied.

Biofeedback
Some individuals learn to control certain body functions such as heart rate, blood pressure, and muscle tension with the help of special machines that indicate how a part or function of the body is responding to stress. Biofeedback is sometimes used to help people learn to relax. Headache patients can use biofeedback techniques to reduce anxiety in order to help them cope with their pain. Usually biofeedback is used in combination with other pain-relief measures.

Acupuncture
In acupuncture, special needles are inserted into the body at certain points and at various depths and angles. Particular groups of acupuncture points are believed to control specific areas of pain sensation. The procedure has been used in China for thousands of years, and elsewhere for a lesser time, to treat many types of pain and as an anesthetic.

Hypnosis
Hypnosis is a trancelike state that can be induced by a person trained in the special technique. During hypnosis a person is very receptive to suggestions made by the hypnotist. To relieve pain, the hypnotist may suggest that when the person "wakes up" pain will be gone. Some cancer patients have learned methods of self-hypnosis that they use to control pain. However, the effectiveness of hypnosis for pain relief is unpredictable. (See also ACUPUNCTURE; BIOFEEDBACK; FATIGUE, FEAR OF; HYPNOSIS; PHANTOM LIMB PAIN; TRANQUILIZERS.)
(Source: American Cancer Society.)

painful sexual intercourse, fear of
See DYSPAREUNIA, FEAR OF.

Pamelor See NORTRIPTYLINE.

Pan See PANIC.

panic, panic attacks, and panic disorder Panic attacks strike some individuals with little warning and for no apparent reason. Panic attacks strike mostly women in their childbearing years. About 4,000,000 to 10,000,000 individuals in the United States experience panic attacks each year.

Panic and panic attacks cover many discomforts, including an abrupt surge of anxiety with a feeling of impending doom that quickly peaks. Panic may be elicited by particular stimuli or by thinking about it. Also, it may occur unpredictably and spontaneously without any cues. A panic attack is not like ordinary anxiety and nervousness most people feel before a job interview or giving a speech. Symptoms of a panic attack include lightheadedness, dizziness, rubbery legs, difficult breathing, a racing, palpitating heart, and choking and tingling sensations.

The word panic is derived from the name of the god the Greeks worshipped as their god of flocks, herds, pastures, and fields, known as Pan. The Greek word for "all" is also *pan*. Man was dependent on Pan to make the flocks fertile; Pan himself was a lustful creature known for his ability to reproduce. Pan's shape was that of a goat; a goat could traverse fields and dart through herds of cattle. Pan, the goat god, loved to scare people. He would dart out of the woods and frighten passersby, often in dark forests and at night. He would make eerie noises. The fright he created was known as "panic." Later, Pan fell out of favor because the Christian church portrayed the devil with the goat god's features; his two horns symbolized the philosophy of devil worship.

Nearly all severe phobics (except some blood and food phobics) have phobic panic, making it difficult to classify phobias according to the presence of panic. During phobic panic, nearly all phobics feel changes in heart rate, tense muscles, and sweaty palms. Spontaneous panic is most common in agoraphobia and in panic disorder without agoraphobia. However, between thirty-three percent and seventy percent of agoraphobics do not have panic. Spontaneous panic also can be elicited by taking amphetamine or caffeine and during WITHDRAWAL from opiates and BARBITURATES.

Nearly all phobics and individuals who have OBSESSIVE–COMPULSIVE DISORDER, panic disorder, generalized anxiety disorder (GAD), and severe depression experience panic at some time or other. (See also AGORAPHOBIA; ANXIETY DISORDERS; PHOBIA.)

Marks, Isaac M., *Fears, Phobias and Rituals* (New York: Oxford University Press, 1987).

panphobia Also known as panophobia, pantophobia, and pamphobia. A fear of anything and everything. Panphobia may be a form of ANXIETY rather than a true phobia.

paper, fear of Fear of paper is known as papyrophobia. This fear may include touching paper, seeing paper, being cut by the edge of paper, or even thinking about paper. Fear of paper may extend to wrapping paper, wallpaper, or drawing paper. It may be a fear of the paper itself or of writing or printing on paper. Fear of paper is classified as a SIMPLE PHOBIA, because it is a fear of one thing. (See also PHOBIA.)

papyrophobia Fear of paper. (See also PAPER, FEAR OF.)

paradoxical intention A technique used to treat phobias. The phobic individual is instructed to think strongly and imagine himself in his phobic situation or facing the feared object. He is asked to magnify his fear reactions, such as rapid breathing in an actual phobic situation. Paradoxical intention is based on an understanding of the effects of anticipatory anxiety and the self-fulfilling prophecy. The goal of paradoxical intention is to teach individuals that they can control symptoms instead of allowing symptoms to control them; reverse the instinctive avoidance of the feared object, situation, or event; and break the cycle through which anticipatory anxiety produces symptoms. (See also ANTICIPATORY ANXIETY; EXISTENTIAL THERAPY; FLOODING.)

paradoxical therapy A method of therapy for phobias developed by VIKTOR

FRANKL (1905–), a German-born American psychiatrist. In this method, the phobic individual magnifies his fear reactions, such as heavy breathing or sweating in an actual fearful situation, under the direction of a psychotherapist. Doing so enables the individual to see his symptoms objectively, particularly if he is able to see humor in the situation and laugh at himself. It also undoubtedly desensitizes the patient to the sensations of the body that occur with anxiety. (See also BEHAVIOR THERAPY; IMPLOSIVE THERAPY; PARADOXICAL INTENTION.)

paraliphobia Also known as paralipophobia and hypengyophobia. Fear of neglecting duty, obligations, or responsibility. (See also RESPONSIBILITY, FEAR OF.)

paranoid Relating to a mental disorder characterized primarily by delusions. Paranoid delusions may include grandiosity or persecution. The word comes from the Greek word meaning "derangement" or "madness." In psychiatric terms, paranoid ideation is thinking, in less than delusional proportions, involving suspiciousness or the belief that one is being harassed, persecuted, or unfairly treated. In some instances the term is used when the therapist is unsure of whether the disturbances are actually delusional. There are some aspects of paranoid thinking in AGORAPHOBIA and other phobic syndromes in which the individual wrongly believes that he is being watched or observed. (See also IDEAS OF REFERENCE; SENSITIVE IDEAS OF REFERENCE.)

paranoid delusions See DELUSIONS; PARANOID.

paranormal cognition See EXTRASENSORY PERCEPTION (ESP).

paraphobia See SEXUAL PERVERSIONS, FEAR OF.

parasites, fear of Fear of parasites is known as parasitophobia or phthiriophobia. This fear may extend to any tiny organism such as a virus, bacterium, or fungus that lives in or on another organism (the host) and at some time in its life takes all or part of its nourishment from the host. Some people fear that they may become infested with parasites but do not believe that they are currently infested. Some who believe that they are hosting parasites pick, scratch, and tear their skin until they develop sores out of fear of the damage the parasites will do. They may display bits of skin as examples of the parasites.

Fears of parasites are not totally unfounded,, as some parasites are harmful to one's health and cause disease. Parasites may exist in the intestinal tract, where they have access to predigested food. Hookworms and tapeworms are examples. Parasites elsewhere in the body can damage cells, block organ ducts, cause toxic or allergic reations, and stimulate the host's tissue to a point where abnormal growths are formed. (See also CONTAMINATION, FEAR OF; DISEASE, FEAR OF; GERMS, FEAR OF.)

parasitophobia Fear of parasites. (See also PARASITES, FEAR OF.)

parents-in-law, fear of Fear of parents-in-law is known as soceraphobia. (See also RELATIVES, FEAR OF.)

parnate See TRANYLCYPRAMINE.

parthenophobia Fear of girls, or specifically of virgins. (See also GIRLS, FEAR OF; SEXUAL FEARS; VIRGINS, FEAR OF.)

parties, fear of going to Fear of going to parties is a SOCIAL PHOBIA. Some individuals fear making a bad impression, fear meeting new people, and fear being in a new situation. Some worry about criticism and ridicule of their appearance or speech. Although this is a fairly common fear in adolescence, for many individuals the fear continues into adulthood. Various forms of behavior therapy have been successful in treating many social phobics. (See also PHOBIA.)

pathophobia Fear of disease or illness. (See also DISEASE, FEAR OF.)

patroiophobia Fear of heredity. (See also HEREDITY, FEAR OF.)

Pavlov, Ivan Petrovich (1849–1936) A Russian physiologist known for his theories of learning based on conditioning techniques. Pavlov was trained in physics, chemistry, and medicine; his major interests were the physiology of digestion and how digestion was controlled by the nervous system. While experimenting with dogs, Pavlov noticed that gastric and salivary secretions occurred in connection with a specific noise made during the preparation of food. This observation led to further experiments (pairing a bell with food) from which he developed the concepts of differentiation between stimuli, UNCONDITIONED RESPONSE, and conditioned reflex, and the inducement as well as elimination of experimental neuroses in animals. Later, when he focused on human neuroses, Pavlov developed the theory that neuroses, including some fears and phobias, are due to an imbalance between the excitatory and inhibitory functions of the cortex. (See also CONDITIONED RESPONSE; CONDITIONED STIMULUS.)

Kleinknecht, Ronald A., *The Anxious Self* (New York: Human Sciences Press, 1986).

Pavlovian conditioning A pattern of learning discovered near the end of the nineteenth century by Russian physiologist IVAN P. PAVLOV. (See also AVERSION THERAPY; CLASSICAL CONDITIONING.)

pavor nocturnus See NIGHT TERRORS; NIGHTMARES.

pavor scleris See BAD MEN, FEAR OF.

peanut butter Fear of peanut butter sticking to the roof of the mouth is known as arachibutyrophobia. This fear is related to fears of SWALLOWING and GAGGING. Spreading peanut butter on an apple slice prevents it from sticking.

peccatiphobia Fear of sinning or wrongdoing. Also known as peccatophobia. (See also SIN, FEAR OF.)

pediaphobia Fear of dolls or small figures. This fear may also extend to a fear of small children or infants who look like dolls. (See also DOLLS, FEAR OF.)

pediculosis Fear of lice. (See also LICE, FEAR OF.)

pedophobia Fear of children, dolls, or infants. (See also CHILDREN, FEAR OF; DOLLS, FEAR OF; INFANTS, FEAR OF.)

peladophobia Fear of bald people or of becoming bald oneself. (See also BALD PEOPLE, FEAR OF.)

pellagra, fear of Fear of pellagra is known as pellagraphobia. Pellagra is a chronic disease caused by niacin deficiency and characterized by skin eruptions, digestive and nervous disturbances, and eventual mental deterioration. (See also ILLNESS PHOBIA.)

pellagrophobia Fear of pellagra. Individuals with this fear may take large doses of niacin in an effort to combat their feared disease. (See also PELLAGRA, FEAR OF.)

peniaphobia Fear of poverty. (See also POVERTY, FEAR OF; RUIN, FEAR OF.)

penis, contour through one's clothes, fear of Fear of the contour of a penis being visible through clothes is known as medectophobia. (See also SEXUAL FEARS.)

penis captivus, fear of Fear of having one's penis held tightly by the female's vaginal muscles during sexual intercourse. This fear may be related to the male's fear of castration and to female castration impulses. It is possible for a female to deliberately produce strong spasmodic vaginal muscle tightening around the penis during intercourse, but this usually is not harmful to the penis. (See also CASTRATION ANXIETY; SEXUAL FEARS.)

penis, fear of erect Fear of an erect penis is known as ithyphallophobia or medorthophobia. (See also PENIS, CONTOUR THROUGH ONE'S CLOTHES, FEAR OF; SEXUAL FEARS.)

penis fear Fear of penises is known as phallophobia. These fears usually relate to anxiety regarding social judgment about the size of one's penis or social embarrassment about having an erection in public. (See also PENIS, FEAR OF ERECT; PSYCHOSEXUAL FEARS.)

pentheraphobia Fear of one's mother-in-law. (See also MOTHER-IN-LAW, FEAR OF.)

people, fear of Fear of people, or of human beings or human society, is known as anthropophobia. Manifestations of this PHOBIA at its extreme would involve complete avoidance of people. (See also SOCIAL PHOBIA.)

performance anxiety Performance anxiety, or stage fright, is a form of SOCIAL PHOBIA. Performance anxiety is a persistent, irrational fear of exposure to scrutiny in certain situations, particularly public speaking and musical, dramatic, or other types of performances. Some musicians are more prone to anxiety than performers in other disciplines because musicians have spent many years practicing by themselves, away from people. Actors, however, even though they train with other people, still may experience extreme performance anxiety when they appear before the public.

Some individuals experience performance anxiety in activities that are not scrutinized by the public, such as doing mechanical work or taking tests. Individuals who have this fear worry about doing something over which they might become embarrassed or humiliated. They tend to "catastrophize," or worry about what might happen in the worst possible cases. Catastrophizing thoughts might include: "I think I'm going to faint," "I don't think I will be able to get through to the end without cracking up," "I'm almost sure to make a dreadful mistake, and that will ruin everything," "I mustn't think about the possibility of making a mistake, or else I'll get into a state," "I don't feel in control of the situation; anything might happen," or "I think I'm going to be sick."

Symptoms may involve features of anxiety attacks, including dry mouth, lump in the throat, faintness, palpitations, rapid pulse, trembling, sweating, stomach upset, frequent urination, and inability to move. Some will avoid the situations, and some overcome these feelings and go through with their performance.

Treatment

Treatment includes positive thinking, with the individual—for example, a musician—repeatedly telling himself or herself, "I know I'm good and have prepared well for this; I'll go on and make them sit up and notice me," "I've prepared properly, so even if I do lose concentration for a bit my fingers can play the notes automatically," or "This concert is really going to be exciting."

Others use a mixed strategy—for example, thinking, "I will just concentrate on the music and ignore everything else," "I will just concentrate on staying relaxed," or "It's not the audience I worry about, it's my colleagues—if I mess it up, they are sure to notice."

To overcome audience sensitivity, some individuals use cognitive coping statements such as: "I will pretend the audience is not there and that it is a rehearsal," "The audience have paid their money; if I mess up I will be letting them down," or "I am in control; this tenseness I feel is an ally."

Learning to cope with performance anxiety includes cognitive therapy and repeated exposure to an audience. Experience before an audience, for most performers, tends to reduce anxieties over time. However, it is difficult to determine whether the performances themselves enable people to be more comfortable or whether the most anxious performers, such as musicians, leave the field because of their anxieties.

Drug treatment

Because many antianxiety drugs (such as benzodiazepines) cause drowsiness, other medications have been sought to combat performance anxiety. Beta-blockers have been tried with some degree of success. This class of drugs inhibits the activity of some NEUROTRANSMITTERS that are often associated with producing the physical symptoms of anxiety. The drug most often used in studies has been PROPRANOLOL. It has been helpful for musicians, public speakers, pilots, students taking examinations, and athletes. Preliminary studies have indicated that propranolol should be taken in a single dose just before exposure to the situation about which the individual feels anxious. However, some beta-blockers are not safe for individuals who have ASTHMA or other lung disorders, cardiovascular disease, diabetes, or hypothyroidism.

In a study begun in 1988 at the Laboratory for the Study of Behavioral Medicine, Stanford University Medical Center, performance anxiety was treated in a program that combines counseling with the use of buspirone (trade name: Buspar), a new nonaddictive, nonsedating antianxiety medication. Buspirone, however, takes three to four weeks of use to become effective as an antianxiety agent. (See chart following.) (See also ANXIETY; BUSPIRONE; STAGE FRIGHT.)

Behavior Observed in Performance Anxiety

Paces
Sways
Shuffles feet
Knees tremble
Extraneous arm and hand movement (swings, scratches, toys, etc.)
Arms rigid
Hands restrained (in pockets, behind back, clasped)
Hand tremors
No eye contact
Face muscles tense (drawn, tics, grimaces)
Face "deadpan"
Face pale
Face flushed (blushes)
Moisten lips
Swallows
Clears throat
Breathes heavily
Perspires (face, hands, armpits)
Voice quivers
Speech blocks or stammers

Adapted from Davison and Neale's *Abnormal Psychology* (New York: John Wiley, 1986).

Harvard Medical School Mental Health Letter (November 1987), p. 8.
Goodkind, Mike, "Researcher Seeks Cure to Music Jitters," Stanford University Medical Center, (Jan. 6, 1988), news release.
Steptoe, A. and H. Fidler, "Stage Fright in Orchestral Musicians: A Study of Cognitive and Behavioral Strategies in Performance Anxiety," *British Journal of Psychology,* 78(1987), pp. 241–249.

Perls, Frederick (Fritz) (1893–1970) A German-born American psychotherapist. Perls left Germany in 1934 and founded the South African Institute of Psychoanalysis. He developed many revisions of classical psychoanalytic theory and was the first person to use the term gestalt therapy in the title of a book. In 1946, with his wife, Laura, Perls founded the New York Institute for Gestalt Therapy, where GESTALT THERAPY training was developed, and a second institute in Cleveland. Perls moved to California and conducted much of his work from the Esalen Institute. Perls used the term phobic attitude to describe behavior patterns involving disruptions in awareness of and attention to present experiences, such as having fantasies to escape an uncomfortable current reality.

personal filth, fear of Fear of personal filth is similar to a fear of being dirty, which is known as automysophobia. This is a common fear of those who have obsessive–compulsive disorder. (See also CONTAMINATION, FEAR OF; DIRT, FEAR OF.)

personal odor, fear of Fear of personal odor is known as bromidrophobia. This may relate to BODY ODOR, odor from soap, hair, perfume, clothing, or shoes, or anything else about the person. Some individuals fear personal odors from themselves; other individuals fear personal odors from others.

personality disorders Patterns of relating to other people, perceiving, and thinking that are deeply ingrained, inflexible, and maladaptive. Such patterns are severe enough to cause the individual anxieties or distress or to interfere with normal functioning. Usually personality disorders are recognizable by adolescence or earlier, continue through adulthood, and become less obvious in middle or old age. The American Psychiatric Association's *Diagnostic and Statistical*

Personality Disorders

Disorder	Description
Histrionic (formerly hysterical personality)	Behaves in an exhibitionistic, immature manner, superficially charming and seductive, but after a relationship is established may become demanding and self-absorbed. Despite sexual flirtatiousness, is often naïve and sexually unresponsive.
Dependent	Does not want to have responsibility or to make decisions; nonassertive, lacking in self-confidence; difficulty being alone.
Passive–aggressive	Resists demands of others by noncompliance, inaction and procrastination; is forgetful, and makes weak excuses and apologies, never expressing true resentment and anger.
Compulsive	Has restricted ability to express warm and tender emotions. Preoccupied with rules, order, and detail.
Avoidant	Shows extreme sensitivity to rejection, ridicule, or disapproval. Avoids close personal attachments even though desires affection and acceptance.

Theories About Personality Disorders

Theorist	Type	Emphasis	Viewpoint	Goal	Methods	Therapy
Freud	Traditional (Psychoanalytic)	Emotions, Biological Instincts, Unconscious Processes	(Biological) Intra-psychic	Explaining/ Helping	Case Histories	Psychoanalysis
Erikson	Traditional (Psychoanalytic)	Emotions, Biological Instincts, Unconscious Processes, (Conscious Processes)	(Biological) Intra-psychic Social	Explaining/ Helping	Case Histories	Psychoanalysis
Jung	Traditional (Jungian Psychoanalytic)	Emotions, (Biological Instincts), Unconscious Processes	(Biological) Intra-psychic Religious	Explaining/ Helping	Case Histories	Jungian Psychoanalysis
Adler	Traditional (Psychoanalytic/ Humanistic)	Emotions, (Biological Instincts), Conscious Processes	(Biological) Intra-psychic Social	Explaining/ Helping	Case Histories (Experiments)	Adlerian Psychoanalysis/ Humanistic
Trait Theorists	Traditional	Underlying Traits or Dispositions	(Biological) Intra-psychic	Describing/ Predicting	Tests	Psychoanalysis/ Humanistic
Rogers	Personologist (Humanistic)	Cognitions, Conscious Processes, Self-Actualization	Intra-psychic	Explaining/ Helping	Case Histories (Experiments)	Humanistic
Maslow	Personologist (Humanistic)	Cognitions, Conscious Processes, Self-Actualization	Intra-psychic	Explaining/ Helping	Case Histories	Humanistic
Murray	Personologist	Cognitions, Conscious Processes, Themas	Intra-psychic Social/Behavioral	Helping/ Predicting	Case Histories, Personality Tests	Humanistic
Skinner	Personologist (Behaviorist)	Learned Responses, (Denies Conscious & Unconscious Processes)	Social/Behavioral	Helping/ Predicting	Experiments	Behavior Modification
Social Learning Theorists (Bandura)	Personologists	Perceptions, Cognitions, Conscious Processes	Intra-psychic Social/Behavioral	Helping/ Predicting	Experiments	Cognitive Behavior Modification

James V. McConnell, *Understanding Human Behavior* (New York: Holt, Rinehart and Winston, 1986).

Manual of Mental Disorders categorizes personality disorders into three clusters:

Cluster A: Paranoid, schizoid, and schizotypal personality disorders. Individuals who have these disorders often appear odd or eccentric.

Cluster B: Antisocial, borderline, histrionic, and narcissistic personality disorders. Individuals who have these disorders often appear dramatic, emotional, or erratic.

Cluster C: Avoidant, dependent, obsessive–compulsive, and passive–aggressive personality disorders. Individuals who have these disorders often appear anxious or fearful.

The DSM-III-R also lists another category, "personality disorder not otherwise specified," that can be used for other specific personality disorders or for mixed conditions that do not qualify as any of the specific personality disorders. (See also charts that follow.) See AVOIDANT PERSONALITY DISORDER; BORDERLINE PERSONALITY DISORDER; DEPENDENT PERSONALITY DISORDER; OBSESSIVE–COMPULSIVE DISORDER; PARANOID.)

American Psychiatric Association, *Diagnostic and Statistical Manual of Mental Disorders* (Washington, DC: American Psychiatric Association, 1987).

personality types See JUNG.

pertofrane See DESIPRAMINE.

phagophobia Fear of eating or swallowing. (See also ANOREXIA NERVOSA; EATING, FEAR OF; FOOD, FEAR OF; SWALLOWING, FEAR OF.)

phalacrophobia Fear of becoming bald. (See also BALD, FEAR OF BECOMING.)

phallic stage In psychoanalysis, the third stage of psychosexual development, usually between ages three and six, when the child first focuses sexual feeling on the genital organs and masturbation becomes a source of pleasure. According to Sigmund Freud, the penis becomes the center of attention for both boys and girls. During the phallic phase or stage, the boy experiences sexual fantasies toward his mother and rivalry toward his father, both of which he eventually gives up due to castration fear. Similarly, the girl experiences sexual fantasies toward the father and hostility toward the mother, due to rivalry and blaming her for being deprived of a penis, but gives up these feelings when she becomes afraid of losing the love of both parents. According to the American psychoanalyst Erik Erikson (1902–), if the child does not successfully advance out of the phallic stage into the genital stage, he or she experiences guilt and role fixation or inhibition, leading to later anxieties. (See also CASTRATION ANXIETY; DEVELOPMENTAL STAGES; ERIKSON, ERIK; GENITAL STAGE; OEDIPUS COMPLEX.)

phallic symbol In psychoanalysis, any object that resembles or represents the penis. Structures that are longer than they are wide may be symbolic of the penis in dreams or in daily life. Examples include trees, skyscrapers, cigars, pencils, snakes, flutes and other musical instruments such as clarinets or trombones, motorcycles, airplanes, hammers, and many other similarly shaped objects. (See also CASTRATION ANXIETY; PHALLIC STAGE; SEXUAL FEARS; SYMBOLS, FEAR OF.)

phallophobia Fear of the penis, especially an erect penis. (See also CASTRATION ANXIETY; GENITALS, FEAR OF MALE; PHALLIC STAGE; SEXUAL FEARS.)

phantom limb pain Individuals who have had a limb (or a breast) removed by surgery may still experience pain as if it were coming from the absent limb. Doctors are not sure why this occurs, but phantom limb pain exists and is not imaginary. Individuals experiencing this kind of pain become anxious, irritable, and nervous because they often do not understand what is happening to them. There is no single method of relieving phantom pain in individuals who experience it, but the least invasive method seems to be relaxation techniques. (See also PAIN, ANXIETY AND DEPRESSION IN.)

pharmacophobia Fear of taking drugs or medicine. (See also DRUGS, FEAR OF TAKING.)

pharmacotherapy See DRUGS.

phasmophobia Fear of GHOSTS.

phenelzine A potent ANTIDEPRESSANT drug and MONOAMINE OXIDASE INHIBITOR (MAOI) also known by the tradename Nardil. Phenelzine is used for relief of moderate to severe DEPRESSION in adults. It is not used for mild depression or depression that is an appropriate response to temporary stress. Individuals taking phenelzine (and other drugs in the MAOI class) must be careful to avoid foods containing TYRAMINE, which is present in hard cheese, red wines, and many other foods and beverages, because tyramine and the MAO inhibitors may interact to cause high blood pressure.

Greist, J. H. and J. W. Jefferson, *Depression and Its Treatment: Help for the Nation's #1 Mental Problem* (Washington, DC: American Psychiatric Association, 1984).

phengophobia Fear of daylight or sunlight. (See also DAYLIGHT, FEAR OF; SUNLIGHT, FEAR OF.)

phenothiazine A class name for a group of drugs used to relieve psychotic symptoms and now considered major tranquilizers. They were once thought to be safe. Permanent neurological damage has been linked to long-term use of phenothiazines. Their molecular structure, like that of the tricyclic drugs, consists of three fused rings. (See also ANTIDEPRESSANTS; DRUGS; TRICYCLIC ANTIDEPRESSANTS.)

philemaphobia, philematophobia Fear of kissing. (See also KISSING, FEAR OF.)

philophobia Fear of love. (See also LOVE, FEAR OF.)

phobia A phobia is an irrational, intense fear of a person, object, situation, sensation, experience, thought, or stimulus event that is not shared by the consensual community and is thus out of proportion to any danger. The individual cannot easily explain or understand the phobia, has no voluntary control over the anxiety response, and seeks to avoid the dreaded situation or stimulus.

The following chart gives some examples of a few types of phobias.

Not all phobias can be neatly classified because phobias of almost any situation can occur and may be associated with almost any other psychological symptom. However, when phobias occur as the dominant symptom, the condition is called a phobic state, phobic reaction, or phobic disorder. According to the American Psychiatric Association's *Diagnostic and Statistical Manual of Mental Disorders* (third edition, revised), phobias are classified as restricted or limited avoidance; AGORAPHOBIA, a form of panic disorder, is extensive avoidance.

Simple phobias

The essential feature of a simple phobia is a persistent, irrational fear of, and compelling desire to avoid, specific objects or situations. Simple phobia is characterized by a relatively specific fear of an object or a situation. The range of stimuli that may elicit a fearful response is narrower than in other phobic disorders. Simple phobias are therefore sometimes also referred to as specific phobias.

The category of simple phobias contains an endless list of fears, as almost any object or situation can be phobic for a given individual. This is evident in this encyclopedia

Examples of Types of Phobias

Animals	Hematophobia; hemophobia—blood
Entomophobia—insects	Pyrexeophobia; febriphobia—fever
Apiphobia; melisophobia—bees	Molysmophobia; mysophobia—contamination
Arachneophobia—spiders	Traumatophobia—injury
Batrachophobia—frogs	Vaccinophobia—vaccinations
Equinophobia—horses	*Social*
Ichthyophobia—fish	Aphephobia; haptephobia—being touched
Musephobia; murophobia—mice	Catagelophobia—ridicule
Ophidiophobia—snakes	Ereuthophobia—blushing
Ornithophobia—birds	Graphophobia; scriptophobia—writing
Zoophobia—animals	Kakorrhaphiophobia—failure
Natural Phenomena	Scopophobia—being looked at
Acluophobia; nyctophobia—night, darkness	Xenophobia—strangers
Acrophobia; hysophobia—heights	*Miscellaneous*
Anemophobia—wind	Ballisphobia—missiles
Astraphobia—lightning	Barophobia—gravity
Aurophobia—northern lights	Claustrophobia—confinement
Brontophobia; keraunophobia—thunder	Dementophobia—insanity
Ombrophobia—rain	Dextrophobia—objects to the right
Potomophobia—rivers	Erythrophobia—the color red
Siderophobia—stars	Harpaxophobia—robbers
Blood-Injury-Illness	Levophobia—objects to the left
Algophobia; odynophobia—pain	Pediophobia—dolls
Belonephobia—needles	Trichopathophobia; trichophobia—hair
Dermatophobia—skin lesions	

by the number of entries covering different phobias. Commonly recognized specific phobias are certain modes of transportation, such as driving, driving across bridges, or flying. Public speaking seems to be the most common phobic situation in the population. Heights and darkness seem to be the most common simple phobias. Other common phobic objects or situations include harmless animals such as dogs and cats, thunderstorms, darkness, and heights. All fears that do not fit into other phobic groups are categorized as simple phobias.

The individual with a simple phobia experiences physiological symptoms and behavior typical of many phobic disorders. However, because these fears are so specific, usually the individual can avoid contact with the phobic object, especially in instances in which the likelihood of a confrontation with the feared object or situation is low, as in snake phobias. On the other hand, individuals who fear common situations, such as elevators or heights, may not be able to avoid these stimuli easily.

Individuals with animal phobias usually only have symptoms in the presence of, or anticipated presence of, their phobic objects. Snakes, spiders, and birds have been the most reported animal phobias. Animal phobias are more prevalent among women.

Blood and injury phobias are special types of simple phobias. Unlike other phobias, which cause increased pulse and other physiological signs of arousal, blood and injury phobias produce lower pulse and blood pressure and bring on fainting spells.

The majority of simple phobias begin at any age. However, certain phobias are more common among certain age groups. For example, infants often fear loud noises and strangers. Children commonly fear darkness

Classification of Phobias

	Animal Phobias	Agoraphobia	Social Phobias	Miscellaneous	School Phobia
Frequency	Rare	Common	Not uncommon	Not uncommon	Not uncommon
Sex incidence	95% women	75% women	60% women	50% women	More common in girls
Onset age	Childhood	After puberty	After puberty	Anytime	Childhood
Associated symptoms	Few	Multiple—general anxiety, depression, panic	Few	Not determined	Nausea, vomiting, diarrhea
Psychophysiology	Normal	High arousal	High arousal	Not determined	Not determined

From Davison and Neale's *Abnormal Psychology: An Experimental Clinical Approach* (New York: John Wiley, 1974), p. 138.

Categories of Phobias

Specific External Stimuli	Specific and General Situations	Specific Internal Concerns
Snakes	*Agoraphobia Complex:*	Illness
Rats	open places, crowds, stores, streets,	Death
Horses	shopping, planes, restaurants,	Cancer
Thunder	churches	Accidents
Lightning		Venereal Disease
Heights	*Confined or Closed Places*	
Knives	*Social Complex:*	
Boats and Water	public speaking, meeting people,	
Surgery	social gatherings	
	Travel Complex	
	driving, flying	

and injections. Fears of animals are common in preschool children around age five. Fear of aging occurs most commonly in people over age 50.

While the age of onset of different phobias varies widely, the average age at which patients seek treatment is age 24, according to Isaac Marks (1969).

How simple phobias start is not well understood. Researchers differ in their explanations; some report that direct conditioning—for example, a traumatic event—is an important factor, while others say that indirect learning experiences or exposure to negative instructions and vicarious experiences are also influential. Many individuals who have simple phobias do not recall the origin of their fear. Treatment of the phobic symptom, however, does not have to wait until the origin is uncovered.

Some simple phobias do not last long and improve as the individual gets older. Phobias in this category include doctors, injections, darkness, and strangers. However, fears of heights, storms, and enclosed places usually last longer. Fears of animals that are prevalent in children between the ages of nine and 11 remain with many girls after age 11 but disappear in most boys.

There are differences of opinions regarding effects of family influences on specific fears. While some experts say that the majority of simple phobics come from families in which no other member of the family shares the same fear, some studies have found relatively strong associations between the fears of mothers and children. Many simple phobics are dependent or anxious individuals, and their family backgrounds may have contributed to these characteristics.

Social phobia

Individuals who have social phobias have excessive anxiety in social situations such as parties, meetings, interviews, restaurants, making complaints, writing in public, eating at restaurants, and interacting with the opposite sex, strangers, and aggressive individuals. They often fear situations in which they believe they are being observed and evaluated, such as eating, drinking, speaking in public, driving, etc.

Social phobia may be associated with fears of negative evaluation or embarrassing public behavior, such as making mistakes, being criticized, making a fool of oneself, sweating, fainting, blushing, speaking poorly, vomiting, or being rejected. Individuals with these phobias usually avoid the specific situations that they fear. Some individuals will participate in the activity only when they cannot be seen, for example, swimming in the dark.

Social phobias usually begin in late adolescence or early adulthood, although the range for onset is from 15 to 30. Usually social phobias are accompanied by heightened levels of generalized anxiety.

Some social phobias begin developing over many months or years, but sometimes a precipitating event can be determined. Some social phobics attribute their fears to direct conditioning, some to vicarious factors, and some to instructional and informational factors. Direct negative learning experience may play an important role

Parental behavior may have some influence on social phobias. For example, parents who have few friends and are socially anxious in the presence of others may influence their children to react in similar ways. Also, the presence of anxiety in children is often associated with verbal punishment and criticism by parents.

Unlike specific or simple phobias, which tend to diminish as the individual grows into puberty and young adulthood, social phobias persist. Many such individuals have traits that interfere with social and marital adjustment. Some have ongoing problems with generalized anxiety, dependence, authority, and depression.

Social phobias often persist on a continuous basis, unlike agoraphobia, which tends to be episodic. Sometimes improving and sometimes worsening during periods of depression, social phobias also differ from the fears of crowds that agoraphobics suffer. Social phobics fear observation by individuals, while agoraphobics partly fear the masses of the crowds and feelings that might occur in crowds such as loneliness, separateness, or lack of identity.

Mixed and other classifications

Phobias of internal stimuli

These are phobias within the individual with no external stimuli that can be avoided to reduce fear. Examples are fears of cancer, heart disease, venereal disease, and death. Fears of this type are often characteristic of depressive illnesses; in such cases, they improve when the depression improves. Illness phobias occur in both sexes. Some of these fears may be regarded as an extreme form of hypochondria.

Obsessive phobias

These are fears that are disproportionate to the demands of the situation, cannot be explained by the individual, and are beyond voluntary control. Examples are fears of harming people or babies, fears of swearing, of fears of contamination that lead to obsessive hand-washing. Such phobias usually occur along with other obsessive–compulsive disorders. (See also AGORAPHOBIA ANXIETY; DIAGNOSTIC AND STATISTICAL MANUAL OF MENTAL DISORDERS; DIAGNOSTIC CRITERIA; FAMILY PATTERNS; HYPOCHONDRISM; OBSESSIVE–COMPULSIVE DISORDERS; PANIC; PHOBIC ANXIETY; PHOBIC CHARACTER; PHOBIC DISORDERS; PHOBIC REACTION; SOCIAL PHOBIA.)

Adams, Henry E. and Patricia B. Sutker, *Comprehensive Handbook of Psychopathology* (New York: Plenum Press, 1984).

Turner, Samuel, *Behavioral Theories and Treatment of Anxiety* (New York: Plenum Press, 1984).

Marks, Isaac M., "The Classification of Phobic Disorders" *British Journal of Psychiatry,* 116(1970), pp. 377–386.

Barlow, David H., "Phobia," in *Encyclopedia Americana* (Danbury, CT: Grolier, 1984).

phobias, history of Avoidance reactions and symptoms of phobias have been recognized throughout ancient and modern civilizations and in many parts of the world. Although phobic symptoms and anxieties had been observed and described over the centuries, detailed analysis and more scientific understanding of these conditions evolved and advanced rapidly during the later half of the 20th century.

The term "PHOBIA" derives from the Greek word *phobos,* which means fear, panic, terror, and flight. The word *phobos* comes from the name of the ancient Greek deity Phobos, who provoked fear and panic in enemies.

Early events

Throughout history, phobic reactions have been noted by writers. Hippocrates (460–377 B.C.) may have been one of the first to describe morbid fears when he wrote about a phobic individual who seemed to fear heights, precipices, and flute music:

> He would not go near a precipice, or over a bridge or beside even the shallowest ditch, and yet he could walk in the ditch itself.
>
> When he used to begin drinking, the girl flute-player would frighten him; as soon as he heard the first note of the flute at a banquet, he would be beset by terror. He used to say he could scarcely contain himself when night fell; but during the day (when there were people about him) he would hear this instrument without feeling any emotion.

William Shakespeare (1564–1616), in *A Merchant of Venice,* wrote of cat phobia: "Some, that are mad if they behold a cat."

Robert Burton (1577–1640), an English clergyman, scholar, and writer, wrote in *Anatomy of Melancholy* (1621) about fear of going away from the safety of home (perhaps describing AGORAPHOBIA):

> Montanus speaks of one that durst not walk alone from home, for fear that he would swoon, or die. . . . A second fears every man he meets will rob him, quarrel with him or kill him. A third dares not venture alone for fear he . . . should be sick. . . . Another dares not go over a bridge, come near a pool, rock, steep hill, lye in a chamber where cross beams are for fear he be tempted to hang, drown or precipitate himself. If he be in a silent auditory, as at a sermon, he is afraid he shall speak aloud unawares, something indecent and unfit to be said. If he be locked in a close room, he is afraid of being stifled for want of air, and still carries bisket, acquavitae, or some strong waters about him, for fear of being sick; or if he be in a throng, middle of a church or multitude, where he may not well get out, he is so misaffected.

Much fearful behavior historically was attributed to witchcraft, demonology, and evil spirits. Indeed, Robert Burton characterized the changes that took place during the 17th century when he wrote, " 'Tis a common practice of some men to go first to a witch, then to a physician; if one cannot, the other shall; if they cannot bend Heaven, they will try Hell."

John Bunyan (1628–1688), English preacher and writer and author of *The Pilgrim's Progress,* noted his own fear of bells ringing and church steeples:

> Now, you must know, that before this I had taken much delight in ringing, but my conscience beginning to be tender, I thought such practice was but vain, and therefore forced myself to leave it, yet my mind hankered; wherefore I should go to the steeple house, and look on it, though I durst not ring. But I thought this did not become religion yet I forced myself, and would look on still; but quickly after, I stand under a main beam, that lay overthwart the steeple, from side to side, thinking there I might stand sure, but then I should think again, Should the bell fall with a swing, it might first hit the wall, and then rebounding upon me, might kill me for all this beam. This made me stand in the steeple door; and now, thought I, I am safe enough; for if a bell should then fall, I can slip out behind these thick walls, and so be preserved not withstanding.
>
> So, after this, I would yet to go see them ring, but would not go farther than the steeple door; but then it came into my head, How, if the steeple itself should fall? And this thought, it may fall for aught I know, when I stood and looked on, did continually so shake my mind, that I durst not stand at the steeple door any longer, but was forced to flee, for fear the steeple should fall upon my head.

Bunyan demonstrated a common feature of phobias: their tendency to spread. At first, he feared just the straight fall of the bell, then its bouncing course, and finally the complete crashing destruction of the whole steeple.

In 1794, Samuel Johnson indicated a fear of death and crowded places when he asked to be excused from jury duty because he came "very near fainting . . . in all crowded places."

In 1789, Benjamin Rush, American physician and author, published an article in which he gave his definition of phobia: "I shall define phobia to be a fear of an imaginary evil, or an undue fear of a real one." He then listed 18 species of fear named according to the object of excessive fear or aversion, such as dirt or rats.

However, the word phobia appeared in psychiatric literature only after the middle of the nineteenth century. (Prior to that, it was used by Celsus to denote a fear of rabies.) It was used then in the same sense it is today, meaning an intense fear out of proportion to the apparent stimulus. These fears cannot be explained or reasoned away, and phobic individuals avoid the feared situations wherever possible.

As understanding of the working of the mind advanced during the 19th century, and particularly the latter part of the 19th century, phobias were described increasingly in psychiatric literature. The term agoraphobia was introduced in 1872, in Otto Westphal's (1824–1902) classic paper describing three agoraphobic cases:

> . . . impossibility of walking through certain streets or squares or possibility of so doing only with resultant dread of anxiety . . . no loss of consciousness . . . vertigo was excluded by all patients . . . no hallucinations nor delusions to cause the strange fear . . . agony was much increased at those hours when the particular streets dreaded were deserted and the shops closed. The subjects experienced great comfort from the companionship of men or even an inanimate object, such as a vehicle or a cane. The use of beer or wine also allowed the patient to pass through the feared locality with comparative comfort. One man even sought, without immoral motives, the companionship of a prostitute as far as his own door . . . some localities are more difficult of access than others; the patient walking far in order not to traverse them . . . Strange to say, in one instance, the open country was less feared than sparsely housed streets in town. Case three also had a dislike to crossing a certain bridge. He feared he would fall into the water . . . In two cases the onset of the

> disease had been sudden; in the third the fear had been gradually increasing for a number of years. In two of the cases there was no hereditary predisposition to mental or nervous disease; in the third case a sister was epileptic and ancestors had had some peculiar seizures.

Westphal labeled his cases "agoraphobia" because the state of the patients was characterized principally by a dread or "phobia" in streets or public places, like "the *agora*" (Greek word for "market"). He commented that the thought of the feared situation frequently was as distressing as the situation itself. Writers in France, England, and Germany commented on Westphal's paper and contributed information of their own to the increasing body of literature about this syndrome. Within the next century, researchers and therapists recognized that fear of fear was a central concept in agoraphobia.

During the late 18th and early 19th century, imaginative naming was in vogue, perhaps in emulation of Linnaeus (1707–1778), the Swedish botanist and originator of the system of biologic taxonomic classification and nomenclature. For several decades after Westphal, many types of phobias were described and named; many names are still in use and can be found in this encyclopedia.

However, with names given to various phobias, confusion increased. Naming phobias led to the idea of a unitary disease entity, phobia, in spite of the appearance of phobic manifestations in many different kinds of clinical cases. Early authors were aware of the strikingly unreasonable quality of the fears, of the frequent chronicity and fluctuating intensity of the symptoms, or apparently "spontaneous" changes, or the circumscribed yet occasionally progressive nature of the pathology.

Then, in 1895, Henry Maudsley (1835–1918), British psychiatrist and author, included all phobias under the heading of *melancholia* and advised against the trend of giving a special name to each variety of phobic situation, as many phobias often were noticed together or successively in the same individual.

Sigmund Freud's writing and theorizing at the end of the 19th century contributed to the stimulation of interest in the causes and treatment of anxieties and phobias.

In 1895, Sigmund Freud wrote "Obsessions and Phobias: Their Psychical Mechanism and Their Aetiology." In this paper, he distinguished the two by suggesting that with phobias the emotional state is always one of morbid anxiety, while in the obsessions, other emotional states such as doubt or anger may occur. Freud emphasized that the origin of phobias was anxiety and that the source was derived from symbols of unconscious fantasies and conflicts. The symbolism always concerned an unacceptable aggressive or sexual impulse, regardless of the individual's personality or previous experience. Freud classified phobia as an anxiety neurosis or a form of hysteria, and his original idea was that the phobia is an attempt to deal with anxiety by substitution and by displacement of anxieties that are foreign to the ego. Freud suggested that phobia relates to objects that have unconscious symbolic meanings and represent regressions to earlier infantile fears and anxieties, usually centered around Oedipal conflicts. To him, the object always symbolized some sexual anxiety, and every phobia, therefore, was invested with some element of sexual anxiety. He believed a phobia was a symbolic expression of repressed feelings and the punishment linked to them in the unconscious. Freud distinguished between common phobias, such as snakes and death, and specific phobias of circumstances (such as going outside) that do not inspire fear in normal individuals.

Many psychotherapists have built upon Freud's ideas, accepting some, modifying others, and adding new understanding to the mechanisms of anxiety, fears, phobias, obsessive–compulsive behavior, and depression.

Most descriptions of OBSESSIVE–COMPULSIVE DISORDERS include some phobias. The converse is also true, and modern authorities (e.g., Chambless and Goldstein) believe that phobias are closely related to obsessive–compulsive disorders and are operationally and dynamically similar to them.

In 1903, Pierre Janet (1859–1947), French psychologist, classified neurotic disorders in two major divisions. To him, hysteria denoted disturbances in sensation, movement, and consciousness; these are still considered characteristic symptoms of that syndrome. Psychasthenia, on the other hand, included most of the other so-called neurotic phenemonena, such as phobias, anxiety, obsessions, depression, and others.

One of Janet's patients is of historical interest because, a quarter of a century before Janet presented him to his students, the patient had been examined by Legrand du Saulle, another French psychologist, when he was studying the problem of agoraphobia. Janet wrote:

> He was about 25, when there started what he himself called "the trouble with spaces." He was crossing the Place de la Concorde (alone, it should be noted) when he felt a strange sensation of dread. His breathing became rapid and he felt as if he were suffocating; his heart was beating violently and his legs were limp, as if half-paralyzed. He could go neither forwards nor backwards, and he had to exert a tremendous effort, bathed in sweat, to reach the other side of the square. From the time of that first episode on, he took a great dislike to the Place de la Concorde and decided that he would not risk going there again alone. However, a short while after the same sensation of anxiety recurred on the Invalides Bridge, and then in a street, which though it was narrow, seemed long and was quite steep.

Although the patient had had temporary relief of his symptoms while he was under Legrand du Saulle's care,

> His illness was not cured and continued to develop slowly. The anxiety he would experience whenever he had to venture out into a place that was at all open was so severe that it became impossible for him to control it, and he was no longer able to cross any square. Some dozen years ago he had to escort a young girl to her house. As long as he was with her everything was all right, but when she had left him, he was unable to go back home. Five hours later, noticing that though it was getting dark and was raining, he had not yet returned, his wife became alarmed and went out in search of him. She found him ashen and shivering with cold on the edge of the Place des Invalides, which he had been completely unable to cross.
>
> After this unpleasant experience, he was not allowed to go out alone, which was exactly what he wanted, since his attacks could thus be controlled. Whenever he came to a square, he would begin to tremble and breathe heavily, and develop tics. He repeated the phrase: "Mama, Rata, bibi, bitaquo. I'm going to die." His wife had to hold him tightly by his arm, and then he would calm down and cross the square without further incident. His wife has to accompany him absolutely everywhere now, even when he goes to the toilet.

In 1913, Emil Kraepelin (1856–1926), a German psychiatrist, included a chapter on irrepressible ideas and irresistible fears in his textbook. He regarded personality factors as by-products of a diseased brain or faulty metabolism. Later these organic interpretations were largely overturned by others who took a more psychodynamic approach, although, as evidenced by the massive research effort directed to use of DRUGS, biological views still predominate.

Development of theories and therapies

Developments in the latter half of the 20th century led to increased knowledge about anxiety and phobic disorders and new directions in treating them. The treatment of choice, in most therapy settings, focuses on helping people cope with phobic reactions in their lives. In many therapeutic settings, therapists use an integrated perspective to treat phobic people. While each perspective offers value, none explains all the phenomena that various individuals experience. While some psychiatrists suggest that phobias are maintained by unconscious conflicts remaining unconscious, other psychotherapists focus on the avoided behavior and thoughts of the individual, such as catastrophic misinterpretation of danger.

Some suggest that phobias are derived from conditioned experiences, and that the phobic object may have been part of a traumatic situation. On this basis, any object has an equal potential to become a phobic stimulus. Some say that certain phobic responses may be learned though imitating the reactions of others, or vicarious learning. Another theory is that phobic reactions are learned by the positive consequences that follow (for example, soothing attention from a parent of a school-phobic child). This type of learning is called operant conditioning.

Those who take a biological perspective suggest that a biological function may contribute to anxieties, phobias, panic attacks, and obsessive–compulsive behaviors; all organisms may have been generally prepared by evolutionary history to acquire fears of certain things more than others, such as snakes, spiders, and the dark.

Today, millions of people have some form of anxiety disorder. Anxiety is currently described as a cluster of symptoms that does not imply any theory of causation. While psychoanalysis had been used as a treatment for anxiety disorders, in many cases, understanding the source of the anxiety did not necessarily make the anxieties and unwanted behaviors go away. Thus many questioned the effectiveness of psychoanalysis. In the late 1950s and early 1960s, BEHAVIOR THERAPY developed. The shift of behavioral therapies for phobias is probably most attributable to the work of Joseph Wolpe and his classic work on RECIPROCAL INHIBITION, as described in his book *Psychotherapy by Reciprocal Inhibition* (1959). Early behavior researchers speculated that they could be effective by looking at an individual's symptoms, working with them, and systematically desensitizing them by gradual exposure. Through a wide variety of behavior-therapy techniques, thousands of individuals have learned that they do not have to be victims of anxiety.

Theories of behavioral therapy suggest that a phobia is a learned response and therefore can be unlearned. Behavioral therapists use techniques that involve gradually exposing the individual to whatever is feared. Exposure may take place in real life or in the person's imagination. For example, a person with a fear of heights may imagine himself on a higher and higher hill without anxiety; gradualness of exposure is an important factor.

It is now understood that phobic and obsessive–compulsive disorders are two very different conditions, although they both have anxiety as a common symptom. Also, psychophysiological measures in the study of anxiety disorders were expanded, making it possible to distinguish certain groups of phobias that have clinical correlates. Thus, in addition to talking therapy, current therapy may now include periodic examinations of cardiovascular, pulmonary, endocrine, or neurological changes, as well as pharmacologic aspects. State-of-the-art technology in medical and pharmacological research is used as a diagnostic and therapeutic tool. The advent of relatively safe, appropriate drugs to relieve anxieties has been an adjunct that has enabled many individuals to work effectively with therapists or with self-help to overcome phobias, anxieties, panic disorders, and obsessive–compulsive behaviors.

Interaction between psychotherapy and biology is increasingly better understood. Researchers now believe that coupled with the medical, scientific, and technological advances, the future of treatment of phobic individuals will continually lean more toward self-help. Many self-help techniques and self-help groups have been developed in recent years. One example is body awareness, which many phobic individuals learn through use of biofeedback. With such techniques, individuals—particularly those who have panic attacks—learn concrete, rapid tools for relaxation and objective ways to validate their relaxation skills if they doubt their ability to relax. Further, individuals learn to develop general increased self-confidence and learn to control the power of stress. Therapy for phobias, in most cases, concentrates on helping the individual focus on the present, switching from thoughts to sensations, facing fears realistically, becoming more assertive, expressing anger when appropriate, and using anxiety constructively. (See also ANTIDEPRESSANTS; ANXIETY DISORDERS; ANXIETY DRUGS; STRESS; SYSTEMATIC DESENSITIZATION; WOLPE, JOSEPH.)

Marks, Isaac M., *Fears, Phobias and Rituals* (New York: Oxford University Press, 1987).

Marks, Isaac M., "The Classification of Phobic Disorders," *British Journal of Psychiatry*, 116(1970), pp. 377–386.

Chambless, Dianne L. and Alan J. Goldstein, *Agoraphobia: Multiple Perspective on Theory and Treatment* (New York: John Wiley and Sons, 1982).

Errara, Paul, "Some Historical Aspects of the Concept, Phobia," *The Psychiatric Quarterly* (April 1962), pp. 325–336.

Lewis, Aubrey, "A Note on Classifying Phobia," *Psychological Medicine*, 6(1976), pp. 21–22.

Bromberg, Walter, "History of Treatment of Mental Disorders," in Albert Deutsch (editor-in-chief), *The Encyclopedia of Mental Health* (New York: Franklin Watts, 1963).

Goldstein, A. and B. Stainback, *Overcoming Agoraphobia: Conquering Fear of the Outside World* (New York: Viking Penguin, 1987).

Pioneers in Criminology (Montclair, NJ: Patterson-Smith, 1972).

Phobia Society of America, The (PSA) The Phobia Society of America (PSA), founded in the late 1970s, is a national, nonprofit organization that promotes the welfare of people with phobias and related anxiety disorders. Its members include people with the disorders and their support persons, health professionals who study and treat the disorders, and other concerned individuals.

PSA promotes public awareness of the nature of the disorders and their effects on people's lives; facilitates advances in the understanding and treatment of the disorders; promotes communication and mutual support among phobics; assists those with phobias and related anxiety disorders in getting appropriate treatment and developing self-help skills; and serves as an advocate for its constituents with public and institutional leaders and policymakers.

PSA publishes the *National Treatment Directory for Phobias and Related Anxiety Disorders*, a newsletter, pamphlets, books, and cassettes. PSA also sponsors an annual conference for laypersons and professionals and facilitates local support groups.

For information contact:
The Phobia Society of America
133 Rollins Avenue, Suite 4B
Rockville, MD 20952
Telephone: (301) 231-9350

phobic anxiety A response of mind and body that the individual experiences only in the actual or imagined presence of the feared object, person, or situation. According to the American Psychiatric Association, there may be a sudden onset of intense apprehension and terror, feelings of unsteadiness, unreality, impending doom, dying, going crazy, or doing something uncontrolled. Also, there may be shortness of breath, sensations of choking and smothering, chest pain or discomfort, hot or cold flashes, faintness, and trembling. Freud applied the term to a type of anxiety that stems from unconscious sources but is displaced to objects or situations such as open areas, insects, or bridges that represent the real fear while posing little if any actual dangers in themselves. Behavioral theories emphasize the conditioned-associative learning that produces a bond between triggering stimuli and the response of anxiety. (See also ANXIETY; PANIC ATTACK; PHOBIA; PHOBIC DISORDERS.)

Turner, Samuel, *Behavioral Theories and Treatment of Anxiety* (New York: Plenum Press, 1984).

phobic character Extremely inhibited, fearful persons. This term was coined by OTTO FENICHEL (1899–1946), an Austrian psychoanalyst, to apply to some individuals who resort to defense mechanisms of phobic reactions such as projection, displacement, and avoidance when facing internal conflicts. In a more generic use, the term would describe a shy, socially inhibited person who lacks assertive and expressive skills and reports excessive anxiety in his or her life, particularly in social contact situations. (See also PHOBIA; PHOBIC ANXIETY; PHOBIC DISORDERS; PHOBIC REACTION.)

phobic disorders A group of disorders in which the significant features are persistent and irrational fears of specific objects, activities, or situations that result in a compelling desire to avoid the dreaded object, activity, or situation. The individual recognizes the fear as excessive or unreasonable in proportion to the actual dangerousness of the object, activity, or situation. Such feelings are so intense that they interfere with everyday functioning and are often a significant source of distress.

According to Stewart Agras (1969), about 77 out of 1,000 people suffer from some type of phobic disorder. Fears of illness or injury are the most common fears, while agoraphobia is the most frequent phobia for which individuals seek treatment.

The American Psychiatric Association, in *Diagnostic and Statistical Manual of Mental Disorder,* says: "Irrational avoidance of objects, activities, or situations that have an insignificant effect on life adjustment is commonplace. For example, many individuals experience some irrational fear when unable to avoid contact with harmless insects or spiders, but this has no major effect on their lives. However, when the avoidance behavior or fear is a significant source of distress to the individual or interferes with social or role functioning, a diagnosis of a phobic disorder is warranted."

Phobic disorders also used to be called phobic neuroses, but the "neuroses" classification was dropped in the DSM-III-R. (See also ANXIETY DISORDERS; DIAGNOSTIC AND STATISTICAL MANUAL OF MENTAL DISORDERS; SEPARATION ANXIETY; SEXUAL FEARS.)

Agras, W.S. et al., "The Epidemiology of Common Fears and Phobias," *Comparative Psychiatry,* 10(1969), pp. 151–156.

Adams, Henry E. and Patricia B. Sutker, *Comprehensive Handbook of Psychopathology* (New York: Plenum Press, 1984).

phobic neuroses See PHOBIC DISORDERS.

phobic reaction A group of persistent, intense, irrational, dominating fears that interfere with everyday life. Autonomic symptoms such as stomach upset and acutely distressing feelings may mount to panic proportions when the individual faces a phobic situation. Phobic situations that cause such reactions usually arise from traumatic or vicarious experiences. (See also PHOBIC DISORDERS.)

phobophobia Fear of fears (See also FEAR.)

Phobos A Greek god who provoked terror and flight in one's enemies. The word "phobia" is derived from the name Phobos.

phonophobia Fear of noise, talking, speaking aloud, or one's own voice. (See also NOISE, FEAR OF; ONE'S OWN VOICE, FEAR OF; SPEAKING ALOUD, FEAR OF; TALKING, FEAR OF.)

phonophobia Fear of telephones. (See also TELEPHONES.)

photoalgia Fear of pain in the eye.

photoaugiaphobia Fear of glaring lights. Also known as photoaugiophobia. (See also GLARING LIGHTS, FEAR OF.)

photographed, fear of being The fear of being photographed, common in certain traditional ethnic groups such as American Indians and gypsies, is an extension of the belief that an individual's soul exists in his or her reflection. Being photographed puts the subject in the power of the photographer and may cause harm or even death.

Modern believers in magic and witchcraft have even more to fear from being photographed. Twentieth-century wizards and sorcerers have adapted and intensified the practice of using a doll in injure someone by attaching a photograph of the victim to the doll. (See also MIRRORS, FEAR OF.)

Daniels, Cora Linn and C.M. Stevans, *Encyclopedia of Superstitions, Folklore and the Occult Sciences of the World* (New York: Gale Research, 1971), "Photograph."

Cavendish, Richard (ed.), *Man, Myth and Magic* (New York: Marshall Cavendish, 1983), "Imitative magic."

photophobia Fear of light. More commonly, however, the term for photophobia refers to an organically determined hypersensitivity to light that results in severe pain and tearing in the eyes when the individual is exposed to light. This may occur during many acute infectious diseases. (See also LIGHT, FEAR OF; LIGHT AND SHADOW, FEAR OF.)

phronemophobia Fear of thinking.

phthiriophobia Fear of lice or parasites. (See also LICE, FEAR OF; PARASITES, FEAR OF.)

phthisiophobia Fear of tuberculosis. This word is derived from the obsolete word (phthisis) for tuberculosis, which comes from the Greek word *phthisis* or *phthiein* meaning "to decay." (See also TUBERCULOSIS, FEAR OF.)

pilots, fears of See FLYING, FEAR OF.

Pinel, Philippe (1745–1826) A French psychiatrist and pioneer in humane treatment for the mentally ill who influenced current treatment for anxieties and mental disorders. Upon completion of his medical degree, Pinel's interest in psychiatry was strengthened by a friend's sudden plunge into madness and death. Against great opposition, Pinel removed chains and fetters from the inmates of the Bicetre hospital outside Paris. Suspected of harboring enemies of the French revolution, he was saved by one of his own patients, an army captain. His writings stressed his two fields of interest: moral medicine and the classification of mental disorders. Pinel served as a consulting physician to Napoleon.

Howells, John G. and Livia Osborn, *A Reference Companion to the History of Abnormal Psychology* (Westport, CT: Greenwood Press, 1984).

pins and needles, fear of Fear of pins and needles is known as belonephobia or enetophobia. The phrase "being on pins and needles" refers to feelings of anxiety, apprehension, and tension. (See also ACUPUNCTURE, FEAR OF; ANXIETY; NEEDLES, FEAR OF.)

places, fear of Fear of specific places is known as topophobia. This fear may be related to fears of landscapes, rivers, lakes, or specific geographic areas. (See also LAKES, FEAR OF; LANDSCAPE, FEAR OF; RIVERS, FEAR OF.)

placebo A preparation containing the form of treatment but not the substance; that is, a pretense of treatment without the actual ingredients being there. A placebo may be prescribed or administered to cause the phobic individual to believe he or she is receiving treatment. Placebo effects include the psychologic and physiologic benefits as well as undesirable reactions that reflect the individual's expectations. For example, if the individual believes that a medication will reduce anxiety, it probably will.

Placebos also influence the effects of psychotherapy. For example, research in psychotherapy includes placebo groups in the research design in order to determine the proportion of people who get better just because they think they are receiving a treatment. Surprisingly, depending on the research method and types of treatment presented, between 30 percent and 70 percent of people will significantly improve with just placebo treatment. Similar results have been obtained in drug research.

These results suggest that a powerful internal and personal energy is available to people who "suffer" from mental disorders that can produce positive change and growth. (See also DRUGS.)

placophobia Fear of tombstones. (See also CEMETERIES, FEAR OF; DEATH, FEAR OF; TOMBSTONES, FEAR OF.)

plague, fear of the Fear of the plague has been one of mankind's greatest fears of disease. There are several types of plague, including bubonic plague, which is characterized by the appearance of buboes, or swollen lymph glands of the armpits and groin, and pneumonic plague, which is the only type that is spread by means of airborne particles. In 14th-century Europe, the plague was referred to as the Great Dying or the Great Pestilence, the Black Death or Black Plague, and it killed about one out of every four persons, or 25,000,000 people. At other times in history, millions of others have died of plague throughout the world. The disease is still feared, although deaths from it are relatively rare.

Plague still occurs in parts of the world, particularly in Africa, South America, and the southwestern United States. In 1986, 10 cases were reported in the United States.

The bacteria that cause plague are usually transmitted to humans though the bites of fleas. The bacteria was identified in 1854 by Alexandre Yersin, a French bacteriologist. The carrier flea may be carried by a rat or other rodent; fleas carried by humans and dogs usually do not harbor the disease. The best way to reduce fear of the plague is through control of rodents and fleas. The risk increases when unsanitary conditions encourage the increase of the rodent population, such as during wartime or flood conditions. Military personnel and others who must live in areas where sanitary conditions are poor receive a vaccine to prevent infection.

Plague has always been highly feared because of the death rate among persons who contract the disease. Symptoms, which include infections in various glands, fever, chills, coughing, vomiting, and bleeding from the gastrointestinal tract, usually peak within a few days to a week. The term "black plague" came about because of dark purplish or black spots that appear on the skin.

At various times in the past the plague was thought to be caused by many sources, including unfavorable astrological combinations and contaminations by witches. Historically, different approaches have been taken to control the spread of the plague. One of these was quarantine, or keeping ill individuals confined at home. This led to contamination of others in the household. Passengers and goods arriving on ships were also quarantined at times.

Fears of the plague have been reduced during the last half of the 20th century because antibiotic drugs, including streptomycin and tetracyclines, and sulfa drugs help to control the disease. Epidemiologists now understand how the disease is spread and can take appropriate measures to prevent it.

In the 1980s, autoimmune deficiency syndrome (AIDS) has been called the plague of the 20th century because of its rapid spread and the extensive physical devastation that results in the death of its victims. AIDS, which still has no cure, is now becoming just as feared as the plague was in earlier centuries.

plants, fear of Fear of plants is known as botanophobia. Some fear plants because they believe that plants consume oxygen needed by man; some fear the allergies and skin rashes plants cause. Others fear plants because of personal associations. There is an old superstition about leaving flowers in the rooms of sick persons at night. Flowers and plants, according to this superstition, were the hiding places for evil spirits who at night, under cover of darkness, would take possession of the sick person and inflict harm.

pleasure, fear of Fear of pleasure is known as hedonophobia. Some individuals who have guilt feelings about themselves fear enjoying themselves and hence fear pleasure. Some cannot enjoy an activity or event themselves because others less fortunate than they cannot do what they are doing. (See also GUILT, FEAR OF.)

pluviophobia Fear of rain. (See also RAIN, FEAR OF.)

pnigophobia, pnigerophobia Fear of being smothered or of choking. The word is derived from the Greek word *pnigos,* meaning "choking." (See also CHOKING, FEAR OF; SMOTHERING, FEAR OF.)

pocrescophobia Fear of gaining weight. (See also WEIGHT GAIN, FEAR OF.)

poetry, fear of Fear of poetry is known as metrophobia. Some individuals have fearful and even aversive feelings about poetry because of its basic nature and because of the way it is taught and analyzed. In classical times, Spartans banned certain types of poetry because they thought it promoted effeminate and licentious behavior. The rhyme and figurative language of poetry is odd and distracting to some people. Frequently, poetry contains words, allusions, and obscurely stated thoughts and feelings that are confusing or incomprehensible to people who lack a scholarly, academic background.

Brooks, Cleanth and Robert Penn Warren, *Understanding Poetry* (New York: Holt, Rinehart and Winston, 1976).

International Encyclopedia of the Social Sciences (New York: Macmillan, 1968), "Censorship."

poetry as therapy for anxiety Like MUSIC THERAPY, poetry therapy—the treatment of ANXIETY by the patient's reading or writing poetry—can help an anxious or fearful individual communicate feelings he or she might not otherwise be able to express. Poetry helps the individual uncover and release emotions that previously may have been repressed, consciously or unconsciously, and thus reduce anxiety and fears. In reading poetry, the individual realizes that someone else feels as he does; he feels less alone with his anxieties and fears. Making up poetry gives an individual a chance to express ideas in an indirect manner. Poetry therapy is used as an adjunct to other forms of therapy. It can be used in group or individual therapy.

Poetry therapy, like MUSIC THERAPY, has been used since antiquity. Chants of magicians and faith healers may be thought of as poetry because of their repetitions. It is said that ancient Egyptian chants were written on papyrus and then eaten by the patient in order that he or she might benefit from the power of the words.

The Association for ..oetry Therapy was founded during the late 1960s.

pogonophobia Fear of beards or of men wearing beards. (See also BEARDS, FEAR OF.)

poinephobia Fear of punishment. (See also PUNISHMENT, FEAR OF.)

pointing the finger, fear of Some individuals fear pointing at their own body to show a place that is diseased or weak and fear pointing at their own body when talking about where another person is diseased; the fear is that the pointing individual will get the same complaint in the same place.

A second fear regarding pointing the finger relates to pointing the finger at someone else. Children are taught not to point their finger at anyone. This notion goes back to early times when man worshipped the phallus, which was the source of life. Man feared the outstretched finger as the image of the male organ, and thus the finger could prove equally productive in the creation of both good and evil. In primitive society, the phrase "to point the finger" became synonymous with killing a person. (See also POINTS, FEAR OF.)

Brasch, R., *Strange Customs* (New York: David McKay, 1976).

Daniels, Cora Linn and Stevans, C.M., *Encyclopedia of Superstitions, Folklore and the Occalt Sciences of the World* (Detroit: Gale Research Company, 1971).

points, fear of Fear of points or pointed objects is known as aichmophobia or aichurophobia. This fear may relate to a fear of pins and needles or a fear of sticks. From a psychoanalytic point of view, pointed objects may be phallic symbols, and thus fear of pointed objects may be a sexual fear. Since pointed objects are also capable of inducing painful stimulation, with experience these can become aversive stimuli that trigger ANXIETY and AVOIDANCE.

poison, fear of Fear of poison is known as iophobia, toxiphobia, toxophobia, and toxicophobia. Fear of poison may be related to a fear of contamination, germs, or dirt. (See also BEING POISONED, FEAR OF; CONTAMINATION; FEAR OF; OBSESSIVE–COMPULSIVE DISORDER.)

poisoned, fear of being See BEING POISONED, FEAR OF.

police, fear of Individuals who have a fear of police and police personnel may fear authority, punishment, or entrapment. It is usual for those who break the law to fear police, because they probably fear being caught. Those who exceed the speed limit while driving fear being seen by police because they may have to pay a fine for their violation or go to court to defend themselves. However, when an individual becomes very anxious every time he sees a uniformed police officer, it may actually be a phobia that causes physiological effects such as rapid breathing, dizziness, and gastrointestinal symptoms. Some individuals who fear police fear that if they are apprehended, they will be subjected to extensive questioning and perhaps prison. Thus a fear of police may also be a fear of loss of control over one's own destiny. (See also AUTHORITY, FEAR OF.)

politicians, fear of Fear of politicians is known as politicophobia. Those who fear politicians may fear authority or regimentation or fear hearing untruths and exaggerations. (See also AUTHORITY FEAR OF.)

politicophobia Fear of politicians. (See also POLITICIANS FEAR OF.)

pollution, fear of Fear of environmental pollution may come from the fear of bad health effects brought on by exposure to polluted air or water. Anxiety may be increased by an individual's personal lack of control over his exposure to pollution and his inability to avoid the many pollutants founds in everyday life, such as exhaust from cars, wastes from industry, smoke from cigarettes, and toxins in drinking water. Some individuals deal with fears of pollution by using avoidance behavior, such as refusing to live in or travel to big cities, where pollution is more prevalent. Fear of air pollution may lead some individuals to develop agoraphobia. (See also ACID DEW, FEAR OF; ACID RAIN, FEAR OF; AGORAPHOBIA, FEAR OF; SMOKING FEAR OF.)

poltergeist, fear of Poltergeists are supernatural spirits that are heard but not seen. *Polter* is the German word for noise, *geist* for spirit. Poltergeists terrorize their victims by rapping, scratching, banging, speaking, whistling, and singing. Victims have reported seeing volleys of stones thrown by unseen hands and large pieces of furniture moved by an invisible force. Poltergeists pull off bedclothes and dump the occupants out of bed. The disappearance and reappearance of small household objects is thought to be the work of a poltergeist. Poltergeists are also blamed for breaking glass and china, and setting fires.

While poltergeists have been called ghosts and DEMONS, they seem to be resistant to the rite of EXORCISM and are considered by some to be a type of nature spirit, such as an elf.

Research has shown that poltergeists typically are associated with adolescent girls with high intelligence and usually excessive fantasy life and little self-awareness. Fraud or simply the tendency of teenagers to play pranks or the neurotic impulse to engage in irrational behavior are also factors, especially in view of the nature of poltergeist behavior. However, in some cases, responsible people have been reported to have eliminated these possibilities through careful observation. There is a theory that certain individuals, particularly the adolescent or the mentally unstable, may have uniquely intense powers of mind of which they themselves are unaware. These pressures, according to the theory, may build into a force that can perform what appear to be the supernatural acts typical of poltergeists. Because of these observations and theories, poltergeists have been called "the only demon left commanding even limited acceptance among the credulous."

Hill, Douglas and Pat Williams, *The Supernatural* (New York: Hawthorne Books, 1965), p. 8493.

Robbins, Rossell Hope, *The Encyclopedia of Witchcraft and Demonology* (New York: Crown, 1974).

Cavendish, Richard, *Man, Myth and Magic* (New York: Marshall Cavendish, 1983), "Poltergeist."

polyphobia Fear of many things is known as polyphobia. Many phobic individuals have more than one phobia and hence are polyphobic.

ponophobia Fear of work or fatigue is known as ponophobia. (See also FATIGUE, FEAR OF; WORK, FEAR OF.)

porphyrophobia Fear of the color purple. This may be related to a fear of colors in general. (See also COLORS, FEAR OF.)

Positron Emission Tomography (PET) A BRAIN IMAGING TECHNIQUE. Using PET, researchers can measure blood flow in areas of the brain that are thought to control panic and anxiety reactions. Differences in blood flow between the two hemispheres of the brain are probably connected with differences in metabolic rates and reflect differences in the activity levels of nerve cells of the two sides. PET is useful in assessing the amount of psychoactive drug in various parts of the brain, as well as physiological abnormalities.

Fischman, Joshua, "The Anxious Brain," *Psychology Today* (April, 1985), p. 29.

possession, fear of Psychological ailments were often ascribed to possession by DEMONS or evil spirits in many primitive cultures. Until the end of the 17th century, some ANXIETY disorders were considered demoniacal possessions, and treatments included beating and exorcism. Modern VOODOO beliefs include notions that possession by evil spirits can result in violent mental and physical symptoms. (See also EVIL EYE, FEAR OF THE; VOODOO, FEAR OF.)

postcoronary bypass anxiety See CORONARY BYPASS ANXIETY, POSTOPERATIVE.

postpartum anxiety Many women experience postpartum anxiety, or depression after childbirth or delivery. Many women have "weepy" spells and feel somewhat "blue" at this time. Even though a woman may be elated with her new baby, some of the mild depression can be attributed to the letdown after months of eager anticipation. Also, a woman's anxiety may come about because she feels fearful of being a parent, fears being a failure as a parent, feels less loving toward her baby than she thinks she should, and feels less sexually attractive to her mate because her body has not regained its normal shape. The woman may also feel a loss of self-esteem if she has gone from a job outside the home into full-time motherhood. Because of the demands of the new baby she may feel exhausted, overwhelmed with chores, and deprived of sleep and may fear the chronic fatigue that seems to accompany her new status. Also, any tensions between the couple that existed before the birth of a baby may worsen after the baby's arrival in the household.

Hormonal changes after the birth of a baby may also affect a woman's mood. For example, rapidly plummeting estrogen and progesterone can lead to hot flashes and irritability, similar to the phenemona associated with menopause. Additionally, sleep deprivation caused by frequent waking during the night by the baby can lead to irritability and depression.

The degree to which a woman experiences postpartum depression also depends on her support system, including her husband, family, and additional caretaker for the baby. Also, the baby's temperament may affect her mood. For example, if the baby is colicky and cries frequently, she may become anxious and irritable. If the baby is calm, she will feel like a better mother and experience less anxiety. (See also CHILDBIRTH, FEAR OF; DEPRESSION; PREGNANCY, FEAR OF.)

(Holt, Linda H., M.D., Skokie, Illinois; personal interview.)

posttraumatic stress disorder (PTSD) PTSD, also known as shell shock, battle fatigue, and war neurosis, affects hundreds of thousands of individuals who have survived the trauma of natural disasters such as EARTHQUAKES, accidental disasters such as airplane crashes, and war, and, according to current thinking, the effects of abuse or neglect as a child or adult. PTSD is not confined to war and catastrophe victims. There is growing concern that living in poverty, in ghettos, and in high-crime areas can produce ANXIETY and PANIC as a form of PTSD.

Psychiatrists estimate that several hundred thousand of the 3.5 million men and women who served in the Vietnam War are affected by PTSD. Veterans of heavy combat are more likely to suffer from PTSD.

Although its symptoms can occur soon after the event, PTSD often surfaces several months or even years later. Symptoms include repeated episodes of reexperiencing the traumatic event. This can happen in sudden, vivid memories accompanied by very painful emotions. The memory can be so strong that the individual thinks he or she is actually experiencing the traumatic event again. When a person has a severe flashback, he or she is in a dissociative state, which sometimes can be mistaken for sleepwalking. Sometimes the reexperience occurs in NIGHTMARES that are powerful enough to awaken the person screaming in terror. Individuals with PTSD often develop insomnia in an attempt to avoid the dreaded DREAMS. At times, the reexperience comes as a sudden, painful rush of emotions that seems to have no cause. These emotions often include grief, anger, or intense fear. Individuals say these emotional experiences occur repeatedly, much like memories or dreams about the traumatic event. PANIC ATTACK and ANXIETY often result from PTSD experiences.

These may result from the extreme fear the individual felt during the traumatic event that remained unresolved during later events in his or her life. During the panic attack, the throat tightens, breathing and heart rate increase, and feelings of dizziness and nausea are present.

Avoidance behavior also occurs. This affects the individual's relationships with others, because he or she often avoids close emotional ties with family, colleagues, and friends. At first the person feels numb, has diminished emotions, and can complete only routine, mechanical activities. Later, when reexperiences of the event begin, the individual alternates between the flood of emotions caused by the reexperience and the inability to feel or express emotions at all. Some individuals who have PTSD say they cannot feel emotions, especially toward those to whom they are closest; or, if they can feel emotions, often they cannot express them. As the avoidance continues the person seems to be bored, cold, or preoccupied.

Some individuals also might avoid situations that remind them of the traumatic event. For example, a survivor of an airplane crash might overreact in another plane as it seems to descend too rapidly. Some—particularly war veterans—avoid accepting responsibility for others because they think they failed in ensuring the safety of those killed or injured during battle. Others who have PTSD may have poor work records and poor relationships with their family and friends. Some have trouble concentrating or remembering current information. Drug and alcohol addiction is high among war veterans. War veterans may become suddenly irritable or explosive without provocation. This may result from remaining feelings of exploitation by superiors during the war or anger over their helplessness as they waited for orders or fulfilled illogical orders.

Some war veterans and others who have PTSD are always on guard for danger. As a result they have exaggerated startle reactions. War veterans may revert to their war behavior when they hear noises such as backfiring cars or fireworks, which are similar to the sound of battle.

Some who have PTSD feel guilty because they survived the disaster when others did not. In combat veterans, this guilt may be worse if they witnessed or participated in behavior that was necessary to survive but is unacceptable in society. Such guilt can contribute to depression as the individual begins to look on himself as unworthy, a failure, or a person who violated his own prewar values.

Therapists can help individuals who have PTSD work through the trauma and pain and resolve their unexpressed grief. Among the treatments is individual psychotherapy. PTSD results, in part, from the difference between the individual's personal values and the reality that he witnessed during the traumatic event. Psychotherapy helps the individual examine his or her values and how his or her behavior and experience during the traumatic event violated them. The goal is resolution of the conscious and unconscious conflicts that were thus created. Additionally, the individual works to build his or her self-esteem and self-control, develop a good and reasonable sense of personal accountability, and renew a sense of integrity and personal pride.

Therapists may recommend family therapy because spouses' and children's behavior may affect and be affected by the individual suffering PTSD. Spouses and children report their loved one does not communicate, show affection, or share in family life. The therapist can help family members learn to recognize and cope with the range of emotions each feels. They do this by learning good communication, parenting, and stress-management techniques.

Another effective therapy for PTSD involves "rap" groups, in which survivors of similar traumatic events are encouraged to share their experiences and reactions. In doing so, group members help one another realize that many people have done the same thing and felt the same emotions. That, in turn, helps the individual realize that he or she is not uniquely unworthy or guilty. Over time, the individual reevaluates himself or herself and others and can build a new view of the world and redefine a positive sense of self. (See also ANXIETY DISORDERS; AVOIDANCE BEHAVIOR; DISSOCIATION; FEAR.)

(This article adapted from material provided by the American Psychatric Association.)

potamophobia Fear of rivers or of sheets of water. (See also RIVERS, FEAR OF; SHEETS OF WATER, FEAR OF.)

poverty, fear of Fear of poverty is known as peniaphobia. (See also RUIN, FEAR OF.)

precipices, fear of Fear of precipices is known as cremnophobia. This fear may be related to fears of heights, high places, and falling.

pregnancy, fear of Some women fear becoming pregnant, not becoming pregnant, and pregnancy itself, for a wide range of reasons. Some unmarried women fear conceiving and bearing a child out of wedlock. Some women, although married, do not want to be burdened with a child; some fear the pain of childbirth, and some fear that they might die during pregnancy or childbirth. Thus fears of pregnancy stem from both psychological and physical sources. Some women fear being taken over by their pregnancy, as if they had no other purpose than to produce a child. They fear feeling victimized by motherhood, as though the child inside them is a parasite. While many women are delighted with the first fetal movement, some find it a frightening indication that they are harboring a separate life. Many women fear the interruption in their work and physical activity brought about by pregnancy. Some women fear that their physical appearance while pregnant will become comical and that they will not be attractive to their husbands and to men in general. A pregnant woman sometimes extends this fear to a feeling that she will never return to her original physical appearance. Some women fear a loss of interest in sexual activity during pregnancy, while others fear an increased interest in sexual activity.

Pregnant women often have intense dreams and fantasies about the child they are carrying. Some women fear that they are losing their minds. Mood swings during pregnancy, sometimes triggered by hormonal changes, disturb many women and their husbands. Well-meant advice and anecdotes from other women can also be a source of anxiety.

Many women become anxious and embarrassed by the physical symptoms associated with pregnancy. Morning sickness, food cravings, frequent urination, water retention, bloating, and swollen breasts are frequent complaints. First-time mothers fear that they may not be able to recognize the first movements of the fetus and as a result may fear that the baby is abnormal or dead. Although most mothers fear weight gain during pregnancy, others may feel that they are not gaining enough. Recent findings about the effects on the fetus of the mother's smoking and alcohol consumption have caused many pregnant women to abstain out of fear that they will have an unhealthy baby.

Clumsiness increases during the last months of pregnancy and, in addition to being unpleasant in itself, makes women fearful of accidents. Some men and women fear that intercourse during pregnancy will harm the fetus. Others may feel uneasy during intercourse in the belief that the fetus is watching and aware of what they are doing.

Some fears related to pregnancy have changed in recent years because of technology, changing social attitudes, and changes in society. The fear of unwanted pregnancy has been reduced by the variety of birth-control techniques. Motherhood without marriage has become more socially acceptable in some circles. Couples who are fearful of an inability to conceive now have hope because of modern medical advances, including in vitro fertilization and artificial insemination. In spite of legal complications, surrogate motherhood is also gaining some degree of acceptance. Women who have delayed motherhood into their late thirties or early forties because of their own or their husbands' careers or because of the attraction of the single life face diminished fertility and greater anxiety about the possibility of birth defects that come with increased maternal age. Amniocentesis (testing the amniotic fluid to detect abnormalities in the fetus) allays some fears of women who postpone motherhood. Fears of bearing a monster and fears of childbirth itself are related fears. (See also BEARING A MONSTER, FEAR OF; CHILDBIRTH FEAR OF.)

de Beauvoir, Simone, *The Second Sex* (New York: Modern Library, 1968).

Eisenberg, Arlene, Heidi Eisenberg Murkoff and Sandee Eisenberg Hathaway, *What to Expect When You're Expecting* (New York: Workman, 1984).

premenstrual syndrome (PMS), fear of Fear of the physical and mental symptoms of anxiety and tension that some women experience before getting their menstrual periods. Many women fear the discomfort associated with PMS, which may include water retention, tender breasts, headaches, body aches, food cravings, lethargy, and depression. Causes of premenstrual syndrome have not been determined and vary from woman to woman. The symptoms that occur several days before menstruation seem to be related to the interplay of hormones between ovulation and the beginning of menstruation.

Many fears about PMS are grounded in actual fact; some may be due to inhibitions and unpleasant associations. Sufferers of PMS sometimes fear that they are going crazy. Some women resent the regular loss of several days a month to PMS. Even nonsufferers dread the fact that a genuine emotional response or complaint may be chalked up to hormones. Since menstruation is not a subject that is discussed freely, many women feel isolated or misunderstood because they suffer in silence. Women are anxious and fearful about the possibility of hostile or even violent interaction with husbands, lovers, children, or employers because of PMS. Statistics on occupational and automobile accidents show that women are more likely to be clumsy, inattentive, and unable to judge distances just before their periods. Students fear that they may have to take an exam that will affect their scholastic records and ultimately their career at this time. Women fear that other occasions when they want to be at their best, such as employment interviews or athletic events, will fall just before menstruation. Since resistance to infection is lowered before the onset of menstruation, a woman has more reason to fear illness just before her period.

Until recently, the medical attitude that the discomfort of PMS was all in the mind has tended to increase rather than decrease anxiety. While attitudes are changing and PMS is a recognized physical condition, there is still some reluctance to take it seriously. Although there is no single successful treatment for PMS, many doctors now regard it as a challenging problem in need of solution. A variety of treatments such as hormones, vitamins, analgesics, and diuretics have been tried with varying degrees of success. (See also MENSTRUATION, FEAR OF.)

Lever, Judy and Michael G. Brush, *Pre-menstrual Tension* (New York: McGraw-Hill, 1981).

Dawood M. Yusoff, John L. McGuire and Laurence Demers, *Premenstrual Syndrome and Dysmenorrhea* (Baltimore: Urban & Scharzenberg, 1985).

prepared fears A theory that individuals may be biologically prepared to develop certain fears and less prepared to develop others. Humans may be prepared for conditioned fear responses to certain stimuli that once evoked danger in our evolutionary cycle. An ability to readily develop fear to these stimuli helped our ancestors avoid such stimuli and therefore survive. This theory helps explain the disproportionately high number of certain phobias, such as snakes and small animals.

Researchers who have tested the preparedness theory of fears and phobias say that prepared fears are easily acquired with as little as a single conditioning trial. Once developed they will be quite resistent to extinction, and the prepared conditioned fear is not easily reduced by the information, for example, that spiders are not likely to be harmful. The theory was proposed by Martin Seligman, a research psychologist, in 1972. (See also CAUSALITY.)

Seligman, M.E.P., "Phobias and Preparedness," in M.E.P. Seligman and J.L. Hager (eds.), *Biological Boundaries of Learning* (New York: Appleton-Century-Crofts, 1972), pp. 451–462.

prevalence of phobias and anxieties
The total number of cases of phobias and anxieties at any given time. Phobias, fears, and anxieties are the most prevalent psychological disturbance in modern society. More than 10 percent of the U.S. adult population is affected by these conditions, qualifying for the diagnosis of anxiety disorder as defined by the American Psychiatric Association in DIAGNOSTIC AND STATISTICAL MANUAL OF MENTAL DISORDERS. Additionally, another 10 percent experience distressingly high levels of anxiety that interfere with their daily lives, although not severe enough to qualify for diagnosis.

Two nationwide surveys were conducted in the mid-1980s to substantiate the prevalence figures for phobias among adults in the U.S. In 1983, E.H. Uhlenhuth et al. found 5.5 percent of the adult population qualified for the diagnosis of phobia. A second study by L.N. Robins et al. in 1984 reported phobia prevalence at 7.8, 9.4, and 23.3 percent in different cities.

Anxiety neurosis may affect about 2.0 to 4.7 percent of the population. There are estimates that up to 14 percent of patients who visit cardiologists may suffer from anxiety states.

When the prevalence of anxiety states is added to that of common phobias and fears, it appears that as much as 20 percent of the population suffers from some form of significant fear or anxiety problem. More than 90 percent have at some time in their lives experienced at least one specific fear, but of lesser proportions. (See also AGE DISTRIBUTION; ANXIETY; PHOBIA.)

Robins, L.N. et al., "Lifetime Prevalence of Specific Psychiatric Disorders in Three Sites," *Archives of General Psychiatry,* 41 (1984), pp. 949–958.

Uhlenhuth, E.H. et al., "Symptom Checklist Syndromes in the General Population," *Archieves of General Psychiatry,* 40 (1983), pp. 1167–1173.

Kleinknecht, Ronald A., *The Anxious Self* (New York: Human Sciences Press, 1986).

primal scene A term used by psychoanalysts to denote the real or fancied observation by the infant of parental or other heterosexual intercourse. Some therapists have suggested that such an experience, whether real or imagined, gives rise to later anxieties. (See also PRIMAL THERAPY; PSYCHOANALYSIS.)

primal scream therapy See PRIMAL THERAPY.

primal therapy A technique developed by ARTHUR JANOV (1924–), an American psychologist and author of *The Primal Scream*. Primal therapy, also known as primal scream therapy, treats neuroses, including anxieties and phobias, by encouraging the individual to relive basic or "primal" traumatic events and discharge painful emotions associated with them. Such events may have led to development of the anxieties and phobias and frequently involve feelings of abandonment or rejection experienced in infancy or early childhood. During therapy the individual may cry, scream, or writhe in agony and later experience a sense of release and freedom from "primal pain."

primal trauma An early-life situation that the individual perceived as painful that is presumed to be the basis for anxieties later in life (See also ANXIETY.)

primary gain The basic internal psychological benefit that the individual derives from having a phobic condition, anxiety, or emotional illness. If the individual develops mental symptoms defensively in largely unconscious ways to cope with or to resolve unconscious conflicts, then the symptoms provide a relief to the individual's system by reducing conflict between UNCONSCIOUS and defensive forces. The need for such gain may be the reason why a phobic condition or emotional problem develops. In contrast, secondary gain is that which is obtained from a symptom of an illness or phobia one already has. The term primary gain is derived from psychoanalytic and psychodynamic theories that emphasize the role of unconscious forces in ANXIETY. (See also AGORAPHOBIA; SECONDARY GAIN.)

primeisodophobia Fear of losing one's virginity. (See also VIRGINITY, FEAR OF LOSING ONE'S.)

Prince, Morton (1854–1929) American psychiatrist and neurologist who studied hysteria, multiple personality, and hallucination. Prince worked with and modified concepts of SIGMUND FREUD and PIERRE JANET, with whom he had studied in Europe, to develop his own method of psychotherapy, which included the use of HYPNOSIS.

Howells, John G. and M. Livia Osborn, *A Reference Companion to the History of Abnormal Psychology* (Westport, CT: Greenwood Press, 1984).

proctophobia Fear of rectal diseases or anything having to do with the rectum. (See also RECTAL DISEASES, FEAR OF; RECTUM, FEAR OF.)

progesterone A HORMONE secreted by females during the luteal phase of the menstrual cycle (after ovulation). Progesterone may partially explain why more women than men have panic attacks and why some women suffer most from anxiety prior to menstruation. The same factors may help explain PREMENSTRUAL SYNDROME (PMS), which is characterized by many of the symptoms exhibited during PANIC ATTACKS: anxiety, irritability, nausea, headaches, and lightheadedness. (See also POSTPARTUM DEPRESSION.)

progress, fear of Fear of progress is known as prosophobia. This fear may be related to fears of novelty, newness, and innovation, and to technophobia and computer phobia. (See also NEWNESS, FEAR OF.)

projection A DEFENSE MECHANISM the individual uses unconsciously to reject ideas or thoughts that are emotionally unacceptable to the self and attribute (project) them to others. Interpersonally, this is called blame as well as projection. This mechanism is a common form of protection with children. Unfortunately, it often remains in place into adulthood. The use of blame prevents the individual from making any significant personal changes. In phobias, an individual is projecting danger onto neutral objects or situations.

prophylactic maintenance Administration of drugs that may prevent or reduce the risk of recurrence of symptoms of a disorder. For example, lithium is taken by some individuals who have MANIC–DEPRESSIVE DISORDER to prevent recurrence of symptoms. Some beta-blocking drugs are taken by some headache sufferers to prevent occurrence of HEADACHES. Individuals who take drugs for these purposes should be carefully monitored by a physician to adjust dosage and watch for possible adverse affects. (See also BETA-BLOCKING AGENTS; LITHIUM.)

propranolol A drug within the family of medications known as beta-adrenergic blocking agents, beta-blocking agents, or BETA BLOCKERS. It is commonly used to treat high blood pressure, migraine headaches, angina, and some heart conditions. Propranolol is also used in some cases to reduce symptoms of anxiety, such as rapid heartbeat (tachycardia), sweating, and general tension. It has been used successfully to help control symptoms of stage fright and fears of public speaking. Because it has few side effects, many tolerate it well. But there are some possible side effects, including dizziness, unusually slow pulse, insomnia, diarrhea, cold hands and feet, and numbness and/or tingling of fingers to toes. Propranolol should not be taken by individuals who have chronic lung disease, asthma, diabetes, or certain heart diseases, or by individuals who are severely depressed.

Propranolol and other beta blockers are sometimes prescribed for individuals who have MITRAL VALVE PROLAPSE (MVP), and for individuals who fear having rapid heartbeat.

Wilson, R. Reid, *Don't Panic: Taking Control of Anxiety Attacks* (New York: Harper & Row, 1986).

Goldstein, Alan, *Overcoming Agoraphobia: Conquering Fear of the Outside World* (New York: Viking Penguin, 1987).

propriety, fear of Fear of propriety is known as orthophobia.

prosophobia Fear of progress. (See also PROGRESS, FEAR OF.)

prostitutes, fear of Fear of prostitutes is known as cyprianophobia. Fears of the practice of prostitution are a mixture of social, religious, and individual fears. Some men fear getting diseases from prostitutes, while others think that prostitutes are evil, without personal moral standards, and hence to be feared. Today, of course, this fear is also compounded by the possibility of acquiring Autoimmune Deficiency Syndrome (AIDS) from prostitutes. Businessmen and neighborhood residents fear prostitution because it damages the area where they live and conduct legitimate businesses. Prostitutes are a reminder of the negative influences in society, including unemployment, child abandonment, and broken families. Prostitution seems to increase in times of war and social disorder.

Women who contemplate prostitution as a form of employment have their own fears. For example, they may fear arrest or fear becoming victims of violence or venereal disease. Many prostitutes fear addiction to drugs or alcohol. Prostitutes may fear total control by a pimp and fear being in a situation they cannot control. On the other hand, in very repressive societies, women have become prostitutes out of fear of the life of the ordinary wife and mother who has no independence, freedom, or rights.

As prostitution is often associated with other criminal activities, men may fear violence, theft, blackmail, and arrest. A woman may fear the involvement of her husband or lover with a prostitute because of the possibility of transmission of disease to her and the possibility that he may become emotionally involved with the prostitute.

Prostitution is as much a product of fear as a cause of fear. In the past, it was a form of contraception for couples who did not want more children. Men patronized prostitutes out of a fear that sex was a distasteful duty for a "good" women. Men who are afraid to ask a wife or lover to act on unusual sexual preferences feel comfortable with prostitutes, as do some men who want assistance with sexual dysfunction. Men may also turn to prostitutes out of fear of intimacy and the usual romantic and domestic demands of a relationship with a woman. (See also SEXUAL FEARS.)

de Beauvoir, Simone, *The Second Sex* (New York: Modern Library, 1968).

Bullough, Vern and Bonnie Bullough, *Prostitution, An Illustrated Social History* (New York: Crown, 1978).

protriptyline An antidepressant medication also used to relieve symptoms of HEADACHES that may arise from anxieties rather than organic causes. (See also ANTIDEPRESSANTS.)

psellismophobia Fear of stuttering (See also STUTTERING FEAR OF.)

pseudoscientific terms, fear of Fear of pseudoscientific terms is known as hellenologophobia.

psychiatrist Psychiatrists are physicians (medical doctors with an M.D. degree) specializing in mental/emotional treatment and research. Some psychiatrists tend to view mental "disorders" as chemical or biological in their source and hence medical in nature.

By virtue of their medical degree, psychiatrists can prescribe medications and conduct medically defined procedures (such as electroconvulsive shock therapy) and can admit patients to hospitals. (See also PSYCHIATRY, SCHOOLS OF.)

psychiatry, schools of There are several theoretical frames of reference that have influenced and still influence psychiatrists' methods of treatment. The schools offer various explanations of how psychiatric symptoms or disorders develop, how they interfere with functioning, and how and why they can be changed by therapeutic interventions. (See also AVERSION THERAPY; BEHAVIORISM; CLASSICAL CONDITIONING; DESENSITIZATION; ERIKSON ERIK; EXISTENTIAL ANALYSIS; FREUD, SIGMUND; MORENO, JACOB; PAVLOV, IVAN; RANK, OTTO; REICH, WILHELM; SKINNER, FREDERICK BURRHUS; WOLPE, JOSEPH.)

psychoactive drug A chemical compound that has a psychological effect and alters mood or thought processes. A tranquilizer is an example of a psychoactive drug. Some psychoactive drugs may be prescribed for individuals under treatment for phobias. (See also ANTIDEPRESSANTS; DRUGS; MAJOR TRANQUILIZER; MINOR TRANQUILIZER.)

psychoanalysis A therapy developed by Sigmund Freud that streses free association, dream analysis, transference, and the modification of defenses to allow the conscious expression of unconscious impulses, memories, emotions, experiences, etc. Psychoanalytic theory has had a powerful impact on our culture, art, movies, literature, advertising, child-rearing practices, views of mental and emotional disorders, and therapy. Anxiety was a key component of the therapy and the theory of human behavior. Psychoanalysis in theory was instrumental in developing anxiety as a diagnostic category.

Schools of Psychiatry

I. Reconstructive
   A. Psychoanalysis—Sigmund Freud
   B. Neo-Freudian, modifications of psychoanalysis
      1. Active analytic techniques—Sandor Ferenczi, Wilhelm Stekel, the Chicago school (especially Franz Alexander and Thomas French)
      2. Analytic play therapy—Anna Freud, Melanie Klein
      3. Analytical psychology—Carl Jung
      4. Character analysis, orgone therapy—Wilhelm Reich
      5. Cognitive—Jean Piaget
      6. Developmental—Erik Erikson
      7. Ego psychology—Paul Federn, Eduardo Weiss, Heinz Hartmann, Ernst Kris, Rudolph Loewenstein
      8. Existential analysis—Ludwig Binswanger
      9. Holistic analysis—Karen Horney
      10. Individual psychology—Alfred Adler
      11. Transactional analysis—Eric Berne
      12. Washington cultural school—Harry Stack Sullivan, Erich Fromm, Clara Thompson
      13. Will therapy—Otto Rank
   C. Group Approaches
      1. Orthodox psychoanalytic—S.R. Slavson
      2. Psychodrama—Jacob L. Moreno
      3. Psychoanalysis in groups—Alexander Wolf
      4. Valence systems—Walter Bion

II. Behavioral and humanistic—Joseph Wolpe
   1. Client-centered (non-directive)—Carl Rogers
   2. Conditioning, behavior therapy, behavior modification
      a. aversion therapy—N.V. Kantorovich, Joseph R. Cautela
      b. behaviorism—John B. Watson
      c. classical conditioning—Ivan Pavlov, Joseph Wolpe, Thomas Stampfl
      d. operant conditioning—Burrhus F. Skinner, Teodoro Ayllon, Ogden R. Lindsley
      e. sexual counseling—William Masters, Virginia Johnson
      f. systematic desensitization—Joseph Wolpe
   3. Cognitive behavior—Aaron Beck
   4. Family therapy—Nathan Ackerman
   5. Gestalt—Wolfgang Kohler, Kurt Lewin, Fritz Perls
   6. Logotherapy—Victor Frankl
   7. Psychobiology (distributive analysis and synthesis)—Adolf Meyer
   8. Zen (satori)—Alan Watts

---

psychodiagnostics Psychodiagnostics is concerned with the methods used to diagnose mental and emotional disorders, including anxiety and phobias. Classification of mental disorders allows researchers to conduct scientific experiments and helps therapists to choose the most appropriate course of treatment.

The process of labeling and discriminating between disorders is largely arbitrary and subjective. The DIAGNOSTIC AND STATISTICAL MANUAL OF MENTAL DISORDERS, produced by the American Psychiatric Association, is periodically updated and revised to include reforms in the field. For example, the current edition (3rd ed., rev.) includes a multiaxial system of classification that forces a diagnostician to take a broader range of information into account when diagnosing a client.

The DSM includes many related disturbances in the "anxiety disorders" category. The first are the phobic disorders, followed by panic disorder, which includes generalized anxiety disorder, obsessive–compulsive disorder, and posttraumatic stress disorder. Demand for further reform of the DSM continues. Suggestions for changes include further study into the validity of the system, a modification of definitions, new organization, and a further increase in the number of conditions a person must fulfill before a diagnosis is reached. (See also DIAGNOSIS; DIAGNOSTIC CRITERIA.)

psychodrama A therapeutic technique in which individuals act out, or watch others act out, personal problems, including phobias and anxieties. Psychodrama is a type of group therapy that evolved in Vienna in the early part of the 20th century. Individuals create their own plays mirroring their personal problems and conflicts. Psychodramatic methods are applicable to many types of phobic individuals and may be used by therapists to help individuals overcome specific phobias or general anxieties. (See also ROLE PLAYING.)

psychophobia See MIND, FEAR OF THE.)

psychologic tests Tests commonly used for diagnostic purposes. Following are some commonly used tests and their uses.

psychologist In most states, a psychologist has a Ph.D. degree from a graduate program in PSYCHOLOGY. After World War II, psychologists began to perform psychotherapy for "mental illness" (up until the 1950s, psychotherapy was claimed to be a medical procedure) and now possess all the privileges of a mental-health professional in the form of licensing, insurance reimbursement, hospital privileges, and expert-witness designation.

Psychology, like medicine, has many areas of specialization. These include child, developmental, school, clinical, social, and industrial. The Ph.D. degree requires training in research skills. Clinical psychologists take further training in psychodiagnosis and psychotherapy and require supervision and an internship experience, as does psychiatry.

psychology The study of all behavior as part of the total life process. This includes the sequence of development, inherited and environmental factors, social interactions, conscious and unconscious mental processes, mental health and disorder, bodily systems associated with behavior, observation, testing and experimental study of behavior, and the application of psychological information to fields such as employment, education, and consumer behavior.

There are more than 20 subdivisions in the American Psychological Association's designated areas of specialization. Some of them are clinical, child, industrial, social, cognitive, animal-experimental, medical psychology, etc. (See also BEHAVIOR THERAPY.)

psychosexual anxieties Psychosexual anxieties are disorders caused by mental attitudes about sexuality and physical conditions involving sexuality. Some anxieties are caused more by psychological attitudes while others come from physical aspects. Many psychosexual anxieties may have arisen because of new sexual freedoms that many individuals discovered in the latter decades of the 20th century. Sexual activity between men and women, unmarried as well as married, seemed to increase for a number of reasons, First, improved methods of contraception in the form of the birth-control pill became available. Secondly, previously known SEXUALLY TRANSMITTED (venereal) DISEASES, most notably SYPHILIS and gonorrhea, were curable with penicillin and other drugs.

During the last two decades of the 20th century, an increasing number of new sexually transmitted diseases (STDs) appeared, causing psychosexual anxieties that differed from previously recognized generalized SEXUAL FEARS. For example, when an individual discovers, feels, or suspects a genital lesion,

Table of Psychologic Tests

Test	Type	Assesses	Age of Patient	Output	Administration
Bayley Scales of Infant Development	Infant development	Cognitive functioning and motor development	1–30 months	Performance on subtests measuring cognitive and motor development	Individual
Bender Visual-Motor Gestalt Test	Projective visual-motor development	Personality conflicts Ego function and structure Organic brain damage	5–Adult	Patient's reproduction of geometric figures	Individual
Benton Visual Retention Test	Objective performance	Organic brain damage	Adult	Patient's reproduction of geometric figures from memory	Individual
Cattell Infant Intelligence Scale	Infant development	General motor and cognitive development	1–18 months	Performance on developmental tasks	Individual
Children's Apperception Test (CAT)	Projective	Personality conflicts	Child	Patient makes up stories after viewing pictures	Individual
Draw-A-Person **Draw-A-Family** **House-Tree-Person**	Projective	Personality conflicts Self-image (DAP) Family perception (DAF) Ego functions Intellectual functioning (DAP) Visual-motor coordination	2–Adult	Patient's drawings on a blank sheet of paper	Individual
Frostig Developmental Test of Visual Perception	Visual perception	Eye-motor coordination Figure ground perception Constancy of shape Position in space Spatial relationships	4–8 years	Performance on paper-and-pencil test measuring five aspects of visual perception	Individual or group

Gesell Developmental Schedules	Preschool development	Cognitive, motor, language and social development	1–60 months	Performance on developmental tasks	Individual
Halstead-Reitan Neuropsychological Battery and Outer Measures	Brain functioning	Cerebral functioning and organic brain damage	6–Adult	Various subtests measure aspects of cerebral functioning	Individual
Illinois Test of Psycholinguistic Ability (ITPA)	Language ability	Auditory-vocal, visual-motor channels of language; receptive, organizational, and expressive components	2–10 years	Performance on 12 subtests measuring various dimensions of language functioning	Individual
Michigan Picture Stories	Defensive structure	Personality conflicts	Adolescent	Patient makes up stories after viewing stimulus pictures	Individual
Minnesota Multiphasic Personality Inventory (MMPI)	Paper and pencil; personality inventory	Personality structure Diagnostic classification	Adolescent-Adult	Personality profile reflecting some dimensions of personality Diagnosis based upon actuarial prediction	Group
Otis Quick Scoring Mental Abilities Tests	Intelligence	Intellectual functioning	5–Adult	Performance on verbal and nonverbal dimensions of intellectual functioning	Group
Rorschach	Projective	Personality conflicts Ego function and structure Defensive structure Thought processes Affective integration	3–Adult	Patient's associations to inkblots	Individual

Table of Psychologic Tests (*Continued*)

Test	Type	Assesses	Age of Patient	Output	Administration
Senior Apperception Test (SAT)	Projective	Personality conflicts	Over 65	Patient makes up stories after viewing stimulus pictures	Individual
Stanford-Binet	Intelligence	Intellectual functioning	2–Adult	Performance on problem solving and developmental tasks	Individual
Tasks of Emotional Development (TED)	Projective	Personality conflicts	Child and Adolescent	Patient makes up stories after viewing stimulus pictures	Individual
Thematic Apperception Test (TAT)	Projective	Personality conflicts	Adult	Patient makes up stories after viewing stimulus pictures	Individual
Vineland Social Maturity Scale	Social maturity	Capacity for independent functioning	0–25+ years	Performance on developmental tasks measuring various dimensions of social functioning	Interview patient or guardian of patient, occasional self-report
Wechsler Adult Intelligence Scale (WAIS)	Intelligence	Intellectual functioning	16–Adult	Performance on 10 subtests measuring various dimensions of intellectual functioning	Individual
Wechsler Intelligence Scale for Children (WISC)	Intelligence	Intellectual functioning Thought processes Ego functioning	5–15	See above	Individual
Wechsler Preschool Primary Scale of Intelligence (WPPSI)	Intelligence	Intellectual functioning Thought processes Ego functioning	4–6½ years	See above	Individual

Reprinted with permission from *American Psychiatric Glossary* (Washington, DC: American Psychiatric Association, 1988).

he or she may lose interest in sexual intercourse or at least restrain himself/herself for fear of infecting the partner. Another situation is the concern faced by the innocently infected partner of an individual with a sexually transmitted disease who has had intercourse outside a stable relationship. The innocent partner may realize the implications of the STD but may not want to face the reality of the diagnosis.

Under the stress of having a sexually transmited disease, a person may become angry, anxious, or depressed. Anger may be directed at the physician consulted as well as the person who transmitted the infection. Professionals in clinics specializing in sexually transmitted disease deal with this kind of anxiety by letting the individual voice his or her feelings and later by reassurance. In some individuals, anxiety is so severe that a short course of antianxiolytic medication is given.

GUILT and DEPRESSION over a sexually transmitted disease are not uncommon. In some cases, antidepressant medications are given. Many conditions, such as genital herpes, pelvic inflammatory disease, acute epididymitis, and hepatitis B, may cause anger, anxiety, guilt, and depression.

Physical symptoms of gonococcal and nongonococcal urethritis may be more easily and rapidly treated than the psychological symptoms. Resuming intercourse soon after tests indicate cure may help to heal the psychological wound that one or both partners in a stable relationship feel. Unfortunately, nongonococcal urethritis may be recurrent, and the patient may be told not to resume intercourse until the inflammation clears. This advice may may put an extra strain on a relationship.

Pelvic pain and pain during sexual intercourse (dyspareunia) usually interfere with satisfactory sexual intercourse. Pelvic inflammatory disease also causes pain during intercourse and may lead to infertility. Along with dealing with a woman's feelings of loss of health and fertility, a physician may see the couple together to identify problems that have occurred because one or both partners has had sex with others, and to discuss the anger and resentment the woman feels if it is the man who has had casual sex (this is often the case).

Genital herpes may occur in one partner in a relationship when the other has never knowingly had the infection. Both may be confused about where the infection came from and may be angry, accusatory, or resentful of the other partner. Discussion guided by a trained therapist enables the couple to face the facts together. Such a couple should discuss whether herpes, once healed, might disturb further sexual relationships (usually not).

Women and homosexual men who have had anorectal herpes may develop maladaptive behavior after the primary attack. Vaginismus (tightening of the vaginal muscles) and anospasm (tightening of the anus muscles) may continue long after the ulcers have healed. SYSTEMATIC DESENSITIZATION (for example, using the partner's finger as a dilator) often is successful in overcoming this problem in a few sessions with an appropriately trained sex therapist.

Frequent recurrences of genital candidiasis (yeast infection) may leave both partners confused, frustrated, and angry about the supposed source of the problem. If the relationship is unstable, symptoms may assume dimensions out of proportion to the signs. Trichomonas vaginalis and Gardnerella vaginalis often involve offensive vaginal discharges, which may cause loss of interest by the male partner. After treatment the odor may disappear, but the woman may have lost confidence in herself, and the man may mistake the normal musky vaginal odor for the previous abnormal odor. The couple may need reassurance from a physician or sex therapist.

Syphilis, whether congenital or acquired, is feared by many people as "worse than cancer." Congenital syphilis that occurs in later life may devastate an individual when he or she realizes the implication of the disease with respect to his or her parents.

An individual who has a sexually transmitted disease or whose partner is unfaithful may lose interest in intercourse, particularly with the partner concerned. Loss of libido may be due to anxiety, depression, or just loss of interest in the partner. Individuals who are undergoing treatment for a sexually transmitted disease should discuss with their physician their attitudes about resuming sexual relations. Counseling with short-term psychotherapy may help the individual return to normal sexual function.

Some individuals may complain of symptoms of a sexually transmitted disease yet not have any illness. Some who have had an infection retain the symptoms after the infection has been cleared up with appropriate medication. Penile and urethral itching, penile and perineal pain, testicular pain, and pelvic pain may either be psychosomatic or represent symptoms of reactive sexually transmitted diseases.

Many individuals visit sexually transmitted disease clinics for checkups because they fear having acquired an STD. Some continue to believe or fear that they have contracted an infection in spite of extensive and frequent reassurance. Some of these individuals may have delusions of venereal disease, which are fixed ideas that the individual cannot be talked out of (found in schizophrenic disorders, psychotic depression, and monosymptomatic delusions), and phobias or obsessional fears. Individuals who have a fixed belief of venereal disease should be referred for psychotherapy. (See also SEX THERAPY; SYPHILIS, FEAR OF; VENEREAL DISEASE, FEAR OF.)

Adapted with permission from: Goldmeier, David, "Psychosexual Problems," in *ABC of Sexually Transmitted Diseases* (London: British Medical Association, 1986), pp. 51–52.

psychosis A severe mental disorder characterized by gross impairment in reality testing. A psychotic (one who has a psychosis) incorrectly evaluates the accuracy of his or her perceptions and thoughts and makes incorrect inferences about external reality, even in the face of contrary evidence. The term psychotic does not apply, however, to minor disortions of reality that involve matters of relative judgment. For example, a depressed individual who lacks self-esteem and underestimates his or her achievements would not be described as psychotic, whereas one who believes that he or she has caused a natural catastrophe would be so described. (See also NEUROSIS; SCHIZOPHRENIA.)

psychosurgery Sometimes called lobotomy, defined by the American Psychiatric Association Task Force on Psychosurgery as: "Surgical intervention to sever fibers connecting one part of the brain with another or to remove, destroy or stimulate brain tissue with the intent of modifying or altering disturbances in behavior, thought content, or mood for which no organic pathological cause can be demonstrated by established tests or techniques." The term "neurosurgery" is preferred when referring to the relief of pain due to organic diseases. The major type of psychosurgery is the prefrontal lobotomy or lesioning of the prefrontal area of the brain from the rest of the brain. Such surgeries, although rare, have been performed on anxiety patients to relieve these symptoms. However, there is no evidence that this surgery has any demonstrable effect on anxiety, panic, phobia, or agoraphobia.

Psychosurgery is still considered an experimental procedure that can be performed only after exhaustive attempts to modify thought, mood, or behavior. It is not at all appropriate with anxiety problems.

psychotherapy A treatment of PHOBIA, ANXIETY, or mental disorder through a corrective experience resulting from the interaction between a trained therapist and the individual. (See also BEHAVIOR THERAPY; PSYCHIATRY; PSYCHOLOGY.)

psychrophobia Fear of being cold or of any cold thing. Also known as frigophobia (See also COLD, FEAR OF.)

pteronophobia Fear of feathers or of anything bearing feathers or having a featherlike appearance. This fear is related to fear of birds, chickens, and other feathered things. (See also BIRDS, FEAR OF; FEATHERS, FEAR OF; WINGED THINGS, FEAR OF.)

public speaking, fear of See PERFORMANCE ANXIETY; SOCIAL PHOBIA.

punishment, fear of Fear of punishment is known as poinephobia. This fear may relate to a fear of wrongdoing and getting caught, as well as telling untruths.

puppet therapy for anxieties and phobias Use of puppets in therapy for ANXIETIES and phobias enables individuals, particularly CHILDREN, to express ideas and thoughts that they otherwise might think of as unacceptable to discuss with a therapist. The most popular kind of puppet in therapy is the one held on the hand because it is easy to manipulate and encourages spontaneity. Puppet therapy is also useful in FAMILY THERAPY: As each member of the family manipulates a puppet, a family's interactions can be enacted on an imaginary but representative level.

In puppet therapy, some puppets are realistic and some are fantasy figures. Based on the patient's choice of puppet, therapists can learn a great deal about such characteristics as aggression, caring, fearfulness, and the nature of conflicts. (See also CHILDHOOD ANXIETIES, FEARS, AND PHOBIAS.)

purple, fear of Fear of the color purple is known as porphyrophobia. This fear may be related to the fear of colors in general. The color purple is also associated with AIDS and homosexuality. (See also COLORS, FEAR OF.)

pyrexiophobia Fear of having a fever. Also known as pyrexeophobia and febriphobia. (See also FEVER, FEAR OF.)

pyrophobia Fear of fire, watching fires, or that one will start fires. (See also FIRES, FEAR OF.)

R

rabies A virus-produced disease that destroys the brain nerve cells in both humans and animals. Rabies is also called hydrophobia (also the name for fear of water); fear of rabies is known as cynophobia, kynophobia, and lyssophobia. Although the dog is the most common transmitter of rabies, many domestic and wild animals such as cats, wolves, foxes, raccoons, bats, horses, and skunks may also carry it. People who fear rabies avoid outdoor activities such as hiking and camping. After a person has been bitten and infected by an animal carrying the virus, it usually takes twenty to ninety days for symptoms to develop. During the early part of the disease, the individual may be restless and anxious. The sight of water will produce throat spasms, pain, and fear of water. At this stage convulsions and delirium may occur, and the disease is almost always fatal in two to ten days. Immediate medical care after a dog or animal bite can be lifesaving. Cleansing of the bitten area removes much of the virus. Treatment consists of seven to fourteen daily injections, depending on the severity of the exposure. (See also HYDROPHOBOPHOBIA.)

Andelman, Samuel L., *The New Home Medical Encyclopedia* (New York: Quadrangle, 1973).

radiation, fear of Fear of radiation is known as radiophobia. Some individuals fear harmful health effects from radiation.

They fear that overexposure to rays may cause sterility, mutations, and damage to internal organs. These are legitimate fears but, if carried to extremes, or in the absence of radiation, are phobias. Some individuals fear radiation from emissions from color television sets, as well as from nuclear bombs.

Radiation has many beneficial characteristics that phobics overlook. Radioactivity in the form of X rays has been used for many years to diagnose and treat people for many injuries and diseases. Use of radiation has expanded to the use of radioisotopes to trace metabolic systems in the body, and to direct use of rays to treat cancer. Many elements, including radium and radioactive cobalt, are used to produce radiation for diagnostic and therapeutic purposes. (See also X RAYS, FEAR OF.)

radiophobia Fear of radiation or of X rays. (See also RADIATION, FEAR OF; X RAY, FEAR OF.)

radon, fear of An invisible radioactive gas emitted naturally by soil and rock containing uranium. Radon is colorless and odorless. Radon becomes diluted when emitted into outdoor air but seeps into homes, largely through cracks in the foundation, through some building materials and in sump pump and floor drain openings, where it may collect to dangerous levels. Radon is also present in groundwater used to supply drinking water. Fear of radon became prevalent during the 1980s when it was realized that inhaling the gas over a long period of time may cause lung cancer.

Individuals who are most fearful of radon are usually also fearful of air pollutants in general. They may fear disease and particularly fear developing cancer. Hypochondriacs, or those who believe they have symptoms or diseases, are another group of individuals who are likely to be fearful of radon.

According to the U.S. Environmental Protection Agency, 5,000 to 20,000 of the 135,000 U.S. lung-cancer deaths that occur each year can be attributed to radiation from indoor radon. Although radon in drinking water is a less serious risk than the radon seeping through the soil, this source of the pollutant is still estimated to contribute 30 to 600 excess lung-cancer deaths annually in the United States.

Those who want to allay their fears can detect the presence of this gas with appropriate detection kits; some communities perform home inspections for radon. Radon is measured in picocuries, a measurement of radioactivity. As of 1987, the EPA's federal standard was four picocuries of radioactive radon per liter of air.

Obviously, the fear of radon gases is not a phobia, since it is not an irrational fear. In this sense, it is in a group with many rational fears that people in a culture experience, such as fear of violence, crime, nuclear war, and radiation. If a significant amount of the individual's life is preoccupied with thoughts, anxieties, and ways to avoid such events, it comes closer to qualifying as a phobic reaction. (See also AIR POLLUTION, FEAR OF; CANCER, FEAR OF; DISEASE, FEAR OF; RADIATION, FEAR OF.)
Science News, (August 15, 1987), p. 105.

railroads, fear of Fear of railroads and trains is known as siderodromophobia. Some individuals may fear railroads because of the motion involved in riding on them. Others may fear them because they move fast and may not be able to stop for an object or person in their path. (See also MOTION, FEAR OF; TRAINS, FEAR OF.)

rain Fear of rain is known as ombrophobia and pluviophobia.

rape, fear of Fear of rape is known as virgivitiphobia. (See also GIRLS, FEAR OF; SEXUAL FEARS.)

Rank, Otto (1884–1939) An Austrian psychoanalyst. Rank broke away from

Sigmund FREUD and Freud's teachings to emphasize short-term therapy and the birth trauma, which he believed was the root of neuroses, such as phobias and anxieties. He aimed his therapy at eliminating the effects of trauma, especially anxiety and dependence, and helping the individual achieve constructive independence and trusting relationships. Rank believed that once the individual's "primal anxiety" (known as "life fear") was uncovered, the analyst could concentrate on helping the individual look forward to the process of separation by gradually undoing the individual's reliance on him. The aim of this separation was to inspire the successive stages of what Rank called "the wills of life," which would enable the individual to become a fully integrated personality. The emphasis on "wills" led Rank's theory of neurosis to become known as "will therapy." This system directs attention to present functioning potential as opposed to the Freudian emphasis on the unconscious past. (See also ADLER, ALFRED; BIRTH FEAR; JUNG, CARL; WILL THERAPY.)

Rational emotive therapy (RET)

A therapy developed by Albert Ellis, an American psychologist (1913–). Also known as rational psychotherapy, rational emotive therapy (RET) is based on the premise that emotional problems are primarily caused by irrational attitudes and beliefs about oneself, others, and the world at large. This therapy helps the individual focus more clearly on specific irrational patterns of thought that produce unwanted ANXIETIES and PHOBIAS disturbing behavior. RET emphasizes that individuals are responsible for creating their own disturbing emotions, and that they are capable of rearranging their thoughts and beliefs in more rational ways that will reduce and eliminate anxieties and fears. Individuals are taught to "depropagandize" themselves in order to confront difficulties in a logical way. Action-oriented, RET makes use of many techniques that work toward the practical aim of creating significant philosophical, emotional, and behavioral changes. The aim of RET is to help individuals integrate their intellectual and experiential processes, to enhance their growth and creativity, and to rid themselves of unproductive and self-defeating habits.

Ellis wrote a book, *Growth Through Reason* in which he details techniques used in rational emotive therapy. He is noted for describing RET as an ABCD process: A refers to an antecedent event that the individual usually thinks causes C, the emotional or behavioral consequent. Ellis points out that, in fact, it is our beliefs (B) that produce negative emotions and behavior. So individual beliefs may form an imperative (must, have to), catastrophic thought (wouldn't it be terrible) or exaggerated outcome event. It is these irrational beliefs that are the immediate cause of anxiety. Proper emotional or behavioral response requires depropagandizing (D) to bring thinking or internal beliefs into line with reality and the true nature of the situation. (See also BEHAVIOR MODIFICATION; BEHAVIOR THERAPY.)

Lande, Nathaniel, *Mindstyles/Lifestyles* (Los Angeles: Price/Stern/Sloan Publishers, 1976).

rationalization A DEFENSE MECHANISM. The individual uses rationalization as an unconscious way to attempt to justify or make consciously tolerable by plausible means feelings, behavior, or motives that otherwise would be intolerable. Rationalization differs from conscious evasion. (See also PROJECTION.)

rational psychotherapy See RATIONAL EMOTIVE THERAPY.

Rat Man, case of In a well-documented case, SIGMUND FREUD treated a young man who was tormented by anxieties and thoughts of harm to others and to himself. His most horrifying thoughts were of a form of torture involving rats eating at the anus being applied to his father and the woman he loved. Probing further, Freud found that the death of the man's father had occurred after he had imagined his death. Freud thought that the young man had developed a belief in what he termed "omnipotence of thought," a feeling that thinking about an occurrence could magically bring it about.

Schur, Max, *Freud: Living and Dying* (New York: International Universities Press, 1972).

rats, fear of Fear of rats as well as mice is known as murophobia. This is a common fear. Rats are repugnant to many individuals for many reasons. Rats destroy food and carry disease. Rat bites may lead to rat-bite fever, a serious disease causing fever, chills, infection of the lymph glands, headache, swelling of the spleen, and other symptoms, including a rash. Prompt treatment with penicillin and other antibiotics reduces the danger of death. Bubonic plague, one of the oldest and most feared diseases in the world, begins with a bacillus carried by the rat flea, carried on the rat. The flea spreads the infection from rat to rat and from rat to man. Murine typus is another disease that fleas and rats transmit. Although there is reason to be careful about rats (due to the potential problems described above), phobias are exaggerated reactions often accompanied by preoccupations and associated excessive avoidance. In his book *1984,* George Orwell gave his main character, Winston, this fear. Winston was forced to face his feared objects in an effort to make him change his political outlook. (See also ANIMALS, FEAR OF; MICE, FEAR OF; PLAGUE, FEAR OF THE; RAT MAN, CASE OF.)

Andelman, Samuel L., *The New Home Medical Encyclopedia* (New York: Quadrangle, 1973).

real anxiety Anxiety caused by a true danger posed by the external environment. The term was used by Freud; also known as reality anxiety or objective anxiety.

reality therapy A form of BEHAVIOR-MODIFICATION THERAPY. Reality therapy tries to help the individual get more closely in touch with the real world around him by providing assistance in learning new ways of fulfilling needs in real-life situations, such as managing anxieties and phobias. The method was developed by William Glasser, a Los Angeles psychiatrist, along with Dr. G.L. Harrington. In reality therapy, the individual is treated not as a patient with a disease stemming from some past crisis, but rather as someone needing guidance in facing the present conditions of his reality. Attention is directed to both present and future behavior with little emphasis on the past. (See also BEHAVIOR THERAPY.)

Lande, Nathaniel, *Mindstyles/Lifestyles* (Los Angeles: Price/Stern/Sloan Publishers, 1976).

rebirthing A type of holistic therapy developed in the early 1970s by Leonard Orr. Rebirthing has been used to relieve anxiety disorders and many types of emotional and physical problems. Rebirthing is a breathing technique based on the belief in a connection between mind and matter. Persons who practice rebirthing with a trained rebirther as a teacher learn to inhale and exhale without pausing in between, emphasizing a longer inhale and a very brief exhale. Orr believed that after rebirthing has been carried out for about an hour, the person's thoughts will move from their focus on breathing to negative images and feelings from their past. As breathing continues these negative images are released, allowing the person to make decisions and take action in the present without the burden of unhealthy former belief systems. Powerful negative images may be connected with a person's birth, and the name "rebirthing" comes from the letting go of these.

Corsini, Raymond J. (ed.), *Encyclopedia of Psychology* (New York: John Wiley, 1984).

reciprocal inhibition, law of A principle based on the logical and physiological fact that two opposing emotions cannot be experienced at the same time, useful in combating many fears and emotions. For example, soldiers forget their fear when they are angry during combat. Many persons overcome the fear of flying by focusing on the pleasure they will derive during their good time at the end of the flight. Those who have elevator phobia manage to take the elevator up to their place of work because they enjoy thinking about what they will buy with their paycheck.

The term was introduced by Joseph WOLPE (1915–), a pioneering psychiatrist in the use of behavior therapy. Wolpe's original book *Psychotherapy by Reciprocal Inhibition,* lead to the practical use of behavioral techniques with adults and children and accelerated the growth of behavior therapy. The principle of reciprocal inhibition is the basis of such widely diverse techniques as systematic desensitization (relaxation is the incompatible response to anxiety), assertive training (assertion is incompatible with fear and inhibition), and sexual responsiveness (treatment of impotence by introducing gradual sexual arousal to inhibit performance anxiety). (See also ANXIETY; ASSERTIVE TRAINING; BEHAVIOR THERAPY; COUNTERCONDITIONING; DESENSITIZATION; FEAR; PHOBIA; SOTERIA; SYSTEMATIC DESENSITIZATION.)

Goodwin, Donald W., *Phobia: The Facts* (Oxford: Oxford University Press, 1983).

rectal diseases, fear of Fear of rectal diseases is known as protophobia, proctophobia, and rectophobia. The rectum is a short passage in the lower intestines between the colon and the anal canal through which solid digestive wastes are discharged. Infections and disorders of the rectum usually include those of the anal canal or the lower (sigmoid) colon. Some individuals fear infections in the rectum or damage to its tissues or muscles during a bowel movement or during childbirth. Excessive strain during childbirth may result in a fistula (abnormal passage) from the rectum to the vagina, or other types of fistulas. Some individuals fear developing rectal hemorrhoids, and some who have them fear injuring themselves and seeing blood. Rectal disease fears may extend to fear of having bowel movements, of having pain during bowel movements, or of injuring oneself during a bowel movement. There are also obsessions about anal activity and appearance of buttocks.

rectophobia Fear of rectal disease. (See also RECTAL DISEASES, FEAR OF.)

red colors, fear of Fear of red colors is known as erythrophobia and ereuthophobia. This may be related to a fear of blood or a fear of blushing in public. Some individuals become fearful when they see another individual wearing red clothing. Some who have this phobia may avoid wearing or being near anything red. (See also BLOOD AND BLOOD-INJURY, FEAR OF; BLUSHING, FEAR OF; COLORS, FEAR OF.)

regression Reversion to behavior appropriate during an earlier developmental stage. Regression is a defense mechanism the individual uses when threatened with anxiety-producing situations or internal conflicts. The regression may be general and long-standing, or it may be temporary and situation-specific. Individuals may react with earlier behaviors, such as fear, crying, thumbsucking, or temper tantrums, to gain attention or to force others to solve their problems. In working with phobic individuals, some therapists may encourage regression to determine the initial cause of the individual's phobic behavior. In psychoanalysis, regression is encouraged so that analyst and analysand can get in touch with the past. Individuals are also encouraged to regress in certain types of group therapy, such as primal therapy and rebirthing.

Reich, Wilhelm (1897–1957) An Austrian-American psychoanalyst. Reich was influenced by Sigmund FREUD but developed his own approaches to therapy for anxieties known as Reichian therapy, orgonomy, vegetotherapy, and CHARACTER ANALYSIS. Orgone energy was Reich's term for Freud's concept of psychic energy, or libido. He viewed Freud's concept of fixation as CHARACTER ARMOR. Reich suggested that neuroses, including anxieties and phobias, develop because of lack of complete release of orgone energy (life energy), and he believed that sexual climax within a genital union offered such a release. Reich worked on muscle groups to weaken the individual's defenses, release repressed emotions, and mobilize energy in a productive way. Reich, who came to the United States in 1933, died in the Lewisburg Penitentiary, where he had been imprisoned for selling unapproved medical devices.

Reich, W., *Character Analysis* (New York: Orgone Institute, 1945).

Zusne, Leonard, *Biographical Dictionary of Psychology* (Westport, CT: Greenwood Press, 1984).

Reik, Theodor (1888–1970) Austrian-born American psychoanalyst. Of all the various offshoots of classic Freudian psychoanalysis, Reik's thinking remains closest to the Freudian style. However, Reik differed with Freud over the cause of neuroses and anxieties, which he saw as stemming from the pre-Oedipal stage of the individual's life. Reik focused on the infant stage of human growth and emphasized the collaboration between therapist and individual in exploring infancy. Reik identified three components as the causes of neuroses: lack of mothering, quality of mothering, and quantity of mothering. While all were crucial to the development of the "adjusted" person, he saw the quality of mothering as most important. Reik is the author of *The Search Within* and *Listening with the Third Ear;* the latter is a description of the intuitive process. Many of the cases he presented were people who had anxiety problems.

reinforcement A procedure to change the likelihood or frequency of a phobic response or fearful behavior pattern. Reinforcement increases the strength of a conditioning or other learning process. In CLASSICAL CONDITIONING, reinforcement is the repeated association of the CONDITIONED STIMULUS with the UNCONDITIONED STIMULUS. In OPERANT CONDITIONING, reinforcement refers to the reward given after a correct response that strengthens the response or the punishment given after an incorrect response that weakens that response.

Longman Dictionary of Psychology and Psychiatry (New York: Longman, 1984).

rejection, fear of Fear of rejection is part of most SOCIAL PHOBIAS. It is a fear of being socially excluded or criticized, which would produce considerable emotional pain and self-degradation. For example, the avoidance of social situations may take obvious forms, such as extreme SHYNESS, avoidance of meeting new people, or fear of parties and crowds or it may take more subtle forms, such as avoidance of elevators and freeways. Individuals with extreme fear of rejection generally have a low sense of self-esteem. (See also SEXUAL FEARS.)

relatives, fear of Fear of relatives is known as syngenesophobia. While extended families offer emotional and practical support, they are also promoters of fears and anxieties. Dependency and intrusiveness often are major issues in family anxieties. One's own family, as well as one's in-laws, often create anxieties and tensions for individuals at all ages and stages of life. Grandparents, while loving, may intrude in the upbringing of grandchildren by spoiling them, disciplining them in ways unacceptable to their parents, or siding with the child against his or her parents. Adult children may also burden their parents with unwanted babysitting responsibilities. Longer life spans are creating situations in which several generations of a family live with responsibilities of caring for elderly relatives. Some middle-aged individuals feel anxieties because they are the "sandwich" generation, with responsibilities to their own children as well as to their elderly parents.

Anxieties regarding relatives often arise because of nepotism in employment in both family-owned and non–family owned organizations. Hiring and promotion of relatives may create anxieties and resentments from both other relatives and from other unrelated employees. Family-owned businesses often suffer because of the emotional stresses and strains inherent in the family relationship, and family members suffer because they feel locked into a certain way of life due to the nature of the business.

Issues related to inheritance also promote extended family anxieties and friction. One member may fear that another received more than he or she deserved from an estate. Positions of responsibility such as executor or trustee of a will also promote jealousy and conflicts. Occasions such as weddings, reunions, and holidays bring buried resentments and fears to the surface in some families, and situations that should be pleasant become filled with anxiety and tension.

Because of the high incidence of child abuse, some parents may fear leaving their children with relatives. (See also CHILD ABUSE, FEAR OF; "GENERATIONAL" ANXIETIES; FATHER-IN-LAW, FEAR OF; INCEST, FEAR OF; MOTHER-IN-LAW, FEAR OF.)

Becker, Benjamin M. and Fred Tillman. *The Family Owned Business* (Chicago: Commerce Cleaning House, 1975).

Klemer, Richard H., *Marriage and Family Relationships* (New York: Harper and Row, 1970).

Kraizer, Sherryll Kerns, *The Safe Child Book* (New York: Delacorte Press, 1983).

Spock, Benjamin, *Raising Children in a Difficult Time* (New York: W.W. Norton, 1974).

relaxation therapy A group of techniques to reduce arousal used to treat many anxieties and phobias. Relaxation training is an important aspect of anxiety-management training, stress inoculation, and various self-help approaches to the reduction of anxieties and phobias. Relaxation training is aimed at reducing the individual's level of response to stressful situations and helping him or her develop a less stressful response pattern. The therapy is based on the concept that muscle relaxation, as a physiological state, is incompatible with anxiety, and that parasympathetic arousal can inhibit low levels of sympathetic arousal.

BIOFEEDBACK can be used to indicate the individual's pattern of arousal. Other methods to teach an individual relaxation are breathing exercises, muscle tensing followed by muscle relaxation, meditation, and imagery. Some therapists give individuals prerecorded tapes or exercises to use between therapy sessions.

Relaxation training, also known as autogenic training and progressive relaxation, was pioneered during the 1930s and further developed during the 1950s. American psychiatrist Joseph WOLPE, in his early work with SYSTEMATIC DESENSITIZATION, emphasized progressive relaxation. (See also RECIPROCAL INHIBITION.)

Turin, A.C. and S.N. Lynch, "Comprehensive Relaxation Training," in R.J. Corsini (ed.), *Handbook of Innovative Psychotherapies* (New York: Wiley, 1981).

religious ceremonies, fear of Fear of religious ceremonies is known as teletophobia. Such fears may be based on individual and/or historical concerns. Some people fear and dislike religious ritual because they were forced into meaningless, rigid observances as children. Others feel that an ethical, moral attitude toward religious practice, such as the observance of the Golden Rule, is more meaningful to them, and that ceremonies actually get in the way. Some fear religious ceremonies outside their own religious or ethnic group because they appear threatening, incomprehensible, or even ridiculous. Historically, Protestants have been fearful and distrustful of religious ceremony. One of the purposes of the Reformation movement was to cleanse the church of what were considered superstitious pagan elements represented in ceremonial behavior. (See also HOLY THINGS, FEAR OF; RELIGIOUS OBJECTS, FEAR OF; RITUAL.)

Spinks, G. Stephens, *Psychology and Religion* (Boston: Beacon Press, 1963).
Thomas, Keith, *Religion and the Decline of Magic* (New York: Scribner, 1971).
Thoules, Robert H., *An Introduction to the Psychology of Religion* (London: Cambridge University Press, 1971).

religious objects, fear of Fear of religious objects or holy objects is known as hierophobia or hagiophobia. The awe- and fear-inspiring attributes of religious objects is evident in such customs as swearing on a Bible, which originated in the medieval church and is still in practice today. The individual tells the truth out of the fear that God will punish perjury in this life or the next. Some Protestants also fear and dislike religious objects, which they associate with what were considered pagan, superstitious practices of the Catholic church. (See also RELIGIOUS CEREMONIES, FEAR OF; SUPERNATURAL, FEAR OF.)

Thomas, Keith. *Religion and the Decline of Magic* (New York: Scribner 1971).

repeating (as a ritual) Many individuals, out of fear of not doing an act correctly or sufficiently, become compulsive and ritualistic about repeating certain activities. For example, an individual may repeat stirring a cup of coffee a fixed number of times or washing a glass a number or times. About 40 percent of those who have OBSESSIVE–COMPULSIVE DISORDER experience repeating as a RITUAL.

repression A defense mechanism by which one pushes impulses and thoughts into the unconscious. (See also PSYCHOANALYSIS.)

reptiles, fear of Fear of reptiles is known as ophidiophobia or batrachophobia. Ophidiophobia refers more to snakes; batrachophobia refers more to lizards and frogs. (See also FROGS, FEAR OF; SNAKES, FEAR OF; TOADS, FEAR OF.)

reserpine An old tranquilizer, not commonly used. (See also DRUGS; TRANQUILIZERS.)

resistance An individual's efforts to obstruct the process of therapy. Resistance, a basic concept in PSYCHOANALYSIS, led Sigmund FREUD to develop his fundamental rule of FREE ASSOCIATION, the need for neutrality on the part of the therapist, and recognition that the UNCONSCIOUS could be reached only by indirect methods. Freud viewed resistance primarily as the ego's efforts to prevent unconscious material from coming into the conscious; later, he considered resistance as a DEFENSE MECHANISM. Other therapeutic disciplines regard resistance in different ways. For example, behavior therapists view resistance from a social-learning point of view. Some behavior therapists explain both repression and resistance in terms of avoidance learning. When certain thoughts are repeatedly associated with painful experiences, such as situations that produce anxieties or fears, they become aversive. Strategic therapists and social influence theorists design strategies to overcome the individual's resistance to the therapist, to the process of treatment, and to the loss of symptoms. (See also BEHAVIOR THERAPY.)

Walrond-Skinner, S., *A Dictionary of Psychotherapy* (London: Routledge and Kegan Paul, 1986), pp. 298–299.

respiration relief therapy A form of treatment that emphasizes respiration training and the use of respiratory relief (exhalation) as an antagonist to anxiety induced by specific phobias. There is some evidence that respiratory relief paired with presentation of a feared stimulus can produce extinction of the anxiety response.

respondent conditioning Also known as CLASSICAL CONDITIONING or Pavlovian conditioning. Respondent conditioning is the eliciting of a response by a stimulus that usually does not elicit that response. The response (salivation or a change in heart rate) is one that is brought about by the autonomic nervous system. A previously neutral stimulus is repeatedly presented just before an unconditioned stimulus that normally elicits that response. When the response subsequently occurs in the presence of the previously neutral stimulus, it is called a conditioned response, and the previously neutral stimulus a CONDITIONED STIMULUS. (See also CONDITIONED RESPONSE; CONDITIONING.)

Psychiatric Dictionary (New York: American Psychiatric Press, 1984).

response properties Qualities of reactions to fearful situations that help therapists differentiate fear from anxiety. In differentiating fear and anxiety, therapists consider the duration and intensity of response. If a source of threat is vague and not predictable, the response might last longer and be more pervasive, keeping the individual in a state of chronic arousal, apprehension, or anxiety. However, fear is considered a response to a more specific, predictable source, and though it would be more acute, the episode might end quickly. A more intense reaction is considered fear; less intense, anxiety.

The following table further explains differentiation between fears and anxieties. (See also ANXIETY; FEAR; STIMULUS PROPERTIES.)

Rachman, S.J., *Fear and Courage*, (San Francisco: W.C. Freeman, 1978).

Levitt, E., *The Psychology of Anxiety*, (Hillsdale, NJ: Lawrence Erlbaum Associates, 1980).

responsibility, fear of Fear of responsibility is known as hypengyophobia or hypeigiaphobia. Some individuals who have depressive disorders fear responsibility because they have a sense of self-worthlessness and inadequacy. Some individuals who have agoraphobia fear responsibility because they cannot make themselves go out to work or to social activities. Those who blame others for these reactions or situations are avoiding personal responsibilities.

retirement, fear of Fear of retirement is a contemporary fear of many individuals as they grow older. The time of life when a person leaves his work or profession and devotes most of his time to leisure activities should be a time of enjoyment and reflection. For many individuals, however, retirement becomes a time filled with anxieties and fears of the future, including fear of aging, fear of death, health anxieties, and fears of being alone without spouse, family, or friends. Some fear the loss of purpose, direction, and fulfillment they gained from working, as well as the loss of income.

Differentiating Fear and Anxiety

Response Properties	Fear	Anxiety
Response components	Behavioral Cognitive Physiological	Behavioral Cognitive Physiological
Duration	Elicited by specific stimuli Short duration	Elicited by generalized stimuli Long-lasting
Intensity	More intense	Less intense

Many people who reach retirement age (usually considered in the upper sixties and beyond) suffer from diseases of older age, including heart disease, lung disorders, vision and hearing disabilities, diabetes, and neurological difficulties. Some individuals experience psychological and social problems connected with retirement that are medically related. The subsequent depression many people experience may require psychotherapy or drug therapy.

Some individuals fear feeling useless and fear boredom after they retire; men may experience this feeling more than women.

Individuals can relieve some of the stresses and anxieties of retirement by keeping in mind the following:

1. Don't wait until later to work on major fears such as traveling or being alone that would restrict retirement activity.
2. Prepare for retirement by planning financially. The further ahead you plan, the more realistic and prepared you will be.
3. Prepare psychologically by developing hobbies and interests that will support retirement.
4. Begin to detach from work, begin to see that your self-esteem does not have to be tied to a title or job activity. The better you feel about yourself the easier it will be to retire.
5. Develop meaningful retirement activities. See where you can contribute and give to others. Retirement tied to giving is much more rewarding.
6. Everything changes. This is a dynamic of life. You have to be able to let go of the past. Forgiveness is the key here.
7. Change emotions tied to illness. Seek help in resolving chronic emotional states (such as anxiety, depression, and fears).
8. Change your diet in both the type and quantities of food. As you age, your body will need fewer calories, less fat, less protein.

(See also AGING, FEAR OF; BOREDOM, FEAR OF; DEATH, FEAR OF; HEART ATTACK, ANXIETY FOLLOWING; HEART ATTACK, FEAR OF.)

"Any Cure for Retirement Phoba?" *Modern Maturity* (February–March 1988), p. 9.

reverse psychology A general term that covers techniques to encourage instead of discourage symptoms of phobia or anxiety as a way of helping an individual ultimately resolve them. These techniques may be categorized as behavioral, such as flooding and negative practice; psychodynamic, such as paradoxical intention or implosion; and cognitive, such as therapeutic double bind, symptom prescription, and paradox. (See also BEHAVIOR THERAPY; FLOODING; IMPLOSION; NEGATIVE PRACTICE; PARADOXICAL INTENTION.)

Rabkin, R., *Strategic Psychotherapy* (New York: Basic Books, 1977).

rhabdophobia Fear of being beaten or punished with a rod, or fear of a rod. (See also BEATEN, FEAR OF BEING; RODS, FEAR OF; STICKS, FEAR OF.)

rhypophobia Fear of filth or dirt. (See also DIRT, FEAR OF; FILTH, FEAR OF.)

rhytiphobia Fear of getting wrinkles. (See also WRINKLES, FEAR OF.)

ridicule, fear of Fear of ridicule is known as catagelophobia or katagelophobia. Ridicule may take the form of unfavorable comments on one's appearance, behavior, or viewpoints. Some agoraphobics are afraid to venture out because they fear being ridiculed by people they meet in the street. Some telephone phobics are afraid to speak on the telephone because they fear that the caller will ridicule their speech mannerisms.

Individuals who lack self-confidence fear ridicule. Those who have depressive disorder feel a lack of self-worth and thus believe that others will ridicule them.

risk taking, fear of Fear of taking risks includes fears of gambling, of making decisions, of making errors, and of new things. People who fear taking risks prefer the security of known places and situations. Such individuals may fear losing control by taking risks. Those who fear losing money, for example, avoid risky investments such as the stock market. (See also CHANGE, FEAR OF; DECISIONS, FEAR OF; CAMBLING, FEAR OF; NEW THINGS, FEAR OF.)

ritual In psychopathology, a distorted or elaborate activity that an individual repeats as part of his or her daily routine. Individuals who have OBSESSIVE–COMPULSIVE DISORDERS commonly include some rituals in their routine—for example, frequent hand-washing or constant checking. Some individuals seek treatment to free themselves of the rituals, even though keeping up with the ritualistic behavior relieves their anxieties to some extent.

There are, of course, also rituals of daily life that are not indications of abnormalities and may actually have benefits in relieving anxieties. This type of ritual has been defined as "a symbol that is acted out" and "an agreed-upon pattern of movement"; such rituals are part of social, educational, religious, and athletic events. Rituals such as the use of good manners serve a positive social purpose as protection from aggressive, antisocial behavior. Religious rituals reduce feelings of guilt because of their cleansing, purifying quality. Rite-of-passage rituals, such as the engagement and marriage ceremony, provide a way to reduce the anxieties inherent in passing from one phase of life to another. Funeral rites provide companionship for the survivors and an organized way to behave at a time of grief and crisis. As rituals tend to be traditional, they also satisfy a need many people feel for a sense of continuity with the past and an avoidance of newness. Rituals make use of unique clothing and objects and exaggerated, repetitious, or unusual language to intensify communication, focus the attention of leader and participants, and exclude outside distractions.

Rituals may also promote fear and anxiety. Individuals may feel inhibited or anxious about conforming to certain types of rigid group-behavior patterns. Rituals that have become empty and meaningless or that are observed too rigidly may promote disaffection and disillusionment in individuals who perceive them as either time-wasting or tension-producing.

Sandmel, Samuel, *A Little Book on Religion for People Who Are Not Religious* (Chambersburg, PA: Wilson Books, 1975), p. 124.

Mitchell, Leonel, *The Meaning of Ritual* (New York: Paulist Press, 1977).

International Encyclopedia of Psychiatry, Psychology and Neurology (New York: Van Nostrand, 1977).

Lorenz, Konrad, "Habit, Ritual and Magic," pp. 18–34 in Richard Schechner and Mady Schuman (eds.), *Ritual, Play and Performance* (New York: The Seabury Press, 1976).

rivers, fear of Fear of rivers is known as potamophobia. Those who have this fear may fear being near or on a river (in a boat or swimming), seeing a picture or movie of a river, or even thinking about a river. This fear is related to fear of water and also to fear of landscape. (See also LANDSCAPE, FEAR OF; WATER, FEAR OF.)

robbers, fear of Fear of robbers is known as harpaxophobia. In modern urban centers this is a very real fear, as crime rates increase along with the population and social problems that come along with crowded conditions, a high cost of living, and lack of jobs for all who wish to work. Fear of robbers motivates many individuals to have elaborate burglar-alarm systems at their homes and places of businesses and several locks on their doors. Fear of robbers is a contemporary fear of many children. This takes the form of fearing being accosted on the street or that someone will enter their home.

rods, fear of being beaten with Fear of being beaten or punished with a rod or stick is known as rhabdophobia. The word rhabdophobia is derived from the Greek word *rhabdos,* or rod. Those who have this phobia fear injury as well as embarrassment and loss of control in the situation. Some who fear police fear being beaten with the policeman's rod. (See also PUNISHMENT, FEAR OF; STICKS, FEAR OF.)

Rogers, Carl (1902–1987) An American psychologist. Rogers was a major early contributor in the movement known as phenomenology or client-centered therapy. He was instrumental in identifying the critical features of the PSYCHOTHERAPY encounter. These features, which apply to all therapies, include consequence on the therapist's part, unconditional positive regard ("prizing" of the client), "empathetic understanding" (being in the frame of mind of the client), and communication of these qualities to the client.

Rogers considered clients as unique persons with unique perceptions, and he took psychotherapeutic techniques out of the area of disease and extended its use to normally functioning persons. Many phobic individuals now participate in groups based on Rogers's theories of self-actualization. His work has influenced all therapies and enriched the psychotherapeutic encounter. (See also BEHAVIOR THERAPY.)

role playing A technique used in PSYCHOTHHERAPY in which the client acts according to a role that is not his or her own. Role playing is used in a variety of ways. For example, it can help a therapist determine how anxious or phobic individuals react to certain important social roles and how they see themselves in social situations. Role playing can help the individual gain insight into the conduct of others. It can also help the individual gain CATHARSIS, or release from phobic or other anxiety symptoms. (See also BEHAVIOR THERAPY.)

rolfing A deep massage technique. Rolfing is named for its originator, Ida Rolf (1896–1979), a biochemist at the Esalen Institute in California. Rolfing is based on the theory that muscle massage will relieve both physical and psychic pain. It is one of many BODY THERAPIES used to help treat individuals who have anxieties and phobias.

room full of people, fear of Fear of being in or entering a room full of people is known as koinoniphobia. Individuals who have this SOCIAL PHOBIA may also have agoraphobia, and vice versa. Some individuals may fear ridicule by others, fear being closed in without escape, or fear some type of social embarrassment, such as having to use the bathroom, fainting in front of others, vomiting, or being watched while they eat.

Rorschach, Hermann (1884–1922) A Swiss psychiatrist and psychoanalyst, developer of the RORSCHACH TEST. Rorschach developed an unstructured stimulus in the form of his inkblot test to help individuals reveal unconscious or traumatic information. The Rorschach test, the first of a series of projective tests (tests that present ambiguous stimuli onto which the individual projects his or her own meaning) is still widely used.

Rorschach test A PSYCHOLOGICAL TEST developed by the Swiss psychiatrist Hermann Rorschach (1884–1922); also referred to as the inkblot test. An individual taking the test is encouraged to disclose conscious and unconscious personality traits and emotional conflicts by associating inkblots with objects, things, and situations.

For example, a severely phobic individual might see fearful objects in the inkblots.

rose petals Historically, rose petals and their perfume have been thought to have curative powers for many illnesses, including anxieties, worries, and disorders of the nervous system. Their efficacy has never been proven, however.

ruin, fear of Fear of ruin or being ruined is known as atephobia. This fear may refer to financial or social ruin and may also apply to a fear of looking at historical ruins, or even ruins after a contemporary disaster, such as a fire or flood. This was a common fear during and following the Great Depression. (See also POVERTY, FEAR OF.)

rum phobia This phobia was mentioned by Benjamin Rush (1745–1813), an American physician and author known as the father of American psychiatry. "The Rum Phobia is a very rare distemper. I have known only five instances of it in the course of my life. The smell of rum, and of spirituous liquors of all kinds, produced upon these persons, sickness and distress. If it were possible to communicate this distemper as we do the smallpox, by inoculation, what an immense revenue would be derived from it by physicians, provided every person in our country who is addicted to the intemperate use of spirits were compelled to submit to that operation!"

Runes, D.D. (ed.), *The Selected Writings of Benjamin Rush* (New York: The Philosophical Library, 1947).

rumination The act of persistently being excessively anxious about, worrying about, thinking about, and pondering one concern for an inordinate period of time. Ruminations produce anxiety and are repetitive, intrusive thoughts or OBSESSIONS about some aspect of one's life, such as fear of CONTAMINATION, fear of harming others, or fear of not doing certain tasks correctly. The thoughts may be evoked by external cues or come out of the blue. Ruminations impair concentration and are hard to drive out of one's mind. Rumination is a common symptom of OBSESSIVE–COMPULSIVE DISORDER. (See also CONTAMINATION, FEAR OF; THOUGHT STOPPING; WORRYING.)

rupophobia Fear of filth or dirt. Also known as rypophobia. (See also DIRT, FEAR OF; FILTH, FEAR OF.)

Russia, fear of Fear of Russia, the Russian language, and things relating to the Russian culture is known as Russophobia.

Russophobia Fear of Russia, the Russian language, and things relating to the Russian culture.

rust, fear of Fear of rust is known as iophobia.

S

Sachs, Hans (1881–1947) An Austrian psychiatrist and follower of SIGMUND FREUD. Sachs headed the Berlin Psychoanalytic Institute and trained many leading psychoanalysts. He was a faculty member of the Harvard Medical School; his writings include interpretation of dreams and the application of PSYCHOANALYSIS to literature and art. He was instrumental in furthering psychoanalytic thought and treatment in the U.S.

sacred things, fear of Fear of sacred things is known as heirophobia. This fear includes holy or religious objects. The individual suffering from such a fear would avoid churches, shrines, museums, etc., where particular objects are displayed. Often this fear is quite specific, involving "holy" people or objects (such as crosses) that evoke anxiety. (See also HOLY OBJECTS, FEAR OF; RELIGIOUS OBJECTS, FEAR OF.)

sarmassophobia Fear of love play. (See also LOVE PLAY, FEAR OF; SEXUAL FEARS.)

Satan, fear of Fear of Satan is known as Satanophobia. People fear manifestations of Satanic interests, such as symbols, rituals, and possibly unknown destructive forces. The name Satan derives from the ancient Hebrew word for devil. Early men believed that the harmful forces of nature were demons and evil spirits, and they blamed such demons for all their troubles. In the Old Testament, Satan is not God's opponent; rather, he searches out the sins of men and accuses mankind before God. In the Apocrypha, Satan is the author of all evil and rules over a host of angels. In the New Testament, other names for Satan are devil, enemy, and Beelzebub. In the Middle Ages, Satan usually was represented with horns, a tail, and cloven hooves. (See also DEMONS, FEAR OF; DEVIL, FEAR OF; VOODOO, FEAR OF.)

Field Enterprises, *The World Book Encyclopedia* (Chicago: Field Enterprises Educational Corp., 1971), vol. D, p. 141.

Satanophobia Fear of Satan. This term also refers to fear of devils in general, and of demons. (See also DEMONS, FEAR OF; DEVILS, FEAR OF; SATAN, FEAR OF.)

scabies, fear of Fear of scabies (also popularly known as the "seven-year itch") is known as scabiophobia. Tiny PARASITES, known as *Sarcoptes scabiei* and popularly known as the itch mite, are responsible for scabies, or "the itch." The mite looks like a white dot. The female burrows into the skin and creates a tunnel in which she lays eggs, resulting in a minute, narrow mark on the skin. Some individuals who are allergic to the mite and its secretions may also have tiny blisters, pus, or other blemishes. Eggs hatch in about a week; larvae appear and then develop into burrowing and egg-laying mites and spread over the body. The "seven-year itch" reached a peak of infestation during World War II, but since then the incidence has dropped dramatically due to new pesticides and improved sanitation. Because it is less common now, this fear is more of historical than practical interest. (See also PARASITES, FEAR OF.)

scabiophobia Fear of scabies or the "seven-year itch." (See also SCABIES, FEAR OF.)

"scared stiff" During extreme fear, many people become "scared stiff," or "frozen with fear." These terms refer to a paralyzed conscious state with abrupt onset and end. This type of fear reaction has been reported by survivors of attacks by wild animals, shell-shocked soldiers, and rape victims. Characteristics of being "frozen with fear" include an inability to move (tonic immobility), body shaking, an inability to scream or call out, numbness or insensitivity to pain, and sensations of feeling cold. This term also refers to an involuntary erection that may occur under intense fear. (See also POSTTRAUMATIC STRESS DISORDER.)

Marks, Isaac M., *Fears, Phobias and Rituals* (New York: Oxford University Press, 1987), pp. 68–69.

scatophobia Fear of fecal matter. The word is derived from the Greek *skatos,* meaning "dung." (See also BOWEL MOVEMENTS, FEAR OF; FECAL MATTER, FEAR OF.)

scelerophobia Fear of attack and harm by wicked persons, such as burglars and robbers. These "fears" have increased in prevalence and intensity such that fear of attack and harm by wicked persons are among the greatest fears of children today. Certainly, media programs with graphic depictions of violence have contributed to this increase. (See also BAD MEN, FEAR OF; BURGLARS, FEAR OF.)

Schiller, Friedrich (1759–1805) See SPIDERS, FEAR OF.

schizophrenia A mental illness with characteristic psychotic symptoms involving withdrawal from reality, delusions, hallucinations, and characteristic disturbances in affect and form of thought. The word schizophrenia is derived from the New Latin terms for "split mind" *(schizo+phrenia).* Schizophrenia begins gradually, creating inner turmoil, and symptoms worsen to become severe distortions in perception, speech, and thoughts.

Symptoms include some of the following:

- Paranoid delusions, which are unshakable personal thoughts that convince the individual that others are plotting against him or her (delusions of persecution).
- Delusions that one's thoughts are "broadcast" outside one's head so others can hear them.
- Delusions that outside forces are controlling thoughts, inserting them into the individual's head or removing them from the individual's mind (delusions of influence).
- Hallucinations in which voices threaten, insult, or command the victim. Hallucinations may occur less commonly in any of the senses.
- Emotions that are blunted or inappropriate to the situation, such as laughing or smiling inappropriately.

The symptoms of schizophrenia come and go, and sufferers have periods when they can function normally. Chronic or process schizophrenia, however, is a progressive deterioration of the mental processes. Schizophrenia almost always begins in adolescence or early adulthood. Some sufferers experience only one episode (reactive), while others have repeated episodes throughout their lives. Some phobics and their families worry about the development of schizophrenia. An examination by a psychiatrist is necessary to have an appropriate diagnosis. Once diagnosed, treatment is essential.

Treatment generally combines therapies because the disease is so complex. Antipsychotic medications usually relieve the hallucinations and delusions. Psychotherapy helps victims understand their disease and assists in learning to distinguish reality from distorted perceptions. Family therapy helps spouses, parents, or siblings learn about the disease and helps the individual live in the community. Family therapies seem to be crucial to successful treatment.

Much of the progress in treating schizophrenia results from medications. Fifty-five percent of the persons who have schizophrenia who do not take medications will suffer a relapse within two years of being discharged from a psychiatric facility. The relapse rate for victims who do take medications is 20 percent.

Schizophrenia affects 1.5 million Americans and accounts for 40 percent of all days in institutionalized, long-term care. (By comparison, heart disease accounts for 27 percent of long-term care days.)

Aside from the pain the individual suffers, the other real tragedy of schizophrenia is the effect on families. Often family members are burdened with a stubborn, confused, and marginally socialized young adult schizophrenic who, though not capable of independent life, is able to attend school part-time, drive a car, and meet people. Family members find themselves in the postion of caretakers, often intervening at acute episodes when crises occur. There is little community or professional support for these families.

A tragic consequence of reduced financing of professional support for schizophrenics is that many have been forced to live on their own, usually as "street people." Current estimates are that 30 percent to 50 percent of the homeless are mentally ill, with a large proportion suffering from schizophrenia. (See also CLOZAPINE; GOING CRAZY, FEAR OF; PSYCHOSIS.)

American Psychiatric Association, "Facts about Schizophrenia," (Washington, DC: American Psychiatric Association 1987).

school phobia School phobia is known as scolionophobia. School phobia is an exaggerated fear of going to school, or, more correctly, of leaving home or parents (separation fear). While many children show anxiety about school at one time or another, school phobics show frequent or long-standing fear and refusal to go to school.

In some individuals, school phobia develops from fears connected either with school or with the home. Some may have an irrational dread of some aspect of the school situation, such as fear of a teacher, principal, classmate, or examination. For most, however, the school phobia may be part of a SEPARATION ANXIETY syndrome.

School phobia is more common in elementary-school children than adolescents and is equally common in both sexes. According to the American Psychiatric Association, the extreme form of the disorder, involving school refusal, begins most often around ages eleven and twelve. The school-phobic child may be above average intelligence and average or above in achievement. Such children may otherwise be well-behaved and come from intact families with close-knit, concerned, caring parents. The disorder seems more common in some families on a transgenerational basis than in the general population. It occurs in children of every socioeconomic group and is not directly related to academic abilities.

In many children, this phobia develops after some life stress, such as a loss of a relative or pet through death, an illness of the child or a relative, or a change in the child's environment, such as a change of school or neighborhood.

In most cases, a school-phobic child should be treated as early as possible because fear of school interrupts the child's academic as well as social development. Also, the long-range outlook may depend on appropriate, early management. If school phobia becomes chronic, the phobic pattern of avoidance may continue into later life and be harder to control as the child gets older.

The child's phobia to school may or may not be overt. Young children may not verbalize reasons for refusing to go to school, while older children may attribute their fears to some specific aspect of school life. Often, school phobics are detected when they show physiologic symptoms on school days that are not present on weekends and holidays. Such symptoms may include headache, nausea, anorexia, vomiting, diarrhea, abdominal pain, feeling faint, sore throat, and others. There may be a lot of crying. The child may complain of being too ill to attend school, but when the mother says the child can stay home, symptoms often disappear. Often, when such children are sent to school despite complaints, the symptoms persist until the school nurse sends the child home.

There is a difference between truancy and school phobia. The truant stays away from both school and home; he avoids or leaves in order to pursue pleasures elsewhere. He keeps his truancy secret from his parents. On the other hand, the school phobic usually spends school hours at home, draws family attention to his problem, and may be ashamed to have others know about it. School-phobic children may refuse to see former friends or relatives to avoid explaining their difficulties in school or their absence from school, and the school phobic, unlike the truant, usually does not exhibit any other delinquent behavior. Researchers have found that the school-phobic child is likely to "fade into the woodwork," or even quietly disappear from school.

According to the American Psychiatric Association, school phobia is not included among its classification of phobic disorders because it has unique features and is characteristically associated with childhood.

Some authorities relate school phobia to separation anxiety, in which the child may have a combination of unconscious, unresolved hostility and feelings of dependency in his relationship with his mother, and at the same time, a fear of separation from her. This psychiatriatic viewpoint suggests that because the child unconsciously fears abandonment by the mother, he does not express his hostility toward her. He unconsciously fears that harm will come to the mother while he is in school and that if he stays home he can prevent his own destructive wishes from coming true. Behavioral viewpoints emphasize the parents' role in acquisition and maintenance of this behavior. Specifically, parents often reinforce school refusal subtly (or not so subtly) by complying with the child's wish to avoid (not wanting to "hurt" the child) or by a wanting the child home (usually as a companion). Under stress, the child engages in refusal and thereby avoids school (and any stresses there) and receives a good deal of attention and sympathy. Some children become violent toward an individual who forces separation.

Experts differ on whether school phobia is a true phobia or should more properly be called *school refusal* and be considered a part of separation anxiety. Those who say it is a true phobia base their opinion on the fact that anxiety, originating from the child's fear of being separated from mother, is displaced to another object—the school and details of school life.

Not all school refusal is due to separation anxiety. When separation anxiety does account for school refusal, the child experiences difficulty being separated from home or family for a variety of purposes; school attendance is only one of them. In a true school phobia, the child fears the school situation, whether or not he is accompanied by the parent.

Some children have very specific, identifiable fears relating to school, and when these are determined and confronted, specific avenues may be taken to make the child more comfortable about attending school. For example, being bullied on the school bus, being teased about appearance or clothing, reciting in class, undressing in front of other children for gym, and going to the bathroom without privacy may be contributory factors to school phobia.

In a 1979 study, adolescent school phobics listed characteristics of the school that enabled them to function in it. First and foremost was the presence of an adult who was reliable and understanding. Next was flexibility in the school. They did not want to be hopelessly trapped in a particular classroom at a given time and did not want to have to experience anguish in returning after absence. They appreciated the involvement of their personal therapist with the school and its staff.

Treatment

The type of help to seek depends on the child, the initial symptoms, the attitudes of parents, and school authorities. Efforts of parents and teachers with encouragement, indulgences, or even coercion may prove unsuccessful. If there has been a *real* event that frightened the child, such as a bully in the playground or an incident with an authority figure, parents and teachers can deal with this without involving a therapist.

In many cases, however, therapists can help the child, parents, and teachers. Treatment procedures vary, depending on the therapist, the age of the child, the duration of symptoms, the child's family situation, and other factors. Generally, school phobias are treated as interpersonal problems, rather than with the deconditioning techniques used with many other phobias, although management strategies are essential to achieve a positive outcome.

Therapists generally encourage returning to school as soon as possible so that the phobia does not become even stronger. However, others view early return to school as only a temporary solution that puts pressure on the child and makes him even more anxious.

Some therapists advocate use of pharmacological ANTIDEPRESSANT therapy for school phobics. This treatment originated when it was found that the antidepressant IMIPRAMINE relieves the panic attacks of AGORAPHOBIA, and many agoraphobics have a history of school phobia. The theory is that drug therapy, under careful supervision, enables the child to relearn behavior patterns and reorient attitudes, and when successful, the new behaviors will take over after the drug is no longer administered.

In some cases, lengthy psychotherapy is helpful for the child and the family. Some therapy programs involve support groups consisting of children, parents, and teachers who meet together to discuss their common problem and work out solutions. In one study, a group of adolescent school phobics reported that the existence of the group and the relaxation and comfort it provided was important to them. They appreciated sharing anxieties and garnering support from one another. Members of the group found that it was consoling to them to know that some of their fellow students were acutely sensitive to their problems and had parallel experiences that they customarily worked hard to hide. Some of the group members had fears related to being out of control and to having no power over their own school experience. Researchers found that it was important for students to exercise as much personal power as they could and learn to be masters of their own fate in school and outside it. (See also CHILDHOOD ANXIETIES, FEARS, AND PHOBIAS; DEPRESSION; DEPRESSION, ADOLESCENT.)

International Encyclopedia of Psychiatry, Psychology, Psychoanalysis, and Neurology. (New York: Van Nostrand Reinhold, 1977).

American Handbook of Psychiatry (New York: Basic Books, 1977).

Diagnostic and Statistical Manual of Mental Disorders (Washington, DC: American Psychiatric Association, 1981), pp. 50–53.

DuPont, Robert L. (ed.), *Phobia* (New York: Brunner/Mazel, 1982), pp. 182–191.

Goodwin, Donald W., *Phobia, the Facts* (London: Oxford University Press, 1983).

Marks, Isaac, *Fears and Phobias* (London: Heinemann Medical, 1969).

Diamond, Stanley C., "School Phobic Adolescents and a Peer Support Group," *The Clearing House* (Nov. 1985), pp. 125–126

Sarafino, Edward P., *The Fears of Childhood* (New York: Human Sciences Press, 1986).

Coolidge J.C., "School Phobia," in J.D. Noshpitz (ed.), *Basic Handbook of Child Psychiatry* (New York: Basic Books, 1979).

Speling, M., "School Phobia," pp. 129–157 in *The Major Neuroses and Behavior Disorders in Children* (New York: Jason Aronson, 1974).

Schopenhauer, Arthur (1788–1860) A German philosopher who described blind will as the ultimate reality and sought release from suffering through the contemplation of works of art and an ethic of sympathy. It is said that he lived on the first story, because he dreaded fire. He is also said to have feared his hairdresser. (See also HAIRCUT, FEAR OF HAVING A.)

Hyslop, T.B., *The Great Abnormals* (Ann Arbor: Gryphon, 1971).

scolionophobia SCHOOL PHOBIA.

sciaphobia, sciophobia Fear of shadows. (See also SHADOWS, FEAR OF.)

scoleciphobia Fear of worms. (See also WORMS, FEAR OF.)

scopophobia, scoptophobia Fear of being stared at. (See also BEING LOOKED AT, FEAR OF; STARED AT, FEAR OF BEING.)

scotomaphobia Fear of blind areas in the visual field

scotophobia Fear of darkness. (See also DARKNESS, FEAR OF.)

scratched, fear of being Fear of being scratched is known as amychophobia.

screen memory A memory that the individual consciously tolerates to cover up a related remembrance that would be emotionally painful if recalled. Apparently, these memories are repressed or suppressed due to their painful or frightening nature and emerge only when the anxiety begins to lessen.

scriptophobia Fear of writing in public. This social phobia prevents many individuals from being able to write checks, use bank cards, or vote. When scriptophobics anticipate having to be seen writing, they experience physiological symptoms of heart palpitations, shortness of breath, trembling hands, sweating, and dizziness. Financial transactions have to be preplanned so that purchases can be made with cash (e.g., at grocery stores), or so that others do not see the individual writing (such as filling out deposit slips at home). Many rely on others to handle all financial matters involving writing. Some scriptophobics can cope better with writing in public when a trusted friend or relative is with them.

Many scriptophobic individuals also have other social anxieties, especially if they think they are being watched while doing some tasks and are afraid of doing something wrong, looking funny (by shaking or trembling), and becoming embarrassed. Scriptophobia represents a generalized fear of negative evaluation by others. Scriptophobia has been treated successfully with behavior therapy, graded exposure, and cognitive restructuring. (See also BEHAVIOR THERAPY; COGNITIVE RESTRUCTURING; PHOBIA; SOCIAL ANXIETY; SOCIAL PHOBIA.)

Birren, M. et al., "In Vivo Exposure vs. Cognitive Restructuring in the Treatment of Scriptophobia," *Behavior Research and Therapy,* 19(1981), pp. 525–532.

Chhabra, S. and Dorothy Fielding, "The Treatment of Scriptophobia by In Vivo Exposure and Cognitive Restructuring," *Journal of Behavior Therapy and Experimental Psychiatry,* 16:3(1985), pp. 265–269.

sea, fear of Fear of the sea is known as thalassophobia. This fear may relate to a fear of water, fear of drowning, fear of waves, or fear of a particular type of landscape, such as the seashore, or just the sea's empty vastness and distance from land. It may also be related to a fear of salty water. (See also DROWNING, FEAR OF; LAKES, FEAR OF; WATER, FEAR OF; WAVES, FEAR OF.)

seasonal affective disorder (SAD) Seasonal affective disorder (SAD) is a syndrome characterized by severe seasonal mood swings. Researchers at the National Institute of Mental Health began studying and defining the syndrome in the early 1980s. In 1987 it was included in the *Diagnostic and Statistical Manual of Mental Disorders.*

Typically, SAD sufferers become clinically depressed with the approach of winter. In addition to gaining weight, oversleeping, and feeling listless, they feel anxious and irritable, withdraw socially, and lose interest in sex. As spring approaches depression subsides and behavior returns to normal.

Latitude appears to be as important as season. The incidence and severity of SAD increase with distance from the equator, peaking at around 40 degrees north.

Researchers roughly estimate the number of SAD victims in the U.S. at between 450,000 and 5,000,000. The syndrome afflicts about four times as many women as men and usually appears in the early twenties. However, the malady has been diagnosed in children as young as age nine.

Researchers suspect there may be a genetic factor involved in SAD, because more than two thirds of those with the syndrome have a close relative with a mood disorder. The role of the absence or presence of light in seasonal mood shifts is unclear. One theory attributes the disorder to a disturbance in the body's natural clock, resulting in an abnormal production of melatonin, a hormone manufactured in the brain, and serotonin, a chemical that helps transmit nerve impulses.

Light therapy, in which the individual is exposed to artificial light with five to ten times the intensity of indoor lighting, has helped some SAD sufferers. (See also AFFECTIVE DISORDERS; CLIMATE, FEAR OF; DEPRESSION; MOOD.)

Toufexis, Anastasia, "Dark Days, Darker Spirits," *Time* (January 11, 1988), p. 66.

secondary gain An obvious advantage that an individual gains from his or her PHOBIA or anxiety disorder. Family and friends may be more protective and more attentive and may release the individual from responsibility. For example, agoraphobics experience secondary gains of having someone willing to accompany them outdoors and to do errands and other chores for them. (See also AGORAPHOBIA; PRIMARY GAIN; SICK ROLE.)

sedative A substance, such as a drug or herb, that relieves nervousness, anxiety, or irritability, sometimes to the point of inducing sleep. A sedative acts by depressing the CENTRAL NERVOUS SYSTEM. The degree of sedation depends on the agent, size of dose, method of administration (for example, oral or intravenous), and the physical and mental condition of the individual. A sedative used as a relaxant in small doses may be used to induce sleep with larger doses. BARBITURATES are common examples of sedative drugs used in this way.

selaphobia Fear of flashing lights. This fear is often related to anxiety produced by excessive stimulation. For example, car headlights at night, crowds of people, and confusing buildings are all situations that involve stimulation and may provoke anxiety in an anxiety-prone individual. (See also FLASHING LIGHTS, FEAR OF.)

selenophobia Fear of the moon. (See also MOON, FEAR OF; NIGHT, FEAR OF.)

self, fear of Fear of oneself is known as autophobia. (See also BEING ONESELF, FEAR OF.)

self-efficacy (SE) The concept that one can perform adequately; self-confidence. This concept as it relates to phobias and anxieties was researched during the 1970s by Albert Bandura, an American psychologist at Stanford University. SE measures how likely one believes one would be to succeed if one attempted a task. Such a rating can be used before, during, or after treatment for phobias. The SE rating correlates highly with performance in a behavioral test just after the rating. In phobics asked to rate SE concerning a phobic task, SE is low before treatment and rises after individuals improve with exposure treatment.

SE at the end of treatment may be the major mediator of fear reduction. However, a better way to increase SE is by exposure, the same procedure that reduces fear. In experiments, SE correlated highly not only with performance of a frightening task, but also with the fear expected during it. In one experiment with 50 snake-phobic students, most refused to try to hold the snake because they were frightened, not because they felt inept. They were certain that they could hold the snake if they really "had to." If a task is frightening, SE reflects an individual's willingness (rather than ability) to do it. When willingness rises, there is less anticipated fear.

SE can predict psychological changes achieved by different modes of treatment. Expectations of personal efficacy determine whether coping behavior will begin, how much effort will be expended, and how long it will be sustained in the face of aversive experiences. Persistence in activities that are subjectively threatening, but in fact relatively safe, produces, through experiences of mastery, further enhancement of self-efficacy and corresponding reductions in defensive behavior.

Individuals derive expectations of self-efficacy from four main sources: performance accomplishments, vicarious experience, verbal persuasion, and physiological states. The more dependable the experiential sources, the greater the changes in perceived self-efficacy.

Marks, I.M., *Fears, Phobias and Rituals* (New York: Oxford University Press, 1987), pp. 500–501.

Bandura, Albert, ''Self-Efficacy: Toward a Unifying Theory of Behavioral Change,'' *Psychological Review,* 84:2(1977), pp. 191–215.

self-esteem The positive light in which one regards one's self. Many studies have been done on the effects of degree of self-esteem on psychological state. Early studies showed that negative stressors contribute to low self-esteem, and more recent work connects ANXIETY to low self-esteem, since it, too, is a negative stressor. For example, test-taking anxiety could lead to a lower self-esteem because the anxious person worries about performance on a test. This may lead the person to question his or her abilities and look at him or herself in a negative light.

Generally, individuals who have high self-esteem tend to be less anxious than those who have low self-esteem. (See also MASLOW, ABRAHAM; PERFORMANCE ANXIETY; TEST ANXIETY.)

self-fulfilling prophecy A belief that helps bring about its own fulfillment. For example, a feared event sometimes is brought about by predicting that it will happen. A student may worry that he or she will be extremely anxious during an examination or performance and will fail. The expectation plays a part in the result. On the other hand, self-fulfilling prophecy can work in a positive way. For example, in therapy, the phobic individual's expectation that the therapist will be helpful enables him or her to benefit from the therapeutic situation. The mystics talk about this phenomenon as the ''law of manifestation.'' (See also COUNTERPHOBIA; FAMILY MYTH; PARADOXICAL INTENTION.)

self-help Self-help means exactly what it says, to help one's self. Therapists want their clients to be able to function independently and therefore must teach some self-management techniques to those willing and able to use them. Self-help can be helpful for a number of psychological disturbances. For example, it is widely used by phobics who need to control their reactions to a particular stimulus. A therapist might teach the individual how to relax and breathe deeply when confronted with the object. Once mastered, the individual can do this independently, eliminating the need for constant outside support. Highly anxious people are trained to help themselves by repeating calming statements or by inducing previously practiced states of tranquility.

One form of self-help is known as focusing, in which the individual learns how to establish the problem in his or her mind, to feel the problem, and to let the answer form in consciousness. In this way, people learn to function more independently.

There are a number of questionnaires available for individuals to use on a self-help basis. From these questionnaires, an individual can get some idea of how severe their fear or phobia actually is. The Fear Questionnaire and the Sex Questionnaire are examples of such questionnaires. The Obsessive–Compulsive Checklist can help an individual determine which activities of daily living are compulsive or ritualistic. (See also

BEHAVIOR THERAPY; EXPOSURE THERAPY; TERRAP.)

Freidman, N., "On Focusing," *Journal of Humanistic Psychology* (Winter 1986), pp. 103–116.

self-rating scales Measurements of phobic reactions as reported by the phobic individuals themselves. Self-rating scales or questionnaires are used by researchers and therapists, often to assess the extent of the phobia and also to measure the success of therapy after therapy is underway, and perhaps again after therapy has been concluded. Self-rating scales are particularly useful in working with agoraphobic individuals, as such people are fearful of many varied situations. Scales have been devised for individuals to indicate, for example, on a scale from 0 to 8, "how much" they "would avoid" or "would not avoid" certain situations. Likewise, questionnaires are used to assess fears relating to AGORAPHOBIA, which might include traveling alone by bus or train, walking alone in busy streets, going into crowded stores, going alone far from home, and being in large open places. Although there is some controversy among researchers regarding the usefulness of self-rating scales because of their lack of specificity, most agree that the scales have a place when used in combination with other assessment techniques that sample behavior and physiological reactions directly. (See also SELF-HELP.)

Seligman, Martin (1942–) An American psychologist and author working in the areas of phobias, LEARNED HELPLESSNESS and depression, the nature vs. nurture question, and classical and instrumental conditioning. Seligman, currently affiliated with the University of Pennsylvania, is the author of *Helplessness; on Depression, Development and Death* (San Francisco: W.C. Freeman, 1975).

American Men and Women of Science: Social and Behavioral Sciences (New York: Bowker, 1978).

semen, fear of Fear of semen is known as spermophobia or spermatophobia. This reaction is usually a variation of "germ" or contamination fears of obsessive–compulsive individuals. (See also PSYCHOSEXUAL ANXIETIES; SEXUAL FEARS; SPERM, FEAR OF.)

sensitive ideas of reference Sensitive ideas of reference or ideas of reference are the fears that actions and words of other people refer to oneself when in fact they do not. An example is the repeated idea that all the people in a room are talking about one as one enters. These fears are common in delusions of persecution experienced by paranoid schizophrenics. They are also common in people who are exceptionally self-involved, fearful, and sensitive to rejection or alienation by others.

sensory deprivation Being cut off from usual external stimuli without opportunity for perception through the senses. This may occur accidentally or experimentally. For example, there is sensory deprivation with the loss of hearing or eyesight, or with physical isolation, such as when one is lost in a snowstorm. In some psychological experiments, such as sleep research, subjects are placed in rooms in which day and night are indistinguishable. Sensory deprivation can lead to ANXIETY, PANIC, DELUSIONS, DEPRESSION, and HALLUCINATIONS.

separation anxiety A fear experienced when an individual contemplates being taken or is actually taken from someone to whom he or she has an attachment. Separation fears are evident in school phobias and have been implicated as a factor in AGORAPHOBIA. Freud discussed separation anxieties in his work and noted this fear as a causative factor in many forms of neuroses. Freud himself had separation anxieties.

Separation anxiety is normal for infants who show fear and apprehension when they are removed from their mother or surrogate mother, or when approached by strangers. Separation is seen as the first step toward individuation, personal responsibility, and psychological maturity.

Prolonged separation often is followed by reactions of protest, detachment, and despair. First the child cries, screams, and struggles to find its caregiver, then seems oblivious to the separation, and finally becomes inactive and perhaps depressed. The sequence is similar to what occurs in acute mourning after bereavement, except that grief tends to start with numbness.

Upon reunion following separation, infants are often angry with their caregivers and may avoid or even attack them; when picked up, the infant may be unresponsive at first.

Adolescents and adults show signs of separation anxiety in times of disaster. People search for one another and cling together, as companionship reduces fear. For example, children sometimes want to cling to parents and sleep with them after a tornado hits. The fact that adult phobics' fears are greatly reduced by the presence of companions is a remnant of infant separation anxiety. (See also BIRTH TRAUMA; CHILDHOOD ANXIETIES, FEARS, AND PHOBIAS; LITTLE HANS; SCHOOL PHOBIA; SOTERIA.)

Marks, Isaac M., *Fears, Phobias and Rituals* (New York: Oxford University Press, pp. 140–141.)

seplophobia Fear of decaying matter. (See DECAYING MATTER, FEAR OF.)

sermons Fear of sermons is known as homilophobia. (See also RELIGIOUS OBJECTS, FEAR OF.)

serotonin A NEUROTRANSMITTER substance found in the central nervous system, blood, nerve cells, and other tissues. The substance was identified during the 1950s as 5-hydroxytryptamine (5-HT); it is also known as hydroxytryptamine. Serotonin is derived from tryptophan, an essential amino acid widely distributed through the body and in the brain. Serotonin functions as a smooth-muscle stimulator and constrictor of blood vessels. Serotonin is involved in circuits that influence sleep and emotional arousal and is indirectly involved in the psychobiology of DEPRESSION. One theory suggests low levels of serotonin as a factor in causing depression. Some ANTIDEPRESSANT drugs increase the levels of serotonin and norepinephrine, other neurotransmitters. (See also DRUGS.)

serum prolactin See LACTATE-INDUCED ANXIETY.

Sex Anxiety Inventory (SAI) A specific-fear questionnaire developed by R. Klorman et al. in 1974. The respondent selects one of two response alternatives on the 25-item questionnaire indicating his or her view concerning sex. Researchers reported that scores on the SAI were related to respondents' actual sexual experiences; those with less sex anxiety reported more sexual activity. (See also PYSCHOSEXUAL ANXIETIES; SEX THERAPY; SEXUAL FEARS.) See chart that follows.

Sample Items from the Sex Anxiety Inventory

Sex:
- a. Can cause as much anxiety as pleasure.
- b. On the whole is good and enjoyable.

I feel nervous:
- a. About initiating sexual relations.
- b. About nothing when it comes to members of the opposite sex.

When I awake from sexual dreams:
- a. I feel pleasant and relaxed.
- b. I feel tense.

When I meet someone I'm attached to:
- a. I get to know him or her.
- b. I feel nervous.

Ronald A. Kleinknecht, *The Anxious Self* (New York: Human Sciences Press, 1986), p. 103.

Kleinknecht, Roland A., *The Anxious Self* (New York: Human Sciences Press, 1986).
Klorman, R. et al., "Psychometric Description of Some Specific-fear Questionnaires," *Behavior Therapy,* 5(1974), pp. 401–409.
Janda, L.H. and K.E. O'Grady, "Development of a Sex Anxiety Inventory," *Journal of Consulting and Clinical Psychology,* 48(1980), pp. 169–175.

sexophobia Fear of the opposite sex. (See also OPPOSITE SEX, FEAR OF.)

sexual abuse, fear of Fear of sexual abuse is known as agraphobia or contrecct-ophobia. (See also SEXUAL FEARS.)

sexual anxiety See PSYCHOSEXUAL ANXIETIES; SEX THERAPY, SEXUAL FEARS.

sexual fears Fears in human love life impair sexual responding so that erotic responses to partners are weakened. Common fears of women include fearing that their vaginas are too tight for insertion of their partners' penises, that they will experience pain during intercourse, and that they will not experience orgasm as often as they desire. Common fears of men include that they will not have an erection, that they cannot maintain an erection long enough during intercourse to achieve orgasm, that they maintain an erection but do not ejaculate, and that they ejaculate sooner than desired.

There are many causes for sexual fears and anxieties. In males, inadequate sexual performance is often due to fear of the same (either through self-judgment—"observer" effect—or perceived rejection or criticism of the partner). Anxiety may either prevent or weaken erection or, more commonly, lead to premature ejaculation. Thus a vicious cycle of fear, failure, and then more fear develops. Fear has these effects only if it is stronger than the sexual excitation. In females, sexual fear may be caused by many things, ranging from the sight of a penis to fear of penetration, to the belief that she will be punished for indulging in sexual pleasure; some men share this last fear. The term frigidity is often applied to women's sexual inadequacies. Frigidity, in actuality, covers situations from a complete inability to be aroused to a failure to reach a climax even when sexual excitement is very high. When a woman has a general inhibition of sexual response, it is often caused by anxiety. Some sexual fears may have origins in relatively trivial situations, such as having been frightened in the act of masturbation, or more serious ones, such as a history of sexual molestation.

Treatment of sexual fears depends on the severity of the fear, the extent to which it interferes with one's functioning, and the perceived cause of the fear. Sexual anxieties are treated with many therapies, including BEHAVIOR THERAPY, in which techniques including DESENSITIZATION are used.

Paraphilias are various sexual deviations that involve sexual arousal by uncommon or bizarre stimuli. FETISHES are one form of paraphilia. A fetishist is almost always a male, and he derives sexual arousal from some inanimate object—such as women's shoes, underwear, etc.—or some specific nongenital part of a person, such as locks of hair, feet, ankles, fingers, etc. Transvestism (cross-sex dressing), incest, pedophilia (sexual gratification through physical and sexual contact with prepubertal children), voyeurism (peeping), and exhibitionism (exposure of genitals) are common forms of paraphilias.

Psychoanalytic theory generally considers the paraphilias as defensive functions that ward off castration anxiety about normal sexual behavior. These views have been challenged by learning theorists, who prefer a theory of stimulus association as explanatory. (See also CLASSICAL CONDITIONING; DYSPAREUNIA, FEAR OF; PSYCHOSEXUAL ANXIETIES; SEX THERAPY.)

Wolpe, Joseph, *Our Useless Fears* (Boston: Houghton Mifflin, 1981).

sex therapy Approaches that focus on eliminating or alleviating sexual anxieties and improving the sexual relationship of a couple. Sex therapy is based on two general principles: teaching the couple about normal sexual behavior and reducing their sexual anxiety by having the individuals in treatment gradually engage in increasingly intimate sexual relations.

Sexual anxieties and dysfunction are treated most effectively with behavioral approaches. Sex therapy is often a part of marital therapy. The goal of sexual therapy is to help individuals overcome traditional taboos and lack of communication regarding the topic of sex and to desensitize anxiety and retrain faulty behavior patterns. Anxiety is often an inhibitor to sexual behavior, and consequently most sex therapies focus on anxiety-reduction skills along with enhancement of sexual arousal and intimacy.

Sex therapy can help overcome fears as well as problems in men and women. There are techniques to help men who cannot achieve or maintain an erection, for anxiety about premature ejaculation, and for failure to ejaculate. Therapy techniques can help women who fear or have vaginal spasms (vaginismus) each time penetration is attempted, and those who do not have orgasm (ANORGASMIA) or who fear this. Success rates in behavior-therapy treatment of individuals who have sexual anxieties are high, particularly in treatment of premature ejaculation, vaginismus, and anorgasmia.

In the late 1960s and early 1970s, Masters and Johnson researched sexual dysfunction and its treatment; their therapeutic program is the basis for many approaches developed later by other researchers. According to Masters and Johnson, treatment must be conjoint—directed to the couple's relationship and carried out by a male-and-female co-therapy pair; the relationship between therapists and couple is considered a primary therapeutic factor. Other therapists have modified these guidelines to treat individuals without a partner as well as couples seeking help. In some cases, surrogate partners are used.

Before sex therapy is initiated, therapists exclude obvious causes of anxieties and problems, such as physical disease, drug abuse, alcoholism, and severe depression. Therapists encourage the couple to become educated about sexual matters, learn to discuss them freely, be able to touch each other's bodies without fear or shame ("sensate focusing"), and experiment gradually until they reach a point where they can both be aroused, satisfied, and reach a climax. Sexual anxiety subsides through increasing the partners' contact with each other's bodies. Couples are encouraged to learn a sexual vocabulary so that they can talk about sexual intercourse with the proper terminology and better describe their sexual feelings to each other. Couples in sex therapy often are encouraged to read descriptive books about sex that include diagrams of the genitals and individuals having sexual intercourse in different positions. In many cases, couples are advised to set aside a period of 15 minutes several times a week to learn to give each other pleasure without moving toward sexual intercourse. Couples are advised to practice "sensate focusing," which involves mutual touching, caressing, and massaging, but avoidance of the genitals and breasts. The aim of sensate focusing is to enable the couple to feel comfortable caressing each other's nude bodies. (See also DYSPAREUNIA, FEAR OF; PSYCHOSEXUAL ANXIETIES; SEXUAL FEARS.)

Walrond-Skinner, S., *A Dictionary of Psychotherapy* (London: Routledge & Kegan Paul, 1986).

Marks, Isaac M., *Living with Fear* (New York: McGraw-Hill, 1978).

sexual intercourse, fear of Fear of sexual intercourse is known as coitophobia, erotophobia, and genophobia. (See also PSYCHOSEXUAL ANXIETIES; SEXUAL FEARS; SEXUALLY TRANSMITTED DISEASES, FEAR OF.)

sexual intercourse, fear of painful Fear of painful vaginal sexual intercourse is known as dyspareunia. (See also DYSPAREUNIA, FEAR OF; MENOPAUSE, FEAR OF; PSYCHOSEXUAL ANXIETIES; SEXUAL FEARS.)

sexual love, fear of Fear of sexual love is known as erotophobia. (See also PSYCHOSEXUAL ANXIETIES; SEXUAL FEARS.)

sexual perversions, fear of Fear of sexual perversions is known as paraphobia. (See also SEXUAL FEARS.)

sexually transmitted diseases (STDs), fear of Many people fear sexually transmitted diseases (STDs) because such diseases cause discomfort, may lead to infertility, and may be life-threatening. Sexually transmitted disease is the term given to a group of diseases that affect both men and women and are generally transmitted during sexual intercourse. Historically, SYPHILIS and gonorrhea have been well-known; they were referred to as VENEREAL DISEASES long before the term STD was coined during the latter part of the 20th century. There are several STDs that are feared because they have become notably widespread during the 1980s. These include herpes, chlamydia, and hepatitis B, as well as pubic lice, genital warts, and other vaginal infections. Syphilis and gonorrhea are still prevalent and, some sources say, on the increase due to the upswing in other concurrent STDs.

Fears of acquiring an STD have led many formerly sexually active individuals to seek fewer sexual partners. Fears of STD are prevalent among individuals who are widowed or divorced and who begin seeking new partners after their loss, as well as among never-married individuals. Such fears have also increased the use of condoms, as condoms are thought to reduce the likelihood of spreading most STDs.

Herpes

Herpes (technically known as Herpes simplex or herpes virus hominus) is feared because one cannot tell if a partner has herpes, and there is no known cure (as of 1988) for herpes. Herpes is more common in women than in men. Herpes outbreaks cause either single or multiple blisters that occur on mucous membranes such as lips or vagina. Herpes simplex I causes most oral "cold sores." Herpes simplex II causes most vaginal herpes. Transmission can occur when a herpes blister comes in contact with any mucous membrane or open cut or sore. Herpes is most often transmitted through sexual intercourse and can also be transmitted during mouth–genital contact, or with manual contact during heterosexual or homosexual relations.

In its active stage, herpes can be debilitating. Herpes recurs, and often attacks occur when the previously infected individual is under stress, fatigued, or has another illness. Women who know that they have the herpes infection are fearful of giving birth to a baby who may also have herpes, as the infection can be transmitted to the baby during the birth process. Women who have active vaginal herpes blisters are routinely given Cesarean sections.

Many individuals who have herpes take drugs to relieve the pain of the blisters and prophylactically (as a preventive) to reduce the severity of future attacks.

Chlamydia

Chlamydia is two or three times more common than gonorrhea (see below) but less well-known. It is only in the latter quarter of the 20th century that information about this disease has appeared in the medical and popular press. Chlamydia is feared because untreated symptoms in women can lead to infections in the Fallopian tubes and uterus (pelvic inflammatory disease). The disease affects men and women, but women are less likely to notice symptoms in early stages.

The signs in women are unusual vaginal discharge, irregular bleeding, bleeding after intercourse, or deep pain during and after intercourse. Men may notice clear, mucus-like discharge from the penis and burning during urination. Chlamydia is treated with antibiotics, and sexual partners must be treated to avoid a ping-pong effect of reinfection. Thus when one individual discovers that he or she has it, anxieties arise regarding informing the partner(s) and urging treatment.

Hepatitis B
This infection may develop about two months after sexual activity. It usually is acquired during sexual intercourse with an individual from a part of the world in which sanitation is poor and the disease has a high prevalence. People who are fearful of acquiring hepatitis B can receive an immunization against it.

Pubic lice
Some individuals who fear germs or bugs may also fear pubic lice. These are tiny bugs, also known as "crab lice" or "crabs," that burrow into the skin and suck blood. They thrive on hairy parts of the body, including the pubic mound, outer lips of the vulva, underarms, the head, and even eyebrows and eyelashes. Eggs take from seven to nine days to hatch; persons infected may notice itching in one to three weeks after exposure. The most direct way of acquiring pubic lice is through sexual or close physical contact with an infected person's body. However, pubic lice can also be transmitted by shared towels or bedsheets. Some people fear sleeping in the bedding in which another person has slept for this reason. Pubic lice is commonly treated with a standard pesticide (known in the United States as Kwell) that is also a standard treatment for head lice. Those who have pubic lice (or live in the same household with someone who has them) fear reinfection or unknowingly infecting others, and they often become zealous about washing towels and bedding with disinfectant, such as household bleach, in boiling water, and drying the items in a hot dryer to be sure of killing off the unhatched eggs of the lice.

Genital warts.
Warts, or small bumps on the mucous membrane of the vulva, the clitoral hood, in the perineum, inside the vagina, in the anus, on the penis, or in the urinary tract may be genital warts. They cause discomfort and anxiety to the sufferer and may be particularly painful during sexual intercourse or when the sufferer wears tight clothing. Genital warts are caused by a sexually transmitted virus and can be removed by a physician. Genital warts are particularly feared by women because certain strains of the wart virus have been implicated as a cause of cervical cancer. To reduce anxieties regarding transmission of the wart virus, if either partner has a history of genital warts, a condom should be used during sexual intercourse.

Gonorrhea and syphilis
Gonorrhea, while treatable, is feared by many people because complications include pelvic inflammatory disease, joint pains, heart disease, liver disease, meningitis, and blindness. Gonorrhea has been referred to as the "dose," "clap," or "drip." Gonorrhea is treated with large doses of penicillin, usually injected, often with follow-up doses of oral antibiotics. During the latter part of the 20th century, many cases of penicillin-resistant gonorrhea have appeared, making the disease more fearsome than during the years when penicillin was hailed as the "magic bullet" against the disease. Because there are fewer symptoms in women than men, usually gonorrhea is detected later in women. In a woman, the gonorrhea germs travel to the uterus, Fallopian tubes, and ovaries. As

the disease advances she may notice abdominal pain. Males may notice painful urination and pus discharge from the penis.

Detection of gonorrhea historically has caused anxieties for many people because anyone diagnosed with gonorrhea should inform recent partners so that they can obtain treatment.

Syphilis, though less common than gonorrhea, is feared because of serious complications that occur when untreated. Syphilis has been known as "syph," "pox," and "bad blood." Treatment with penicillin or other antibiotics is usually effective during the early stages of the disease and will prevent complications. Treatment is difficult in the later stages of the disease.

Other diseases

Many women fear acquiring vaginal infections because the vagina becomes red, swollen, and very tender. Women fear the intense itching that accompanies infections and the pain that occurs with any friction, such as during sexual intercourse. One commonly known infection is trichomonas, which is caused by microscopic, parasitic organisms that live in small numbers in the vagina. The organisms, known as trichomonads, also live under the foreskin of a man's penis or in the urethra, usually without producing any symptoms. Medications are available to combat this infection. However, a treated individual must inform his or her sexual partner so that the partner can also be treated. Imparting such information may cause anxiety on the part of the treated person who must inform the other partner as well as the one who hears about the need for treatment.

Yeast infections (monilia) are not necessarily sexually transmitted diseases, but the organisms also live in the vagina and under the foreskin of the penis and can be transmitted during sexual intercourse. Many women, however, have yeast infections without having had sexual intercourse. In fact, some women fear taking certain antibiotic drugs because a fairly well-known side effect of such drugs is the onset of a monilia infection.

Bacterial infections can also be transmitted during sexual intercourse; these are treatable with sulfa creams or oral antibiotics.

Autoimmune deficiency syndrome

AIDS has become a widely known and feared sexually transmitted disease during the latter part of the 20th century. The AIDS virus is known to be transmitted by direct exchange of body fluid, such as semen or blood.

Reducing fears of acquiring an STD

While some STDs seem to be increasing in prevalence, individuals can reduce their fears of these diseases by taking certain precautions:

1. Have a monogamous relationship. Have sexual contact with only one partner who limits contact to you only.
2. Look your partner over. Ask about any suspicious-looking discharges, sores, or rashes.
3. Be clean. Partners should bathe before and after sexual intercourse. Wash with soap and water.
4. Use condoms. Condoms provide some (though not complete) protection against STDs. However, the condom must be put on before sexual activity begins and not removed until the end of the activity.
5. Use foam, a diaphragm with spermicides, or sponge spermicides, which kill many infectious agents; these should be used in addition to the condom.
6. Avoid the "ping pong" effect of infection. If one partner has an STD,

the other partner must be informed and treated at the same time to avoid reinfection.

(See PSYCHOSEXUAL FEARS.)

Kahn, Ada P. and Linda Hughey Holt, *Midlife Health: Every Woman's Guide to Feeling Good* (New York: Facts On File, 1987).

shadows, fear of Fear of shadows is known as sciaphobia or sciophobia. This fear may be related to the fear of LIGHT AND SHADOWS, or of twilight.

Shakespeare, William (1564–1616) English writer and dramatist. The powers of anxiety and fear were of concern to Shakespeare, whose reputation for greatness rests on his ability not only as a dramatist, but also as a psychologist.

A central theme in Shakespeare's *Macbeth* is the overwhelming strength and control of fear on the human mind. Beginning with the witches' mysterious prediction of greatness, glory and danger for Macbeth, fear, mixed with ambition, becomes a self-fulfilling prophecy, corrupting him and his wife and eventually leading to their doom.

The contrast between light and dark and the frightening qualities of each are recurring Shakespearean themes. Several of his characters are attracted to dark and find light disturbing. Before he falls in love with Juliet, Romeo, brokenhearted over another young woman, is described by his father:

Away from light steals home my heavy son,
And private to his chamber pens himself.
Shuts up his windows, locks fair daylight out,
And makes himself an artificial night.

(*Romeo and Juliet,* Act I, scene I)

To other characters, however, the dark of the night is menacing, a cloak for evil. As he contemplates the murder of his uncle and stepfather, the king, Hamlet remarks:

'Tis now the very witching time of night,
When churchyards yawn and hell itself breathes out
Contagion to this world; now could I drink hot blood,
And do such bitter business as the day
Would quake to look on.

(*Hamlet,* Act III, scene 2)

Although Shakespeare's comedies frequently end with weddings, his characters often display strong fears about marriage. *As You Like It* contains the cynical observation that:

Men are April when they woo, December when they wed.
Maids are May when they are maids, but the sky changes when they are wives.

(*As You Like It,* Act IV, scene 1)

Two of Shakespeare's best known characters are tortured by anxiety. Hamlet's anxious indecision about avenging his father's death brings him to his own tragic end. Goaded by Iago's insinuations about Desdemona's fidelity, Othello is in a truly conflicted state: wanting to know and yet fearing the truth.

Halio, Jay L., "Anxiety in Othello," *Costerus: Essays in English and American Language and Literature* 1(1972), pp. 123–31.

Maguin, Jean-Marie, "Shakespeare et Les Terreurs de la Nuit," *Actes du Colloque Organise par la Centre de Recherches sur l'Angleterre des Tudors a la Regence de L'Univ. de Lille* (Vilenuve d'Ason, 1985).

Nelson, Timothy, "The Rotten Orange: Fears of Marriage in Comedy from Shakespeare to Congreve," *Southern Review: Literary and Interdisciplinary Essays, South Australia* 8(1975), pp. 205–226.

Rama Moorthy, P., "Fear in Macbeth," *Essays in Criticism, a Quarterly Journal of Literary Criticism* 23(1973), pp. 154–166.

Rothenberg, Alan, "Infantile Fantasies in Shakespeare Metaphor III: Photophobia," *Psychoanalytic Review* (Summer 1977), pp. 173–202.

Waldeck, Peter, "Anxiety, Tragedy and Hamlet's Delay," in Holzberger, William G and Waldeck, Peter (eds.), *Perspectives on Hamlet* (Lewisburg, PA: Bucknell U. Press, 1975).

shaking, fear of Because they fear shaking in front of other people, some phobic individuals will not eat in front of others, walk past a line of people, or sit facing another passenger in a bus or train. Some fear public speaking or appearing in front of an audience out of a fear of shaking. Some fear that their hands will shake when they write and so avoid writing anything in front of others. Those who have this fear usually fear going into banks, because they are often asked to sign their name in the course of a transaction. As a practical matter, many who have a fear of shaking rarely do shake in public. Fear of shaking is a SOCIAL PHOBIA and is often overcome with behavior-modification techniques involving exposure therapy. (See also PHOBIA.)

shaping A BEHAVIOR-MODIFICATION technique derived from OPERANT CONDITIONING. Shaping involves gradual and systematically reinforced responses toward a long-range desired new behavior. Shaping, also known as behavior-shaping, approximation conditioning, or reinforcement of successive approximations, was devised by B.F. SKINNER, an American psychologist. (See also BEHAVIOR THERAPY.)

sharp objects, fear of Fear of sharp objects, such as knives, is known as belonophobia. (See also KNIVES, FEAR OF.)

sheets of water, fear of Fear of sheets of water is known as potamophobia. This fear may be related to fear of very heavy rain, rivers, or lakes. (See also LAKES, FEAR OF; RAIN, FEAR OF; WATER, FEAR OF.)

shellfish, fear of Fear of shellfish is known as ostraconophobia. This fear may relate to eating shellfish, getting a disease from them, or to seeing them, thinking of them, or even seeing a picture of them. (See also CONTAMINATION, FEAR OF.)

shell shock A term used during World War I to denote many mental disorders presumed due to experience in battle. The term ''combat fatigue'' was applied to the same syndrome of effects. More recently, the group of battle-related disorders is referred to as POSTTRAUMATIC STRESS DISORDER.

shock, fear of Fear of shock is known as hormephobia. This fear relates both to electrical shock and the shock one receives, for example, at hearing extremely bad news. (See also ELECTRICITY, FEAR OF.)

shock treatment An inaccurate and obsolete term for electroconvulsive treatment.

shopping, fear of Fear of shopping may be associated with AGORAPHOBIA as well as a fear of being seen in public. Fear of shopping may also be related to a more underlying fear of spending money or fear of POVERTY. Individuals who fear shopping may lack confidence to make correct purchases or correctly count out money and change or fear coming in contact with STRANGERS. Individuals who have a low sense of self-esteem and a negative body image may fear or avoid shopping for clothes because doing so forces them to confront their appearance, which in turn may make them feel anxious. (See also BODY IMAGE, FEAR OF; SOCIAL PHOBIA; STRANGERS, FEAR OF.)

short-term-anxiety-provoking-psychotherapy A brief therapy technique lasting for three to four months or from 12 to 16 sessions used to help anxious individuals who are unable to make satisfactory relationships and whose disturbance originates in unresolved Oedipal conflicts, separation difficulty, grief reaction, and other problems. The treatment is often used with young adults. The basis for the therapy is to help individuals gain insight into the roots of their disturbances and thereby relieve their distress. The therapy includes establishing a therapeutic alliance with the therapist, active use of anxiety-provoking confrontation, and clarification to penetrate the individual's resistance. Presumably, through a corrective emotional relationship, the individual can resolve disturbances that may have arisen from early unsatisfactory relationships with parents.

shot, fear of being Fear of being shot involves a fear of violence, injury, and death. The fear has existed since man invented firearms. However, fears of being shot in the latter part of the twentieth century, particularly in the United States, have become more realistic in many places. In 1986, firearms were used in three out of five murders and in twenty-one percent of all aggravated assault cases. Guns are more frequently used in killings between individuals unknown to each other than in cases involving acquaintances. Homicides involving guns are more frequent in the South than in the North. Victims of fatal shootings are most likely to be male, specifically men in their twenties.

Individuals who fear being the victim of criminal or accidental gunshot wounds have formed a strong gun-control movement in the United States, although there are many opponents to it. Assassinations of prominent figures and random irrational killings have caused fearful speculation that the American inner city will begin to resemble the Wild West, where owning and carrying a gun was standard behavior.

Encyclopedia of Crime and Justice (New York: Free Press, 1983).

Pasternack, Stefan A., *Violence and Victims* (New York: Spectrum, 1975).

Uniform Crime Reports of the United States (Washington, DC: Government Printing Office, 1987).

Shriek, The A painting depicting a panic attack. (See also MUNCH, EDVARD; PANIC ATTACK.)

shyness Shyness is a symptom of social anxiety, related to a fear of being unfavorably evaluated by others. Shyness can be observed in several ways. Physically, the shy person may blush and perspire. Emotionally, he or she may feel anxious and insecure. The shy person may think that no one wants to talk to him or her, or that no one likes him or her. A shy person's behavior may actually help to discourage social intercourse, because shy people tend to keep their heads down and even avoid eye contact with others. Shyness may bring on a lack of social relationships, or a distorted view of social relationships, causing the shy person to feel the anxieties of loneliness and emotional unfulfillment.

Shyness may be related to social phobia; social phobia involves fear of scrutiny from other people and leads to gaze aversion and avoidance of eating, drinking, blushing, speaking, writing, or eliminating in their presence.

Almost everyone experiences shyness at some time, especially "situational shyness," which arises in such uncomfortable social situations as meeting new people or going for a job interview. The term "dispositional shyness" describes a pervasive personality trait, which can be long-lasting or correlated to a particular stage of life, especially adolescence.

Shyness may be handled in different ways, depending on the individual's personal system of DEFENSE MECHANISMS. While it may cause some persons to withdraw and become quiet in social situations (introversion), shyness may encourage others to behave more aggressively in public, trying to cover up their shyness by being "the life of the party" (extroversion).

It is not uncommon for extroverted shy people to become performers or public figures, handling their shyness by keeping themselves in controlled, structured situations, performing well-rehearsed roles in familiar situations. (See chart following.) (See

Shyness Reactions

Physiological Reactions	Overt Behaviors	Thoughts and Feelings
Blushing	Silence	Self-consciousness
Perspiration	Avoidance of others	Concern about impression on others
Increased pulse	No eye contact	
Heart pounding	Avoidance of action	Concern for social evaluation
Butterflies in stomach	Low speaking voice	Unpleasantness of situation

also BLUSHING, FEAR OF; PERFORMANCE ANXIETY; STAGE FRIGHT.)

Marks, Isaac M., *Fears, Phobias and Rituals* (New York: Oxford University Press, 1987).

Zimbardo, Phillip, *Psychology and Life* (Glenview, IL: Scott, Foresman, 1985).

sick role The protected position an individual who is anxious, phobic, or considered not well assumes or is put in by family and friends. The sick role may give the individual so labeled the advantages of attention and support, emotional and financial, that he or she might not otherwise have. The individual in the sick role may not be motivated to improve because he or she fears removal of attention (a powerful reinforcer). Some individuals who have AGORAPHOBIA are encouraged in the sick role because their families do chores and errands for them, enabling the phobic individuals to perpetuate their agoraphobic (avoidance) tendencies. The sick role may have positive effects on a family, in that it causes family members to become more cohesive. (See also FAMILY MYTH; PRIMARY GAIN; SECONDARY GAIN.)

side effects Reactions or results that follow administration of a drug that are not related to the particular and desired effect of the drug. For example, side effects (such as dizziness, warmth on parts of the body, paradoxical anxiety) can occur after an individual takes an antianxiety or antidepressant drug. Side effects occur for many reasons, including as a result of interaction between drugs and opposing or additive effects; of an individual's allergy to certain substances; or of a drug's interaction with food. (See also ADVERSE DRUG REACTIONS.)

siderodromophobia Fear of railroads, trains, or traveling by train. The word is derived from the the Greek word *sideros,* meaning "iron," and *dromos,* meaning "course" or "running." (See also MOTION, FEAR OF; RAILROADS, FEAR OF; TRAINS, FEAR OF.)

siderophobia Fear of the stars or evil that might come from stars. (See also HEAVEN, FEAR OF; STARS, FEAR OF.)

SIDS See SUDDEN INFANT DEATH SYNDROME.)

sign An indication of the existence of a disorder. A sign is usually objective evidence and is observed by the examiner or another person rather than reported by the individual. For example, a sign of a panic attack might be visible rapid breathing. A sign should be contrasted with a SYMPTOM, which is a phenomenon reported by the individual himself or herself. The term behavior sign is often used. (See also DIAGNOSIS.)

signal anxiety A form of ANXIETY that functions as an early warning system. Signal anxiety, a concept from psychoanalytic theory, comes from the normal ability to anticipate a potentially threatening situation, either from internal or external sources, and to deploy emergency defenses against it before the anxiety intensifies. Such defenses might be fight, flight, or giving in. Signal anxiety may progress to a full ANXIETY ATTACK or even to a PANIC attack if the individual does not pay attention to the early warning or if available defenses are insufficient.

simple phobia A simple PHOBIA is a persistent irrational, intense fear of and compelling desire to avoid specific objects or situations. Simple phobias are sometimes referred to as specific phobias.

Almost any object or situation can be phobic for a given individual. All fears that do not fit into other phobic groups are generally categorized as simple phobias. Examples of common simple phobias include driving across bridges, flying, harmless animals such as dogs and cats, heights, darkness, and thunderstorms. (See also DIAGNOSTIC CRITERIA; PHOBIC ANXIETY; PHOBIC DISORDERS.)

sin, fear of Fear of sin is known as hamartophobia, harmatophobia, enissophobia, enosiophobia, peccatiphobia, and peccatophobia. (See also SINNING, FEAR OF.)

Sinequan See DOXEPIN.

single, fear of staying Fear of staying single is known as anuptaphobia. Many people fear remaining single because they view the world as being populated by couples. They find themselves feeling like a "fifth wheel" when they are in the company of couples. The fear of being single is a fear of being considered socially somewhat different than most other people. The fear also includes a fear of growing old and being alone.

single-room occupancy and phobias In a study of a rehoused poverty population in New York City in 1960, many individuals, particularly women, who previously had lived in very close, crowded quarters developed fears of being alone in a room. Panic and fears developed as soon as the families were moved into new homes in new neighborhoods. Some of the mothers could not sleep without close contact with their children or another adult and returned to their old sleeping arrangements. Although the new apartments had several rooms, they would use only a single room. Women showed phobias of traveling outside of the apartment and were fearful of doing anything alone. They returned to their old neighborhoods for shopping. Some children developed school phobias.

Social workers explained that these phobic reactions included feelings of helplessness that were relieved when the women were within close proximity of others. (See also ALONE, FEAR OF BEING.)

Perman, J.M., "Phobia as a Determinant of Single-Room Occupancy," *American Journal of Psychiatry* (Nov. 1966), pp. 609–613.

sinistrophobia Fear of things to the left or left-handedness. (See also LEFT, THINGS TO THE, FEAR OF.)

sinning, fear of Fear of sinning is known as peccatiphobia. Fear of sinning has been a strong disciplinary force in religious history. In the church of the middle ages through the 17th century, sinful acts were expected to bring direct retribution from God in the form of illness or natural disaster. Scientific explanations for these phenomena and a more sophisticated sense of the forces of history lessened but did not eliminate this belief in a cause-and-effect relationship between sinful acts and direct punishment.

Although 20th-century people are concerned with feelings of GUILT (which is the internal form of punishment), the consciousness of specific acts as being sinful seems greatly reduced. Society has become less God-fearing, more secular, and more inclined to depend on law enforcement of a behavioral code than religious discipline. (See also CONSCIENCE.)

Sandmel, Samuel, *A Little Book on Religion (for People Who Are Not Religious)* (Chambersburg, PA: Wilson Books, 1975).

Thomas, Keith, *Religion and the Decline of Magic* (New York: Scribner, 1971).

Sinophobia Fear of CHINA, the Chinese language, and things relating to the Chinese culture.

sitophobia Fear of eating or fear of food. (See also EATING, FEAR OF; FOOD, FEAR OF.)

sitting, fear of Fear of sitting is known as cathisophobia, kathisophobia, and thaasophobia. Some individuals who are very anxious and very restless are fearful of sitting or of sitting for very long periods of time. This fear may relate to a fear of one's lap or holding something on one's lap.

skin cancer, fear of Many individuals fear skin cancer because it can be painful and disfiguring. Skin cancer often occurs on the face and is visible to others, causing the victim anxieties and self-consciousness as well as discomfort. Out of fear of skin cancer, many individuals now avoid suntanning and even being in the sun. Some fearful people cover themselves from head to toe while outdoors on a sunny day. Many people use cream or lotion sunscreens on exposed portions of their skin to avoid any sunburn.

There are three types of skin cancer: basal-cell carcinoma, squamous-cell carcinoma, and malignant melanoma. Basal-cell carcinoma is the most common. Cells just below the surface of the skin become cancerous. Cell damage usually seems to be caused by long-term exposure to strong sunlight, and many years may pass before skin cancer develops. Unlike other malignant growths, basal-cell carcinoma does not spread to other parts of the body until it has been present a long time.

In squamous-cell carcinoma, underlying skin cells are damaged, leading to the development of a malignant or life-threatening tumor. Years of exposure to strong sunlight seems to be the main cause. If this type of cancer is allowed to develop, it may spread to other parts of the body. But good results have been obtained with early detection and treatment.

Malignant melanoma, the most serious of the types of skin cancer, often spreads through the body.

Anxieties about skin cancer, and the suspicion that any skin defect is a symptom of skin cancer, can usually be alleviated by an examination by a dermatologist. With early detection and early treatment, most skin cancers can be successfully controlled. (See also CANCER, FEAR OF; PAIN AND ANXIETIES; SKIN DISEASE AND SKIN LESION, FEAR OF.)

Kunz, J.R.M. and A.J. Finkel, *The American Medical Association Family Medical Guide* (New York: Random House, 1987).

skin conductance Certain anxiety-inducing, stressful, or pleasant stimuli change the electrical resistance of the skin, particularly the skin on the palms or other areas without hair. The response is produced by unconscious activity of the sweat glands. This effect is known as GALVANIC SKIN RESPONSE (GSR), electrodermal response (EDR), and psychogalvanic reflex (PGR).

skin disease and skin lesion, fear of Fear of skin disease and skin lesions or injury is known as dermatopathophobia, dermatophobia, and dermatosiophobia. Some individuals who fear skin disease also have fears of contamination and germs. Out of fear they avoid touching items that others have touched. Many individuals fear skin diseases and skin injury or skin lesions because such conditions may be uncomfortable as well as disfiguring. Some individuals who have skin diseases are anxious and self-conscious about their appearance and tend to avoid social situations where others may look at them, criticize them, or ask questions. For example, acne in teenagers causes considerable anxiety because the lesions come and go with relative unpredictability, and often a young person will have a flare-up of acne on a socially or academically important and stressful day.

Fears of skin diseases are related to overall fears of injury and illness, to fear of doctors and hospitals, and to fear of needing medical attention.

Skin conditions such as hives and eczema are themselves symptoms of anxiety disorder, and some skin conditions become worse when an individual is in a state of anxiety.

Among the many specific skin disorders different individuals fear are acne, boils and carbuncles, warts, impetigo, cellulitis, eczema, psoriasis, hives, ichthyosis, keloids, lichen planus, abnormal skin pigmentation, vitiligo, pityriasis, chloasma, and moles.

Individuals who become anxious about any symptoms of skin disease should consult their dermatologist before trying commercial preparations. Many prescription drugs are available to relieve skin problems; seeking treatment usually is the first step toward reducing anxieties about a skin problem. (See also ALLERGIC REACTIONS; BUGS, FEAR OF; CONTAMINATION, FEAR OF; FLYING THINGS, FEAR OF; GERMS, FEAR OF, ILLNESS, FEAR OF; INSECTS, FEAR OF; ITCH, FEAR OF; PAIN, ANXIETY AND DEPRESSION IN; PAIN, FEAR OF.)

Kunz, J.R.M. and A.J. Finkel, *The American Medical Association Family Medical Guide* (New York: Random House, 1987).

skin of animals, fear of Fear of the skin of animals is known as dorophobia. This may be related to a fear of textures and a fear of fuzz, or fuzz aversion. It may also be related to a fear of the animals themselves. The classical case of dorophobia was that of Little Albert, who was classically conditioned by JOHN B. WATSON and R. Raynor during the 1920s to fear rabbits. The fear quickly generalized to fur, furry objects, beards, and hair. (See ALBERT B.)

Skinner, Burrhus Frederick (B.F.) (1904–) An American psychologist known as a pioneer in operant behavior-modification techniques of psychotherapy. Skinner's work affected approaches to treatment of anxieties, phobias, and other areas of mental health. He constructed a major learning theory and was an influential spokesman for radical behaviorism. His theory of behavior was based on a deterministic philosophy that included the notion that individuals' behavior and personality are determined by both past and present events and genetic makeup and not by internal influences. He believed that psychologists should focus on behavior that is observable and verifiable and that behavior can be best understood and modified by manipulating its consequences. (See also BEHAVIOR THERAPY.)

SK-Pramine See IMIPRAMINE.)

sleep, fear of Fear of sleep is known as hypnophobia. Fear of sleep may be common in individuals suffering from sleep disorders such as NIGHTMARES, sleeptalking, sleepwalking, and especially narcolepsy. Fear of sleep may be related to the individual's feelings of a loss of control of his actions if he falls asleep. The fear may also be related to a fear of death, as the person may fear NOT WAKING UP. (See also SLEEPTALKING, FEAR OF; SLEEPWALKING, FEAR OF.)

sleep, function of Sleep is an activity that causes many people anxieties as well as fears. Some individuals become anxious if they do not sleep enough, while others become anxious that they sleep too much. Some have difficulty getting to sleep, and some have difficulty staying asleep. Others have difficulty waking up. Sleep disorders are common in many individuals who have anxiety disorders. Those who have depression may have difficulty sleeping or may sleep too much. For many individuals, physical conditions that make them uncomfortable or anxious also interfere with adequate and satisfying sleep. In some people, sleep may be used as an escape from problems and tensions present during waking hours. Lack of adequate sleep may make one feel nervous and jumpy, affect judgment and decision-making abilities, and slow reaction times.

Sleep is a necessary activity that provides a restorative function. During sleep, daily bodily functions such as digestion and waste removal have a chance to rest and recharge. An evolutionary theory regarding sleep suggests that sleep originally allowed humans and animals to conserve energy during the dark hours when it was less practical to hunt for food and harder to escape from danger.

The average adult needs about eight hours of sleep per 24 hours; the need for sleep seems to decrease as the person ages. Individual sleep patterns vary, however, and may be affected by anxiety. An average person may go through his or her sleep cycle about four to six times each night. A sleep cycle consists of stages (known as Stages I, II, III, and IV) in a cycle lasting about 90 minutes followed by a period of rapid eye movement (REM) sleep for about ten minutes. With each cycle, REM periods lengthen. During the last cycle, REM sleep may last for 30 to 60 minutes. Dreaming is most likely to occur during REM sleep. This period is characterized by extensive muscular inhibition; most of the voluntary muscles in the body take on a paralyzed state, and there are bursts of rapid movements of the eye, under the closed eyelid, as if the person were watching something occurring in front

Patterns of Sleep During Lifetime

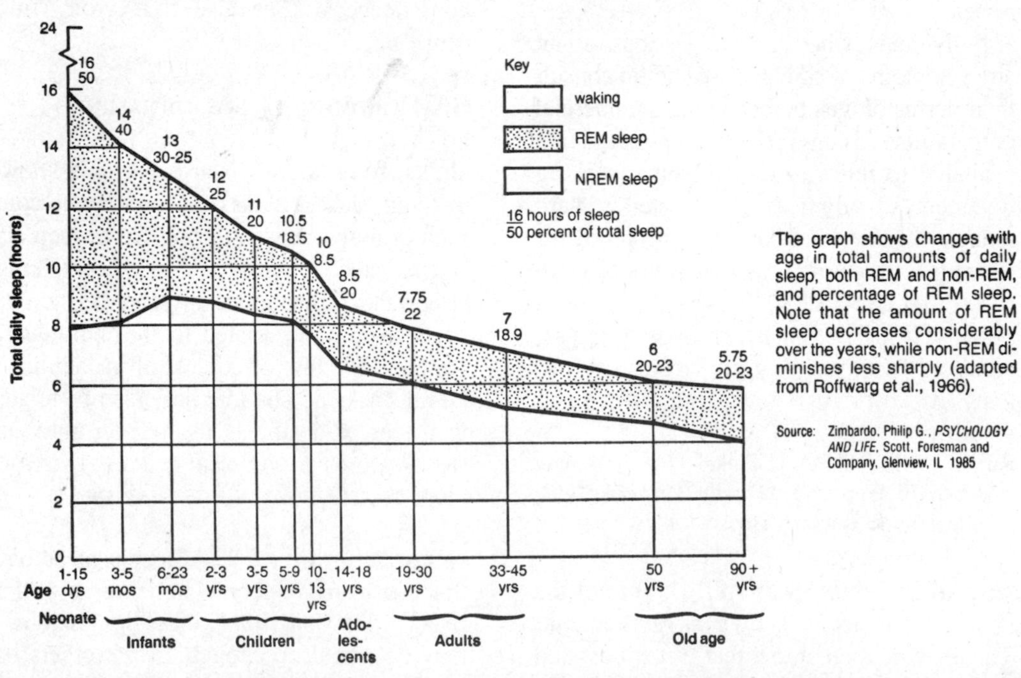

The graph shows changes with age in total amounts of daily sleep, both REM and non-REM, and percentage of REM sleep. Note that the amount of REM sleep decreases considerably over the years, while non-REM diminishes less sharply (adapted from Roffwarg et al., 1966).

Source: Zimbardo, Philip G., *PSYCHOLOGY AND LIFE*, Scott, Foresman and Company, Glenview, IL 1985

of him or her. (See also BEDWETTING; DREAM SYMBOLS; DREAMS, FEAR OF; INSOMNIA; NARCOLEPSY; SLEEPTALKING, FEAR OF; SLEEPWALKING, FEAR OF; WET DREAMS.)

McConnell, James V., Understanding Human Behavior (New York: Holt, Rinehart and Winston, 1986).

Zimbardo, Phillip, *Psychology and Life* (Glenview, IL: Scott, Foresman, 1985).

sleep terror disorder See NIGHT TERRORS.

sleeptalking, fear of Talking during sleep most often occurs during the early and dreamless stages of an individual's sleep cycle. Persons who have a fear of sleeptalking may be anxious that they might reveal personal secrets or feelings to listeners. In actuality, most sleeptalking is related to unemotional subjects. The habit of sleeptalking has not been related to any specific personality traits or disorders. (See also SLEEP, FEAR OF; SLEEP, FUNCTION OF; SLEEPWALKING, FEAR OF.)

sleepwalking, fear of Sleepwalking (somnambulism) episodes occur most often in children between ages nine and twelve, although they may happen at any age in a child's or adult's life. Estimates are that as many as twenty percent of the population has experienced sleepwalking at least once. Individuals who walk during sleep will usually perform some familiar or ritualistic activities such as getting dressed, going to the kitchen for something to eat, or getting into their car. In very unusual cases, persons have been known to board trains and wake up hundreds of miles away from home.

Sleepwalking may run in families and may also be related to other sleep disturbances such as sleeptalking and NIGHT TERRORS. If any individual has had an unpleasant or dangerous experience while sleepwalking, this may lead to a fear of the disorder and may also cause increased anxiety concerning sleeping in general. (See also NIGHTMARES; SLEEP, FEAR OF; SLEEP, FUNCTION OF.)

McConnell, James V., *Understanding Human Behavior* (New York: Holt, Rinehart, and Winston, 1986).

sliding down the drain, fear of
Many young children view their bathwater going down the drain and worry that they, too, might be caught up in the swirling water and disappear down the water pipe. Commonly, children who have this fear accept the explanation that they are too big to fit in the drain. This fear usually disappears by age five. (See also CHILDHOOD ANXIETIES, FEARS, AND PHOBIAS.)

slime, fear of Fear of slime is known as blennophobia or myxophobia. Individuals who have this fear may fear eating certain foods, such as oysters, or touching or even looking at certain animals, such as frogs and snakes. The fear may also be related to a fear of contamination by dirt or filth. (See also CONTAMINATION, FEAR OF; DIRT, FEAR OF; FILTH, FEAR OF.)

slips of the tongue, fear of Many individuals fear slips of the tongue, or saying one thing when they mean to say something else. Fear of making such slips is based on the interpretation given to these remarks by SIGMUND FREUD, and they are known as "Freudian slips." It was through the study of slips of the tongue and dreams that Freud formulated his theory of psychic functioning. The Freudian view is that the speaker said exactly what he or she really meant to say. These slips may be the emergence of an unconscious wish or a failure to repress the unconscious desire. Everyone interchanges words frequently, usually without any meaning, but for some social phobics, who fear being heard talking or fear talking with others, this fear is enough to keep them away from social situations. Slips of the tongue often happen when a person is distracted or preoccupied with some stressful situation. (See also SHYNESS; SOCIAL PHOBIA; SPEAKING, FEAR OF.)

slowness, compulsive A symptom of OBSESSIVE–COMPULSIVE DISORDER in which individuals take a very long time to do everyday actions. It may take them several hours to bathe, get dressed, and eat their breakfast. When they go out, it may take a long time for them to cross a street because they check and recheck traffic in all directions before setting forth.

small objects Fear of small objects is known as microphobia or tapinophobia. Individuals who fear small objects may fear particular objects, such as figurines, rocks, marbles, and other objects.

smells, fear of Fear of smells is known as osmophobia. Because the sense of smell is closely related to emotions and motivation, the fear of smells may cause anxieties for many individuals.

Unpleasant odors are often precursors to certain anxiety attacks and epileptic seizures. Certain cases of mass hysteria have supposedly been triggered by peculiar smells or other changes in the environment that frightened many people at the same time.

The fear of a particular smell may be related to an individual's previous unpleasant experience with it. Individuals may fear smelling cooking odors or body odors (their own or those of others). Some may fear smelling smoke. Several primary categories of smells have been identified, including musky, floral, peppermint, ether (dry-cleaning fluid), pungent (vinegar), and putrid (rotten eggs). Most smells experienced in daily life are a combination of two or more of these categories. (See also BODY ODOR, FEAR OF.)

smoking, fear of Smoking of cigarettes, pipes, and cigars is most often feared because of its negative health effects on the smoker. Negative health effects have also been attributed to "secondhand smoke," or the sidestream smoke from the smoker's materials that others unwillingly inhale. In 1987, statistics from the Coalition on Smoking and Health indicated that 350,000 Americans die yearly from cigarette smoking-related diseases.

Although smoking oneself or being near another who is smoking may cause anxiety, many individuals use smoking itself as a means of relieving tension. Smokers often cite the act as a "nervous habit," providing oral gratification and giving them "something to do with their hands." Smokers addicted to the nicotine in tobacco need to smoke to relieve the anxiety caused by their withdrawal between cigarettes. At one time, smoking was looked upon as a sign of maturity and was considered chic, relieving anxiety by raising the smoker's level of confidence and self-esteem. As smoking has become less socially acceptable, however, this has changed, and the more negative image now associated with smoking may actually add to the smoker's anxiety level. Fear of becoming addicted to smoking may keep some individuals from ever starting to smoke. (See also DRUG DEPENDENCE; TOBACCO, FEAR OF.)

smothering, fear of Fear of smothering is known as pnigophobia. Smothering to phobic individuals may mean having their air supply cut off in a closed, crowded space, such as an elevator, in which they fear that there may not be enough air for everyone to breathe. Also, such individuals may fear having their faces covered with blankets, masks for anesthesia, or other items that may interfere with their breathing. (See also CHOKING, FEAR OF; SUFFOCATION, FEAR OF.)

Snake Questionnaire (SNAQ) A questionnaire devised by R. Klorman et al. in 1974 to measure fear of snakes. The questionnaire is composed of 30 statements concerning snakes to which the respondents answer "true" or "false." Statements concern the areas of avoidance of situations where snakes might be present, physical responses felt while in the presence of a snake, and thoughts one might have about snakes. (See also SNAKES, FEAR OF.)

See chart that follows.

Kleinknecht, Ronald A., *The Anxious Self* (New York: Human Sciences Press, 1986).

Klorman, R. et al., "Psychometric Description of Some Specific-fear Questionnaires," *Behavior Therapy,* 5(1974), pp. 401–409.

Sample Items from SNAQ

	True	False
I avoid going to parks or on camping trips because there may be snakes about.	___	___
I shudder when I think of snakes.	___	___
Some snakes are very attractive to look at.	___	___
I enjoy watching snakes at the zoo.	___	___

Ronald A. Kleinknecht, *The Anxious Self* (New York: Human Sciences Press, 1986), p. 102.

snakephobia See SNAKES, FEAR OF.

snakes, fear of Fear of snakes is known as ophidiophobia, ophiophobia, ophiciophobia, and herpetophobia. Fear of snakes is a nearly universal fear among humans as well as animals. Many people fear snakes because of their fangs and the possibility of receiving a fatal snakebite. Many people cannot tell a poisonous snake from a nonpoisonous one and hence fear any snakebite. Also, many people consider snakes slimy and hence disgusting. Some fears of snakes are realistic. In the U.S. and Europe, poisonous snakes include the Eastern diamondback rattlesnake, the Western diamondback rattlesnake, and the European viper (adder).

There is evidence that the vast majority of people who fear snakes have had no direct contact with them. This would suggest a genetic trigger or possibly cultural attitudes conditioning the reaction.

Fear of snakes usually comes with age because small children evidence less fear. In 1928, two American psychologists, H.E. Jones and M.C. Jones, conducted an experiment in which they placed children of various ages in an enclosure with a large, harmless snake and observed their reactions. Children up to the age of two did not show fearful reactions, but those who were three and four years old looked cautious and hesitant. Those over age four showed definite signs of fear. In 1933, Ernest Holmes reported that fear of snakes was shown more frequently by children between the ages of two and four than before or after that age.

In 1965, two British psychologists, Morris and Morris, found that dislike of snakes increases from age four to age six, at which stage it was present in one-third of British children, and then declines to the age of 14. Isaac Marks, in *Fears and Phobias* (1969), commented: "This prevalence is striking when one considers how small the actual danger is from snakes in the British Isles." Children may learn that snakes are dangerous from reading or from their parents. It may be that individuals exposed to a snake for the first time are not frightened by the snake itself, but rather by the writhing movements of the snake.

Researchers have considered the effects of viewing distance on fear of snakes. In a Northampton, Massachusetts study, phobic subjects made magnitude estimations of the intensity of fear felt when viewing a snake at distances from 2.5 to 15.0 feet. Heart rate, skin conductance, and respiration were also measured throughout each 20-second viewing period. A control group of nonphobic subjects made magnitude estimates of perceived nearness for the empty snake box at the same test distances. Judged fear was inversely proportional to distance. Heart rate and skin conductance decreased signficantly for phobics as viewing distance increased.

In psychoanalysis, the snake is a symbol for the penis and is identified with sexual energies. The snake symbol appears frequently in dreams and in primitive rites and art productions, in which it may represent life.

In psychologic, symbolic terms, snakes represent life energy itself. For this reason, snakes carry multivalencies—guardians of life, health, wisdom, immortality, and mystery as well as destruction, illness, temptation, and the principle of will (potentially) inherent in all worldly things. Furthermore, the snake is seen as a symbol of transformation. For example, the ancient Mayan myth tells of the snake (nature principle) climbing the tree, leaping and catching the bird (spirit principle) to become transformed into a "winged serpent."

Probably, the best SYMBOLISM of the serpent is that of the Kundalini, a progressive movement of the life energy through movement of the six Chakras (energy centers of the body in eastern Indian tradition).

The serpent in the Garden of Eden is seen as the life force bringing man into consciousness from unconsciousness. In consciousness, there is fear because man develops awareness of relationships.

In the caduceus, the design of the rod and serpent traditionally used as a medical emblem, there is recognition of illness and health as coexisting in the individual. Of all medical symbols, the serpent is among the most outstanding and widely used. According to mythological tales and records found in excavations and shown by artifacts, the ancients actually used serpents in their healing arts. Before man began recording, he observed the serpent periodically shedding his skin, gliding gracefully along the ground, disappearing into the earth, and then reappearing. These actions fascinated early man, and gradually the powers of wisdom, rejuvenation, convalescence, and long life were attributed to the serpent. (See also PHOBIA; SIMPLE PHOBIAS.)

Teghtsoonian, Robert and Randy O. Frost, "The Effects of Viewing Distance on Fear of Snakes," *Journal of Behavior Therapy and Experimental Psychiatry,* 13:3(1982), pp. 181–190.

Kahn, Ada P., "From Serpent Healing . . . to AMRA Symbol," *Medical Record News* (February 1970), pp. 24–34.

Goodwin, Donald W. *Phobias: The Facts* (Oxford: Oxford University Press, 1983).

Kleinknecht, Ronald A., *THE ANXIOUS SELF* (New York: Human Sciences Press, 1986).

Jones, H.E. and M.C. Jones, "Fear," *Childhood Education,* 5(1928), pp. 135–143.

Marks, Isaac M., *Fears and Phobias* (New York: Academic Press, 1969).

snow, fear of Fear of snow is known as chionophobia. Because snow is associated with the harshness and sterility of winter, it has come to symbolize death, poverty, and suffering. In the myths of some cultures, the end of the world is predicted to occur in winter, preceded by a barrage of snow. In folk tales, snow has been personified as a beautiful, alluring woman who leads her victims to their doom.

There are realistic reasons for fear of snow. Snow causes falls, traffic accidents, and collapsing roofs. Blizzards can create drifts as high as 30 feet. Victims of a white-out during a snowstorm suffer from loss of balance and sense of direction because snow blurs the horizon and landscape and cancels shadows. Avalanches, which may travel at speeds of 50 miles per hour, cause death and destruction not only because of the actual weight and force of the snow, but also because of sudden air-pressure changes preceding and following. The sudden melting of large amounts of snow may create destructive floods.

Halford, Ingrid, *The Guinness Book of Weather Facts and Feats* (London: Guinness Superlatives, 1982).

Jobes, Gertrude, *Dictionary of Mythology, Folklore and Symbols* (New York: Scarecrow Press, 1961).

Cavendish, Richard (ed.); *Man, Myth and Magic* (New York: Marshall Cavendish, 1983), "Winter."

soceraphobia Fear of parents-in-law. (See also FATHER-IN-LAW, FEAR OF; MOTHER-IN-LAW, FEAR OF; RELATIVES, FEAR OF.)

social anxiety Social anxieties involve relationships with other people and one's feelings about them. This concept was once referred to as "interpersonal anxiety." Most people have some social anxieties, such as wanting to be liked and accepted, to avoid criticism, to conform when conformity is desirable, and to be deemed competent. Social anxieties include a wide range of feelings, including worrying about what to wear for an occasion, apprehension upon entering a roomful of strangers, or worries about eating in front of other people. When these situations become so difficult for an individual that he or she begins to avoid them, they are considered phobias. (See also BLUSHING; PHOBIA; SHYNESS; SOCIAL PHOBIA.)

social phobia Fear being evaluated, criticized, censured, embarrassed, or in some way punished in social settings by the reactions of others. Social phobias are the most common phobias. Social phobics fear acting or looking stupid, and thus they avoid doing many activities of daily life when and where they can be seen by others. Social phobias include eating, drinking, speaking, urinating, blushing, or vomiting in the presence of others. Social phobics fear that their hands tremble or shake as they eat or write and tend to avoid restaurants, banks, and other public places. They often avert their eyes when talking to another person. Some social phobics have been known to cross the street to avoid greeting someone they know. Social phobics are fearful of attending parties, particularly with people they do not know.

Many social phobics have had lifelong shyness and introverted habits. Usually social phobias begin after puberty and peak in the late teems. Social phobias are equally common among men and women. Many agoraphobics have social phobias, and many social phobics have minor agoraphobic symptoms.

The incidence of social phobias in two urban populations over a six-month period ranged from 0.9 to 1.7 percent for men and 1.5 to 2.6 percent for women. These figures are derived from self-reports and screening questions in community surveys. The percent of socially phobic individuals who seek treatment are much lower than these incidence figures. Significant depressive symptoms are also associated with social phobias. (See also AGORAPHOBIA; PHOBIA.)

Marks, Isaac M., *Fears, Phobias and Rituals* (New York: Oxford University Press, 1987).

society, fear of Fear of society in general is known as sociophobia. This fear may be related to AGORAPHOBIA. Many individuals who have several SOCIAL PHOBIAS may also be categorized as sociophobics. (See also PHOBIA.)

sociophobia Fear of society or people in general. (See also SOCIETY, FEAR OF.)

sodium lactate infusions See LACTATE-INDUCED ANXIETY.

solitude, fear of Fear of solitude is known as autophobia, eremophobia, eremiophobia, ermitophobia, and isolophobia. (See also ALONE, FEAR OF BEING; OLD, FEAR OF GROWING.)

solo phobia See ALONE, FEAR OF BEING.

soteria A term that describes the disproportionate comfort some individuals get from the presence of certain objects or situations. The word comes from the Greek *soteria,* which refers to festive entertainment given on a person's recovery from illness or escape from danger. Examples of soterias are the toys and stuffed animals young children carry around with them and the talismans and charms many adults wear. Phobic individuals often develop a soterial attachment to an object that reduces their fear. For example, some get comfort from carrying a bottle of smelling salts with them; some are comforted by the knowledge that they have a supply of sedative drugs in their pocket, even if they don't actually take the drug.

The best known contemporary soteria is the "Linus blanket," the security blanket named for the cartoon-strip character in Charles Schultz's "Peanuts." A soteria has also been called a transitional object. Loss of a soteria usually produces grief.

Marks, Isaac M., *Fears, Phobias and Rituals* (New York: Oxford University Press, 1987).

sophophobia Fear of learning. (See also LEARNING, FEAR OF; SCHOOL PHOBIA.)

sounds, fear of Fear of sounds is known as acousticophobia. This may relate to specific sounds, sound in general, or noise. Parents become anxious when they hear cries of fear or pain from their infants. Many people become fearful when they hear others screaming in agony or panic (for example, hearing other children crying after receiving shots or hearing women in labor). The sound of buzzing bees arouses fear in many people. (See also NOISE, FEAR OF.)

Marks, Isaac M., *Fears, Phobias and Rituals* (New York: Oxford University Press, 1987).

sourness, fear of Fear of sourness or a sour taste is known as acerophobia or acerbophobia. This fear may relate to a fear of taste in general. (See also TASTE, FEAR OF.)

space phobia Fear of falling when one perceives space without nearby support, often occurring with increased age and decreased mobility and flexibility. Space phobics need visual boundaries rather than physical support to walk or drive across open spaces. Space phobia affects more women than men. Although there are many overlapping characteristics of space phobia and AGORAPHOBIA, there are characteristics that distinguish the two. Usually space phobia begins after age 40 and agoraphobia in early adulthood. In space phobia, the individual has intense fears of falling; this usually does not occur in agoraphobia. Space phobics, unlike agoraphobics, rarely have accompanying depression, nonsituational anxiety or panic, or personality difficulties. Space phobics often have diverse cardiovascular or neurological disorders; some progress until the individuals are confined to a wheelchair.

Space phobics respond less well to treatment by exposure in vivo than do agoraphobics. (See also FALLING, FEAR OF.)

Marks, Isaac M., *Fears, Phobias and Rituals* (New York: Oxford University Press, 1987).

spacephobia Fear of outer space. (See also OUTER SPACE, FEAR OF; SPACE TRAVEL, FEAR OF.)

space travel, fear of Fear of traveling in space is a fear of the unknown. Outer space seems dark, still, and mysterious. Modern man realizes that a highly organized system of technology is necessary to sustain life in outer space and also fears that our current system may not be adequate. The classic film of the late 1960s, *2001, A Space Odyssey,* explored the fears of relying on fallible technology in space as well as other frightening aspects of space travel, including isolation, keeping physically and mentally stimulated in a limited environment, and the possibility of encountering the unknown.

The explosion of the space shuttle *Challenger* in 1986 created a new realization of the risks of space travel and a rethinking of the U.S. manned space flight program. (See also OUTER SPACE, FEAR OF; UNKNOWN, FEAR OF.)

Newlon, Clarke, *1001 Questions Answered about Space* (New York: Dodd, Mead, 1962).

World Book, Inc. *World Book Encyclopedia* (Chicago: World Book, 1987), "Space Travel."

speaking, fear of Fear of speaking, a social phobia, is known as laliophobia. This fear may be related to a fear of speaking out loud or speaking over the telephone or fear that one may use the wrong words, have an ineffective tone of voice, or sound powerless. Other fears related to speaking include hearing the sound of one's own voice and stuttering. Public speaking is one of the most prevalent fears among adults. (See also PUBLIC SPEAKING; FEAR OF; SHYNESS; SLIPS OF THE TONGUE, FEAR OF; SPEAKING ALOUD, FEAR OF; STUTTERING, FEAR OF.)

speaking aloud, fear of Fear of speaking out loud is known as phonophobia. This fear may be related to the fear of hearing one's own voice, of stuttering, or of having a poor voice quality. Muteness and aphonia (inability to speak louder than a whisper) may result as traces of avoidance. (See also PUBLIC SPEAKING, FEAR OF; SHYNESS; SLIPS OF THE TONGUE, FEAR OF; SOCIAL PHOBIA; STUTTERING, FEAR OF.)

speaking in public, fear of See PUBLIC SPEAKING, FEAR OF.

specific fear inventories Tests to determine information about an individual's specific fears. Psychologists have developed tests in questionnaire form regarding fears of death, dentistry, sex, spiders, mutilation, social anxiety, test anxiety, acrophobia, agoraphobia, and other fears. These scales can be used to assess the various features associated with a feared object or situation and the various ways in which an individual might respond.

Typical scales are: Death Anxiety Scale (DAS), Spider Questionnaire (SPQ), Mutilation Questionnaire (MQ), Social Anxiety Inventory (SAI), Test Anxiety Scale (TAS), Acrophobia Questionnaire (APQ), and Agoraphobic Questionnaire Cognitions. (See also SEX ANXIETY INVENTORY; SNAKE QUESTIONNAIRE.)

Kleinknecht, Ronald A., *The Anxious Self* (New York: Human Sciences Press, 1986).

specific phobias Specific phobias are phobias that are restricted to only one situation or object, such as darkness, heights, elevators, closed spaces, or animals. Agoraphobics often have fears of closed places, but that does not mean that all persons who fear closed places are agoraphobic. The gender incidence of specific phobias is approximately equal, except animal phobics are largely women. Onset of specific phobias varies from early childhood to old age. The exceptions are animal and blood phobias, which tend to begin in early childhood.

Most specific phobias are treated successfully by exposure therapy. (See also ANIMAL PHOBIAS; BLOOD AND BLOOD-INJURY PHOBIAS; PHOBIA; SIMPLE PHOBIAS; SOCIAL PHOBIA.)

Marks, Isaac M., *FEARS, PHOBIAS AND RITUALS* (New York: Oxford University Press, 1987).

specters, fear of Some individuals fear specters, or ghosts, because they are supernatural phenomena and involve a fear of the unknown. A specter may be the appearance of a living person at a time or place where he or she could not logically be or the ghost of someone who has died. (See also GHOSTS, FEAR OF.)

Drury, Nevill, *Dictionary of Mysticism and the Occult* (San Francisco: Harper and Row, 1985).

spectrophobia Fear of specters or fear of ghosts. (See also GHOSTS, FEAR OF; SPECTERS, FEAR OF.)

speed, fear of Fear of speed is known as tacophobia. This fear may relate to fear of driving fast, walking fast, or doing any sport activity fast, such as skating or bicycling. The fear may be related to a fear of motion. (See also MOTION, FEAR OF.)

sperm, fear of See SPERMATOPHOBIA.

spermatophobia, spermophobia Fear of semen is known as spermatophobia.

(See also GERMS, FEAR OF; SEXUAL FEARS.)

spheksophobia Fear of wasps. (See also WASPS, FEAR OF.)

spiders Fear of spiders is known as arachnophobia or arachenophobia. Spider phobia, like other insect phobias, tends to be stimulus-specific in that the frightened person will usually respond to particular characteristics over others. Common stimulus properties that trigger anxiety are size, color, and texture of the spider. Individuals who have severe spider phobia have to fumigate their homes regularly, wash all fruits and vegetables completely, and check incoming bags and other receptacles where spiders might hide. They are usually unable to picnic or stay in strange hotels or houses, and they generally maintain a strong vigilance outside. The exact incidence of spider phobias is not known, but clinically it is not one of the more common phobias.

Spiders have many symbolic meanings such as a sinister face, evil, death and life, and the feminine mode. Spider phobics, however, are not responding to the symbolic qualities.

The fear of spiders may be almost instinctive, a case of what scientists call "prepared learning." For example, the sight of a spider triggers a rapid heartbeat and the "FIGHT OR FLIGHT" response, which thousands or more years ago might have served to protect us. In response to this fear most people's brains manufacture and release into the bloodstream natural tranquilizers called endorphins. These natural painkillers temper the fear and allow the majority of people to react calmly to the sight of the spider. A failure to release endorphins may be the cause of excessive fear of spiders.

British researchers have used fear of spiders to demonstrate that the meaning of a word associated with a feared situation can interfere with one's ability to name the color in which the word is printed. In a study, 75 spider phobics and 18 nonphobics were asked to name colors of words written on cards. One set of cards contained spider-related words, such as "spider," "creepy," "hairy," "legs," and "crawl."

Researchers also included unrelated words such as "cars" and "effort." Both the phobics and nonphobics averaged about 78 seconds to name the color of 200 comparison words. When the phobics looked at "spider words," they slowed down to 92 seconds per 100 words, compared with the nonphobics' rate of 76 seconds per 100. Later, the researchers wanted to know if the spider phobics could name the color of the words faster after several "DESENSITIZATION" sessions. In their sessions, phobics began by examining dead spiders or spider fragments, gradually worked up to live specimens, and even handled them. Fourteen of the original phobics had four treatment sessions and 14 did not. Researchers found that the "desensitized" phobics improved much more over their original performance than did the comparison group of phobics.

Johann Christoph Friedrich von Schiller (1759–1805), German dramatist, editor, and writer, is said to have feared and hated spiders so much that the fear made him physically sick.

Young children may be encouraged to fear spiders as they repeat the well-known nursery rhyme:

Little Miss Muffet
Sat on a tuffet
Eating her curds and whey.
There came a big spider
Who sat down beside her
And frightened Miss Muffet away.

(See also BEHAVIOR THERAPY.)

Goodkind, Mike, "Spider Fear May be Drug Related," (Stanford University Medical Center News Bureau, June 12, 1987).

Lowe, Geoff, "Spider Talk," *Psychology Today* (December 1986).

von Wolzogen, Caroline, *Schillers' Leben* Stuttgart: Tubinger, 1951), p. 33.

spirits, fear of Those who fear spirits may fear evil spirits, such as the EVIL EYE, demons, or the spirits of deceased persons. Those who believe that the spirits of the dead can communicate with living persons are called spiritualists. Scientists and others have challenged the claims of spiritualists. Some who have attended seances, or meetings in which a dead person's spirit supposedly returns and makes known its presence, say that people are tricked into believing in the return of spirits. According to one explanation, the table in a seance room moves not by any action of the spirit of the deceased, but by the unconscious hand pressure of living persons sitting around it. Nevertheless, there are individuals who fear the spirits of deceased persons and fear the spirits will return in some way to harm them. (See also DEMONS, FEAR OF; EVIL EYE, FEAR OF; GHOSTS, FEAR OF.)

sport anxiety While sports and athletic games give many people satisfaction and relief from stress, for many others, sports lead to anxieties, fears, and avoidance. An example is a young child involved in a highly organized team sport (often known in the United States as "little league") in which his parents have much interest invested, almost to the point of vicariously playing on the field while watching their children. Such a child may become fearful of losing the game and not pleasing the parents, being ridiculed, or being rejected. Fears developed in this way may remain with a person into adult life.

Adults who wish to excel in their chosen sport but do not may suffer frustration and anxiety because of lack of ability and fear or embarrassment when they are watched by others. Some who fear losing may avoid the sport, even though it was once a source of great personal satisfaction.

Some sports participants have the same feelings of anxiety before a game or a match as speakers and performers; physical symptoms include "butterflies" in the stomach, gastrointestinal upset, vomiting, headache, lightheadness, and dizziness. Usually these symptoms subside entirely as soon as the participant begins his or her activity. For some, this "nervous anticipation" becomes part of the routine of getting ready for the sport.

Practical anxieties relating to sports include fears of injury, such as fear of injuring a limb and not being able to play, or fear of injury during a game, such as football, in which the risks of being thrown to the ground and trampled are great. There are specific fears within every sport; for example, in tennis, a player may fear being hit in the eye with a ball; in hockey, there may be a fear of being hit with a puck. When the fear leads to avoidance of the sport, the fear becomes a phobia. Mild fear may actually be helpful and may encourage the player to use caution and to react quickly and effectively.

Other fears associated with sports include fear of crowds, fear of noise, and fear of motion. (See also PERFORMANCE ANXIETY; STAGE FRIGHT.)

spying, fear of See BUGGING, FEAR OF.)

stage fright A fear of speaking or performing to an audience is a common ANXIETY. Stage fright is also known as topophobia, or PERFORMANCE ANXIETY. This is a type of panic that affects people in many kinds of situations where they are being evaluated, such as making a speech, playing a musical instrument, or even attending a social affair. Stage fright is related to a fear of making a mistake in front of others, looking foolish or uncertain, etc. Actors, politicians, executives, and others who regularly are in the spotlight often are afflicted. Some anxiety is natural and may even enhance performance, because anxiety pumps more adrenaline into the body's system, making one more alert and motivated. However, when the pressure becomes extreme, the effects on physical and emotional well-being can be destructive. Migraine headaches, skin and gastrointestinal problems, hot and cold flashes, and hypertension can be typical reactions. As anxiety mounts the individual may become increasingly involved with overcoming it, which depletes energy needed to think, concentrate, and be creative. When the anxiety becomes worse, it can become a phobia. The phobic person may then avoid any situation that might provoke fears.

A typical treatment program gradually reintroduces phobics to stressful situations to help them gain confidence and develop skills one step at a time as they learn to deal with the situation. The starting point is wherever the each individual feels comfortable. (See also PHOBIA; SOCIAL PHOBIA.)

Adapted with permission from "Fear Breaker," The Phobia Society of America, vol. 4, no. 2 (Summer 1985).

stages of development See DEVELOPMENTAL STAGES.

stairs, climbing, fear of Fear of stairs is known as climacophobia. This fear may be related to fears of falling, injury, heights, or high places.

Standardized Behavioral Avoidance Tests (SBATs) Tests used by researchers in AGORAPHOBIA. Researchers have used several different SBATs in assessing the behavioral component of agoraphobia. Examples include driving a car along a progressively more difficult route and assessment of behavior in various areas of functioning, including shopping, driving, crowds, and restaurants.

One useful SBAT for agoraphobics involves the "behavioral walk." This involves a walking course divided into approximately equidistant units. For example, the course might be 1.2 km long and divided into 20 stations that present feared stimulus elements. Individuals are instructed to walk along the course and return when they either complete the course or are unable to proceed further. The major dependent variable from this measure is the number of stations completed. Subjective anxiety ratings and heart rate can be monitored at each station with a portable unit. (See also BARLOW, DAVID H.; INDIVIDUALIZED BEHAVIOR AVOIDANCE TESTS.)

Himadi, William G. et al., "Assessment of Agoraphobia—II, Measurement of Clinical Change," *Behavior Research and Therapy*, 24:3(1986), pp. 321–332.

standing, fear of Fear of standing is known as stasiphobia or stasophobia. The fear may be related to a fear of falling or of injury. (See also BLOCQ'S SYNDROME; FALLING, FEAR OF; INJURY, FEAR OF.)

stared at, fear of being Fear of being stared at is known as scopophobia, scoptophobia, and opthalmophobia. (See also BEING LOOKED AT, FEAR OF.)

stars, fear of Fear of stars is known as siderophobia. The fear that man's fate is written in the stars is ancient. Primitive man thought that gods made their home in the stars. The science of astrology, which began in Mesopotamia in the 5th century B.C. gave rise to the fear that human destiny was controlled by the heavenly bodies. In the Egyptian Hellenistic period, a complex set of writings described man's subjection to the demonic powers of stars. An Egyptian scriptural text, *Poimandres,* described how the soul could be saved and ascend to the highest heaven. These beliefs turned into the doctrine of Gnosticism, which portrayed Christ as the deliverer from the power of the stars and the star announcing his birth as the herald of a new order. Astrology continues to attract adherents. (See also ASTROLOGY, FEAR OF.)

Daniels, Cora Linn and C.M. Stevans, *Encyclopedia of Superstitions, Folklore, and the Occult Sciences of the World* (Detroit: Gale Research, 1971), "Stars, Planets, Constellation."

state anxiety A term used to differentiate types of ANXIETY. State anxiety, also called A-state, is a temporary and changing emotional state involving feelings of tension and apprehension and increased autonomic nervous system activity. It is a response to a specific situation that the individual perceives as threatening, but the response changes as the situation changes. Examples of state anxiety are the unpleasant feelings one experiences when taking an examination or facing a new and strange situation. When the situation is over or one becomes accustomed to it, the anxiety disappears. State anxiety may be contrasted with TRAIT ANXIETY, an integral part of a personality that causes consistent anxiety. The concept of state anxiety was first expressed in 1961 by Raymond B. Cattell, an American psychometrician, and subsequently researched by Charles Spielberger, an American clinical psychologist, and colleagues in 1970. (See also FEAR; PHOBIA.)

Catell, R.B. and I.H. Scheirer, *The Meaning and Measurement of Neuroticism and Anxiety* (New York: Ronald Press, 1961).

Spielberger, C.D. et al., *The State-Trait Anxiety Inventory* (Riverside, CA: Consulting Psychologists Press, 1970).

State-Trait Anxiety Inventory (STAI) A psychological test developed about 1970 to research anxiety. Use of the test has led to advances in understanding of anxiety. The test differentiates between STATE ANXIETY, also known as A-state, in which the ANXIETY is a temporary and changing response to a situation, and trait anxiety, which is an ongoing personality trait.

The STAI A-Trait portion includes 20 statements relating to anxiety and tension and their opposites. Respondents indicate on a scale ranging from 1 to 4 how often each statement generally pertains to them. The STAI A-Trait is considered reliable and valid. There is also a version of the STAI for children known as the STAIC. (See also EYSENCK PERSONALITY INVENTORY; FEAR; TAYLOR MANIFEST ANXIETY SCALE; TRAIT ANXIETY.)

Spielberger, C.D. et al., *The State-Trait Anxiety Inventory* (Riverside, CA: Consulting Psychologists Press, 1970).

Kleinknecht, Ronald A., *The Anxious Self* (New York: Human Sciences Press, 1986).

staurophobia Fear of crucifixes. (See also CRUCIFIX, FEAR OF.)

stasiphobia See STANDING, FEAR OF.

stealing, fear of Fear of stealing is known as cleptophobia or kleptophobia. Some fear that they will steal something themselves and be caught and punished. Fear of stealing may be related to a fear of punishment, fear of sin, or fear of GUILT. Some fear that others will steal from them; some fear robbers. (See also PUNISHMENT, FEAR OF; ROBBERS, FEAR OF; SINNING, FEAR OF.)

steep places, fear of Fear of steep places or cliffs is known as cremnophobia. This fear may be related to fears of falling, injury, heights, or looking at high places. (See also FALLING, FEAR OF; HEIGHTS, FEAR OF.)

stepfather, fear of Fear of a stepfather, or of stepfathers in general, is known as vitricophobia. Some stepchildren experience frightening or unpleasant behavior from their stepfathers because of the tension and guilt he may feel about the breakup of his previous marriage and responsibilities to his own children. A stepfather may seem to favor his own children because they live elsewhere and he puts time aside to visit and entertain them while his stepchildren are taken for granted as part of his everyday life.

A stepfather may exhibit jealousy toward his stepchildren because he would prefer to have their mother to himself. Because of his own insecurity, he may encourage stepchildren to say negative things about their real father.

Some stepchildren fear that a stepfather will try to replace their real father. On the other hand, some children who have lost their father or have a poor relationship with him may have such high expectations of the stepfather that they become hostile when he is unable to meet them. Stepfathers who have no children of their own may be uncomfortable with their new family responsibilities and may set standards, such as of household neatness and quiet, that are impossible to maintain in a home with children.

Stepchildren may also feel fear and resentment toward their stepfather because his relationship with their mother reveals her sexual nature, something most children prefer to ignore.

Studies show that some stepchildren have reason to fear mistreatment from stepfathers. Sexual abuse of stepdaughters is a frequent problem. The stepfather surrogate, the live-in boyfriend, is also the culprit in some cases of physical child abuse. (See also CHILD ABUSE, FEAR OF; RELATIVES, FEAR OF.)

Getzoff, Ann and Carolyn McClenahan, *Step Kids, a Survival Guide for Teenagers in Stepfamilies* (New York: Walker, 1984).

Hawkins, Paula, *Children at Risk* (Bethesda, MD: Adler and Adler, 1986), p. 73.

Kraizer, Sherryll Kerns, *The Safe Child Book* (New York: Delacorte Press, 1983). p. 38.

stepmother, fear of Fear of stepmother, or of stepmothers in general, is known as novercaphobia. The cruel fairy-tale stepmother may be a healthy projection of a child's negative feelings about his or her real mother that are more easily handled as fantasy at a certain stage in the child's development. However, the stepmother image may interfere when stepmother and stepchild meet in real life. Stepmothers may become so anxious to avoid the cruel stepmother image that they discipline their own children but are lenient with their stepchildren, thus ultimately disrupting the household. At the other extreme, some stepmothers favor their own children and are harsh or negligent with their stepchildren. Some negative behavior toward stepchildren may arise from the stepmother's wish to have perfect children to prove that she is the ideal mother. The new stepmother may also feel anxious and pressured to love her stepchildren immediately and, finding that she does not, may convince herself that they are not lovable at all.

When a stepmother takes over, stepchildren may experience anxiety caused by a different household routine, different cooking, and a different value system being applied to homework, neatness, clothing, and other domestic matters. Competition for the father's time and attention and a feeling that the stepmother is trying to replace their real mother may lead to resentment. Stepmothers who have no children of their own may be disturbing to their stepchildren because of their lack of skill and familiarity with domestic problems. (See also RELATIVES, FEAR OF.)

Bettelheim, Bruno, *The Uses of Enchantment, The Meaning and Importance of Fairy Tales* (New York: Alfred A. Knopf, 1976).

Getzoff, Ann and Carolyn McClenahan, *Stepkids, a Survival Guide for Teenagers in Stepfamilies* (New York: Walker, 1984).

sticks, fear of Fear of sticks is known as rhabdophobia. This fear may be related to fears of being beaten or to sexual fears, since to some a stick or rod may be a phallic symbol. (See also BEATING, FEAR OF; SEXUAL FEARS; SYMBOLS, FEAR OF.)

stigiophobia See STYGIOPHOBIA.

stillness, fear of Fear of stillness is known as eremiophobia. This is related to fears of solitude and of being alone. (See also ALONE, FEAR OF BEING; SOLITUDE, FEAR OF.)

stimulus properties In differentiating between FEAR and ANXIETY, some therapists describe fear and anxiety in terms of stimulus properties, which include *identifiability, specificity, and predictability* of the source that brings on a response. Fear is considered a response to a clearly identifiable and circumscribed stimulus, whereas with anxiety, although it is a similar response, the stimulus to which the individual is responding is unclear, ambiguous, and/or pervasive. If a response occurs to a stimulus that is a *realistic* threat and therefore useful, it is said to be fear. Conversely, if a response is elicited by a stimulus that is not seen as a realistic or consensual threat and is therefore irrational and not useful, it is called anxiety. Another factor that differentiates fear from anxiety is the predictability of the source of the threat to which the individual responds. When an object or situation provides a signal of danger or threat and is therefore predictable, the state experienced is called fear. For example, the response of a person in the middle of a thunderstorm who worries about being struck by a lightning bolt would be considered fear because the stimulus is clearly identifiable and predictable and the threat is realistic. (See also PHOBIA; RESPONSE PROPERTIES.)

Seligman, Martin, *Helplessness: On Depression, Development, and Death* (San Francisco: W.C. Freeman, 1975).
Kleinknecht, Ronald A., *The Anxious Self* (New York: Human Sciences Press, 1986).

stings, fear of Fear of stings is known as cnidophobia. This fear involves being stung by any type of insect, such as a mosquito, bee, or wasp. Some individuals with severe allergies to stings of particular insects have realistic fears of their reactions to stings. When there is no such justification and when the fear becomes so extreme that it disrupts normal daily life, it has become a phobia. Manifestations of this phobia would involve avoidance of areas, time of day, and weather that is associated with stinging insects. For example, one would not picnic or walk out of doors in warm, balmy weather when bees are likely to be active. (See also BEES, FEAR OF; WASPS, FEAR OF.)

stooping, fear of Fear of stooping is known as kyphophobia. This fear may be related to fears of falling, of injury, such as to the back, or of dizziness, which may be brought on by change of posture. (See also FALLING, FEAR OF; INJURY, FEAR OF.)

stories, fear of Fear of stories or myths is known as MYTHOPHOBIA.

storms, fear of Many people fear storms, which may involve lightning, thunder, rain, hail, or snow. While most people do not fear personal injury from the storm, they do fear the unknown causes of the storm, and the unknown consequences. Being near or in a storm leaves one feeling out of control. The power of the storm may overwhelm some people and thus make them fearful. While some individuals become fearful during a storm, others have phobic reactions just at the suggestion of a storm, or at the sight of little rain, or a little snow. Some avoid going outdoors when any kind of storm is predicted. Some will pull down their window shades or close the shutters on

Similarity and Difference Between Fear and Anxiety

Stimulus Properties	Fear	Anxiety
Identifiability	Clear	Unclear/Ambiguous
Specificity	Discrete/Circumscribed	Pervasive
Predictability	Predictable	Unpredictable
Rationality of Threat	Rational	Irrational

their house when they expect any kind of storm. Some fear hurricanes or tornadoes and do not venture outdoors even in seasons in which hurricanes or tornadoes never occur. Some individuals only fear storms when they have to be traveling through them, such as driving through a blizzard or riding on a train during a rainstorm. Some fear only one type of storm, while others fear all types of storms.

Fears of lightning, thunder, rain, snow, or storms in general are classified as simple phobias or specific phobias. (See also CLIMATE, FEAR OF; LIGHTNING, FEAR OF; RAIN, FEAR OF; SNOW, FEAR OF; THUNDER, FEAR OF.)

strangers, fear of The fear of unknown persons is known as xenophobia or zenophobia. The term refers to individuals as well as entire groups of people, such as those from another country.

Fear of strangers is normal in infants between six and 12 months old. The infant learns to recognize a familiar combination of forehead, eyes, and nose that elicits the smile response, and this in turn elicits parental care. An unfamiliar face will frighten the infant and probably make him or her cry.

Other mammals and birds also fear strangers. Chimpanzees, for example, begin fearing strangers at about the same time in life as the human infant.

Stranger fear in human infants may be an evolutionary remnant reflecting widespread abuse and even infanticide by strangers during prehistoric times. (See also SEPARATION ANXIETY.)

Goodwin, Donald W., *Phobias: The Facts* (Oxford: Oxford University Press, 1983).

Marks, Isaac M., *Fears, Phobias and Rituals* (New York: Oxford University Press, 1987), p. 23.

streets, fear of Fear of streets is known as agyiophobia. Individuals who are fearful of streets may be afraid of getting hit by a vehicle or afraid of crowds. Many agoraphobics are afraid of streets because they will be seen by others there. (See also AGORAPHOBIA; STREETS, CROSSING.)

streets, crossing Fear of crossing streets is known as dromophobia. (See also AGORAPHOBIA; STREETS, FEAR OF.)

stress See STRESS MANAGEMENT.

stress inoculation This is a concept and therapeutic strategy to prevent anxiety developed by American psychologist Donald MEICHENBAUM (1940–) that represents an analogue at the psychological/behavioral level to immunization on the biological level. Individuals are given practice with mild stress to modify beliefs and self-statements in order to be more successful and less resistive. The stress situations are then gradually increased in difficulty. Training involves an educational phase (to observe and learn to modify self-statements), rehearsal phase (direct action and cognitive coping), and the application phase (cognitive/somatic skills and strategies are developed).

stress management Appropriate management of stress in one's life is necessary to avoid anxieties. Stress, a feeling of being tired, jittery, nervous, or anxious, occurs when there are many demands upon an individual or changes in his or her life. Because people are social beings and interact daily with others and also face constant changes throughout the life cycle, stress is part of life. Stress is a feeling of being tired, jittery, nervous, or anxious.

Stress is an individualized physical and/or emotional response and may come from internal or external sources. The level of a person's tolerance for stress depends on his or her physiological condition, past experiences, perceptions of situations, and how he or she has learned to adapt. Examples of physical stresses are illness, excessive cold or heat, lack of sufficient oxygen, confinement, dietary insufficiencies, and trauma. Examples of emotional stresses are pressure, conflict, frustration, excessive emotions, or delayed satisfaction of needs. Emotional stress can occur when one is faced with making decisions or deadlines, or after the loss of a loved one, which produces a major change in one's life. Death of a spouse is one of the most stressful situations an individual faces. Next seems to be divorce and marital separation. Other highly stressful personal situations include personal injury or illness, marriage, being fired from a job, marital reconciliation, retirement, pregnancy, sex difficulties, business readjustments, changes in financial state, taking out a mortgage or loan for a major purchase, children leaving home, trouble with in-laws, change in residence, school, or church, or change in sleeping or eating habits. (See the social readjustment rating scale chart that follows at the end of this entry.)

Individuals who are exposed to stress for long periods of time respond with what has been called the general adaptation syndrome (GAS). So named by Hans Selye, a Canadian endocrinologist (1907–1982), the syndrome consists of an "alarm reaction," a "stage of resistance," and finally a "stage of exhaustion." The individual is alerted to stress, pauses to appraise it, and then attempts to make adjustments. When he realizes he cannot adapt, his body may show damage or disease, or his personality may begin to disintegrate.

Stress causes certain changes in the structure and chemical composition of the body. The NERVOUS SYSTEM and the ENDOCRINE (hormonal) SYSTEM are especially important in maintaining resistance during stress. Some studies indicate that many emotional disturbances and some common diseases such as HIGH BLOOD PRESSURE, ULCERS, HEADACHES, and ASTHMA may be at least partly due to failure to adapt to stress.

When managed appropriately, stress can be useful. Stress is an adaptive mechanism that helps people ward off danger and solve problems. Many health-care professionals have developed techniques and methods to help people cope with stress, using both older and more ancient methods as well as new biophysiological and psychological methods. The best approach to solving stress-caused complications is to prevent the stress buildup in the first place. Some cultures have relatively well-defined methods of preventing the buildup of stress. For example, in India, children at early ages are taught meditation. When used appropriately, this seems to work well on the biophysiological system in reducing stress. In China, children as well as older adults practice Tai chi ch'uan, a martial art and form of stylized, meditative exercise characterized by methodically slow circular and stretching movements to balance bodily energy.

(See also ANXIETIES; HEART ATTACK, ANXIETY FOLLOWING; HEART ATTACK, FEAR OF; MEDITATION; MOVING, FEAR OF; SLEEP, FUNCTION OF; STROKE, FEAR OF; TRANSCENDENTAL MEDITATION; ULCERS AND ANXIETY.)

The following charts can help individuals manage stress.

The ABCs of managing stress

A Awareness:
Be aware of the stress factors in your life. Take inventory of the issues and problems that cause stress.

B Balance:
A series of steps in which the individual tries to balance the effects of uncomfortable or destructive stress with areas that give gratification and relief from stress.

C Choice:
Recognition that, in most instances, the individual has an element of choice. Most people in highly stressful situations have the capacity to help themselves. Sometimes, when an individual feels out of control of the situation or feels trapped, choice is not easy.

How to reduce daily accumulations of stress

The following can be modified to meet each individual's situation. The underlying principle is a series of routines that allow one to intervene with the stresses and strains in life.

1. Exercise. Calisthenics, tennis, swimming, and other sports help clear the mind. Those who are not athletic can take a walk. Try and walk briskly for 20 to 40 minutes each day.
2. Take frequent breaks from work or at-home projects. Move away from your desk, work site, or immediate chore as often as possible.
3. Take vacations. Short vacations may be better than long ones because they give one more frequent breaks in the regular routine.
4. Eat a balanced diet. Do not overeat and become overweight. Limit your intake of alcohol.
5. Get enough sleep. If you don't sleep six to eight hours a night, and if you don't awake feeling well-rested most days, help is available for you.
6. Develop a sense of humor and use it to help you face each day.
7. Allow time for the unexpected. Don't schedule yourself so tightly that an unexpected use of time becomes a major stress.
8. Learn to say "no." Don't become overinvolved to the point where you feel stressed and become anxious about your use of time. Know your priorities. Take steps to change or solve what you can and do not worry about the rest.
9. Set aside a quiet time and place for yourself each day. This can be while you are walking, or a time for quiet reading and private thinking.
10. Be aware of tense muscles and learn to relax them.

Adapted with permission from "Stress Management," by Harold Visotsky, M.D., professor and chairman, Department of Psychiatry and Behavioral Science, Institute of Psychiatry, Northwestern Memorial Hospital, Chicago, Illinois; in "A Lifetime of Health" (Pamphlet, 1987).

string, fear of Fear of string is known as linonophobia.

stroke A term that, when used alone, refers to a cerebrovascular accident, or accident in the brain and blood vessels. Many individuals fear having a stroke when they have any form of chest pain or breathlessness. Some individuals wrongfully consider strokes synonymous with heart attacks. Some individuals fear that their anxieties will bring on a stroke. Many individuals fear having a stroke themselves or fear seeing another individual who has had a stroke because a stroke can cause some permanent impairment of the muscles, limbs, ability to speak, or perceptual abilities. Fear of seeing a stroke victim may be related to a fear of body deformities. The fear of viewing a person who has had a stroke may come from a fear of contagion.

Strokes occur when the blood flow to the brain is interrupted, either by blocking of large or small arteries or veins or by bleeding from a blood vessel into brain tissue. A stroke can also be provoked by an aneurysm, a bulging out of a weakened part of a wall of a blood vessel. An aneurysm may cause mental and physical disturbances of the nervous system by pressing against nearby brain cells, or the bulge may break open and bleed

The Social Readjustment Rating Scale

Major life changes can be predictive of physiological or psychological disturbances within two years of the change. The Social Readjustment Rating Scale quantifies the probability of having a disturbance within two years.

Events	Scale of Impact	Events	Scale of Impact
Death of spouse	100	Son or daughter leaving home	29
Divorce	73	Trouble with in-laws	29
Marital separation	65	Outstanding personal achievement	28
Jail term	63	Spouse begins or stops work	26
Death of close family member	63	Begin or end school	26
Personal injury or illness	53	Change in living conditions	25
Marriage	50	Revision of personal habits	24
Fired at work	47	Trouble with boss	23
Marital reconciliation	45	Change in work hours or conditions	20
Retirement	45	Change in residence	20
Change in health of family member	44	Change in schools	20
Pregnancy	40	Change in recreation	19
Sex difficulties	39	Change in church activities	19
Gain in new family member	39	Change in social activities	18
Business readjustment	39	Taking out a mortgage or loan for a lesser purchase	17
Change in financial state	38	Change in sleeping habits	16
Death of close friend	37	Change in number of family get-togethers	15
Change to different line of work	36	Change in eating habits	15
Change in number of arguments with spouse	35	Vacation	13
Taking out a mortgage or loan for a major purchase	31	Christmas	12
Foreclosure of mortage or loan	30	Violations of the law	11
Change in responsibilities at work	29		

Note: Scores of 200 or more are associated with stress reactions at a much higher incidence than scores below 200.

into tissues. In older persons, minor aneurysms or narrowing of blood vessels in the brain may cause "little strokes," particularly in individuals whose circulatory system is already impaired. During these attacks, the individual may have symptoms of anxiety, mental confusion, forgetfulness, irritability, irrational behavior, or headaches.

Strokes come on suddenly, usually reaching a peak within seconds or minutes or a few hours. The stroke victim may collapse, lapse into a coma, or remain conscious with little or no pain or discomfort. Among the many signs of stroke are blindness in one or both eyes or in half of one eye, loss of an ability to smell, dizziness, or reduction of feeling in various parts of the body, a stiff neck, and difficulty in swallowing. When an individual appears to be having a stroke, he should be kept quiet and not moved until a physician arrives. (See also HEART ATTACK, ANXIETY FOLLOWING; HEART ATTACK, FEAR OF.)

stuttering, fear of Fear of stuttering is known as psellismophobia and laliophobia. The word stammering is used interchangeably with stuttering and refers to a nonfluency of speech. An individual who stutters has an interrupted flow of words or an inability to articulate certain sounds or repetitions of certain sounds. The speech pattern may be explosive or there may be occasional hesitations. An individual's speech difficulty may be aggravated by situations that arouse anxieties or fears of self-consciousness. Some individuals who have difficulties with speech may avoid certain situations, such as speaking aloud in a community meeting or going to social occasions, because they are fearful that they will stutter when they speak to others. Many forms of speech therapy help individuals overcome their stutters and their fears of stuttering. Also, behavior therapy can help individuals overcome anxieties and phobias about specific situations that bring on stuttering. (See also BEHAVIOR THERAPY; SPEAKING, FEAR OF; SPEAKING ALOUD, FEAR OF.)

stygiophobia, styiophobia Fear of hell. The word is derived from the Latin *stygius,* pertaining to the river Styx, the river that surrounds Hades, the underworld of Greek mythology. (See also HELL, FEAR OF.)

subsconscious An obsolete term for the unconscious as well as the preconscious, which meant remembrances that could be recalled with effort. (See also FREUD, SIGMUND; UNCONSCIOUS.)

Subjective Units of Distress (SUDS scale) A standard ANXIETY scale used in BEHAVIOR THERAPY. The scale is a way of quantifying people's feelings of fear and thus provides a way to monitor or assess an individual's responses and make comparisons among people. The individual is asked to think of the worst anxiety and call it the maximum anxiety, or a rating of 100. Being absolutely calm is given a rating of 0. All other fears are ranked in between. The same scale is used later on during therapy to determine the strengths of the person's reactions during desensitization and after treatment. Following are some descriptions of anxiety that an individual may use to equate with the various levels on the scale:

0	No anxiety at all; complete calmness
1–10	Very slight anxiety
10–20	Slight anxiety
20–40	Moderate anxiety; definitely unpleasant feeling
40–60	Severe anxiety; considerable distress
60–80	Severe anxiety; becoming intolerable
80–100	Very severe anxiety; approaching panic

(See also BEHAVIOR MODIFICATION.)

Wolpe, Joseph, *Our Useless Fears* (Boston: Houghton Mifflin, 1981).

sublimation A defense mechanism. Individuals use sublimation unconsciously by diverting instinctual drives, such as sexual or aggressive drives, which may be unacceptable, into personally and socially acceptable channels. Such channeling of energy may protect the individual from the anxiety the original drive might produce and also usually brings the individual satisfactions, such as acceptance and recognition from others. An example of an individual who uses sublimation constructively is one who has exhibitionistic tendencies who becomes a choreographer. While this term is used in PSYCHOANALYSIS, it is also common in psychological vocabularies. The broader use of the term refers to the focusing of one's energy, frustration, anxiety, etc. on an activity that comes to dominate one's life. For example, an active, achievement-oriented person might sublimate their energies into sports and fitness, working out or competing on a regular basis. (See also FREUD, SIGMUND.)

success, fear of Some individuals have a fear of success that causes them anxieties while they are striving for an objective and after they achieve it. Fear of success is closely related to fear of failure. The individual who fears achieving success fears being a failure at another plateau, or that he will not be able to fulfill expectations at the higher level. Some find that striving for success, but not quite reaching it, is tolerable; but when an anxious individual imagines himself successful, the level of stress becomes intolerable and turns into fear. Some who fear success fear that success will put them in another academic, social, or athletic class and that they will lose the friendship and comradeship of their peers. Some fear that they will not be conforming to their group if they are successful. Fear of success is related to a fear of RISK TAKING and a fear of CRITICISM. (See also FAILURE, FEAR OF.)

succubus A female demon, evil spirit, or devil who seduces men while they sleep and causes noctural seminal emissions. Historically, succubi were thought to cause abnormal behavior. Individuals feared the succubus because she brought on nightmares and a feeling that something heavy was on one's chest during the night, causing suffocation and exhaustion; the dreamer usually remembered the episode with anxiety and fear upon awakening. (See also DEMONS, FEAR OF; INCUBUS; WITCHES AND WITCHCRAFT, FEAR OF.)

Sudden Infant Death Syndrome (SIDS), fear of Parents of infants fear Sudden Infant Death Syndroms (SIDS) because of its mysteriousness and unpredictability. The exact cause of SIDS, which ends the lives of sleeping infants between the ages of two and four months without warning, is unknown. Physicians believe that each case may be a product of a variety of causes, such as viruses, abnormally small air passages, or momentary interruptions of breathing during sleep. Premature infants and black infants are more likely to be affected, but perfectly healthy babies of affluent white families are also victims. Parents of SIDS babies have at times been treated with suspicion of abuse or neglect by health and law-enforcement professionals. Having a baby taken by Sudden Infant Death may make parents neurotic and overprotective toward surviving children.

"The SIDS Mystery," *Stanford Medicine* (Fall 1987).

Welch, Wayne, "Why Did My Baby Have to Die?" *Louisville Courier and Times Magazine,* (August 15, 1971).

suffocation, fear of Fear of suffocation or smothering is known as pnigophobia. Suffocation means an inability of the body tissues to receive oxygen due to primary failure of the respiratory system to draw adequate amounts of air and oxygen into the lungs. Fears of suffocation may be related to many other fears, such as being buried alive, being in a crowded room, being in an elevator, being in a small, enclosed space, or even being in a bus, train, or airplane. Individuals who fear suffocation may actually have symptoms of suffocation, even though they are breathing in adequate air and oxygen. Symptoms of suffocation are dizziness, along with lethargy and drowsiness, and finally unconsciousness. If no oxygen is administered, there will first be brain damage and then death. (See also BURIED ALIVE, FEAR OF BEING; CHOKING, FEAR OF.)

suggestion The influence a therapist exercises over an individual in a therapeutic setting to accept an attitude or belief. Suggestion may be given to the individual who is anxious or phobic during a conscious state or may be given during a state of HYPNOSIS. Suggestion is used during many forms of BEHAVIOR THERAPY.

suicide, adolescent The stresses in adolescents, with their ANXIETIES and tendencies to react impulsively, have increased suicide rates among this age group dramatically. The rapidly increasing number of adolescent suicides is frightening to parents, social workers, and therapists. The rate of suicide for this age group has nearly tripled during the past 20 years (in the United States), making it the second leading cause of death among adolescents (after automobile accidents).

Many attempts at suicide by young people arise from the combination of long-standing anxieties and FEARS coupled with a triggering event. Young people who commit or consider suicide often are depressed. DEPRESSION is often associated with biological and chemical changes in the body. Severely depressed young people may have trouble with parents, siblings, friends, or authority. They may develop suicidal thoughts from a perceived loss of love or rejection by important individuals in their lives. Their depression may take the form of ANGER and resentment with exaggerated GUILT. Chronic fears about sexual identity or intellectual and physical inferiority, as well as anxiety about parents' expectations and peer acceptance, burden many young people.

Indications of problems

Some behavioral changes associated with adolescent depression may indicate serious problems, particularly if more than one sign is present and persists over an extended period of time. These conditions include:

- Decreased appetite
- Interrupted or changed sleep patterns
- Avoidance of friends and normal social activities
- Angry outbursts, tearfulness, or increased touchiness
- Withdrawn, uncommunicative behavior
- Marked personality change from outgoing to isolative, or from quiet to extremely active
- Frequent physical complaints or fatigue
- Use of drugs, alcohol, or self-abusive behavior (includes intentional reckless driving)
- Preoccupation with death
- Obsessive fear of nuclear war
- Irrational, bizarre behavior
- Overwhelming sense of guilt or shame
- Feelings of sadness, hopelessness, or despair
- A suicide attempt, or threat, is the most serious of warnings.

Prevention

The apparently normal period following a SUICIDE threat or attempt is critical. Young people need help during this time and should be encouraged to talk about feelings. They need someone to listen to them but not to lecture at them. They need reassurance that suicidal thoughts are not a sign of being a bad person. Adolescents can go to peer support groups, school counselors trained to work with such problems, community mental health centers, crisis intervention centers, hospital emergency rooms, or psychiatric units.

A potentially suicidal adolescent may need professional counseling to deal with his or her thoughts and feelings. A depressed young person needs assistance in increasing SELF-ESTEEM and improving perceptions of the world to learn to cope with reality. Help is available in the form of PSYCHOTHERAPY as well as drug therapy.

Troubled adolescents have many community resources available to help them. A place to begin is the National Mental Health Association, which acts as a national referral center (in the United States) for troubled adolescents. The NMHA is composed of parents of children with psychological problems, as well as professionals and concerned citizens who work to promote better mental health.

Parents, teachers, or young people may contact:

National Mental Health Association
1021 Prince Street
Alexandria, VA 22314-2971
Phone: (703) 684-7722

(See also ANTIDEPRESSANTS.)

(Adapted with permission from the National Mental Health Association, Alexandria, Virginia.)

suicide, fear of Taking one's own life. Some individuals who have anxieties and phobias fear that they will kill themselves. Some fear heights because they are afraid that they will feel compelled to jump from a high place. The same may be true of some bridge phobics and even some who fear flying in an airplane. Some individuals whose parent or other relative committed suicide may fear that they will feel compelled to do so, too. However, suicide does not run in the family; it is an individual pattern.

Many who contemplate suicide have an overwhelming feeling of rejection and lack of love and affection in their lives. Individuals who commit suicide often suffer from depression and have deep feelings of hopelessness or helplessness. The attempt at suicide may be brought on by a wish for revenge against the world, for being reunited with an individual who has died, or for instilling guilt in a person who has rejected him or her. Some individuals make threats of suicide in an attempt to dominate and control a spouse or parent or to force favorable treatment. Studies reveal that the suicidal person gives many clues and warnings of his or her contemplated intentions. Such individuals are often confused, alienated, and self-condemning. (See also DEATH; DEPRESSION; DYING, FEAR OF; HIGH PLACES, FEAR OF; SUICIDE, ADOLESCENT.)

Sullivan, Harry Stack (1892–1949) An American psychiatrist. A dissenter from Sigmund FREUD, Sullivan defined personality as "the relatively enduring pattern of recurrent interpersonal situations which characterize a human life." He noticed that individuals sometimes used language as a defense mechanism or form of "distortion" rather than as a common ground for communication. He said this "verbal shield" was caused by low self-esteem, which results in anxiety. Sullivan defined anxiety as a physiological and psychological reaction learned in early childhood. He was instrumental in setting up the World Federation of Mental Health and the UNESCO committee investigating the causes of tension among a variety of cultures. (See also HORNEY, KAREN; PSYCHOANALYSIS.)

sun and sunlight, fear of Fear of sun and sunlight is known as heliophobia and phengophobia. Early men feared the sun because they recognized it as a source of life and worshiped it as the supreme deity. Men paid homage and brought offerings to the sun. They watched the sun and its daily movement across the sky with awe, puzzlement, and terror. They were frightened by the sun's decrease of power in winter; they feared that the sun might die and cause them to freeze to death. A solar eclipse caused the fear that the end of the world had come.

In modern times, the sun is feared as a cause of cancer. Dermatologists and oncologists have repeatedly warned that excessive exposure to sunlight without appropriate covering or use of sunscreen puts people at great risk for developing skin cancers, some of which can be disfiguring or even fatal. (See also AGORAPHOBIA; DEPRESSION; ILLNESS, FEAR OF; SEASONAL AFFECTIVE DISORDER.)

Brasch, R., *Strange Customs* (New York: David McKay, 1976).

superego In psychoanalysis, superego is the part of the personality representing society's standards, and it determines one's own standards of right and wrong as well as our aims and aspirations. The superego is popularly referred to as the conscience.

superego anxiety Anxiety that occurs from the anticipation of feeling guilty. An individual is aware that if he violates his own moral standards, his SUPEREGO, or conscience, will let him know by imposing (usually uncomfortable) feelings of guilt or shame. In thinking about the unpleasant guilt that he will experience after committing the transgression, the person may feel tense and anxious, possibly enough to prevent him from carrying out his planned actions.

supernatural, fears of Belief in the supernatural with the accompanying fears and sense of terror has been common in many societies. Fears of the supernatural start in the child's vivid imagination and continue into later life; such fears are often associated with and prompted by religions, which use them as methods of discipline and social control. Natural disaster and misfortune, the behavior of wild animals, and the attempt to explain the fate of the soul after death contribute to fears of the supernatural.

As society becomes more scientific and rational and beliefs in the supernatural decrease, stories of the supernatural have become more popular; the supernatural has become a popular subject for novels and films. Supernatural themes allow an escape from the relative security of modern life. Continuing interest in horror stories indicates that people have a capacity to enjoy being frightened. There is a communal quality about the horror story, because a sense of shared terror brings people together, and children may fear the dark, monsters, and other frightening beings less when they are organized into plots.

Interest in the supernatural has heightened in modern times around concerns of death. For example, the dying are isolated in hospitals and cared for by professionals at the time of death. In becoming less a part of life, death has become more remote and mysterious. In spite of modern skepticism, superstitions and half beliefs linger. Frightening stories about the supernatural may be an acceptable way to express and contain these fears. Stories about supernatural, frightening situations may be a type of catharsis and drugless hallucinogen.

The study of death (thanatology) has become a legitimate area of science.

Hill, Douglas and Pat Williams, *The Supernatural* (New York: Hawthorn Books, 1965).

Sarafino, Edward P., *The Fears of Childhood* (New York: Human Sciences Press, 1986).

Sullivan, Jack (ed.), *The Penguin Encyclopedia of Horror and the Supernatural* (New York, Viking, 1986).

supportive psychotherapy Psychotherapy that reinforces the individual's defenses and helps the individual suppress disturbing ideas. Supportive PSYCHOTHERAPY may utilize such techniques as suggestion, reeducation, and reassurance to help an individual face his fears, phobias, or anxieties. Unlike PSYCHOANALYSIS, this type of therapy does not look into the historical antecedents to an individual's emotional conflicts.

suppression Conscious efforts to control and conceal experiences, impulses, thoughts, feelings, or acts that are unacceptable to the individual. Some individuals who have specific phobias have suppressed experiences that surface later in life as phobias of situations or objects. Also, these suppressed experiences lead to the development of patterns (e.g., chronic emotional expression) that can trigger anxiety and panic disorders. (See also REPRESSION.).

surgical operations (or surgical incisions), fear of Fear of surgical operations is known as ergasiophobia or tomophobia. This fear may extend to any medical procedure that uses operations, instruments, and manipulation, especially cutting and suturing. An individual may be phobic about having an operation himself or herself or of hearing about someone else's operation. A fear of surgical operations may be related to fears of doctors, hospitals, or death. Some individuals have grown up with a fear of surgical operations because they are aware that an older member of their family or someone they knew died during surgery, and they equate surgery with death from an early age. In recent years, knowledge about hospital-induced infections has caused many individuals to fear having anything to do with hospitals and surgery. Some individuals may fear particular types of surgery, such as hysterectomy. (See also DEATH, FEAR OF; DISEASE, FEAR OF; DOCTORS, FEAR OF; HOSPITALS, FEAR OF; ILLNESS, FEAR OF.)

suriphobia Fear of mice. (See also MICE, FEAR OF.)

surmontil See TRIMIPRAMINE.

surveillance, fear of See BUGGING, FEAR OF; SPYING, FEAR OF.

swallowing, fear of Fear of swallowing is known as phagophobia. Some individuals feel that they have a lump in their throat and find it difficult to swallow when they are very anxious. Muscles of the throat may actually go into spasm, and the individual may make some choking sounds. Fear of swallowing is a SOCIAL PHOBIA and may cause phobic individuals to avoid being seen while they are eating. The fear of swallowing is also related to the feeling of having a "lump in the throat" (globus hystericus). (See also EATING, FEAR OF; FOOD, FEAR OF; GLOBUS HYSTERICUS.)

swastika, fear of The swastika causes fear and terror in modern societies because of its association with Hitler and the horrors of the Holocaust preceding and during World War II. Hitler adopted the emblem in 1920, taking it from a badge on the helmets of the German Baltic Corps, which in turn had copied it from the distinguishing mark of the Finnish air force.

The swastika is one of man's earliest and most universal symbols, representing the wheel of the sun as it rolls across the skies, advancing by its feet, or short protrusions at the four ends of its spikes. The term swastika is of Sanskrit derivation, and the sign may have originated in India. The word—derived from two words, *su* meaning good, and *asti*, meaning being—was meant to express and promote good fortune. Throughout history, there have been a variety of meanings attributed to the symbol. For example, some cultures interpreted the emblem sexually, claiming that the joining of two bent lines at their center symbolized the sexual union of the male and female. Thus the emblem became a magic symbol in the promotion of fertility. In Scandinavian countries, the swastika represented the hammer of Thor, the god of thunder and lightning. A similar symbol is also seen in American Indian art.

Brasch, R., *Strange Customs* (New York: David McKay, 1976).

sweating, fear of Fear of sweating is a SOCIAL PHOBIA. Some individuals avoid crowds, being in close contact with others in elevators, and even eating in restaurants because they fear that they will sweat and look ridiculous. They may also worry about giving off an offensive odor and staining their clothing. They fear attracting attention to themselves. Some women who suffer from HOT FLASHES fear that others will notice while they are having a hot flash. Many individuals who have a low sense of self-esteem worry that others will hold them in even less regard if they sweat at an unpredictable time. Social phobias, such as fear of sweating, are often treated successfully with BEHAVIOR MODIFICATION techniques and exposure therapy. (See also PHOBIA.)

swimming, fear of Fear of swimming may be a SOCIAL PHOBIA in that many who fear swimming fear being seen in their bathing suits by others, fear criticism about their body shape, and fear that they may look ridiculous while swimming or approaching the pool or body of water. Fear of swimming may also come from a fear of water or a fear of drowning. Some fear being out of control if a wave or the undertow overtakes them while swimming in an ocean or large lake. Some individuals are comfortable standing in a pool or body of water but fear swimming; some can float or swim but fear putting their face in the water while they do so. For many, a fear of swimming can be overcome by taking lessons and learning to use appropriate breathing techniques while in the water. For others, behavior modification techniques may be effective. (See also PHOBIA; WATER, FEAR OF.)

switch process The transition between DEPRESSION and mania or mania and depression in BIPOLAR DISORDER. Individuals switching into mania from depression usually experience a moderate depressive period followed by a brief, relatively normal period, but with reduction in total sleep and REM sleep. In the switch into depression, individuals go through several stages: mania, hypomania, a short period of changeable mood and activity, and finally deep depression, characterized by helplessness, hopelessness, and total feelings of self-inadequacy. (See MANIC–DEPRESSIVE ILLNESS; SLEEP, FUNCTION OF.)

symbolism, fear of Fear of symbolism is known as symbolophobia. Many personal fears can be produced by phobic stimuli. Individuals may fear the symbols themselves with or without understanding their unconscious representation. For example, water has been viewed symbolically as a representation of the mind. Going underwater—the "deep dive," for example, in *Moby Dick*—is symbolic of going into the unconscious or going into the "dark side."

Jung, to a greater degree than FREUD, explored the enduring and universal evolutionary aspects of symbols. JUNG used the word "archetype" to designate universal symbols that possess constancy and efficiency and can force the way to psychic evolution. These ready-made systems of images are inherited, powerful, instinctive guides to creative action and growth. The deeper significance of these archetypes are secret and require an opening to the beyond or unknown. Some archetypes are the mother, father, wise man, warrior, magician, etc.

Freud viewed symbolism in dreams as important in understanding concealed unconscious wishes or conflicts. In the English school of psychoanalysis, also known as the Kleinian school, symbol formation was viewed as an essential prerequisite of early normal development. Investigations by Melanie KLEIN (1882–1960), an Austrian psychoanalyst, led to an understanding of how symbolism helps the child construct his internal world at an early age. The infant's transference of interest from his subjective world to the outside world of external reality begins with symbols. For example, the baby regards objects as symbolizing others, if there is some resemblance between them. The baby's fingers symbolize the breast when the breast is not available, and the symbol serves as a bridge to the actual object.

Behavior therapists acknowledge that symbolism distinguishes between radical objective theorists who are not interested in mediating processes and those who view congitions and imagery as mediating between the stimulus and response in the behavioral sequence that governs human behavior. The development of language presupposes an ability to utilize symbols and symbolization. (See also COLLECTIVE UNCONSCIOUS; LITTLE HANS.)

symbolophobia Fear of symbolism (See also SYMBOLISM.)

symbiosis A relationship that reinforces the dependency of two persons on each other. Symbiosis is a normal and expected relationship between a mother and a child. Symbiosis also occurs between two individuals when one is an agoraphobic and is totally dependent on the other and will not go out unless accompanied by the other. (See also AGORAPHOBIA.)

symmetrophobia Fear of symmetry. (See also SYMMETRY.)

symmetry Fear of symmetry is known as symmetrophobia. Symmetry is a relationship of characteristic equivalence or balance. It is an exact correspondence of form and configuration on opposite sides of a dividing line or plane or about a center or axis. An example of fear of symmetry is an individual's compulsion to rearrange furniture so that end tables are not exactly the same distance from a couch, or so that identical lamps are not placed equidistant from a chair. A compulsion to rearrange pictures on a wall in a random fashion rather than in a row or equidistant from each other is another example of fear of symmetry.

sympathetic nervous system One of two major divisions of the AUTONOMIC NERVOUS SYSTEM, and the one that prepares an individual for fighting, fleeing, action, or sexual climax. During a PHOBIC REACTION, the sympathetic nervous system becomes quickly activated. The sympathetic nervous system tends to excite or arouse one by speeding up the contractions of the blood vessels, slowing those of the intestines, and increasing the heartbeat to prepare the body for exertion, emotional stress, and extreme cold, while the parasympathetic nervous system tends to depress many bodily functions. These two divisions of the autonomic nervous system coordinate to control bodily activities and respond appropriately to physical and psychological challenges. When an individual wants to be aroused (such as when fleeing from fear) the sympathetic system speeds up and the parasympathetic system slows down. When one wants to relax, the parasympathetic system increases its activities and the sympathetic system slows down.

The sympathetic nervous system consists of a group of 22 neural centers on or close to the spinal cord. From these 22 centers fibers connect to all parts of the body, including the sweat glands and tiny blood vessels near the surface of the skin. When one is suddenly afraid, the sympathetic nervous system activates the following physiological responses:

- Heart pumps more blood to the brain and muscles and to the surface of the skin
- Breathing becomes faster and harder
- Blood-sugar level becomes elevated
- Digestion slows down
- Skin perspires to remove waste products created by exertion and to keep one cool
- Pupils in the eyes open up to let in more light
- Controls orgasm and ejaculation during sexual arousal

(See also HYPERVENTILATION.)

symptom Evidence of a disorder as noticed personally by the individual afflicted with it. For example, phobic individuals report that they experience rapid heartbeat and a tight feeling in their chest when they view their feared object. A symptom is usually distinguished from a SIGN, which is a manifestation of a disorder that is noticed on an objective, observable basis by another person, such as a therapist or physician. However, in common usage, the word symptom often includes objective signs of disordered conditions as well. (See also DIAGNOSIS; SYNDROME.)

symptom substitution Development of a SYMPTOM to replace one that has been removed after therapy. An example of symptom substitution is replacement of one phobia with another. Some therapists, including dynamic therapists, who oppose behavioral therapy techniques, argue that such therapy's removal of a symptom, such as a phobia, without addressing the "underlying cause" will result in the emergence of a new substitute symptom. Behaviorists have found no evidence for this hypothesis and have successfully treated phobias without adverse effects. Since symptom substitution is a major corollary of the medical or dynamic model of behavioral pathology, the lack of evidence for the occurrence of symptom substitution calls into question the medical model. (See also BEHAVIOR THERAPY; HYPNOSIS; MEDICAL MODEL; SUGGESTION.)

syndrome A group of symptoms that occur together that constitute a recognizable condition, either physical or mental. Syndrome is also called symptom complex or disease entity. For example, the group of symptoms exhibited by agoraphobics is known as the agoraphobic syndrome. "Syndrome" is less specific than "disorder" or "disease," which generally implies a specific cause or disease process. In the American Psychiatric Association's *Diagnostic and Statistical Manual of Mental Disorders,* most disorders are considered syndromes.

American Psychiatric Association, *Diagnostic and Statistical Manual of Mental Disorders* (Washington, D.C.: American Psychiatric Association 1987).

syngenesophobia Fear of relatives. (See also RELATIVES, FEAR OF.)

syphilis, fear of See SEXUALLY TRANSMITTED DISEASES.

syphilophobia Fear of syphilis. Also known as syphilidophobia. (See also SEXUALLY TRANSMITTED DISEASES; VENEREAL DISEASE, FEAR OF.)

systematic desensitization A behavioral therapy procedure that is highly effective in the treatment of excessive emotional states such as anxiety and anger. It originated with Joseph Wolpe, who used in vivo and imaginal desensitization with his patients and reported over 80 percent recovery rates for a variety of anxiety, phobic, and emotional reactions. The essence of systematic desensitization is the gradual exposure of an individual to components of a feared situation while he or she is relaxed. Systematic desensitization is the major treatment procedure for phobias and agoraphobia. Exposure may occur in imagination or self-visualization or in actuality (in vivo). Systematic desensitization is best applied with the help of a skilled therapist. Once relaxation skills are mastered (which takes five to six weeks), a hierarchy involving gradually more intimate (and reactive) triggering stimuli is developed, and imaginal or in vivo exposure is started. Systematic desensitization is a highly effective treatment method for simple phobias. The cure rate for simple phobias is about 80 percent to 85 percent with 12 to 15 sessions. Social phobias, agoraphobia, and panic require more patience, time, and skill in using systematic desensitization. These reactions also usually require in vivo exposure rather than imaginal to be effective. (See also AGORAPHOBIA; BEHAVIOR THERAPY.) See chart.

Difficulties Some Individuals Experience During Systematic Desensitization

Following are some of the difficulties phobic individuals learn to overcome during systematic desensitization.

Difficulties during relaxation:
- Sleepiness
- Poor concentration
- Fear of losing control
- Muscular relaxation without mental relaxation
- Severe anxiety and depression

Problems of imagery:
- Inability to obtain images
- Dissociation of anxiety
- Dilution of image to more protective setting
- Intensification of image to panic proportions

Misleading hierarchies:
- Irrelevant hierarchies
- Fluctuating hierarchies

Relapse of desensitized phobias

Lack of cooperation

Life situation influences outside treatment

systematic rational restructuring A form of psychotherapy. The individual is encouraged to imagine and talk about anxiety-provoking situations in a realistic way during the therapy session and thus reduce his anxieties. (See also BEHAVIOR THERAPY; SYSTEMATIC DESENSITIZATION.)

T

taboos Collective beliefs shared by members of a culture about danger, such as the notion that bad luck will occur after walking under a ladder. Other taboos concern religious beliefs, such as not eating meat or working on holy days. Cultural taboos sometimes contribute to individuals' fears and anxieties.

tacophobia (tachophobia) Fear of speed. (See also SPEED, FEAR OF.)

tachycardia Rapid, intensive heartbeat, often associated with a fearsome situation or high levels of ANXIETY that occur during phobic attacks and PANIC ATTACKS. Tachycardia is not dangerous to the person's health but, if persistent, should be checked by a physician. (See also PANIC; PANIC DISORDER; SYMPATHETIC NERVOUS SYSTEM.)

taeniophobia Fear of tapeworms is known as taeniophobia or teniophobia. (See also TAPEWORMS, FEAR OF.)

t'ai chi ch'uan A Chinese martial art and form of stylized, meditative exercise, characterized by methodically slow circular and stretching movements planned to rebalance bodily energy. Practitioners of t'ai chi ch'uan usually perform their routines early in the morning to keep themselves anxiety-free during the day.

talking, fear of Fear of talking is known as glossophobia, laliophobia, lalophobia, and phonophobia. Fear of talking may be a SOCIAL PHOBIA in that the individual is afraid to speak up in a crowd, fears embarrassment, or fears saying something ridiculous or inappropriate. Also, fear of talking may relate to fear of hearing the sound of one's own voice or a fear of stuttering. (See also ONE'S OWN VOICE, FEAR OF; STUTTERING, FEAR OF; TELEPHONES, FEAR OF.)

tandamine An antidepressant drug. (See also ANTIDEPRESSANTS, NEW.)

tapeworms, fear of Fear of tapeworms is known as taeniophobia or teniophobia. Some individuals fear tapeworms because they can cause disease and discomfort. Tapeworms, a member of the class Cestoda, are a parasite of man and other vertebrates. If a human or animal eats improperly cooked pork or beef containing worm larvae, the digestive juices of the consumer free the larvae; the young parasites then attach themselves to the new host's intestinal lining and develop into adults. Treatment is either by surgery or drugs. Reinfection is possible unless the victim practices proper hygiene. Thoroughly cooking all meat and fish products will also eliminate the possibility of infection. (See also WORMS, FEAR OF.)

taphophobia (taphephobia) Fear of being buried alive is known as taphophobia. These terms also refer to fears of graves and tombs. See BURIED ALIVE, FEAR OF BEING; GRAVES, FEAR OF; TOMBS, FEAR OF.

tapinophobia Fear of small objects. (See also SMALL OBJECTS, FEAR OF.)

tardive dyskinesia An impairment of voluntary movement brought upon by years of taking neuroleptic drugs (drugs that block transmission at dopamine synapses). These medications are normally given to schizophrenics and include a wide range of drugs, but all of them have in common the fact that they block transmission at dopamine synapses. Typical symptoms of tardive dyskinesia include tremors and involuntary movements of the mouth and tongue. This condition persists long after drug withdrawal and sometimes worsens even after treatment is suspended. It is believed that the blocked dopamine synapses become hypersensitive to any dopamine that does reach them, leading to these uncontrollable behaviors. (See also SCHIZOPHRENIA; THORAZINE.)

taste, fear of Fear of taste is known as geumaphobia, geumophobia, or geumatophobia. Individuals may fear certain tastes because of their associations with past experiences or situations that caused anxieties. The fear also may be generalized to other foods in the particular taste category. For example, a child who becomes nauseous after eating a lemon for the first time, or who is always given lemons to eat by a feared authority figure, may grow to associate lemon with discomfort and begin to fear not only this taste but any sour-tasting food.

There is a disorder known as gustatory agnosia, in which food becomes tasteless or even has a disgusting taste. Individuals who have this condition may also lose their ability to smell or may find that formerly pleasant odors are offensive. With an inability to smell, they may fear that they are unaware that they are eating or drinking something that formerly caused them anxieties. (See also EATING, FEAR OF; FOOD, FEAR OF; SWALLOWING, FEAR OF.)

tattoos, fear of Many individuals who fear tattoos do so because ornamental tattooing can produce tumors, or individuals may develop allergic skin reactions to some of the color pigments used. Those who fear contamination or infection may fear those problems from needles used in tattooing. The most common infections from needles are hepatitis and AIDS (autoimmune deficiency syndrome).

Some fear tattooing because it seems to be a permanent coloration of the skin. Because the pigment in a tattoo extends deep into the skin, its removal, by any method, is likely to leave a scar. Small tattoos can be removed by excision, leaving a small, minimal scar. Dermabrasion (skin planing) is also used to make the tattoo fainter.

Others may fear tattoos because the tattoos depict their phobic object, such as butterflies, lips, or the word "mother." (See also CONTAMINATION, FEAR OF; NEEDLES, FEAR OF.)

Taylor Manifest Anxiety Scale (TMAS) A scale used by therapists to assess trait ANXIETY and useful in helping individuals who have phobias understand themselves better and deal with their phobias. The TMAS was one of the first self-report ("paper and pencil") scales designed specifically to measure anxiety. The scale was adapted by Janet Taylor in the early 1950s from the Minnesota Multiphasic Personality Inventory, a multifactorial personality scale.

The test is a reliable, valid, and economical means to determine levels of anxiety; it has been used to test effects of anxiety on learning and conditioning and in hundreds of clinical and experimental studies of anxiety. Janet Taylor believed that anxiety was a drive or motivating force and that persons with high drive, or high anxiety, would develop conditioned responses more rapidly than low-anxiety or low-drive subjects. (See also EYSENCK PERSONALITY INVENTORY; STATE-TRAIT ANXIETY INVENTORY.)

Taylor, J.A., "A Personality Scale of Manifest Anxiety," *The Journal of Abnormal and Social Psychology,* 48(1953), pp. 285–290. 48 (1953): 285–290.

technology, fear of Fear of technology is known as technophobia. Many individuals fear technological devices in modern society. For example, some individuals look with fear upon computers, highly technical telephone answering systems, and even videocassette recorders. Some individuals become very anxious when faced with a set of instructions that are supposed to be easy for the average individual to follow. Another aspect of technophobia is the fear that machines will be able to do what people do now. Fear of robots is part of this fear. (See also COMPUTER PHOBIA.)

technophobia Fear of technology. (See also TECHNOLOGY, FEAR OF.)

teeth, fear of Fear of teeth is known as odonophobia. (See also DENTAL ANXIETY.)

teleology In psychology and psychiatry, teleology is the concept that mental processes have purposes and are directed toward goals. Within this concept, behavior, including phobic or avoidant behavior, can be explained in terms of purposes as contrasted with causes. Alfred ADLER's emphasis on ideals and goals that the individual chooses for self-fulfillment is a teleological approach, as is Carl JUNG's concentration on religious and moral values and on development of individual purposes.

telephone, fear of the Some individuals fear talking on the telephone. Others fear the ringing of a telephone, perhaps because they fear hearing bad news. Some are afraid to pick up the phone and answer it because they fear that they will say something that will be criticized by the listener. Some experience a great deal of anxiety if they have to pick up the telephone to inquire about a job, place an order, or make any kind of an inquiry. Some individuals feel that they are powerless when speaking to another person by telephone, because when deprived of visual clues, such as body language, they feel they cannot control the response they will get. Some express anxiety that they are intruding on the person they are calling and can never seem to find a "good" time to place their call. Others are fearful of using the telephone because doing so reminds them of overhearing conversations their parents had, of listening when they should not have been, or of hearing something specifically traumatic. Individuals who have telephone phobia experience symptoms of nervous stomach and sweaty palms, which are typical anxiety reactions. Many telephone phobics are motivated to overcome their phobia because they realize that the telephone can be a bridge between themselves and someone about whom they care and between themselves and necessary services. Individuals who have overcome this phobia have suggested rehearsing the conversation before making the call, writing down what they want to say when they call, or standing up while speaking into the telephone. Behavior therapy techniques can be helpful for telephone phobics. (See also BEHAVIOR THERAPY.)

teletophobia Fear of religious ceremonies. (See also RELIGIOUS CEREMONIES, FEAR OF; CHURCHES, FEAR OF.)

television, role of in phobias Television can be a powerful source of observational learning for both children and adults. Children observe models of fearful behavior on television, such as people who are afraid of the dark and of harmless animals. Television presents many unrealistic and exaggerated situations in cartoon form that can frighten children, such as goblins, dragons, and vampires. Children may later think about these situations, dream about them, and even develop night terrors because of what they have seen. Crime programs make children as well as adults fearful of criminal attack, and news programs that report murders, arson, and robberies reinforce the notion that these events are more frequent than they actually are. (See also CHILDHOOD ANXIETIES, FEARS, AND PHOBIAS.)

Sarafino, Edward P. *The Fears of Childhood* (New York: Human Sciences Press, 1986).

TENS (transcutaneous nerve stimulation) See PAIN, ANXIETY AND DEPRESSION IN.

teratophobia Fear of deformed people or of bearing a monster. Some women develop this fear while pregnant. Others fear becoming pregnant because of this fear. (See also BEARING A MONSTER, FEAR OF; DEFORMED PEOPLE, FEAR OF.)

termites, fear of Fear of termites (also known as white ants) is known as isopterophobia. The word *termites* applies to many antlike insects which feed on wood and are highly destructive to trees and wooden structures. Individuals who fear termites actually may fear being buried alive if the termites cause collapse of the buildings in which they live.

TERRAP The TERitorrial APprehansiveness Program (TERRAP) is a multifaceted approach to treatment of AGORAPHOBIA and panic attack syndromes. TERRAP was founded in 1965 by Arthur B. Hardy, M.D., of Menlo Park, CA, together with a number of agoraphobic patients. By 1988, there were over 35 TERRAP centers in the United States.

Before acceptance into a TERRAP program, an individual is evaluated and diagnosed during a private consultation with a psychotherapist, at which time decisions about the need for medication are made. However, many people arrive at the program already addicted, for example, to imipramine, alprazolam, or combinations of several drugs. Many individuals who enter the TERRAP program have seen several therapists without result.

Following are the basic principles of TERRAP:

1. A 20-session program. Each session addresses a separate complication regarding phobias. Education is emphasized, because the individuals who have a problem must understand what they have, why they have it, and what they can do to assure the best possible results for recovery.
2. A pre-group. This is preparatory to going into the main therapy group. In the pre-group, individuals ask basic questions, learn about what they will be doing, and prepare for the basic treatment in a group. Pre-group is led by ex-phobics who have recovered using the TERRAP method and offers group support, information, and skill building. Homework is required. Participants then join the regular treatment group, which also serves as an ongoing support group during therapy.
3. Anxiety attacks are considered a response to some noxious stimuli. Participants learn to recognize the stimuli that trigger the anxiety reactions. This is referred to as "stimulus hunting."
4. Participants learn relaxation exercises and calming procedures in order to decrease excessive anxiety and tension. This includes use of progressive muscular relaxation exercises, visual clues such as pictures, colors, decorations, pleasant sights, sounds (such as favorite music), smells (such as perfume), tastes, and tactile sensations (such as hugging, soft fur, or movement such as rocking in a rocking chair)—all of which are natural tranquilizers.
5. Once the fundamentals have been accomplished, participants are ready for DESENSITIZATION. Desensitization

procedures include the use of BIOFEEDBACK, pictures of the noxious stimuli (providing an opportunity to face the fear in a safe setting), mental desensitization (bringing to mind anxiety-producing situations, alternating with pleasant thoughts and thus relaxing mentally at the thought of them), and IN VIVO DESENSITIZATION with the entire group, as demonstrated by a trained guide.

6. Fieldwork is available individually with a trained guide who is a recovered phobic. This consists of going out into the natural situation accompanied by a trained field worker who assists in the implementation of the program.
7. Treatment includes spouse participation. Spouses can be particularly helpful with in vivo desensitization. Spouses are educated about the problem, how they can help, and what they may do that makes the problem worse (if that is the case). Marriage counseling is available when necessary. Agoraphobia frequently creates tension between spouses, and help is almost always needed to assist in resolving marital conflicts.
8. Participants learn to chart their progress on graphs during goal-setting sessions, which are highly motivating.
9. Participants learn self-talk to help them develop realistic, logical, positive, and practical thinking and offset their ever-present negative thoughts. Self-talk consists of positive coping statements.
10. Participants learn ASSERTIVENESS TRAINING to correct the tendency to please others and to enable them to speak up for themselves to get what they want.
11. Participants learn the principles of problem solving and apply those principles to conflict resolution.
12. Participants experience emotional breakthroughs about halfway through the program. Breakthroughs are part of recovery, and by understanding and allowing their feelings to emerge, people can learn to accept and understand their feelings better, as well as reduce their intensity.
13. Participants are prepared in advance for the inevitable setbacks that occur to almost all recovering people. Participants are taught what to do about setbacks, so they do not become panicky when and if they happen.
14. Medication, when and if needed, is available. Medication is always carefully monitored to assure best results and to avoid addiction.
15. Participants return to the support group for continued association with recovered phobics and to allow time to consolidate their gains from the treatment group. This makes recovery as lasting and permanent as possible. The support group utilizes field trips, networking, buddy systems, distance trips, driving practice, lecture sessions, and video tapes.
16. Advanced goal setting and individual and group therapy continue to be available if necessary.
17. Follow-up interviews are used for information and research.

(See also PHOBIA.)

(Arthur B. Hardy, M.D., Menlo Park, California.)

test anxiety Fear of taking tests is common among individuals of all ages, but it is particularly noticeable in students. Test anxiety may be related to a desire for perfectionism and fear of failure. Outside of academic settings, individuals face many test situations in everyday life, including tests for acquiring a driver's license, medical tests, and tests as part of employment applications. Desensitization programs have been used to treat test anxiety with varying degrees of success. (See also ANXIETY.)

Hudesman, John et al., "Desensitization of Test-Anxious Urban Community College Students and Resulting Changes in Grade Point Average: A Replication," *Journal of Clinical Psychology* 40:1(1984), pp. 65–67.

testophobia Fear of taking tests. (See also TEST ANXIETY.)

testosterone A male HORMONE produced by the testes that stimulates development of male reproductive organs, including the prostate, and secondary features, such as the beard and bone and muscle growth. Testosterone stimulates the male sexual drive. Testosterone level usually decreases in men during ANXIETY and stress. (See also STRESS MANAGEMENT.)

textophobia Fear of certain fabrics. (See also FABRICS, FEAR OF CERTAIN.)

textures, fear of certain Some people have aversions to fuzzy surfaces, such as certain carpets, tennis balls, peach skins, or the skins of kiwi fruit. Some avoid suede, velvet, corduroy, or other fabrics, or shiny buttons. Usually aversions to textures make the individual uncomfortable but do not elicit phobic reactions.

tetanophobia Fear of lockjaw or tetanus. (See also LOCKJAW, FEAR OF; TETANUS, FEAR OF.)

tetanus, fear of Fear of tetanus is known as tetanophobia. Tetanus is an acute infectious disease caused by a toxin produced in the body by *Clostridium tetani*. Tetanus is commonly called lockjaw. (See also LOCKJAW, FEAR OF.)

thaasophobia Fear of sitting down. (See also SITTING, FEAR OF.)

thalassophobia Fear of the sea, ocean, or other large body of water. (See also SEA, FEAR OF.)

thanatophobia Fear of death. (See also DEATH, FEAR OF.)

theaters, fear of Fear of theaters is known as theatrophobia. Individuals who fear theaters may do so because they feel closed in and unable to get out easily. They may be agoraphobics and may also be afraid of crowds, suffocation, fire, or being far from a bathroom. Some people fear being in the center section of a theater and will not go unless they can be assured of an aisle seat. They may fear contamination from the seat or the back of the seat. Some individuals who fear head lice fear that they will contract them while sitting in a theater seat (as well as in a bus or train). (See also AGORAPHOBIA.)

theatrophobia Fear of theaters. (See also THEATERS, FEAR OF.)

theologicophobia Fear of theology. (See also THEOLOGY, FEAR OF.)

theology, fear of Fear of theology is known as theologicophobia. Some people fear theology because explanations of theological concepts are often made in specialized and obscure terms. Some believers with a mystical or personal approach to religion resent the scholarly application of theological thinking. Such individuals become anxious when they try to analyze and categorize religious ideas because the structured academic approach interferes with their personal sense of contact with God. (See also GOD, FEAR OF; RELIGION, FEAR OF.)

Sandmel, Samuel, *A Little Book on Religion (For People Who Are Not Religious)* Chambersburg, PA: Wilson Books, 1975).

theophobia Fear of God. (See also GOD, FEAR OF.)

Thematic Apperception Test (TAT) A personality diagnostic test. The TAT may be useful in giving therapists information about an anxious or phobic individual, because in doing the test, the individual projects attitudes, feelings, conflicts, and personality characteristics. Individuals are asked to make up stories with a beginning, middle, and end about a series of pictures; then the therapist looks for common themes in the stories. Scoring is primarily subjective. (See also PERSONALITY TYPES.)

thermophobia Fear of heat or of being too warm. (See also HEAT, FEAR OF.)

thieves, fear of Fear of thieves or burglars is known as cleptophobia, kleptophobia, and harpaxophobia. Because of high crime rates in modern urban areas, many individuals have become excessively fearful of burglars and muggers. Antidotes to this fear seem to include burglar-alarm systems, training in self-defense techniques, and carrying weapons (although the last may be illegal in many places).

things that go bump in the night, fear of This term has contemporary meaning in referring to fears of strange noises in the dark. There is an anonymous Scottish prayer, presumed to have been used popularly during the 1800s:

> From ghoulies and ghosties and long-leggety beasties
> And things that go bump in the night,
> Good Lord, deliver us!

Bartlett, John (Ed.), *Bartlett's Familiar Quotations*, 15th ed. (Boston: Little Brown, 1980).

third force The term given to approaches to psychotherapy that include HUMANISTIC PSYCHOLOGY and existential and experiential therapies. Many individuals who have anxieties and phobias are helped by such techniques. The term is used to contrast these approaches from the "first force" of psychoanalysis and the "second force" of behavior therapy. Leaders of third-force therapy have included Abraham Maslow, Carl Rogers, Gordon Allport, and Kurt Goldstein. In general, third-force therapy emphasizes direct experience, the here-and-now, responsibility for oneself, group interactions, personal growth rather than symptom alleviation or adjustment, and self-exploration and self-discovery. (See also EXISTENTIAL THERAPY; GESTALT THERAPY; REALITY THERAPY.)

thirteen, fear of the number Fear of the number thirteen, or of having thirteen people at a table, is known as tridecaphobia, tredecaphobia, and triskaidekaphobia. Individuals who fear the number 13 may fear any situation or event involving this number, such as a house number, floor of a building, apartment or office number, or the 13th day of the month. Because this is such a common fear, many buildings have omitted labeling the 13th floor as such. (Residents of the 13th floor are less anxious believing that they live on the 14th floor.)

thorazine Trade name for chlorpromazine, one of the MAJOR TRANQUILIZERS and a member of the penothiazine group of drugs. There is a history of its use for anxiety during the 1950s, but it was replaced by anxiety-specific drugs. Thorazine is no longer considered appropriate for treatment of anxiety problems.

thought stopping A cognitive BEHAVIOR THERAPY technique developed by Joseph WOLPE. The therapist asks the phobic or anxious individual to recognize fear-producing thoughts. When the individual begins to verbalize or produce these undesirable thoughts, he is asked to interrupt them with an internal shout of "stop." Eventually the individual learns to control and reduce the incidence of such thoughts. Thought stopping is also useful in treating smoking and sexual deviations. (See also REINFORCEMENT.)

thumb sucking, fear of Some parents fear that their infant's habit of thumb sucking will lead to infection or a malformed mouth. Young infants put anything they can into their mouths, and as they get older they usually grow out of the habit of thumb sucking. However, parents who have fears of contamination or germs may worry that their infant will contract a disease because of something on his or her fingers. Fears about thumb sucking may be related to fears of nail biting. (See also CONTAMINATION, FEAR OF; GERMS, FEAR OF.)

Bugelski, B. Richard and Anthony M. Graziano, *Handbook of Practical Psychology* (Englewood Cliffs, NJ: Prentice-Hall, 1980), p. 274.

thunder, fear of Fear of thunder is known as brontophobia, ceraunophobia, keraunophobia, and tonitrophobia. (See also THUNDERSTORMS, FEAR OF.)

thunderbolt, fear of Fear of a thunderbolt is known as keraunosophobia. (See also THUNDERSTORMS, FEAR OF.)

thunderstorms, fear of Fear of thunderstorms is known as astraphobia. Individuals who fear thunderstorms listen intently to weather forecasts and may call their local weather bureau with questions. Such individuals will avoid going outdoors when thunderstorms are predicted. Some phobics hide in a closet or under a bed during a thunderstorm, and some become incontinent as a result of their fear. Some fear the noise of the thunder, and others fear injury or death. (See also THUNDER, FEAR OF; THUNDERBOLT, FEAR OF.)

tic A tic is a frequent involuntary muscle spasm. A person with a tic is known as a tiquer. Tics can occur in any muscle group, but the ones most noticeable to others involve the facial muscles, such as the eyelids or the lips. Additionally, tics may also be vocal, involving sudden, uncontrollable, loud sounds. The individual who has a tic may not be aware of it until someone else points it out. On the other hand, once an individual knows that he has a tic, he may become very anxious and embarrassed about it and may even avoid people, becoming a social phobic. Some people associate tics with nervousness and anxiety, and to some extent this is correct. Tics may disappear in time as the individual becomes more relaxed. Tics are treated with therapy to determine the conditions causing the anxiety, then with behavioral methods of relaxation training and SYSTEMATIC DESENSITIZATION. Tics are characteristic of Gilles de la TOURETTE SYNDROME, a disorder of the nervous system; they can also be brought about by certain drugs. (See also BEHAVIOR THERAPY.)

Bugelski, B. Richard and Anthony M. Graziano, *Handbook of Practical Psychology* (Englewood Cliffs, NJ: Prentice-Hall, 1980), p. 274.

tied up, fear of being Fear of being tied up is known as merinthophobia. This fear may relate to fears of burglars, of violent crime, of being out of control, and of helplessness. The fear may also relate to a sexual fear, as being tied up is sometimes involved in certain sadomasochistic sexual practices. (See also BOUND, FEAR OF BEING; BURGLARS, FEAR OF; SEXUAL FEARS.)

time, fear of Fear of time is known as CHRONOPHOBIA. This fear relates to fear of time passing, either too slowly or too rapidly; free time, either too much or too little; or running out of time.

timidity A lasting tendency to show fearful behavior. (See also SHYNESS; SOCIAL PHOBIA.)

toads, fear of The toad has a long history as an object of fear and superstition. It has been viewed as a repulsive, warty creature as well as a favorite item in witchcraft. Ozark Mountain–area residents once feared that killing toads would cause cows to give blood instead of milk. Others feared, erroneously, that they would break out in warts if they touched toads. (See also FROGS, FEAR OF.)

Brasch, R., *Strange Customs* (New York: David McKay, 1976).

tobacco, fear of Modern fears of tobacco are related to the evidence that smoking is a risk factor in the development of many types of cancer, lung diseases, and heart disease. Historically, in certain parts of Russia the tobacco plant was feared because some individuals believed that it was inhabited by the devil. (See also DEVIL, FEAR OF; SMOKING, FEAR OF.)

Daniels, Cora Linn and Prof. C.M. Stevans, *Encyclopedia of Superstitions, Folklore and the Occult Sciences of the World* (Detroit: Gale Research, 1971).

tocophobia Fear of childbirth. (See also CHILDBIRTH, FEAR OF.)

Tofranil See IMIPRAMINE.

token economy, use in therapy A procedure used in a BEHAVIOR THERAPY technique called OPERANT CONDITIONING; tokens are given as rewards for constructive behavior, then are exchanged for special items and privileges. Token economies, usually used with hospitalized or institutionalized individuals (but also used in group therapy), may be effective in changing symptomatic behavior in individuals who have anxieties, fears, and phobias. When reinforcement is used consistently after appropriate behaviors, and inappropriate behaviors are ignored, the preferred behaviors will tend to increase in frequency and the unwanted behaviors begin to decline. Unfortunately, many institutions inadvertently reinforce inappropriate, undesired behaviors, and thus the token economy is as much a means of training staff in how to effectively respond to behavior as it is in changing patients' behavior.

Davison, Gerald C. and John M. Neale, *Abnormal Psychology* (New York: John Wiley, 1986).

Tolman, Edward Chase (1886–1959) American psychologist known primarily for his behavioral learning theory. Believing in "purposive behavior," Tolman espoused that an individual's actions were affected by his perception of the situation (such as the perception of danger to a phobic individual), the goal involved, and his own expectations. Tolman believed that behavior is purposeful or goal-directed. Expectations are cognitive events involving bits of knowledge concerning the nature of the goal-object and the means to the goal.

tombs, fear of The common fear of tombs relates to the fear of being buried alive, of suffocation, and of death. (See also BURIED ALIVE, FEAR OF; SUFFOCATION, FEAR OF.)

tombstones, fear of Fear of tombstones is known as placophobia. This fear is related to a fear of cemeteries and, indirectly, to a fear of death. (See also CEMETERIES, FEAR OF; DEATH, FEAR OF.)

tomophobia Fear of surgical operations. (See also SURGICAL OPERATIONS, FEAR OF.)

tonitrophobia Fear of thunder. (See also THUNDER, FEAR OF; THUNDERBOLT, FEAR OF; THUNDERSTORMS, FEAR OF)

toothache, fear of Having a toothache causes everyone to feel a certain amount of anxiety and uneasiness. However, fear of a toothache extends beyond just the pain in the mouth. Some individuals fear any kind of PAIN. Many people fear having a toothache because they fear going to the DENTIST. Some fear that they will need an INJECTION if the dentist does any drilling as preparation for filling a cavity in a tooth. Some fear the drilling, or even the sound of the drill. Some who have blood or injury phobia fear that they will see blood during the visit to the dentist, or that they may receive further injury in the course of treatment. Some fear having a tooth pulled. Some fear toothaches because going to the dentist means confinement in the dental chair. During treatment for the toothache, they will be covered with a waterproof apron and may have any number of devices working in their mouth at one time. All these prospects make some individuals fearful because there will be no easy escape from the situation once they are in it. Anxiety sometimes arises when the individual is uncertain which tooth is hurting. A visit to the dentist, even if one is fearful of dentists and dentistry, will do much to allay the fear aroused by a toothache. Dentists today have many techniques to help fearful patients relax enough and to treat dental problems with a minimum of pain. (See also DENTAL FEARS; PAIN, ANXIETY AND DEPRESSION IN; PAIN, FEAR OF.)

topological vs. functional approach See MEDICAL MODEL.

topophobia Fear of certain places. This term also refers to a fear of being on the stage, or STAGE FRIGHT. (See also PLACES, FEAR OF.)

tornadoes, fear of Fear of tornadoes is known as lilapsophobia. (See also HURRICANE, FEAR OF; THUNDER, FEAR OF; THUNDERBOLT, FEAR OF; THUNDERSTORMS, FEAR OF.)

touched, fear of being Fear of being touched is known as haphephobia; haptephobia; hapnophobia; aphephobia, haptophobia; and thixophobia. This fear may relate to a fear of contamination or to a sexual fear.

Tourette syndrome Gilles de la Tourette syndrome is a movement disorder characterized by repeated, involuntary, rapid movements of various muscle groups and by vocal tics, such as barks, sniffs, or grunts. It was first described by the French physician Georges Gilles de la Tourette in 1885. The cause of the disorder is unknown. The syndrome is a lifelong disorder that often begins during adolescence with eye spasms. Tourette individuals and members of their families may have an increased incidence of compulsive rituals and agoraphobia, although the role of these disorders in the disease is not understood. (See also AGORAPHOBIA; OBSESSIVE–COMPULSIVE DISORDER.)

Marks, Isaac M., *Fears, Phobias and Rituals* (New York: Oxford University Press, 1987).

toxicophobia, toxiphobia, and toxophobia, Fear of poison. (See also POISON, FEAR OF.)

trains, fear of Fear of trains is known as siderodromophobia. Some people fear long waits for trains. Others fear trains for their noise, motion, or speed. Individuals who fear trains may fear being in an enclosed space, feel trapped on a train, or fear becoming ill and being seen by others with no place to take refuge. Some fear trains if there are no toilet facilities available. Fear of trains is fairly common among agoraphobics. However, trains may be less frightening if they stop frequently at stations and have corridors and a toilet. If there are toilets, though, some people may fear being seen entering the toilet booth. (See also ENCLOSED PLACES, FEAR OF; MOTION, FEAR OF; SPEED, FEAR OF; WAITS, FEAR OF LONG.)

trait anxiety A general, persistent pattern of responding with ANXIETY. Trait anxiety resembles timidity and indicates a habitual tendency to be anxious over a long period of time in many situations, also known as A-trait. The person with a high A-trait perceives more situations as threatening than a person who is low in A-trait. Phobic individuals are high in A-trait. The term is used in research projects to differentiate between types of anxieties. For example, American psychologist Charles Spielberger (1927–) has developed an instrument to measure A-trait vs. A-state anxiety, the latter being more situational and varied over time. (See also STATE ANXIETY; STATE-TRAIT ANXIETY INVENTORY (STAI).)

Spielberger, C.D. et al., *The State-Trait Anxiety Inventory* (Riverside, CA: Consulting Psychologists Press, 1970).

Kleinknecht, Ronald A., *The Anxious Self* (New York: Human Sciences Press, 1986).

trait theorists See PERSONALITY DISORDERS (chart).

tranquilizers Tranquilizers are pharmacological agents that act on the emotional state of the individual, quieting or calming the person without affecting clarity of consciousness. As a class of drugs, tranquilizers can be divided into two groups: antianxiety agents (called ANXIOLYTICS or ''minor'' tranquilizers) and antipsychotic drugs (called neuroleptics or ''major'' tranquilizers).

Antianxiety agents (Minor tranquilizers)
BENZODIAZEPINE compounds such as DIAZEPAM and ALPRAZOLAM are generally favored over SEDATIVES (such as BARBITURATES) for relief of ANXIETY. Phenothiazines (which are antipsychotic drugs) are sometimes used to relieve anxiety, although their side effects are a major drawback. A group of drugs known as BETA-ADRENERGIC BLOCKERS (e.g., PROPRANOLOL) may also have some effectiveness in relieving anxiety.

Antipsychotic drugs (Major tranquilizers; neuroleptics)
The neuroleptic drugs have gone a long way in advancing psychiatric health care. They are often used to maintain an individual's psychiatric state at a level to allow some enjoyment of life. There are four main subgroups of neuroleptic drugs: the PHENOTHIAZINES, the butyrophenones, the thioxanthenes, and the nearly obsolete rauwolfia alkaloids. Most of these drugs have major side effects and physiological effects with prolonged use. (See also HYPNOTICS; MEPROBAMATE; TARDIVE DYSKINESIA.)

Merck & Co., *The Merck Manual* (Rahway, NJ: Merck & Co., 1972).

transactional analysis (TA) A type of group therapy developed by Eric Berne, a Canadian-born American psychoanalyst (1910–1970). TA is based on his theory of personality structure. According to Berne, the personality is made up of three constructs: the parent, the adult, and the child, which correspond in a general way to Freud's superego, ego, and id. The parent ego state can be nurturing or critical (''I love you,'' ''You should . . .''); the adult is practical and evaluative, taking in information and making rational decisions; and the child is primarily made up of feelings, expressing them naturally, as they occur, or adaptively, as they have been socialized.

In TA, group members make determined efforts to change their patterns of communications (or ''transactions'') with others by engaging in ''games'' and role-playing scenarios that manipulate the way they choose to use their different ego states. Berne believed that transactions were frequently set up to satisfy only one person's needs, not allowing for mutual fulfillment. This unhealthy pattern can stem from an individual's fear of presenting the true self to another person and risking rejection.

Berne also stressed that each person is responsible for accepting himself and his own feelings (I'm OK), and realizing that other people must do the same (You're OK). He believed that psychological disturbance would occur when the personality was inappropriately dominated by the parent, adult, or child ego state.

The essence of TA therapy is to help the individual develop psychological independence and identity, marked by awareness of self and others and spontaneity and intimacy in his or her life-style rather than the more common human coping attributes of manipulation and self-defeating behavior.

TA sees anxiety as the outcome of faulty life-style, hence the focus is on modification of life-style rather than specific symptoms. For example, Eric Berne, in his book about transactional analysis *(Games People Play)*, did not make one reference to anxiety in the subject index.

McConnell, James V. *Understanding Human Behavior* (New York: Holt, Rinehart and Winston, 1986).

Zimbardo, P., *Psychology and Life* (Glenview, IL: Scott Foresman, 1985).

Bootzin, R. et al., *Psychology Today* (New York: Random House, 1983).

transcendental meditation (TM) A type of MEDITATION developed in the early 1960s by Maharishi Mahesh Yogi. Some individuals find relief from their anxieties in TM. In TM, the individual sits quietly with eyes closed and focuses his attention solely on the verbal repetition of a special sound or "mantra." The person practicing TM usually spends about twenty minutes, twice a day, engaged in meditation. This process of focused attention should have the effect of taking the person's mind away from his anxieties and worries, helping him to relax. TM claims benefits of reducing anxiety and aggression and possibly changing certain body states by slowing metabolism and heart rate and lowering blood pressure.

Zimbardo, P., *Psychology and Life* (Glenview, IL: Scott Foresman, 1985).

Bootzin, R. et al., *Psychology Today* (New York: Random House, 1983).

transcutaneal nerve stimulation (TENS) See PAIN, ANXIETY AND DEPRESSION IN.

transference A process through which the individual displaces to the therapist feelings, attitudes, and attributes of a significant attachment figure from the past, usually a parent, and then responds to the therapist accordingly. In a general way, transference refers to the tendency to transfer to the current relationship with the therapist feelings and emotions that belonged to a past relationship. An understanding and resolution of transference is a necessary part of all psychoanalytic therapies. FREUD believed that transference was a necessary part of analysis because new forms of the old conflicts could be brought to consciousness, where they could be relieved, understood, and worked through to a more satisfactory resolution. During this process, the sources for anxieties and phobic behaviors are often discovered. Transference thus becomes a major aspect of psychoanalytic work. (See also COUNTERTRANSFERENCE; PSYCHOANALYSIS.)

transfusion, fear of blood See BLOOD TRANSFUSION, FEAR OF.

transitional object An object an infant selects because of its anxiety-reducing qualities, such as a "security blanket" or soft doll. The child perceives that the transitional object acts as a defense against outside threats and is especially important at bedtime or during periods of regression to an earlier phase of development. The term was introduced by Donald W. WINNICOTT, an English pediatrician and psychoanalyst, in the early 1950s. (See also SOTERIA.)

tranylcypromine A potent ANTIDEPRESSANT drug and MONOAMINE OXIDASE INHIBITOR (MAOI). Also known by the tradename Parnate, tranylcypromine is used for relief of severe depression.

Greist, J.H. and J.W. Jefferson, *Depression and Its Treatment: Help for the Nation's #1 Mental Problem* (Washington, DC: American Psychiatric Association, 1984).

trauma Real or imaginary incidents that occur and affect the individual's later life and ability to cope with anxieties. FREUD believed that all neurotic illnesses were the result of early psychological trauma. The term *trauma* comes from the Greek word meaning "wound." In medicine, the word trauma refers to a violent shock or severe wound. Traumatic stress is associated with phobia onset in about 3 percent of cases, with panic disorder in about 4 percent of cases, and with OBSESSIVE–COMPULSIVE DISORDER in more than 10 percent of cases.

traumatophobia Fear of injury. (See also INJURY, FEAR OF.)

travel, fear of Fear of travel is known as hedonophobia or hodophobia. Individuals who are afraid to travel are likely to be fearful of new things and new places. They may also have a fear of moving. Generally, agoraphobics fear traveling. Also, some individuals who fear airplanes, trains, or moving vehicles fear traveling. (See also FLYING, FEAR OF; TRAINS, FEAR OF.)

trazodone An antidepressant drug with relatively few side effects. Trazodone is sometimes prescribed (in countries where clomipramine is not available) for OBSESSIVE–COMPULSIVE DISORDER. The side effects of trazodone are tolerable for most patients, with excessive sedation being a problem for a small proportion of patients. A side effect is priapism in males, in which the penis becomes erect and will not detumesce (lose its erection). Trazodone is also sometimes used to treat symptoms of headaches not due to organic causes. (See also ANTIDEPRESSANTS, NEW; DEPRESSION; HEADACHES.)

LaPierre, Y.D., "New Antidepressant Drugs," *Journal of Clinical Psychiatry* (August 1983), pp. 41–44.

trees, fear of Fear of trees is known as dendrophobia. Individuals who fear trees may fear certain landscapes, may fear being hit on the head with apples, acorns or other falling objects, or may fear blossoms or fruit from the trees. Some individuals fear seeing trees with leaves turning brown; this may represent a fear of death to them. In mythology and legends, trees were considered special, mysterious places because they gave shade and shelter; wood from trees enabled man to build fires, homes, and bridges, and the fruit of trees fed man and animals. Trees were a link from earth to heaven, and tree worship was an early form of religion. The common practice to "touch wood" for luck is a carryover from tree worship. Early believers tried to summon friendly spirits by knocking on the trunks of the tree. (See also SUPERNATURAL, FEARS OF.)

Brasch, R., *Strange Customs* (New York: David McKay, 1976).

trembling, fear of Fear of trembling is known as tremophobia. Individuals who fear trembling in themselves are afraid that others will notice and be critical or frightened. Some people who have trembling hands due to disease, such as Parkinson's, fear that if they are seen trembling they will appear helpless. Some who fear trembling in others are afraid that the other individual may have a contagious disease or may act violently. (See also SOCIAL PHOBIA.)

tremophobia Fear of trembling. (See also TREMBLING, FEAR OF.)

triazolam A drug in the BENZODIAZEPINE class, commonly used to induce sleep.

trichinophobia Fear of trichinosis. (See also TRICHINOSIS, FEAR OF).

trichinosis, fear of Fear of trichinosis is known as trichinophobia. Trichinosis is caused by eating undercooked pork containing *Trichinella spiralis.* In the early stages, symptoms of trichinosis are diarrhea, nausea, colic, and fever, and later, stiffness, pain, swelling of the muscles, fever, sweating, and insomnia. Some individuals avoid eating certain foods because of this fear. (See also EATING, FEAR OF; FOOD, FEAR OF.)

trichophobia Fear of hair is known as trichophobia. (See also HAIR, FEAR OF.)

trichopathophobia Fear of hair disease is known as trichopathophobia. (See also HAIR, FEAR OF; HAIR DISEASE, FEAR OF.)

tricyclic drug One of a group of ANTIDEPRESSANTS whose molecular structure is characterized by three fused rings. Tricyclic DRUGS are effective primarily in alleviating ENDOGENOUS DEPRESSION. Imipramine, one of the tricyclic antidepressive drugs, has been used extensively for treatment of panic disorder. While results are mixed, it does seem to be effective in the short run with a small percentage of people who have panic reactions.

trifluoperazine An antianxiety and antipsychotic drug that may be effective for short-term treatment of generalized nonpsychotic anxiety for individuals in whom other drugs, such as BENZODIAZEPINES, are not effective. A common trade name for trifluoperazine is Stelazine. Use of trifluoperazine is always closely monitored by a physician, as high doses of the drug may cause persistent TARDIVE DYSKINESIA (an impairment of voluntary movement brought upon by years of taking neuroleptic drugs that block transmission at dopamine synapses.) (See also ANXIETY DRUGS.)

trimipramine A TRICYCLIC ANTIDEPRESSANT drug, also known by the tradename surmontil. (See also ANTIDEPRESSANTS; DEPRESSION.)

Triptafen See AMITRIPTYLINE.

Triptizol See AMITRIPTYLINE.

triskaidekaphobia Fear of the number thirteen. (See also THIRTEEN, FEAR OF THE NUMBER.)

tropophobia Fear or moving or of making changes. (See also CHANGE, FEAR OF; MOVING, FEAR OF; NEWNESS, FEAR OF.)

trypanophobia Fear of injections. (See also INJECTIONS, FEAR OF; NEEDLES, FEAR OF.)

tuberculosis, fear of Fear of tuberculosis is known as tuberculophobia, or phthisiophobia. Tuberculosis is an infectious disease caused by *Mycobacterium tuberculosis,* or the tubercle bacillus. The disease is characterized by formation of tubercles, or pockets of infection, in the tissues throughout the body. Persons who have tuberculosis tend to cough, spreading moist particles of the TB germ into the air. Some of these particles continue floating in the air until they enter the respiratory passages of another person and find their way down to the lungs to cause common tuberculosis. The germ may remain dormant for many years before making the individual ill. The bacillus responsible for tuberculosis was identified in 1882, but it was not until 1944 that the drug streptomycin was found, which was effective against tuberculosis. Now that most forms of tuberculosis are treatable, the disease is not as feared as it once was. During the 19th and the early part of the 20th century, tuberculosis was feared by many. Individuals who had tuberculosis were often isolated or sent to sanitariums where they could be outdoors; even before the discovery of streptomycin, it was known that the tubercle bacillus is killed by exposure to sunlight. Tuberculosis was always more common among families subject to poor housing, overcrowding and generally substandard health conditions, although it has affected all socioeconomic groups because of contagion.

The word tuberculosis, used alone, has

come to mean pulmonary, or lung, tuberculosis. However, the infection may take hold elsewhere in the body. When it does, the problem is identified by the area it affects: tuberculosis of the bones, intestinal tuberculosis, tuberculous meningitis (in the brain), tuberculous peritonitis (in the membrane surrounding the abdomen), or tuberculosis of the urinary tract. (See also DISEASE, FEAR OF; HEALTH ANXIETY; ILLNESS PHOBIA.)

tuberculophobia Fear of tuberculosis. Also known as phthisiophobia.

twins, fear and phobias in Studies of panic disorders in families and among twins suggest that such disorders may have a genetic basis. Individuals who have relatives with panic attacks are more likely to suffer similar attacks than are those with no such family history. Identical twins, who have exactly the same genetic makeup, are more likely to both suffer from panic attacks than are fraternal twins, who share the same environment are genetically no more similar than other siblings.

Through studying twins, researchers have determined that some fears and phobias may have genetic contributions. In a study of 15 pairs of identical twins reared apart, University of Minnesota researchers found three sets of twins with multiple phobias. Two siblings were afraid of water and heights and had claustrophobia. Three other pairs of twins shared a single phobia. One of these pairs, although separated soon after birth, worked out the same solution to their water phobia: they waded into the ocean backward, averting their eyes from the surf. Researchers speculate that evolution selected genes for such fears because they conferred a survival advantage on early man. For example, avoiding heights and water helped them avoid falling off cliffs and drowning.

Genes may make individuals more sensitive to their environment. At the Medical College of Virginia, where 3,798 pairs of identical and fraternal twins were examined, identical twins were found to have a higher concordance than fraternal twins for anxiety and depression. While these results are interesting and suggestive, scientifically acceptable twin studies are rare and usually consist of too few subjects to allow one to generalize the results.

Begley, S., A. Murr, K. Springer, J. Gordon and J. Harrison, "All About Twins," *Newsweek*, (November 23, 1987), p. 58.

Fishman, Scott M. and David V. Sheehan, *Psychology Today* (April 1985), pp. 26–32.

Type A behavior pattern See CORONARY-PRONE TYPE-A BEHAVIOR.

tyramine A substance found in some foods that may contribute to causing HEADACHES and may interfere with the effectiveness of certain ANTIDEPRESSANT medications. Tyramine affects the constriction or expansion of blood vessels. This reaction to certain foods occurs only in about thirty percent of people who have migraine headaches. Since there is no way to know whether an individual is in this sensitive group, physicians generally recommend that all migraine sufferers and individuals who take MAO (MONOAMINE OXIDASE) INHIBITORS as mood elevators for depression avoid ripened cheeses, including Cheddar, Emmentaler, Gruyere, Stilton, Brie, and Camembert (cottage, cream, and some processed cheeses are permitted), herring, chocolate, vinegar (except white vinegar), anything fermented, pickled, or marinated, sour cream, yogurt, nuts, peanut butter, seeds, pods of broad beans (lima, navy, pinto, garbanzo, and pea), any foods containing large amounts of monosodium glutamate (Oriental foods), onions, and canned figs.

Kahn, Ada P., *Headaches* (Chicago: Contemporary Books, 1983).

tyrants, fear of Fear of tyrants is known as tyrannophobia. Many individuals who have survived such an oppressive environment develop this fear.

tyrannophobia Fear of tyrants. (See also TYRANTS, FEAR OF.)

U

UFOs, fear of Individuals and groups of people often become anxious when they think they see unidentified flying objects (UFOs). Anxieties about sightings of UFOs are related to the times. For example, in the 20th century, when space travel became a reality, there was increased speculation about life on other planets, and some came to fear invasion by alien beings. However, in the Middle Ages, when dragon shapes were seen in the clouds or a fiery cross was sighted in the sky, people feared divine retribution. Fear of UFOs is an example of fear of the unknown, because no one is sure where the UFOs are from or exactly what they are. (See also FLYING THINGS, FEAR OF; UNKNOWN, FEAR OF.)

ulcers Peptic ulcers are a chronic condition in which the lining of the stomach or duodenum (the first part of the small intestine) becomes inflamed as a result of the action of digestive juices on the mucous membranes. Ulcers may also appear in any part of the digestive tract because of irritation from medication, intake of corrosive chemicals, or endocrine disorders. Many psychological factors seem to contribute to the development of peptic ulcers. Tense, hard-driving people appear to be more likely to develop them than more placid individuals. "Ulcer personalities" tend to be ambitious and competitive; these people suppress feelings of frustration, resentment, and anxiety. However, ulcers also occur, though less often, in individuals who are calm. Men over 30 or 40 are more likely than others to suffer from ulcers, although men and women of all ages do have them.

The outstanding symptom of peptic ulcers is pain, which usually occurs at certain regular times and is relieved by eating. Constipation, nausea, vomiting, loss of appetite, and even anemia may sometimes be symptoms. Many people suffer with symptoms for five years or longer without seeking medical advice. Drugs are available to alleviate ulcer symptoms and bring peptic ulcers under control. Antacids, antispasmodics, and sedatives are often part of the treatment. Smoking, use of alcohol, and overexertion may aggravate ulcers and delay healing; individuals who have ulcers are usually advised to abstain from smoking and alcohol. Often psychotherapy is recommended to help reduce anxiety, tension, and anger. (See also STRESS MANAGEMENT.)

unconditional positive regard A term used by client-centered therapists to denote the worth of the individual under treatment. Unconditional positive regard is used interchangeably with the words "ACCEPTANCE" and "prizing" and is viewed as necessary to promote effective psychotherapy. If a person is raised in a situation without unconditional positive regard, he or she is more likely to develop anxieties. For example, phobic individuals often come from families in which they received criticism (the opposite of unconditional positive regard). (See also CLIENT-CENTERED THERAPY; FAMILY THERAPY.)

unconditioned response Behavior that is elicited reliably following an UNCONDITIONED STIMULUS and not based upon learning. Classical CONDITIONING theory views the unconditioned response as automatic and resulting from innate sensory processes not governed by experience. With conditioning (the association of a new stimulus with the unconditioned stimulus) new learning occurs. For example, the sight and smell of food is an unconditioned stimulus for hunger and salivation. With learning by association, words and images (conditioned stimuli) can come to elicit hunger and salivation (conditioned response). Many anxieties are thought to be acquired in this manner so that an apparently neutral stimulus (such a seeing the brake lights on an automobile) may come to elicit anxiety (part of the unconditioned response) because of its association with the trauma and suffering of an automobile accident.

unconditioned stimulus A signal that provokes a response not based on learning. For example, experiments have shown that a child's fear of loud noises could be generalized (transferred) to a white rat. This is done by pairing the presentation of loud noises with the white rat. For effective conditioning, the conditioned stimulus (white rat) must be presented slightly before the onset of the unconditioned stimulus. With repetition, the conditioned stimulus will come to elicit a portion of the unconditioned response. The loud noise was the unconditioned stimulus because it existed before the experiment. Loud noise, falling, certain animals, being out of control, suffocation, and perhaps a few other fears are unconditioned stimuli that elicit the unconditioned response of fear. (See also CONDITIONING; PAVLOV, IVAN; UNCONDITIONED RESPONSE.)

unconscious, the The designation given by Sigmund Freud to a region of the psyche comprising all mental functions and products of which the individual is unaware and which he or she cannot recognize or remember at will. The unconscious in its most simplistic form refers to the availability (or unavailability) of psychic material. Some individuals develop phobias because of unconscious memories. (See also FREUD, SIGMUND; PSYCHOANALYSIS.)

undressing (in front of someone), fear of Fear of undressing in front of someone is known as dishabillophobia. The term also includes the fear of being seen in a less than fully clothed state, or being seen in a state of disarray. There may be some sexual connotations to this fear, insofar as the individual fears being seen in the nude. There also may be an obsession with wanting to be seen only at one's best.

unknown, fear of the Fear of the unknown is a common thread among many phobias and anxieties. For example, fears of death and darkness represent fears of the unknown, as do fears of outer space and the future. Many anxieties in illness conditions are fears of the unknown, as the individual does not know whether medications will work or what complications might occur. Some who fear travelling or doing new activities have these fears because of their fears of the unknown. (See also CANCER, FEAR OF; NEWNESS, FEAR OF; OUTER SPACE, FEAR OF.)

uranophobia Fear of heaven. (See also HEAVEN, FEAR OF.)

urinating, fear of Fear of urinating is called urophobia. This can be a very embarrassing and debilitating fear. It occurs more frequently in men than in women. Fear of urinating usually occurs when others are present when the person wants to or is actually urinating. Some men may be unable to urinate in front of any other person, and many waste time waiting at work and other places until the men's room becomes empty. Some women cannot urinate in any toilet except in their own home. In its extreme form, the fear of urinating with another person nearby necessitates holding in urine through the working day until the home bathroom can be used. The victim often avoids parties, restaurants, and social gatherings that might involve long commitments of time. The fear usually develops as a form of social anxiety and is often traced to adolescent fears of public exposure and possible criticism, which are common in youth.

Some individuals fear that they might urinate when far from a toilet, wet themselves, and be seen by others. Such individuals may visit public toilets frequently and try to urinate so that they will not feel the urge far from a toilet. They may avoid social gatherings where no toilets are readily available. Individuals who become incontinent, or unable to control the flow of their urine, due to illness or injury fear odor and offending others. Urinary incontinence due to physical causes can be treated with medication, surgery, or commercially available adult diapers. Other fears relating to urination can be treated with psychotherapy and/or behavioral therapy quite effectively. DESENSITIZATION, RELAXATION THERAPY, and EXPOSURE THERAPY are generally helpful. (See also DEFECATION, FEAR OF.)

Marks, Isaac, *Living with Fear* (New York: McGraw-Hill, 1978).

urophobia Fear of urinating. (See also URINATING, FEAR OF.)

V

vaccination, fear of Fear of vaccination is known as vacciniophobia. Some people fear vaccination because they fear INJECTION. Some fear NEEDLES or devices that pierce the skin. Some fear unwanted side effects from vaccination. Those who have ILLNESS PHOBIA or fear of CONTAMINATION may fear contamination from the inoculation device. Many people worldwide fear being vaccinated and taking their infants for vaccination because they do not understand what vaccination means.

Andelman, Samuel L. *The New Home Medical Encyclopedia* (New York: Quadrangle books, 1973), vol. 4, pp. 1269–1270.

vacciniophobia Fear of vaccination (See also VACCINATION, FEAR OF.)

Valium An antianxiety drug. Chemically known as DIAZEPAM, Valium is in a class of drugs called BENZODIAZEPINES. It has been used more extensively and for more conditions than any of the other benzodiazepines. (See also ANXIETY DRUGS.)

vampire A fearsome creature that sucks blood, usually at night. There is a deep, archetypal fear of images that can transform from humans to animals and back to human form. Vampires seem to fall into this category of creatures. During the Middle Ages, vampires, like werewolves, were highly feared. The fear that the vampires would come after one during the NIGHT in quest of blood, the only food on which he could survive, brings with it all of the psychological associations with human BLOOD. To be drained of blood is to be drained of strength and one's soul. Offering blood was associated with sacrifice in many cultures; primitive gods demanded blood. Blood, symbolized by wine, plays a part in the Christian communion service. Blood, particularly the blood of a virgin, was considered to have healing properties during the Middle Ages. Warriors drank the blood of their fallen victims.

Blood is also a sexual symbol, directly associated with MENSTRUATION and less directly with SEMEN. The vampire's bite of a sleeper, usually of the opposite sex, is linked closely with a kiss. In *The Vampire Myth,* James Twitchell described this aspect of the vampire as a symbol: "The myth is loaded with sexual excitement; yet there is no mention of sexuality. It is sex without genitalia, sex without confusion, sex without responsibility, sex without guilt, sex without love—better yet, sex without mention." This quality of the legend created an eager Victorian audience for *Dracula,* since they could read it as an exciting and superficially proper story that both expressed and suppressed their sexual desire, GUILT, and ANXIETY.

The hero of Bram Stoker's *Dracula* described the tension between attraction and revulsion that has made the vampire a significant psychological symbol: There was something about them that made me uneasy, some longing and at the same time some deadly fear. I felt in my heart a wicked burning desire that they would kiss me with those red lips.

Because of this unique combination of qualities, the vampire has been referred to as a "psychic sponge" and "a kind of incestuous, necrophilous, oral-anal-sadistic-all-in-wrestling match." The historical inspiration for Stoker's Count Dracula was Vlad the Impaler, a 15th-century ruler of Wallachia, who was a cruel and violent man, but not a vampire. The concept of a bloodsucking evil spirit goes back to antiquity, but the vampire as thought of today emerged in 16th-century eastern Europe, where the Magyar term *vampir* came into use. The vampire legend spread throughout Europe and was taken up by literary figures such as Goethe, Baudelaire, Byron, and Dumas. *Dracula* was published in 1897 and subsequently adapted for the stage and then the screen, with Bela Lugosi playing the evil count. Over 200 vampire films have been produced throughout the world. An upsurge of interest in vampires in the 1970s produced still more vampire-related plays, films, books, and music.

Centuries ago, certain practical situations involving DEATH and BURIAL may have contributed to fears about vampires. As premature burial was a possibility before the days of modern technology to confirm death, live bodies were sometimes actually interred. Incidents of multiple deaths from the PLAGUE and less-than-formal burials added to these fears. Actual cases of body snatching in eras when corpses were not available for medical research also contributed to the belief that some dead bodies did not stay in their proper places.

Unusual cases of deviant individuals who desire human blood further reinforced vampire fears. Elizabeth Bathory, a Hungarian countess, tortured and killed over 600 young women, partly for her own perverse enjoyment and partly from the belief that their blood would prolong her youth and beauty. More common psychological deviations that endorsed a belief and fear of vampires were necrophagia (eating dead bodies), necrosadism (mutilation of dead bodies), and necrophilia (sexual intercourse with a corpse).

Historically, superstitions have led many people to believe in and fear vampires. Many cultures follow rituals resulting from beliefs that CORPSES will wander freely from their GRAVES with ill intentions toward the living, particularly relatives, unless proper precautions are taken. Suicides, excommunicants, and criminals were thought to be assured of this fate after death.

Fear of vampires may also symbolize a type of human relationship that is both attractive and frightening. A particularly magnetic individual can influence and hold others in his power, draining away talent, energy, and individuality for his own purposes.

The vampire's superhuman strength, capacity to live forever, and ability to create other vampires at will appeal to the basic human fear of death and desire for eternal life. However, those who fear vampires also believe that the vampire is vulnerable. They believe that silver, a CRUCIFIX, or garlic can ward off a vampire, and that one can end the eternal existence of a vampire by driving a stake through his heart, if he can be found sleeping in his coffin. (See also SUPERNATURAL, FEAR OF; WEREWOLVES, FEAR OF; WITCHES AND WITCHCRAFT, FEAR OF.)

"Dracula Lives!" *Newsweek* (October 21, 1977), pp. 74–75.

Leatherdale, Clive, *Dracula, the Novel and the Legend* (Wellingborough, Northamptonshire: Antiquarian Press, 1985), pp. 145–175.
Cavendish, Richard (ed.) *Man, Myth and Magic* (New York: Marshall Cavendish, 1983), "Vampire."
Masters, Anthony, *The Supernatural History of the Vampire* (New York: Putnam, 1972), pp. 3–39.
Ronay, Gabriel, *The Truth about Dracula* (Briarcliff, NY: Stein and Day, 1979), pp. 58–67, 93–136.
Robbins, Russell, *Encyclopedia of Witchcraft and Demonology* (New York: Crown, 1959), "Vampire."
Stoker, Bram, *Dracula* (London: Constable, 1897).

vasovagal response See BLOOD AND BLOOD-INJURY PHOBIA; FAINTING.

vegetables, fear of Fear of vegetables is known as lachanophobia. This fear may be related to fears of certain foods or fear of eating things that have grown in the ground. Some individuals who fear pollution in the air or water may fear eating vegetables. (See also FOODS, FEAR OF; POLLUTION, FEAR OF.)

vehicles, fear of Fear of vehicles is known as amaxophobia or ochophobia. This fear may relate to driving a car or riding in a car or other form of transportation such as trains, boats, buses, and airplanes. This phobia may be part of a fear of motion or a fear of being in an enclosed place. Sometimes the fear relates to being away from a safe place (such as home) or a fear of losing emotional or psychological control in front of others. (See also AUTOMOBILES, FEAR OF; FLYING, FEAR OF; MOTION, FEAR OF; TRAINS, FEAR OF.)

Campbell, Robert J., *Psychiatric Dictionary* (New York: Oxford University Press, 1981).

venereal disease, fear of Fear of venereal disease is known as cypridophobia, cypriphobia, and venereophobia. A venereal disease is a SEXUALLY TRANSMITTED DISEASE (STD). Individuals who have a phobia of venereal disease may also fear prostitutes and sexual activity. The outbreak of autoimmune deficiency syndrome (AIDS) in the 1980s has increased many persons' fears of sexually transmitted diseases and has caused them to take measures to prevent their spread. (See also PROSTITUTES, FEAR OF; SEXUAL INTERCOURSE, FEAR OF; SEXUALLY TRANSMITTED DISEASES, FEAR OF; SYPHILIS, FEAR OF.)

venustaphobia Fear of beautiful women (See also WOMEN, FEAR OF.)

verbophobia Fear of words. (See also WORDS, FEAR OF.)

verminophobia Fear of worms. (See also WORMS, FEAR OF.)

vertigo, fear of Fear of vertigo is known as illyngophobia. Vertigo is an anxiety response to a situation and also the medical term that refers to dizziness. Dizziness is a common symptom of many phobics, such as those who fear heights, looking over cliffs, bridges, elevators, and riding in automobiles. Many agoraphobics experience dizziness when venturing out alone or to places they fear. Fear of dizziness is known as dinophobia.

Individuals who experience vertigo because of phobias should sit, lie down, or brace themselves. Sitting with one's head between one's legs is a good precaution if one thinks he or she may lose consciousness, but it may not stop the dizziness. Behavior therapies sometimes help individuals who experience dizziness because of phobic reactions. (See also ACROPHOBIA; AGORAPHOBIA; DIZZINESS, FEAR OF; HEIGHTS, FEAR OF.)

vestiphobia Fear of clothing, either one's own or that of another. Some individuals fear particular items of clothing, such as textured items, silk or velvet garments, undergarments, or a particular style of clothing. (See also CLOTHING, FEAR OF.)

viloxazine An antidepressant drug. (See also ANTIDEPRESSANTS; ANTIDEPRESSANTS, NEW; DEPRESSION.)

virgins, fear of Fear of virgins is known as parthenophobia. (See also YOUNG GIRLS, FEAR OF.)

virginity, fear of losing Fear of losing one's virginity is known as esodophobia or primeisodophobia. Attitudes toward retaining virginity until marriage have changed with the new morality of the 1960s and 1970s, but the experience of defloration may still be frightening for many reasons. Women's fears are in part a product and reflection of male anxiety. In many cultures, men have wanted to marry virgins as insurance that children from the union will be their own. A male attitude that inexperience is synonymous with purity of mind encourages the feeling that a virgin bride will more truly belong to her husband. Male fear of defloration has arisen from the feeling that sexual intercourse, particularly with a virgin, will rob a man of his strength and put him in the woman's power. Loss of virginity may be more directly frightening to a woman because of the threat of pain and pregnancy and also the fear of appearing inexperienced or awkward. Defloration also represents a sudden, radical change, a break with the past that is the end of girlhood.

Horney, Karen, *Feminine Psychology* (New York: W.W. Norton, 1967).
de Beauvoir, Simone, *The Second Sex* (New York: Modern Library, 1968).

virgivitiphobia Fear of rape. (See also RAPE, FEAR OF.)

vitricophobia Fear of a stepfather. (See also STEPFATHER, FEAR OF.)

Vivactil See PROTRIPTYLINE.

vomiting, fear of Fear of vomiting is known as emetophobia. Fear of vomiting is considered a social phobia. Some individuals fear that they might vomit in public or that they may see others vomiting. Some individuals who have this phobia avoid any situation that is remotely likely to provoke vomiting in themselves or in others, such as going on a boat or riding in a car. (See also FOOD, FEAR OF; NAUSEA; SWALLOWING, FEAR OF.)

voodoo, fears in Voodoo is a religion and set of related superstitions that include many different magical figures and frightening beliefs. Witches, sorcerers, medicine men, and priests all have their places in voodoo. At night, believers fear bloodsucking spirits call loupgarous. Noon is frightening, too, because the human shadow, which believers equate with the soul, disappears. The soul, called the *gros bon ange,* or large good angel, is a fragile, easily disturbed link between the body and the conscience, the *ti bon ange* or good little angel. Magical spells aim at the soul in the culture of Haiti, where voodoo was transplanted from African tribal beliefs. Any sort of enmity may be a source for possession by evil spirits resulting in violent mental and physical symptoms.

Believers undertake initiation into voodoo, a type of purified intentional form of possession, as a safeguard against calamity, a way to please ancestral spirits, and a way to get the powerful voodoo spirits known as *loa* on one's side. The initiation procedure is essentially a ritual death, a giving up of the soul, which is imagined to leave the body to be captured in a sacred vessel where it will be protected by the gods and safe from evildoers. The initiate is then considered to be a servant of the *loa,* reborn with a new name. The ceremony, during which the initiate learns the secrets and rites of voodoo, is long and complex, lasting over a month. At the end of this time the initiate is called a *hounsi canzo,* the initiated spouse of the god. On the death of an initiate, a rite called *dessounin* releases his spirits into the water of death and again captures his soul in a sacred vessel to await resurrection.

A fear associated with voodoo belief is the possibility of becoming a ZOMBIE, a walking corpse in the service of the person who has reanimated him. The initiation and *dessounin* rituals are supposed to give some sort of assurance that the initiate's soul is safe from anyone with the magical powers to create a zombie. (See also ZOMBIE, FEAR OF BECOMING A.)

Hill, Douglas and Pat Williams, *The Supernatural* (New York: Hawthorn Books, 1965), pp. 234–267.

Cavendish, Richard (ed.), *Man, Myth and Magic* (New York: Marshall Cavendish, 1983), "Voodoo," "Zombie."

W

waits, fear of long Fear of long waits is known as macrophobia. Long waits are common in modern society; people are asked to wait on the telephone, in stores, at airports, and for one another. Many individuals become inpatient and anxious; some are so fearful of waiting that they will not frequent busy restaurants; they take scheduled transportation so that waits are predictable. This fear may be somewhat related to AGORAPHOBIA, in which individuals do not like to be away from a secure place for very long. Also, some individuals experience a feeling of being trapped while in line, as they cannot leave easily and still maintain their place. (See also TRAINS, FEAR OF.)

waking up, fear of not Fear of not waking up may be related to a fear of death. Many individuals who fear going to bed or going to sleep have this fear. Fear of not waking up is somewhat common in physically ill and elderly persons and in individuals who have anxieties about death. This fear is related to fear of going to sleep. (See also BED, FEAR OF; DEATH, FEAR OF; SLEEP, FEAR OF.)

walking, fear of Fear of walking and/or standing upright is known as basiphobia, basistasiphobia, stasiphobia, and stasibasiphobia. The fear is often related to fear of falling, collapse, and death. (See also BLOCQ'S SYNDROME; STANDING UPRIGHT, FEAR OF.)

war, fear of Fear of war is not a phobia, since it is realistic and quite sane. The fear of war appears to follow an inverse "U" function with age. That is, the fear at very young ages (before age five or so) is low but increases in intensity up to about ages 12 to 14, when it peaks. At late adolescence and young adulthood it declines considerably, and at adulthood it is low relative to economic and health fears.

Studies of junior and senior high school students indicate that fear about nuclear war is intense in about 30 percent of that population. On a worldwide basis, this intensity seems to be steady across countries. If children's fears are ranked, the fear of nuclear war is always second or third. The only item to be ranked consistently higher is the fear of parents dying. The high intensity of this fear together with its pervasive nature would classify fear of nuclear war as a major social stressor to children worldwide. The effects on family life and social and psychological development may become evident soon.

war exposure See POSTTRAUMATIC STRESS DISORDER.

war neuroses See POSTTRAUMATIC STRESS DISORDER.

warlock See WITCHES AND WITCHCRAFT, FEAR OF.

washing, fear of Fear of washing is known as ablutophobia. Usually this refers to fear of washing oneself, or even of thinking of washing oneself. However, it also refers to a fear of viewing another individual washing himself or herself.

wasps, fear of Fear of wasps is known as spheksophobia. Individuals who fear wasps often fear stings, pain, bees, or flying insects in general. (See also BEES, FEAR OF; FLYING THINGS, FEAR OF.)

water, fear of Fear of water is known as aquaphobia and hydrophobia. Fear of water is related to a fear of drowning and a fear of death. In some aquaphobes, this fear extends to bathing, swimming, or seeing or imagining bodies of water or running water. Fear of water is a learned fear. By age three, children are ready to learn to swim, unless they become fearful of water, particularly deep water. Some individuals who fear water may have had a traumatic experience in a pool or other body of water. They may have been cautioned not to go near the water. Some children of water phobics are taught at an early age to also be afraid of the water and consequently grow up fearful. Many individuals are phobic about going into water that is over than their head, even though they know how to swim. Some fear putting their faces in the water and getting water up their nose; when this happens, they have a rapid heartbeat and breathe faster, often inhaling water, which further increases their anxiety. Some individuals avoid boat rides because they are afraid of falling out into deep water. Some panic when flying in an airplane over water. For still others, fear of water may be related to a fear of landscape that includes a body of water. Former aquaphobics advise persons afraid of water to take swimming lessons to become more comfortable in water and to learn to relax and breathe correctly.

The word for fear of water, hydrophobia, may have been the first term using the suffix "phobia" to denote a morbid fear. The term was used by Celsus, a Roman medical authority of the first century A.D., who said of hydrophobia, "There is just one remedy, to throw the patient unawares into a water tank which he has not seen beforehand. If he cannot swim, let him sink under and drink, then lift him out; if he can swim, push him under at intervals so that he drinks his fill of water even against his will; for so his thirst and dread of water are removed at the same time." (See also LAKES, FEAR OF; LANDSCAPES, FEAR OF CERTAIN.)

Celsus, A.C., *Of Medicine,* trans. by J. Grieve. (Edinburgh; Dickson, 1814).

Errara, P., "Some Historical Aspects of the Concept Phobia," *The Psychiatric Quarterly* (April 1962).

Watson, John B. (1878–1958) An American psychologist and founder of BEHAVIORISM. Watson wrote, "Psychology as the behaviorist views it is a purely objective branch of natural science. Its theoretical goal is the prediction and control of behavior. Introspection forms no essential part of its methods, nor is the scientific value of its data dependent upon the readiness with which they lend themselves to interpretation in terms of consciousness." Watson emphasize learned behavior, stimulus–response c n-nections, and CONDITIONING and reg ded behavior as the product of both here y and the environment. He believed tha he task of psychology is to determine hat is instinctive and what is learned. W tson is best known for his article "Psy ology as the Behaviorist Views It" (19 . After leaving psychology he had a s essful career in advertising. (See also ERT B.; RESPONSE; STIMULUS.)

Harre, Rom and Roge amb, *The Encyclopedic Dictionary of P ology* (Cambridge: The MIT Press, 19

waves, fear of Fear of waves is known as cymophobia. This fear may be related to a fear of motion, a fear of water, or a fear of landscapes in which water and leaves are prominent. (See also LANDSCAPE, FEAR OF CERTAIN; MOTION, FEAR OF; WATER, FEAR OF.)

weakness, fear of Fear of weakness is known as asthenophobia. Individuals fear weakness because they fear losing physical, emotional, social, or political control. (See also LOSING CONTROL, FEAR OF.)

wealth, fear of See MONEY, FEAR OF.

weight gain, fear of Fear of gaining weight is known as obesophobia or pocrescophobia. Some individuals who fear gaining weight stop eating, or eat very little, a condition known as ANOREXIA NERVOSA, which is found most often among teenage girls. Some individuals who fear gaining weight practice BULIMIA, or bingeing and purging, in which they gorge themselves and then induce vomiting. Fear of weight gain is related to concerns about one's body image and social fears. (See also EATING DISORDERS.)

weight loss, fear of Fear of losing weight may be related to a fear of illness or a fear of death. Some individuals fear "losing themselves" or disappearing if they lose too much weight. Fear of losing weight may be related to a fear of being out of control of one's body. (See also ANOREXIA NERVOSA; BULIMIA; EATING DISORDERS; LOSING CONTROL, FEAR OF; WEIGHT GAIN, FEAR OF.)

werewolves Some men fear that they will become werewolves, and some people fear that they will be devoured by werewolves. Like satyrs, centaurs, and mermaids, werewolves are a combination of human being and animal. The word werewolf is derived from the Anglo-Saxon term *wer,* or man. Fear of werewolves in the classical world were recorded by Herodotus, Plato, and Pliny. Fear of werewolves developed out of fear of wolves, which are known to be ferocious, cruel, and howling. Werewolves change back and forth between human and animal form. Legends describe different methods of metamorphosis or change. Methods include removal of a hide of human skin, donning of an animal skin under the power of a full moon, rolling on the ground in the nude, and immersion in water. Some legends say that transformation is complete, while others say that in animal form the werewolf has some human characteristics and vice versa. Reversal occurs at daybreak or if the animal is injured or killed. In their animal form, werewolves murder and devour human flesh.

There are many fears and beliefs about the creation of werewolves. The metamorphosis may be voluntary or involuntary. Ritual may be used to call up an evil spirit; some may use fire, or application of a magic ointment to the skin. Some may urinate in a circle under the full moon; some become werewolves because they were conceived under a new moon. Others say that werewolves are created by contact with a magic flower, drinking from a stream where wolves commonly go, from a wolf paw print, eating wolf meat or brains, or making a pact with the devil. Still other origins of werewolves may be heredity, living an evil life, and self-hypnosis.Some say that a priest or saint can turn a living human being into a werewolf, that witchcraft and sorcery can turn an innocent victim into a werewolf, and that evil individuals may return after death as werewolves.

Once a man becomes a werewolf, he can be cured of his affliction through religious exorcism, shedding blood, being addressed by his human name, and abstaining from eating flesh for years. In some legends werewolves can be killed by ordinary means; other stories say that they must be shot with a consecrated silver bullet.

There have been cases of lycanthropy, a mental disorder more common in the past, in which the victim believes himself to be a wolf and runs wild, eats raw meat, rapes, murders, and eats human flesh.

In one anthropological study of the werewolf, researchers suggested that the werewolf image is a product of the COLLECTIVE UNCONSCIOUS, which has recorded a transition in man's evolution from a pastoral, vegetarian society to a meat-eating, possibly cannibalistic, aggressive culture in which males took females by violence. (See also SUPERNATURAL, FEAR OF; WITCHES AND WITCHCRAFT, FEAR OF.)

Campbell, Robert J., *Psychiatric Dictionary* (New York: Oxford University Press, 1981), "Lycanthropy."

Shepard, Leslie (ed.), "Werewolf," in *Encyclopedia of Occultism and Parapsychology* (Detroit: Gale, 1984).

Cavendish, Richard (ed.), *Man, Myth and Magic* (New York: Marshall Cavendish, 1983), "Werewolf" and "Shape Shifting."

West, Ellen A patient of Otto Binswanger (1852–1929), a German psychiatrist. Ellen West had a phobia of being fat. Binswanger published the case history in 1944. The case was significant because it marked the introduction of existentialism into the field of psychotherapy. Ellen was treated in a sanitarium in Switzerland but was declared incurable after two and a half months. On the evening of her return home to her husband, she committed suicide with poison.

Westphal, Carl Friedrich Otto (1833–1890) A German neurologist who studied the fear of open spaces and gave it the name "AGORAPHOBIA." Westphal conducted his studies and research in Berlin and Leipzig, exploring the microscopic pathology of the brain and its relation to mental disorders. He was the first to describe obsessional states and was an innovator in the scientific study of homosexuality.

Howells, John G. and M. Livia Osborn, *A Reference Companion to the History of Abnormal Psychology* (Westport, CT: Greenwood Press, 1984), p. 976.

wet dreams, fear of Fear of wet dreams is known as oneirogmophobia. Wet dreams are nocturnal emissions from the penis while asleep. Some men fear wet dreams because of embarrassment that others might become aware of the problem. Nocturnal emissions are part of normal adolescent development and are brought about by accumulated normal tensions that find release during sleep. (See also DREAMS, FEAR OF; SEXUAL FEARS.)

whirlpools, fear of Fear of whirlpools is known as dinophobia. This fear may be related to a fear of motion or of water. The swirling action of a whirlpool may make the individual feel that he will be swept away; the fear may also represent a fear of being out of control. (See also MOTION, FEAR OF; WATER, FEAR OF.)

whistling, fear of Those who fear whistling may do so because whistling is associated with unseen dangers, such as the sound of wind or the hiss of a snake. Whistling has been associated with the casting of spells and has been called the devil's music. On the other hand, whistling in the dark or in other frightening situations historically has been thought to work a kind of countermagic to keep away evil. In some cultures, if a woman whistles, bad luck is thought to follow. In the theater, newspaper offices, mines, and on shipboard, whistling is thought to bring misfortune. (See also SOUNDS, FEAR OF.)

Daniels, Cora Linn, *Encyclopedia of Superstitions, Folklore and the Occult Sciences* (Detroit: Gale Research, 1971).

de Lys, Claudia *A Treasury of American Superstitions* (New York: Philosophical Library, 1940).

"white coat" hypertension A term referring to high blood pressure caused by anxiety induced by visiting a doctor's office. Some individuals appear to be victims of "white coat" hypertension, a condition in which blood pressure is generally normal but increases when the patient is tested by a doctor. This type of hypertension occurs more frequently among young women than men. Because of this type of anxiety, some patients may be misclassified as hypertensives.

Some individuals' blood pressure may rise in the doctor's office or clinic because they are fearful of doctors or fearful of the surroundings, including laboratories where they might encounter needles or blood-testing devices (particularly if they are phobic about these things).

There may be some aspect of conditioned response involved in "white coat" hypertension, too. When a subject's blood pressure is checked once, it may be high due to anxiety. In a small number of cases, the remembrance that it was high once may lead to anxiety that in turn causes the blood pressure to rise. Some experience a rise in blood pressure just by looking at the blood pressure (sphygmomanometer) cuff. (See also DOCTORS, FEAR OF; HIGH BLOOD PRESSURE, FEAR OF.)

Pickering, Thomas G. et al., "How Common Is White Coat Hypertension?" *Journal of the American Medical Association* (January 8, 1988), pp. 225–228.

white, fear of the color Fear of the color white is known as leukophobia. To some individuals, paleness may represent ill health. White may also symbolize virginity to some individuals who fear virginity or chastity. White may also represent ghosts to those who fear the supernatural. (See also COLORS, FEAR OF.)

wigs, fear of Individuals who are phobic about wigs may become so frightened that they cannot come close to anyone wearing a wig or other false hairpiece. Wigs may be disturbing because they represent artificiality or disguise or because they resemble severed scalps. For some, hair has deep psychological associations. For example, some associate hair with youth, life, the seat of the soul, and strength; lack of hair represents aging, sacrifice, and punishment. Thus they find anything that covers, confines, or substitutes for hair may be distasteful. Fears of wigs may be closely related to fear of hair in general, or fear of damage to the hair. (See also HAIR, FEAR OF.)

Jobes, Gertrude, *Dictionary of Mythology, Folklore and Symbols.* (New York: Scarecrow Press, 1961).

Marks, Isaac M., *Living With Fear* (New York: McGraw-Hill, 1978).

will therapy A form of psychotherapy. Will therapy was introduced by Otto Rank, an Austrian psychoanalyst (1884–1939), in 1936. Rank viewed therapy as a way to free the individual from anxieties and fears and enable him or her to become independent and responsible, take risks, and achieve an ability for self-expression. He viewed life as a struggle to separate oneself psychologically from the mother, just as one is separated physically during birth. Rank viewed human behavior as derived from an innate condition of conflict between patterns of dependence and independence. Fear develops if one pattern predominates. For example, if independence (self-assertion) predominates, fear of isolation, being alone, and losing love develops. Guilt is also a byproduct of independence as individuals perceive themselves rejecting others. Will therapy is also known as Rankian therapy. This viewpoint on therapy has influenced many different approaches to HUMANISTIC PSYCHOLOGY. (See also BIRTH TRAUMA; CHARACTER TRAINING APPROACHES.)

wind, fear of Fear of wind is known as aerophobia or anemophobia. Individuals who fear wind may also fear all movement of air, such as tornadoes and hurricanes. They may fear being out of control and may be afraid that they will be pushed over by a strong wind and not be able to get to safety. They may fear falling or being helpless. Some fear injury from getting particles in their eyes during a windstorm. Some who fear wind also fear all types of inclement weather, such as rain, snow, or sleet. (See also HURRICANE, FEAR OF; TORNADO, FEAR OF.)

wine, fear of Fear of wine is known as oenophobia or oinophobia. Some individuals who fear drinking wine fear becoming intoxicated or alcoholic. They may fear being out of control and perhaps doing something to embarrass themselves or others. (See also INTOXICATION, FEAR OF.)

winged things, fear of Many people fear winged things, such as birds, bats, and flying insects because their quick, unpredictable movements simulate attack. Phobics react to this fear by keeping their houses closed to the point of discomfort, carrying umbrellas, or avoiding the out-of-doors and enclosed spaces where they might become trapped with a flying animal or insect. (See also BATS, FEAR OF; BEES, FEAR OF; BIRDS, FEAR OF; FLYING THINGS, FEAR OF; INSECTS, FEAR OF; WASPS, FEAR OF.)

Kent, Fraser, *Nothing to Fear: Coping with Phobias* (Garden City, NY: Doubleday, 1977).

Melville, Joy, *Phobias and Obsessions* (New York: Coward, McCann and Geoghegan, 1977).

Winnicott, Donald W. (1896–1971) British pediatrician and psychoanalyst considered as a part of the British school of psychoanalysis. He was president of the British Psychoanalytic Society and wrote extensively on the areas of psychoanalysis and child analysis. Winnicott introduced many psychoanalytic viewpoints into his work with children's anxieties, including the concepts of the child's TRANSITIONAL OBJECT (an object an infant selects because of its anxiety-reducing qualities, such as a soft doll or security blanket), the child's relationship with his or her mother, and the importance of maternal holding and mirroring of the infant's emotional states.

witches and witchcraft, fear of Historically, many individuals have feared witches and witchcraft because witches appear to be inherently evil and have mystical powers. Witches usually have been women, but male witches, known as warlocks, have also been feared. The term witchcraft derives from the Saxon word *wicca,* a contraction of witega, a prophet or wise person. Beliefs that have led to persistent fears include the notions that witches can inflict misfortune and a state of demonic possession on their victims, fly through the air, become invisible, appear in spectral form as seductive women or men, eat human flesh and have a mysterious link with animals. Some have believed that witches possessed the power of the EVIL EYE and that they could change winds to adversely affect sailors, cause the neighbor's wheat to rot, control certain animals, and turn themselves into animals. Witches were believed to possess the power to make themselves invisible by means of magic given to them by the devil, and of harming others by thrusting nails into a waxen image representing them. Other beliefs include notions that witches can be identified by marks on their bodies and by the use of tests and ordeals.

Witchcraft was at times associated with religious heresy, condemned in the Bible and by religious authorities. In some cultures, witches were thought to be in league with the Devil, and to have had sexual intercourse with the Devil.

Beliefs in witches have persisted in part because such beliefs were a way to handle social strain and competition in primitive societies. Witchcraft provided a fear inducement for social control and promoted conformity within the society. Witchcraft provided an explanation for misfortune, which, unlike other systems of metaphysical belief, provided an opportunity for redress of wrongs. Beliefs in witches have also served a social and political purpose by punishing incompetent behavior and discouraging begging. (See also DELUSIONS; HALLUCINATIONS; INCUBUS; SUCCUBUS; SUPERNATURAL, FEAR OF.)

Cavendish, Richard, *Encyclopedia of the Unexplained,* (New York: McGraw-Hill, 1974).
Davison, Gerald C. and John M. Neale, *Abnormal Psychology,* (New York: John Wiley, 1986).
Mair, Lucy, "Witchcraft," in Leslie Shepard (Ed.), *Encyclopedia of Occultism and Parapsychology* (Detroit: Gale, 1984).
Keith, Thomas, "Witchcraft," in R. Cavendish (Ed.), *Man, Myth and Magic* (Freeport, NY: M. Cavendish, 1983).

withdrawal effects of addictive substances Many people fear the effects of withdrawing from an addictive substance, whether they are using drugs on a abusive or therapeutic basis. There is a good basis for this fear because a series of symptoms often appears when a drug on which the user is physically dependent is abruptly stopped or severely reduced. Withdrawal symptoms occur most consistently in cases of addiction to central nervous system depressants or narcotics. Symptoms are usually opposite to the usual effects of the drugs (a rebound effect).

Intensity and duration of withdrawal symptoms usually depends on the susceptibility of the individual, properties of the particular drug, and the degree of addiction. Usually, shorter-acting substances, such as heroin, cause more rapidly developing, shorter, and more severe withdrawal symptoms than longer-lasting, more slowly eliminated drugs, such as methadone. If administered during heroin withdrawal, methadone can ease the intensity of the withdrawal experience.

Many people experience withdrawal symptoms after taking tranquilizers and other sedatives on a prescription basis. Withdrawal symptoms from depressants (barbiturates, SEDATIVES, and tranquilizers) may occur within a few hours after the drug is stopped. Physical weakness, anxiety, nausea and vomiting, dizziness, sleeplessness, hallucinations, delirium, delusions, and convulsions may occur as long as three days to a week following withdrawal and may last for many days. Withdrawal from the minor tranquilizers is similar but may take longer to develop. Not all symptoms that emerge after taking tranquilizers are withdrawal effects. Some may be anxiety that was repressed by the medications.

While certain substances, such as stimulant drugs (AMPHETAMINE and CAFFEINE), are considered more psychologically than physically addictive, sudden abstinence may produce withdrawal effects. These may include headache, stomach cramps, lethargy, chronic fatigue, and possibly severe emotional depression.

Individuals taking tricyclic ANTIDEPRESSANTS or MAO inhibitors should be aware that use of these drugs should be tapered off to avoid withdrawal reactions. If symptoms of withdrawal occur, the drugs may be reinstated temporarily and then tapered off even more gradually. The longer the period of use, the likelier there are to be withdrawal effects. (See also ADDICTION, FEAR OF; DEPRESSION; DRUG DEPENDENCE; LITHIUM; MANIC–DEPRESSIVE DISORDER.)

O'Brien, R and S. Cohen, *The Encyclopedia of Drug Abuse* (New York: Facts On File, 1984).

Wolf Man, case of A well-known case of animal phobia, documented in the writings of SIGMUND FREUD. In the case titled "From the History of an Infantile Neurosis," Freud analyzed the reasons for a young man's childhood animal phobia, religious obsession with conflicting blasphemous thoughts, and sudden change to unruly behavior. A key point in the analysis revealed a dream about wolves with fairy-tale symbolism. Using this dream, Freud attributed the young man's mental instability to early sexual experiences and observations and an erotic attachment to his father.

Freud, Sigmund, *The Standard Edition of the Complete Psychological Works of Sigmund Freud,* vol. XVII, (London: Hogarth Press, 1955).

Kaplan, Harold I. and Benjamin J. Sadock, *Comprehensive Textbook of Psychiatry* (Baltimore: Williams and Wilkins, 1985).

Wolpe, Joseph (1915–) An American psychiatrist who discovered that phobics could be desensitized if they were trained to relax and gradually confront the phobia in their imaginations. He developed a theory of "RECIPROCAL INHIBITION" (that two opposing emotions cannot be experienced at the same time) and designed such contemporary therapies as assertiveness training, sexual therapies, and aversive conditioning from this theme.

women, fear of Fear of women is known as gynophobia, gynephobia, and feminophobia. Some men who fear women may have a fear of heterosexual activity or sexual intercourse. From a psychiatric point of view, they may have an unresolved conflict with their own mothers and hence fear all women. They may fear marriage because they will feel confined or limited in their activities. (See also MARRIAGE, FEAR OF; WOMEN, FEAR OF BEAUTIFUL.)

women, fear of beautiful Fear of beautiful women is known as venustaphobia. (See also WOMEN, FEAR OF.)

woods, fear of Fear of woods is known as hylophobia. Some may fear being lost in the woods or being in the woods after dark. They may feel closed in when they are surrounded by tall trees. This fear may be related to fear of trees or fear of landscape that includes wooded areas. (See also LANDSCAPE, FEAR OF; TREES, FEAR OF.)

words, fear of Fear of words is known as verbophobia or logophobia. This may be a fear of hearing words in general or of specific words. Those who have this fear become anxious even at the thought of certain words. Some individuals fear certain words because they fear that they will stammer or stutter when they try to say them. (See also NAMES, FEAR OF; STUTTERING, FEAR OF; TALKING, FEAR OF.)

work, fear of Fear of work is known as ergasiophobia, ergophobia, and ponophobia. The term ergasiophobia also sometimes refers to fear of surgical operations.

worms, fear of Fear of worms is known as vermiphobia or scoleciphobia. Those who have this fear may avoid going into certain places, such as near rivers, swamps, or even out on rainy days because they fear the presence of worms. Fear of worms may be related to a fear of slimy things, slime, or of other small creatures that thrive in the water or ground, such as frogs, toads, and lizards. (See also FROGS, FEAR OF; SLIME, FEAR OF.)

worms, fear of infestation with Fear of infestation with worms is known as helminthophobia or vermiphobia. Some individuals fear eating certain foods, such as pork, because they fear infestation with worms. This fear is related to a fear of contamination and of disease. (See also CONTAMINATION, FEAR OF; GERMS, FEAR OF; PARASITES, FEAR OF; TRICHINOSIS, FEAR OF.)

worrying Worrying is a common expression or symptom of ANXIETY. Persons troubled about a past, present, or future event may worry. Worrying is characterized by a feeling of uneasiness and mental discomfort. Excessive or highly irrational worry may be a symptom of an anxiety disorder. Individuals who have OBSESSIVE–COMPULSIVE DISORDER worry excessively. It is often worry that leads them to perform certain

RITUALS such as repeated hand-washing or checking for locked doors. Individuals who have AGORAPHOBIA are commonly worriers, as are social phobics. Agoraphobics may worry that they will not be able to get to a secure place, while social phobics may worry that they will be seen not looking their best or will find themselves in an embarrassing situation. Furthermore, anxiety sufferers almost always worry in anticipation of a situation in which they may experience anxiety.

Phobics and those who have obsessive–compulsive disorder differ in the ways in which they worry. Phobics have persistent worries around one theme, such as their phobic object or situation, whereas obsessive–compulsives have repetitive worries that lead them to actions (such as checking repeatedly to see that the door is locked). Obsessive–compulsives worry about remote, abstract, and future consequences of contact with an evoking stimuli, while phobics worry more about coming into contact with a specifically feared object or situation. (See RUMINATION; SOCIAL PHOBIA.)

Marks, Isaac M. *Fears, Phobias and Rituals,* (New York: Oxford University Press, 1987).

wrinkles, fear of getting Fear of wrinkles or of getting wrinkles is known as rhytiphobia. The most feared wrinkles are those on the face, particularly around the eyes and mouth. Wrinkles are feared because they are a sign of AGING. Contemporary society places emphasis on youth as a standard of beauty, and many individuals, particularly women, fear losing their attractiveness because of wrinkles. Some who are so motivated seek reconstructive cosmetic surgery to remove wrinkles. (See also AGING, FEAR OF.)

writer's block Nearly all writers suffer from writer's block at some time, and many people fear that it will happen to them. Writer's block is a seeming inability to get started with a writing project, and, specifically, to set words down on paper. Anxiety about writing generally occurs before one begins to write; the hardest part of writing may be putting the first words down. Writer's block often includes many self-doubts. The writer may worry about the validity of his topic, his ability to communicate on paper, and acceptance by teachers, publishers, or readers.

Writer's block is sometimes difficult to recognize because it may hide behind other activities, such as procrastination. At the beginning of a writing project, one often thinks of many things to do except write. Overresearch is another symptom. One can always collect more information, visit one more library, or do one more interview as an excuse for staying away from the desk, typewriter, word processor, or paper and pencil.

The process of writing includes several steps: incubation, planning, research, organization, first draft, incubation, revision, and final draft. Before one starts, one unconsciously develops ideas and insights for the written material. This is the important incubation process. To bring these ideas out of the mind and onto paper and break writer's block, or overcome writer's anxiety, one must reach a state of relaxed, energized concentration in which one sets aside self-criticism and freely expresses creative thoughts.

There are a number of exercises one can perform to help reach the state of energized relaxation. Physical exercise energizes and is conducive to a relaxed state of mind. Meditation and imagery exercises are also very useful in reducing stress and minimizing the self-doubt that obstructs expression. Proper nutrition and enough sleep are similarly important to the writer.

Too much stress can paralyze the writer, and too little stress can lead to apathy. The ideal state of mind, the one that unblocks, is called "eustress," or good stress, by Hans Selye, the Canadian author well known for writing about subjects relating to stress. That middle point in the stress spectrum is the state of relaxed concentration accompanied by energy. Because writing is hard work, one must be in the right mental framework to take risks and have confidence and self-esteem regarding one's own talents.

Another useful measure in avoiding writer's block is staying away from people who are critical of one's work or ideas in the early stage of the writing project. While their criticisms may be helpful later, early in the project criticism may be inhibitory.

A writer is usually his or her own best critic, and also a source of writing anxiety. One cannot get rid of the internal critic, but one can negotiate with it. The aim in any project is to express before you become critical and evaluate. The internal critic wants to evaluate before you put the ideas on paper. To overcome writer's block, try to keep the internal critic hidden until the revision stage.

(Adapted with permission from Sloane, Beverly LeBov. *Town Hall of California Reporter* (March–April 1987), pp. 6–7.

writing, fear of Fear of writing is known as graphophobia. Some fear writing in public and having others observe as they write. They may fear criticism of their handwriting or of their posture while writing. Some fear writing anything at any time, because they do not want to commit their ideas to paper for others to see. Fear of writing is a SOCIAL PHOBIA and can be treated with behavior modification therapy. (See also BEHAVIOR THERAPY.)

X

X rays Fear of X rays is known as radiophobia. Many people refuse to have diagnostic X rays out of fear of harmful effects of radiation. This fear is becoming more prevalent as more people are aware of the possible effects of radiation. Dental X rays are part of routine dental examinations, and chest X rays are often part of routine physical examinations, particularly before admission to a hospital or before a surgical procedure. (See also RADIATION, FEAR OF.)

Xanax An anxiolythic and antidepressant drug. Chemically known as alprazolam, Xanax is a triazolobenzodiazepine belonging to the benzodiazepine class of drugs. It has antianxiety, antidepressant, and antipanic qualities. (See also ALPRAZOLAM; ANXIETY DRUGS; CORONARY BYPASS ANXIETY, POST-OPERATIVE; HEART ATTACK, ANXIETY FOLLOWING.)

xenophobia Fear of strangers. (See also STRANGERS, FEAR OF.)

xerophobia Fear of dryness. (See also DRYNESS, FEAR OF.)

xylophobia Fear of forests. (See also FORESTS, FEAR OF.)

Y

yoga as an anxiety reducer Many individuals attempt to reduce anxieties through yoga, a system of beliefs and practices first described comprehensively in the third century B.C. Yoga is a way to balance energy and thus achieve relaxation, absence of anxiety, and better functioning. The most well-known form of yoga in the United States in Hatha yoga, which emphasizes physical well-being and mental concentration through stretching and breath-control exercises.

Yoga proposes that the human ego produces attachments, dependencies, obsessions, and fantasies that in turn produce anxiety. Meditation reduces the effects of these anxiety-producing mental conditions not by fighting them, but by allowing the meditator to observe them in a state of detachment. Like other meditation techniques, yoga focuses on a higher level of consciousness than the ordinary waking state.

Yoga exercises and postures are based on the observation that an individual's mental state is reflected in his physical posture. Thus exercises are intended to promote self-awareness of the condition of the body. Stimulation of the spinal column and glands is thought to create a feeling of well-being. Concentration on breathing is central to yoga practice; breath control helps the individual conserve and focus energy. (See also TRANSCENDENTAL MEDITATION.)

Hassin, Vijay. *The Modern Yoga Handbook* (Garden City, NY: Doubleday, 1978), pp. 47–52.

Rama, Swami, Rudolph Ballentine and Swami Ajaya, *Yoga and Psychotherapy, the Evolution of Consciousness* (Glenview, IL: Himalayan Institute, 1976), pp. xx–13, 152–157.

young girls, fear of Fear of young girls is known as parthenophobia. (See also GIRLS, FEAR OF.)

Z

Zane, Manuel (1913–) An American psychiatrist and developer of CONTEXTUAL THERAPY, an EXPOSURE-THERAPY technique. Dr. Zane is associate clinical professor of psychiatry at New York Medical College, Valhalla, NY, an associate with White Plains Hospital Medical Center, White Plains, NY, and author of *Your Phobia: Understanding Your Fears through Contextual Therapy* (1984).

zelophobia Fear of jealousy. (See also JEALOUSY, FEAR OF.)

Zen therapy Zen is one of many anxiety-reducing meditative techniques. Some individuals who begin Zen meditation are sufferers from depression who have not found help from other self-help techniques or therapy. Zen has been helpful to many individuals who have a strong sense of their own internal control. Meditation may be effective because extreme emotions produce a hypnotic, exclusive state of mind that meditation helps to break down. Also, meditation helps the individual balance arousal, tranquility, and objective observation of behavior and thoughts.

Zen, derived from the Chinese word for meditation, emerged as a Buddhist movement in seventh-century China and evolved further as a Japanese practice. Two central concepts of Zen are the individual's ability to control his mind and the desirability of a state of detachment. An attitude common to the meditative techniques is that man's usual state of awareness is clouded and distorted with fantasies, emotions, and associations that produce many psychological problems and result from the lack of control of thought processes. Zen meditative techniques known as *zazen* are intended to break through this distortion of perception. Zen meditation is practiced with the eyes open, the back upright and unsupported, the whole body in a firmly balanced position. The *zazan* technique may be a controlled method of breathing or concentration on a *koan,* a nonrational problem put to the meditator by a teacher. An example of a *koan* is the question: "While we know the sound of two hands clapping, what is the sound of one hand clapping?" The meditator is to think about the *koan* but not to force himself if his thoughts wander. He should simply observe his own thoughts in a detached state. The goal of this technique is a breakthrough in thought process. A transcendental state of mind called *satori,* which is beyond thought and language, is the ultimate goal. A meditator who reaches this state is capable of accepting daily experience with a clear mind and without dwelling on the past or events over which he has no control. (See also TRANSCENDENTAL MEDITATION.)

Corsini, Raymond (ed.), *Handbook of Innovative Psychotherapies* (New York: John Wiley, 1981), pp. 470–488.

Goleman, Danile, ''Meditation without Mystery,'' *Psychology Today,* (March 1977), pp. 54+.

Shainberg, Lawrence, ''The Violence of 'Just Sitting,' '' *New York Times Magazine* (October 10, 1976), pp. 16+.

zombie, fear of becoming The fear of becoming a zombie results from the belief that a lifeless corpse can be reanimated by magic and continue a robotlike existence under the control of the person who revived it. The belief is founded in the set of superstitions surrounding the voodoo religion of Haiti, which originated in African tribal tradition. Practitioners of voodoo believe that a voodoo priest can raise a dead corpse from the grave to create a zombie. Thus special burial precautions are taken, such as sewing the mouth of the body closed to prevent the spirit from escaping. Another belief that frightens many people is that a sorcerer can draw out a man's soul, cause his death, and subsequently have him in his power.

A recent expedition to Haiti uncovered a rational explanation for fear of becoming a zombie. Soom voodoo experts know the secret of using a certain kind of poison from the puffer fish. The poison creates a condition simulating death. The victim is buried, exhumed, and, because the poison suppresses the activity of certain areas of the brain, the ''corpse'' continues his existence as a zombie. (See also VOODOO, FEAR OF.)

Cavendish, Richard (ed.), *Man, Myth and Magic,* (New York: Marshall Cavendish, 1983), ''Zombie.''

Encyclopedia of Occultism and Parapsychology (Detroit: Gale Research, 1984), ''Zombie.''

Hill, Douglas and Pat Williams, *The Supernatural,* (New York: Hawthorn Books, 1965), pp. 294–295.

zometapine An antidepressant drug. (See also ANTIDEPRESSANTS, NEW; DEPRESSION.)

zoophobia Fear of animals (See also ANIMALS, FEAR OF.)

BIBLIOGRAPHY

Adams, Henry E. and Patricia B. Sutker, *Comprehensive Handbook of Psychopathology*. New York: Plenum Press, 1984.

Adams, P.L., *Obsessive Children: A Sociopsychiatric Study*. New York: Brunner/Mazel, 1973.

Agras, S., D. Sylvester and D. Oliveau, "The Epidemiology of Common Fears and Phobias," *Comprehensive Psychiatry*, 10(1969):151–156.

Agras, W.S., *Panic: Facing Fears, Phobias and Anxiety*. New York: Freeman, 1985.

———et al., "The Natural History of Phobia: Course and Prognosis," *Archives of General Psychiatry*, 26(1972):315–317.

Agulnik, P.L., "The Spouse of the Phobic Patient," *British Journal of Psychiatry*, 117(1970):59–67.

Aitken, R.C.B. et al., "Identification of Features Associated with Flying Phobias in Aircrew," *British Journal of Psychiatry*, 139(1981):38–42.

———, "Treatment of Flying Phobia in Aircrew," *American Journal of Psychotherapy*, 25:4(1971):530–542.

Akhtar, S. et al., "Phenomenological Analysis of Symptoms in Obsessive–Compulsive Neurosis, *British Journal of Psychiatry*, 127(1975):342–348.

Allport, G.S., "Attitudes," in C. Murchison (ed.), *Handbook of Social Psychology*. Worcester, Mass.: Clark University Press, 1935.

Allsopp, L.F., G.L. Cooper and P.H. Poole, "Clomipramine and Diazepam for Agoraphobia and Social Phobia in General Practice," *Current Medical Research Opinion*, 9(1984):64–70.

Altesman, R.I. and J.O. Cole, "Psychopharmacologic Treatment of Anxiety," *Journal of Clinical Psychiatry*, 44(1983):12–18.

American Medical Association, *AMA Drug Evaluation*. Chicago: American Medical Association, 1980.

American Psychiatric Association, *Diagnostic and Statistical Manual of Mental Disorders*, rev. 3rd ed. Washington, D.C.: American Psychiatric Association, 1988.

———, *Psychiatric Glossary*. Washington, D.C.: American Psychiatric Association, 1988.

Amies, P.L., M.G. Gelder and P.M. Shaw, "Social Phobia: A Comparative Clinical Study," *British Journal of Psychiatry*, 142(1983):174–179.

Angelino, H., J. Dollins and E.V. Mech, "Trends in the Fears and Worries of School Children," *Journal of Genetic Psychology*, 89(1956):263–267.

Appleby, I.L., D.F. Klein, E.J. Sachar and M. Levitt, "Biomedical Indices of Lactate-induced Panic," in D.F. Klein and J.J. Rabkin (eds.), *Anxiety: New Research and Changing Concepts.* New York: Raven, 1981.

Aronson, Marvin L., *How To Overcome Your Fear of Flying.* New York: Hawthorn Books, 1971.

Aronson, Thomas and Camille Logue "On the Longitudinal Course of Panic Disorder," *Comprehensive Psychiatry,* 28:4(July-August 1987), pp. 344–353.

Arrindell, W.A., "A Factorial Definition of Agoraphobia," *Behavior Research and Therapy,* 18(1980):229–242.

———, "Psychological Profile of the Spouse of the Female Agoraphobic Patient," *British Journal of Psychiatry,* 146(1985):405–414.

———, "Marital Adjustment, Intimacy and Needs in Female Agoraphobics and Their Partners," *British Journal of Psychiatry,* 149(1986):592–602.

Arrindell, W.A. and P.M.G. Emmelkamp, "A Test of the Repression Hypothesis in Agoraphobics," *Psychological Medicine* 15(1985):125–129.

Arrindell, W.A., P.M.G. Emmelkamp, A. Monsma and E. Brilman, "Perceived Parental Rearing Practices in Phobic Disorders," *British Journal of Psychiatry,* 143(1983):183–187.

Arrindell, W.A., P.M.G. Emmelkamp and J. Van der Ende, "Phobic Dimensions across Samples, Gender and Nations," *Advanced Behaviour Research and Therapy,* 6(1984):207–254.

Asberg, M., P. Thoren and L. Bertilsson, "Clomipramine Treatment of Obsessive–Compulsive Disorder: Biochemical and Clinical Aspects," *Psychopharmacology Bulletin,* 18(1982):13–21.

Asch, Stuart S., "Claustrophobia and Depression," *Journal of the American Psychoanalytic Association,* 14(1966):711–729.

Ascher, L.M., "Employing Paradoxical Intention in the Treatment of Agoraphobia," *Behavior Research and Therapy,* 19(1981):533–542.

Ashem, B., "The Treatment of Disaster Phobia by Systematic Desensitization," *Behavior Research and Therapy,* 1(1963):81–84.

Azima, A. and E.D. Wittkower, "A Case of Spider Phobia: Treatment with Drugs," *Psychoanalytic Quarterly,* 26(1957).

Babcock, H.H. and D.H. Powell, "Vasovagal Fainting: Deconditioning an Autonomic Syndrome," *Psychosomatics,* 23(1982):969–973.

Baer, B.L., W.E. Minichielli and M.A. Jenika, "Behavioral Treatment in Two Cases of OCD with Concomitant Bipolar Affective Disorder," *American Journal of Psychiatry,* 142(1985):358–360.

Bagby, E., "The Etiology of Phobias," *Journal of Abnormal Psychology,* 17(1922):16–18.

Ba' iracli-Levy, Juliette O., *The Illustrated Herbal Handbook.* New York: Schocken Books, 1974.

Baker, H. and U. Wills, "School Phobia: Classification and Treatment," *British Journal of Psychiatry,* 132(1978):492–499.

———, "School Phobia Children at Work," *British Journal of Psychiatry,* 135(1979):561–564.

Ballenger, James C., *Biology of Agoraphobia.* Washington, D.C.: American Psychiatric Press, 1984.

———, "Panic Disorder and Agoraphobia." Conference on the brain and the heart: Psychiatric Complications of Cardiovascular Disease. Duke University Medical Center, November 14, 1985.

———, "Pharmacotherapy of the Panic Disorders," *Journal of Clinical Psychiatry,* 47:6 (June 1986), pp. 27–32.

Ballenger, J., G. Burrows, R.T. Rubin et al., "Alprazolam Treatment of Agoraphobia/Panic Attacks," *Abstracts of the World Congress of Biological Psychiatry,* (Abstract 302.6, p. 227). Held in Philadelphia, September 1985.

Ballenger, J.C., G. Burrows and R. Swinson, "Alprazolam for Panic Disorder," in *Abstracts of the APA Annual Conference* (Abstract NP83). Held in Dallas, May 1985.

Ballenger, J., R.M. Post, D.C. Jimerson et al., "Neurobiological Correlates of Depression and Anxiety in Normals." In R.M. Post and J.C. Ballenger (eds.), *Neurobiology of Mood Disorders.* London: Williams & Wilkins, 1984.

Ballenger, J.C., R.M. Post, D.C. Jimerson et al., "Norepinephrine and Epinephrine in Agoraphobia," in *Abstracts of the APA Annual Meeting* (Paper 30D, p. 82).

Bamber, J.H., "The Fears of Adolescents," *Journal of Genetic Psychology,* 125(1974):127–140.

———, *The Fears of Adolescents.* London: Academic Press, 1979.

Bandura, A., "Self-Efficacy Determinants of Anticipated Fears and Calamities," *Journal of Personality and Social Psychology,* 45(1983):464–469.

———, "Self-Efficacy: Toward a Unifying Theory of Behavioral Change," *Psychological Review,* 84(1977):191–215.

———, *Principles of Behavior Modification.* New York: Holt, Rinehart & Winston, 1969.

Bandura, A., N.E. Adams and J. Beyer, "Cognitive Processes Mediating Behavioral Change," *Journal of Personality and Social Psychology,* 35(1977):125–139.

Barlow, D.H., "The Causes of Anxiety and Panic Attacks." Albany: The Center for Stress and Anxiety Disorders, Phobia and Anxiety Disorders Clinic, 1987.

———, "The Dimensions of Anxiety Disorders," in H. Tuma and J. Maser (eds.), *Anxiety and Anxiety Disorders.* Hillsdale, N.J.: Erlbaum, 1985.

———, "Couples Treatment for Agoraphobia." Paper presented at the 13th annual convention of the Association for the Advancement of Behavior Therapy, San Francisco, December 1979

Barlow, D., L.R. Hay and M. Mavissakalian, "Couples Treatment of Agoraphobia: Changes in Marital Satisfaction," *Behavior Research and Therapy,* 19(1981):245–255.

Barlow, D.H., G.T. O'Brien and C.G. Last, "Couples Treatment of Agoraphobia," *Behavior Therapy,* 15(1984):41–58.

Barlow, D.H., J. Vermilyea, E.B. Blanchard, B.B. Vermilyea, P.A. Di Nardo and J.A. Cerny, "The Phenomenon of Panic," *Journal of Abnormal Psychology,* 94(1985):320–328.

Barlow, D.H. and M.T. Waddell, "Agoraphobia," in Barlow (ed.), *Clinical Handbook of Psychological Disorders.* New York: Guilford Press, 1985.

Bauer, D.H., "An Exploratory Study of Developmental Changes in Children's Fears," *Journal of Child Psychology and Psychiatry,* 17(1976):69–74.

Beck, A.T., *Cognitive Therapy and the Emotional Disorders.* New York: International Universities Press, 1976.

———, *Depression: Causes and Treatment.* Philadelphia: University of Pennsylvania Press, 1967.

Beck, A.T. and G. Emery, *Anxiety Disorders and Phobias: A Cognitive Perspective.* New York: Basic Books, 1985.

Beck, A.T., A.J. Rush, B.F. Shaw and G. Emery, *Cognitive Therapy of Depression.* New York: The Guildford Press, 1979.

Becker, J., R.M. Doctor, M. Miranda and J. Wallace, "Cognitive-Perceptual Style and Verbal Conditioning," *Journal of Perceptual and Motor Skills,* 32(1971):631–636.

Beidel, D.C., S.M. Turner and C.V. Dancu, "Physiological, Cognitive and Behavioral Aspects of Social Anxiety," *Behavior Research and Therapy,* 23(1985):109–117.

Bennun, Ian, "A Composite Formulation of Agoraphobia," *American Journal of Psychotherapy,* 40:2(April 1986).

Benson, H., *Beyond the Relaxation Response.* New York: Times Books, 1984.

Benson, H., *The Mind/Body Effect.* New York: Simon and Schuster, 1979.

Berg, I., "Teenage School Refusers Grow Up: A Ten-Year Follow-up of 168 Inpatients," *British Journal of Psychiatry,* 147(1985):366–370.

———, "School Phobia in the Children of Agoraphobic Women," *British Journal of Psychiatry,* 128(1976):86–89.

———, "School Phobia—Its Classification and Relationship to Dependency," *Journal of Child Psychology and Psychiatry* 10(1969):123–141.

Berg, I., I.M. Marks and R. McGuire, "School Phobia and Agoraphobia," *Psychological Medicine,* 4(1974):428–434.

Berg, I. and R. McGuire, "Are School Phobic Adolescents Overdependent?" *British Journal of Psychiatry,* 119(1971):167–168.

Berggren, U., A. Linde, "Dental Fear and Avoidance: Two Modes of Treatment," *Journal of Dental Research,* 63(1984):1223–1227.

Bergler, Edmund, "A New Approach to the Therapy of Erythrophobia," *Psychoanalytic Quarterly,* 13(1944).

Bernadt, M.W., T. Silverstone and W. Singleton, "Beta-adrenergic Blockade in Phobic Subjects," *British Journal of Psychiatry,* 137(1980):452–457.

Berney, T., I. Kolvin, S.R. Bhate et al., "School Phobia: Clomipramine and Short-term Outcome," *British Journal of Psychiatry,* 138:(1981):10–118.

Bernsted, L., R. Luggin and B. Petersson, "Psychosocial Considerations of the Premenstrual Syndrome," *Acta Psychiatrica Scandinavia,* 69(1984):455–460.

Bernstein, I.L., and M.M. Webster, "Learned Taste Aversions in Humans," *Physiology and Behavior,* 25(1980):363–366.

Bettelheim, Bruno, *The Uses of Enchantment: The Meaning and Importance of Fairy Tales.* New York: Alfred A. Knopf, 1976.

Bianchi, G.N., "Origins of Disease Phobia," *Australian and New Zealand Psychiatry,* 5(1971):241–257.

Bibb, J.L. and D.L. Chambless, "Alcohol Use and Abuse Among Diagnosed Agoraphobics," *Behavior Research and Therapy,* 24(1986):49–58.

Biran, M. and G.T. Wilson, "Treatment of Phobic Disorders Using Cognitive and Exposure Methods: A Self-efficacy Analysis," *Journal of Consulting and Clinical Psychology,* 49(1981):886–899.

Birren, M., F. Augusto and G.T. Wilson, "In Vivo Exposure vs. Cognitive Restructuring in the Treatment of Scriptophobia," *Behavior Research and Therapy,* 19(1981):525–532.

Bland, K. and R.S. Hallam, "Relationship between Graded Exposure and Marital Satisfaction in Agoraphobics," *Personality and Individual Differences,* 1:(1981):282–287.

Bland, K. and R.S. Hallam, "Relationship between Response to Graded Exposure and Marital Satisfaction in Agoraphobics," *Behavior Research and Therapy,* 19(1981):335–338.

Boersma, K., S. Den Hengst, J. Dekker and P.M.G. Emmelkamp, "Exposure vs. Response Prevention in OC Patients," *Behavior Research and Therapy,* 14(1976):19–24.

Bolton, D., S. Collins and D. Steinberg, "The Treatment of Obsessive–Compulsive Disorder in Adolescence," *British Journal of Psychiatry,* 142(1983):456–464.

Bond, D.D., *The Love and Fear of Flying.* New York: International Universities Press, 1952.

Bonn, J.A., C.P. Readhead and B.H. Timmons, "Enhanced Adaptive Behavioural Response in Agoraphobics Pretreated with Breathing Retraining," *Lancet,* 2(1984):665–669.

Bootzin, Richard R., Elizabeth F. Loftus and Robert B. Zajonc, *Psychology Today*. New York: Random House, 1983.

Boss, Medard, *Existential Foundations of Medicine and Psychology*. New York: Jason Aronson, 1971.

———, *Psychoanalysis and Dasein-analysis*. New York: Basic Books, 1963.

Bowen, R. et al., "Relationship between Agoraphobia, Social Phobia and Blood-Injury Phobia," *Canadian Journal of Psychiatry*, 32(May 1987).

Bower, B., "Post-traumatic Stress Disorder: Hypnosis and the Divided Self," *Science News*, March 26, 1988.

Bowlby, John, *Loss*. New York: Basic Books, 1980.

Brasch, R., *Strange Customs*. New York: David McKay, 1976.

Breier, A., D.S. Charney and G.R. Heninger, "The Diagnostic Validity of Anxiety Disorders and Their Relationship to Depressive Illness," *The American Journal of Psychiatry*, 142(1985):787–797.

———, "Major Depression in Patients with Agoraphobia and Panic Disorder," *Archives of General Psychiatry*, 41(1984):1129–1135.

Breslin, Frances A., Kathryn R., Taylor and Stanley L. Brodsky, "Development of a Litigaphobia Scale: Measurement of Excessive Fear of Litigation," *Psychological Reports*, 58(1986):547–550.

Bromberg, W., *The Mind of Man: A History of Psychotherapy and Psychoanalysis*. New York: Harper and Row, 1959.

Bronson, G.W., "The Fear of Novelty," *Psychological Bulletin*, 69(1968):350–358.

———, "Fear of Visual Novelty: Developmental Patterns in Males and Females," *Developmental Psychology*, 2(1969):33–40.

Brooks, Frank P., "Anxiety and the Gastrointestinal System," pp. 19–21 in *Consequences of Anxiety: Management Strategies for the Primary Care Physician*. A clinical monograph based on a symposium held October 8–11, 1987, Orlando, Florida.

Brooks, J. and M. Lewis, "Infants' Responses to Strangers: Midget, Adult and Child," *Child Development*, 47(1976):323–332.

Brueschke, Erich E., "Case Study I: Application of a 'Decision Priorities' Algorithm to the Diagnosis of Anxiety," pp 37–38 in *Consequences of Anxiety: Management Strategies for the Primary Care Physician*. A clinical monograph based on a symposium held October 8–11, 1987, Orlando, Florida.

Bugelski, B. Richard and Anthony M. Graziano, *The Handbook of Practical Psychology*, Englewood Cliffs, N.J.: Prentice-Hall, 1980.

Buglass, D., J. Clark, A.S. Henderson, N. Kreitman and A.S. Presley, "A Study of Agoraphobic Housewives," *Psychological Medicine*, 7(1977):73–86

Burns, L.E., G.L. Thorpe, A. Cavallaro and J. Gosling, "Agoraphobia Eight Years after Behavioral Treatment," *Behavior Therapy* 17(1986):580–591.

Burrows, G.D., T.R. Newman and B. Davis (eds.), *Anti-anxiety Agents*. New York: Elsevier, 1984.

Burton, R., *The Anatomy of Melancholy*. New York: Farrar & Rinehart, 1927.

Butler, G., A Cullington, M. Munby, P. Amies and M. Gelder, "Exposure and Anxiety Management in the Treatment of Social Phobia," *Journal of Consulting and Clinical Psychology*, 52(1984):642–650.

Cammer, L., *Freedom from Compulsion*. New York: Simon & Schuster, 1976.

Campbell, Robert Jean, *Psychiatric Dictionary*. New York: Oxford University Press, 1981.

Carey, G., "Genetic Influences on Anxiety Neurosis and Agoraphobia," in R.J. Mathew (ed.), *The Biology of Anxiety*. New York: Brunner/Mazel, 1982.

Carey, G. and Gottesman, I., "Twin and Family Studies of Anxiety, Phobic and Obsessive Disorders," in D.F. Klein and J. Rabkin (eds.), *Anxiety: New Research and Changing Concepts*. New York: Raven, 1981.

Carr, D.B. and D.V. Sheehan, "Panic Anxiety: A New Biological Model," *Journal of Clinical Psychiatry*, 45(1984):323–330.

Cattell, R.B. and I.H. Scheirer, *The Meaning and Measurement of Neuroticism and Anxiety*. New York: Ronald Press, 1961.

Catts, S. and N. McConaghy, "Ritual Prevention in the Treatment of Obsessive–Compulsives," *Australian and New Zealand Journal of Psychiatry*, 9(1975):37–41.

Caudill, W. and L.T. Doi, "Interrelations of Psychiatry, Culture and Emotion in Japan," in I. Goldstein (ed.), *Man's Image in Medicine and Anthropology*. New York: International University Press, 1963.

Cavenar, Jesse O. and J. Ingram Walker, *Signs and Symptoms in Psychiatry*. Philadelphia: Lippincott, 1983.

Cavendish, Richard (ed.), *Man, Myth and Magic*. New York: Marshall Cavendish, 1983.

Cellucci, A.J. and P.S. Lawrence, "The Efficacy of Systematic Desensitization in Reducing Nightmares," *Journal of Behavior and Therapy Experimental Psychiatry*, 9:(1979):109–114.

Chambers, J., V.K. Yeragani and M.S. Keshavan, "Phobias in India and the United Kingdom," *Acta Psychiatrica Scandinavica*, 74(1986):388–391.

Chambless, D.L., "The Relationship of Severity of Agoraphobia to Associated Psychopathology," *Behavior Research and Therapy*, 23(1985):305–310.

Chambless, D.L., G.C. Caputo, P. Bright and R. Gallagher, "Fear of Fear in Agoraphobics," *Journal of Consulting and Clinical Psychology*, 52(1984):1090–1097.

Chambless, D.L., E.G. Foa, G.A. Groves and A.J. Goldstein, "Exposure and Communications Training in the Treatment of Agoraphobia," *Behavior Research and Therapy,* 20(1982):219–231.

Chambless, D.L., E.B. Foa, G.A. Groves and A. Goldstein, "Flooding with Brevital in the Treatment of Agoraphobia: Countereffective?" *Behavior Therapy,* 17(1979):243–251.

Chambless, D.L. and A.J. Goldstein (eds.), *Agoraphobia: Multiple Perspectives on Theory and Treatment.* New York: John Wiley, 1983.

———, "Clinical Treatment of Agoraphobia," in M. Mavissakalian and D.H. Barlow (eds.), *Phobia: Psychological and Pharmacological Treatment.* New York: Guildford, 1981.

Charney, D.S., G.R. Heninger and A. Breier, "Noradrenergic Function in Panic Anxiety: Effects of Yohimbine in Healthy Subjects and Patients with Agoraphobia and Panic Disorder," *Archives of General Psychiatry,* 41(1984):751–763.

Charney, D.S., G.R. Heninger and D.D. Redmond, "Yohimbine-induced Anxiety and Increased Noradrenergic Function in Humans: Effects of Diazepam and Clonidine," *Life Sciences,* 33(1983):19–29.

Chazan, M., "School Phobia," *British Journal of Educational Psychology,* 32(1962):109–217.

Chhabra, S. and Dorothy Fielding, "The Treatment of Scriptophobia by In Vivo Exposure and Cognitive Restructuring," *The Journal of Behavior Therapy and Experimental Psychiatry,* 16(1985):265–269.

Cirlot, J.E., *A Dictionary of Symbols.* New York: Philosophical Library, 1962.

Clark, D.M., P.M. Salkovskis and A.J. Chalkley, "Respiratory Control as a Treatment for Panic Attacks," *Journal of Behavior Therapy and Experimental Psychiatry,* 16(1985):23–30.

Clark, E.M. and D.R. Hemsley, "Hyperventilation; Individual Variability and Its Relation to Personality," *Journal of Behavior Therapy and Experimental Psychiatry,* 13(1982):41–47.

Cobb, J.P., R.M. McDonald, I.M. Marks and R.S. Stern, "Marital versus Exposure Treatment for Combined Marital and Phobic Obsessive Problems," *Behavior Analysis and Modification,* 4(1980):3–16.

Cohen, S., "Alcoholism in the Elderly," *Canadian Family Physician,* 34(March 1988).

Cohen, S. and J. Reed "Treatment of 'Nervous Diarrhoea' and Other Conditioned Autonomic Disorders by Desensitization," *British Journal of Psychiatry,* 114(1968):1275–1280.

Cohn, C.F., R.E. Kron and J.P. Brady, "A Case of Blood-Illness-Injury Phobia Treated Behaviourally," *Journal of Nervous and Mental Disorders,* 162(1976):65–68.

Cole, W.C. "Group Psychotherapy As An Aid in the Medical Treatment of Eczema," *Journal of the American Academy of Dermatology,* 18:2(February 1988), pp. 286–291.

Coleman, J., J. Batcher and R. Carson, *Abnormal Psychology and Modern Life.* Glenview, Illinois: Scott, Foresman, 1984.

Connolly, F.H. and M. Gipson, "Dysmorphophobia—A Long-term Study," *British Journal of Psychiatry,* 132(1978):568–570.

Conolly, J., *An Inquiry Concerning the Indications of Insanity.* London: Lawson's, 1964.

Connolly, J. C., R.S. Hallam and I.M. Marks, "Selective Association of Fainting with Blood-Injury-Illness Fear," *Behavior Therapy,* 7(1976):8–13.

Corsini, Raymond J. (ed.), *Encyclopedia of Psychology.* New York: John Wiley, 1984.

Coryell, W., "Obsessive-Compulsive Disorder and Primary Unipolar Depression," *Journal of Nervous and Mental Disorders,* 169(1981):220–224.

Coryell, W., R. Noyes and J. Clancy, "Panic Disorder and Primary Unipolar Depression: A Comparison of Background and Outcome," *Journal of Affective Disorders,* 5(1983):311–317.

Costa, E., "BZ/GABA Interactions: The Neurobiology of Anxiety," in H. Tuma and J. Maser (eds.), in *Anxiety and Anxiety Disorders.* Hillsdale, N.J.: Erlbaum, 1985.

Costello, C.G., "Fear and Phobias in Women: A Community Study," *Journal of Abnormal Psychology,* 91(1982):280–286.

Cowley, D.S., S.R. Dager and D.L. Dunner, "Lactate Panic in Primary Depression," in *Abstracts of the World Congress of Biological Psychiatry* (Abstract 242.1). Philadelphia, September 1985.

Croake, J.W., "Fears of Children," *Human Development,* 12(1969):239–247.

Croake, J.W. and F.H. Knox "The Changing Nature of Children's Fears," *Child Study Journal,* 3(1973):91–105.

Crowe, M.J., I.M. Marks, W.S. Agras and H. Leitenberg, "Time-limited Desensitization, Implosion and Shaping for Phobic Patients," *Behavior Research and Therapy,* 10(1972):319.

Crowe, R.R., "Panic Attacks in Family Members of Patients with Mitral Valve Prolapse," in *Abstracts of APA Annual Conference* (p. 70). Held in Toronto, May 1982.

Crowe, R.R., G. Gaffney and R. Kerber, "Panic Attacks in Families of Patients with Mitral Valve Prolapse," *Journal of Affective Disorders,* 4(1982):121–125.

Crowe, R.R., R. Noyes, D.L. Pauls and D. Slymen, "A Family Study of Panic Disorder," *Archives of General Psychiatry,* 40(1983):1065–1069.

Crowe, R.R., D.L. Pauls, R.E. Kerber and R. Noyes, "Panic Disorders and Mitral Valve Prolapse," pp. 103–116 in D.F. Klein and J. Rabkin (eds.), *Anxiety: New Research and Changing Concepts.* New York: Raven, 1981.

Cummings, J.D., "The Incidence of Emotional Symptoms in School Children," *British Journal of Educational Psychology,* 14(1944):151–161.

———, "A Followup Study of Emotional Symptoms in School Children," *British Journal of Educational Psychology,* 16(1946):163–177.

Curtis, G.C., O.G. Cameron and R.M. Nesse, "The Dexamethasone Suppression Test in Panic Disorder and Agoraphobia," *American Journal of Psychiatry,* 139(1982):1043–1046.

Curtis, G.C. and B. Thyer, "Fainting on Exposure to Phobic Stimuli," *American Journal of Psychiatry,* 140(1983):771–774.

Dackis, C.A., A.L.C. Potash and M.S. Gold, "DST Testing of Depressed Agoraphobics," in *Abstracts of the World Congress of Biological Psychiatry* (No. 148.3). Philadelphia, September 1985.

Daniels, Cora Linn and C.M. Stevans, *Encyclopedia of Superstitions, Folklore and the Occult Sciences of the World.* Detroit: Gale Research Company, 1971.

Davidson, J., M. Swartz, M. Sworck et al., "A Diagnostic and Family Study of Post-traumatic Stress Disorder," *American Journal of Psychiatry,* 142(1985):90–93.

Davis, John M. and David L. Garver, "Psychobiology of Affective Disorders," in *Current Concepts.* Kalamazoo, Michigan: Upjohn Company, 1978.

Davison, Gerald C. and John M. Neale, *Abnormal Psychology.* New York: Wiley & Sons, 1986.

Davison, S., "School Phobia as a Manifestation of Family Disturbance," *Journal of Child Psychology and Psychiatry,* 1(1961):270–287.

Dawson, R.W., "Comparative Contributions of Cognitive Behaviour Therapy Strategies in the Treatment of Speech Anxiety," *Australian Journal of Psychology,* 34(1982):297–308.

Dealy, R.S., D.M. Ishiki, D.H. Avery, L.G. Wilson and D.L. Dunner, "Secondary Depression in Anxiety Disorders," *Comparative Psychiatry,* 22(1981):612–618.

Dean, R.D. and K.M. Whitaker, "Fear of Flying: Impact on the U.S. Air Travel Industry," *Journal of Travel Research,* 21:1(1982).

Delaney, Janice, *The Curse: A Cultural History of Menstruation.* New York: E.P. Dutton, 1976.

Delmonte, M.S. and V. Kenny, "An Overview of the Therapeutic Effects of Meditation," *Psychologia,* 28(1985):189–202.

De Silva, P. and S. Rachman, "Does Escape Behaviour Strengthen Agoraphobic Avoidance?: A Preliminary Study," *Behavior Research and Therapy,* 22(1984):87–91.

———, "Exposure and Fear-Reduction," *Behavior Research and Therapy,* 21(1983):151–152.

Deutsch, Albert and H. Fishman, *The Encyclopedia of Mental Health.* New York: Franklin Watts, 1963.

Devereux, R.B., M.K. Shear, R. Kramer-Fox, N. Hartman, E. Lutas and W.T. Brown, "Mitral Valve Prolapse: An Overview." Paper to APA, Dallas, May 1985.

Doctor, Ronald M., "Pretreatment Survey of Agoraphobics," pp. 203–214 in R.L. DuPont (ed.), *Phobia: Summary of Modern Treatments.* New York: Brunner/Mazel, 1982.

———, "Locus of Control of Reinforcement and Responsiveness to Social Influence," *Journal of Personality,* 39(1971):542–551.

———, "Bias Effects and Awareness in Studies of Verbal Conditioning," *Experimental Research in Personality*, 5(1971):243–256.

Doctor, R.M. and F. Altman, "Worry and Emotionality as Components of Test Anxiety: Replication and Further Data," *Psychological Reports*, 24(1969):563–568.

Doctor, R.M., J. Aponte, A. Burry and R. Welch, "Group Counseling versus Behavior Therapy in Treatment of College Underachievement," *Behavior Research and Therapy*, 8(1970):87–89.

Doctor, R.M. and W. Craine, "The Effects of Social Reinforcement and Generalization on Argot Language Usage of Primary and Neurotic Psychopaths," *Journal of Abnormal Psychology*, 77(1971):175–180.

Doctor, R.M., J.M. Goldenring, E. Chivian et al., "Self-reports of Soviet and American Children on Worry about the Threat of Nuclear War," *Political Psychology*, 9(1988):13–21.

Doctor, R.M. and E. Singer, "Behavioral Intervention Strategies with Child Abusive Parents: A Home Intervention Program," *International Journal of Child Abuse and Neglect* (1979).

Dratcu, L., L. da Costa Ribeiro and H.M. Calil, "Depression Assessment in Brazil," *British Journal of Psychiatry* 150(1987):797–800.

Dunsworth, F.A., "Phobias in Children," *Journal of the Canadian Psychiatry Association*, 6(1961):191–294.

DuPont, R.L. (ed.), *Phobia: A Comprehensive Survey of Modern Treatments*. New York: Bruner/Mazel, 1982.

duSaulle, L., "De l'agoraphobie," *Practicien*, 8(1895)208–210.

Eaton, W.W. and J. McLeod, "Consumption of Coffee and Tea and Symptoms of Anxiety," *American Journal of Public Health*, 74(1984):66–68.

Ehlers, A., J. Margraf, W.T. Roth et al., "Lactate Infusions and Panics in Patients and Controls," *Psychiatric Research*, 17(1986):295–308.

Eitinger, L., "Anxiety in Concentration Camp Survivors," *Australian and New Zealand Journal of Psychiatry*, 3(1969):348–351.

Elmore, R.T., R.W. Wildman, and J.S. Westefeld, "Systematic Desensitization for Blood Phobia," *Journal of Behavior Therapy and Experimental Psychiatry*, 11(1980):277–279.

Emmelkamp, Paul, "Phobias: Theoretical and Behavioral Treatment Considerations," in *The Treatment of Phobic Disorders*. Oxford: Pergamon Press, 1977.

Emmelkamp, P.M.G., "Behaviour Therapy with Adults," in S. Garfield and A. Bergin (eds.), *Handbook of Psychotherapy and Behavior Change*. New York: Wiley, 1986.

———, *Phobic and Obsessive–Compulsive Disorders*. New York: Plenum, 1982.

———, "Self-observation versus Flooding in the Treatment of Agoraphobia," *Behavior Research and Therapy*, 12(1974):229–237.

Emmelkamp, P.M.G., "Agoraphobics' Interpersonal Problems: Their Role in the Effects of Exposure In Vivo Therapy," *Archives of General Psychiatry,* 37(1980):1303–1306.

Emmelkamp, P.M.G. and DeLange. "Spouse Involvement in the Treatment of Obsessive–Compulsive Patients," *Behavior Research and Therapy,* 21(1983):341–346.

Emmelkamp, P.M.G. and M. Felten, "Cognitive and Physiological Changes during Exposure In Vivo Treatment of Acrophobia," *Behavior Research and Therapy,* 23(1985):219–223.

Emmelkamp, P.M.G. and P.P. Mersch, "Cognition and Exposure in Vivo in the Treatment of Agorophobia: Short-term and Delayed Effects," *Cognitive Therapy and Research,* 6(1982):77–88.

Emmelkamp, P.M.G., P.P. Mersch, E. Vissia and M. Van der Helm, "Social Phobia: Cognitive and Behavioral Interventions," *Behavior Research and Therapy,* 23(1985):365–369.

Emmelkamp, P.M.G. and H. van der Heyden, "Treatment of Harming Obsessions," *Behaviour and Analytical Models,* 4(1980):28–35.

Emmelkamp, P.M.G., A. Van der Hout and K. De Vries, "Assertive Training for Agoraphobics," *Behavior Research and Therapy,* 21(1983):63–68.

Emmelkamp, P.M.G. and A. van der Hout, "Failure in Treating Agoraphobia," in Emmelkamp (eds.), *Failures in Behaviour Therapy.* New York: Wiley, 1983.

Emmelkamp, P.M.G. and H. Wessels, "Flooding in Imagination v. Flooding in Vivo in Agoraphobics," *Behavior Research and Therapy,* 13:7(1975).

Enoch, M. David and W.H. Trethowan, *Uncommon Psychiatric Symptoms.* Chicago: Year Book Medical Publishers, 1979.

Errera, Paul, "Some Historical Aspects of the Concept, Phobia," *The Psychiatric Quarterly,* 36(April 1962).

Errera, P. and J.V. Coleman, "A Long-term Followup Study of Neurotic Phobic Patients in a Psychiatric Clinic," *Journal of Nervous and Mental Disorders,* 136(1963):267–271.

Erwin, W.J., "Confinement in the Production of Human Neuroses," *Behavior Research and Therapy,* 1(1963)175–183.

Eysenck, H.J., "A Genetic Model of Anxiety," *Issues in Mental Health Nursing,* 7(1985):159–199.

Eysenck, Hans J., *Behavior Therapy and the Neuroses.* London: Pergamon Press, 1960.

Eysenck, H.J. and Irene Martin, *Theoretical Foundations of Behavioral Therapy.* New York: Plenum Press, 1987.

Eysenck, Hans J. and Michael, *Mindwatching.* Garden City, N.Y.: Anchor Press/Doubleday, 1983.

Fairbank, J.A. and T.M. Keane, "Flooding for Combat-related Stress Disorders," *Behaviour Therapy,* 13(1982):499–510.

Falloon, I., G.G. Lloyd and R.E. Harpin, "Treatment of Social Phobia: Real Life Rehearsal and Nonprofessional Therapist," *Journal of Nervous and Mental Disorders,* 169(1981):180–184.

Fawcett, Jan, "Is Anxiety a Precursor to Suicide?" In *Consequences of Anxiety: Management Strategies for the Primary Care Physician.* A clinical monograph based on a symposium held October 8–11, 1987, Orlando, Florida.

Fawcett, J. and H.M. Kravitz, "Anxiety Syndromes and Their Relationship to Depressive Illness," *Journal of Clinical Psychiatry,* 44(1983):8–11.

Ferguson, Ronald D., "Abstraction Anxiety: A Factor of Mathematics Anxiety," *Journal for Research in Mathematics,* 17(1986):145–150.

Ferrari, Michael, "Fears and Phobias in Childhood," *Child Psychiatry and Human Development,* 17:2(Winter 1986), pp. 75–87.

Festinger, Leon., *A Theory of Cognitive Dissonance.* Stanford, California: Stanford University Press, 1957.

Fischman, Joshua, "The Anxious Pain," *Psychology Today,* (April 1985).

Fisher, L.M. and T.G. Wilson, "Psychology of Agoraphobia," *Behavior Research and Therapy,* 23(1985):97–107.

Fishman, Scott M. and David V. Sheehan, "Anxiety and Panic: Their Cause and Treatment," *Psychology Today* (April 1985).

Foa, E.B. and D.L. Chambless "Habituation of Subjective Anxiety During Flooding in Imagery," *Behavior Research and Therapy,* 16(1978):391–399.

Foa, E.B. and U.G. Foa, "Differentiating Depression and Anxiety: Is It Possible? Is It Useful?" *Psychopharmacology Bulletin,* 18(1982):62–68.

Foa, E.B. and A. Goldstein, "Continuous Exposure and Complete Response Prevention in Obsessive–Compulsive Neurosis," *Behaviour Therapy,* 9(1978):821–829.

Foa, E.B. and M.J. Kozak, "Treatment of Anxiety Disorders: Implications for Psychopathology," pp. 421–452 in A.H. Tuma and J.D. Maser (eds.), *Anxiety and Anxiety Disorders.* Hillsdale, N.J.: Erlbaum, 1985.

Foa, E.B. and G.S. Steketee, "Obsessive–Compulsives: Conceptual Issues and Treatment Interventions," pp. 1–53 in R.M. Hersen et al. (eds.), "*Progress in Behaviour Modification.* New York: Academic, 1979.

Foa, E.B., G. Steketee, J.B. Grayson et al., "Deliberate Exposure and Blocking of Obsessive–Compulsive Rituals," *Behaviour Therapy,* 15(1984):450–472.

Forgione, Albert G. and Frederic M. Bauer, *Fearless Flying.* Boston: Houghton Mifflin, 1980.

Forgione, A.G. and R. Holmberg, "Biofeedback Therapy," in R. Corsini (ed.), *Handbook of Innovative Psychotherapies.* New York: Wiley, 1981.

Frampton, Muriel, *Agoraphobia: Coping with the World Outside.* Wellingborough, Northamptonshire, England: Turnstone Press, 1984.

Frankl, V.E., *Psychotherapy and Existentialism: Selected Papers on Logotherapy.* New York: Simon & Schuster, 1967.

Freeman, Arthur M. et al., "Alprazolam Treatment of Postcoronary Bypass Anxiety," *Journal of Clinical Psychopharmacology,* 6(February 1, 1986).

Friedman, J.H., "Short-term Psychotherapy of 'Phobia of Travel,' " *American Journal of Psychotherapy,* 4(1950):259–278.

Friedman, N., "On Focusing," *Journal of Humanistic Psychology* (Winter 1986), pp. 103–116.

Freud, S., "A Reply to Criticisms on the Anxiety Neurosis," in *Collected Papers,* vol. I, pp. 107–127. London: Hogarth and Institute of Psychoanalysis, 1924–50.

———, "Analysis of a Phobia in a Five-Year-Old Boy," in *Collected Papers,* vol. 3, pp. 149–287. London: Hogarth, 1924–50.

———, "On the Psychical Mechanism of Hysterical Phenomena," in *Collected Papers,* vol. I, pp. 24–26. London: Hogarth, 1924–50.

———, *Totem and Taboo* London: Hogarth, 1955.

Fryrear, J.L., and S. Werner, "Treatment of a Phobia by Videotaped Modeling," *Behaviour Therapy,* 1(1970):391–394.

Gale, E.N. and W.A. Ayer, "Treatment of Dental Phobias," *Journal of the American Dental Association,* 78(1969):1304–1307.

Garssen, B., W. Van Veenedaal and R. Bloemink, "Agoraphobia and the Hyperventilation Syndrome," *Behavior Research and Therapy,* 21(1983):643–649.

Garvey, Michael et al , "Does Situational Panic Disorder Represent a Specific Panic Disorder Subtype?" *Comprehensive Psychiatry,* 28:4(July-August 1987), pp. 329–333.

Garvey, M.J. and V.B. Tuason, "The Relationship of Panic Disorder to Agoraphobia," *Comprehensive Psychiatry,* 25(1984):529–531.

Geer, J.H., "Fear and Autonomic Arousal," *Journal of Abnormal Psychology,* 71(1966):253–255.

Geer, J.M., "The Development of a Scale to Measure Fear," *Behavioral Research and Therapy,* 3(1965).

Gehl, Raymond H., "Indecision and Claustrophobia," *International Journal of Psychoanalysis,* 54(1973).

Gelder, M.E. and I.M. Marks, "Severe Agoraphobia: A Controlled Prospective Trial of Behaviour Therapy," *British Journal of Psychiatry,* 112(1966):309–319.

Gelder, M.E., I.M. Marks and H.H. Wolff, "Desensitisation and Psychotherapy in the Treatment of Phobic States," *British Journal of Psychiatry,* 113(1967):53–73.

Gelder, M.G. and A.M. Mathews, "Forearm Blood Flow and Phobic Anxiety," *British Journal of Psychiatry,* 114(1968):1371–1376.

Gerdes, E.P. and E.J. Guidi, "Anxiety in Patients Awaiting Primary Medical Care," *Medical Care,* 25(1987):913–923.

Ginsberg, G. and I.M. Marks, "Costs and Benefits of Behavioural Psychotherapy: A Pilot Study," *Psychological Medicine,* 7(1977):685–700.

Girodo, M. and J. Roehl, "Coping Preparation and Coping Self-talk During the Stress of Flying," *Journal of Consulting Clinical Psychology,* 46(1978):978–989.

Gittelman, R. and D.F. Klein, "Childhood Separation Anxiety and Adult Agoraphobia," pp. 389–402 in H. Tuma and J. Maser (eds.), *Anxiety and Anxiety-related Disorders.* Hillsdale, N.J.: Erlbaum, 1985.

———, "Relationship between Separation Anxiety and Panic and Agoraphobic Disorders," *Psychopathology,* 17(1984):56–65.

Gittelman-Klein, R. and D.F. Klein, "Controlled Imipramine Treatment of School Phobia," *Archives of General Psychiatry,* 25(1971):204–207.

Goldenring, J.M. and R.M. Doctor. "Teen-age Worry about Nuclear War: North American and European Questionnaire Studies," *International Journal of Mental Health,* 15(1986):72–92.

Goldensen, Robert M. (ed.), *Longman Dictionary of Psychology and Psychiatry.* New York: Longman, 1984.

———, *The Encyclopedia of Human Behavior: Psychology, Psychiatry, and Mental Health.* Garden City, New York: Doubleday, 1970.

Goldfried, M.R. and C. Robins, "On the Facilitation of Self-efficacy," *Cognitive Therapy and Research,* 6(1982):361–380.

Goldstein, A. and B. Stainback, *Overcoming Agoraphobia: Conquering Fear of the Outside World.* New York: Viking Penguin, 1987.

Goldstein, A.J., "Case Conference: Some Aspects of Agoraphobia," *Journal of Behavior Therapy and Experimental Psychiatry,* 1(1970):305–313.

Goldstein, A.J. and D.L. Chambless, "A Reanalysis of Agoraphobia," *Behavior Therapy,* 9(1978):47–59.

Good, B.J. and A.M. Kleinman, "Culture and Anxiety," pp. 297–324 in H. Tuma and J. Maser (eds.), *Anxiety and Anxiety-related Disorders.* Hillsdale, N.J.: Erlbaum, 1985.

Goodkind, M., "Researcher Seeks Cure to Music Jitters." News release, Stanford University Medical Center, January 6, 1988.

Goodwin, Donald W., *Anxiety.* New York: Oxford University Press, 1986.

———, *Phobia.* New York: Oxford University Press, 1983.

Goorney, A.B., "Treatment of Aviation Phobias by Behaviour Therapy," *British Journal of Psychiatry,* 117(1970):535–544.

Goorney, A.B. and P.J. O'Connor, "Anxiety Associated with Flying: A Survey of Military Aircrew Psychiatric Casualties," *British Journal of Psychiatry,* 119(1971):159–166.

Gorman, J.M., J. Askanazi, M.R. Liebowitz et al., "Response to Hyperventilation in a Group of Patients with Panic Disorder," *American Journal of Psychiatry,* 141(1984):857–861.

Gorman, J.M., A.F. Fyer, J. Gliklich et al., "Effect of Imipramine on Prolapsed Mitral Valves of Patients With Panic Disorder," *American Journal of Psychiatry,* 138(1981):977–978.

Gorman, J.M., A.F. Fyer, J. Gliklich, et al. "Mitral Valve Prolapse and Panic Disorder: Effect of Imipramine." pp. 317–326 in D.F. Klein and J.G. Rabkin (eds.), *Anxiety Revisited.* New York: Raven, 1981.

Gorman, J.M., G.F. Levy, M.R. Liebowitz et al., "Effect of Acute Beta-Adrenergic Blockade on Lactate-Induced Panic," *Archives of General Psychiatry,* 40(1983):1079–1082.

Gorman, J.M., J.M. Martinez, M.R. Liebowitz et al., "Hypoglycemia and Panic Attacks," *American Journal of Psychiatry,* 141(1984):101–102.

Graham, D.T., "Prediction of Fainting in Blood Donors," *Circulation,* 23(1961):901–906.

Greenberg, Donna B., Theodore A. Stern and Jeffrey B. Weilburg, "Fear of Choking," *Journal of Family Practice,* 22(1986):547–548.

Greenspon, Lee W., "Anxiety and the Respiratory System," pp. 17–18 in *Consequences of Anxiety: Management Strategies for the Primary Care Physician.* A clinical monograph based on a symposium held October 8–11, 1987, Orlando, Florida.

Greist, J. et al., "Avoidance versus Confrontation of Fear," *Behavior Therapy,* 11(1980):1–14.

Greist, J.H. and G.L. Greist, *Fearless Flying: A Passenger Guide to Modern Airline Travel.* Chicago: Nelson Hall, 1981.

Greist, J.H. and J.W. Jefferson. *Depression and Its Treatment: Help for the Nation's #1 Mental Problem.* Washington, D.C.: American Psychiatric Association, 1984.

Greist, John H., James W. Jefferson and Isaac M. Marks, *Anxiety and Its Treatment: Help is Available.* Washington, D.C.: American Psychiatric Press, 1986.

Grey, S., G. Sartory and S. Rachman, "Synchronous and Desynchronous Changes in Fear Reduction," *Behavior Research and Therapy,* 17(1979):137–147.

Griez, E. and M.A. Van den Hout, "Treatment of Photophobia by Exposure to Co_2-Induced Anxiety Symptoms," *Journal of Nervous and Mental Disorders,* 175(1983):506–508.

Griffin, Suzanne J. and Matthew J. Friedman, "Depressive Symptoms in Propranol Users," *Journal of Clinical Psychiatry,* 47(1986):453+.

Grunhaus, L., S. Gloger and E. Weisstub, "Panic Attacks: A Review of Treatments and Pathogenesis," *Journal of Nervous and Mental Diseases,* 169(1981):608–613.

Gurney, C. et al., "Studies in the Classification of Affective Disorders: II. The Relationship Between Anxiety States and Depressive Illness," *British Journal of Psychiatry,* 121(1972):162–166.

Gurney, C., M. Roth, A. Kerr and K. Schapira, "Treatment and Classification of Anxiety Disorders," *British Journal of Psychiatry,* 117(1970):251–255.

Gustavsson, B., L. Jansson, A. Jerremalm and L.G. Ost, "Therapist Behaviours during Exposure Treatment of Agoraphobia," *Behaviour Modification,* 9(1985):491–504.

Haefely, W., "The Mechanism of Action of Benzodiazepines," *Journal of Psychoactive Drugs* (1983), pp. 1–32.

Hafner, R.J., "Catharsis during Prolonged Exposure for Snake Phobia," *American Journal of Psychiatry,* 135(1978):247–248.

———, "Predicting the Effects on Husbands of Behaviour Therapy for Wives' Agoraphobia," *Behavior Research and Therapy,* 22(1984):217–226.

———, "Behaviour Therapy for Agoraphobic Men," *Behavior Research and Therapy,* 21(1983):51–56.

———, "The Husbands of Agoraphobic Women: Assortative Mating or Pathogenic Interaction?" *British Journal of Psychiatry,* 130(1977):223–239.

———, "The Husbands of Agoraphobic Women and Their Influence on Treatment Outcome," *British Journal of Psychiatry,* 131(1977):289–294.

———, "Fresh Symptoms Emergence after Intensive Behavior Therapy," *British Journal of Psychiatry,* 129(1976):378–383.

Hafner, R.J. and I.M. Marks, "Exposure In Vivo of Agoraphobics: Contributions of Diazepam, Group Exposure, and Anxiety Evocation," *Psychological Medicine,* 6(1976):71–88.

Hafner, R.J. and F. Milton, "The Influence of Propanolol on the Exposure In Vivo of Agoraphobics," *Psychological Medicine,* 7(1977):419–425.

Hafner, R.J. and M.W. Ross, "Predicting the Outcome of Behavior Therapy for Agoraphobia," *Behavior Research and Therapy,* 21(1983):375–382.

Hallam, R.S., *Anxiety: Psychological Perspectives on Panic and Agoraphobia.* New York: Academic, 1985.

Hallam, R.S. and R.J. Hafner, "Fears of Phobic Patients: Factor Analyses of Self-report Data," *Behavior Research and Therapy,* 16(1978):1–6.

Hallstrom, T. and A. Halling, "Prevalence of Dentistry Phobia in an Urban Community Sample," *Acta Psychiatrica Scandinavica,* 70(1984):438–446.

Hand, I., Y. Lamontagne and I.M. Marks, "Group Exposure (Flooding) In Vivo for Agoraphobics," *British Journal of Psychiatry,* 124(1974):588–602.

Hand, I., B. Spoehring and E. Stanik, "Treatment of Obsessions, Compulsions and Phobias as Hidden Couple-counseling," in J.C. Boulougouris and A.D. Rabavilaus (eds.), *Treatment of Phobic and Obsessive–Compulsive Disorders.* Oxford: Pergamon, 1977.

Hand, I. and H.U. Wittchen, *Panic and Phobias.* New York: Springer, Verlag, 1986.

Handley, R., *Anxiety and Panic Attacks: Their Cause and Cure.* New York: Rawson, 1985.

Hardy, G.E. and J.A. Cotterill, "A Study of Depression and Obsessionality in Dysmorphophobia and Psoriatic Patients," *British Journal of Psychiatry,* 140(1982):19–22.

Harre, R. and R. Lamb, *Encyclopedic Dictionary of Psychology,* pp. 457–462. Cambridge, Massachusetts: The MIT Press, 1983.

Hartman, N., R. Kramer, T. Brown and R.B. Devereux, "Panic Disorder in Patients with Mitral Valve Prolapse," *American Journal of Psychiatry,* 139(1982):669–670.

Hartocollis, P., "Psychiatry in Contemporary Greece," *American Journal of Psychiatry,* 123:4(October 1966).

Hay, G.G., "Dysmorphophobia," *British Journal of Psychiatry,* 116:(1970):399–406.

———, "Paranoia and Dysmorphophobia," *British Journal of Psychiatry,* 142(1983):309.

Haynes-Clements, L.A. and A.W. Avery, "A Cognitive–Behavioral Approach to Social Skills Training with Shy Persons," *Journal of Clinical Psychology,* 40(1984):710–713.

Healy, Sean, *Boredom, Self and Culture.* Rutherford N.J.: Fairleigh Dickinson University Press, 1984.

Hellekson, Carla and Norman Rosenthal, "New Light on Seasonal Mood Changes," *Harvard Medical School Mental Health Newsletter* (April 1987).

Henauer, S.A., H.K. Gillespie and L.E. Hollister, "Yohimbine and the Model Anxiety State," *Journal of Clinical Psychiatry,* 45(1984):512–515.

Henderson, R.W., "Forgetting of Conditioned Fear Inhibition," *Learning and Motivation,* 8(1978):16–30.

Hepner, A. and N.R. Cauthen, "Effects of Subject Control and Graduated Exposure on Snake Phobias," *Journal of Consulting and Clinical Psychology,* 43(1975):297–304.

Hill, Douglas and Pat Williams, *The Supernatural.* New York: Hawthorn Books, 1965.

Hibbert, G.A., "Hyperventilation as a Cause of Panic Attacks," *British Medical Journal,* 288(1984):263–264.

Himadi, William G., Robert Boice and David Barlow, "Assessment of Agoraphobic—II, Measurement of Clinical Change," *Behavior Research and Therapy,* 24(1986):321–332.

———, "Assessment of Agoraphobia: Triple Response Measurement," *Behavior Research and Therapy,* 23(1985):311–323.

Hobbs, W.R. et al., "Psychophysiology of Agoraphobia," pp. 65–80 in J.E. Ballenger (ed.), *Biology of Agoraphobia.* Washington, D.C.: American Psychiatric Press, 1984.

Hodgson, R. and S. Rachman, "Desynchrony in Measures of Fear," *Behavior Research and Therapy,* 12(1974):319–326.

Hoehn-Saric, R., "Neurotransmitters in Anxiety," *Archives of General Psychiatry,* 39(1982):735–742.

Hoehn-Saric, R. and V.C. Barksdale, "Impulsiveness in Obsessive–Compulsive Patients," *British Journal of Psychiatry,* 143(1983):177–182.

Hoffman, Paul, "Triskaidekaphobia Can Strike When You're Most Expecting It," *Smithsonian* (February 1987).

Holden, A.E. et al., "Self-Help Manual for Agoraphobia: Preliminary Report of Effectiveness," *Behavior Therapy,* 14(1983):545–566.

Holes, Christina, *Encyclopedia of Superstitions.* London: Hutchinson of London, 1981.

Hollingsworth, C.E. et al., "Long-term Outcome of OCD in Childhood," *American Academy of Child Psychiatry,* 19(1980):134–145.

Hollister, Leo E., "Pharmacotherapeutic Considerations in Anxiety Disorders," *Journal of Clinical Psychiatry,* 47:6(June 1986).

Horne, D.J. deL. and H. McCormack, "Behavioural Psychotherapy for a Blood and Needle Phobic Mastectomy Patient Receiving Adjuvant Chemotherapy," *Behavioural Psychotherapy,* 12(1984):341–349.

Horney, Karen, *Feminine Psychology.* New York: Modern Library, 1968.

Horowitz, M.J. et al., "Signs and Symptoms of Posttraumatic Stress Disorder," *Archives of General Psychiatry,* 37(1980):85–92.

Howard, W.A. et al., "The Nature and Treatment of Fear of Flying: A Controlled Investigation," *Behavioural Therapy,* 14(1983):557–567.

Howells, J.G. and M.L. Osborn, *A Reference Companion to the History of Abnormal Psychology.* Westport, Connecticut: Greenwood Press, 1984.

Hsu, L.K., "Novel Symptom Emergence after Behavior Therapy in a Hypodermic Injection Phobic," *American Journal of Psychiatry,* 135(1978):237–238.

Hudesman, John, Charles Loveday and Nathaniel Woods, "Desensitization of Test Anxious Urban Community College Students and Resulting Changes in Grade Point Average: A Replication," *Journal of Clinical Psychology,* 401(1984):, pp. 65–67.

Hudson, B., "The Families of Agoraphobics Treated by Behaviour Therapy," *British Journal of Social Work,* 4(1974):51–59.

Hugdahl, K. and A-C. Karker, "Biological vs. Experiential Factors in Phobic Conditioning," *Behavior Research and Therapy,* 19(1981):109–115.

Husain, M.Z., "Desensitization and Flooding (Implosion) in Treatment of Phobias," *American Journal of Psychiatry,* 127(1971):1509–1514.

Hyslop, T.B., *The Great Abnormals.* Ann Arbor, Michigan: Gryphon Books, 1971.

Insel, T.R. et al., "Clomipramine and Clorgyline in OCD," *Archives of General Psychiatry,* 40(1983):605–612.

Insel, T.R., E.A. Mueller, I. Alterman et al., "Obsessive–Compulsive Disorder and Serotonin: Is There a Connection?" *Biology and Psychiatry,* 20(1985):1174–1188.

Ishiyama, F.I., "Morita Therapy: Its Basic Features and Cognitive Interventions for Anxiety Treatment," *Psychotherapy,* 23:13(Fall 1986), pp. 375–381.

Jablensky, A., "Approaches to the Definition Classification of Anxiety and Related Disorders in European Psychiatry," pp. 755–758. in H. Tuma and J. Maser (eds.), *Anxiety and Anxiety-related Disorders.* Hillsdale, N.J.: Erlbaum, 1985.

James, I. and I. Savage, "Nadolol, Diazepam and Placebo for Anxiety in Musicians," *American Heart Journal,* 108(1984):1150–1155.

James, J.E., M. Hampton and S.A. Larsen, "Imaginal and In Vivo Desensitization in Agoraphobia," *Journal of Behavioural Therapy and Experimental Psychiatry,* 14(1983):203–207.

Jampolsky, Gerald G., *Good-bye to Guilt.* New York: Bantam Books, 1985.

Janda, L.H. and K.E. O'Grady. "Development of a Sex Anxiety Inventory," *Journal of Consulting and Clinical Psychology,* 48(1980):169–175.

Janet, P., *The Major Symptoms of Hysteria.* New York: Hafner, 1965.

Jennike, M.A., "Dysmorphophobia," Letter to *British Journal of Psychiatry,* 146(1985):326.

Jannoun, L. et al., "Home-based Treatment for Agoraphobia, Replication and Controlled Evaluation," *Behavioural Therapy,* 11(1980):294–305.

Jobes, Gertrude, *Dictionary of Mytyhology, Folklore and Symbols.* New York: Scarecrow Press, 1961.

Johnson, S.B. and B.G. Melamed, "The Assessment and Treatment of Children's Fears," pp. 107–139 in B.B. Lahey and A.E. Kazdin (eds.), *Advances in Child Psychology.* New York: Plenum, 1977.

Johnston, M. et al., "Cumulative Scales for the Measurement of Agoraphobia," *British Journal of Clinical Psychology,* 23(1984):133–143.

Jones, E., *Sigmund Freud: Life and Work.* Garden City, N.Y.: Doubleday, 1961.

Jones, W.H., J.M. Check and S.R. Briggs, *Shyness.* New York: Plenum, 1986.

Joranson, David E., "Pharmacologic Treatment of Anxiety in the Present Medical/Legal Environment," pp. 12–13 in *Consequences of Anxiety: Management Strategies for the Primary Care Physician.* A clinical monograph based on a symposium held October 8–11, 1987, Orlando, Florida.

Kagan, J., "The Fearful Child's Hidden Talents," *Psychology Today* (July 1982), pp. 58–59.

Kahn, Ada P., *Arthritis.* Chicago: Contemporary Books, 1983

———, *Diabetes.* Chicago: Contemporary Books, 1983.

——— *Headaches.* Chicago: Contemporary Books, 1983

———, *High Blood Pressure*. Chicago: Contemporary Books, 1983.

Kahn, Ada P. and Linda Hughey, Holt, M.D., *Midlife Health: Every Woman's Guide to Feeling Good*. New York: Facts On File, 1987.

———, *Menopause: Are the Best Years Ahead?* London: Bloomsbury Publishing, 1987.

Kahn, Rene S. and Herman G.M. Westerberg, "L-5-Hydroxytryptophan in the Treatment of Anxiety Disorders," *Journal of Affective Disorders*, 8(1985):197–200.

Kalish, Richard, "Cemetery Visits," *Death Studies*, 10(1986):55–58.

Kantor, J.S., C.M. Zitrin and S.M. Zeldis, "Mitral Valve Prolapse Syndrome in Agoraphobic Patients," *American Journal of Psychiatry*, 137(1980):467–469.

Kaplan, Harold I. and Benjamin J. Sadock, *Comprehensive Textbook of Psychiatry*. Baltimore: Williams and Wilkins, 1985.

Karabanow, O., "Double-blind Controlled Study in Phobias and Obsessions Complicated by Depression," *International Journal of Medical Research*, 5(1977):42–48.

Kasvikis, Y.G. et al., "Past History of Anorexia Nervosa in Women with Obsessive–Compulsive Disorder," *The International Journal of Eating Disorders*, 5:6(1985), pp. 1069–1075.

Kazdin, A.E. and G.T. Wilson, "Criteria for Evaluating Psychotherapy," *Archives of General Psychiatry*, 35(1978):407–416.

Keane, T.M. and D.G. Kaloupek, "Imaginal Flooding in the Treatment of a Posttraumatic Stress Disorder," *Journal of Consulting and Clinical Psychology*, 50(1982):138–140.

Kelly, D., W. Guirguis, E. Fommer, N. Mitchell-Heggs and W. Sargent, "Treatment of Phobic States with Antidepressants: A Retrospective Study of 246 Patients," *British Journal of Psychiatry*, 116(1970):387–398.

Kelly, W., *Post-Traumatic Stress Disorder and the War Veteran Patient*. New York: Brunner/Mazel, 1985.

Kennedy, W.A., "School Phobia: Rapid Treatment of Fifty Cases," *Journal of Abnormal Psychology*, 70(1965):285–289.

Kent, Fraser, *Nothing to Fear*. Garden City, N.Y.: Doubleday, 1977.

Kent, G., "Anxiety, Pain and Type of Dental Procedure," *Behavioral Research and Therapy*, 22(1984):465–469.

Kerr, T.A., M. Roth and K. Schapira, "Prediction of Outcome in Anxiety States and Depressive Illnesses," *British Journal of Psychiatry*, 124(1974):125–133.

Kerry, R.J., "Phobia of Outer Space," *Journal of the Mental Sciences*, 106(1960):1383–1387.

Kinzie, J.D. et al., "PTSD Among Survivors of Cambodian Concentration Camps," *American Journal of Psychiatry*, 141(1984):645–650.

Kipper, D.A., "Behavior Therapy for Fears Brought on by War Experiences," *Journal of Consulting and Clinical Psychology,* 45(1977):216–221.

Kirk, J.W., "Behavioural Treatment of Obsessive–Compulsive Patients in Routine Clinical Practice," *Behavioral Research and Therapy,* 21(1983):57–62.

Klamer, Richard H., *Marriage and Family Relationships.* New York: Harper and Row, 1970.

Klein, D.F., "Importance of Psychiatric Diagnosis in Prediction of Clinical Drug Effects," *Archives of General Psychiatry,* 16(1967):118–126.

Klein, D.F., C.M. Zitrin, M.G. Woerner and D.C. Ross, "Treatment of Phobias—Behavior Therapy and Supportive Psychotherapy: Are There Any Specific Ingredients?" *Archives of General Psychiatry,* 40(1983):139–145.

Kleinknecht, Ronald A., *The Anxious Self.* New York: Human Sciences Press, 1986.

Kleinknecht, R.A. and D.A. Bernstein, "Assessment of Dental Fear," *Behavior Therapy,* 9(1978):626–634.

Kleinknecht, R.A. et al., "Origins and Characteristics of Fear and Dentistry," *Journal of the American Dental Association,* 86(April 1973), pp. 842–848.

Klepac, R.K., "Treatment of Dental Avoidance by Densensitisation or by Increasing Pain Tolerance," *Journal of Behavioural and Therapeutic Experimental Psychiatry,* 6(1975):307–310.

Klepac, R.K., J. Dowling and G. Hauge, "Reactions to Pain in Dental Avoidance," *Journal of Behavioural Therapy and Experimental Psychiatry,* 13(1982):293–300.

Klepac, R.K., M. McDonald, G. Hang and J. Dowling, "Reactions to Pain among Subjects High and Low in Dental Fear," *Journal of Behavioural Modification,* 3(1980):373–384.

Klerman, Gerald, "Current Trends in Clinical Research in Panic Attacks, Agoraphobia and Related Anxiety Disorders," *Journal of Clinical Psychiatry,* 47:6(June 1986), pp. 37–39.

Klorman, R., "Habituation of Fear: Effects of Intensity and Stimulus Order," *Psychophysiology,* 11(1974):15–26.

Klorman, R., T.C. Weerts and J.E. Hastings, "Psychometric Description of Some Specific Fear Questionnaires," *Behavior Therapy,* 5(1974):401–409.

Ko, G.N., et al., "Panic-induced Elevation of Plasma MHPG in Phobic-anxious Patients: Effects of Clonidine or Imipramine," *Archives of General Psychiatry,* 40(1983):425–430.

Kolvin, I., T.P. Berney and S.R. Bhate, "Classification and Diagnosis of Depression in School Phobia," *British Journal of Psychiatry,* 145(1984):347–357.

Koocher, G.P. et al., "Death Anxiety in Normal Children and Adolescents," *Psychiatric Clinician,* 9(1976):220–229.

Korpell, Herbert S., *How You Can Help: A Guide for Families of Psychiatric Hospital Patients.* Washington, D.C.: American Psychiatric Association, 1984

Kroeger, Robert F., "Levels of Fear or Phobia and a Formal Dental Fear Control Program," *General Dentistry,* 34:3(May-June 1986), pp. 241–242.

Kubler-Ross, Elisabeth, *On Death and Dying.* New York: Macmillan, 1975.

Lader, Malcolm, "The Nature of Clinical Anxiety in Modern Society," *Issues in Mental Health Nursing,* 7(1985):309–334.

———, *Introduction to Psychopharmacology.* Kalamazoo, Michigan: The Upjohn Company, 1980.

———, "Behavior and Anxiety: Physiologic Mechanisms," *Journal of Clinical Psychiatry,* 44(1983):5–10.

Lader, M.H. and I.M. Marks, *Clinical Anxiety.* London: Heinemann Medical, 1971.

Ladouceur, R.L., "Participant Modeling with or without Cognitive Treatment for Phobias," *Journal of Consulting and Clinical Psychology,* 51(1983):942–944.

Lande, Nathaniel, *Mindstyles/Lifestyles.* Los Angeles: Price/Stern/Sloan Publishers, 1976.

Lang, P.J., "Imagery in Therapy: An Information Processing Analysis of Fear," *Behavior Therapy,* 8(1977):862–886.

LaPierre, Y.P., "New Antidepressant Drugs." *Journal of Clinical Psychiatry,* 44:8(August 1983), pp. 41–43.

Lazarus, R.S., *Psychological Stress and the Coping Process.* New York: McGraw-Hill, 1986.

Leckman, J.F., et al., "Increased Risk of Depression, Alcoholism, Panic and Phobic Disorders in Families of Depressed Probands with Panic Disorder," *Archives of General Psychiatry,* 40(1983):1055–1060.

Lee, I., P. Tyrer and S. Horn, "Subliminal, Supraliminal and Faded Phobic Cine-films in the Treatment of Agoraphobia," *British Journal of Psychiatry,* 143(1983):356–361.

Lehman, Heinz, "The Clinician's View of Anxiety and Depression," *Journal of Clinical Psychiatry* (August 1983), p. 3.

Leitenberg, H., W.S. Agras, D.H. Barlow and D.C. Oliveau, "The Contribution of Selective Positive Reinforcement and Therapeutic Instructions to Systematic Desensitization Therapy," *Journal of Abnormal Psychology,* 74(1969):113–118.

Leitenberg, H., S. Agras, R. Butz and J. Wincze, "Relationship between Heart Rate and Behavioral Change during the Treatment of Phobias," *Journal of Abnormal Psychology,* 78(1971):59–68.

Lesser, Ira and Robert Rubin, "Diagnostic Considerations in Panic Disorder," *Journal of Clinical Psychiatry,* 47:6(June 1986), pp. 4–10.

Levin, A.P. et al., "Lactate Induction of Panic," in J.C. Ballenger (ed.), *Biology of Agoraphobia.* Washington, D.C.: American Psychiatric Press, 1984.

Lewis, Aubrey, "A Note on Classifying Phobia," *Psychological Medicine,* 6(1976):21–22.

Lewis, A.J., "The Ambiguous Word 'Anxiety' as Used in Psychopathology," *Israel Annals of Psychiatry and Related Disciplines,* 5(1967):105–121.

Lewis, M. and J. Brooks, *The Origins of Fear.* New York: John Wiley, 1974.

Levitt, E., *The Psychology of Anxiety.* Hillsdale, N.J.: Lawrence Erlbaum Associates, 1980.

Liberthson, R.R., "MVP in Patients with Panic and Other Phobic Amxiety." Paper presented at Upjohn Conference on Biological Considerations in Anxiety Disorders, Boston, December 1983.

Liberthson, R.R. and David Sheehan, "Prevalence of Mitral Valve Prolapse in Patients with Panic Disorders," *American Journal of Psychiatry,* 143:4(April 1986), pp. 511–515.

Lieberman, J.A., R. Brenner, M. Lesser et al., "Dexamethasone Suppression Tests in Patients with Panic Disorder," *American Journal of Psychiatry,* 140(1983):917–919.

Liebowitz, M.R. and D.F. Klein, "Differential Diagnosis and Treatment of Panic Attacks and Phobic States," *Annual Review of Medicine,* 32(1981):583–599.

Liebowitz, M.R., J.M. Gorman A.J. Fyer and D.F. Klein, "Social Phobia," *Archives of General Psychiatry,* 42(1985):729–736.

———, "Assessment and Treatment of Phobic Anxiety," *Journal of Clinical Psychiatry,* 40(1979):486–492.

Lief, H.A., "Sensory Association in the Selection of Phobic Objects," *Psychiatry,* 18(1955):331–338.

Lindsay, S.J.E. and C.J. Busch, "Behaviour Modification in Dentistry: A Review," *Behavioral Psychotherapy,* 9(1981):200–214.

Lloyd, G.G. and H.G. Deaking, "Phobias Complicating Treatment of Uterine Carcinoma," *British Medical Journal* (November 22, 1975), pp. 440–441.

Loehlin, J.C. and R.C. Nichols, "Heredity, Environment and Personality: A Study of 858 Sets of Twins," Austin: University of Texas Press, 1976.

Lowenstein, L.F., "Combined Treatment of School Phobia," *Britisn Journal of Sociology and Clinical Psychiatry,* 2(1983):32–38.

Lubetkin, B., "The Use of a Planetarium in the Desensitization of a Case of Bronto- and Astra-phobia," *Behavior Therapy,* 6(1975):276–277.

Ludwig, Arnold M., *Principles of Clinical Psychiatry.* New York: The Free Press, 1980.

Lum, L.C., "Hyperventilation and Anxiety State," *Journal of the Royal Society of Medicine,* 32(1981):583–599.

Lydiard, R. Bruce, Michele T. Laraia, Elizabeth F. Howell and James C. Ballenger, "Can Panic Disorder Present as Irritable Bowel Syndrome?" *Journal of Clinical Psychiatry,* 47:9(September 1986), pp. 470–473.

Lys, Claud de, *A Treasury of American Superstitions.* New York: Philosophical Library, 1940.

MacAlpine, I., "Syphilophobia," *British Journal of Venereal Disease,* 33(1957):92–99.

Mahoney, Patrick J., *Freud and the Rat Man*. New Haven: Yale University Press, 1986.

Shepard, Leslie (ed.), *Encyclopedia of Occultism and Parapsychology.* Detroit: Gale Research Co., 1984–85.

Malleson, N., "Panic and Phobia: Possible Methods ot Treatment," *Lancet,* 1(1959):225.

Margraf, Jurgen, A. Ehlers and W.T. Roth, "Biological Models of Panic Disorder and Agoraphobia," *Behavior Research Therapy,* 24(1986):553+

Marks, Isaac M., "Agoraphobic Syndrome (Phobic Anxiety State)," *Archives of General Psychiatry,* 23(1970):538–553.

———, "Are There Anticompulsive or Antiphobic Drugs? Review of the Evidence," *British Journal of Psychiatry,* 143(1983):338–347.

———, "Behavioral Psychotherapy in General Psychiatry," *British Journal of Psychiatry,* 150(1987):593–597.

———, "Behavioral Psychotherapy of Adult Neurosis," in A.E. Bergin and S. Garfield (eds.), *Handbook of Psychotherapy and Behavior Change.* New York: John Wiley, 1978.

———, "Behavioural Treatment of Phobic and Obsessive–Compulsive Disorders: A Critical Appraisal," in M. Hersen, R.M. Eisler and P.M. Miller (eds.), *Progress in Behaviour Modification.* New York: Pergamon Press, 1975.

———, "Behavioral Treatment of Social Phobia," *Psychopharmacology Bulletin,* 21(1985):615–618.

———, "The Classification of Phobic Disorders," *British Journal of Psychiatry,* 116(1970):377–386.

———, "Components and Correlates of Psychiatric Questionnaires in Phobic Patients," *British Journal of Medical Psychology,* 40(1967):261–272.

———, "Exposure Treatment," in W.S. Agra (ed.), *Behavior Modification in Clinical Psychiatry.* Boston: Little, Brown, 1978.

———, *Fears and Phobias.* London: Heinemann Medical, 1969.

———, *Fears, Phobias and Rituals.* New York: Oxford University Press, 1987.

———, *Living with Fear.* New York: McGraw-Hill, 1978.

———, "Phobic Disorders Four Years after Treatment," *British Journal of Psychiatry,* 118(1971):683–688.

———, "The Reduction of Fear: Towards a Unifying Theory," *Journal of Canadian Psychiatric Association,* 18(1973):9–12.

———, "Space 'Phobia': A Pseudoagoraphobic Syndrome," *Journal of Neurology and Neurosurgical Psychiatry,* 44(1981):387–391.

Marks, I.M. et al., *Nursing in Behavioural Psychotherapy*. London: Research Series of Royal College of Nursing, 1977.

Marks, I.M. and P. Bebbington, "Space Phobia: Syndrome or Agoraphobic Variant," *British Medical Journal,* 2(1976):345–347.

Marks, I.M., J. Boulougouris and P. Marset, "Flooding v. Desensitization for Phobic Patients: A Cross-over Study," *British Journal of Psychiatry,* 119((1971):353–375.

Marks, I.M., M. Crowe, D. Drewe, J. Young and W.G. Dewhurst, "Obsessive–Compulsive Neurosis in Identical Twins," *British Journal of Psychiatry,* 115(1969):991–998.

Marks, I.M. and M.G. Gelder, "A Controlled Retrospective Study of Behaviour Therapy in Phobic Patients," *British Journal of Psychiatry,* 111(1965):571–573.

———, "Different Onset Ages in Varieties of Phobia," *American Journal of Psychiatry,* 123(1966):218–221.

Marks, I.M., M.G. Gelder and J.G. Edwards, "Hypnosis v. Desensitisation for Phobias: A Controlled Prospective Trial," *British Journal of Psychiatry,* 114(1968):1263–1274.

Marks, I.M., S. Gray, D. Cohen, R. Hill, D. Mawson, E. Ramm and R. Stern, "Imipramine and Brief Therapist-aided Exposure in Agoraphobics Having Self-exposure Homework," *Archives of General Psychiatry,* 40(1983):153–162.

Marks, I.M. and E.R. Herst, "A Survey of 1200 Agoraphobics in Britain," *Social Psychiatry,* 5(1970):16–24.

Marks, Isaac M., M.D., and M.H. Lader, "Anxiety States (Anxiety Neurosis): A Review," *Journal of Nervous and Mental Disorders,* 156(1973):3–18.

Marks, I.M. and A.M. Mathews, "Brief Standard Self-rating for Phobic Patients," *Behavior Research and Therapy,* 17(1979):263–267.

Marks, I.M., R. Viswanathan, M.S. Lipsedge and R. Gardner, "Enhanced Relief of Phobias by Flooding during Waning Diazepam," *British Journal of Psychiatry,* 121(1972):493–505.

Marks, I.M. and C.G.W. Wilks, "Treatment of A Dentist's Phobia of Practising Dentistry," *British Dental Journal,* 147(1979):189–191.

Martin, I., I.M. Marks and M.G. Gelder, "Conditioned Eyelid Responses in Phobic Patients," *Behavior Research and Therapy,* 7(1969):115–124.

Masserman, J.H., *Principles and Practice of Biodynamic Psychotherapy: An Integration*. New York: Thieme/Stratton, 1980.

Masters, John C., Thomas G. Burish, Steven D. Hollon and David C. Rimm, *Behavior Therapy*. New York: Harcourt Brace Jovanovich, 1987.

Mathews, A.M., "Psychophysiological Approaches to the Investigation of Desensitization and Related Procedures," *Psychological Bulletin,* 76(1971):73–91.

Mathews, A.M., M.G., Gelder and D.W. Johnston, *Agoraphobia: Nature and Treatment*. New York: Guilford Press, 1981.

Mathews, A.M., D.W. Johnson, M. Lancashire, M. Munby, P.M. Shaw and M.G. Gelder, "Imaginal Flooding and Exposure to Real Phobic Situations: Treatment Outcome with Agoraphobic Patients," *British Journal of Psychiatry*, 129(1976):362–371.

Mathews, A.M., and V.A. Rezin, "Imaginal Exposure with Dental Phobics," *Behavior Research and Therapy*, 15(1976):321–328.

Mathews, A.M., J. Teasdale, M. Munby, D. Johnson and P.M. Shaw, "A home-based Treatment Program for Agoraphobia," *Behavior Therapy*, 8(1977):915–924.

Maurer, A., "What Children Fear," *Journal of Genetic Psychology*, 106(1965):265–277.

Mavissakalian, M.R., "Agoraphobia: Behavioral Therapy and Pharmacotherapy," pp. 187–211 in B.D. Beitman and G.L. Klerman (eds.), *Combining Psychotherapy and Drug Therapy in Clinical Practice*. New York: Spectrum, 1984.

———(ed.), *Obsessive–Compulsive Disorders: Psychological and Pharmacological Treatments*. New York: Plenum, 1985.

———, "Pharmacologic Treatment of Anxiety Disorders," *Journal of Clinical Psychiatry*, 43(1982):487–491.

Mavissakalian, M.R. and D.H. Barlow, "Assessment of Obsessive–Compulsive Disorders," in D.H. Barlow (ed.), *Behavioral Assessment of Adult Disorders*. New York: Guildford Press, 1980.

Mavissakalian, M. and D.H. Barlow (eds.), *Phobia: Psychological and Pharmacological Treatment*. New York: Guilford Press 1981

Mavissakalian, M. and L. Michaelson, "Agoraphobia: Behavioral and Pharmacological Treatments," *Psychopharmacology Bulletin*, 18(1982):91–103.

———, "Agoraphobia: Therapist-assisted In Vivo Exposure and Imipramine," *Journal of Clinical Psychiatry*, 47(1986):117–122.

———, "Patterns of Psychophysiological Change in the Treatment of Agoraphobia," *Behavior Research and Therapy*, 20(1982):347–356.

———, "Self-directed In Vivo Exposure Practice in Behavioral and Drug Treatments of Agoraphobia," *Behavior Therapy*, 14(1983):505–519.

———, "Tricyclic Antidepressants in Obsessive–Compulsive Disorder," *Journal of Nervous and Mental Disorders*, 171(1983):301–306.

Mavissakalian, M., L. Michelson, D. Greenwald et al., "Paradoxical Intention vs. Self-statement Training of Agoraphobia," *Behavior Research and Therapy*, 21(1983):75–80.

Mavissakalian, M., L. Michelson and R.S. Dealy, "Imipramine versus Imipramine with Programmed Practice for Agoraphobia," *British Journal of Psychiatry*, 143(1983):348–355

Mavissakalian, M., R. Salerni, M.E. Thompson and L. Michelson, "Mitral Valve Prolapse and Agoraphobia," *American Journal of Psychiatry,* 140(1983):1612–1614.

Mazza, Dominic L. et al., "Prevalence of Anxiety Disorders in Patients with Mitral Valve Prolapse," *American Journal of Psychiatry,* 143:3(March 1986), pp. 349–352.

McConnell, James V., *Understanding Human Behavior.* New York: Holt, Rinehart and Winston, 1986.

McDonald, Rita T. and William A. Hilgendorf, "Death Imagery and Death Anxiety," *Journal of Clinical Psychology,* 42:1(January 1986), pp. 87–91.

McDonald, R. et al., "Effects of Self-exposure Instructions on Agoraphobic Outpatients," *Behavior Research and Therapy,* 17(1978):83–85.

McMahon, C., "A Clinical Overview of Syndromes Following Withdrawal of Antidepressants," *Hospital and Community Psychiatry,* 37:9(September 1986), pp. 883–884.

McNally, R.J. and S. Reiss, "The Preparedness Theory of Phobias: The Effects of Initial Fear Level on Safety-signal Conditioning to Fear-relevant Stimuli," *Psychophysiology,* 21(1984):647–652.

McNally, R.J. and G.S. Steketee, "Etiology and Maintenance of Severe Animal Phobias," *Behavior Research and Therapy,* 23(1985):431–435.

McPherson, F.M., L. Brougham and S. McLaren, "Maintenance of Improvement in Agoraphobic Patients Treated by Behavioural Methods—A Four-year Followup," *Behavior Research Therapy,* 18(1980):150–152.

Meichenbaum, D.H., *Cognitive Behavior Modification.* New York: Plenum Press, 1977.

Meikl, S. and M.C. Mitchell, "Factor Analysis of the Fear Survey Schedule with Phobics," *Journal of Clinical Psychology,* 40(1974):44–46.

Melamed, B., "Reduction of Medical Fears: Information Processing and Arousal Level," pp. 205–218 in J.C. Boulougouris (ed.), *Learning Theory Approaches to Psychiatry.* New York: Wiley, 1982.

Melamed, B.G., R.R. Hawes, E. Heiby, and J. Glick, "Filmed Modeling to Reduce Children's Uncooperative Behavior during Dental Treatment," *Journal of Dental Research* (July-August 1975), pp. 797–801.

Melamed, B.G., S.L. Ross, F. Courts et al., "Dentists' Behavior Management as It Affects Compliance and Fear in Pediatric Patients," *Journal of the American Dental Association,* 106(1983):324–330.

Melamed, B.G., D. Weinstein, R. Hawes and M. Katin-Borland, "Reduction of Dental Fear by Filmed Modeling," *Journal of American Dental Association,* 90(1975):822–826.

Melville, Joy, *Phobias and Obsessions.* New York: Coward, McCann and Geoghegan, 1977.

Messer, Joseph V., "Anxiety and Cardiovascular Disease in the Primary Care Setting," pp. 25–27 in *Consequences of Anxiety: Management Srrategies for the Primary Care Physician.* A clinical monograph based on a symposium held October 8–11, 1987, Orlando, Florida.

Meyer, Bernard C., 'Notes on Flying and Dying," *Psychoanalytic Quarterly,* 2(1983):327.

Michelson, Larry et al., "Self-Directed in-vivo Exposure—Treatment of Agoraphobia," *Behavior Therapy,* 17(1986):91–108.

Michelson, L. and L.M. Ascher, "Paradoxical Intention in the Treatment of Agoraphobia and Other Anxiety Disorders," *Journal of Behaviour Therapy and Experimental Psychiatry,* 15(1984):215–220.

Michelson, L. and M. Mavissakalian, "Psychophysiological Outcome of Behavioral and Drug Treatments of Agoraphobia," *Journal of Consulting Clinical Psychology,* 53(1985):229–236.

Miller, L.C., C.L. Barret and E. Hampe, "Phobias of Childhood," in A. Davids (ed.), *Child Personality and Psychopathology: Current Topics*. New York: Wiley, 1974.

Miller, M.L., "On Street Fear," *International Journal of Psychoanalysis,* 34(1953):232–252.

Milton, F. and J. Hafner, "Outcome of Behavior Therapy for Agoraphobia in Relation to Marital Adjustment," *Archives of General Psychiatry,* 36(1979):807–811.

Mineka, S., "The Frightful Complexity of the Origins of Fears," in J.B. Overmier and F.R. Brush (eds.), *Affect, Conditioning and Cognition: Essays on the Determinants of Behavior*. Hillsdale, N.J.: Erlbaum, 1986.

Minuchin, S., *Families and Family Therapy*. London: Tavistock, 1974.

Monteiro, W., I.M. Marks, H. Noshirvani and S. Checkley, "Normal Dexamethasone Suppression Test in Obsessive–Compulsive Disorder," *British Journal of Psychiatry,* 148(1986):326–329.

Monteiro, W, I.M. Marks and E. Ramm, "Marital Adjustment and Treatment Outcome in Agoraphobia," *British Journal of Psychiatry,* 146(1985):383–390.

Moore, B.E. and B.D. Fine, *A Glossary of Psychoanalytical Terms and Concepts*. Washington, D.C.: American Psychoanalytic Association, 1968.

Moran, C. and G. Andrews, "The Familial Occurrence of Agoraphobia," *British Journal of Psychiatry,* 146(1985):262–267.

Morreall, John, *Taking Laughter Seriously*. Albany: State University of New York, 1983.

Morris, R.J. and T.R. Kratochwil, *Treating Children's Fears and Phobias: A Behavioral Approach*. New York: Pergamon General Psychology Series, 1983.

Morris, R.J. and K.H. Magrath, "Therapist Warmth in Contact Desensitization of Acrophobia," *Journal of Consulting Clinical Psychology,* 47(1979):786–788.

Morrison, J.M., *Your Brother's Keeper*. Chicago: Nelson-Hall, 1981.

Mullaney, J.A. and C.J. Trippett, "Alcohol Dependence and Phobias: Clinical Description and Relevance," *British Journal of Psychiatry,* 135(1979):565–573.

Munjack, D.J., "Onset of Driving Phobias," *Journal of Behavior Therapy and Experimental Psychiatry,* 15(1984):305–308.

Munjack, D.J. and H.B. Moss, "Affective Disorder and Alcoholism in Families of Agoraphobics," *Archives of General Psychiatry,* 38(1981):869–871.

Munjack, D.J. et al., "Imipramine vs Propanolol for Panic Attacks: A Pilot Study," *Comprehensive Psychiatry,* 25(1985):80–89.

Murray, E. and F. Foote, "The Origins of Fear of Snakes," *Behavior Research Therapy,* 17(1979):489–493.

Naud, J., J.M. Boisvert and Y. Lamontagne, "Treatment of Firearm Phobia by Flooding In Vivo and Motor Activity," *Journal of Behavior Therapy and Experimental Psychiatry,* 4(1973):407–409.

Ndetei, D.M. and A. Vadher, "Pattern of Anxiety in a Cross-Cultural Hospital Population," *Acta Psychiatrica Scandinavica,* 70(1984):69–72.

Neftel, K.A. et al., "Stage Fright in Musicians: Effect of Beta Blockers," *Psychosomatic Medicine,* 44(1982):461–469.

Neki, J.S., "Psychiatry in South-East Asia, ' *British Journal of Psychiatry,* 123(1973):257–269.

Neshkes, Robert E. and Leo E. Hollister, "Cardiovascular Side Effects of Antidepressant Agents," excerpted from symposium on "Psychiatric Problems in the Elderly" (Pfizer, Inc.), January 1987.

Nesse, R.M. et al., "Endocrine and Cardiovascular Responses during Phobic Anxiety," *Psychosomatic Medicine,* 47:1(July-August 1985).

Nesse, R.M. et al., "Urinary Catecholamines and Mitral Valve Prolapse in Panic-anxiety Patients," *Psychiatric Research,* 14(1985):67–75.

Neuman, F., *Fighting Fear: An Eight-week Guide to Treating Your Own Phobias.* New York: Macmillan, 1985.

Nichols, K. and I. Berg, "School Phobia and Self-evaluation," *Journal of Child Psychology and Psychiatry,* 11(1970):133–141.

Nichols, K.A., "Severe Social Anxiety," *British Journal of Medical Psychology,* 47(1974):301–306.

Nimmer, W.H. and R.A. Kapp, "A Multiple Impact Program for the Treatment of Injection Phobias," *Journal of Behavior Therapy and Experimental Psychiatry,* 5(1974):257–258.

Norton, G.R. et al., "Characteristics of People with Infrequent Panic Attacks," *Journal of Abnormal Psychology,* 94(1985):216–221.

Noyes, R., D. Chaudry and D.V. Domingo, "Pharmacologic Treatment of Phobic Disorders," *Journal of Clinical Psychiatry,* 47:9(September 1986), pp. 445+.

Noyes, R. et al., "Diazepam and Propranolol in Panic Disorder and Agoraphobia," *Archives of General Psychiatry,* 41(1984):287–292.

Oates, J.K. and J. Gomez, "Venereophobia," *British Journal of Hospital Medicine,* 31(1984):435–436

O'Brien, G.T., D.H. Barlow and C.G. Last, "Changing Marriage Patterns of Agoraphobics as a Result of Treatment," pp. 140–152 in R. Dupont (ed.), *Phobias*. New York: Brunner/Mazel, 1982.

O'Brien, Robert and Sidney Cohen, *The Encyclopedia of Drug Abuse*. New York: Facts On File, 1984.

O'Connor, P.J., "Phobic Reaction to Flying: Historical Background," *Proceedings of Royal Society of Medicine*, 63(1970):877–878.

Ohman, A., M. Fredrikson and K. Hugdahl, "Towards an Experimental Model for Simple Phobic Reactions," *Behavior Analysis Modality*, 2(1978):97–114.

Ohman, A., U. Dimberg and L-G Ost, "Animal and Social Phobias: Biological Constraints on Learned Fear Responses," in S. Reiss and R. R. Bootzin (eds.), *Theoretical Issues in Behavior Therapy*. New York: Academic, 1984.

Ost, L-G., "Behavioral Treatment of Thunder and Lightning Phobias," *Behavior Research and Therapy*, 16(1978):197–207.

Ost, L-G, and K. Hugdahl, "Acquisition of Agoraphobia, Mode of Onset and Anxiety Response Patterns," *Behavior Research and Therapy*, 21(1983):612–631.

———, "Acquisition of Phobias and Anxiety Response Patterns in Clinical Patients," *Behavior Research and Therapy*, 19(1981):439–447.

———, "Acquisition of Blood and Dental Phobia and Anxiety Response Patterns in Clinical Patients," *Behavior Research and Therapy*, 23(1985):27–34.

Ost, L-G, A. Jerremalm and J. Johansson, "Individual Response Patterns and Different Behavioral Treatments of Social Phobia," *Behavior Research and Therapy*, 19(1981):1–16.

Ost, L-G, A. Jerremalm and L. Jansson, "Individual Response Patterns and Different Behavioral Treatments of Agoraphobia," *Behavior Research and Therapy*, 22(1984):697–707.

Ost, L-G, J. Johansson and A. Jerremalm, "Individual Response Patterns and Different Behavioral Treatments of Claustrophobia," *Behavior Research and Therapy*, 20(1982):445–460.

Ost, L-G. et al., "Exposure In Vivo vs Applied Relaxation for Blood Phobia," *Behavior Research and Therapy*, 22(1984):205–216.

Ost, L-G, U. Sterner and I-L Lindahl, "Physiological Responses in Blood Phobics," *Behavior Research and Therapy*, 22(1984):109–117.

Ostrow, David, "The New Generation of Antidepressants: Promising Innovations or Disappointments?" *Journal of Clinical Psychiatry*, 46:10(October 1985), pp. 24–29.

Owen, John A., "Alprazolam: A New Benzodiazepine Appropriate for Anxiety Disorders," *Hospital Formulary*, 18(1983):10.

Palgi, P., "Persistent Traditional Yemenite Ways of Dealing with Stress in Israel." *Mental Health Society*, 5(1978):113–140.

Paolino, A., *Agoraphobia (Fear of Fear)*. Fort Tilden, N.Y.: Apollo, 1984.

Parker, G., "Reported Parental Characteristics of Agoraphobics and Social Phobics," *British Journal of Psychiatry,* 135(1979):555–560.

Pasnau, R. (ed.), *Anxiety and the Anxiety Disorders.* Washington, D.C.: American Psychiatric Press, 1984.

Paul, Steven M., "Biochemical Basis of Anxiety," in *Consequences of Anxiety: Management Strategies for the Primary Care Physician.* A clinical monograph based on a symposium held October 8–11, 1987, Orlando, Florida.

Pecknold, J.C. et al., "Does Tryptophan Potentiate Clomipramine for Agoraphobics and Social Phobics?" *British Journal of Psychiatry,* 140(1982):484–490.

Perman, J.M., "Phobia as a Determinant of Single-Room Occupancy," *American Journal of Psychiatry,* 123:5(November 1966), pp. 609–613.

Persons, J.B. and E.B. Foa, "Processing of Fearful and Neutral Information by Obsessive–Compulsives," *Behavior Research and Therapy,* 22(1984):259–265.

Persson, G. and C.L. Nordlund, "Agoraphobics and Social Phobics: Differences in Background Factors, Syndrome Profiles and Therapeutic Response," *Acta Psychiatrica Scandinavica,* 71(1985):148–159.

Philips, H.C., "Return of Fear in the Treatment of a Fear of Vomiting," *Behavior Research and Therapy,* 23(1985):45–52.

Phillips, J.P.N., "Essay-writing Phobia in Undergraduates." *Behavior Research and Therapy,* 24(1986):603–604.

Pickering, Thomas G. et al., "How Common Is White Coat Hypertension?" *Journal of the American Medical Association,* 259:2(January 8, 1988), pp. 225–228.

Prigatano, C.P. and H.J. Johnston, "Autonomic Nervous System Changes Associated with a Spider Phobic Reaction," *Journal of Abnormal Psychology,* 83(1974):169.

Pynoos, Robert S. et al., "Life Threat and Post-Traumatic Stress in School Age Children," *Archives of General Psychiatry,* 44(December 1987).

Quitkin, F.M. et al., "Phobic Anxiety Complicated by Drug Dependence and Addiction," *Archives of General Psychiatry,* 27(1972):159–162.

Rachman, S., "Agoraphobia: A Safety-Signal Perspective," *Behavior Research and Therapy,* 22(1984):59–70.

———, *Fear and Courage.* San Francisco: W.H. Freeman, 1978.

———, *The Meaning of Fear.* Baltimore: Penguin Books, 1974.

———, "The Modification of Agoraphobia Avoidance Behaviour: Some Fresh Possibilities," *Behavior Research and Therapy,* 21(1983):567–574.

———, *Phobias: Their Nature and Control.* Springfield, Illinois: Charles C. Thomas, 1968.

Rachman, S., J. Cobb, S. Grey, B. McDonald, D. Mawson, G. Sartory and R. Stern, "The Behavioral Treatment of Obsessional–Compulsive disorders, with and without Clomipramine," *Behavior Research and Therapy,* 17(1979):467–478

Rachman, S. and R. Hodgson, "Synchrony and Desynchrony in Fear and Avoidance," *Behaviour Research and Therapy,* 12(1974):311–318

Rachman, S., R. Hodgson and I.M. Marks, "Treatment of OCD by Modelling and Flooding In Vivo," *Behavior Research and Therapy,* 11(1973):463–471.

Raguram, R. and A. Bhide, "Patterns of Phobic Neurosis: A Retrospective Study," *British Journal of Psychiatry,* 147(1985):557–560.

Rainey, J.M. et al., "A Comparison of Lactate and Isoproterenol Anxiety States," *Psychopathology,* 17(1984):74–82.

Ramsay, R.W. and R. Noorbergen, *Living with Loss.* New York: William Morrow, 1981.

Rangtell, L., "The Analysis of a Doll Phobia," *International Journal of Psychoanalysis,* 33(1952): 43.

Rapee, Ronald, "Differential Response to Hyperventilation in Panic Disorder and Generalized Anxiety Disorder," *Journal of Abnormal Psychology,* 95(1986):27.

Rapoport, J., R. Elkins and E. Mikkelsen, "Chlorimipramine in Adolescents with Obsessive–Compulsive Disorder," *Psychopharmacology Bulletin,* 16(1980):61–63.

Rapoport, J. et al., "Dietary Choice and the Effects of Caffeine Challenge in Children," *Archives of General Psychiatry,* 41(1984):1073–1079.

Raschka, L.B., "The Incubus Syndrome," *Canadian Journal of Psychiatry,* 24(1979):549–553.

Razani, J., "Treatment of Phobias by Systematic Desensitization," *Archives of General Psychiatry,* 30(1974):291–296.

Redlich, Fredrich C. and Daniel X. Freedman, *The Theory and Practice of Psychiatry.* New York: Basic Books, 1966.

Reich, Wilhelm, *Character Analysis.* New York: Orgone Institute, 1945.

Reiss, S. et al., "Anxiety Sensitivity, Anxiety Frequency and the Prediction of Fearfulness," *Behavior Research and Therapy,* 24(1986):1–8.

Reynolds, D.K., *Naikan Therapy: Meditation for Self Development.* Chicago: University of Chicago Press, 1983.

Ricciuti, H.N., "Fear and Social Attachments in the First Year of Life," in M. Lewis and L.A. Rosenblum (eds.), *The Origins of Fear.* New York: Wiley, 1974.

Rimm, D., D. Briddell, M. Zimmerman and G. Caddy, "The Effects of Alcohol and the Expectancy of Alcohol on Snake Fear," *Addictive Behavior,* 6(1981):47–51.

Rimm, D.C., L.H. Janda, D.W. Lancaster, M. Nahl and K. Dittmar, "The Origin and Maintenance of Phobias," *Behavior Research and Therapy,* 15(1977):231–238.

Rizzo, P.A., S.M. Spadaro, G. Albani and C. Morocutti, "Contingent Negative Variation and Phobic Disorders," *Neuropsychobiology,* 9(1983):73–77.

Robbins, Rossell Hope, *The Encyclopedia of Witchcraft and Demonology.* New York: Crown, 1974.

Robins, L.N., J.E. Helzer and M. Weissman, "Lifetime Prevalence of Specific Psychiatric Disorders in Three Sites," *Archives of General Psychiatry,* 4(1984):949–958.

Rogerson, H.L., "Venereophobia in the Male," *British Journal of Venereal Disease,* 27(1951):158–159.

Rohrbaugh, M. and D.C. Ricci, "Paradoxical Enhancement of Learned Fear," *Journal of Abnormal Psychology,* 75(1970):210–216

Roper, G., S. Rachman and I.M. Marks, "Passive and Participant Modelling in Exposure Treatment of OCD," *Behavior Research and Therapy,* 13(1975):271–279.

Rose, R.J. and W.B. Ditto, "A Developmental Genetic Analysis of Common Fears from Early Adolescence to Early Childhood," *Child Development,* 54(1983):361–368.

Rosenthal, T.L. and A. Bandura, "Psychological Modeling: Theory and Practice," in S.L. Garfield and A.E. Bergin (eds.), *Handbook of Psychotherapy and Behavior Change: An Empirical Analysis.* New York: Wiley, 1978.

Ross, J., "The Use of Former Phobics in the Treatment of Phobias," *American Journal of Psychiatry,* 136(1980):715–717.

Roth, M., "Agoraphobia, Panic Disorder and Generalized Anxiety Disorder: Some Implications of Recent Advances," *Psychiatric Development,* 2(1984):31–52.

Roth, M. and C. Argyle, "Panic Attacks in Phobic and Generalized Anxiety and Depression," in *Abstracts of the World Biological Psychiatry Congress* (Abstract 113.2). Philadelphia, 1985.

Rubin, Rhea Joyce, *Bibliotherapy Sourcebook.* Phoenix: Oryx Press, 1978.

Rubinow, D.R. and P. Roy-Byrne, "Premenstrual Syndromes: Overview from a Methodologic Perspective," *American Journal of Psychiatry,* 141(1984):163–172.

Rush, Benjamin, *The Selected Writings of Benjamin Rush,* edited by D.D. Runes. New York: The Philosophical Library, 1947.

Rutner, I.T., "Effects of Feedback and Instructions on Phobic Behavior," *Behavior Therapy,* 4(1973):338–348.

Rycroft, Charles, *A Critical Dictionary of Psychoanalysis.* Harmondsworth, Middlesex, England: Penguin Books, 1986.

Ryle, J.A., "Nosophobia," *Journal of Mental Science,* 94(1948):1–17.

Salkovskis, P.M., D.R.O. Jones and D.M. Clark, "Respiratory Control in the Treatment of Panic Attacks: Replication," *British Journal of Psychiatry,* 148(1986):526–532.

Salkovskis, Paul M. and H. Warwick, "Morbid Preoccupations, Health Anxiety and Reassurance: A Cognitive–Behavioral Approach to Hypochondriasis," *Behavior Research and Therapy,* 24(1986):597–602.

Sarafino, Edward P., *The Fears of Childhood.* New York: Human Sciences Press, 1986.

Sartory, G., S. Richman and S. Grey, "Return of Fear: The Role of Rehearsal," *Behavior Research and Therapy,* 20(1982):123–133.

Schapira, K, T.A. Kerr and M. Roth, "Phobias and Affective Illness," *British Journal of Psychiatry,* 117(1970):25–32.

Schapira, K., M. Roth, T.A. Kerr and C. Gurney, "The Prognosis of Affective Disorders: The Differentiation of Anxiety from Depressive Illness," *British Journal of Psychiatry,* 121(1972):175–181.

Scharfstein, Steven S., "The Economics of Anxiety," in *Consequences of Anxiety: Management Strategies for the Primary Care Physician.* A clinical monograph based on a symposium held October 8–11, 1987, Orlando, Florida.

Scherer, M.W. and C.Y. Nakamura, "A Fear Survey Schedule for Children (FSS-FC)," *Behavior Research and Therapy,* 6(1968):173–182.

Schraeder, P.L., R. Pontzer and T.R. Engel, "A Case of Being Scared to Death," *Archives of Internal Medicine,* 143(1983):1793–1794.

Schultz, J. and W. Luthe, *Autogenic Training: A Psychophysiological Approach in Psychotherapy.* New York: Grune and Stratton, 1959.

Schwartz, Barry, *Psychology of Learning and Behavior.* New York: W.W. Norton, 1978.

Scott, Donald and Richard Hirschman, "Psychological Aspects of Dental Anxiety in Adults," *Journal of the American Dental Association,* 104(January 1982), pp. 27–31.

Seligman, Martin, *Helplessness: On Depression, Development, and Death.* San Francisco: W.C. Freeman, 1975.

———, "Phobias and Preparedness," *Behavior Therapy,* 2(1971):307–320.

Shafar, S., "Aspects of Phobic Illness—A Study of 90 Personal Cases," *British Journal of Medicine and Psychology,* 49(1976):221–236.

Shapiro, M.B., I.M. Marks and B. Fox, "Phobic and Affective Symptoms in an Individual Psychiatric Patient," *British Journal of Social and Clinical Psychology,* 2(1963):81–93.

Shaw. O., "Dental Anxiety in Children," *British Dental Journal,* 139(1975):134–139.

Shaw, P., "Three Behavior Therapies for Social Phobia," *British Journal of Psychiatry,* 134(1979):620–623.

Shear, M.K., "Pathophysiology of Panic: Review of Pharmacologic Provocative Tests and Monitoring Data," *Journal of Clinical Psychiatry,* 47:6(June 1986, Supplement)

Shear, M.K., R.B. Devereux, R. Kramer-Fox, J.J. Mann and A. Frances, "Low Prevalence of Mitral Valve Prolapse in Patients with Panic Disorder " *American Journal of Psychiatry,* 141(1984):302–330

Sheehan, D.V., *The Anxiety Disease.* New York: Scribner, 1984

Sheehan, D.V., J. Ballenger and G. Jacobsen, "Treatment of Endogenous Anxiety," *Archives of General Psychiatry,* 37(1980):51–59

Sheehan, D.V. and K.H. Sheehan, "The Classification of Phobic Disorders," *International Journal of Psychiatric Medicine,* 12(1982):243–266.

Sheehan, D.V. et al., "Panic Attacks and the Dexamethasone Suppression Test," *American Journal of Psychiatry,* 140(1983):1063–1064.

———, "Some Biochemical Correlates of Panic Attacks with Agoraphobia and Their Response to a New Treatment," *Journal of Clinical Psychopharmacology,* 4(1984):66–75

Sher, K.J., J.O. Frost and R. Otto, "Cognitive Deficits in Compulsive Checkers *Behavior Research and Therapy,* 21(1983):357–363

Shine, K.I., "Anxiety in Patients with Heart Disease," *Psychosomatics,* 25(1984):27–31.

Shoben, E.J. and L. Borland, "An Empirical Study of the Etiology of Dental Fears," *Journal of Clinical Psychology,* 10(1954):171–174.

Silverman, I. and J.H. Geer, "The Elimination of Recurrent Nightmare by Desensitisation of a Related Phobia," *Behavior Research and Therapy,* 6(1968):109–112.

Sim, M. and H. Houghton, "Phobic Anxiety and Its Treatment," *Journal of Nervous and Mental Disorders,* 143(1966):484–491.

Sinnott, A., B. Jones and A.S. Fordham, "Agoraphobia: A Situational Analysis," *Journal of Clinical Psychology,* 37(1981):123–127

Smail, P. et al., "Alcohol Dependence and Phobic States: I A Prevalence Study," *British Journal of Psychiatry,* 144(1984):53–57

Snaith, R.P., "A Clinical Investigation of Phobias," *British Journal of Psychiatry,* 114(1968):673–698.

Snyder, S.H. and S.J. Peroutka, "Antidepressants and Neurotransmitter Receptors," in R.M. Post and J.C. Ballenger (eds.), *Neurobiology of Mood Disorders.* Baltimore: Williams & Wilkins, 1984.

Solyom, L., B. Ledwidge and C. Colyom, "Delineating Social Phobia," *British Journal of Psychiatry,* 149(1986):464–470.

Spielberger, C.D., R. Gorsuch and R. Lushene, *The State-Trait Anxiety Inventory.* Riverside, California: Consulting Psychologists Press, 1970.

Spina, Joseph, "Fear of Cataract Extraction," *Clinical Gerontologist,* 2:4(Summer 1984), pp. 68–70

Spinks, G. Stephens, *Psychology and Religion.* Boston: Beacon Press, 1968.

Stampfl, T.G. and D.J. Levis, "Essentials of Implosion Therapy: A Learning Theory Based on Psycho dynamic Behavioral Therapy," *Journal of Abnormal Psychology,* 72(1967):496–503.

Steptoe, A. and H. Fidler, "Stage Fright in Orchestral Musicians: A Study of Cognitive and Behavioral Strategies in Performance Anxiety," *British Journal of Psychology,* 78(1987):241–249.

Sterba, Edith, "Excerpt from the Analysis of a Dog Phobia," *The Psychoanalytic Quarterly,* 4:(1935), pp. 135–160.

Stern, R. and I.M. Marks, "Brief and Prolonged Flooding: A Comparison in Agoraphobic Patients," *Archives of General Psychiatry,* 28(1973):270–276.

Stern, R.S., I.M. Marks, D. Mawson and D.K. Luscombe, "Clomipramine and Exposure for Compulsive Rituals: II. Plasma Levels, Side Effects and Outcome," *British Journal of Psychiatry,* 136(1980):161–166

Stern, T.A., "The Management of Depression and Anxiety Following Myocardial Infarction," *The Mount Sinai Journal of Medicine* (October 1985).

Stockwell, R., P. Smail, R. Hodgson and S. Canter, "Alcohol Dependence and Phobic States. II: A Retrospective Study," *British Journal of Psychiatry,* 144(1984):58–63.

Stratton, J.G., D.A. Parker and J.R. Snibbe, "Posttraumatic Stress in Police Officers Involved in Shootings," *Psychology Reports,* 55(1984):127–131.

Suess, W.M., A.B. Alexander, D.D. Smith, H.W. Sweeney and R.J. Marion, "The Effects of Psychological Stress on Respiration: A Preliminary Study of Anxiety and Hyperventilation," *Psychophysiology,* 17(1980):535–40.

Suinn, R.M., *Fundamentals of Behavior Pathology.* New York: John Wiley, 1975.

Suinn, R.M. and F. Richardson, "Anxiety Management Training: A Non-specific Behavior Therapy Program for Anxiety Control," *Behavior Therapy,* 2(1971):498–510.

Talbot, M., "Panic in School Phobia," *American Journal of Orthopsychiatry,* 27(1951):286–295

Taylor, J.A., "A Personality Scale of Manifest Anxiety," *Journal of Abnormal and Social Psychology* 48(1953):285–290.

Tearnan, B.H., M.J. Telch and P. Keefe, "Etiology and Onset of Agoraphobia: A Critical Review,' *Comparative Psychiatry,* 25(1984):51–62.

Teghtsoonian, Robert and Randy O. Frost, "The Effects of Viewing Distance on Fear of Snakes, ' *Journal of Behavior Therapy and Experimental Psychiatry,* 13(1982)·181–190

Telch, M.J., B.H. Tearnan and C.B. Taylor, "Antidepressant Medication in the Treatment of Agoraphobia: A Critical Review," *Behavior Research and Therapy,* 21(1983):505–517.

Teja, J.S., R.L. Narang and A.K. Aggarwal, "Depression across Cultures," *British Journal of Psychiatry,* 119(1971):253–260.

Terhune, W.B., "The Phobic Syndrome," *Archives of Neurological Psychiatry,* 62(1949):162–172.

———, "The Phobic Syndrome: Its Nature and Treatment," *Journal of Arkansas Medical Society,* 58(1961):23–236.

Thomas, C.S., "Dysmorphophobia: A Question of Definition," *British Journal of Psychiatry,* 144(1984):513–516.

Thoren, P. et al., "Clomipramine Treatment of Obsessive–Compulsive Disorders: I," *Archives of General Psychiatry,* 37(1980):1281–1285.

Thorpe, G.L. and L.E. Burns, *The Agoraphobic Syndrome.* New York: Wiley, 1983.

Thorpe, G L., E.G. Freedman and J.D. Lazar, "Assertiveness Training and Exposure In Vivo for Agoraphobics," *Behaviour Psychotherapy,* 13(1985):132–141.

Thouless, Robert H., *An Introduction to the Psychology of Religion.* Cambridge: Cambridge University Press, 1971.

Thyer, B.A., "Alcohol Abuse among Clinically Anxious Patients," *Behavior Research and Therapy,* 24(1986):357–359.

Thyer, B.A. and G.C. Curtis, "The Effects of Ethanol Intoxication on Phobic Anxiety," *Behavior Research and Therapy,* 22(1984):599–610.

Thyer, B.A., R.M. Nesse, O.G. Cameron and G.C. Curtis, "Agoraphobia: A Test of the Separation Anxiety Hypothesis," *Behavior Research and Therapy,* 23(1985):75–78.

Thyer, B.A., J.D. Papsdorf and P. Wright, "Physiological and Psychological Effects of Acute Intentional Hyperventilation," *Behavior Research and Therapy,* 22(1984):587–590.

Thyer, B.A., R.T. Parrish, G.C. Curtis, R.M. Nesse and O.G. Cameron, "Ages of Onset of DSM-III Anxiety Disorders," *Comprehensive Psychiatry,* 26(1985):113–122.

Tollefson, Gary D., "Pharmacologic and Nonpharmacologic Treatment of Anxiety," pp. 34–36 in *Consequences of Anxiety: Management Strategies for the Primary Care Physician.* A clinical monograph based on a symposium held October 8–11, 1987, Orlando, Florida.

Torgersen, S., "Childhood and Family Characteristics in Panic and Generalized Anxiety Disorders," *American Journal of Psychiatry,* 143:5(May 1986).

———, "Genetic Factors in Anxiety Disorders," *Archives of General Psychiatry,* 40(1983):1085–1089.

———, "Hereditary Differentiation of Anxiety and Affective Neuroses," *British Journal of Psychiatry* 146(1985):530–534.

———, "The Nature and Origin of Common Phobic Fears," *British Journal of Psychiatry,* 134(1979):343-351.

Tuma, A.H. and J.D. Maser, *Anxiety and the Anxiety Disorders*. Hillsdale, N.J.: Erlbaum, 1985.

Turin, A.C. and S.N. Lynch, "Comprehensive Relaxation Training," in R.J. Corsini (ed.), *Handbook of Innovative Psychotherapies*. New York: Wiley, 1981.

Turner, R.M., T.R. Giles and R. Marofiote, "Agoraphobics: A Test of the Repression Hypothesis," *British Journal of Clinical Psychology*, 22(1983):75–76.

Turner, R.M., D. Meles and R. DiTomasso, "A Controlled Comparison among Social Phobics, Obsessive–Compulsives, Agoraphobics, Sexual Disorders and Simple Phobics," *Behavior Research and Therapy*, 21(1983):181–183.

Turner, R.M., F.I. Newman and E.B. Foa, "Assessing the Impact of Cognitive Differences in the Treatment of Obsessive–Compulsives," *Journal of Clinical Psychology*, 39(1983):933–938.

Turner, R.M., G.S. Steketee and E.B. Foa, "Fear of Criticism in Washers, Checkers and Phobics," *Behavior Research and Therapy*, 17(1979):79–81.

Turner, Samuel, *Behavioral Theories and Treatment of Anxiety*. New York: Plenum Press, 1984.

Turner, S.M., D.C. Beidel and R.S. Nathan, "Biological Factors in Obsessive–Compulsive Disorders," *Psychological Bulletin*, 97(1985): pp. 430–450.

Turner, S.M. et al., "Fluoxetine Treatment of Obsessive–Compulsive Disorder," *Journal of Clinical Psychopharmacology* (1986).

Turns, Danielle M., "Epidemiology of Phobics and Obsessive–Compulsive Disorders in Adults," *American Journal of Psychotherapy*, 39:3(July 1985).

Uhde, T.W., J.P. Boulenger, R.M. Post et al., "Fear and Anxiety: Relationship to Noradrenergic Function," *Psychopathology*, 17(1984):8–23.

Uhde, T.W., J.P. Boulenger, L. Siever et al., "Drug Challenges in Panic Disorder," in *Abstracts of the Annual Meeting of APA* (Abstract 92D, p. 211). Los Angeles, May 1984.

Uhde, T.W. et al., "Longitudinal Course of Panic Disorder," *Progressive Neuro-Psychopharmacology and Biological Psychiatry*, 9(1985):39–51.

Uhde, T.W., P.P. Roy-Byrne, P.W. Gold, D.R. Rubinow, B.J. Vittone and R.M. Post, "Panic and Depression: Biological Relationships." Paper presented to APA, Dallas, May 1985.

Uhde, T.W., B.J. Vittone and R.M. Post, "Glucose Tolerance Testing in Panic Disorder," *American Journal of Psychiatry*, 141(1984):1461–1463.

Uhlenhuth, E.H., M.B. Balter and G.O. Mellinger, "Symptom Checklist Syndromes in the General Population," *Archives of General Psychiatry*, 40(1983):1167–1173.

Vandereycken, W., "Agoraphobia and Marital Relationship: Theory, Treatment and Research," *Clinical Psychological Review*, 3(1983):317–338.

Van Putten, T. and J. Yager, "Post-traumatic Stress Disorder: Emerging from the Rhetoric," *Archives of General Psychiatry*, 41(1984):411–413.

Van Valkenburg, C., H.S. Akiskal, V. Puzantian and T. Rosenthal, "Anxious Depressions: Comparisons with Panic and Major Depressive Disorders," *Journal of Affective Disorders,* 6(1984):67–82.

Van Valkenburg, C., G. Winokur, D. Behar and M. Lowry, "Depressed Women with Panic Attacks," *Journal of Clinical Psychiatry,* 45(1984):367–369.

Vargo, M.E. and W.M. Batsel, "Reduction of Death Anxiety: Comparison of Didactic, Experiential and Non-conscious Treatments," *British Journal of Medical Psychology,* 57(1984):333–337.

Vermilyea, J.A., R. Boice and D.H. Barlow, "How Do Desynchronous Response Systems Relate to the Treatment of Agoraphobia?" *Behavior Research and Therapy,* 22(1984):615–621.

Vierordt, H., *Medizinisches aus der Geschichte.* Tübingen, Germany: Laupp, 1910.

Visotsky, Harold, "Stress Management," in *A Lifetime of Health.* Chicago: Northwestern Memorial Hospital, 1987.

Volavka, J., F. Neziroglu and J.A. Yaryura-Tobias, "Clomipramine and Imipramine in Obsessive–Compulsive Disorder," *Psychiatric Research,* 14(1985):83–91.

Vontress, C.E., "Existential Anxiety," *American Mental Health Counselors Association Journal,* 8(1986).

Walrond-Skinner, Sue, *A Dictionary of Psychotherapy.* London: Routledge and Kegan Paul, 1986.

Wardle, J., "Dental Pessimism: Negative Cognitions in Fearful Dental Patients," *Behavior Research and Therapy,* 22(1984):553–556.

———, "Fear of Dentistry," *British Journal of Medical Psychology,* 55(1982):119–126.

Wardle, J. and M. Jarvis,."The Paradoxical Fear Response to Blood, Injury and Illness—A Treatment Report," *Behavior Psychotherapy,* 9(1981):13–24.

Watson, J.P. and I.M. Marks, "Relevant and Irrelevant Fear in Flooding: A Crossover Study of Phobic Patients," *Behavior Therapy,* 2(1971):275–395.

Weekes, Claire, *Agoraphobia.* New York: Hawthorn Books, 1976.

———, "A Practical Treatment of Agoraphobia," *British Medical Journal* (May 26, 1973).

———, *Simple, Effective Treatment of Agoraphobia.* New York: Bantam, 1979.

———, "Simple, Effective Treatment of Agoraphobia," *American Journal of Psychotherapy,* 32(1978):357–369.

Weideger, Paula (ed.), *Menstruation and Menopause: The Physiology and Psychology, the Myth and the Reality.* New York: Knopf, 1976.

Weiss, K.J. and D.J. Rosenberg, "Prevalence of Anxiety Disorder among Alcoholics," *Journal of Clinical Psychiatry,* 46(1985):3–5

Weissman, Myrna, "Epidemiology of Anxiety," pp. 5–6 in *Consequences of Anxiety: Management Strategies for the Primary Care Physician.* A clinical monograph based on a symposium held October 8–11, 1987, Orlando, Florida.

———, "The Epidemiology of Anxiety Disorders: Rates, Risks and Familial Patterns," in H. Tuma and J. Maser (eds.), *Anxiety and Anxiety Disorders.* Hillsdale, N.J.: Erlbaum, 1985.

Weissman, M. et al., "Children of Depressed Parents," *Archives of General Psychiatry,* 44(October 1987).

Weissman, M.M., P.J. Leaf, C.E. Holzer and K.R. Merikangas, "Epidemiology of Anxiety Disorders," *Psychopharmacology Bulletin,* 26(1985):543–545.

Weissman, Myrna M. and Kathleen R. Merikangas, "The Epidemiology of Anxiety and Panic Disorders: An Update," *Journal of Clinical Psychiatry,* 47:6(June 1986).

Werner, Arnold et al., *Psychiatric Glossary.* Washington, D.C: American Psychiatric Press, 1984.

Westphal, C., "Die Agoraphobie: Eine Neuropathische Erscheinung," *Arch fur Psychiatrie und Nervenkrankheiten,* 3(1871):138–171, 219–221.

Whitehead, T., *Fears and Phobias.* New York: Arco Publishers, 1983.

Wilks, C.G.W. and I.M. Marks, "Reducing Hypersensitive Gagging," *British Dentistry Journal,* 155(October 22, 1983), pp. 263–265.

Williams, S.L., "On the Nature and Treatment of Agoraphobia," *Progress in Behavior Modification,* 19(1985):109–144.

Williams, S.L., G. Dooseman and E. Kleifield, "Comparative Effectiveness of Guided Mastery and Exposure Treatments for Intractable Phobias," *Journal of Consulting and Clinical Psychology,* 52(1984):505–518.

Williams, S.L. and E. Kleifield, "Transfer of Behavioral Change across Phobias in Multiply Phobic Clients," *Behavior Modification,* 9(1985):22–31.

Williams, S.L. and A. Rappoport, "Cognitive Treatment in the Natural Environment for Agoraphobics," *Behavior Therapy,* 14(1983):299–313.

Williams, S.L., S.M. Turner and D.F. Peer, "Guided Mastery and Performance Desensitization for Severe Acrophobia," *Journal of Consulting Clinical Psychology,* 53(1985):237–247.

Wilson, R.R., *Don't Panic: Taking Control of Your Anxieties.* New York: Harper & Row, 1986.

Wolpe, J., "Behavior Therapy and Its Malcontents, II: Multimodal Eclecticism, Cognitive Exclusivism, and 'Exposure' Empiricism," *Journal of Behavior Therapy and Experimental Psychiatry,* 7(1976):109–116.

———, "Cognition and Causation in Human Behavior and Its Therapy," *American Psychologist,* 33(1978).

———, "Identifying the Antecedents of an Agoraphobic Reaction: A Transcript," *Journal of Behavior Therapy and Experimental Psychiatry,* 1(1970):299–304.

———, *Our Useless Fears.* Boston: Houghton Mifflin, 1981.

———, *Psychotherapy by Reciprocal Inhibition.* Stanford, California: Stanford University Press, 1958.

Woods, Scott W. et al., "Carbon Dioxide Sensitivity in Panic Anxiety," *Archives of General Psychiatry,* 43(1986):900+

Yap, P.M., "Phenomenology of Affective Disorder in Chinese and Other Cultures." CIA Foundation Symposium/Transcultural Psychiatry, London, 1965.

Yaryura-Tobias, Jose A. and Fugen A. Neziroglu, *Obsessive–Compulsive Disorders.* New York: Marcel Dekker, 1983.

Yuksel, S., et al., "Slow versus Rapid Exposure In Vivo of Phobics," *Behaviour Psychotherapy,* 12(1984):249–256.

Yule, W., B. Sacks and L. Hersov, "Successful Flooding Treatment of a Noise Phobia in an Eleven-year-old," *Journal of Behaviour Therapy and Experimental Psychiatry,* 5(1974):209–211.

Zane, M.D., "Contextual Analysis and Treatment of Phobic Behavior as It Changes," *American Journal of Psychotherapy,* 32(1978):338–356.

Zane, M.D. and H. Milt, *Your Phobia: Understanding Your Fears through Contextual Therapy.* Washington, D.C.: American Psychiatric Press, 1984.

Zimbardo, Philip G., *Psychology and Life.* Glenview, Illinois: Scott, Foresman, 1985.

Zitrin, C.M., D.F. Klein and M.G. Woerner, "Treatment of Agoraphobia with Group Exposure In Vivo and Imipramine," *Archives of General Psychiatry,* 37(1980):63–72.

Zitrin, C.M., D.F. Klein, M.G. Woerner and D.C. Ross, "Treatment of Phobias: I. Imipramine and Placebo," *Archives of General Psychiatry,* 40(1983):125–138.

Ziv, Avner, *Personality and Sense of Humor.* New York: Springer Publishing, 1984.

INDEX

A

Abandonment 1
Ablutophobia 1, 67
Abraham, Karl 198, 226
Abreaction 1, 93, 198, 239
Abstraction Anxiety—*See Mathematics; Numbers*
Abu Bakr (573-634) 1
Acarophobia 1, 32
Acceptance 1, 185
Accidents 1-2, 164, 174
Accomodation 2
Acerophobia 2
Acetycholine—*See Lithium*
Achluophobia 2
Acid Dew 2, 25
Acid Rain 2, 25
Acousticophobia 2
Acrophobia 4, 170
ACTH (Adrenocorticotrophic hormone) 4
Action Therapy 4
Active Technique 4
Acupressure 4-5, 218
Acupuncture 5, 131, 218, 299
Adapin—*See Doxepin*
Adaptation 5-6, 116
Adaptive Behavior Scale 5
Addiction 5-6, 24, 26, 55, 108, 272, 427
Adenosine 6, 78, 91
Adenylate Cyclase 6
Adjustment 6
Adler, Alfred (1870-1937) 6, 31, 77, 112, 114, 198, 226, 241, 341, 403
Adler, Arthur 142
Adnazolam 41
Adolescence 137-139, 393-394
Adrenaline 7, 89, 108, 172
Adrenergic System 7
Aelurophobia 8, 25, 93
Aerocrophobia 8
Aeronausiphobia 8, 25
Aerophagia 8
Aerophobia 8, 156
Affective Disorders and Neuroses 8-11, 44, 97, 261, 268, 275, 358—*See also sepcific disorder*
Aging 1, 12, 28, 65, 74, 79, 93, 103, 208, 239, 257, 268, 294
Agism 12
Agitation 12, 26
Agoraphobia 8, 12-24, 28, 53, 56, 166, 301, 360, 370, 379-380, 425
Agraphobia 24
Agras, Stewart 318
Agrizoophobia 24, 32, 34
Agyiophobia 24
Aha, Ah-hah 24-25
Aichmophobia 25
Aichurophobia 25
AIDS (acquired immune deficiency syndrome) 2-3
Ailurophobia 8, 25, 32, 93
Air 25, 120, 156
Air Pollution 2, 25, 195, 251
Airsickness 25
Akathisia 25-26
Albert B. 26, 373, 423
Albuminurophobia 26
Alcohol and Alcoholism 26, 157
Alektorophobia 26, 96
Alexander, Franz (1891-1964) 4, 26-27, 31, 118
Algophobia 27
Alienation 27
Allegron—*See Nortriptyline*
Allergic Disorders 27
Alliumphobia 27
Allodoxaphobia 27
Allport, Gordon Willard (1897-1967) 27, 407
Alone 1, 28, 61, 74, 173, 371
Alpha Adrenergic Blockers—*See Adrenergic Blocking Agents*
Alprazolam (Xanax) 28, 40-41, 54, 78, 117, 272
Alzheimer's Disease 29, 208
AMA—*See American Medical Association*
Amathophobia 28
Amaxophobia 28
Ambivalence 28, 34
American Medical Association (AMA) 3
Amineptine 29, 41
Amitid 29
Amitriptyline (Tryptizol) 29
Amnesia 29
Amnesiophobia 29
Amoxapine 29, 41
Amphetamines 29-30, 57, 108
Amulets 30
Amychophobia 30
Amygdala 30
Anablepophobia—*See Heights*
Analgesics 30-31
Anal Stage 30, 125, 155, 296
Analysand 31
Analysis—*See Psychoanalysis*
Analysis of a Phobia in a Five-Year Old Boy (case study) 256
Anamnesis 31
Anaphylaxis 31
Anatomy of Melancholy, The (book) 31, 106, 312
Androphobia 32, 57
Anemophobia 25
Angina Pectoris 32
Anginophobia 32
Anglophobia 32, 172, 251
Angst 32, 177
Angyal, Andras (1902-60) 32
Anhedonia 32
Animals 11, 24, 26, 30, 32, 34, 88, 94, 154—*See also specific type*
Animism 34, 183
Ankylophobia—*See Joint Immobility*
Anna O. (Bertha Pappenheim) (1859-1936) 1, 34, 86
Anorexia Nervosa 35, 52, 83, 88, 100, 165, 185
Anorgasmia 35
Anthophobia 35
Anthropophobia 35
Antianxiety Drugs 35, 54, 87, 89, 161, 253
Antibiotics 35-36
Anticholinergics 36
Anticipatory Anxiety 300
Anticonvulsives 36, 107
Antidepressants 36-41
Antihistamines 41-42
Antimanic Drugs 42, 162
Antiophobia 43
Antipsychotic Drugs 26, 42, 162
Ants 43
Anutaphobia 43
Anxiety 6, 24, 35, 43-56, 66-67, 76, 78, 86, 89, 109, 117, 263, 284, 296—*See also specific anxiety*
Anxiety Sensitivity Index (ASI) 56
Anxiogenic 56
Anxiolytic Drugs (anxiolytics) 11, 40, 54, 56, 100, 152, 272
Apeirophobia 56
Aphenophobia 56, 75
Apiphobia—*See Bees*
Apocalypse 56, 88, 171
Appetite Suppressants 30, 57
Approach-Avoidance Conflict 57
Approximation Conditioning—*See Shaping*
Aquaphobia—*See Water*
Arachibutyrophobia 57, 302
Arachnophobia 32, 57
Arches 57
Arithmophobia—*See Numbers*
Arrhenophobia 57
Arsonphobia 57
Asendin—*See Amoxapine*
Assertiveness Training 57-58, 70, 343
Asthenic Personality 58
Asthenophobia 58, 182
Asthma 27, 58, 103, 259, 304
Astraphobia 58
Astrology 58
Astrophobia 87
As You Like It (play) 367
Ataraxy 58
Ataxiophobia 58
Atelophobia 59
Atenolol (tenormin) 55, 59
Atephobia 59
Attachment Theory 59, 79, 239
Attention Deficit and Hyperactivity Disorder (ADHD) 59
Attribution Theory 59, 242
Atychiphobia 59
Aulophobia 59
Aura 59
Aurophobia 60

Auroraphobia 60
Authority 60, 89, 322
Autodysomophobia 60
Autogenic Training 27, 60, 83
Autohypnosis 60
Automobiles 28, 60, 278
Automysophobia 60
Autonomic Nervous System (ANS) 7, 60-61, 118, 152, 284
Autonomic Side Effect 61
Autophobia 61, 74
Aventyl—*See Nortriptyline*
Aversion Therapy 61-62, 119, 302, 331
Aviatophobia 62
Avoidance Learning 62
Avoidance Response 63, 174
Avoidant Disorders 54, 63, 307
Ayllon, Teodoro 71, 295

B

Babies 63-64
Bacilli 64
Bacillophobia 64
Bacteria 64
Bacteriophobia 64
Bad Men 64
Baldness 65
Ballistophobia 65
Bandura, Albert 65, 242, 358
Barber's Chair Syndrome 65, 69, 114, 210
Barbiturates 66, 134, 358
Barlow, David H. 24, 54, 66, 240, 384
Barophobia 66
Barren Spaces 66, 94
Basiphobia 67
Basistasiphobia 67
Bateson, Gregory (1904-80) 67, 155
Bathing 1, 67
Bathophobia 67
Bathroom Phobia 67
Batophobia 67
Batrachophobia 67, 198
Bats 67, 195
Battle Fatigue 67
Beards 68, 322
Beating 68
Beauty Shop 68
Beck, Aaron T. 69, 109-110
Bed 69, 106, 207
Bedwetting 61, 69
Bees 69, 89, 108
Behaviorism 70, 104, 269, 331, 423
Behavior Modification 61, 70, 87, 109-110, 113-114, 170, 242, 252, 258, 267, 277, 295, 341-342, 368
Behavior Therapy 4, 10, 22, 24, 55, 58, 62-63, 66, 69-74, 78, 106, 108-110, 115, 118, 125, 132, 142, 192, 204, 247, 252, 271, 274, 277, 283, 287, 291, 301, 316, 333, 338, 341-342, 350, 357, 360, 373—*See also specific therapy*
Belching 75, 192
Belonophobia 76
Bends 76, 153
Benedict, Ruth 226
Benedikt, Moritz (1825-1920) 14
Benzodiazepines 40-41, 54-56, 66, 76, 100
Bereavement 76
Bergler, Edmund 82
Berne, Eric (1910-70) 76, 411
Beta-Blocking Agents 7, 77, 330
Bettelheim, Bruno 77, 183
Beyond The Pleasure Principle (book) 198
Biased Apperception 77
Bible 44, 78
Bibliophobia 78, 84
Bibliotherapy—*See Books*
Binet, Alfred 190
Binswanger, Otto (1852-1929) 425
Biodynamic Psychology 78
Bioenergetics 83
Biofeedback 74, 78, 83, 130, 217, 299, 345
Bipolar Disorder—*See Manic-Depressive Disorder*
Birds 26, 79, 189
Birthdays 79
Birth Trauma 59, 79, 361
Black Cats 79
Bleuler, Eugen (1857-1939) 1, 28, 79, 249
Blocking 80
Blocq, Paul Oscar (1860-96) 80
Blocq's Syndrome 80
Blood 80-81, 132; Pressure 61, 82, 107, 223; Transfusions 82, 412
Blushing 82, 174
Body: Image 83, 100, 368; Odor 60, 83, 293; Therapies 83, 350
Bogeyman 99
Bolshephobia 83
Bolshevism 83
Books 78, 84
Borborygami 84
Borderline Personality Disorder 84, 279, 307
Boredom 85
Boss, Medard 85, 122
Botonophobia 85
Bound—*See Tied-Up*
Bowlby, John 59, 85
Bradycardia 85
Brain: Brainwashing 86, 229; Disease 85, 268; Imaging Techniques 85, 323
Breakdown—*See Nervous Breakdown*
Breuer, Josef (1841-1925) 34, 86, 236
Bridges 86, 202
Bromides 87
Bromidrophobia 87
Bromidrosiphobia 83
Brontophobia 87
Browne, Richard 280
Bugging 87
Bugs 87
Buildings 88
Bulimia 83, 88, 165, 185
Bulls 88
Bunyan, John (1628-88) 313
Bupropion 41, 88
Bureaucracy 60, 88
Burglars 89
Buried Alive 89
Burrow, Trigant (1875-1951) 115
Burton, Robert (1577-1640) 31, 106, 312
Buspar 89
Buspirone 89
Butriptyline 41, 89
Butterflies 89

C

Caffeine 56, 78, 89-91
Cainophobia 91
Cancer 91, 96, 103, 372
Carbon Dioxide 56, 78, 92, 96, 158, 250
Cardiophobia 92
Cardiovascular Symptoms 92
Cargo Anxiety 92
Carnophobia 92
Case Control 92, 110, 258
Castration 67, 92, 124, 171, 303, 307
Catagelophobia 93
Catapedaphobia 93
Cataract Extraction 93
Catastrophic Anxiety 93, 180
Catch-22 (book) 89
Catharsis 1, 4, 34, 93, 239, 350
Cathexis 93
Cathisophobia 93
Catoptrophobia 93
Cats 8, 25, 79, 93, 170, 200
Cattell, Raymond B. 385
Causality 94
Cemeteries 94, 110, 124
Cenophobia 94
Centophobia 94
Central Nervous System 78, 90, 94, 108, 218, 358
Ceraunophobia 95
Cerny, Jerome 54
CHAANGE (self-help organization) 95
Chaetophobia 95
Change 95
Character Analysis and Training 95, 344
Charcot, Jean-Martin (1825-93) 95, 246
Checking (ritual) 96
Cheimaphobia 96
Chemoceptors 78, 92, 96
Chemotherapy 96
Cherophobia 96
Chickens 26, 96
Child Abuse 97, 116, 183
Childbirth 68, 97, 275, 327
Childhood 1, 11, 34, 44, 54, 97-99, 124, 260, 287, 361
Children 99-100
Chins 100, 202
Chionophobia—*See Snow*
Chlamydia 364
Chlordiazepoxide 100, 253
Chloropromazine 100
Choking 32, 58, 100, 152
Cholera 101
Cholesterol 101, 220
Chorophobia 101
Chrematophobia 101
Chromatophobia 102
Chronophobia 103, 106, 163
Churches 103, 166
Cibophobia 103
Circumspection-Preemption-Control (CPC) Cycle 103
Circumstantiality 103
Citalopram 41

Classical Conditioning 104, 238, 252, 292, 302, 331, 344, 347, 362
Claustrophobia 11, 17, 74, 85, 89, 104-106, 114, 170
Claustrophoboid 105
Cleaning (ritual) 105
Cleithrophobia 105
Cleptophobia 106
Cliffs 106, 119
Climacophobia 106
Climate 106, 120, 254, 358
Clinical Psychology 106
Clinophobia 106
Clithrophobia 74, 106
Clocks 106
Clomipramine 106, 292
Clonazepam 107
Clonidine 107
Clothing 107
Clouds 107, 284
Clovaxamine 41, 107
Clozapine 107
Cnidophobia 108
Coaching 108
Cocaine 108
Cockroaches 108
Cognitive Therapy 69, 109-110, 136, 170, 277; Appraisal 109; Dissonance 109; Restructuring 109-110, 357
Cognitive Therapy and the Emotional Disorders (book) 69
Cohort 92, 110, 119, 258
Coimetrophobia 94, 110
Coitophobia 110
Coitus More Ferarum 111
Coitus Oralis 111
Cold 96, 111, 120
Collective Unconscious 111
Colors 102, 107, 111, 339, 343, 426
Combat Fatigue 111
Combined Therapy 111
Cometophobia 112
Comets 112
Commitment Phobia 112, 259
Compensation 6, 112, 241
Complex 6, 112, 241
Compulsion 112
Compulsive Personality 113
Computer Phobia 113, 120, 260
Computer Therapy 113
Concordin—*See Protriptyline*
Condensation 113, 157
Conditioning and Conditioning Therapy 24, 104, 113-114, 252, 295, 423; Conditioned Response 62, 113-114, 238, 302, 347; Conditioned Stimulus (CS) 104, 113-114, 238, 302, 344
Confinement 114, 120
Confrontation 114
Conjoint Therapy 114
Conscience 114, 372
Conscious 114
Consensual Validation 115
Constipation 115, 117
Contamination 25, 43, 64, 75, 97, 109, 115, 124, 251
Contextual Therapy 24, 115, 432
Contingency Management 115, 295
Contrectophobia 116
Contributions to Psychological Theory (book) 253
Control Group 116
Conversational Catharsis—*See Catharsis*
Conversion 116, 236
Coping 109, 116
Coprastasophobia 117
Coprophobia 117
Corners 117
Coronary Bypass Anxiety 117, 220
Corpses 117, 123, 283
Corrective Emotional Experience 27, 117
Correlation 118
Cortisol 118
Co-Therapy 118
Counterconditioning 56, 118, 343
Counterphobia 105, 118, 359
Countertransference 118
Courage to Create, The (book) 266
Covert Modeling 56, 72, 117-118
Covert Sensitization 119
Cremnophobia 119
Crime 65, 119
Crisis Intervention 119
Criticism 27, 119, 152, 182
Crossings 119
Cross Sectional 119
Crowds 120, 127, 172
Crucifixes 120
Crying 120
Cryophobia 120
Crystallophobia 120
Curses 120
Cyberphobia 120
Cyclones 25, 120
Cyclophobia 120
Cyclothymia 9, 120
Cymophobia 121
Cynophobia 32, 121, 154
Cyprianophobia 121
Cypridophobia 121

D

Dampness 121, 230
Dancing 101, 121
Darkness 2, 121
Dasein Analysis 85, 122
Dawn 122, 172
Daylight 122
Daymare 122
Dead Bodies—*See Corpses*
Death and Death Anxiety 76, 81, 94, 99, 123-124, 167
Decapitation 124
Decaying Matter 124
Decidophobia 124
Decisions 2, 124
Deconditioning 125
Defecalgesiophobia 115, 125
Defecation 67, 125, 152
Defense Mechanisms 5, 125, 127, 341, 346, 369-370
Deformity 83, 125, 163, 252
Deipnophobia—*See Dining*
Deja Vu 126
Delusions 42, 60, 126, 237, 246, 360
Dementophobia 127
Demons 127
Demophobia 127
Dendrophobia 127
Denial 127
Densensitization Treatment 72
Dental Anxiety 128-133
Dentophobia—*See Dental Anxiety*
Dependent Personality Disorder 133, 307
Depersonalization 16-17, 27, 85, 133-134
Depression: Causes and Treatment (book) 69
Depression and Depressive Disorders 8-9, 11, 20, 24, 29-31, 35-36, 40-41, 44, 55, 59, 88-89, 107, 110, 134-142, 196, 240, 263, 267, 337—*See also specific depression*
Depth Psychology 142
Depths 67, 142
Dermatopathophobia 142
Dermatophobia 142
Desensitization 1, 4, 74, 101, 118, 125, 142, 193, 331, 362, 382
Desipramine 142
Desyrel—*See Trazodone*
Developmental Stages 30, 125, 142-145, 155, 165, 167-168, 173-174, 192, 202, 307
Devil—*See Satan*
Dexamethasone Suppression Test (DST) 21, 145
Dextrophobia 145
Diabetes 145, 230
Diabetophobia 145
Diagnosis 145-147, 230, 269, 333, 370
Diagnostic and Statistical Manual of Mental Disorders (book) 53, 147, 268-269, 279, 312, 318, 328, 332, 357
Diagnostic Criteria 86, 147-151, 312, 333, 371
Diarrhea 151
Diazepam (Valium) 54, 78, 152
Dibenzepin 41
Didaskaleinophobia 152
Diet 101
Dikephobia 152
Dilbenzepin 152
DiNardo, Peter 54
Dining Conversation 152
Dinophobia 152-153
Diplopiaphobia 152
Dipsophobia 152
Directive Therapy 152
Dirt and Dirtiness 43, 60, 75, 109, 124, 152, 190, 305
Disease 3, 26, 64, 82, 92, 153, 302—*See also specific disease*
Dishabillophobia 153
Disorder 58, 153
Disorientation 153
Displacement 153
Dissociation 153, 279
Diving 76, 153
Dizziness 61, 82, 100, 153
Doctor, Ronald M. 11
Doctors 154, 237
Dogs 121, 154
Dollard, J. 57
Dolls 155
Domatophobia 155
Domical—*See Amitriptyline*
Doorknobs 155
Dopamine 155
Doraphobia 155
Dothiepin (prothiaden) 41, 55, 155

Double-Bind Theory 67, 155
Double-Blind 155
Double Vision 156, 181
Doxepine (sinequan) 55
Drafts 156
Dreams 156, 251
Dream Symbols 157, 251
Drinking 157
Drive Theory 228
Driving 60, 157
Drowning 157
Drugs 7-8, 11, 26, 29-30, 36, 40-41, 61, 66, 76, 100, 107-108, 256, 370—*See also specific drug*; Abuse 108, 158; Dependence 158, 376; Effects 78, 158; Fear of 96, 101, 158-161, 210; Treatment 22, 161-163
Dry Mouth 36, 161
Dryness 162
Dual-Sex Therapy 162
Duncan, Isadora (1878-1927) 163
Duration 163
Dust 28, 163
Dying—*See Death*
Dynamic Theory of Personality, A (book) 253
Dysmorphophobia 68, 83, 163
Dyspareunia 163, 362-363
Dysthymia 9, 164
Dystychiphobia 164

E

Earthquakes 164
Eating and Eating Disorders 35, 83, 88, 101, 119, 165-166, 185, 196
Ecclesiaphobia 166
Echo 166
Ecophobia 166
Eczema 166
EEG (electroencephalograph) 167
Ego 6, 61, 114, 125, 167; Defense Mechanisms 5, 128, 167; Integrity 167, 173
Ego and The Id (book) 198
Ego-Nuclei 204
Eidetic Psychotherapy 167
Eisoptrophobia 167
Ejaculation 167
Elavil—*See Amitriptyline*
Electicism (electric therapy) 166
Electra Complex 92, 112, 168
Electricity 168
Electrocardiogram (EKG) 169, 256
Electroconvulsive Therapy (ECT) 136, 368
Electromyographic Pattern Analysis (EMG) 169
Electrophobia 169
Electroshock Treatment 169
Elevators 105, 114, 169
Ellis, Albert 109, 170, 341
Elurophobia 8, 93, 170
Emetophobia 170
Emotional Deprivation 170
Emotional Flooding Approaches 170
Empty Objects and Areas 94, 170, 203
Encounter Groups 114, 171, 253
Endocrine System 171
End of The World 171
Endogenous Depression 11, 171, 256
Endorphins 4, 172, 218
Eneuresis—*See Bedwetting*
Enissophobia 172
Enochlophobia 172
Entomophobia 172
Eosophobia 172
Epidemic Anxiety 3, 172, 265
Epidemiology 172
Epilepsy 172, 230
Epinephrine 7, 172
Epistaxiophobia 173
Equinophobia 173
Erection 173, 267
Eremophobia 28, 173
Ergasiophobia 173
Ergophobia 173
Ergot 173
Erikson, Eric H. 143, 167, 173, 307, 331
Erotophobia 174
Error 174
Erythrophobia 82, 174
Escalators 174
Escape Behavior 174
Esodophobia 174
ESP—*See Extrasensory Perception*
Eternity 175
Euphobia 175
Eurotophobia 175
Evil Eye 175, 273
Evocative Therapy 175
Examination Phobia—*See Test Anxiety*
Excrement—*See Feces*
Exercise 176
Exhaustion 176
Existential Therapy 6, 114, 122, 176-177, 196, 257, 266, 300; Analysis 176, 331; Movement 32; Neurosis 176
Exogenous Depression 11, 171, 177
Exorcism 177
Exposure Therapy 4, 72, 178-181, 283, 287, 432
Extrasensory Perception (ESP) 181
Eyeglasses 181
Eyes 75, 156, 181
Eysenck, Hans Jurgen 71, 74, 181-182, 266
Eysenck Personality Inventory 181-182

F

Fabrics 182, 199
Failure 59, 182
Fainting 58, 81, 182
Fairies 182
Fairy Tales 34, 182-183
Falling 86, 142, 183
Family and Family Therapy 2, 81, 87, 108, 112, 178, 183-184, 204, 223, 339, 359, 370
Fantasies 68, 92, 185
Fat 185
Father-in-Law 185
Fatigue 185
Fear 185-186—*See also specific fear*
Fear Survey Scale (FSS) 186-189
Feathers 97, 189
Febriphobia 189
Feces 117, 176, 189
Feedback 189
Felinophobia 8, 93, 189
Feminophobia 190
Fenichel, Otto (1899-1946) 93, 175, 190, 253, 318
Ferenczi, Sandor 4
Festinger, Leon 109
Fetishes 190
Fever 189-190
Fibriphobia 190
Fight Response 190
Filth—*See Dirt*
Fire 57, 190
Fish 191
Fitness Anxiety 191
5-Hydroxytroptophan 191
Fixation 191-192
Flashing Lights 192
Flatulence 75, 192
Flight Response 190
Flooding 4, 24, 72, 170, 180, 193, 238, 283, 287, 300
Floods 43, 192
Flowers 35, 193
Fluoxetine 41, 193
Flutes 193
Fluvoxamine 41, 193
Flying 8, 25, 62, 105, 107, 114, 185, 193-195
Flying Things 26, 68-69, 79, 89, 112, 195
Fog 195, 224
Folk Healers 195
Food 35, 101, 103, 196, 283
Foreigners 196
Forests 196
Foundations for a Science of Personality (book) 32
Framingham Type A Scale 196
Frankl, Viktor 176-177, 196, 257, 301
Free Association 196, 346
Freedom 197
Freedom and Destiny (book) 266
Free-Floating Anxiety 197
French, Thomas 4
Freud, Anna (1895-1982) 197-198
Freud, Sigmund (1856-1939) 2, 7, 31, 33-34, 80, 86, 112, 125, 128, 143, 173, 190, 197-198, 211, 226, 236, 246-247, 253, 256, 289-290, 296, 314, 329, 331, 341, 346, 351, 375, 398, 413, 417
Frigidity 35, 93, 198
Frigophobia 198
Frogs 67, 198
Fromm, Erich (1900-80) 198, 259
Frost 199
Functional Approach 199, 267
Functional Autonomy 27
Fur 199
Fuzz Aversion 62, 182, 199

G

GABA—*See Gamma-Amino Bytyric Acid*
Gagging 132, 199, 259
Gaiety 96, 200
Galeophobia 8, 25, 93, 200
Gallophobia 196, 200, 251
Galvanic Skin Response (GSR) 47, 200, 372

Gambling 200
Gamma Amino Butyric Acid (GABA) 78
Gamophobia 201
Garlic 27, 201
Gastrointestinal Symptoms 115, 152, 201
Gatophobia 8, 25, 93, 201
Gelder, Michael 11
Geliophobia 201
Gender Identity Disorder 201
Gender Role 201
Generalized Anxiety Disorder (GAD) 52-53, 107, 148, 201
Generational Anxiety 201
Geniophobia 100, 202
Genitals: Female 175, 189, 202; Male 202
Genital Stage 202, 296, 307
Genital Warts 365
Genophobia 202
Genuphobia 202
Gephyrophobia 202
Gerascophobia 202
Germanophobia 202, 251
Germs 64, 75, 102, 124, 202
Gerontophobia—*See Aging*
Gestalt Therapy 170, 177, 203, 222, 305, 407
Geumaphobia 203
Ghosts 203
Girls 204
Glaring Lights 204
Glass 120, 204, 230, 283
Glasser, William 204, 212, 342
Globus Hystericus 204
Glover, Edward (1888-1972) 204
Goal 204
Goal Attainment Scaling (GAS) 205
Goblins 205
God 205-206
Goethe, Johann Wolfgang von (1749-1832) 181, 206
Gold 60, 207
Goldstein, Kurt 228, 407
Gonorrhea—*See Sexually Transmitted Diseases; Venereal Disease*
Good News 175, 207
Graded Exposure 357
Graphophobia 207
Graves 207
Gravity 66, 207
Greece 142, 208
Greisinger, Wilhelm (1817-68) 208, 296
Grief 208
Growing Old—*See Aging*
Growth Through Reason (book) 341
Guilt 125, 134, 208, 239, 337, 371
Gull, Sir William 35
Gunshot 273, 369
Gymnophobia 209
Gynephobia 209
Gynophobia 57

H

Habit Strength 209, 228
Hadephobia 209
Hagiophobia 209
Hair 65, 95, 209; Cutting 66, 209, 356; Disease 95, 210
Halloween 210
Hallucinations 42, 108, 126, 190, 210, 281, 298, 360
Hallucinogen 210
Hamartophobia 210
Hamilton Anxiety Scale 47
Hamilton Depression Scale 211
Hamlet (play) 367
Handwringing 211
Hangover 26
Hans, Little—*See Little Hans*
Hansen, G. Armauer 252
Haphephobia 75, 212
Happiness 96, 212
Haptephobia 75
Hardy, Arthur B. 212, 404
Harpaxophobia 212
Harrington, G. Leonard 204, 212, 342
Harris' Syndrome 212
Hathaway, Starke Rosecrans (1903-84) 212, 271
Hawthorne Effect 212
Headaches 26, 29, 60, 82, 142, 167, 173, 212-219, 234, 330
Heart: Attacks 32, 82, 117, 219-220, 231; Disease 92, 101, 220; Rate 169, 220
Heat 220
Heaven 220
Hedonophobia 221
Heidegger, Martin (1889-1976) 122
Heights 11, 67, 86, 169, 221
Heliophobia 221
Hell 221
Hellenologophobia 222
Heller, Joseph 89
Helminthophobia 222
Helplessness 222, 252
Helplessness; on Depression, Development and Death (book) 360
Hematophobia 222
Hepatitis B 365
Here and Now Approach 203, 222
Heredity 222
Heresyphobia 222
Herpes 364
Herpetophobia 222
Heterophobia 223, 225
Heterosexuality 223
Hex 223
Hierarchy of Needs 223, 228, 264
Hierophobia 223
High Objects 67, 224
High Places 93, 224
Himadi, William 54
Hippocrates (460-377 B.C.) 44, 224, 279
Hippophobia 224
HIV—*See Human Immuno Virus (HIV)*
Hoarding 224
Hobgoblin 224
Hodophobia 224
Holistic Therapy 342
Holmes, Ernest 377
Holy Things 78, 103, 224
Home 166, 224, 228
Homichlophobia 224
Homilophobia 225
Homophobia 225
Homosexuality 3, 225, 236, 364
Hormephobia 225
Hormones 225-226
Horney, Karen (1885-1952) 44, 47, 67, 142, 199, 226, 395
Horses 173, 224, 226
Hospitals 154, 226
Hot Flashes 227
Hughes, Howard (1905-76) 228
Hull, Clark Leonard (1884-1952) 209, 228, 252
Human Beings 228
Human Immuno Virus (HIV) 82
Humanistic Psychology 32, 228, 407
Humor 228-229
Huntington's Chorea 230, 256
Hurricanes 230, 254
Hyalophpbia 230
Hydrargyophobia 230
Hydrophobia 230
Hydrophobophobia 230, 339
Hygrophobia 121, 230, 273
Hylephobia 230
Hylophobia 230, 265
Hypengyophobia 230
Hyperactivity—*See Attention Deficit*
Hyperinsulinism 230, 235
Hypersensitive 132, 259
Hypertension 81
Hyperthyroidism 230, 235
Hyperventilation 56, 78, 92, 101, 153, 231-233
Hypnophobia 233
Hypnosis 35, 73, 95, 131, 218, 233-234, 270, 299
Hypnotics 234
Hypoanalysis—*See Depth Psychology*
Hypochondriasis 3, 44, 153, 234, 238
Hypoglycemia 21, 212, 214, 235
Hypomanic Episodes 9
Hypothalamus 235
Hypothyroidism 235, 256
Hypsiphobia 235
Hypsosophobia—*See Acrophobia; Heights*
Hysterectomy 235
Hysteria and Hysterical Disorders 30, 95, 116, 127, 236

I

Iatrogenic Homosexuality 236
Iatrogenic Illness 237
Iatrophobia 154, 237
Ice 120, 237
Icthyophobia—*See Fish*
Id and Id Anxiety 6, 167, 237
Ideaphobia 237
Ideas 237
Ideas of Influence 237
Ideas of Reference 237, 301
Idee Fixe 237, 246
Identity 106
Illness 3, 7, 64, 82, 101, 153, 156, 237, 302—*See also specific illness*
Illyngophobia 238
Imagery 291; 299
Imipramine 55, 238
Imperfection 59, 238
Implosion and Implosive Therapy 72, 170, 180, 301
Impotence 239

Imprinting 239
Incest 239
Incontinence 239
Incubation 239
Incubus 240
India 142, 240
Individualized Behavior Avoidance Tests (IBATS) 23-24, 240
Individual Psychology 6, 240
Infants 241
Infection 124, 241
Inferiority Complex 6, 241
Infinity 56, 241
Informed Consent 241
Inhibition 241
Injection 241-242
Injury 2, 242
Inkblot Tests—*See Rorschach Test*
Innate Behavior 242
Innovation 242, 285
Inoculation 242
Insanity 127, 206, 242, 260
Insects 88-89, 172, 242
Insight 4, 242
Insomnia 90-91, 108, 242-243
Integrity Groups 95, 244
Interpersonal Anxiety 244
Interpretation of Dreams, The (book) 198
Intoxication—*See Alcoholism*
In Vivo Desensitization 244
In Vivo Therapy 244
Iophobia 244, 351
Iprindole 41, 244
Iproniazid 244
Irrational Beliefs 245
Irritable Bowel Syndrome 115, 152, 192, 201, 245, 284
Isocarboxazid 55, 245
Isolation 245
Isolophobia 246
Isoproternol Infusion 56
Isoterophobia 246
Itch 246
Ithyphallophobia 246

J

Janet, Pierre (1859-1947) 96, 126, 237, 246, 290, 315, 329
Janimine—*See Imipramine*
Janov, Arthur 246, 329
Jealousy 246
Johnson, William 162, 363
Joint Immobility 34, 238
Jones, Ernest A. (1879-1958) 246
Jones, H. E. 377
Jones, Mary Cover (1896-1987) 247, 377
Jumping 93, 247
Jung, Carl (1875-1961) 6, 31, 80, 111, 142, 157, 198, 247, 253, 341, 398, 403
Justice 247

K

Kainophobia 247
Kakorrhaphiophobia 247
Katagelophobia 247
Kathisophobia 248
Kelly, George A. (1905-67) 103
Kempf, Edward (1885-1971) 225
Kempf's Disease—*See Homosexual Panic*
Kenophobia 248
Keraunophobia 58, 248
Kidney Disease 26, 248
Kinesophobia 248, 277
Kissing 248, 308
Klein, Melanie (1882-1962) 248, 398
Kleinknecht, Donald 57
Kleptophobia 248
Kloman, R. 361, 376
Knees 202, 248
Knives 25, 249
Kohler, Edward 203
Koinoniphobia—*See Room*
Kolpophobia 249
Koniophobia 249
Kraepelin, Emil (1856-1926) 80, 249, 296, 315
Kubler-Ross, Elisabeth 208
Kymophobia 249
Kynophobia 249
Kyphophobia 249

L

Lachanophobia 249
Lactate-Induced Anxiety 78, 92, 96, 249-250, 274
Lakes 191, 250
Laliophobia 250
Landscapes 57, 66, 127, 250
Lang, Peter 186
Languages 250
Large Objects 251
Latent Content 251
Laughter 251
Lavatories, Public 251
Lazarus, Arnold 278
Lead Poisoning 251
Learned Helplessness 70, 184, 222, 251, 360
Learning and Learning Theory 252
Lentizol—*See Amitriptyline*
Leprophobia 252
Leprosy 252
Leukophobia 252
Leukotomy 252, 256
Levophobia 252
Lewin, Kurt (1890-1947) 252
L-5-Hydroxtrytophan 249
Libido 190, 247, 253
Librium 100, 253, 272
Lice 253
Light 122, 253—*See also specific type*
Lightning 58, 107, 253—*See also Thunder*
Ligyrophobia 254
Lilapsophobia 254
Limbic System 30, 254
Limnophobia 254
Lindsley, Ogden 71, 295
Linonophobia 254
Listening with The Third Ear (book) 344
Lithium and Lithium Therapy 2, 10, 40, 42, 137, 254-256, 263, 330
Litigaphobia 256
Little Albert—*See Albert B.*
Little Hans 34, 93, 211, 226, 256, 267, 361
Lizards 256
Lobotomy 256
Locked In 74
Lockjaw 256
Locus Ceruleus 21, 79, 92, 158, 256, 285
Locus of Control 257
Lofepramine 41, 257
Logophobia 257
Logotherapy 257
Lonely 257
Longitudinal Study 92, 110, 119, 258
Looked At 74, 94
Looking-Glass Self 258
Looking Ridiculous 152, 258
Lorazepam 55
Lorenz, Konrad 239
Loss of Control 97, 164, 176, 181, 258
Lost 258
Love 258
Love and Will (book) 266
Love Play 259, 352
Ludiomil—*See Maprotiline*
Luiphobia 259
Lump In The Throat 259
Lung Disease 102-103, 259
Lygophobia 259
Lying 183, 259
Lyssophobia 260

M

Macbeth (play) 367
Machinery 260
Macrophobia 260
Magic 30, 58, 260
Magical Thinking 260
Maharishi Mahesh Yogi 412
Maieusiophobia 260
Malaxophobia 261
Mania 261
Maniaphobia 261
Manic-Depressive Disorders 11, 40, 42, 241, 254, 261-263, 275, 296, 330
Manic Episodes 9, 263, 275
Manifest Content 251
Man's Search of Himself (book) 266
MAOIs—*See Monoamine Oxidase Inhibitors*
Maprotiline 41, 263
Marijuana 264
Marks, Isaac M. 11, 18, 264, 290, 310, 377
Marplan—*See Isocarboxazid*
Marriage 201, 264
Marsilid—*See Iproniazid*
Maslow, Abraham Harold (1908-70) 223, 228, 264, 359, 407
Masserman, Jules Homan 78
Mass Hysteria 3, 265, 280
Masters, William 162, 363
Masturbation 265
Material Things 265
Mathematics Anxiety 265, 289
Maudsley, Henry (1835-1918) 314

Maudsley Marital Questionnaire (MMQ) 19, 24, 266
Maudsley Personality Inventory (MPI) 266
May, Rollo 32, 177, 228, 266
McKinley, John Charnley (1891-1950) 271
Mead, Margaret (1901-78) 100, 226
Meaning of Anxiety, The (book) 266
Meat 92, 266
Mechanophobia—*See Machinery*
Medectophobia 303
Medical Model 31, 266
Medical Psychotherapists, American Board of 28-29
Medicina Musica (book) 280
Medicine 267
Meditation and Meditation Therapy 95, 267
Medomalacophobia 267
Medorthophobia 267
Megalophobia 251, 267
Meichenbaum, Donald 109, 267, 388
Melancholia 31, 267
Melissophobia 69, 268
Melitracen 41, 268
Memories and Memory Loss 31, 268
Men 32, 57, 268
Meningitophobia 85, 268
Menopause 228, 236, 268
Menophobia 268
Menstruation 268-269, 328
Mental Disorders 269—*See also specific disorder*
Merchant of Venice (play) 312
Mercurial Medicines 230, 269
Merinthophobia 85, 269
Merital—*See Nominfensine*
Mesmer, Franz Anton (1734-1815) 270
Mesmerism 270
Metallophobia 270
Meteorphobia 112, 270
Methyphobia 26, 270
Metrophobia 270
Meyer, Adolf (1866-1950) 31, 270
MHPG (3-Methoxy 4-Hydroxy Phenylethylene Glycol) 270
Mianserin 41, 271
Mice 271, 279
Microbes 271
Microphobia 271
Migraine Headaches—*See Headaches*
Milieu Therapy 271
Miller, Neil 57
Mind 271
Minnestota Multiphasic Personality Inventory (MMPI) 271
Mirroring 272
Mirrors 93, 272-273
Misophobia 273
Missiles 65, 273
Mist 273
Mites 274
Mitral Valve Prolapse (MVP) 21, 79, 92, 274, 330
Mnemophobia 274
Modeling 4, 70, 72, 131, 252, 274, 292
Molysmophobia 274
Money 102, 274
Monoamine Oxidase Inhibitors (MAOIs) 8, 36-37, 55, 79, 107, 137, 245, 274, 292
Monopathophobia 274
Monophobia 275
Monotony 275
Monstrosities 275
Mood and Mood Disorders 8, 275, 358
Moon 275
Moreno, Jacob Levi (1889-1974) 171, 276, 331
Morita, Shoma (1874-1938) 276
Morita Therapy 95, 276, 280
Mother-in-Law 277
Motion 25, 121, 164, 277
Motivation 252, 277
Motorphobia 60, 278
Movement—*See Motion*
Moving 95, 125, 278
Mowrer, O. Hobart (1902-82) 69, 244, 285
Muggers 65
Mullaney, J. A. 19
Multimodal Behavior Therapy 278
Multiple Personality Disorder 278
Munch, Edvard (1863-1944) 279, 369
Murophobia 279
Music and Music Theraphy 279-280, 321
Musophobia 32, 280
Myctophobia 280
Myrmecophobia 43, 280
Mysophobia 280
Mythophobia 183, 280
Myxophobia 280

N

Naikan Therapy 95, 280
Names 281
Narcolepsy 281
Narcosynthesis—*See Depth Psychology*
Nardil—*See Phenhelzine*
Narrowness 32, 86, 281
National Institutes of Mental Health (NIMH) 282
National Mental Health Association 282
Nausea 282, 284
Nebulaphobia 283
Needles—*See Pins and Needles*
Negative Ambition 283
Negative Practice 283, 348
Neglect of Duty 283
Nelophobia 283
Neopharmaphobia 283
Neophobia 95, 283
Neophophobia 284
Nerves and Nervousness 89, 284; Breakdown 284
Neurosis 57, 82, 113, 116, 126, 134, 155, 284, 338
Neurosis and Treatment: A Holistic Theory (book) 32
Neurotic Paradox 62, 285
Neurotransmitters 7, 21, 79, 92, 155, 158, 173, 285, 288, 304, 361
Newness 91, 242, 285
Night and Night Terrors 2, 121, 286-287—*See also specific terror*
Nightmares 287
Nisoxetine 41, 287
Noctiphobia 287
Noise 2, 254, 287
Nomatophobia 287
Noradrenergic Mechanisms 79
Noradrenergic System—*See Locus Ceruleus*
Norepinephrine 79, 254, 274, 285, 288
Norpramin—*See Desipramine*
Nortriptylene 288
Nosebleeds 173, 288
Nosemaphobia 288
Nosocomephobia 288
Nosophobia 288
Nostophobia 288
Novelty 91, 94, 288
Novercaphobia 289
Noxiptiline 41, 289
Nuclear Weapons 289
Nucleomitophobia 289
Nudity 281, 289
Nudophobia—*See Nudity*
Numbers 265, 289, 407
Numerophobia 289
Nyctophobia 2, 289

O

Obesophobia 289
Objective Anxiety 289
Obsessions 18, 289
Obsessive-Compulsive Disorder 1, 27, 35, 43, 52-53, 87-88, 96, 105-106, 150, 191, 228, 290-292
Ochlophobia 292
Ochophobia 60, 292
Odonophobia 292
Odors 60, 83, 87, 201, 305
Odynesphobia 294
Oedipus Complex 92, 112, 294, 307
Oenophobia 294
Oikophobia 294
Olfactophobia 294
Ombrophobia 294
Ommatophobia 294
Oneirogmophobia 294
Oneirophobia 156, 294
Oneself 75, 294
Onomatophobia 294
Open Door Association, The 295
Open Places 94
Open Spaces—*See Agoraphobia*
Operant Conditioning 70, 73-74, 109, 116, 192, 252, 295, 344, 368
Operant Shaping 295
Ophidiophobia 32, 295
Ophthalmophobia 295
Opinions 27, 295
Opposite Sex 295, 362
Optophobia 296
Oral Stage 165, 296
Orderliness (ritual) 296
Organic Approach 208, 249, 296
Ornithophobia 79, 296
Orr, Leonard 296, 342
Orthophobia 296
Osmophobia 296
Osphreisiophobia 83, 297
Ostraconophobia 297
Ouranophobia 297
Outer Space 297
Overanxious Disorder 54

Oxazepum 55
Oxprenolol (trasicor) 55

P

Pagophobia 297
Pain and Pain Anxiety 27, 30, 103, 297-299
Pamelor—*See Nortriptyline*
Pamphobia 56
Panic and Panic Disorders 3, 18, 24, 44, 49, 51, 56, 79, 82, 90-92, 96, 101, 107, 122, 128, 149, 157, 207, 249, 264, 274, 299-300, 360, 369
Panphobia 56, 300
Pantophobia 56
Paper 300
Pappenheim, Bertha—*See Anna O.*
Papyrophobia 300
Paradoxical Intention 257, 300, 348, 359
Paradoxical Therapy 300
Paraliphobia 301
Paranoia 87, 108, 127, 237, 262, 301, 307
Paranoid Delusions—*See Delusions*
Paranormal Cognition—*See Extrasensory Perception (ESP)*
Paraphobia—*See Sexual Perversions*
Parasites 64, 301, 352
Parasitophobia 301
Parasympathetic Nervous System 254
Parents-In-Law 301
Parnate—*See Tranylcypramine*
Parthenophobia 301
Parties 302
Pathophobia 302
Patroiophobia 302
Pavlov, Ivan Petrovich (1849-1936) 62, 71, 104, 113-114, 252, 302, 331, 417
Pavlovian Conditioning 74, 302
Pavor Nocturnus—*See Nightmares; Night Terrors*
Pavor Scleris—*See Bad Men*
Peanut Butter 57
Peccatiphobia 302
Pediaphobia 302
Pediculosis 302
Pediophobia 155
Pedophobia 302
Peladophobia 65, 302
Pellagra 302
Pellagrophobia 302
Peniaphobia 303
Penis 303
Pentheraphobia 277, 303
People 35, 228, 303, 350
Performance Anxiety 27, 47, 55, 77, 282, 303-305, 359
Perls, Frederick (Fritz) S. (1893-1970) 170, 177, 203, 305
Personality: A Psychological Interpretation (book) 27
Personality and Personality Disorders 58, 63, 85, 113, 120, 133, 237, 240, 247, 266, 271, 305-307—*See also specific disorder*
Pertofrane—*See Desipramine*
Phagophobia 35, 307
Phalacrophobia 65, 307
Phallic Stage 143, 296, 307
Phallic Symbol 59, 307
Phallophobia 303, 307
Phantom Limb Pain 299, 307
Pharmacophobia 308
Pharmacotherapy—*See Drugs*
Phasmophobia—*See Ghosts*
Phenelzine (nardil) 55, 308
Phengophobia 308
Phenothiazine 308
Philemaphobia 308
Philophobia 308
Phobia and Phobic Disorders 11, 24, 34, 78, 308-318, 381—*See also specific phobia*
Phobia Society of America, The (PSA) 317
Phobophobia 28, 318
Phobos 318
Phonophobia 2, 166, 318
Photoalgia 319
Photoaugiaphobia 319
Photography 319
Photophobia 319
Phronemophobia 319
Phthiriophobia 319
Phthisiophobia 319
Pilots 319
Pinel, Philippe (1745-1826) 319
Pins and Needles 76, 319
Placebo 116, 320
Places 320
Placophobia 320
Plague 320-321
Plants 85, 321
Pleasure 221, 321
Pluviophobia 321
Pnigophobia 321
Pocrescophobia 321
Poetry 270, 280, 321
Pogonophobia 68, 322
Poinephobia 322
Pointing The Finger 322
Points 25
Poison and Poisoning 75, 322
Police 322
Politicians 322
Politicophobia 323
Pollution 25, 323
Poltergeist 323
Polyphobia 323
Ponits 322
Ponophobia 323
Porphyrophobia 323
Positive Emission Tomography (PET) 250, 291, 323
Positive Reinforcement 70
Possession 324
Postcoronary Bypass Anxiety—*See Coronary Bypass Anxiety*
Postpartum Anxiety 324
Postpartum Depression 329
Posttraumatic Stress Disorders (PTSD) 52, 54, 56, 67, 111, 124, 150, 273, 287, 324-326, 352, 368
Potamophobia 326
Poverty 326, 351
Precipices 119, 326
Pregnancy 68, 97, 326-327
Premature Ejaculation 363
Premenstrual Syndrome (PMS) 79, 225, 256, 327, 329
Prepared Fears 328
Primal Scene 328
Primal Scream, The (book) 246, 329
Primal Scream Therapy—*See Primal Therapy*
Primal Therapy 79, 83, 170, 246, 329
Primal Trauma 329
Primary Gain 236, 329, 370
Primeisodophobia 329
Prince, Morton (1854-1929) 14, 329
Principles of Topological Psychology (book) 253
Prison Neurosis 103
Proctophobia 329
Progesterone 329
Progress 329
Projection 329, 341
Prophylactic 256
Prophylactic Maintenance 330
Propranolol (inderal) 55, 304, 330
Propriety 330
Prosophobia 330
Prostitutes 121, 330
Protriptyline 331
Psellismophobia 331
Pseudoscientific Terms 331
Psychiatric Association, American 29, 53
Psychiatry 29, 331
Psychoactive Drug 331
Psychoanalysis 4, 31, 86, 122, 136, 152, 191, 197, 204, 226, 331-332, 346, 351
Psychoanalysis and Dasein Analysis (book) 85
Psychoanalytic Theory of Neuroses, The (book) 190
Psychobiology 31
Psychodiagnostics 332
Psychodrama 142, 276, 333
Psychologic Tests 333-336
Psychology 106, 333—*See also specific type*
Psychology of Personal Constructs 103
Psychophobia 333
Psychosexual Anxieties 3, 175, 198, 202, 225, 333-338, 360-361, 367
Psychosexual Stages 168
Psychosis 156, 338
Psychosurgery 338
Psychotherapy 2, 22, 31, 73, 87, 106, 118, 122, 162, 240, 338, 350—*See also specific therapy*
Psychotherapy by Reciprocal Inhibition (book) 71, 316, 343
Psychrophobia 339
Pteronophobia 339
Pubic Lice 365
Public Speaking—*See Performance Anxiety; Social Phobia*
Punishment 339
Puppet Therapy 339
Pyrexiophobia 339
Pyrophobia 339

R

Rabies 230
Radiation 68, 339
Radiophobia 340
Rado, Sandor (1870-1972) 186

Radon 340
Railroads 340
Rain 107, 340
Rank, Otto (1884-1939) 79, 198, 331, 340, 426
Rape 340
Rational Emotive Therapy (RET) 170, 341
Rationalization 341
Rational Psychotherapy—*See Rational Emotive Therapy*
Rat Man 341
Rats 342
Ray, Sondra 296
Raynor, R. 373
Real Anxiety 342
Reality Testing 167
Reality Therapy 204, 212, 342
Reality Therapy: A New Approach to Psychiatry (book) 204
Rebirthing 83, 342
Rebirthing in The New Age (book) 296
Reciprocal Inhibition 71, 74, 118, 228, 316, 342, 345, 428
Rectal Diseases 329, 343
Rectophobia 343
Redmone, Eugene 257
Regression 143, 343
Reich, Wilhelm (1897-1957) 95, 170, 331, 343
Reik, Theodor (1888-1970) 283, 344
Reinforcement 116, 344
Rejection 344
Relatives 185, 344—*See also specific relative*
Relaxation Training and Therapy 56, 60, 83, 132, 345
Religion 78, 345, 406
Religious Objects 346, 351
Repeating (ritual) 346
Repression 29, 346
Reptiles 346
Reserpine 346
Resistance 346
Respiration Relief Therapy 346
Respondent Conditioning 347
Response Properties 44, 53, 347
Responsibility 230, 347
Retirement 1, 12, 347-348
Reverse Psychology 348
Rhabdophobia 348
Rhine, J. B. 181
Rhypophobia 348
Rhytiphobia 348
Ridicule 93, 183, 348
Risk Taking 200, 349
Rituals 55, 224, 239, 290
Rivers 349
Robbers 65, 349, 407
Rods 193
Rogers, Carl (1902-87) 106, 228, 350, 407
Role Playing 333, 350
Rolf, Ida (1896-1979) 350
Rolfing 83, 350
Romeo and Juliet (play) 367
Roosevelt, Franklin Delano (1882-1945) 185
Rorschach, Hermann (1884-1922) 350
Rorschach Test 350
Rose Petals 351
Rotter, Julian 257
Ruin 59, 351
Rum 351
Rumination 351
Rupophobia 351
Rush, Benjamin (1745-1813) 28, 80, 94, 154, 292, 351
Russophobia 251, 351
Rust 351

S

Sachs, Hans (1881-1947) 351
Sarmassophobia 352
Satanophobia 143, 352
Scabies 352
Scabiophobia 352
Scared Stiff 186, 352
Scatophobia 352
Scelerophobia 89, 352
Schiller, Johann Christoph Friedrich von (1759-1805) 353, 382
Schizoaffective Disorder 9
Schizophrenia 9, 27, 30, 32, 42, 79, 107, 127, 207, 237, 296, 353-354
School 59, 99, 139, 152, 354-356, 361
Schools Without Failure (book) 204
Schopenhauer, Arthur (1788-1860) 191, 210, 356
Schultz, Johannes 60
Sciaphobia 356
Sclerophobia 64
Scoleciphobia 356
Scolionophobia—*See School Phobia*
Scopophobia 75, 356
Scotomaphobia 356
Scotophobia 357
Scratched 30, 357
Screen Memory 357
Scriptophobia 357
Sea 357
Search Within, The (book) 344
Seasonal Affective Disorder (SAD) 11, 106, 137, 357
Secondary Gain 7, 80, 184, 236, 358, 370
Sedatives 6, 40, 66, 87, 91, 100, 358—*See also specific sedative*
Selaphobia 358
Selenophobia 358
Self 358
Self-Efficacy (SE) 65, 358
Self-Esteem 114, 258, 359
Self-Fulfilling Prophecy 359
Self-Help 22, 359-360
Self-Rating Scales 360
Seligman, Martin 222, 251, 328, 360
Semen 360
Sensate Focus 363
Sensitive Ideas of Reference 301, 360
Sensory Deprivation 360
Seperation Anxiety 54, 59, 74, 76, 85, 99, 170, 354, 360, 388
Seplophobia 361
Sermons 361
Serotonin 285, 288, 361
Serum Prolactin—*See Lactate-Induced Anxiety*
Sex Anxiety Inventory (SAI) 361
Sex Therapy 35, 338, 361, 363
Sexual Fears and Anxieties 173, 253, 295, 303, 307, 330, 333—*See also specific sexual terms*; Sexophobia 362; Sexual Abuse 24, 116, 362; Sexual Intercourse 93, 111, 121, 163, 363-364; Sexual Love 174, 364; Sexually Transmitted Diseases 3, 241, 259, 364-367; Sexual Perversions 364
Shadows 367
Shakespeare, William (1564-1616) 312, 367
Shaking 368
Shaping 368
Sharp Objects 368
Shellfish 368
Shell Shock 67, 368
Shock 225, 368
Shock Treatment 368
Shopping 368
Short-Term-Anxiety-Provoking-Psycho therapy 368
Shriek, The (painting) 279, 369
Shyness 11, 258, 369
Sick Role 116, 370
Side Effects 370
Siderodromophobia 370
Siderophobia 370
SIDS—*See Sudden Infant Death Syndrome*
Signal Anxiety 47-49, 370
Simple Phobia 53-54, 147, 371
Sin 172, 371
Sinequan—*See Doxepin*
Single-Room Occupancy 371
Sinistrophobia 371
Sinophobia 100, 251, 372
Sitophobia 372
Sitting 93-94, 107, 372
Skin and Skin Diseases 67, 142, 372-373
Skinner, Burrhus Frederick 71, 74, 252, 295, 331, 368, 373
SK-Pramine—*See Imipramine*
Sleep and Sleep Disorders 69, 91, 167, 281, 287, 373-375—*See also specific disorder*; Sleeptalking 69, 375; Sleepwalking 69, 375
Sliding Down The Drain 375
Slime and Slimy Things 198, 375
Slips of The Tongue 375
Slowness 376
Small Objects 1
Smells 2, 62, 376
Smoking 376
Smothering 376
Snakephobia 11, 377-378
Snake Questionnaire (SNAQ) 376
Snow 378
Soceraphobia 379
Social Anxiety 357, 379
Social Phobia 52, 70, 74, 83, 114, 121, 148, 166, 282, 311, 344, 350, 368
Society 379
Sociophobia 379
Sodium Lactate 56
Sodium Lactate Infusions—*See Lactate-Induced Anxiety*
Solitude 28, 61, 379
Solo Phobia—*See Alone*
Sophophobia 252, 380
Soteria 379
Sounds 380

Sourness 2, 380
Space Phobia 183, 380
Space Travel 380
Spalding, D. A. 239
Speaking 294, 381
Specters 381
Spectrophobia 381
Speed 381
Sperm—*See Spermatophobia*
Spermatophobia 381
Spheksophobia 382
Spiders 57, 88, 382
Spielberger, Charles 385
Spirits 383
Sports Anxiety 282, 383
Spying 383
Stage Fright 304, 383
Stairs 106, 384
Stampfl, Thomas 238
Standardized Behavioral Avoidance Tests (SBATs) 384
Standing 67, 384
Stared At 181, 384
Stars 384
Stasiphobia—*See Standing*
State Anxiety 44, 53, 385
State-Trait Anxiety Inventory (STAI) 182, 385
Staurophobia 385
Stealing 106, 385
Steep Places 385
Stekel, Wilhelm 4
Stepfather 385
Stepmother 386
Sticks 386
Stigiophobia—*See Stygiophobia*
Stillness 386
Stimulants 162
Stimulus Properties 44, 53, 387
Stings 69, 108, 387
Stooping 387
Stories 387
Storms 11, 87, 254, 387—*See also specific type*
Strangers 388
Streets 119, 388
Stress 4, 10; Inoculation 109, 117, 267, 388; Management 56, 103, 139, 208, 388-390
String 254, 390
Stroke 390-391
Studies in Hysteria (book) 34
Stuttering 391
Stygiophobia 392
Subjective Units of Distress (SUDS Scale) 392
Sublimation 392
Subsconscious 392
Success 392
Succubus 157, 240, 393
Sudden Infant Death Syndrome (SIDS) 63, 97, 393
Suffocation 393
Suggestion 393
Suicide 10-11, 393-395
Sullivan, Harry Stack (1892-1949) 115, 142, 395
Sun and Sunlight 395
Superego 6, 26, 112, 114, 167, 237, 395; Anxiety 167, 395
Superiority Complex 241
Supernatural 120, 127, 396
Supportive Psychotherapy 396
Suppression 396
Surgical Operations 173, 396
Suriphobia 397
Surmontil—*See Trimipramine*
Surveillance 397
Swallowing 35, 397
Swastika 397
Sweating 397
Swimming 397
Switch Process 398
Symbiosis 398
Symbolism 34, 59, 79, 88, 273, 378, 398
Symbolophobia 398
Symmetrophobia 398
Symmetry 399
Sympathetic Nervous System 200, 274, 399
Symptom 370, 399; Substition 399
Syndrome 400
Syngenesophobia 400
Syphilis—*See Sexually Transmitted Diseases; Venereal Disease*
Syphilophobia 400
Systematic Desensitization 55, 71, 117, 124, 131, 239, 317, 337, 345, 400
Systematic Rational Restructuring 401

T

Taboos 401
Tachycardia 85, 401
Tacophobia 401
Taeniophobia 401
T'ai Chi Ch'uan 401
Talking 54, 401
Tandamine 41, 401
Tapeworms 401
Taphophobia 401
Tapinophobia 401
Tardive Dyskenesia 107, 401
Taste 2, 62, 203, 402
Tattoos 402
Taurophobia 88
Taylor, Janet 402
Taylor Manifest Anxiety Scale 182, 287, 402
Technology 113, 402
Technophobia 403
Teeth 403
Teleology 247, 403
Telephone 403
Teletophobia 403
Television 403
TENS (Transcutaneous Nerve Stimulation)—*See Pain*
Teratophobia 68, 404
Termites 404
TERRAP (Territorrial Apprehansiveness Program) 404-405
Test Anxiety 139, 359, 405
Testophobia 406
Testosterone 406
Tetanophobia 256, 406
Tetanus 406
Textophobia 406
Textures 406
Thaasophobia 406
Thalassophobia 406
Thanatophobia 406
Theaters 406
Theatrophobia 406
Thematic Apperception Test (TAT) 407
Theologicophobia 406
Theology—*See Religion*
Theophobia 205, 407
Thermophobia 407
Thieves—*See Robbers*
Things That Go Bump In The Night 407
Third Force 407
Thorazine 100, 407
Thorndike, Edward Lee 252
Thought Stopping 407
Three Essays on The Theory of Sexuality (book) 198
Thumb Sucking 408
Thunder and Thunderstorms 87, 95, 107, 408
Tic 408
Tied Up 85, 408
Time 85, 103, 408
Timidity 408
Toads 408
Tobacco 409
Tocophobia 409
Tofranil—*See Imipramine*
Token Economy 295, 409
Tolman, Edward Chase (1886-1959) 252, 409
Tombs 409
Tombstones 94, 124, 409
Tomophobia 409
Tonitrophobia 409
Toothache 132, 409
Topophobia 24, 410
Tornadoes 410
Totem and Taboo (books) 198
Touch 25, 56, 75, 410
Tourette, Georges Gilles de la 410
Tourette Syndrome 410
Toxicophobia & Toxocophobia 75, 410
Trains 28, 410
Trait Anxiety 44, 53, 410
Tranlycypromine (parnate) 55
Tranquilizers 11, 36, 42, 58, 134, 252, 261, 272, 411—*See also specific type*
Transactional Analysis (TA) 76, 411
Transcendental Meditation (TA) 267, 412
Transcutaneal Nerve Stimulation (TENS) 412
Transference 118, 412
Transfusions—*See Blood Transfusions*
Transitional Object 412
Tranylcypromine 412
Trauma 413
Traumatophobia 413
Travel 95, 224, 413
Trazodone 41, 413
Trees 127, 413
Trembling 413
Tremophobia 413
Triazolam 413
Trichinophobia 413
Trichinosis 413
Trichopathpophobia 414
Trichophobia 414
Tricyclic Antidepressants (TCAs) 29, 36-37, 55, 106, 137, 142, 156, 238, 256, 263, 288, 414

Trifluoperazine 414
Trimipramine 414
Trippett, C. J. 19
Triptafen—*See Amitriptyline*
Triptizol—*See Amitriptyline*
Triskaidekaphobia 414
Tropophobia 95, 278, 414
Tryanophobia 414
Tuberculophobia 203, 415
Tuberculosis 259, 319, 414
Twins 415
Type A Behavior Pattern 415
Tyramine 8, 308, 415
Tyrannophobia 415
Tyrants 415

U

UFOs 416
Ulcers 416
Unconditional Positive Regard 1, 416
Unconditioned Response (UCR) 104, 302, 416
Unconditioned Stimulus 344, 417
Unconscious 237, 329, 346, 417
Undressing 153, 417
Unknown, Fear of the 241, 417
Unmarried 43, 371
Uranophobia 417
Urinating 67, 417
Urophobia 418

V

Vaccination 418
Vacciniophobia 418
Valium 55, 135, 152, 272, 418
Vampire 418-419
Vasovagal Response 182
Vegetables 249, 420
Vehicles 28, 420
Venereal Diseases 121, 338, 364-365, 420
Venustaphobia 420
Verbophobia 420
Vermilyea, Bonnie 54
Vermilyea, James 54
Verminophobia 420
Vertigo 8, 238, 420
Vestiphobia 420
Viloxazine 41, 421
Virgins and Virginity 174, 204, 329, 421
Virgivitiphobia 340, 421
Vitricophobia 421
Vivactil—*See Propriptyline*
Vogt, Oskar 60
Vomiting 170, 421
Voodoo 120, 155, 223, 421-422

W

Waddell, Maria 54
Waiting 257, 422
Waking Up 69, 422
Walking 67, 422
War 422
War Exposure—*See Posttraumatic Stress Disorder*
Warlock 423
War Neurosis—*See Posttraumatic Stress Disorder*
Washing 423
Wasps 423
Water 67, 76, 230, 368, 423
Watson, John Broadus (1878-1958) 26, 68, 70-71, 104, 252, 373, 423
Waves 25, 121, 424
Weakness 58, 424
Wealth—*See Money*
Weight 424
Werewolves 424-425
West, Ellen 185, 425
Westphal, Alexander Karl Otto (1863-1941) 14
Westphal, Carl Friedrich Otto (1833-90) 425
Wet Dreams 157, 425
Whirlpools 425
Whistling 425
White Coat Hypertension 82, 154, 426
Wigs 426
Will Therapy 95, 341, 426
Wind 8, 25, 120, 426
Wine 427
Winged Things 427
Winnicott, Donald W. (1896-1971) 427
Witches and Witchcraft 30, 427—*See also Voodoo*
Wolf Man 427
Wolpe, Joseph 71, 93, 142, 186, 226, 247, 252, 316, 343, 345, 407
Women 190, 209, 428-429
Woods 429
Words 257, 429
Work 429
Worms 1, 222, 356, 429
Worrying 429
Wrinkles 430
Writer's Block 430
Writing 431

X

Xanax 55, 135, 220, 431
Xenophobia 196, 431
Xerophobia 431
X-Rays 68, 340
Xylophobia 431

Y

Yersin, Alexandre 320
Yoga 431
Yoshimoto, Isshin 280
Young Girls 432

Z

Zane, Manuel 72, 115, 432
Zelophobia 432
Zenophobia 196
Zen Therapy 432
Zimelidine 41
Zombie 120, 433
Zometapine 41, 433
Zoophobia 32, 433